D0597226

GERMAN WINE GUIDE

By *Armin Diel* and *Joel Payne*

ABBEVILLE PRESS PUBLISHERS

NEW YORK LONDON PARIS

CONSELL FRANKFURT
See the Light!
Discover Riesling.
Crisp & Dry. It Brings out the Flavour of Today's Lighter Meals.
GERMAN WINES LIGHT AND ELEGANT
naturally

Table of Contents

Preface

This is the sixth annual edition of our German guide, the first to be published in English. In that time the German wine industry has matured considerably. A new generation of young winemakers has emerged that is determined to change the international perception of German wines. This guide is intended to give them a voice.

At the end of the 19th century German Rieslings from the Mosel and the Rheingau were the most expensive wines in the world, commanding prices higher than those of the top growths in Bordeaux. Although the quality of the finest wines remained high, the fall from zenith to nadir took less than 50 years. Only two decades ago German wines were synonymous for cheap, sweet plonk. Even today some well-heeled German wine lovers still prefer to drink French.

Since then dry wines have become immensely popular in Germany, heralding a rebirth in national pride for the quality of wines "made in Germany." At the same time it created a schism for the producers. In the German market many estates sell only dry wines; on the export market, nothing but delicately sweet Spätlese and Auslese. Nonetheless, as beer and spirit consumption wanes, wine sales are booming; and today's generation is also willing to spend more money on finer wines, creating new markets for quality oriented producers. Wine lovers have always sworn by the varietal Riesling. The wine consumer has tended to acknowledge its inherent quality, but not to buy it. This guide's mission is to bring the two poles closer together.

Everyone in Germany realizes, although politicians are loathe to discuss it in public, that their future cannot lie in exporting Liebfrauenmilch. Total volumes are down significantly in recent years, but a quarter of Germany's annual wine production is still exported at prices that barely cover the costs of production. Few shippers can seriously speak of a return on investment. Labor costs are so high that the producers must increasingly concentrate on their unique sales proposition, which is clearly the expression of pure Riesling fruit from the finest sites. The collective world of wine is changing quickly, obliging even modest estates to produce better wines or perish. Today no producer can sit on his laurels and expect his clientele to remain faithful forever. The buyer wants a product that is unique, well made and eminently quaffable. Quality on the one hand, value for money on the other, have become the bottom line, and the consumer benefits.

In the past generation the more intellectual German wines have lost their clientele to the simple pleasures of "off-dry" Chardonnay. More educated wine lovers are now beginning to even the score. The "Anything But Chardonnay" movement is growing, and overly oaked wines are being lambasted, but fashions die hard. Interestingly enough, the average consumer has always loved the product, but not the packaging; he has enjoyed the style of well-made Riesling, but not the name. Studies have shown that wine buyers prefer off-dry Rieslings to other white wines, but producers know that any bottle labeled Riesling is difficult to sell. Why else would the Australians flog their Rieslings as "dry white" in a Burgundy bottle. From a marketing point of view this is, you might say, nothing other than the same old wine in a brand new bottle, but the wine is eternally young.

The finest vineyards for Riesling in Germany are extremely steep. Most of the work must be done by hand, making it very expensive. However, the consumer finds it so difficult to wade through the information on the often gothic labels that he is seldom able to distinguish the wheat from the chaff. Bottle designers and a myriad of artist's labels have made the task even more difficult.

For six years we have endeavored to simplify buying strategies with this guide. That so many readers feel that we have succeeded makes it easier for us to bear the occasional criticism of those estates who feel that they have not been sufficiently praised. But wine, in particular German wine, is not a public relations gimmick. As the German Wine Institute has stated for years, it's the quality of the wine in the glass that counts!

With our best wishes and "Prost!"

Armin Diel

Joel B. Payne

About This Book…

We have tried to keep this book as simple as possible, so that every reader will be able to find the wines that he wants to drink from a producer that he admires. Obviously the easiest thing to do for any reader unfamiliar with German wine is to look at the lists on pages 26 to 27 and buy only from the best estates. Even easier would be to buy nothing other than the select group of top wines listed on pages 30 to 43. Unfortunately, few of the finest wines are produced in quantity. Lots of 360 bottles are not uncommon; lots of 12,000 the exception. Thus, many of these wines will be difficult to find.

The 13 wine-growing regions, which are presented in alphabetical order, are our point of departure. Although we refer to English names in the introductions, we have left the German names as the headlines, as these are the names that will appear on the labels.

Similarly, the individual producers are portrayed exactly as they are known in German – with ä, ö, ü and ß – in alphabetical order within their respective growing region. Because many of the obscure German names are difficult to decipher, we have highlighted the defining letter for each estate in order to make the search easier. This is clearly better than presenting the producers in the order of their ranking, as such a list is provided both on pages 26 to 27 and, for each region, in the introduction to the corresponding chapter. Anyone who is not able to find a particular producer or wine should search for the name in the index of estates or individuals listed at the end of the guide.

Any ranking of producers is always a subjective matter, and often one of contention. In our assessment we have endeavored to provide an accurate picture of how each individual estate has performed over the last five vintages. Thus, on the one hand, a given estate may appear highly rated in light of a poor performance in 1996 or 1997. On the other hand, another producer with excellent results in one of those vintages may appear underrated, generally owing to the fact that the estate has at most two vintages of that quality under its belt. The criteria for the ranking of the individual estates are provided on page 24.

The telephone and fax numbers we have listed are valid for calls within Germany. Anyone phoning from abroad should use his own international access number, plus Germany's national code of 49 and delete the first 0 of the area code for the village. To date, few of the German estates are online, but where applicable we have also included e-mail and homepage addresses.

In the presentation of the growing regions and individual estates, we have left the vineyard sizes in hectares. One hectare equals approximately 2.5 acres. Similarly, we have left the yields in hectoliters per hectare, which is the common standard in Europe. For those not familiar with this measure, we provide the following vague conversions as a guide:

35 hl/ha	2 tons/acre
50 hl/ha	3 tons/acre
68 hl/ha	4 tons/acre
85 hl/ha	5 tons/acre

Any given producer's yields are an average. Thus an estate may produce an average of 60 hectoliters per hectare, while having yields of 75 or 80 hectoliters for its simple liter bottling but only 30 hectoliters per hectare for the finest wines. More importantly, the average consumer has been misled by the French vaunting their low productions. Except for the top estates, their claims seldom bear close scrutiny.

In the line "Member" we have tried to include any reference to organizations that have international significance. The most prominent is the VDP, a club that unites the majority – albeit not all – of Germany's best producers. There is also the Barrique Forum, which, as the name implies, is a group of producers promoting the use of oak barrels for a richer style of wine. Many of the best producers of Burgundian varietals are members of this forum. Most of the other names such as Naturland, Bioland and BÖW are organizations insuring the organic production of their members' wines. The remaining groups such as Charta or the Bernkastler Ring have, although their members are carefully chosen, primarily local significance.

The presentation of the individual wines from any given estate has been restricted, by and large, to the 1996 and 1997 whites and 1995 and 1996 reds that are currently in the market. Although we have tried to include most of every estate's finest wines, the selection is often no more than a fraction of the total number produced. Many of the finest late harvest Rieslings are bottled in halves, which is noted as 0.375 liters after the price. All wines have been presented exactly as they are mentioned on the German label, using the German names for the grape varieties. The red wines have, additionally, been separated from the whites in order to make them more easily recognizable.

Although it may be frustrating, we have chosen to print the cellar door prices in German marks as listed in each estate's current consumer price list. These are the prices that you, the reader, would pay, were you to purchase the wines directly at the estate, as any other German client does. Given freight costs, customs and excise taxes, retailer margins and value added taxes, these may vary widely from what you will see on your local shelf. Nonetheless, they do provide a frame of reference.

German wines can be sublime at low alcoholic strengths. As this is rather unusual, we have included a mention of total alcohol for all wines. The German Wine Institute is right in promoting the theme "naturally light," for a Spätlese from the Mosel at 8.5% is a far different animal from the New World Chardonnay at 14%. Both have their merits, and both their clientele, but no other country in the world produces top-notch quality at such low levels of alcohol.

The description and scoring of each wine is our personal judgement. We do not pretend to be totally objective. We have been tasting most wines from almost all of the producers in Germany from every vintage for more than a decade and hope to have provided the reader with an accurate picture of each wine's intrinsic quality. In order to save space, and thus present a wider range of wines, we have deleted all tasting notes.

This book has traditionally based all wine scores on a 20-point scale, which is the scholastic rating system used in France that has become one of the two standards widely used in Germany (the other being that from 1 to 5, like the A to F used in America). In order to make the scoring in this guide more understandable for an international public, we have translated the scores into the 100-point scale used in America. The criteria for scoring are provided on page 24.

Given the fact that we are presenting only the finest wines from a select group of estates, this guide's apparently low scoring of many wines may appear disheartening. This is, however, a misunderstanding. European educators have traditionally been very strict. There is no political correctness that requires teachers to give every child a pass, much less an A. Most children in Germany are tickled pink to take home Cs, marks above 90 are rare, 95 is almost unheard of and 100 essentially never given. More disheartening for the consumer, though, is the fact that there are seldom more than a few thousand bottles of the highly scored wines produced. You will have to search out a merchant who specializes in German wines to find any of them.

Lastly, the recommended drinking dates are only tentative. It is very difficult to predict how a given wine will develop, but the reader should not lay down wines that he could have been drinking. Further, today's consumer tends to prefer fresh, youthful fruit rather than the complexities of bottle aging. For this reason we have been very conservative in our estimations. Many of the wines will probably age better than stated in this guide.

Germany's 13 wine regions an

Rheinhessen	**26,330 hectares**	**Baden**	**15,759 hectares**
22% Müller-Thurgau		30% Müller-Thurgau	
13% Silvaner		29% Spätburgunder	
9% Riesling		9% Grauburgunder	
Pfalz (Palatinate)	**23,488 hectares**	**Mosel-Saar-Ruwer**	**11,985 hectares**
21% Riesling		54% Riesling	
19% Müller-Thurgau		21% Müller-Thurgau	
11% Portugieser		9% Elbling	

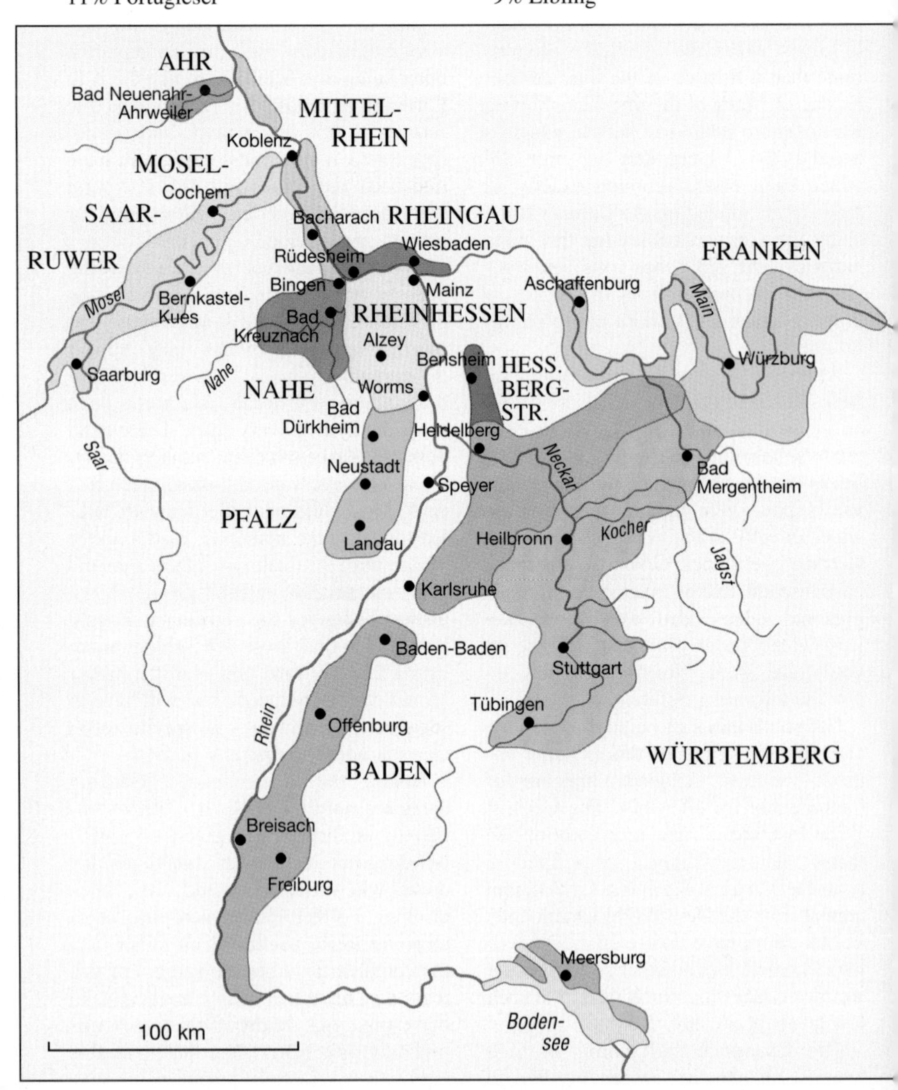

Regions

heir principal grape varieties

Württemberg **11,196 hectares**
24% Riesling
23% Trollinger
16% Schwarzriesling

Franken (Franconia) **6,087 hectares**
42% Müller-Thurgau
21% Silvaner
12% Bacchus

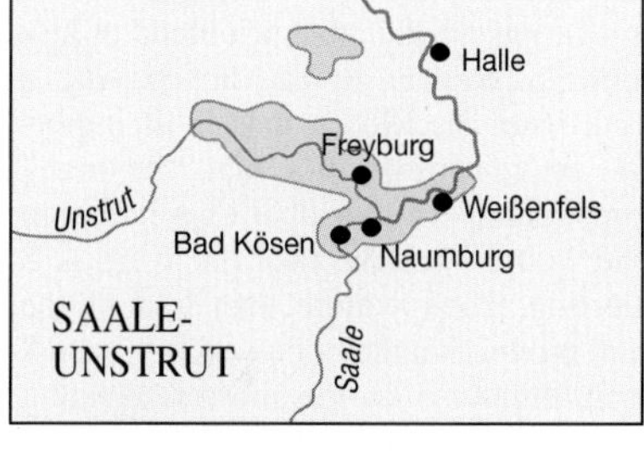

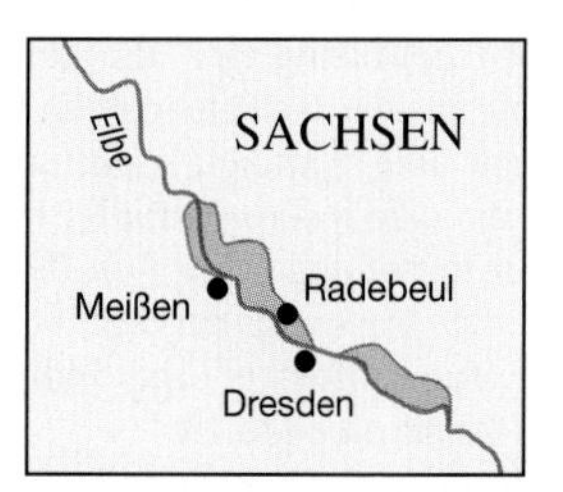

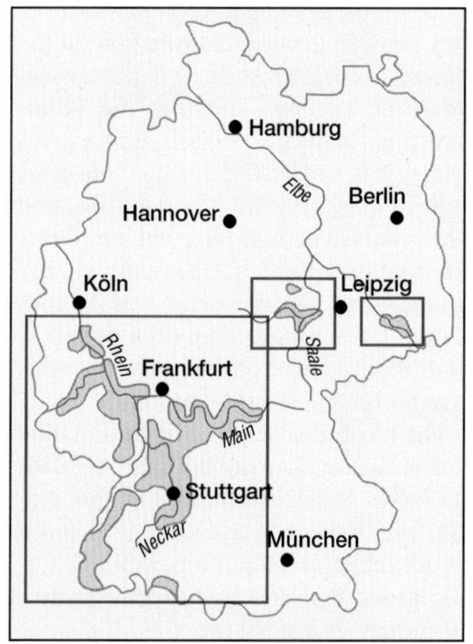

Nahe **4,586 hectares**
26% Riesling
21% Müller-Thurgau
10% Silvaner

Rheingau **3,230 hectares**
81% Riesling
10% Spätburgunder
3% Müller-Thurgau

Mittelrhein **610 hectares**
74% Riesling
8% Müller-Thurgau
5% Kerner

Saale-Unstrut **520 hectares**
25% Müller-Thurgau
11% Silvaner
11% Weißburgunder

Ahr **517 hectares**
55% Spätburgunder
15% Portugieser
9% Riesling

Hessische Bergstraße **454 hectares**
56% Riesling
12% Müller-Thurgau
8% Grauburgunder

Sachsen (Saxony) **352 hectares**
21% Müller-Thurgau
16% Riesling
12% Weißburgunder

Germany **105,114 hectares**

White wine grapes:
22% Riesling
21% Müller-Thurgau
7% Silvaner
7% Kerner

Red wine grapes:
7.4% Spätburgunder
4.5% Portugieser
2.5% Dornfelder
2.4% Trollinger

Germany's Wine Terminology

German wine labels present the average consumer with such a welter of information that most duck for cover. Hugh Johnson's humorous remark that he was surprised that there was no chair for German labels at any leading university remains valid; but the terminology is well defined and meticulously regulated by the federal government. The problem is that such precise definitions can be confusing and are often even misleading for the average consumer, who may find it easier to buy a used car than a German wine. On the opposite page is an exposition of what information is provided on any given label. As a guide through this labyrinth, we offer further suggestions on this in the following pages.

Vintages are terribly important in a country that is as far north as Germany, but it would be ludicrous to give a single value to the quality of any given year for all of Germany. Winter frosts, problems during flowering, hail, cold summers, rainy autumns and disease can vary enormously from region to region. We have tried to provide a frame of reference on page 15, but this cannot begin to describe the quality of the wines from any given producer. Some make excellent wines in poor vintages, others poor wines in great vintages.

Few consumers have any understanding whatsoever about the names of individual villages, much less vineyards. Even in Germany not many buyers would be able to differentiate between a Wehlener Sonnenuhr, one of the Mosel's finest vineyards, and the Piesporter Michelsberg, a name for a *Großlage* that describes not a site but an enormous viticultural conglomeration with Piesport at its center. Already this duel between single vineyards and *Großlage,* which is the German name for an amalgam that few if any consumers understand, has producers, lawyers and legislators at loggerheads. That *Großlage* are a legal form of consumer deception is clearly evident; but there are also numerous individual villages mentioned on labels that provide the buyer no assurance whatsoever of any perceivable quality either, and even some vineyards within prestigious villages should perhaps remain unspoken. Anyone interested in the debate on classifying Germany's prestigious sites should read page 16. Suffice it to say that today, the word with the most meaning on any label is that of the producer!

Germany is known abroad for its Rieslings, and rightly so; but there are a myriad of other grape varieties grown, which may or may not appear on the label. Usually a wine with no mention of any variety on the label is a blend of less noble parentage. If you are buying a wine from the Mosel, it is most important to remember this fact, for many shippers rely on consumer expectation to lead you to believe that the wine is a Riesling. Today, more than half of the total production there, however, is not. A short discourse on the more interesting varieties is found on page 12.

Equally confusing are the different *Prädikate,* for the consumer often thinks that words like *Kabinett, Spätlese* and *Auslese* indicate a flavor profile. In fact, they refer to nothing other than the ripeness of the grapes at harvest. A more detailed description of the individual terms is found on page 13.

The terms *trocken* (dry) and *halbtrocken* (off-dry), are very precise, for they provide detailed information on the amount of residual sugar in a given wine. However, without knowing the corresponding acidity, alcohol and extract levels, it is impossible for the consumer to have a true picture of the flavor. And who wants to be bothered with all of this information? Further, the lack of any indication of flavor creates similar confusion. Do the wines then taste sweet? A short discussion of profiles of wine styles is to be found on page 14.

The most precise piece of information concerning quality on any label remains the name of the producer. For this reason, we have listed Germany's finest estates on pages 26 to 27 as well as a further group that provides excellent value for money on page 44.

The Wine Label

German wine labels are so detailed that hardly anyone can make sense of them. The following are pointers that should help provide a better understanding of the labels.

Obligatory information:

1. **Producer or bottler**. The use of the words Schloß, Burg, Kloster and Domäne is reserved for producers who bottle their own production. Wine estates use the term "Gutsabfüllung" to denote an estate bottling. Cooperatives may only write "Erzeugerabfüllung."
2. The **official control number** (the A.P.Nr. for "Amtliche Prüfnummer") is obligatory for all quality wines. The reference number assembles various pieces of information. In this example the number 7 represents the region where the wine was tested, 763 the village, 19 the estate, 20 the sequential number used only for this bottling and 93 for the year of the tasting. The next wine presented from this estate would bear the number 21.
3. The **place** where the producer or bottler is located must be indicated.
8. The **volume** of wine contained in the bottle.
9. The name of the **wine region** is obligatory for all quality wines.
10. The **alcoholic** strength of the wine.

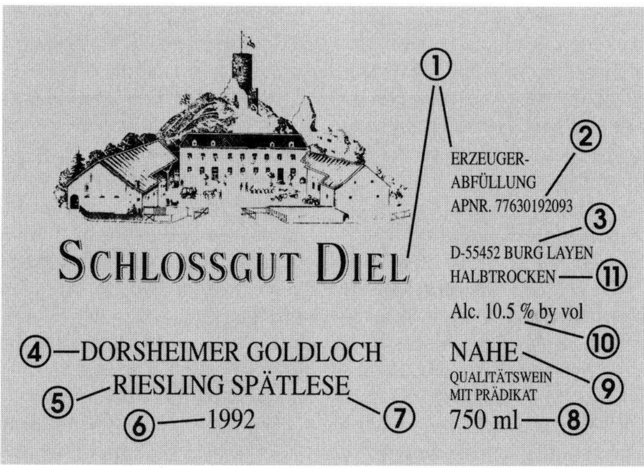

Optional information:

4. The name of the **village and the vineyard** (see page 16) where the grapes for this wine were grown. These are not to be confused with the similar sounding but completely fictitious names of the "Großlage," which are wines blended across the whole of a sub-region and thus give no specific guarantee of origin.
5. **Grape variety** (see page 12) or varieties from which the wine was produced.
6. The **vintage year** in which the wine was grown. In the case of an ice wine picked in early January 1997, the label must indicate the year as 1996! If no year is specified, this would suggest that the wine is a blend of several vintages.
7. The **"Prädikat"** (see page 13) is based on the sugar content of the grapes. The so-called must weight indicates the natural potential alcoholic content of the wine. A "Qualitätswein" may be chaptelized; one with "Prädikat" may not. In northerly regions such as the Mosel the required must weight levels are set lower than in warmer, more southerly regions such as Baden.
11. **Taste:** trocken means "dry;" halbtrocken means "off-dry;" no indication usually means that the wine is "sweet" (see page 14).

It's All in the Grapes

The names of the grape varieties for every wine presented are in the German original, as these are the names that you will see on the labels. Many of the new cultivars are not even worth mentioning; few of the important varieties, however, are unfamiliar to the wine lover.

Riesling is without any doubt Germany's single most important contribution to the world of fine wine. Nowhere is it more widely planted; nowhere does it achieve such heights of quality. Now covering over 23,000 hectares, it is Germany's most widely planted grape. Although consumers have yet to understand its complexity, journalists are unanimous in their praise: a Riesling from the Mosel is almost ethereal, one from the Rheingau stately, those from the Palatinate exude a luxuriant lushness.

Müller-Thurgau still occupies some 20 percent of the vineyard area, but its star is waning. A cross between Riesling and Silvaner, it can produce interesting wines with nutty aromas and crisp fruit. However, it is usually planted on inferior sites and overcropped. The best wines from this varietal are found in Franconia.

In the 19th century **Silvaner** was the most widely planted variety. With seven percent of the total vineyard area, it is still the third most popular grape. Like Müller-Thurgau, it is usually overcropped on inferior sites, where it produces a simple wine for daily consumption. In better vineyards, though, it can produce wines of distinct character. The finest are found in Franconia and Rheinhessen.

Of the new cultivars, both **Kerner** with seven and **Bacchus** with over three percent of the vineyard area are the most important in terms of volume. However, they seldom produce wines worth mentioning. At their best, **Scheurebe** (3,500 hectares) and **Rieslaner** can be excellent. The former in the hands of a vintner such as Fuhrmann-Eymael can be exhilarating. The later, planted on only some 70 hectares, is known principally for its sumptuous late harvest wines.

More classical are **Gewürztraminer** (850 hectares) and **Muskateller** (only 80 hectares). The fact that they are both irregular in yield and aromatic in style has done little to promote their popularity. However, they are regaining merited recognition, as much less noble but more widely planted varieties such as **Faberrebe**, **Morio Muskat** and **Huxelrebe** cede ground.

The trend towards varieties with aromatic components paired with lower acidity has also taken root in Germany. **Grauburgunder** or **Grauer Burgunder** – Pinot Gris or Pinot Grigio – has long had a loyal following in Baden and now covers some 2,500 hectares. **Weißburgunder** or **Weißer Burgunder** – Pinot Blanc or Pinot Bianco – has doubled its plantation area in ten years to 2,000 hectares. Now that it has been approved by the authorities, **Chardonnay** is also beginning to be more widely planted. The lower Pfalz and the Kaiserstuhl produce the best wines from these three varieties, as is seen on pages 32 and 33.

Red wines have become extremely popular in Germany in the last ten years. Their area has grown by 5,000 hectares, so that red grapes now occupy some 20 percent of the total surface planted. It is true that few of the wines pass international muster, and most of these are too expensive, but it would be short-sighted to overlook this development.

With 7,500 hectares, **Spätburgunder** – Pinot Noir – remains not only the most noble but also the most widely planted red wine grape variety in Germany. The finest examples from the Ahr, Palatinate or Kaiserstuhl can hold their own with fine *village,* in some cases *premier cru* qualities from Burgundy. Most of the better reds from Germany are made from this grape, as is seen on pages 30 and 31.

Varieties such as **Portugieser**, **Trollinger** and **Schwarzriesling** are of no international significance; nor is the popular **Dornfelder**, which has doubled its share of the vineyard area in the past ten years, probably due to its dependable yields and deep color. On the other hand, the lesser known **Lemberger** and **Sankt Laurent** merit more serious attention.

What Is the “Prädikat?”

The most difficult word to understand on any label is that of the *Prädikat*, such as *Spätlese* or *Auslese*, which is not a flavor profile but merely a measure of the natural sugar content of the grape juice at the time of harvest. The so-called must weight is measured by using a spectrometer or hygrometer and recorded in *Oechsle*. Better producers also measure the grape acidity and flavor, but the sugar level is an important factor in determining when to harvest.

The scales describing must weights begin with the *Tafelwein*, which is not allowed to mention the name of the region, village or vineyard on the label. *Landwein* may mention only the region of production. Although a number of barrel-aged wines from Burgundian varieties are sold as *Tafelwein*, only one top grower – Karl Heinz Johner in Baden – markets the whole of his production as *Tafelwein*. Suffice it to say that good *Tafelwein* and *Landwein*, unlike the *vino da tavola* in Italy, are rare in Germany.

The large majority of Germany's finest wines are *Qualitätsweine*, or quality wines. All are marketed bearing the name of the growing region and may – but need not – mention the village and vineyard where they were harvested. Simple quality wines may be chaptalized and will carry the word *Qualitätswein* only in the fine print on the label; *Qualitätswein mit Prädikat*, which must be fermented as it was harvested, will emphasize the individual *Prädikat* on the label. In ascending order of ripeness the *Prädikate* have the following meanings.

Kabinett is in theory the lightest of the *Prädikatswein*, which means that it generally has the lowest alcoholic strength. At their finest, such wines are off-dry in style and embody a beautiful example of what the Mosel and Nahe are capable of producing: light wines with a perfect balance of residual fruit sugar and natural acidity. However, there are neither limits set on residual sugars nor upper limits on alcohol. This means that some light wines may be quite sweet while others are totally dry; still others with higher alcoholic levels might be declassified as *Kabinett*. Nonetheless, at their best, they are a fine example of Germany's slogan “naturally light.”

Spätlese represents the next level of ripeness. The term, meaning late harvest, signifies that mature grapes were allowed to remain on the vines longer to reach higher sugar concentrations. Generally slightly sweeter, these wines are synonymous with an exquisite style of Riesling from the Rheingau. The dryer *Spätlese* from the Palatinate and Baden, however, are popular in Germany today.

The German term *Auslese* means selective harvest. These wines are made from individual bunches of grapes culled late in harvest that have higher must weights than the *Spätlese*. Although some producers vinify a small part of these grapes in a dry or off-dry style for their German clientele, almost all of the *Auslese* found in the export market are sweet, succulent and refreshing. The finest examples will have a gold cap or long gold cap to distinguish the higher quality. The use of these capsules, however, is not defined by law, but left to the discretion of each producer.

Beerenauslese translates literally as selected grapes. Generally affected by botrytis, the individual grapes plucked from the late harvested bunches have high concentrations of sugar and produce lusciously sweet wines that age marvellously well; but because these wines have low alcohol and high residual sugar levels, it is important that they retain their natural acidity to insure that they remain lively, balanced and delicate.

Trockenbeerenauslese means dry berry selection, referring to the shrivelled grapes that have been fully concentrated by botrytis. The word *trocken* defines the individual berry and not the wine, which is the ultimate dessert nectar.

Eiswein is made from grapes that are harvested during a deep frost and crushed while frozen. Thus the sugars, extract and acidity are highly concentrated, providing the wine with a pungent vivacity that makes it almost eternal.

Much as the *Prädikat* describes the natural sugar content of the grapes at the time of harvest, the terms *trocken* and *halbtrocken* indicate the total amount of sugar in the finished wine at the time of bottling. Theoretically this information should provide the consumer with an accurate frame of reference to determine flavor; but while the residual sugar in a wine is important in determining flavor profile, it is not a sufficient factor. In short, residual sugar should not be confused with sweetness in a wine.

Nor should residual sugar be confused with chaptalization, which involves enriching a wine by the addition of sugar before or during fermentation to raise alcoholic levels. This is done in moderate climates to make the resulting wines more palatable. Given their higher natural acidity, German wines are generally better balanced by residual fruit sugars left in the finished wines.

The word *trocken* on the label, which means dry, signifies that the wine in the bottle has less than nine grams of residual sugar. Few buyers, though, understand what this means and take the word dry at face value. However, if the wine has low levels of acidity and higher levels of alcohol and glycerol, both of which have a sweetening effect, it may taste slightly sweet. Thus a dry Riesling Kabinett from the Mosel can taste sour, while a dry Grauburgunder Spätlese from Baden might seem slightly sweet.

In Germany, where the consumer wants to see *trocken* on the label, they generally prefer the wine to taste off-dry. Fans of bone dry wines are – world wide – almost an extinct species. Fewer and fewer truly dry wines are being produced; more and more off-dry wines being consumed. This has been the key to success for both the Californian Chardonnays and Chilean Cabernet Sauvignons. It is indispensable for a fine German Riesling.

Halbtrocken, or off-dry, indicates that the wine has more than nine but less that 18 grams of residual sugar. Again, the consumer is generally unable to make any sense of the numbers and assumes that the wine will be off-dry in flavor. However, an off-dry Riesling Spätlese from the Mittelrhein might taste puckeringly dry, while an off-dry Weißburgunder Auslese from the Palatinate will be decidedly sweet.

Even more confusing is the fact that no flavor description on the label does not mean that the wine must be sweet, for both *trocken* and *halbtrocken* – although generally used – are optional, not mandatory terms. Further, even a Riesling Auslese from the Saar produced in a vintage with high natural acidity like 1996 may turn out to be more than dry enough for many palates.

Years ago, the individual *Prädikate* were by and large sufficient to provide the consumer with the information on flavor profiles that he needed to make his buying decisions: the *Kabinette* were light and off-dry in style; the *Spätlesen* had a bit more depth and were generally off-dry to slightly sweet in style; the *Auslesen* were delicious dessert wines, that nonetheless remained lively and refreshing. Further, the consumer knew that the vintage would shade the style of each *Prädikat*. The 1953s, for example, were unctuous, the 1954s more lean.

By codifying this impression of flavors, the German wine laws of 1971 left a loophole for producers who wanted to take advantage of consumer expectations. Grape varieties were developed that brought consistent yields of ripe grapes in marginal sites which could be marketed as *Spätlese* and *Auslese*. To a certain extent this makes sense for a northerly region like Germany, but the new laws did not take into account the role of the site, variety or total physiological ripeness in guaranteeing quality. As the *Prädikat* measures only the sugar content of the grape at harvest, the new laws have unwittingly tarnished the image of the terms *Kabinett, Spätlese* and *Auslese*. For this reason many wine lovers would like to see these terms used only for select noble varieties in each growing region. Given the current political climate, it is unlikely that the laws will change.

Vintage Chart

The Vintages in the Growing Regions

(5 grapes) Outstanding

(4 grapes) Excellent

(3 grapes) Good

(2 grapes) Average

(1 grape) Poor

Vintages are important in a country that is as far north as Germany, but it is impossible to give a single value to the quality of any given year for all of the 13 growing regions. On the whole, however, the last ten years have brought a string of above average vintages unparalleled in German history. We have tried to provide a frame of reference using the grape symbols of this book, but this will not describe the quality of the wines from any given producer. Some make excellent wines even in poor vintages, others poor wines in great vintages.

	1988	1989	1990	1991	1992	1993	1994	1995	1996	1997
Ahr	4	3	4	2	3	4	4	4	3	5
Baden	4	4	4	2	3	4	3	3	4	4
Franken	4	3	5	2	4	4	4	2	3	4
Hessische Bergstraße	3	3	5	2	4	4	3	3	4	3
Mittelrhein	3	5	4	3	4	5	4	3	4	3
Mosel-Saar-Ruwer	4	4	5	3	4	4	5	4	4	4
Nahe	3	4	5	3	4	5	4	4	4	4
Pfalz	4	3	5	3	4	4	4	3	5	4
Rheingau	4	3	5	3	4	5	4	4	4	3
Rheinhessen	4	3	4	2	4	4	3	3	4	3
Saale-Unstrut	1	1	2	2	3	2	3	2	1	2
Sachsen	1	1	2	2	3	2	3	2	1	2
Württemberg	3	4	4	2	3	4	3	3	3	3
	1988	1989	1990	1991	1992	1993	1994	1995	1996	1997

The Classification Debate

For the average consumer the *Prädikat* is the most important bit of information on the label. In theory this rewards those producers who reduce their yields and take the risks of harvesting late. However, there is no similar hierarchy for grape varieties nor vineyard sites, all of which are viewed as inherently equal. It is thus possible to cultivate a high-yielding, early ripening varietal such as Müller-Thurgau in a poor site and produce an *Auslese* almost every year. Whether the wine has flavor, style or character matters little to the legislator. On the other hand, a diligent grower who plants Riesling in the steepest sites on the Mosel will produce only small quantities of *Auslese* thrice in a decade.

Few claim that the two wines bear comparison, but finding a way to give the intrinsically better *Auslese* some individual distinction has been difficult. Almost everyone agrees that grape variety, yield and soil are important factors in determining quality, but the debate over a vineyard classification has stirred an enormous controversy.

A few estates already market their standard wines with the name of the region, their better wines with the name of the village and their finest growths with the individual site. This was once the norm in Germany. Even today no law prohibits a producer from selling his wines in this fashion, but the law neither obliges his neighbors to do the same nor permits anyone to vaunt the quality of the top sites as a *grand cru*.

The debate as to who should determine which sites are *grand cru* is a political mine field. Most of the proposals rest their case in some form on the classification systems of the authorities in the last century that set higher tax rates for the best sites, an inherent recognition of quality. To date, however, the VDP estates of the Nahe are the only producers who have actually introduced anything that resembles a valid classification. Granted, it has no legal repercussions, but it is a pragmatic approach to a common goal in today's political turmoil. The producers have renounced the use of *Großlage*, agreed to market only their Rieslings with the names of the top sites, severely limited their yields and imposed higher levels of ripeness.

The debate began in the Rheingau, where a group of producers – with the aid of local authorities and the university in Geisenheim – delineated a map of the finest sites in the region. Although almost everyone agrees that this classification is by and large correct, the back-biting began only minutes after the map was published. Anyone whose property was not granted *grand cru* status joined the lynch mob; and as only about 20 percent of the surface area was anointed, most dissented. It is in the nature of quality to be elitist, but without a majority the proposition was dead in its tracks.

The situation is equally unclear in Rheinhessen and in the Palatinate, where only a handful of estates have any interest in producing *grand crus*. The spadework has been done in delineating the sites, but there is no consensus as how to surmount the legislative hurdles or make the concept clear to the consumer.

On the Mosel, where a classification would make the most sense, the problem is even more acute. Whereas an estate like that of Dr. Loosen would love to see its finest sites given a legal status, a producer like Egon Müller wants no part in the debate. As long as some leading estates remain mute, nothing is likely to happen.

Although several groups are shaping classification systems, one thing is certain: it will be a long time before any new status is given official recognition. Indeed, the German winegrowers guild would rather prefer a term like *classic* than *grand cru*. The consumer should base his buying strategies more on the estate's reputation than that of the vineyard sites, which is why we have organized this guide in that fashion. A great wine is determined in part by the vineyard, in part by the vintage and to a large part by the talent of the individual producer. No wine will be better than the ability of the grower to produce it.

BADEN IS PASSION
Give time – take time. Go into depth and collect new experiences: great wines in small oak barrels. Pinot noir, Pinot gris or Chardonnay – from Baden co-operatives. Soigné with passion, served with pride. A discreet Barrique note in the concert of aromas. And a finish that invites to taste again.
BADISCHER WEIN®
von der Sonne verwöhnt

Each year the authors pay tribute to those producers who have earned special praise: Some are the epitome of Germany's long wine-making tradition; others shine as rising stars; still others merit recognition as promising talent. Restaurant owners and sommeliers who contribute to Germany's wine culture are also given well-deserved attention.

Gerhard Biffar, Weingut Josef Biffar
Deidesheim, Pfalz
Discovery of the year 1994

Stéphane Gass
Restaurant "Schwarzwaldstube"
Baiersbronn-Tonbach
Sommelier of the year 1997

Bernhard Breuer, Weingut Georg Breuer
Rüdesheim, Rheingau
Rising star of the year 1996

Wilhelm Haag, Weingut Fritz Haag
Brauneberg, Mosel
Winemaker of the year 1994

Joachim Heger, Weingut Dr. Heger
Ihringen, Baden
Rising star of the year 1998

Peter Jost
Weingut Toni Jost – Hahnenhof
Bacharach, Mittelrhein
Rising star of the year 1995

Norbert Holderrieth
Geheimrat J. Wegeler Erben
Oestrich-Bernkastel-Deidesheim
Estate Manager of the year 1997

Dieter L. Kaufmann
Restaurant "Zur Traube," Grevenbroich
Wine list of the year 1996

Horst Kolesch
Weingut Juliusspital
Würzburg, Franken
Estate Manager of the year 1996

Marie-Helen Krebs
Restaurant "Marcobrunn"
Schloß Reinhartshausen
Eltville-Erbach, Rheingau
Sommelier of the year 1998

Matthias Müller
Weingut Heinrich Müller
Spay, Mittelrhein
Discovery of the year 1998

Helmut Mathern
Weingut Oskar Mathern
Niederhausen, Nahe
Discovery of the year 1997

Egon Müller
Weingut Egon Müller – Scharzhof
Wiltingen, Saar
Winemaker of the year 1998

Dr. Manfred Prüm
Weingut Joh. Jos. Prüm
Bernkastel-Wehlen, Mosel
Winemaker of the year 1996

Willi Schaefer
Weingut Willi Schaefer, Graach, Mosel
Rising star of the year 1997

Dr. Carl-Ferdinand von Schubert
and Alfons Heinrich
Gutsverwaltung von Schubert
Maximin Grünhaus, Ruwer
Winemaker of the year 1995

Hans-Günter Schwarz
Weingut Müller-Catoir
Neustadt-Haardt, Pfalz
Estate Manager of the year 1998

Thomas Seeger
Weingut Seeger, Leimen, Baden
Discovery of the year 1996

Alexander Spinner
Weingut Schloß Neuweier
Baden-Baden, Baden
Discovery of the year 1995

H. B. Ullrich
Historic Hotel "Krone"
Rüdesheim-Assmannshausen
Wine list of the year 1998

Alfred Voigt
Restaurant "Residence"
Essen-Kettwig
Sommelier of the year 1996

Johannes van Toorn
Restaurant "Die Ente vom Lehel"
Wiesbaden
Wine list of the year 1997

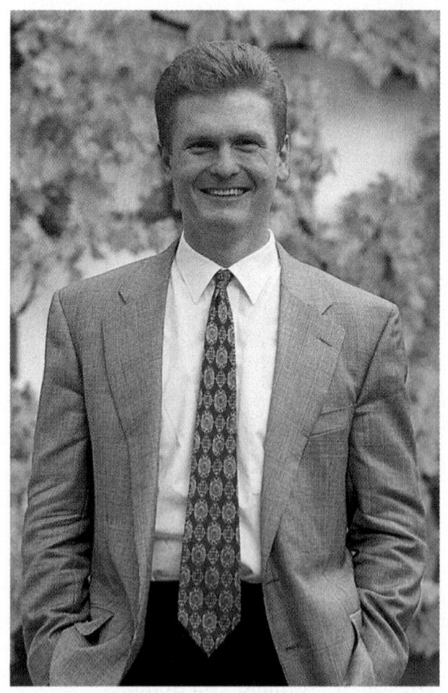

Wilhelm Weil
Weingut Robert Weil, Kiedrich, Rheingau
Rising star of the year 1994 and
Winemaker of the year 1997

Helmut Dönnhoff
Weingut Hermann Dönnhoff
Oberhausen, Nahe
Winemaker of the year 1999

Heinfried and Gerold Pfannebecker
Weingut Michel-Pfannebecker
Flomborn, Rheinhessen
Discovery of the year 1999

Markus Molitor
Weingut Molitor – Haus Klosterberg
Bernkastel-Wehlen, Mosel
Rising star of the year 1999

Heinrich Hillenbrand
Staatsweingut Bergstraße
Bensheim, Hessische Bergstraße
Estate Manager of the year 1999

Gerhard and Werner Leve
Hotel "Im Engel," Warendorf
Wine list of the year 1999

Hendrik Thoma
Hotel "Louis C. Jacob," Hamburg
Sommelier of the year 1999

Our Rating System

The classification of the estates

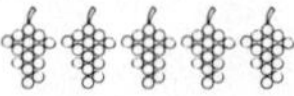

Highest rating: These producers belong to the world's finest.

Excellent estates: These producers are among Germany's best.

Very good producers, known for their consistently high quality.

Good estates, offering better than average quality.

Reliable producers that offer well-made standard quality.

In their classification system, the authors judge the quality performance of each individual estate over the last five to ten vintages. Special attention, however, is given to the development over the last two or three years.

At the beginning of each chapter a list of **other notable producers** has been included. These are also reliable estates, offering standard wines that do not merit further attention in this guide. They are, however, better than the majority of the rest of the producers in their given region.

The classification of the wines

100

A perfect wine that is worth its weight in gold.

95 to 99

Superlative wines from excellent vintages that will age marvellously. Showing complexity, depth and character, these wines are generally very expensive.

90 to 94

Excellent wines from very good vintages with fine aging potential. Fine expressions of their region, they seldom come cheap.

85 to 89

Very good wines with fine balance that should age quite well. These wines often offer excellent value for money.

80 to 84

Good wines that are better than average. When inexpensive, they offer a good deal.

70 to 79

Average wines for daily consumption. For wine lovers, though, they seldom offer any drinking pleasure.

The recommended **drinking dates** (🍷) are only estimates. The average consumer will not want to lay the wines down for a longer period of time, but many will age better than stated in this guide.

Given Germany's reputation for wines that are naturally light, the alcoholic content of all wines has been included in the descriptions.

The **prices** printed in this guide are the cellar door prices in marks, as listed in each estate's consumer price list. Although shelf prices may vary widely, they do provide a frame of reference. Estates that produce wines that offer excellent value for money are given special attention on page 44.

GERMAN WINES LIGHT AND ELEGANT
naturally

Germany's Best Estates

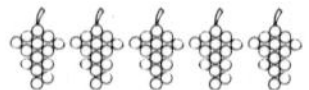

Highest rating: These producers belong to the world's finest

FRITZ HAAG
Brauneberg, *Mosel-Saar-Ruwer*

EGON MÜLLER
Wiltingen, *Mosel-Saar-Ruwer*

JOH. JOS. PRÜM
Bernkastel-Wehlen, *Mosel-Saar-Ruwer*

VON SCHUBERT
Grünhaus-Mertesdorf, *Mosel-Saar-Ruwer*

WEIL
Kiedrich, *Rheingau*

BREUER
Rüdesheim, *Rheingau*

DÖNNHOFF
Oberhausen, *Nahe*

DR. HEGER
Ihringen, *Baden*

KARTHÄUSERHOF
Eitelsbach, *Mosel-Saar-Ruwer*

KELLER
Flörsheim-Dalsheim, *Rheinhessen*

DR. LOOSEN
Bernkastel, *Mosel-Saar-Ruwer*

MÜLLER-CATOIR
Haardt, *Pfalz*

Excellent estates: These producers are among Germany's best

BERCHER
Vogtsburg-Burkheim, *Baden*

BÜRKLIN-WOLF
Wachenheim, *Pfalz*

CHRISTMANN
Gimmeldingen, *Pfalz*

JOH. JOS. CHRISTOFFEL
Ürzig, *Mosel-Saar-Ruwer*

DEUTZERHOF
Mayschoß, *Ahr*

EMRICH-SCHÖNLEBER
Monzingen, *Nahe*

FÜRST
Bürgstadt, *Franken*

LE GALLAIS
Wiltingen, *Mosel-Saar-Ruwer*

GRANS-FASSIAN
Leiwen, *Mosel-Saar-Ruwer*

GUNDERLOCH
Nackenheim, *Rheinhessen*

REINHOLD HAART
Piesport, *Mosel-Saar-Ruwer*

HEYL ZU HERRNSHEIM
Nierstein, *Rheinhessen*

Schloßgut Diel in Burg Layen (Nahe) has not been rated, since one of the two authors of this wine guide is Armin Diel, the owner of the estate.

Germany's Best Estates

HEYMANN-LÖWENSTEIN
Winningen, *Mosel-Saar-Ruwer*

VON HÖVEL
Konz-Oberemmel, *Mosel-Saar-Ruwer*

HUBER
Malterdingen, *Baden*

JOHANNISHOF
Johannisberg, *Rheingau*

JOHNER
Bischoffingen, *Baden*

JOST
Bacharach, *Mittelrhein*

JULIUSSPITAL
Würzburg, *Franken*

KARLSMÜHLE
Mertesdorf, *Mosel-Saar-Ruwer*

KESSELSTATT
Trier, *Mosel-Saar-Ruwer*

KOEHLER-RUPRECHT
Kallstadt, *Pfalz*

KÜHN
Oestrich, *Rheingau*

KÜNSTLER
Hochheim, *Rheingau*

LAIBLE
Durbach, *Baden*

SCHLOSS LIESER
Lieser, *Mosel-Saar-Ruwer*

MEYER-NÄKEL
Dernau, *Ahr*

MOLITOR
Bernkastel-Wehlen, *Mosel-Saar-Ruwer*

MOSBACHER
Forst, *Pfalz*

S. A. PRÜM
Bernkastel-Wehlen, *Mosel-Saar-Ruwer*

SCHLOSS REINHARTSHAUSEN
Eltville-Erbach, *Rheingau*

SALWEY
Oberrotweil, *Baden*

SANKT URBANS-HOF
Leiwen, *Mosel-Saar-Ruwer*

WILLI SCHAEFER
Graach, *Mosel-Saar-Ruwer*

SCHMITT'S KINDER
Randersacker, *Franken*

SELBACH-OSTER
Zeltingen, *Mosel-Saar-Ruwer*

STAATSWEINGUT
Bensheim, *Hessische Bergstraße*

WEGELER
Oestrich-Winkel, *Rheingau*

WIRSCHING
Iphofen, *Franken*

ZILLIKEN
Saarburg, *Mosel-Saar-Ruwer*

© Armin Faber & Partner

Finest estate-bottled sparkling wine

1990 Spätburgunder Blanc de Noirs Brut
Weingut Rudolf Fürst (Franken)

Finest dry red wine

1996 Assmannshäuser Höllenberg Spätburgunder Spätlese **
Weingut August Kesseler (Rheingau)

Finest dry white Burgunder

1997 Burkheimer Feuerberg Grauer Burgunder Auslese "SE"
Weingut Bercher (Baden)

Finest dry Riesling

1997 Dalsheimer Hubacker Riesling Auslese
Weingut Keller (Rheinhessen)

Finest off-dry Riesling

1997 Hochheimer Hölle Riesling Spätlese
Weingut Künstler (Rheingau)

Finest Riesling Spätlese

1997 Wehlener Sonnenuhr Riesling Spätlese – 34 –
Weingut Joh. Jos. Prüm (Mosel)

Finest Riesling Auslese

1997 Kiedricher Gräfenberg Riesling Auslese Goldkapsel
Weingut Robert Weil (Rheingau)

Finest noble late harvest Riesling

1997 Erdener Treppchen Riesling Beerenauslese
Weingut Dr. Loosen (Mosel)

Best dry red wines of 1996

German red wines were once rarely able to hold their own in tastings against top wines from producers in other countries. In a mere ten years, however, the most ambitious growers have made enormous progress – above all, those producers who understand how to employ *barriques*. The best German Spätburgunders no longer need to shrink from comparison with the world's finest Pinot Noirs.

92

Assmannshäuser Höllenberg Spätburgunder Spätlese **
Weingut Kesseler (Rheingau)

Blauer Spätburgunder "SJ"
Weingut Karl H. Johner (Baden)

91

Birkweiler Kastanienbusch Spätburgunder Auslese
Weingut Dr. Wehrheim (Pfalz)

Großkarlbacher Burgweg Spätburgunder Auslese
Weingut Knipser (Pfalz)

Assmannshäuser Höllenberg Spätburgunder Spätlese ***
Weingut August Kesseler (Rheingau)

Spätburgunder "Reserve"
Weingut Huber (Baden)

Cabernet & Merlot
Weingut Knipser (Pfalz)

Spätburgunder "Reserve"
Weingut Friedrich Becker (Pfalz)

Ihringer Winklerberg Spätburgunder ***
Weingut Dr. Heger (Baden)

Burkheimer Feuerberg Spätburgunder Spätlese "SE"
Weingut Bercher (Baden)

90

Spätburgunder "Grand Duc Select"
Weingut Deutzerhof (Ahr)

89

Dernauer Pfarrwingert Spätburgunder Auslese
Weingut Kreuzberg (Ahr)

Schweigener Sonnenberg Spätburgunder Auslese "Selektion"
Weingut Bernhart (Pfalz)

Spätburgunder "S"
Weingut Meyer-Näkel (Ahr)

Spätburgunder "Philippi RR"
Weingut Koehler-Ruprecht (Pfalz)

Rotwein "Kreation"
Weingut Ernst Dautel (Württemberg)

Best dry red wines of 1995

The best red wines of Germany flourish primarily in Baden and on the Ahr; but in Franken, Württemberg, the Pfalz and the Rheingau interesting wines are also produced. In Baden, the Kaiserstuhl, blessed by sunshine, produces the richest and most powerful red wines. In the far more northerly Ahr, a phenomenal microclimate in its steep vineyards makes it possible to produce Pinot Noir that is reminiscent of fine Burgundy.

91

Spätburgunder "Reserve"
Weingut Huber (Baden)

90

Dernauer Pfarrwingert Spätburgunder Auslese
Weingut Meyer-Näkel (Ahr)

Spätburgunder "B 52"
Weingut Nelles (Ahr)

Spätburgunder Auslese "Grand Duc Goldkapsel"
Weingut Deutzerhof (Ahr)

89

Spätburgunder Auslese "Grand Duc Select"
Weingut Deutzerhof (Ahr)

"Ex flammis orior"
Weingut Fürst zu Hohenlohe-Oehringen (Württemberg)

Spätburgunder "S Goldkapsel"
Weingut Meyer-Näkel (Ahr)

Spätburgunder "Caspar C"
Weingut Deutzerhof (Ahr)

Spätburgunder "S"
Weingut Seeger (Baden)

"Kreation"
Weingut Dautel (Württemberg)

Dernauer Pfarrwingert Spätburgunder Auslese
Weingut Kreuzberg (Ahr)

Zweigeltrebe "Hades"
Weingut Ellwanger (Württemberg)

Blauer Spätburgunder
Weingut Karl H. Johner (Baden)

Spätburgunder "Futura"
Weingut Nelles (Ahr)

Spätburgunder "S"
Weingut Meyer-Näkel (Ahr)

Best dry white Burgunders of 1997

The white Burgundian varieties produced in Germany no longer lead a shadowy existence. The best taste exactly the way dry wines should: mouth filling, balanced and restrained in their acidity. Thanks to their flavorful richness they are ideal accompaniments to food, but because of their body they are seldom drunk on their own.

92

Burkheimer Feuerberg Grauer Burgunder Auslese "SE"
Weingut Bercher (Baden)

91

Ihringer Winklerberg Grauer Burgunder Spätlese ***
Weingut Dr. Heger (Baden)

Guldentaler Rosenteich Grauer Burgunder Auslese
Weingut Schweinhardt (Nahe)

90

Chardonnay Spätlese "S"
Weingut Bercher (Baden)

Weißer Burgunder Spätlese
Weingut Hermann Dönnhoff (Nahe)

Ihringer Winklerberg Weißer Burgunder Spätlese ***
Weingut Dr. Heger (Baden)

Langenlonsheimer Bergborn Chardonnay Auslese
Weingut Schweinhardt (Nahe)

89

Ungsteiner Herrenberg Chardonnay Spätlese
Weingut Pfeffingen – Fuhrmann-Eymael (Pfalz)

Grauer Burgunder "SJ"
Weingut Karl H. Johner (Baden)

Ihringer Winklerberg Chardonnay Spätlese
Weingut Dr. Heger (Baden)

Grauer Burgunder Spätlese
Weingut Hermann Dönnhoff (Nahe)

Flomberger Goldberg Chardonnay Spätlese
Weingut Michel-Pfannebecker (Rheinhessen)

Bürgstadter Centgrafenberg Weißer Burgunder Spätlese
Weingut Rudolf Fürst (Franken)

Best dry white Burgunders of 1996

The best white Burgundian varieties are produced not only in Baden, but also in Rheinhessen and the Pfalz, and can now hold their own against the international competition. Squared off against Tokay d'Alsace or Chardonnay from the celebrated villages of Meursault and Puligny-Montrachet, only the wines of Baden have regularly been able to trade punches.

92

Burkheimer Feuerberg Grauer Burgunder Spätlese "SE"
Weingut Bercher (Baden)

Achkarrer Schloßberg Grauer Burgunder Spätlese ***
Weingut Dr. Heger (Baden)

91

Birkweiler Rosenberg Chardonnay Spätlese
Weingut Dr. Wehrheim (Pfalz)

Ihringer Winklerberg Grauer Burgunder Spätlese ***
Weingut Dr. Heger (Baden)

Burkheimer Feuerberg Weißer Burgunder Spätlese
Weingut Bercher (Baden)

Weißburgunder Spätlese "R"
Weingut Ökonomierat Rebholz (Pfalz)

Niersteiner Hipping Weißer Burgunder Spätlese
Weingut Freiherr Heyl zu Herrnsheim (Rheinhessen)

Malterdinger Bienenberg Weißer Burgunder Spätlese
Weingut Bernhard Huber (Baden)

90

Weißer Burgunder Spätlese
Weingut Hans Lang (Rheingau)

Grauer Burgunder Spätlese
Weingut Schales (Rheinhessen)

Chardonnay
Weingut Hans Lang (Rheingau)

Ihringer Winklerberg Grauer Burgunder Spätlese
Weingut Dr. Heger (Baden)

Burkheimer Feuerberg Grauer Burgunder Spätlese
Weingut Bercher (Baden)

Chardonnay Spätlese
Weingut Bergdolt (Pfalz)

Birkweiler Mandelberg Weißer Burgunder Auslese
Weingut Dr. Wehrheim (Pfalz)

Ihringer Winklerberg Weißer Burgunder Spätlese ***
Weingut Dr. Heger (Baden)

Best dry Rieslings of 1997

Most non-German wine enthusiasts have trouble coming to terms with dry Rieslings, which signify to them at best a mouth-puckering drink that is best avoided. Indeed, in the past, German growers often delivered wines that were all too often sour rather than dry. They ignored the fact that dry wines need richness, that the acidity should not dominate the flavor.

92

Dalsheimer Hubacker Riesling Auslese
Weingut Keller (Rheinhessen)

91

Bacharacher Hahn Riesling Spätlese ***
Weingut Toni Jost (Mittelrhein)

Hochheimer Stielweg Riesling Auslese
Weingut Franz Künstler (Rheingau)

Rüdesheim Berg Schloßberg Riesling "Erstes Gewächs"
Weingut Georg Breuer (Rheingau)

Hattenheimer Wisselbrunnen Riesling "Erstes Gewächs"
Weingut Hans Lang (Rheingau)

Riesling "Selektion"
Weingut Schloß Ortenberg (Baden)

Niederhäuser Rosenberg Riesling Spätlese
Weingut Oskar Mathern (Nahe)

Forster Kirchenstück Riesling Spätlese "Erstes Gewächs"
Weingut Dr. Bürklin-Wolf (Pfalz)

Forster Ungeheuer Riesling Spätlese "Erstes Gewächs"
Weingut Dr. Bürklin-Wolf (Pfalz)

Ruppertsberger Gaisböhl Riesling "Erstes Gewächs"
Weingut Dr. Bürklin-Wolf (Pfalz)

Eitelsbacher Karthäuserhofberg Riesling Auslese "Selection"
Weingut Karthäuserhof (Mosel-Saar-Ruwer)

90

Nackenheimer Rothenberg Riesling "Erstes Gewächs"
Weingut Gunderloch (Rheinhessen)

Rauenthaler Nonnenberg Riesling "Erstes Gewächs"
Weingut Georg Breuer (Rheingau)

Niersteiner Pettental Riesling "Erstes Gewächs"
Weingut Heyl zu Herrnsheim (Rheinhessen)

Deidesheimer Hohenmorgen Riesling Spätlese "Erstes Gewächs"
Weingut Christmann (Pfalz)

Best dry Rieslings of 1996

The Pfalz and the Ortenau region within Baden – as well as the finest sites in Rheinhessen and the Rheingau – offer ideal natural conditions for the production of dry Riesling. Above all, though, the Pfalz has shown consumers in 1995 and 1996 what Riesling vinified in a dry style is capable of achieving. The best have a thoroughly majestic richness without being heavy.

92

Forster Kirchenstück Riesling Spätlese
Weingut Dr. Bürklin-Wolf (Pfalz)

Forster Pechstein Riesling Spätlese
Weingut Dr. Bürklin-Wolf (Pfalz)

91

Forster Ungeheuer Riesling Spätlese
Weingut Dr. Bürklin-Wolf (Pfalz)

Königsbacher Idig Riesling Spätlese
Weingut Christmann (Pfalz)

90

Forster Ungeheuer Riesling Spätlese ***
Weingut Georg Mosbacher (Pfalz)

Ruppertsberger Reiterpfad Riesling Spätlese
Weingut Christmann (Pfalz)

Durbacher Plauelrain Riesling Spätlese "SL"
Weingut Laible (Baden)

Deidesheimer Mäushöhle Riesling Spätlese
Weingut Georg Mosbacher (Pfalz)

Winninger Röttgen Riesling
Weingut Heymann-Löwenstein (Mosel-Saar-Ruwer)

Ruppertsberger Gaisböhl Riesling Spätlese
Weingut Dr. Bürklin-Wolf (Pfalz)

Schloß Johannisberger Riesling Spätlese
Weingut Schloß Johannisberg (Rheingau)

Haardter Herrenletten Riesling Spätlese
Weingut Müller-Catoir (Pfalz)

Kiedricher Gräfenberg Riesling
Weingut Robert Weil (Rheingau)

Erbacher Marcobrunn Riesling Spätlese
Weingut Schloß Reinhartshausen (Rheingau)

Rüdesheimer Berg Schloßberg Riesling
Weingut Georg Breuer (Rheingau)

Best off-dry Rieslings of 1997

The finest wines in this category, which the Germans call "halbtrocken," are a flavorful combination of the full-bodied dry Riesling styles typical of the southern regions and the elegantly fruity styles found in the more northerly areas. On international markets these Rieslings tend to be regarded as dry wines. In fact they contain a touch of residual sugar, which often helps to balance the lively fruity acidity in the wine.

91

Hochheimer Hölle Riesling Spätlese
Weingut Franz Künstler (Rheingau)

Niederhäuser Rosenheck Riesling Spätlese
Weingut Oskar Mathern (Nahe)

Kaseler Kehrnagel Riesling Spätlese
Weingut Patheiger – Karlsmühle (Mosel-Saar-Ruwer)

Heppenheimer Centgericht Riesling Spätlese
Staatsweingut Bergstraße (Hessische Bergstraße)

90

Neefer Frauenberg Riesling Auslese
Weingut Reinhold Franzen (Mosel-Saar-Ruwer)

Merler Königslay-Terrassen Riesling Auslese
Weingut Albert Kallfelz (Mosel-Saar-Ruwer)

Münsterer Dautenpflänzer Riesling Spätlese
Weingut Kruger-Rumpf (Nahe)

89

Zeltinger Sonnenuhr Riesling Auslese
Weingut Molitor – Haus Klosterberg (Mosel-Saar-Ruwer)

Erbacher Michelmark Riesling Spätlese
Weingut Jakob Jung (Rheingau)

Altenbamberger Rotenberg Riesling Spätlese
Gutsverwaltung Niederhausen-Schloßböckelheim (Nahe)

Langenlonsheimer Königsschild Riesling Spätlese
Weingut Tesch (Nahe)

Graacher Himmelreich Riesling Auslese
Weingut Molitor – Haus Klosterberg (Mosel-Saar-Ruwer)

Ungsteiner Herrenberg Riesling Spätlese
Weingut Pfeffingen – Fuhrmann-Eymael (Pfalz)

Best off-dry Rieslings of 1996

The best off-dry Rieslings emerge from the centrally located wine regions of Germany: the Rheingau, the Mittelrhein, and the Nahe as well as from parts of the Mosel, Rheinhessen and the Pfalz. They need not be Spätlese or Auslese and are perfect accompaniments to food. The Kabinetts and simple Qualitätsweine can turn out to be extremely attractive.

91

Bopparder Hamm Feuerlay Riesling Spätlese
Weingut Weingart (Mittelrhein)

Brauneberger Kammer Riesling Auslese
Weingut Paulinshof (Mosel-Saar-Ruwer)

90

Bopparder Hamm Fässerlay Riesling Spätlese
Weingut Lorenz (Mittelrhein)

89

Wachenheimer Gerümpel Riesling Spätlese
Weingut Dr. Bürklin-Wolf (Pfalz)

Münsterer Dautenpflänzer Riesling Spätlese
Weingut Kruger-Rumpf (Nahe)

Forster Pechstein Riesling Spätlese
Weingut Reichsrat von Buhl (Pfalz)

Ruppertsberger Linsenbusch Riesling Spätlese
Weingut Christmann (Pfalz)

Mehringer Zellerberg Riesling Auslese
Weingut Clüsserath-Weiler (Mosel-Saar-Ruwer)

Wehlener Sonnenuhr Riesling Spätlese
Weingut S. A. Prüm (Mosel-Saar-Ruwer)

Schloßböckelheimer Felsenberg Riesling Spätlese
Weingut Crusius (Nahe)

Trittenheimer Apotheke Riesling Auslese
Weingut Ernst Clüsserath (Mosel-Saar-Ruwer)

Ungsteiner Herrenberg Riesling Spätlese
Weingut Pfeffingen – Fuhrmann-Eymael (Pfalz)

Bopparder Hamm Feuerlay Riesling Spätlese
Weingut August Perll (Mittelrhein)

Norheimer Dellchen Riesling Spätlese
Weingut Oskar Mathern (Nahe)

Bensheimer Streichling Riesling Kabinett
Staatsweingut Bergstraße (Hessische Bergstraße)

Best Riesling Spätlese wines of 1997

This fruity, elegant style is viewed by the international market as the quintessence of German Riesling. There are very few grape varieties capable of producing such attractive wines with such low levels of alcohol, a fact much appreciated by the health conscious. On the Mosel, Saar and Ruwer they rarely exceed eight percent of alcohol.

94

Wehlener Sonnenuhr Riesling Spätlese – 34 –
Weingut Joh. Jos. Prüm (Mosel-Saar-Ruwer)

Dalsheimer Hubacker Riesling Spätlese – 26 –
Weingut Keller (Rheinhessen)

Scharzhofberger Riesling Spätlese – 19 –
Weingut Egon Müller – Scharzhof (Mosel-Saar-Ruwer)

Brauneberger Juffer-Sonnenuhr Riesling Spätlese – 7 –
Weingut Fritz Haag (Mosel-Saar-Ruwer)

Maximin Grünhäuser Abtsberg Riesling Spätlese
Gutsverwaltung von Schubert (Mosel-Saar-Ruwer)

93

Wehlener Sonnenuhr Riesling Spätlese – 22 –
Weingut Joh. Jos. Prüm (Mosel-Saar-Ruwer)

Brauneberger Juffer-Sonnenuhr Riesling Spätlese – 14 –
Weingut Fritz Haag (Mosel-Saar-Ruwer)

92

Rüdesheimer Berg Rottland Riesling Spätlese ***
Weingut Johannishof (Rheingau)

Niederhäuser Kertz Riesling Spätlese
Weingut Oskar Mathern (Nahe)

Hallgartener Jungfer Riesling Spätlese Goldkapsel
Weingut Prinz (Rheingau)

Graacher Domprobst Riesling Spätlese
Weingut Willi Schaefer (Mosel-Saar-Ruwer)

Wiltinger Schlangengraben Riesling Spätlese
Weingut Sankt Urbans-Hof (Mosel-Saar-Ruwer)

Hattenheimer Wisselbrunnen Riesling Spätlese Goldkapsel
Weingut Hans Lang (Rheingau)

Hochheimer Kirchenstück Riesling Spätlese
Weingut Franz Künstler (Rheingau)

Ürziger Würzgarten Riesling Spätlese
Weingut Dr. Loosen (Mosel-Saar-Ruwer)

Best Riesling Spätlese wines of 1996

The Riesling Spätlese wines from the Mosel, Saar and Ruwer, as well as from the Mittelrhein, Nahe and Rheingau, taste particularly elegant. In the Rheinhessen, the Ortenau and the Pfalz they exhibit more body. The best wines in this category, which can be quite lively when young, easily age in bottle for ten years and more.

94

Kiedricher Gräfenberg Riesling Spätlese
Weingut Robert Weil (Rheingau)

93

Niersteiner Oelberg Riesling Spätlese – 9 –
Weingut J. u. H. A. Strub (Rheinhessen)

Dalsheimer Hubacker Riesling Spätlese – 26 –
Weingut Keller (Rheinhessen)

Piesporter Goldtröpfchen Riesling Spätlese
Weingut Reinhold Haart (Mosel-Saar-Ruwer)

92

Piesporter Goldtröpfchen Riesling Spätlese
Weingut Sankt Urbans-Hof (Mosel-Saar-Ruwer)

Ürziger Würzgarten Riesling Spätlese
Weingut Dr. Loosen (Mosel-Saar-Ruwer)

Forster Jesuitengarten Riesling Spätlese
Weingut Bassermann-Jordan (Pfalz)

Ürziger Würzgarten Riesling Spätlese
Weingut Joh. Jos. Christoffel Erben (Mosel-Saar-Ruwer)

Hochheimer Domdechaney Riesling Spätlese
Domdechant Wernersches Weingut (Rheingau)

91

Hochheimer Kirchenstück Riesling Spätlese
Weingut Franz Künstler (Rheingau)

Bopparder Hamm Feuerlay Riesling Spätlese
Weingut Heinrich Müller (Mittelrhein)

Brauneberger Juffer-Sonnenuhr Riesling Spätlese – 14 –
Weingut Fritz Haag (Mosel-Saar-Ruwer)

Hochheimer Domdechaney Riesling Spätlese
Weingut W. J. Schäfer (Rheingau)

Maximin Grünhäuser Abtsberg Riesling Spätlese
Gutsverwaltung von Schubert (Mosel-Saar-Ruwer)

Wiltinger Braune Kupp Riesling Spätlese
Weingut Le Gallais (Mosel-Saar-Ruwer)

Scharzhofberger Riesling Spätlese
Weingut Egon Müller – Scharzhof (Mosel-Saar-Ruwer)

Best Riesling Auslese wines of 1997

The finest wines in this category are quite noticeably sweet; but they attain their true elegance and harmony due to their stylish and racy play of acidity. This is a style of Riesling that has never been matched, let alone surpassed, outside Germany. Its admirers know that patience is required, as Riesling Auslese wines often do not show their full complexity and elegance until they have attained considerable bottle age.

96

Kiedricher Gräfenberg Riesling Auslese Goldkapsel
Weingut Robert Weil (Rheingau)

Dalsheimer Hubacker Riesling Auslese ***
Weingut Keller (Rheinhessen)

Erdener Prälat Riesling Auslese lange Goldkapsel – 36 –
Weingut Dr. Loosen (Mosel-Saar-Ruwer)

Graacher Domprobst Riesling Auslese
Weingut Willi Schaefer (Mosel-Saar-Ruwer)

Scharzhofberger Riesling Auslese Goldkapsel
Weingut Egon Müller – Scharzhof (Mosel-Saar-Ruwer)

Brauneberger Juffer-Sonnenuhr Riesling Auslese Goldkapsel – 13 –
Weingut Fritz Haag (Mosel-Saar-Ruwer)

Oberhäuser Brücke Riesling Auslese Goldkapsel
Weingut Hermann Dönnhoff (Nahe)

95

Riesling Auslese
Weingut Peter Jakob Kühn (Rheingau)

Nackenheimer Rothenberg Riesling Auslese Goldkapsel
Weingut Gunderloch (Rheinhessen)

Rüdesheimer Berg Rottland Riesling Auslese
Weingut Johannishof (Rheingau)

Eitelsbacher Karthäuserhofberg Riesling Auslese Goldkapsel – 35 –
Weingut Karthäuserhof (Mosel-Saar-Ruwer)

Brauneberger Juffer-Sonnenuhr Riesling Auslese Goldkapsel – 9 –
Weingut Fritz Haag (Mosel-Saar-Ruwer)

Scharzhofberger Riesling Auslese – 21 –
Weingut Egon Müller – Scharzhof (Mosel-Saar-Ruwer)

Lieser Niederberg Helden Riesling Auslese *** – 10 –
Weingut Schloß Lieser (Mosel-Saar-Ruwer)

Serriger Schloß Saarsteiner Riesling Auslese lange Goldkapsel
Weingut Schloß Saarstein (Mosel-Saar-Ruwer)

Wiltinger Braune Kupp Riesling Auslese Goldkapsel
Weingut Le Gallais (Mosel-Saar-Ruwer)

Best Riesling Auslese wines of 1996

There is no doubt that outstandingly elegant wines come from the Mosel, Saar and Ruwer. Nonetheless the Rheingau, Nahe and parts of the Rheinhessen and Pfalz are capable of producing full-bodied Riesling Auslese wines with a piquant but fruity acidity. Wine lovers around the world have learned to treasure these rarities and recognize their unique character by paying the appropriate prices.

98

Kiedricher Gräfenberg Riesling Auslese Goldkapsel
Weingut Robert Weil (Rheingau)

96

Dalsheimer Hubacker Riesling Auslese ***
Weingut Keller (Rheinhessen)

Scharzhofberger Riesling Auslese Goldkapsel
Weingut Egon Müller – Scharzhof (Mosel-Saar-Ruwer)

95

Heppenheimer Centgericht Riesling Auslese
Staatsweingut Bergstraße (Hessische Bergstraße)

Erdener Prälat Riesling Auslese Goldkapsel
Weingut Dr. Loosen (Mosel-Saar-Ruwer)

Piesporter Goldtröpfchen Riesling Auslese – 11 –
Weingut Reinhold Haart (Mosel-Saar-Ruwer)

Brauneberger Juffer-Sonnenuhr Riesling Auslese lange Goldkapsel
Weingut Fritz Haag (Mosel-Saar-Ruwer)

Ürziger Würzgarten Riesling Auslese Goldkapsel
Weingut Dr. Loosen (Mosel-Saar-Ruwer)

Riesling Auslese
Weingut Peter Jakob Kühn (Rheingau)

Brauneberger Juffer-Sonnenuhr Riesling Auslese Goldkapsel – 12 –
Weingut Fritz Haag (Mosel-Saar-Ruwer)

Bernkasteler Doctor Riesling Auslese lange Goldkapsel
Weingut Wwe. Dr. H. Thanisch – Erben Thanisch (Mosel-Saar-Ruwer)

94

Forster Ungeheuer Riesling Auslese "Classic"
Weingut Reichsrat von Buhl (Pfalz)

Graacher Domprobst Riesling Auslese
Weingut Willi Schaefer (Mosel-Saar-Ruwer)

Trittenheimer Apotheke Riesling Auslese Goldkapsel – 11 –
Weingut Grans-Fassian (Mosel-Saar-Ruwer)

Wehlener Sonnenuhr Riesling Auslese Goldkapsel
Weingut Joh. Jos. Prüm (Mosel-Saar-Ruwer)

Best noble late harvest Rieslings of 1997

These outstanding wines are produced from overripe, dried grapes that have concentrated both the sweetness and acidity of their juice. Particularly rare are the ice wines, which can be produced only after a severe frost. The more they are tweaked by their acidity, the more piquant is their expression of flavor. These treasures of German wine culture are among the most long-lived wines on earth.

98

Erdener Treppchen Riesling Beerenauslese
Weingut Dr. Loosen (Mosel-Saar-Ruwer)

Scharzhofberger Riesling Trockenbeerenauslese
Weingut Egon Müller – Scharzhof (Mosel-Saar-Ruwer)

Riesling Beerenauslese
Weingut Peter Jakob Kühn (Rheingau)

Würzburger Stein Riesling Trockenbeerenauslese
Staatlicher Hofkeller (Franken)

Dalsheimer Hubacker Riesling Trockenbeerenauslese
Weingut Keller (Rheinhessen)

96

Dalsheimer Hubacker Riesling Eiswein
Weingut Keller (Rheinhessen)

Winninger Riesling Trockenbeerenauslese
Weingut Reinhard und Beate Knebel (Mosel-Saar-Ruwer)

Geisenheimer Rothenberg Riesling Trockenbeerenauslese
Gutsverwaltung Geheimrat J. Wegeler Erben (Rheingau)

Kiedricher Gräfenberg Riesling Trockenbeerenauslese Goldkapsel
Weingut Robert Weil (Rheingau)

Ürziger Würzgarten Riesling Trockenbeerenauslese
Weingut Dr. Loosen (Mosel-Saar-Ruwer)

Winninger Röttgen Riesling Beerenauslese
Weingut Heymann-Löwenstein (Mosel-Saar-Ruwer)

Kiedricher Gräfenberg Riesling Eiswein
Weingut Robert Weil (Rheingau)

Oberhäuser Brücke Riesling Eiswein
Weingut Hermann Dönnhoff (Nahe)

Ruppertsberger Reiterpfad Riesling Trockenbeerenauslese
Weingut Geheimer Rat Dr. von Bassermann-Jordan (Pfalz)

Ürziger Würzgarten Riesling Eiswein
Weingut Joh. Jos. Christoffel Erben (Mosel-Saar-Ruwer)

Best noble late harvest Rieslings of 1996

Although Rieslaner and Scheurebe can be quite good, the most elegant nobly sweet wines of Germany are produced from the Riesling grape. These exceptional wines are produced in all the German wine regions, but the most sought-after examples come from the Rheingau, the Mosel, Saar and Ruwer, the Nahe, the Pfalz and Rheinhessen. These rarities develop over decades before attaining their full perfection.

99

Oberhäuser Brücke Riesling Eiswein – 28 –
Weingut Hermann Dönnhoff (Nahe)

Kiedricher Gräfenberg Riesling Trockenbeerenauslese
Weingut Robert Weil (Rheingau)

98

Kiedricher Wasseros Riesling Eiswein
Weingut Robert Weil (Rheingau)

Kiedricher Gräfenberg Riesling Beerenauslese Goldkapsel
Weingut Robert Weil (Rheingau)

Eltviller Sonnenberg Riesling Eiswein
Weingut Freiherr Langwerth von Simmern (Rheingau)

Geisenheimer Kläuserweg Riesling Eiswein
Weingut Prinz von Hessen (Rheingau)

Forster Ungeheuer Riesling Trockenbeerenauslese
Weingut Reichsrat von Buhl (Pfalz)

Heppenheimer Centgericht Riesling Eiswein
Staatsweingut Bergstraße (Hessische Bergstraße)

Dalsheimer Hubacker Riesling Eiswein Goldkapsel
Weingut Keller (Rheinhessen)

Scharzhofberger Riesling Eiswein
Weingut Egon Müller – Scharzhof (Mosel-Saar-Ruwer)

Riesling Trockenbeerenauslese
Weingut Peter Jakob Kühn (Rheingau)

Riesling Eiswein
Weingut Peter Jakob Kühn (Rheingau)

Kiedricher Gräfenberg Riesling Eiswein
Weingut Robert Weil (Rheingau)

Oberhäuser Brücke Riesling Eiswein – 27 –
Weingut Hermann Dönnhoff (Nahe)

Wines for Bargain Hunters

These estates produce wines with excellent value for money. Some wines might be expensive, but the consumer will generally find the best price here.

HESSISCHE BERGSTRASSE

Staatsweingut Bergstraße, Bensheim

❊

MITTELRHEIN

Toni Lorenz, Boppard
Heinrich Müller, Spay
August Perll, Boppard
Walter Perll, Boppard
Weingart, Spay

❊

RHEINGAU

J. B. Becker, Walluf
Hupfeld, Oestrich-Winkel
J. Jung, Erbach
Kanitz, Lorch
Knyphausen, Erbach
Kühn, Oestrich
Hans Lang, Hattenheim
Josef Leitz, Rüdesheim
W. J. Schäfer, Hochheim
Weingut der Stadt Eltville

❊

MOSEL-SAAR-RUWER

Beulwitz, Mertesdorf
Kurt Hain, Piesport
Kees-Kieren, Graach
Knebel, Winningen
Merkelbach, Ürzig
Meulenhof, Erden
Piedmont, Konz
Walter Rauen, Detzem
Reuscher-Haart, Piesport
Josef Rosch, Leiwen
Sankt Urbans-Hof, Leiwen
Willi Schaefer, Graach
Selbach-Oster, Zeltingen
Studert-Prüm, Wehlen

NAHE

Hermann Dönnhoff, Oberhausen
Emrich-Schönleber, Monzingen
Göttelmann, Münster-Sarmsheim
Königswingert, Guldental
Kruger-Rumpf, Münster-Sarmsheim
Lötzbeyer, Feilbingert
Oskar Mathern, Niederhausen
Joh. Bapt. Schäfer, Burg Layen
Schäfer-Fröhlich, Bockenau
Willi Schweinhardt, Langenlonsheim
Sitzius, Langenlonsheim
Tesch, Langenlonsheim

❊

RHEINHESSEN

Gunderloch, Nackenheim
Keller, Flörsheim-Dalsheim
Kissinger, Uelversheim
Meiser, Gau-Köngernheim
Michel-Pfannebecker, Flomborn
Posthof, Stadecken-Elsheim
Sankt Antony, Nierstein
Schales, Flörsheim-Dalsheim
Scherner-Kleinhanß, Flörsheim-Dalsheim
Franz Karl Schmitt, Nierstein
Georg Albrecht Schneider, Nierstein
Heinrich Seebrich, Nierstein
Staatliche Weinbaudomäne, Oppenheim
J. u. H. A. Strub, Nierstein

❊

PFALZ

Gerhard Klein, Hainfeld
Koehler-Ruprecht, Kallstadt
Meßmer, Burrweiler
Münzberg, Godramstein
Rebholz, Siebeldingen

German Wine Guide

The Regions, the Producers, the Wines

Germany's best red wines?

The history of the Ahr valley as a wine producing region dates back to the eighth century. The Ahr is now home to 500 hectares of vines. Between the Rhine and the Eifel mountains, the vineyards stretch some 25 kilometers from the Altenahrer Eck to the Heimersheimer Kapellenberg. The picturesque landscape clearly shows that the lower Ahr valley, with its basalt cones and gardenlike appearance, is quite different geologically from the precipitous and narrowly winding middle Ahr valley. There the steep vineyards cling tightly to the craggy cliffs, where they are laid out in terraces beneath the wooded hilltops. Soils, cliffs and vineyard walls, made from dark gray slate, retain the heat of the sun and reflect that warmth onto the vines during the night.

The consequence of this greenhouse effect is that, despite the northerly latitude, the region enjoys a Mediterranean microclimate with astonishingly high average temperatures. The most expressive wines of the valley derive from the meager slate slopes above the villages of Marienthal, Dernau and Mayschoß. Downstream, where the majority of the vines are grown, the slopes are less steep, the temperatures cooler and the wines exhibit both less weight and character.

1996 was a small vintage in terms of quantity, and a difficult one in terms of quality. Several producers brought little more than thirty hectoliters per hectare into their cellars, but low yields alone are no guarantee for quality, and only a handful of the Pinot Noirs produced in that vintage, in particular those of Deutzerhof, will age gracefully. The 1997s are infinitely better, but production is even lower. The red wines surpass the outstanding quality of the 1995s and are probably the finest wines that the valley has ever produced. While quality in 1996 was less consistent from cellar to cellar, the excellent 1997s and well balanced 1995s more or less made themselves. "Whoever made mediocre wine in those two vintages should look for another job," declared Werner Näkel, one of the region's top growers, after the last harvest.

That three or four of the estates on the Ahr know what they are doing is shown in a glance at our list of Germany's finest red wines. Nine of the fifteen top wines from the 1995 vintage came from the Ahr valley, partly due to the fact that 1995 was a difficult year in both Baden and Württemberg. But even in a difficult vintage for the Ahr like 1996, three of the finest German red wines came from this small region. The best wines from the Ahr can be compared with most of the *villages* and even some of the better *premiers crus* of Burgundy. While those of the Meyer-Näkel estate are very similar

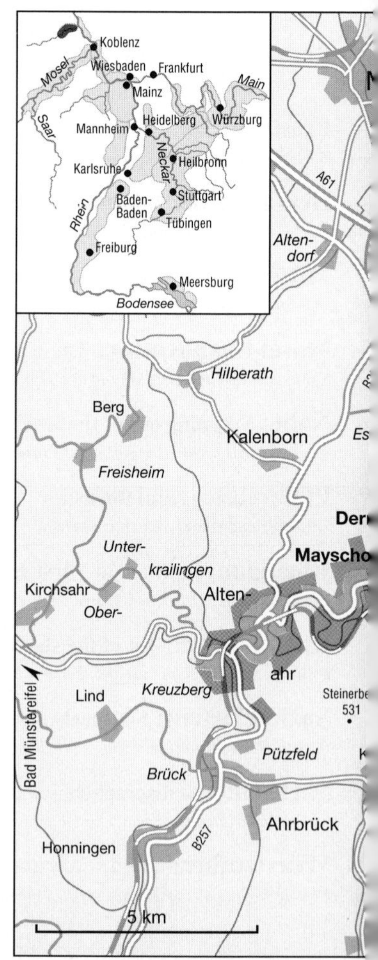

in style to those of Volnay, Deutzerhof has a more robust approach that is reminiscent of the finest Pinot Noir from the New World. Up and coming is also the estate of Toni Nelles.

Yet all three are now charging prices not that far from those demanded by their Burgundian colleagues, sometimes even more. Be that as it may, of the some 75 producers in the region, only six or seven merit much attention; for even at the smaller estates, which are often run as a hobby, bargains are non-existent. And because of demand, the cooperatives, which account for at least 80 percent of the total production, are also able to charge high prices for, at best, modest quality. The only exception being that of Mayschoß-Altenahr, which has been improving steadily in the past three vintages.

85 percent of the vineyards are planted with red varieties; but the term "Red wine paradise" should apply only to Spätburgunder, which accounts for less than half of the total production.

During the Napoleonic era, Ahr wines enjoyed great success in a rosé style. But in those days most producers sought even greater profit by selling sparkling wines. In England, the "Sparkling Wine from Walporzheim" was particularly prized and once fetched prices comparable to those of the best champagne.

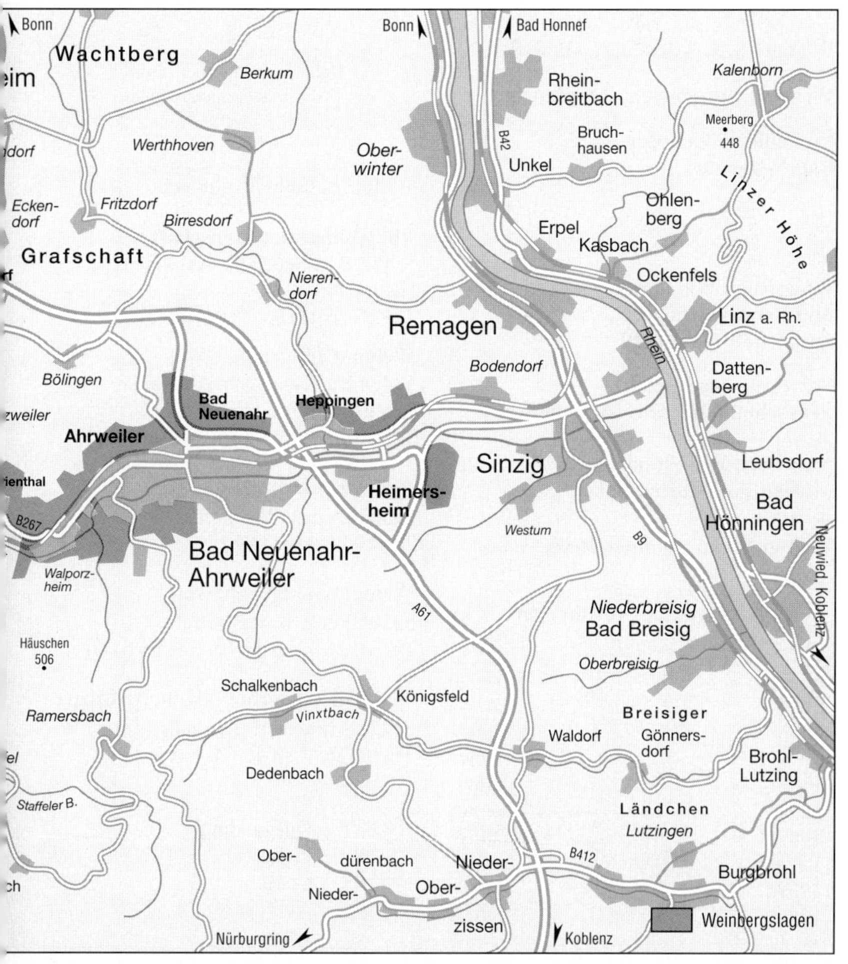

The leading estates of the Ahr

Weingut Deutzerhof – Cossmann-Hehle, Mayschoß

Weingut Meyer-Näkel, Dernau

Weingut Kreuzberg, Dernau

Weingut Nelles, Heimersheim

Weingut J. J. Adeneuer, Ahrweiler

Weingut Burggarten, Heppingen

Weingut Sonnenberg, Bad Neuenahr

Brogsitters Weingüter und Privatsektkellerei, Grafschaft-Gelsdorf

Winzergenossenschaft Mayschoß-Altenahr, Mayschoß

Staatliche Weinbaudomäne Marienthal, Marienthal

Weingut Jean Stodden, Rech

Vintage chart for the Ahr

vintage	quality	drink
1997	🍇🍇🍇🍇🍇	till 2003
1996	🍇🍇🍇	now
1995	🍇🍇🍇🍇	till 2002
1994	🍇🍇🍇🍇	now
1993	🍇🍇🍇🍇	now
1992	🍇🍇🍇	now
1991	🍇🍇	now
1990	🍇🍇🍇🍇	now
1989	🍇🍇🍇	now
1988	🍇🍇🍇🍇	now

Rating scale for the estates

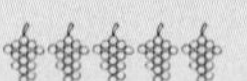

Highest rating: These producers belong to the world's finest.

Excellent estates: These producers are among Germany's best.

Very good producers, known for their consistently high quality.

Good estates, offering better than average quality.

Reliable producers that offer well-made standard quality.

Other notable producers

Ahr-Winzergenossenschaft
53474 Bad Neuenahr-Ahrweiler, Heerstraße 91–93
Tel. (0 26 41) 9 47 20, Fax 94 72 94

Weingut Lingen
53474 Bad Neuenahr-Ahrweiler, Teichstraße 3
Tel. (0 26 41) 2 95 45

Weingut Erwin Riske
53507 Dernau, Wingertstraße 26
Tel. (0 26 43) 84 06

Weingut Jakob Sebastian
53506 Rech, Brückenstraße 2
Tel. (0 26 43) 9 36 10, Fax 93 61 61

Weingut Weilerhof – Hubert Knieps
53474 Ahrweiler, Bossandstraße 13
Tel. (0 26 41) 3 42 64, Fax 3 40 74

🍇🍇🍇🍇🍇 : Outstanding
🍇🍇🍇🍇 : Excellent
🍇🍇🍇 : Good
🍇🍇 : Average
🍇 : Poor

WEINGUT J. J. ADENEUER

Owner: Frank and Marc Adeneuer
Winemaker: Frank Adeneuer
53474 Ahrweiler, Max-Planck-Straße 8
Tel. (0 26 41) 3 44 73, Fax 3 73 79
Directions: A 61 Köln–Koblenz, exit Ahrweiler
Sales: Marc Adeneuer
Opening hours: Mon.–Fri. 9 a.m. to 6 p.m., Sat. 10 a.m. to 3 p.m.
Sun. by appointment
History: The family has been making wine for 500 years

Vineyard area: 8.5 hectares
Annual production: 80,000 bottles
Top site: Walporzheimer Gärkammer
Soil types: Weathered slate
Grape varieties: 85% Spätburgunder, 10% Portugieser, 3% Frühburgunder, 2% Dornfelder
Average yield: 65 hl/ha
Best vintages: 1995, 1996, 1997
Member: VDP

In 1984 the brothers Frank and Marc Adeneuer took over their family's run-down estate. Since then they have steadily been making more of its potential. The cellars have been modernized and the property enlarged by almost three hectares. The brothers are particularly proud of the red wines they make from their exclusively owned Walporzheimer Gärkammer, the tiniest single vineyard in all of Europe. Thanks to its excellent microclimate, it is often possible to harvest fully ripened Auslese from this site. Since the 1994 vintage the Adeneuers' wines have been growing in stature. With the exception of the two Auslese, the 1995s were perhaps a touch austere and tannic. The 1996s, if not great, were quite good for the vintage. The 1997s are arguably the best wines the two have ever produced. If this trend continues, the Adeneuers may soon compete in the big leagues.

——— Red wines ———

1996 Spätburgunder
trocken "JJA"
16 DM, 13%, 🍷 till 2000 **84**

1997 Bachemer Karlskopf
Frühburgunder Auslese trocken
33 DM, 13%, 🍷 now **84**

1996 Spätburgunder
Auslese trocken "N°1"
33 DM, 13%, 🍷 now **84**

1996 Bachemer Karlskopf
Frühburgunder trocken
20 DM, 13%, 🍷 till 2000 **86**

1996 Walporzheimer Gärkammer
Spätburgunder Spätlese trocken
23 DM, 12.5%, 🍷 till 2000 **86**

1995 Walporzheimer Gärkammer
Spätburgunder Auslese trocken
32 DM, 13%, 🍷 now **86**

1995 Spätburgunder
Auslese trocken "N°1"
32 DM, 13%, 🍷 till 2000 **86**

1996 Walporzheimer Gärkammer
Spätburgunder Auslese trocken
33 DM, 13%, 🍷 till 2000 **88**

1997 Walporzheimer Gärkammer
Spätburgunder Spätlese trocken
25 DM, 13%, 🍷 till 2002 **89**

1997 Spätburgunder
Auslese trocken "N°1"
33 DM, 13%, 🍷 till 2002 **89**

BROGSITTER'S WEINGÜTER UND PRIVATSEKTKELLEREI

Owner: Hans-Joachim Brogsitter
Manager: Elmar Sermann
Winemaker: Markus Hallerbach
53501 Grafschaft-Gelsdorf, Max-Planck-Straße 1
Tel. (0 22 25) 91 81 11, Fax 91 81 12
e-mail: brogsitters-weingueter@t-online.de
Directions: A 61 Köln–Koblenz, exit Ahrweiler, follow the B 267 to Walporzheim
Sales: Christel Müller and Harald Gerhard
Opening hours: Mon.–Fri. 8 a.m. to 8 p.m., Sat. 9 a.m. to 3 p.m.
Restaurant: "Sanct Peter" with Vinothek, open from 9 a.m. to midnight
Specialties: Sauerkraut soup, homemade smoked meats, venison from the Eifel
History: Once the estate of the cathedral in Cologne

Vineyard area: 30 hectares
Annual production: 120,000 bottles
Top sites: Walporzheimer Alte Lay and Domlay, Ahrweiler Forstberg and Rosenthal, Neuenahrer Sonnenberg and Schieferlay
Soil types: Weathered slate, loess and loam
Grape varieties: 63% Spätburgunder, 18% Portugieser, 8% Frühburgunder, 6% Dornfelder, 5% Riesling
Average yield: 58 hl/ha
Best vintages: 1994, 1996, 1997

In recent years the Brogsitter estate has expanded its cask cellar and invested in its vineyards. The progress is noticeable with the 1996 and 1997 wines, which are more successful than the rather simple 1995s. Documents from A.D. 600 first make mention of an estate called "St. Peter" that belonged to the Frankish kings and later became part of the Benedictine monastery at Prüm in the Eifel. In 1246 the estate was given to the trust fund serving the Cologne Cathedral. From then on the estate was considered the "pearl of the cathedral Treasury," for the clergy also enjoyed drinking after Mass the fiery Burgunder wines produced here. After the Second World War the Brogsitter family acquired the estate, which is today the core of a large mail order business. The wines can also be found at the family's "Sanct Peter" restaurant. Although always clean and well made, they are seldom worth their price.

——— Red wines ———

1996 Walporzheimer Alte Lay
Spätburgunder Auslese trocken "Ad Aram"
38 DM, 14%, 🍷 now — **77**

1996 Frühburgunder
trocken "Ad Aram"
30 DM, 13%, 🍷 now — **80**

1996 "Cuvée Ad Aram"
trocken
32 DM, 13%, 🍷 now — **80**

1996 Spätburgunder
trocken "Ad Aram"
34.50 DM, 13.5%, 🍷 till 2000 — **82**

1996 Spätburgunder
trocken "Ad Aram"
37.50 DM, 13%, 🍷 now — **82**

1997 Ahrweiler Silberberg
Frühburgunder Auslese trocken
38 DM, 13%, 🍷 till 2000 — **84**

WEINGUT BURGGARTEN

Owner: Paul Schäfer
Winemaker: Paul Schumacher
53474 Heppingen,
Landskroner Straße 61
Tel. (0 26 41) 2 12 80, Fax 7 92 20
Directions: A 61, exit Bad Neuenahr-Ahrweiler, towards Heppingen
Sales: Paul-Josef and Gitta Schäfer
Opening hours: Mon.–Fri. 8 a.m. to 6 p.m., Sat. and Sun. 10 a.m. to 1 p.m.
Restaurant: Open from Easter to Pentecost and in Sept. and Oct., 5 p.m. to 10 p.m., except Mon.

Vineyard area: 15 hectares
Annual production: 60,000 bottles
Top sites: Neuenahrer Sonnenberg, Ahrweiler Ursulinengarten, Heppinger Burggarten
Soil types: Loess, loam, gravel and volcanic stone
Grape varieties: 60% Spätburgunder, 12% Domina, 10% each of Portugieser and Dornfelder, 5% Frühburgunder, 3% Riesling
Average yield: 55 hl/ha
Best vintages: 1993, 1995, 1997

Paul Schäfer used to deliver his grapes to the local cooperative. In 1989 he began vinifying a proportion of his own harvest in the facilities of the former wine growers' association in Heppingen. By 1995 he had already achieved major successes in regional wine competitions. Spurred on by these prizes, Paul Schäfer is keen to maintain the level of quality at his winery. From the 1995 vintage it was a rosé that appealed to us the most. Although Schäfer presented a perfectly respectable collection of wines from the difficult 1996 vintage, they seemed less successful. Due to improvements in the cellar, the 1997s have more weight and stature than anything that he has produced to date. Only a handful of estates on the Ahr did a better job with this excellent vintage. Even his liter bottlings are appealing.

Red wines

1997 Neuenahrer Sonnenberg
Frühburgunder trocken
18 DM, 13%, 🍷 now **82**

1997 Heppinger Burggarten
Spätburgunder trocken
13.50 DM/1.0 liter, 12.5%, 🍷 now **82**

1997 Heppinger Burggarten
Spätburgunder trocken
20 DM, 13%, 🍷 till 2000 **84**

1997 Neuenahrer Sonnenberg
Dornfelder trocken
18 DM, 12%, 🍷 till 2000 **84**

1997 Ahrweiler Ursulinengarten
Spätburgunder Auslese trocken
26 DM, 13.5%, 🍷 till 2000 **84**

1995 Neuenahrer Sonnenberg
Spätburgunder Auslese trocken
26 DM, 12.5%, 🍷 till 2000 **84**

1997 Spätburgunder
trocken "Signatur"
17 DM, 12.5%, 🍷 till 2000 **84**

1997 Neuenahrer Sonnenberg
Spätburgunder Auslese trocken
28 DM, 13.5%, 🍷 till 2000 **86**

WEINGUT DEUTZERHOF – COSSMANN-HEHLE

Owner: Hella and Wolfgang Hehle
Winemaker: Wolfgang Hehle
53508 Mayschoß
Tel. (0 26 43) 72 64, Fax 32 32
Directions: A 61 Köln–Koblenz, exit Altenahr
Sales: Hella and Wolfgang Hehle
Opening hours: By appointment
History: Owned by the family for over 400 years

Vineyard area: 7.5 hectares
Annual production: 50,000 bottles
Top sites: No vineyard designations, with the exception of top Rieslings from Altenahrer Eck
Soil types: Weathered slate with loess
Grape varieties: 62% Spätburgunder, 15% Riesling, 13% Dornfelder, 6% Portugieser, 2% each of Frühburgunder and Chardonnay
Average yield: 58 hl/ha
Best vintages: 1995, 1996, 1997
Member: VDP, Deutsches Barrique Forum

Under the direction of Wolfgang Hehle, who married into the family, this old estate has achieved nationwide recognition in the last three years. The 1994 vintage was very good; and although they appear to be maturing quickly, this ambitious estate made an even greater effort with the 1995s. The finest 1996s reach the same high level of quality. The 1997s are the finest wines he has ever made. The formula seems a simple one, though nowhere else is it so scrupulously pursued as here. In the choicest vineyards the pruning is severe and there are multiple pickings during the harvest to insure maximum maturity. In addition Hehle vinifies part of the crop in open fermenters; and his use of wood is more successful every year. In terms of style his Spätburgunders are somewhat more powerful and perhaps less delicate than those of his colleague Werner Näkel, but in terms of sheer quality they leave nothing to be desired.

——— Red wines ———

1996 Spätburgunder
trocken "Caspar C"
29 DM, 13%, 🍷 till 2000 **88**

1996 Altenahrer Eck
Spätburgunder Auslese trocken
65 DM, 13%, 🍷 till 2002 **89**

1997 Spätburgunder
trocken "Caspar C"
30 DM, 12,5%, 🍷 till 2002 **89**

1995 Spätburgunder
Auslese trocken "Grand Duc Select"
48 DM, 13%, 🍷 till 2000 **89**

1995 Spätburgunder
Auslese trocken
"Grand Duc Select Goldkapsel"
138 DM, 13%, 🍷 till 2002 **90**

1997 Altenahrer Eck
Spätburgunder Auslese trocken
65 DM, 13%, 🍷 till 2002 **90**

1996 Spätburgunder
Auslese trocken "Grand Duc Select"
48 DM, 13%, 🍷 till 2002 **90**

1997 Spätburgunder
Auslese trocken "Grand Duc Select"
48 DM, 13%, 🍷 till 2003 **92**

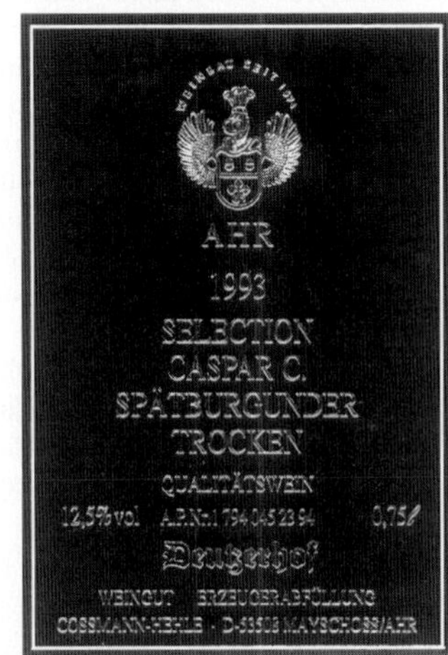

WEINGUT KREUZBERG

Owner: Ludwig Kreuzberg
Winemaker: Hermann-Josef Kreuzberg
53507 Dernau, Benedikt-Schmittmann-Straße 30
Tel. (0 26 43) 16 91, Fax 32 06
Directions: A 61 Köln–Koblenz, exit Bad Neuenahr-Altenahr, five kilometers towards Altenahr
Sales: Thomas Kreuzberg
Opening hours: Mon.–Fri. 8 a.m. to 6 p.m., in summertime to 9 p.m. Sat. and Sun. 10 a.m. to 3 p.m.
Restaurant: At the estate
Open May to Oct. from 3 p.m. to 11 p.m., except Mon. and Tue.

Vineyard area: 8 hectares
Annual production: 50,000 bottles
Top sites: Neuenahrer Schieferlay and Sonnenberg, Dernauer Pfarrwingert
Soil types: Slate and weathered grey slate, partly with loess and loam
Grape varieties: 72% Spätburgunder, 10% Portugieser, 7% Frühburgunder, 6% Dornfelder, 4% Riesling, 1% other varieties
Average yield: 64 hl/ha
Best vintages: 1993, 1996, 1997

This family estate of almost eight hectares has developed into one of the most esteemed properties of the Ahr valley. The credit for this must certainly go to winemaker Hermann-Josef Kreuzberg, whose 31-year-old brother Ludwig now manages the estate. As in the past, this estate continues to cultivate a somewhat old-fashioned style, which can sometimes entail a rather robust acidity; some wines would certainly benefit from a greater use of new oak. While other estates have long given up on the traditional classification of German wines, Kreuzberg in 1995, 1996 and 1997 released a number of excellent dry Auslese. Despite their conventionality, they solidify the estate's reputation for quality. However, we see a greater future in the more well balanced, slightly wooded style of Pinot that they market as "Devon."

Red wines

1997 Neuenahrer Schieferlay
Spätburgunder Auslese trocken
34 DM, 13.5%, ♀ till 2001 **88**

1996 Dernauer Pfarrwingert
Spätburgunder Auslese trocken
33 DM, 13%, ♀ till 2002 **88**

1997 Spätburgunder
trocken "Devon"
29 DM, 13%, ♀ till 2001 **88**

1996 Dernauer Pfarrwingert
Spätburgunder Auslese trocken
33 DM, 13%, ♀ till 2003 **89**

1997 Dernauer Pfarrwingert
Spätburgunder Auslese trocken
39 DM, 13.5%, ♀ till 2002 **89**

1997 Neuenahrer Sonnenberg
Frühburgunder Auslese trocken
32 DM, 14%, ♀ till 2001 **89**

1995 Dernauer Pfarrwingert
Spätburgunder Auslese trocken
30 DM, 13%, ♀ till 2000 **89**

1997 Spätburgunder
trocken "Devon" Goldkapsel
42 DM, 13.5%, ♀ till 2003 **89**

WINZERGENOSSENSCHAFT MAYSCHOSS-ALTENAHR

Manager: Rudolf Mies
Winemaker: Rolf Münster
53508 Mayschoß, Ahrrotweinstraße 42
Tel. (0 26 43) 9 36 00, Fax 93 60 93
Directions: A 61 Köln–Koblenz, exit Bad Neuenahr, towards Altenahr
Sales: Rudolf Stodden
Opening hours: Mon.–Fri. 8 a.m. to 6:30 p.m., Sat.–Sun. 9 a.m. to 7 p.m.
History: Oldest cooperative in Germany
Worth seeing: Old cask cellars, wine museum

Vineyard area: 112 hectares
Number of members: 280
Annual production: 1 million bottles
Top sites: Mayschosser Mönchberg, Burgberg and Laacherberg, Altenahrer Eck, Ahrweiler Daubhaus, Neuenahrer Sonnenberg
Soil types: Weathered slate, partly with loess and loam
Grape varieties: 47% Spätburgunder, 28% Riesling, 11% Müller-Thurgau, 9% Portugieser, 5% other varieties
Average yield: 70 hl/ha
Best vintages: 1995, 1996, 1997

In 1868 dire economic necessity persuaded 18 winegrowers on the Ahr to band together and found the first German wine cooperative, the "Mayschoss Growers' Association." Today it comprises 280 members, who plant 112 hectares along the Ahr. Above all it's their Rieslings that show style and polish. Their red wines, on the other hand, are more often artisanal in style. Nonetheless their more scrupulous selections show that they can do a good job with Spätburgunder. At present no other Ahr cooperative can hold a candle to the performance of the Mayschoss Growers' Association. Indeed, only a few of the private estates can match their quality.

1997 Altenahrer Eck
Riesling Eiswein
98 DM/0.375 liter, 9.5%, 🍷 till 2002 **84**

1996 Mayschosser Laacherberg
Riesling Eiswein
98 DM/0.375 liter, 11.5%, 🍷 till 2006 **88**

——— Red wines ———

1997 Spätburgunder
trocken
11.50 DM, 12.5%, 🍷 now **80**

1997
trocken
15 DM, 12%, 🍷 now **82**

1997 Spätburgunder
trocken "Klassiker"
15.50 DM, 12.5%, 🍷 now **82**

1997 Spätburgunder
halbtrocken "12 Trauben"
25 DM, 12%, 🍷 now **82**

1995 Spätburgunder
trocken "Edition Ponsard 6"
27.50 DM, 12%, 🍷 till 2000 **84**

1997 Spätburgunder
trocken "12 Trauben"
25 DM, 13%, 🍷 till 2000 **84**

1997 Spätburgunder
trocken "Edition Ponsard"
25 DM, 13%, 🍷 till 2000 **84**

1997 Bad Neuenahrer Sonnenberg
Spätburgunder Auslese trocken
30 DM, 13%, 🍷 till 2001 **86**

WEINGUT MEYER-NÄKEL

Owner: Werner Näkel
53507 Dernau, Hardtbergstraße 20
Tel. (0 26 43) 16 28, Fax 33 63
Directions: A 61 Köln–Koblenz, exit Bad Neuenahr, towards Altenahr
Sales: Werner Näkel
Opening hours: By appointment

Vineyard area: 10 hectares
Annual production: 70,000 bottles
Top sites: Dernauer Pfarrwingert, Bad Neuenahrer Sonnenberg, Ahrweiler Riegelfeld and Ursulinengarten
Soil types: Weathered slate, partly with loess and loam
Grape varieties: 73% Spätburgunder, 12% Frühburgunder, 10% Dornfelder, 5% Riesling
Average yield: 48 hl/ha
Best vintages: 1995, 1996, 1997
Member: VDP

Werner Näkel, always relaxed and smiling, has an exemplary understanding of the need to allow his best Spätburgunder to age in oak barrels until at least the autumn following the previous harvest. His 1995 Spätburgunders have remarkable depth of color, as well as a tannic structure that one only rarely encounters on the Ahr. Moreover, our subsequent tastings have shown that these wines are evolving well and have even improved in quality. Näkel's 1996s were, given the difficult vintage, not quite as good as his best 1995s. His finest 1997s, on the other hand, are stunning. Can German red wine be better than this? Näkel also knows how to make very good Spätburgunder rosé, as he has been demonstrating for years with his perfectly balanced "Illusion." He has also made great strides with his Rieslings, as his delicious 1996 ice wine proves.

1996 Riesling
Eiswein
150 DM/0.375 liter, 9%, ♀ till 2010 **95**

Red wines

1996 Spätburgunder
trocken "Blauschiefer"
28 DM, 13%, ♀ till 2000 **87**

1996 Bad Neuenahrer Sonnenberg
Spätburgunder trocken "G"
19 DM, 12.5%, ♀ till 2000 **88**

1997 Dernauer Schieferlay
Frühburgunder trocken
30 DM, 13.5%, ♀ till 2001 **89**

1995 Spätburgunder
trocken Goldkapsel "S"
42 DM, 13.5%, ♀ till 2003 **89**

1995 Spätburgunder
trocken "S"
35 DM, 13%, ♀ till 2003 **89**

1996 Spätburgunder
trocken "S"
42 DM, 13%, ♀ till 2001 **89**

1995 Dernauer Pfarrwingert
Spätburgunder Auslese trocken
38 DM, 13,5%, ♀ till 2002 **90**

1997 Dernauer Pfarrwingert
Frühburgunder Auslese trocken
54 DM, 13%, ♀ till 2002 **90**

1997 Spätburgunder
trocken "S"
42 DM, 13%, ♀ till 2003 **91**

1997 Dernauer Pfarrwingert
Spätburgunder Auslese trocken Goldkapsel
60 DM, 13,5%, ♀ till 2004 **93**

WEINGUT NELLES

Owner: Thomas Nelles
Manager: Andreas Engelmann
53474 Heimersheim,
Göppinger Straße 13
Tel. (0 26 41) 2 43 49, Fax 7 95 86
Directions: A 61 Köln–Koblenz, exit Bad Neuenahr
Sales: Thomas Nelles
Opening hours: Mon.–Fri. 9 a.m. to noon and 2 p.m. to 6 p.m.
Sat. 10 a.m. to noon
Restaurant: Weinhaus Nelles, Tel. (0 26 41) 68 68, open from 11 a.m. to 10 p.m., except Mon.
Specialties: Local fare
History: The family has been making wine for over 400 years

Vineyard area: 5 hectares
Annual production: 35,000 bottles
Top sites: Heimersheimer Landskrone
Soil types: Weathered slate, grey slate, loess and loam
Grape varieties: 43% Spätburgunder, 25% Portugieser, 14% Riesling, 9% Grauburgunder, 6% Domina, 3% Frühburgunder
Average yield: 53 hl/ha
Best vintages: 1994, 1995, 1997
Member: VDP

In their annually published harvest records the Nelles family refer to a tax register of the nearby Castle at Landskrone dating from 1479, in which Peter Nelis is cited as the tenant of a vineyard. This date is displayed today in large letters on each of the estate's labels. In the past few years Thomas Nelles has done everything possible – using traditional methods – to extract the best from his vineyards. Since 1993 quality has improved dramatically. The finest 1995s are top notch. After an at best respectable showing in 1996 he bounced back with a pair of superb 1997s. If this trend continues, Nelles will be on his way to the head of his class. For everyday consumption he also produces three refreshing summer wines. The "Ruber" is a genuine Spätburgunder at a fair price.

Red wines

1997 Spätburgunder
trocken "Ruber"
17 DM, 12.5%, ♀ till 2000 — **84**

1996 Spätburgunder
trocken "B 47"
31 DM, 12%, ♀ now — **84**

1995 Spätburgunder
Auslese trocken
21 DM, 13%, ♀ now — **86**

1996 Spätburgunder
trocken "B 52"
41 DM, 12.5%, ♀ till 2001 — **87**

1995 Spätburgunder
trocken "B 45"
23 DM, 13%, ♀ till 2000 — **88**

1995 Spätburgunder
trocken "Futura"
21 DM/0.5 liter, 12.5%, ♀ till 2000 — **89**

1997 Spätburgunder
trocken "B 48"
33 DM, 13%, ♀ till 2002 — **89**

1995 Spätburgunder
trocken "B 52"
31 DM, 13%, ♀ till 2001 — **90**

1997 Spätburgunder
trocken "B 52"
45 DM, 13%, ♀ till 2003 — **91**

WEINGUT SONNENBERG

Owners: Görres and Linden families
Manager: Manfred Linden
53474 Bad Neuenahr, Heerstraße 98
Tel. (0 26 41) 67 13, Fax 20 10 37
Directions: A 61 Köln–Koblenz, exit Bad Neuenahr
Sales: Manfred and Birgit Linden
Opening hours: Mon.–Fri. 9 a.m. to 6 p.m., Sat. 10 a.m. to 2 p.m. Sun. 10 a.m. to noon
Restaurant: Five weeks a year in the spring and in the fall
Specialties: Homemade meats and cheeses

Vineyard area: 5 hectares
Annual production: 45,000 bottles
Top sites: Neuenahrer Sonnenberg and Schieferlay, Ahrweiler Silberberg
Soil types: Weathered grey slate with loess and loam
Grape varieties: 65% Spätburgunder, 13% Portugieser, 5% Riesling, 4% each of Kerner and Frühburgunder, 9% other varieties
Average yield: 94 hl/ha, only 60 hl/ha for the Burgunders
Best vintages: 1994, 1995, 1997

Since Manfred Linden set out on his own in 1981 in the old Sonnenberg courtyard, he has given up a great deal of his former security to throw himself into the uncertain life of an estate owner. After only five years the former automobile mechanic received a federal gold medal for his quality. Today he sells only a small amount of his wine with the name of the village, has partly relinquished vineyard designations and has even introduced an Ahr Valley country wine as an "honest house wine," as he calls it. The large number of different wines has been reduced to a sensible scale. The 1996 range of wines left us with the impression that the level of quality was improving. The 1997s not only confirm this trend, they are the best wines he has ever produced. If you are looking for a reliable Spätburgunder from the Ahr, you'll be in good hands at this estate.

Red wines

1996 Neuenahrer Schieferlay
Spätburgunder trocken
14.50 DM, 12.5%, ♀ till 2000 **82**

1995 Neuenahrer Sonnenberg
Spätburgunder Spätlese trocken
21 DM, 12%, ♀ now **84**

1997 Neuenahrer Schieferlay
Spätburgunder trocken
15 DM, 13%, ♀ now **84**

1996 Spätburgunder
trocken
24 DM, 13%, ♀ till 2000 **84**

1997 Ahrweiler Ursulinengarten
Frühburgunder Auslese trocken
32 DM, 12.5%, ♀ till 2000 **84**

1997 Neuenahrer Schieferlay
Spätburgunder Spätlese trocken
25 DM, 13%, ♀ till 2000 **86**

1997 Neuenahrer Sonnenberg
Spätburgunder Auslese trocken
35 DM, 14%, ♀ till 2001 **86**

1997 Spätburgunder
trocken "Tradition"
24 DM, 13.5%, ♀ till 2001 **86**

STAATLICHE WEINBAU-DOMÄNE MARIENTHAL

Owner: State of Rheinland-Pfalz
Director: Wolfgang Frisch
Manager: Siegmund Lawnik
Winemakers: Lorenz Jakoby, Roland Sebastian
53507 Marienthal, Klosterstraße 3
Tel. (0 26 41) 9 80 60, Fax 98 06 20
Directions: A 61 Köln–Koblenz, exit Bad Neuenahr-Ahrweiler, towards Altenahr
Opening hours: Mon.–Fri. 8 a.m. to noon and 1 p.m. to 4:30 p.m.
Worth seeing: Ruins of the old cloister and their gardens, old wine cellar in the Augustinian monastery from the 12th century

Vineyard area: 18.5 hectares
Annual production: 100,000 bottles
Top sites: Ahrweiler Rosenthal and Silberberg, Walporzheimer Kräuterberg, Pfaffenberg and Alte Lay, Marienthaler Klostergarten (sole owners)
Soil types: Weathered slate, grey slate, loess with gravel subsoil
Grape varieties: 61% Spätburgunder, 14% Portugieser, 6% Domina, 5% Dornfelder, 3% Frühburgunder, 11% other varieties
Average yield: 61 hl/ha
Best vintages: 1995, 1996, 1997
Member: VDP

The State Domaine, located in the former Augustinian monastery in Marienthal, is one of the largest and best-known estates of the region, lying in a beautiful side valley of the Ahr. After modest wines from three successive vintages, the estate managed to bottle more attactive wines in 1994. The predominately dry red wines were aged in old oaken casks. Cleanly made, they are nonetheless very conservative – sometimes even old fashioned – in style. The 1995s, 1996s and 1997s were poured in the same mold. Always pleasant to drink, they do not begin to develop the great potential of the vineyards. Rumor has it that the estate may soon be privatized.

Red wines

1997 Marienthaler Stiftsberg
Spätburgunder halbtrocken
13 DM, 11.5%, 🍷 now **80**

1996 Marienthaler Klostergarten
Spätburgunder Spätlese trocken
23 DM, 12.5%, 🍷 now **82**

1995 Marienthaler Klostergarten
Spätburgunder Spätlese trocken
21 DM, 11%, 🍷 till 2000 **82**

1996 Spätburgunder
trocken
18 DM, 13%, 🍷 now **82**

1996 Marienthaler Klostergarten
Frühburgunder trocken
38 DM, 13%, 🍷 now **84**

1995 Walporzheimer Kräuterberg
Spätburgunder Spätlese trocken
20 DM, 12.5%, 🍷 now **84**

1996 Walporzheimer Kräuterberg
Spätburgunder Auslese trocken
28 DM, 13%, 🍷 now **84**

1995 Ahrweiler Silberberg
Spätburgunder Auslese trocken
45 DM, 12.5%, 🍷 now **86**

WEINGUT JEAN STODDEN

Owner: Gerhard Stodden
53506 Rech, Rotweinstraße 7–9
Tel. (0 26 43) 30 01, Fax 30 03
Directions: A 61 Köln–Koblenz, exit Bad Neuenahr, towards Altenahr
Sales: Dr. Birgitta Stodden
Opening hours: Mon.–Fri. 9 a.m. to 6 p.m., Sat. 10 a.m. to 5 p.m.
History: The family has been making wine since 1573
Worth seeing: Art gallery in the Vinothek

Vineyard area: 6.5 hectares
Annual production: 45,000 bottles
Top sites: Recher Herrenberg, Neuenahrer Sonnenberg
Soil types: Weathered slate, partly with loess and loam
Grape varieties: 83% Spätburgunder, 8% Riesling, 7% Portugieser, 2% other varieties
Average yield: 47 hl/ha
Best vintages: 1994, 1995, 1997

Out of love for his native land Gerhard Stodden took over his family's wine estate in the upper Ahr valley in 1975. Since then he has been carefully pursuing considered improvements: he shuns insecticides and chemical fertilizers; yields are limited by rigorous pruning and thinning in the summer, all with the aim of producing richer wines. Only indigenous yeasts are used during fermentation; some wines are left unfined, while others are simply clarified with pure egg white. Since 1989 Stodden has been aging his red wines in small wooden barrels and marketing them with the modern label "JS." The 1995 red wines were the best to date. In the more difficult vintage of 1996 he was not able to maintain that standard. Since 1997 he has been aided by an oenologist from Dijon, which we hope will bring a further improvement in quality. In the estate's distillery, founded in 1928, Stodden also produces marc, fine and fruit brandies.

1997 Recher Herrenberg
Riesling Kabinett halbtrocken
17 DM, 13%, ♀ now **80**

1997 Recher Herrenberg
Riesling Auslese trocken
35 DM, 12.5%, ♀ now **82**

——— Red wines ———

1996 Recher Herrenberg
Spätburgunder trocken
16 DM, 13%, ♀ till 2000 **80**

1996 Spätburgunder
trocken "Vis-à-Vis"
25 DM, 12.5%, ♀ till 2000 **80**

1995 Spätburgunder
trocken "Selektion JS"
25 DM, 13%, ♀ till 2000 **82**

1996 Spätburgunder
trocken "J"
25 DM, 13%, ♀ now **82**

1996 Spätburgunder
Auslese trocken "JS"
42 DM, 13%, ♀ till 2000 **84**

1995 Recher Herrenberg
Spätburgunder Auslese trocken
"Selektion JS"
48 DM, 12.5%, ♀ till 2002 **86**

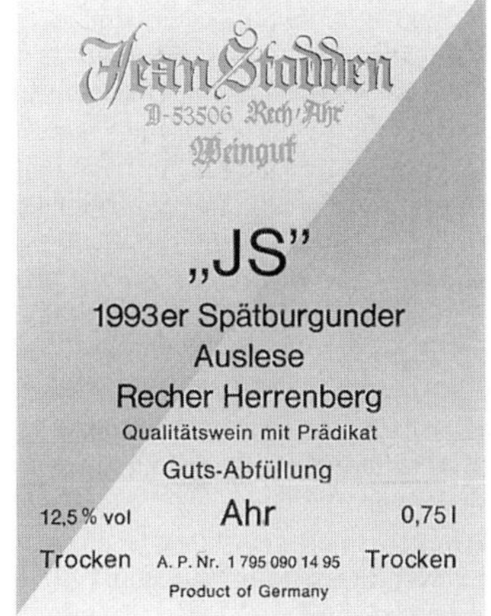

The sun also rises

When wine lovers speak of Baden, they generally mean the Kaiserstuhl. And there are a number of very good reasons for this: the Kaiserstuhl is the warmest growing zone within Germany and its climate imbues the wines with an enormous depth and warmth of fruit. This is reflected in the advertising slogan of Baden's growers: "Drenched in sunshine."

It would be foolish, though, to speak of Baden as a unified region. The almost 16,000 hectares of vines are divided among eight districts, stretching from Franken to Lake Constance; and there are considerable differences with regard to microclimate, soil properties and slope inclination which mold the diverse and hardly comparable wine styles of each region. Whereas Silvaner from the Tauber valley is easily confused – not only because of the bottle – with a wine from Franken, a Riesling from the Ortenau, which occupies barely eight percent of Baden's vineyards, resembles a Riesling from the Pfalz. Whereas the Burgundian varieties planted in the Kaiserstuhl definitely taste Alsatian in style, the Gutedel from the neighboring Markgräflerland, which accounts for some ten percent of the total vineyard area, expresses itself with an audibly Swiss accent.

Some 120 cooperatives – 12,430 hectares owned by 30,000 adherents – account for 80 percent of Baden's wine production. 400 other wineries crush the rest. For decades the *Genossenschaft*, as the cooperatives are called in German, were drowning in Müller-Thurgau, but over the past ten years they have made considerable progress, both in terms of marketing and quality. Their self-confidence has increased enormously, and the prices they demand for special ranges of wines are creeping ever closer to those of noted private producers. Yet apart from the custom-packed prestige wines, the overall quality offered by the cooperatives remains modest.

After two rather ordinary years, nature delivered Baden with 1996 and 1997 two excellent vintages. 1998 also looks promising. But in fact, Baden has not been as sun drenched of late as the famous slogan would have us believe. Great vintages, like 1988, 1989, and 1990, were followed, save for 1993, by a string of mediocre crushes. "At least as far as the red wines are concerned," says Bernhard Huber with conviction, "1996 is the best vintage since 1990." The white wines, too, were both powerful and stylish. Karl Heinz Johner speaks of "aromas of grapefruit" as being the characteristic signature of the 1996 whites, which indeed have a backbone of robust acidity. His 1997s are more luscious and supple, but almost as fine in terms of sheer quality.

After the excesses of the 1980s, the growers have reduced their yields to an average of about 90 hectoliters per hectare in the 1990s. In 1996 climatic conditions limited them to only 70 hectoliters, in 1997 to only 60. These two small crops have many growers worried that they will not be able to satisfy demand and thus lose a part of their traditional clientele. In fact, some of the most sought-after estates harvested scarcely 40 hectoliters per hectare, so that many of their wines were already sold out before they were bottled.

The finest producers brought in only a fraction of Baden's total crop in 1996, but over 80 percent of their production was harvested with the Prädikats Kabinett, Spätlese and Auslese, which was way above the average. It's from these grapes, mainly in the Ortenau and the Kaiserstuhl, that the finest wines of the vintage were produced. The 1996 Grauburgunder Spätlese "SE" from Bercher and Grauburgunder Spätlese*** from Dr. Heger were two of the most outstanding dry white wines from Burgundian varieties in the whole of Germany in that vintage.

1997, on the other hand, brought a plethora of very rich wines that often lacked the acidic structure to carry their weight. Palate-numbing Auslesen with 15 percent alcohol were not uncommon, but the two best wines were again from Bercher and Heger, who continue to make the finest wines from the Kaiserstuhl. Less successful this year were the Rieslings from the Ortenau, in particular those of Andreas Laible. After several stunning vintages, he remained on the sidelines as Schloß Ortenberg and Schloß Neuweier showed what they were capable of doing with that variety in a difficult year.

All producers have high hopes for their 1996 red wines, most of which are only just now beginning to unfold. The 1997s, too, are already being highly touted. Barrel samples of the later vintage confirm this optimism. 1998 also looks promising. Karl Heinz Johner's 1996 Pinot Noir "SJ" was the most ethereal red wine of that vintage, but Bercher and Heger also produced excellent Spätburgunder. However, it is the oak-aged 1995 reds that are now on the market and, despite yields of barely 60 hectoliters per hectare, Mother Nature hardly gave winemakers the quality to produce excellent red wines in that vintage. Rampant rot squelched all hopes for what might have been a great year. Few wines can compare with the best from the Ahr or Württemberg. However, Seeger with his 1995 Spätburgunder "S" has shown once again that he knows how to make fine red wines. And Bernhard Huber's Spätburgunder Reserve – which also made a splash in a blind tasting of first-class Burgundy organized by the "Grand Jury Européen" – put all other 1995s in the shade!

Dr. Heger continues reigning supreme among the top estates in Baden. Each of his 1996s, from the Kabinett to the Trockenbeerenauslese, was a masterpiece. His 1997s are of similar caliber. This is a label that you can literally buy blind! Just behind in quality is the Bercher estate and, although his past two years' performances have been a bit erratic, Karl Heinz Johner. Close behind is Wolf-Dietrich Salwey, who always produces highly individualistic wines. Bernhard Huber, who is gradually obtaining more elegance in his rich oaky wines, has also moved to the top of the class; and the wines of Reinhold Schneider from Endingen have also dramatically improved in the past three vintages.

The leading estates of Baden

Weingut Dr. Heger, Ihringen

Weingut Bercher, Vogtsburg-Burkheim

Weingut Bernhard Huber, Malterdingen

Weingut Karl H. Johner, Bischoffingen

Weingut Andreas Laible, Durbach

Weingut Salwey, Oberrotweil

Weingut Abril, Bischoffingen

Weingut Schloß Neuweier, Baden-Baden

Weingut Schloß Ortenberg, Ortenberg

Weingut Reinhold und Cornelia Schneider, Endingen

Weingut Seeger, Leimen

Winzergenossenschaft Achkarren, Vogtsburg-Achkarren

Weingut Bercher-Schmidt, Oberrotweil

Weingut Blankenhorn, Schliengen

Weingut Hermann Dörflinger, Müllheim

Durbacher Winzergenossenschaft, Durbach

Weingut Freiherr von und zu Franckenstein, Offenburg

Weingut Freiherr von Gleichenstein, Oberrotweil

Weingut Thomas Hagenbucher, Sulzfeld

Joachim Heger, Ihringen

Weingut Ernst Heinemann & Sohn, Ehrenkirchen-Scherzingen

Weingut Albert Heitlinger, Östringen-Tiefenbach

Weingut Reichsgraf und Marquis zu Hoensbroech, Angelbachtal-Michelfeld

Schloßgut Istein, Istein

Weingut Kalkbödele, Merdingen

Franz Keller Erzeugergemeinschaft Schwarzer Adler, Oberbergen

Winzergenossenschaft Königschaffhausen, Königschaffhausen

Weingut Konstanzer, Ihringen

Weingut Lämmlin-Schindler, Mauchen

Weingut Heinrich Männle, Durbach

Weingut Michel, Achkarren

Weingut Gebrüder Müller, Breisach

Weingut Hartmut Schlumberger, Laufen

Weingut Stigler, Ihringen

Gräflich Wolff Metternich'sches Weingut, Durbach

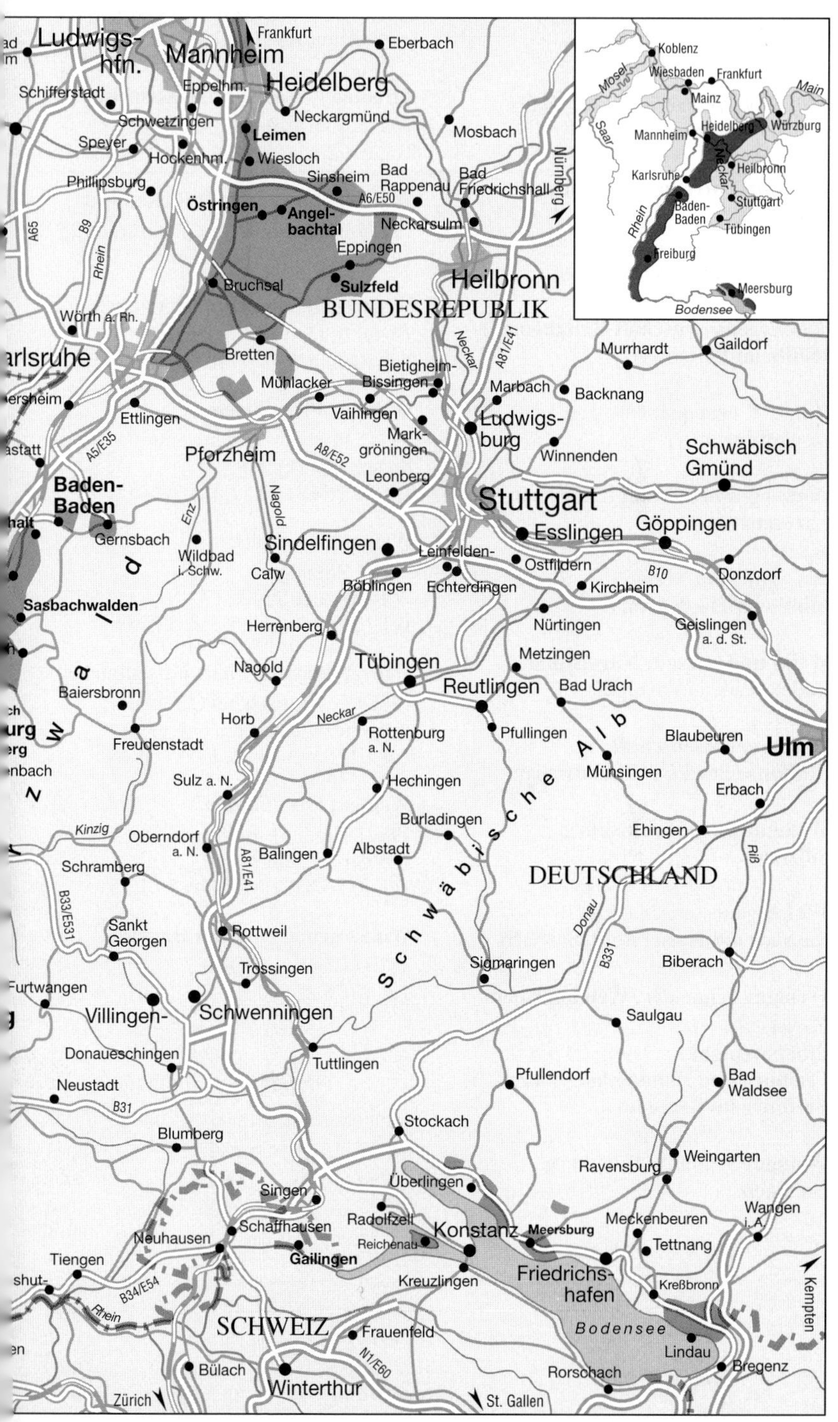
Ludwigs-hfn.
Mannheim
Heidelberg
Frankfurt
Eberbach
Schifferstadt
Eppelhm.
Neckargmünd
Schwetzingen
Leimen
Mosbach
Speyer
Hockenhm.
Wiesloch
Phillipsburg
Sinsheim
Bad Rappenau
Bad Friedrichshall
Nürnberg
A6/E50
Östringen
Angelbachtal
Neckarsulm
A65
B9
Rhein
Eppingen
Bruchsal
Sulzfeld
Heilbronn
BUNDESREPUBLIK
Wörth a. Rh.
Neckar
A81/E41
Murrhardt
Gaildorf
Karlsruhe
Bretten
Bietigheim-Bissingen
Mühlacker
Marbach
Backnang
Ettlingen
Vaihingen
Ludwigsburg
Markgröningen
A5/E35
A8/E52
Pforzheim
Winnenden
Schwäbisch Gmünd
Baden-Baden
Leonberg
Stuttgart
Nagold
Enz
Gernsbach
Esslingen
Göppingen
Sindelfingen
Wildbad i. Schw.
Leinfelden-Echterdingen
Ostfildern
Calw
B10
Donzdorf
Böblingen
Kirchheim
Sasbachwalden
Herrenberg
Nürtingen
Geislingen a. d. St.
Metzingen
Nagold
Tübingen
Reutlingen
Bad Urach
Baiersbronn
Neckar
Horb
Rottenburg a. N.
Pfullingen
Blaubeuren
Ulm
Freudenstadt
Münsingen
Sulz a. N.
Hechingen
Erbach
Burladingen
Ehingen
Kinzig
Oberndorf a. N.
Albstadt
Balingen
Riß
Schramberg
A81/E41
DEUTSCHLAND
B33/E531
Sankt Georgen
Rottweil
Donau
Schwäbische Alb
Schwarzwald
Sigmaringen
B331
Biberach
Trossingen
Furtwangen
Villingen-Schwenningen
Saulgau
Donaueschingen
Tuttlingen
Pfullendorf
Neustadt
B31
Bad Waldsee
Stockach
Blumberg
Weingarten
Ravensburg
Überlingen
Singen
Wangen i. A.
Radolfzell
Meckenbeuren
Schaffhausen
Konstanz
Meersburg
Neuhausen
Reichenau
Tettnang
Gailingen
Tiengen
Friedrichshafen
Kreuzlingen
Kreßbronn
Kempten
B34/E54
Rhein
SCHWEIZ
Frauenfeld
Bodensee
Lindau
N1/E60
Bülach
Winterthur
Rorschach
Bregenz
Zürich
St. Gallen
Koblenz
Mosel
Wiesbaden
Frankfurt
Main
Mainz
Saar
Mannheim
Heidelberg
Würzburg
Karlsruhe
Neckar
Heilbronn
Baden-Baden
Stuttgart
Rhein
Tübingen
Freiburg
Meersburg
Bodensee

Alde Gott Winzergenossenschaft, Sasbachwalden

Weingut Aufricht, Meersburg

Winzergenossenschaft Bischoffingen, Bischoffingen

Winzergenossenschaft Britzingen, Müllheim-Britzingen

Hofgut Consequence, Bischoffingen

Winzergenossenschaft Ehrenstetten, Ehrenstetten

Weingut Emil Marget, Müllheim-Hügelheim

Wein- und Sektgut Nägelsförst, Baden-Baden (Varnhalt)

Winzergenossenschaft Pfaffenweiler EG, Pfaffenweiler

Weingut Burg Ravensburg, Sulzfeld

Winzergenossenschaft Sasbach am Kaiserstuhl, Sasbach

Weingut Schneider, Weil am Rhein

Staatsweingut Freiburg und Blankenhornsberg, Freiburg im Breisgau

Weingut Schloß Staufenberg, Durbach

🍇🍇🍇🍇🍇 : Outstanding
🍇🍇🍇🍇 : Excellent
🍇🍇🍇 : Good
🍇🍇 : Average
🍇 : Poor

Other notable producers

Affentaler Winzergenossenschaft
77815 Bühl-Eisental, An der B 3
Tel. (0 72 23) 98 98-0, Fax 98 98 30

Winzergenossenschaft Bickensohl
79235 Bickensohl, Neulindenstraße 25
Tel. (0 76 62) 93 11-0, Fax 93 11 50

Winzergenossenschaft Bötzingen
79268 Bötzingen, Hauptstraße 13
Tel. (0 76 63) 93 06-0, Fax 93 06 50

Weingut Peter Briem
79241 Ihringen-Wasenweiler, Kaiserstuhlweg 10
Tel. (0 76 68) 52 57, Fax 9 44 06

Weingut Brodbeck
79268 Bötzingen, Wasenweiler Straße 17–19
Tel. (0 76 63) 65 65, Fax 5 00 05

Winzergenossenschaft Fessenbach
77654 Fessenbach bei Offenburg, Am Winzerkeller 2
Tel. (07 81) 3 20 06, Fax 3 62 78

Weingut Otto Fischer
79331 Nimburg-Bottingen, Auf der Ziegelbreite 4
Tel. (0 76 63) 17 47, Fax 5 01 75

Winzergenossenschaft Hagnau
88709 Hagnau, Im Hof 3
Tel. (0 75 32) 10 30, Fax 13 41

Vintage chart for Baden

vintage	quality	drink
1997	🍇🍇🍇🍇	till 2001
1996	🍇🍇🍇🍇	till 2002
1995	🍇🍇🍇	now
1994	🍇🍇🍇	now
1993	🍇🍇🍇🍇	now
1992	🍇🍇🍇	now
1991	🍇🍇	now
1990	🍇🍇🍇🍇	now
1989	🍇🍇🍇🍇	now
1988	🍇🍇🍇🍇	now

Weingut Helde & Sohn
79361 Jechtingen, Emil-Gütt-Straße 1
Tel. (0 76 62) 61 16, Fax 61 60

Weingut Hügle
79341 Kenzingen-Bombach,
Kirchberghof
Tel. (0 76 44) 12 61, Fax 40 54

Weingut Bernd Hummel
69254 Malsch, Oberer Mühlweg 5
Tel. (0 72 53) 2 71 48, Fax 2 57 99

Winzergenossenschaft Jechtingen
79361 Jechtingen, Winzerstraße 1
Tel. (0 76 62) 93 23-0, Fax 82 41

Winzergenossenschaft Kappelrodeck
77876 Kappelrodeck,
Waldulmer Straße 41
Tel. (0 78 42) 3 00 63, Fax 87 63

Winzergenossenschaft Kiechlinsbergen
79346 Endingen, Herrenstraße 35
Tel (0 76 42) 90 41-0, Fax 90 41 41

Kellerei Friedrich Kiefer
79356 Eichstetten, Bötzinger Straße 13
Tel. (0 76 63) 10 63, Fax 39 27

Weingut Klumpp
76646 Bruchsal,
Heidelberger Straße 100
Tel. (0 72 51) 1 67 19, Fax 1 05 23

Weingut Knab
79346 Endingen, Hennengärtle 1
Tel. (0 76 42) 61 55, Fax 61 55

Weingut Landmann
79112 Freiburg-Waltershofen
Umkircher Straße 29
Tel. (0 76 65) 67 56, Fax 5 19 45

Winzergenossenschaft Laufen
79295 Sulzburg, Weinstraße 48
Tel. (0 76 34) 56 05-0, Fax 56 05 20

Weingut Andreas Männle
77770 Durbach, Heimbach 12
Tel. (07 81) 4 14 86, Fax 4 29 81

Weingut Marget
79423 Heitersheim, Hauptstraße 43
Tel. (0 76 34) 22 54, Fax 3 56 58

Bezirkskellerei Markgräflerland
79588 Efringen-Kirchen, Winzerstraße 2
Tel. (0 67 28) 91 14-0, Fax 29 26

Winzergenossenschaft Neuweier-Bühlertal
76534 Baden-Baden, Mauerbergstraße 32
Tel. (0 72 23) 96 87-0, Fax 5 20 74

Weingut Reiner Probst
79235 Achkarren, Castellbergstraße 21
Tel. (0 76 62) 3 29, Fax 2 29

Schloß Rheinburg
78262 Gailingen, Büsinger Straße
Tel. (0 77 34) 60 66, Fax 21 18

Weingut Freiherr Roeder von Diersburg
77749 Diersburg, Kreisstraße 20
Tel. (0 78 08) 22 21, Fax 22 26

Weingut Gregor und Thomas Schätzle
79235 Schelingen,
Heinrich-Kling-Straße 38
Tel. (0 76 62) 94 61-0, Fax 94 61 20

Weingut Dr. Schneider
79379 Müllheim-Zunzingen,
Rosenbergstraße 10
Tel. (0 76 31) 29 15, Fax 1 53 99

Tauberfränkische Winzergenossenschaft Beckstein
☞ *See below, page 115*

Weingut Wilhelm Zähringer
79423 Heitersheim, Hauptstraße 42
Tel. (0 76 34) 10 25, Fax 10 27

Weingut Julius Zotz
79423 Heitersheim, Staufener Straße 1
Tel. (0 76 34) 10 59, Fax 47 58

WEINGUT ABRIL

Owner: Hans-Friedrich Abril
79235 Bischoffingen, Talstraße 9
Tel. (0 76 62) 2 55, Fax 60 76
Directions: A 5 Frankfurt–Basel, exit Riegel, towards the Rhine
Opening hours: Mon.–Fri. 8 a.m. to noon and 2 p.m. to 6 p.m.
Sat. by appointment
History: Has been making wine for eight generations
Worth seeing: Traditional house from 1803, collection of corkscrews

Vineyard area: 6.6 hectares
Annual production: 40,000 bottles
Top sites: Bischoffinger Enselberg, Bischoffinger Steinbuck
Soil types: Stony weathered volcanic soil with loess and loam
Grape varieties: 30% each of Spätburgunder and Grauburgunder, 15% Müller-Thurgau, 9% Silvaner, 6% Riesling, 5% Weißburgunder, 5% other varieties
Average yield: 55 hl/ha
Best vintages: 1995, 1996, 1997

Many of Hans-Friedrich Abril's best wines are grown in the heart of the Enselberg vineyard, where he owns almost a hectare of land. Traditionally the red wines were the highlight of each vintage; in the past few years the white wines have gained in stature, due to a number of measures he has undertaken: he introduced whole-cluster pressing, ferments the must using temperature control and allows the malolactic fermentation to remove rough edges from the wines. This had a particularly positive effect on the 1996s, which were naturally higher in acidity than the 1995s. Nonetheless the alcoholic level of some of the wines is unsettling. In spite of his efforts, Auslese with 15 percent make a somewhat rustic impression, for they lack elegance and harmony. The 1997s are much more refreshing, but should be consumed before the 1996s.

1997 Schelinger Kirchberg
Grauer Burgunder Kabinett trocken
10 DM, 13%, 🍷 now **84**

1997 Bischoffinger Enselberg
Weißer Burgunder Spätlese trocken
16 DM, 13.5%, 🍷 till 2000 **86**

1997 Bischoffinger Steinbuck
Grauer Burgunder Spätlese trocken
16 DM, 13.5%, 🍷 till 2000 **86**

1996 Bischoffinger Rosenkranz
Silvaner Spätlese trocken
14 DM, 12%, 🍷 till 2000 **86**

1996 Bischoffinger Enselberg
Riesling Spätlese trocken
13.50 DM, 12.5%, 🍷 till 2000 **86**

1997 Bischoffinger Enselberg
Chardonnay Auslese trocken
31.50 DM, 15%, 🍷 till 2002 **86**

1996 Bischoffinger Steinbuck
Grauer Burgunder Spätlese trocken
14.50 DM, 13%, 🍷 till 2000 **88**

Red wines

1996 Bischoffinger Enselberg
Spätburgunder Auslese trocken
38 DM, 15%, 🍷 till 2003 **86**

1995 Bischoffinger Enselberg
Spätburgunder Auslese trocken
36 DM, 13.5%, 🍷 till 2005 **88**

WINZERGENOSSENSCHAFT ACHKARREN

Manager: Waldemar Isele
Winemaker: Anton Kiefer
79235 Achkarren, Schloßbergstraße 2
Tel. (0 76 62) 9 30 40, Fax 82 07
Directions: A 5, exit Bad Krozingen or Riegel, towards Breisach
Sales: Florian Graner
Opening hours: Mon.–Fri. 8 a.m. to 12:30 p.m. and 1:30 p.m. to 5:30 p.m. Sat. 9 a.m. to 1 p.m., or by appointment with Ms. Kind
History: The cooperative was founded in 1929
Worth seeing: Kaiserstühler Wine Museum

Vineyard area: 155 hectares
Number of adherents: 320
Annual production: 1.7 million bottles
Top sites: Achkarrer Schloßberg and Castellberg
Soil types: Weathered volcanic soils as well as loess and loam
Grape varieties: 40% Grauburgunder, 22% Spätburgunder, 21% Müller-Thurgau, 7% Weißburgunder, 6% Silvaner, 4% other varieties
Average yield: 70 hl/ha
Best vintages: 1995, 1996, 1997

Achkarren belongs to the elite villages of the Kaiserstuhl; and the cooperative has traditionally been the leading producer there. A few estates from neighboring villages sell wines from sites in Achkarren, but almost no one from the village itself has managed to market their own wines with any success. The cooperative's wines from the difficult 1994 vintage indicated that the growers from Achkarren had set their sights somewhat higher. This trend continued with the 1995 vintage; and although the 1996s didn't disappoint us, the growers should have been able to extract more from the excellent harvest. The 1997s were marginally better, but in spite of the improved quality of the dessert wines, the full potential of the magnificent vineyards of this cooperative has yet to be tapped.

1996 Achkarrer Schloßberg
Weißer Burgunder Spätlese trocken
"Bestes Faß"
17 DM, 13%, ♀ now **82**

1997 Achkarrer Schloßberg
Grauer Burgunder Spätlese trocken
"Bestes Faß"
17.50 DM, 13.5%, ♀ till 2000 **84**

1996 Achkarrer Schloßberg
Chardonnay Spätlese trocken
"Bestes Faß"
17 DM, 13%, ♀ now **84**

1997 Achkarrer Schloßberg
Weißer Burgunder Spätlese trocken
"Bestes Faß"
21.50 DM, 13.5%, ♀ till 2001 **86**

1996 Achkarrer Schloßberg
Muskateller Eiswein
40 DM/0.375 liter, 8%, ♀ till 2007 **89**

1996 Achkarrer Schloßberg
Scheurebe Eiswein "Bestes Faß"
45 DM/0.375 liter, 9%, ♀ till 2006 **89**

1996 Achkarrer Schloßberg
Ruländer Trockenbeerenauslese
"Bestes Faß"
45 DM/0.375 liter, 10.5%, ♀ till 2005 **89**

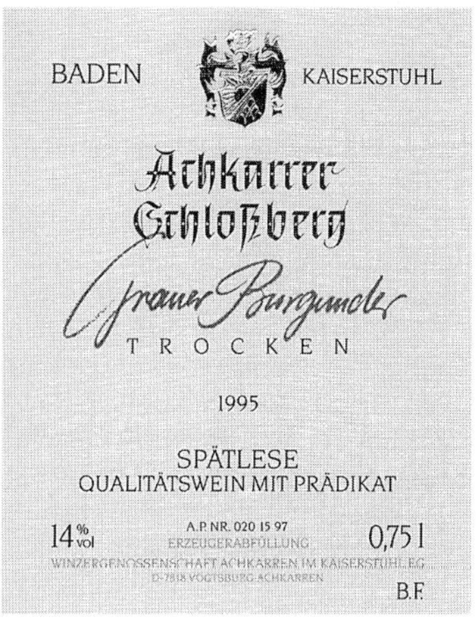

BADEN
KAISERSTUHL
Achkarrer
Schloßberg
Grauer Burgunder
TROCKEN
1995
SPÄTLESE
QUALITÄTSWEIN MIT PRÄDIKAT
14 % vol
A.P. NR. 020 15 97
ERZEUGERABFÜLLUNG
0,75 l
WINZERGENOSSENSCHAFT ACHKARREN IM KAISERSTUHL EG
D-7818 VOGTSBURG-ACHKARREN
B.F.

ALDE GOTT WINZERGENOSSENSCHAFT

Manager: Bruno Spinner
Winemaker: Hermann Bähr
77887 Sasbachwalden, Talstraße 2
Tel. (0 78 41) 2 02 90, Fax 20 29 18
Directions: A 5 Frankfurt–Basel, exit Achern, follow the road signs
Sales: Bruno Spinner and Friederich Wäldele
Opening hours: Mon.–Fri. 7:30 a.m. to noon and 1:30 p.m. to 6 p.m.
Sat. 8:30 a.m. to noon, 8:30 a.m. to 5 p.m. from May to Oct.
Sun. 1 p.m. to 5 p.m. from May to Oct.
History: Founded in 1948

Vineyard area: 230 hectares
Number of adherents: 416
Annual production: 2.2 million bottles
Top site: Sasbachwaldener Alde Gott
Soil types: Rocky weathered granite
Grape varieties: 60% Spätburgunder, 16% Riesling, 14% Müller-Thurgau, 5% Grauburgunder, 5% other varieties
Average yield: 72 hl/ha
Best vintages: 1993, 1996, 1997

The legend goes that the name of "Alde Gott" – Old God – derives from a lonely man's exclamation at the sight of a survivor after the end of the Thirty Years' War: "The Old God lives!" The 1995 white wines from this cooperative, which was founded 50 years ago, left much to be desired; nor were the 1996s much better. Even the red wines, which play an important role here, were a bit heavy and often seem somewhat contrived; but, being soundly crafted, they are clearly superior in quality to the white wines. The 1997s are much better across the board than anything this cooperative has bottled recently. In addition, the change of name from Winzergenossenschaft Sasbachwalden to Alde Gott, the name of their largest single vineyard, should also help the growers with their marketing.

1997 Sasbachwaldener Alde Gott
Riesling Kabinett trocken
10.50 DM, 10.5%, 🍷 now **80**

1996 Sasbachwaldener Alde Gott
Riesling Kabinett trocken
10.50 DM, 10%, 🍷 now **80**

1997 Sasbachwaldener Alde Gott
Grauer Burgunder Spätlese trocken
15.90 DM, 12.5%, 🍷 now **82**

1997 Sasbachwaldener Alde Gott
Riesling Spätlese trocken
13.50 DM, 11.5%, 🍷 till 2000 **82**

1997 Sasbachwaldener Alde Gott
Weißer Burgunder Spätlese trocken
15.90 DM, 13%, 🍷 now **82**

1996 Sasbachwaldener Alde Gott
Grauer Burgunder Spätlese trocken
15 DM, 12.5%, 🍷 now **82**

——— Red wines ———

1996 Sasbachwaldener Alde Gott
Spätburgunder Auslese
29.90 DM, 12%, 🍷 now **77**

1997 Sasbachwaldener Alde Gott
Spätburgunder Spätlese trocken
15.90 DM, 12.5%, 🍷 till 2000 **82**

1996 Sasbachwaldener Alde Gott
Spätburgunder Spätlese trocken
15 DM, 13%, 🍷 till 2000 **82**

BADEN

1996er Sasbachwaldener
Alde Gott
Spätburgunder Rotwein
Qualitätswein · trocken
0,75 l A. P. Nr. 046.26.97 *12,5 % vol*
Erzeugerabfüllung Alde Gott Winzergenossenschaft eG
D-77887 Sasbachwalden/Baden

WEINGUT AUFRICHT

Owners: Robert and Manfred Aufricht
Winemaker: Herbert Senft
88709 Meersburg am Bodenseee
Tel. (0 75 32) 61 23 and 24 27, Fax 24 21
Directions: B 31, between Meersburg and Hagnau
Sales: Aufricht family
Opening hours: Mon.–Fri. 8 a.m. to 6:30 p.m., Sat. and Sun. 10 a.m. to 4 p.m.

Vineyard area: 12.5 hectares
Annual production: 90,000 bottles
Top sites: Meersburger Sängerhalde and Fohrenberg
Soil types: Sandy loam with much limestone
Grape varieties: 40% Spätburgunder, 20% Müller-Thurgau, 15% Grauburgunder, 10% Weißburgunder, 5% Chardonnay, 5% Auxerrois, 5% other varieties
Average yield: 70 hl/ha
Best vintages: 1995, 1996, 1997

Now in the hands of the fifth generation, the heart of this old estate lies in a vast sloping vineyard with southern exposure in a nature reserve on the shores of Lake Constance. The owners' personal preference for dry wines that work well with food means that almost all of them are fermented to complete dryness. The troika of Robert and Manfred Aufricht plus Herbert Senft has done a decent job over the past three years. The white wines are variable in quality, although even the better examples are rather light and marked by a tart acidity. The red wines, albeit somewhat commercial, are considerably more attractive. These wines may not compare with those from the Kaiserstuhl, but no one on Lake Constance is doing a better job.

1997 Meersburger Sängerhalde
Weißer Burgunder trocken "Classic"
15.90 DM, 12.5%, ♀ now **77**

1997 Meersburger Sängerhalde
Auxerrois trocken
15.90 DM, 12%, ♀ now **80**

1997 Meersburger Sängerhalde
Grauer Burgunder trocken
15.90 DM, 12.5%, ♀ now **80**

1996 Meersburger Sängerhalde
Grauer Burgunder trocken
16 DM, 12.5%, ♀ now **80**

1996 Meersburger Sängerhalde
Auxerrois trocken
16 DM, 12%, ♀ now **82**

——— Red wines ———

1997 Meersburger Sängerhalde
Spätburgunder trocken "Classic"
15.90 DM, 12.5%, ♀ now **80**

1996 Meersburger Sängerhalde
Spätburgunder trocken "Classic"
20 DM, 13%, ♀ till 2000 **80**

1996 Meersburger Sängerhalde
Spätburgunder trocken "Sophia"
20 DM, 13%, ♀ till 2000 **80**

1996 Meersburger Sängerhalde
Spätburgunder trocken
25 DM, 13%, ♀ till 2000 **82**

WEINGUT BERCHER

Owners: Eckhardt and Rainer Bercher
79235 Burkheim, Mittelstadt 13
Tel. (0 76 62) 2 12 and 60 66, Fax 82 79
Directions: A 5 Karlsruhe–Basel, exit Riegel, towards Endingen-Vogtsburg
Sales: The two Bercher families
Opening hours: Mon.–Sat. 9 a.m. to 11:30 a.m. and 1 p.m. to 6 p.m. or by appointment
History: The estate has been owned by the family for nine generations

Vineyard area: 21 hectares
Annual production: 140,000 bottles
Top sites: Burkheimer Feuerberg and Schloßgarten, Sasbacher Limburg, Jechtinger Eichert
Soil types: Weathered volcanic soil and loess
Grape varieties: 42% Spätburgunder, 15% Grauburgunder, 14% Weißburgunder, 12% Riesling, 5% each of Müller-Thurgau and Chardonnay, 7% other varieties
Average yield: 50 hl/ha
Best vintages: 1994, 1996, 1997
Member: VDP, Deutsches Barrique Forum

This beautifully situated winery in the heart of Burkheim on the western edge of the Kaiserstuhl can trace its history back to the 16th century. The property has always been consistent in quality and offered reliable wines throughout the range, from simple liter bottlings to exquisite Spätlese. Today the estate is one of Baden's finest producers. After the somewhat disappointing 1995s, the Berchers bounced back with excitingly elegant 1996s and stunningly concentrated 1997s. Although many of these wines will need time before they are ready to drink, potential buyers shouldn't delay. In the spring of 1997 one third of the flowering buds were severely damaged by frost; the wines will now have to be allocated more sparsely than usual to accommodate the demand.

1997 Burkheimer Feuerberg
Grauer Burgunder Spätlese trocken
23 DM, 13.5%, ♀ till 2000 **88**

1996 Burkheimer Feuerberg
Chardonnay Spätlese trocken "SE"
32 DM, 12.5%, ♀ till 2002 **89**

1996 Burkheimer Feuerberg
Grauer Burgunder Spätlese trocken
22 DM, 13%, ♀ till 2002 **90**

1997 Burkheimer Schloßgarten
Muskateller Spätlese trocken
25 DM, 12.5%, ♀ till 2003 **91**

1996 Burkheimer Feuerberg
Weißer Burgunder Spätlese trocken
20 DM, 13%, ♀ till 2002 **91**

1997 Chardonnay
Spätlese trocken "SE"
33 DM, 12.5%, ♀ till 2002 **91**

1996 Burkheimer Feuerberg
Grauer Burgunder Spätlese trocken "SE"
30 DM, 13%, ♀ till 2000 **92**

1997 Burkheimer Feuerberg
Grauer Burgunder Auslese trocken "SE"
36 DM/0.375 liter, 14%, ♀ till 2003 **92**

——— Red wine ———

1996 Burkheimer Feuerberg
Spätburgunder Spätlese trocken "SE"
48 DM, 13%, ♀ till 2003 **91**

WEINGUT BERCHER-SCHMIDT

Owners: Beate Wiedemann-Schmidt and Franz Wilhelm Schmidt
Winemaker: Franz Wilhelm Schmidt
79235 Oberrotweil, Herrenstraße 28
Tel. (0 76 62) 3 72, Fax 62 33
Directions: A 5 Karlsruhe–Basel, exit Riegel, towards the Rhine
Sales: Beate Wiedemann-Schmidt and Annemarie Wiedemann
Opening hours: Mon.–Fri. 9 a.m. to 6 p.m., Sat. and Sun. by appointment

Vineyard area: 10 hectares
Annual production: 60,000 bottles
Top sites: Oberrotweiler Henkenberg, Eichberg and Käsleberg, Bischoffinger Enselberg and Steinbuck, Burkheimer Feuerberg
Soil types: Weathered volcanic soil, loess and loam
Grape varieties: 31% Spätburgunder, 26% Grauburgunder, 15% Weißburgunder, 13% Müller-Thurgau, 4% Silvaner, 3% Riesling, 8% other varieties
Average yield: 55 hl/ha
Best vintages: 1995, 1996, 1997

This estate has been known for its wines since the beginning of this century. In 1985 the artist Beate Wiedemann-Schmidt – who has a spacious studio in what was formerly a dilapidated barn at her disposal since 1994 – and her husband, Franz Wilhelm Schmidt, joined the family business. After the convincing collection of wines from the 1993 vintage, the 1994s came across as simpler and just a touch rustic. With the far lower yields of the 1995 vintage, Franz Wilhelm Schmidt obtained more elegance in his wines. The 1996s have better substance, but malty fruit and in some cases a rather tart acidity on the finish. The 1997 whites are not much better. Be that as it may, Schmidt is a reliable craftsman, and his wines are a sound choice for everyday drinking.

1997 Oberrotweiler Käsleberg
Weißer Burgunder Spätlese trocken
16.90 DM, 13%, ♀ now **80**

1997 Bischoffinger Steinbuck
Grauer Burgunder Spätlese trocken
17.90 DM, 13%, ♀ till 2000 **82**

1997 Bischoffinger Enselberg
Chardonnay Spätlese trocken
19.90 DM, 12.5%, ♀ till 2000 **82**

1996 Oberrotweiler Käsleberg
Weißer Burgunder Spätlese trocken
16 DM, 12.5%, ♀ now **82**

1997 Oberrotweiler Henkenberg
Ruländer Spätlese
13.90 DM, 12.5%, ♀ till 2000 **82**

1996 Bischoffinger Enselberg
Riesling Spätlese trocken
10 DM/0.375 liter, 11.5%, ♀ till 2000 **84**

1996 Oberrotweiler Eichberg
Grauer Burgunder Spätlese trocken
16 DM, 13.5%, ♀ now **84**

1997 Bischoffinger Enselberg
Riesling Auslese
15 DM/0.375 liter, 12%, ♀ till 2002 **86**

WINZERGENOSSENSCHAFT BISCHOFFINGEN

Manager: Michael Oxenknecht
Winemaker: Werner Haßler
79235 Bischoffingen,
Bacchusstraße 14
Tel. (0 76 62) 9 30 10, Fax 93 01 93
Directions: A 5 Frankfurt–Basel, exit Riegel, towards the Rhine
Sales: Emil Pfistner
Opening hours: Mon.–Fri. 8 a.m. to 5:30 p.m., Sat. 8:30 a.m. to 12 a.m. Or by appointment with Ms. Weber or Mr. Johner
Restaurant: Weinstube “Steinbuck” Open daily except Tue.
Specialties: Regional fare

Vineyard area: 225 hectares
Number of adherents: 288
Annual production: 2.2 million bottles
Top sites: Bischoffinger Enselberg, Steinbuck and Rosenkranz
Soil types: Weathered volcanic soil and loess terraces
Grape varieties: 33% Spätburgunder, 26% Müller-Thurgau, 23% Grauburgunder, 8% Silvaner, 5% Weißburgunder, 5% other varieties
Average yield: 80 hl/ha
Best vintages: 1993, 1995, 1997

Although almost one third of the vineyards of this old cooperative on the southwest side of the Kaiserstuhl are planted with Müller-Thurgau, the growers of Bischoffingen have earned their reputation with more classical wines made from Grauburgunder and Spätburgunder. In the last few vintages they have produced specially selected wines from low-yielding old vines of these varieties; these “Selections,” as they are called, are aged in new oak. After a fine performance with the 1995 vintage, the growers did less well in 1996. The wines were well made, but they scarcely bear closer scrutiny. The Trockenbeerenauslese was the exception that proves the rule. Our first tasting of the 1997s proved more refreshing; and the finest wines are still in cask.

1997 Bischoffinger Rosenkranz
Gewürztraminer Spätlese trocken
15 DM, 13.5%, ♀ now **80**

1996 Bischoffinger Enselberg
Grauer Burgunder Spätlese trocken “Selektion”
17.50 DM, 13.5%, ♀ till 2000 **82**

1997 Bischoffinger Steinbuck
Ruländer Auslese
18 DM, 10.5%, ♀ till 2003 **84**

1996 Bischoffinger Enselberg
Ruländer Eiswein
64.30 DM, 8.5%, ♀ till 2006 **86**

1995 Bischoffinger Rosenkranz
Weißer Burgunder Trockenbeerenauslese
40 DM/0.5 liter, 9%, ♀ till 2006 **91**

——— Red wines ———

1996 Spätburgunder
trocken “BB”
12.50 DM, 12.5%, ♀ till 2000 **82**

1996 Bischoffinger Enselberg
Spätburgunder trocken
29.80 DM, 12.5%, ♀ till 2000 **84**

1997 Bischoffinger Steinbuck
Spätburgunder Spätlese trocken
14.80 DM, 12.5%, ♀ till 2002 **84**

WEINGUT BLANKENHORN

Owner: Rosemarie Blankenhorn
Manager: Fritz Deutschmann
79418 Schliengen, Baslerstraße 2
Tel. (0 67 35) 8 20 00, Fax 82 00 20
Directions: A 5 Freiburg–Basel, exit Müllheim, 8 kilometers to Schliengen
Sales: Rosemarie Blankenhorn
Opening hours: Mon.–Fri. 8 a.m. to noon and 2 p.m. to 6 p.m., Sat. 9 a.m. to 1 p.m. or by appointment
History: Founded in 1847 by Johann Blankenhom
Worth seeing: The old Thurn & Taxis post station
Restaurant: Tel. (0 76 35) 82 25 90
Managed by Thomas and Renate Vierk, open from 11 a.m. to 3 p.m. and 5 p.m. to midnight, except Mon.

Vineyard area: 20 hectares
Annual production: 170,000 bottles
Top sites: Schliengener Sonnenstück, Auggener Schäf
Soil types: Loess and loam
Grape varieties: 30% Gutedel, 25% Spätburgunder, 10% each of Grauburgunder and Weißburgunder, 5% each of Riesling, Chardonnay and Müller-Thurgau, 10% other varieties
Average yield: 60 hl/ha
Best vintages: 1993, 1995, 1997
Member: VDP

When the vivacious Rosemarie Blankenhorn took over this estate from her parents, she cancelled all grape contracts with neighboring growers and decided to concentrate on making wines solely from her own vineyards. With her winemaker Fritz Deutschmann she embarked onto uncharted waters. Although the wines produced in the Markgräflerland rarely attain the body and complexity of those from the Kaiserstuhl, this new team is getting things off to a fine start. The 1995s were very appealing; a touch more fruit and less acidity would have done wonders for the 1996s. The 1997s are the finest wines that they have bottled to date and prove that it is possible to make fine wines in this part of Baden.

1996 Auggener Schäf
Gutedel Kabinett trocken
9.50 DM, 11%, 🍷 now **80**

1997 Schliengener Sonnenstück
Grauer Burgunder Spätlese trocken
18 DM, 13.5%, 🍷 now **80**

1996 Schliengener Sonnenstück
Gewürztraminer Spätlese trocken
17 DM, 12%, 🍷 till 2002 **80**

1996 Schliengener Sonnenstück
Weißer Burgunder Kabinett trocken
13 DM, 11.5%, 🍷 now **82**

1996 Schliengener Sonnenstück
Grauer Burgunder Kabinett trocken
13 DM, 11.5%, 🍷 now **82**

1997 Schliengener Sonnenstück
Chardonnay Spätlese trocken
30 DM, 13%, 🍷 till 2002 **84**

1997 Schliengener Sonnenstück
Grauer Burgunder Beerenauslese
52 DM/0.375 liter, 15%, 🍷 till 2007 **84**

1997 Schliengener Sonnenstück
Riesling Spätlese
18 DM, 12%, 🍷 till 2002 **86**

1997 Schliengener Sonnenstück
Weißer Burgunder Auslese
41 DM/0.375 liter, 14%, 🍷 till 2003 **86**

1996 Schliengener Sonnenstück
Riesling Eiswein
99 DM/0.375 liter, 9%, 🍷 till 2006 **88**

Blankenhorn
Gutedel 1997

WINZERGENOSSENSCHAFT BRITZINGEN

Manager: Achim Frey
Winemaker: Hermann Zenzen
79379 Müllheim-Britzingen,
Markgräfler Straße 25–29
Tel. (0 76 31) 1 77 10, Fax 40 13
Directions: A 5 Karlsruhe–Basel, exit Bad Krozingen or Müllheim
Sales: Matthias Oettlin
Opening hours: Mon.–Fri. 9 a.m. to 12:30 p.m. and 2 p.m. to 6 p.m.
Sat. 9 a.m. to 12:30 p.m.
History: Founded in 1950

Vineyard area: 178 hectares
Number of adherents: 210
Annual production: 1.6 million bottles
Top sites: Britzinger Sonnhole, Britzinger Rosenberg, Badenweiler Römerberg
Soil types: Loess and loam with a rich rocky limestone subsoil
Grape varieties: 39% Gutedel, 19% Spätburgunder, 17% Müller-Thurgau, 10% Weißburgunder, 15% other varieties
Average yield: 80 hl/ha
Best vintages: 1995, 1996, 1997

Founded in 1950, the cooperative in Britzingen drew attention to itself with its first vintages. Blind tastings of wines from neighboring cooperatives continue to confirm this impression. Nonetheless, we were often left wondering why the growers so overdid the use of new oak when their wines have so much naturally lively fruit to offer. The 1996 collection of wines left a tad to be desired. The 1997s were much better balanced and are certainly the finest wines that we have tasted from this cooperative in some time. In the Markgräflerland only the cooperatives of Pfaffenweiler and Ehrenstetten play in the same league.

1997 Britzinger Sonnhole
Weißer Burgunder Kabinett trocken "Exklusiv"
16 DM, 12.5%, ♀ till 2000 **80**

1997 Britzinger Sonnhole
Grauer Burgunder Spätlese trocken
11 DM, 14%, ♀ now **80**

1996 Britzinger Sonnhole
Weißer Burgunder Spätlese trocken
17 DM, 12.5%, ♀ now **82**

1996 Britzinger Sonnhole
Grauer Burgunder Spätlese trocken
17 DM, 12.5%, ♀ now **82**

1997 Britzinger Sonnhole
Weißer Burgunder Spätlese trocken "Exklusiv"
17.50 DM, 13%, ♀ till 2000 **82**

1997 Britzinger Sonnhole
Ruländer Beerenauslese
32 DM/0.375 liter, 9.5%, ♀ till 2005 **86**

——— Red wines ———

1996 Badenweiler Römerberg
Cabernet Sauvignon-Merlot trocken
33 DM, 13%, ♀ now **80**

1996 Britzinger Rosenberg
Spätburgunder trocken
17 DM, 13%, ♀ now **82**

1996 Britzinger Rosenberg
Spätburgunder trocken
22 DM, 13.5%, ♀ now **84**

HOFGUT CONSEQUENCE

Owners: Manfred and Eva Maria Schmidt
79235 Bischoffingen, Talstraße 15
Tel. (0 76 62) 9 40 87, Fax 9 40 86
Internet: www.ecovin.de.hofgut-consequence
Directions: A 5 Frankfurt–Basel, exit Riegel, towards the Rhine
Opening hours: Mon.–Sat. 2 p.m. to 8 p.m. or by appointment

Vineyard area: 5.8 hectares
Annual production: 17,000 bottles
Top sites: Vineyard designations are not used
Soil types: Weathered volcanic soil with loess terraces
Grape varieties: 30% Blauer Spätburgunder, 21% Müller-Thurgau, 7% Grauburgunder, 6% Silvaner, 36% other varieties
Average yield: 30 hl/ha
Best vintages: 1996, 1997
Member: BÖW

Before they made their "leap into independence" in 1994, Manfred and Eva Maria Schmidt were members of the cooperative in Bischoffingen. At the same time they committed themselves to organic viticulture in their vineyards. Even though many of the wines are harvested as Spätlese, quality levels are not specified as such on the labels. Moreover, any information about vineyard sites is omitted. Extremely low yields play an important part in achieving the quality level displayed in these wines, which certainly belong to the best of any produced by organic growers in Germany. If Manfred and Eva Maria Schmidt would tone down their use of over-extraction and new oak, this estate could become one of the finer producers in the region.

1996 "Creation No. 1"
trocken
8 DM, 11.5%, ♀ now **80**

1997 Rivaner
trocken
13.50 DM, 12.5%, ♀ now **82**

1997 Silvaner
trocken
19.50 DM, 13.5%, ♀ till 2000 **82**

1996 Rivaner
trocken
12 DM, 12%, ♀ now **82**

1997 Weißer Burgunder
trocken
19.50 DM, 14%, ♀ till 2000 **84**

1996 Weißer Burgunder
trocken
16.50 DM, 13%, ♀ till 2000 **84**

1997 Grauer Burgunder
trocken
19.50 DM, 14%, ♀ till 2002 **86**

1996 Grauer Burgunder
trocken
18 DM, 13%, ♀ till 2000 **86**

——— Red wines ———

1997 Spätburgunder Weißherbst
trocken
19.50 DM, 13.5%, ♀ now **84**

1996 Spätburgunder
trocken
22.50 DM, 13%, ♀ now **82**

WEINGUT HERMANN DÖRFLINGER

Owner: Hermann Dörflinger
79379 Müllheim, Mühlenstraße 7
Tel. (0 76 31) 22 07, Fax 41 95
Directions: A 5 Karlsruhe–Basel, exit Müllheim
Sales: Hermann and Doris Dörflinger
Opening hours: Mon.–Fri. 8 a.m. to noon and 1:30 p.m. to 6 p.m.
Sat. 8 a.m. to 4 p.m.
Worth seeing: Barrel cellar

Vineyard area: 18 hectares
Annual production: 130,000 bottles
Top Sites: Müllheimer Reggenhag, Pfaffenstück, Römerberg and Sommerhalde
Soil: Chalky loess and sandy loam
Grape varieties: 48% Gutedel, 15% Spätburgunder, 11% Weißburgunder, 10% Grauburgunder, 16% other varieties
Average yield: 67 hl/ha
Best vintages: 1993, 1996, 1997

Even at the time when sweet wines were the rage in Baden, Dörflinger fermented his wines to total dryness. In fact he earned his reputation as a champion of uncompromisingly dry wines. After a slump in quality in 1995, Dörflinger was back on form with his 1996s. His courage in leaving the grapes on the vine until well into late autumn paid off handsomely. Admittedly these wines lacked weight, but they had a lively freshness and an elegance that was lacking in the previous vintage. That collection thrust him into the forefront of the Markgräflerland estates and set the stage for his finely balanced range from the 1997 vintage. Few in the Markgräferland make better wines today than Hermann Dörflinger.

1997 Müllheimer Reggenhag
Chardonnay Kabinett trocken
16.50 DM, 12.5%, ♀ now **80**

1996 Müllheimer Sonnhalde
Weißer Burgunder Kabinett trocken
11.50 DM, 12%, ♀ till 2000 **82**

1997 Müllheimer Reggenhag
Gewürztraminer Spätlese trocken
14 DM/0.5 liter, 14%, ♀ now **82**

1997 Müllheimer Reggenhag
Gewürztraminer Auslese trocken
20.50 DM/0.5 liter, 15%, ♀ till 2000 **82**

1996 Müllheimer Sonnhalde
Grauer Burgunder Kabinett trocken
12 DM, 12%, ♀ till 2000 **84**

1997 Müllheimer Reggenhag
Weißer Burgunder Spätlese trocken
15.50 DM, 13%, ♀ till 2000 **84**

1997 Müllheimer Sonnhalde
Grauer Burgunder Spätlese trocken
20.50 DM, 13.5%, ♀ now **84**

1997 Badenweiler Römerberg
Weißer Burgunder Spätlese trocken
20.50 DM, 13.5%, ♀ till 2002 **86**

——— Red wine ———

1997 Müllheimer Sonnhalde
Spätburgunder Spätlese trocken
18.50 DM, 13%, ♀ till 2001 **80**

DÖRFLINGER
1996er
GUTEDEL
MÜLLHEIMER REGGENHAG
TROCKEN
Gutsabfüllung · A.P.Nr. 274 07 97 · Qualitätswein · 11% vol. · RZ 1 g/l · 0,75 ltr
Weingut Hermann Dörflinger D-79379 Müllheim/Baden/Markgräflerland

DURBACHER WINZERGENOSSENSCHAFT

Manager: Konrad Geppert
Winemaker: Josef Wörner
77770 Durbach, Nachweide 2
Tel. (07 81) 9 36 60, Fax 3 65 47
Directions: A 5 Karlsruhe–Basel, exit Appenweier or Offenburg-Süd
Sales: Günter Lehmann, Ulrich Litterst
Opening hours: Mon.–Fri. 8 a.m. to noon and 1:30 p.m. to 6 p.m., Sat. 9 a.m. to noon, Sun. 10 a.m. to noon
Or by appointment with Ms. Benz
History: Founded in 1928

Vineyard area: 320 hectares
Number of adherents: 310
Annual production: 3 million bottles
Top sites: Durbacher Ölberg, Plauelrain, Kochberg and Steinberg
Soil types: Weathered granite
Grape varieties: 40% Spätburgunder, 24% Riesling, 20% Müller-Thurgau, 7% Clevner, 6% Grauburgunder, 3% other varieties
Average yield: 79 hl/ha
Best vintages: 1993, 1996, 1997

The slopes around Durbach are steep, precipitous, rocky and almost impossible to cultivate. Of the 450 hectares of vineyards in the village, 320 are managed by the cooperative. The distinction of these sites is readily apparent in the exquisite Rieslings; but the Spätburgunders too, in better vintages, merit respect. In 1996 the growers of Durbach gave a stunning performance – all the wines were rich in extract as well as typical of their varietal origin; moreover, the skillful use of new wood was a tribute to their cellarmaster. The dessert wines were exemplary! The 1997s were also quite good, but not as fine as winemaker Josef Wörner would have us believe. Nonetheless, the growers here have few peers among the cooperatives in Germany.

1997 Durbacher Plauelrain
Chardonnay Spätlese trocken
20 DM, 12.5%, ♀ now **80**

1996 Durbacher Plauelrain
Klingelberger (Riesling) Spätlese trocken
13.50 DM, 11.5%, ♀ till 2002 **82**

1997 Durbacher Steinberg
Weißer Burgunder Auslese trocken
25 DM/0.5 liter, 14.5%, ♀ till 2000 **82**

1996 Durbacher Kochberg
Grauer Burgunder Spätlese trocken
13.50 DM, 12.5%, ♀ till 2000 **84**

1997 Durbacher Plauelrain
Riesling Auslese trocken
22 DM/0.5 liter, 13%, ♀ till 2002 **84**

1996 Durbacher Plauelrain
Chardonnay Auslese trocken
35 DM/0.5 liter, 14%, ♀ till 2004 **86**

1997 Durbacher Plauelrain
Riesling Auslese
20 DM/0.5 liter, 10%, ♀ till 2002 **86**

1996 Durbacher Plauelrain
Gewürztraminer Beerenauslese
66 DM/0.5 liter, 9.5%, ♀ till 2010 **89**

Red wines

1997 Durbacher Kochberg
Spätburgunder Auslese trocken
28 DM/0.5 liter, 13.5%, ♀ till 2001 **80**

1996 Durbacher Kochberg
Spätburgunder trocken
10.50 DM, 13%, ♀ till 2002 **84**

WINZERGENOSSENSCHAFT EHRENSTETTEN

Manager: Franz Herbster
Winemaker: Norbert Faller
79238 Ehrenstetten, Kirchbergstraße 9
Tel. (0 76 33) 9 50 90, Fax 5 08 53
Directions: A 5 Karlsruhe–Basel, exit Freiburg-Süd, towards Staufen
Opening hours: Mon.–Fri. 8 a.m. to 6 p.m., Sat. 9 a.m. to noon
History: Founded in 1952

Vineyard area: 130 hectares
Number of adherents: 250
Annual production: 1.1 million bottles
Top site: Ehrenstetter Oelberg
Soil types: Loess, loam and rocky limestone
Grape varieties: 34% Gutedel, 30% Müller-Thurgau, 28% Burgundian varieties, 8% other varieties
Average yield: 78 hl/ha
Best vintages: 1993, 1996, 1997

Fifteen kilometers south of Freiburg, Ehrenstetten is an ancient village in the Markgräflerland that was first mentioned in written documents in 1139. Last year the cooperative, founded in 1952, made a name for itself with its fresh and fruity "Chasslie," a wine to be consumed in its youth. This name combines a reference to Chasselas, the French name for the region's most characteristic grape varietal Gutedel, and the "sur lie" concept, which refers to the practice of leaving the wine to age on its fine lees, as is commonly done with Muscadet. With the 1996 vintage, which the growers here considered to be their best ever, Franz Herbster and Norbert Faller demonstrated steady craftsmanship: the whole collection was most appealing. A welcome surprise in our tastings in southern Baden, the 1997s are of similar quality!

1997 Ehrenstetter Oelberg
Grauer Burgunder Spätlese trocken
18 DM, 13.5%, ♀ till 2000 **82**

1996 Ehrenstetter Oelberg
Weißer Burgunder Spätlese trocken
18 DM, 12.5%, ♀ till 2000 **82**

1996 Ehrenstetter Oelberg
Chardonnay trocken
24 DM, 12.5%, ♀ till 2000 **84**

1997 Ehrenstetter Oelberg
Gutedel Spätlese trocken
14 DM, 13.5%, ♀ now **84**

1996 Ehrenstetter Oelberg
Chardonnay Spätlese trocken
24 DM, 14%, ♀ till 2000 **84**

1996 Ehrenstetter Oelberg
Gewürztraminer Eiswein
32 DM/0.5 liter, 11%, ♀ till 2003 **86**

Red wines

1997 Ehrenstetter Oelberg
Spätburgunder Kabinett trocken
13.50 DM, 12.5%, ♀ till 2000 **80**

1996 Ehrenstetter Oelberg
Spätburgunder trocken
24 DM, 13%, ♀ till 2000 **84**

WEINGUT FREIHERR VON UND ZU FRANCKENSTEIN

Owner: Freiherr von und zu Franckenstein
Leased and managed by Hubert Doll
77654 Offenburg, Weingartenstraße 66
Tel. (07 81) 3 49 73, Fax 3 60 46
Directions: A 5 Frankfurt–Basel, exit Offenburg, towards Zell-Weierbach
Sales: Hubert and Lioba Doll
Opening hours: Mon.–Fri. 9 a.m. to noon and 2 p.m. to 6 p.m.
Sat. 9 a.m. to 1 p.m. or by appointment

Vineyard area: 12 hectares
Annual production: 80,000 bottles
Top sites: Zell-Weierbacher Neugesetz and Abtsberg, Berghauptener Schützenberg
Soil types: Weathered granite, loess and loam
Grape varieties: 38% Riesling, 14% Müller-Thurgau, 15% Spätburgunder, 20% Grauburgunder, 8% Weißburgunder, 5% other varieties
Average yield: 49 hl/ha
Best vintages: 1993, 1994, 1997
Member: VDP

On the outskirts Offenburg lies the property of the Franckenstein family, who trace their activity as wine producers back to 1517. They also manage the neighboring vineyards in Zell-Weierbach. In 1978 the calm and single-minded Hubert Doll came here from the nearby village of Durbach to manage the estate; since 1985 he has leased the property from the baron, so that he can run everything as he sees fit. The Rieslings produced here generally show delicate elegance. The 1995s, however, did not come up to the standard of the 1994s; the 1996s were a touch more successful. Light and tart, the wines have shown somewhat better in each tasting. Nonetheless, none quite match earlier splendors. The 1997s are much better and almost on par with the excellent 1993s and 1990s.

1996 Berghauptener Schützenberg
Riesling Kabinett trocken
12 DM, 10.5%, ♀ till 2000 **82**

1996 Berghauptener Schützenberg
Chardonnay Kabinett trocken
13.50 DM, 12%, ♀ now **84**

1997 Zell-Weierbacher Neugesetz
Riesling Spätlese trocken
18.50 DM, 12%, ♀ till 2001 **84**

1997 Berghauptener Schützenberg
Chardonnay Spätlese trocken
18.50 DM, 13%, ♀ till 2000 **84**

1997 Zell-Weierbacher Neugesetz
Traminer Spätlese trocken
18.50 DM, 13%, ♀ till 2000 **84**

1996 Zell-Weierbacher Neugesetz
Riesling Spätlese trocken
13.50 DM/0.5 liter, 12%, ♀ till 2002 **84**

1996 Zell-Weierbacher Neugesetz
Traminer Spätlese
16 DM/0.5 liter, 11.5%, ♀ till 2002 **84**

1997 Zell-Weierbacher Abtsberg
Grauer Burgunder Spätlese trocken
18.50 DM, 13%, ♀ till 2002 **86**

1996 Zell-Weierbacher Abtsberg
Grauer Burgunder Spätlese trocken
16 DM, 12.5%, ♀ till 2000 **86**

WEINGUT FREIHERR VON GLEICHENSTEIN

Owner: Hans-Joachim Freiherr von Gleichenstein
General Manager: Franz Orth
Winemaker: Frank Müller
79235 Oberrotweil, Bahnhofstraße 12
Tel. (0 76 62) 2 88, Fax 18 56
Directions: A 5 Frankfurt–Basel, exit Riegel via Endingen
Sales: Freiherr von Gleichenstein
Opening hours: Mon.–Fri. 8:30 a.m. to 6 p.m., Sat. and Sun. 9:30 a.m. to noon or by appointment
History: The estate has belonged to the family since 1634
Worth seeing: Old barrel cellar from 1580

Vineyard area: 24 hectares
Annual production: 180,000 bottles
Top sites: Oberrotweiler Eichberg, Henkenberg as well as Käsleberg and Achkarrer Schloßberg
Soil types: Weathered volcanic soil
Grape varieties: 30% Spätburgunder, 20% each of Grauburgunder, Weißburgunder and Müller-Thurgau, 3% Riesling, 7% other varieties
Average yield: 75 hl/ha
Best vintages: 1995, 1996, 1997

Although it has belonged to his family for more than 350 years, Baron Hans-Joachim von Gleichenstein inherited this estate in 1959 in rather desolate conditions. After years of rather mediocre quality, the 1995s set this estate on a new track; the 1996s are the finest they have ever produced. The slate of excellent Spätlese demands little commentary. Even the ordinary wines have improved in quality. The 1997s are equally good. Gleichenstein's use of new wood still needs to be honed; nonetheless, his estate has embarked on a new and laudable course.

1997 Oberrotweiler Eichberg
Chardonnay Kabinett trocken
18 DM, 12.5%, ♀ till 2000 **82**

1997 Oberrotweiler Henkenberg
Grauer Burgunder Spätlese trocken
16 DM, 13%, ♀ till 2000 **84**

1997 Oberrotweiler Eichberg
Weißer Burgunder Spätlese trocken
18 DM, 13.5%, ♀ till 2000 **84**

1997 Achkarrer Schloßberg
Silvaner Spätlese trocken
14 DM, 12%, ♀ till 2000 **86**

1996 Achkarrer Schloßberg
Grauer Burgunder Spätlese trocken
21 DM, 13%, ♀ till 2000 **86**

1996 Oberrotweiler Eichberg
Chardonnay Spätlese trocken
23 DM, 12.5%, ♀ till 2000 **86**

1997 Oberrotweiler Eichberg
Müller-Thurgau Auslese trocken
18 DM, 13.5%, ♀ till 2003 **86**

1996 Oberrotweiler Eichberg
Traminer Spätlese trocken
21 DM, 12.5%, ♀ till 2002 **88**

1995 Amolterer Steinhalde
Weißer Burgunder Eiswein
51.75 DM, 11%, ♀ till 2006 **92**

——— Red wine ———

1997 Oberrotweiler Eichberg
Spätburgunder Spätlese trocken
18 DM, 12.5%, ♀ till 2003 **88**

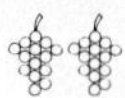

WEINGUT THOMAS HAGENBUCHER

Owner: Thomas Hagenbucher
75056 Sulzfeld, Friederichstraße 36
Tel. (0 72 69) 91 11 20, Fax 91 11 22
Directions: A 5 Frankfurt–Basel, exit Bruchsal, B 293 towards Heilbronn
Opening hours: Mon.–Fri. 6 p.m. to 8 p.m., Sun. 9 a.m. to 3 p.m. or by appointment

Vineyard area: 8 hectares
Annual production: 40,000 bottles
Top sites: No vineyards are specified on the label
Soil types: Stony clay, loess, gravel
Grape varieties: 27% Riesling, 17% Schwarzriesling, 12% Weißburgunder, 5% Spätburgunder, 11% Grauburgunder, 21% Müller-Thurgau, 4% Chardonnay, 3% Lemberger
Average yield: 54 hl/ha
Best vintages: 1993, 1996, 1997

After technical training in a number of countries, including France and Switzerland, Thomas Hagenbucher established his own estate in 1992 in Sulzfeld, a small village in the Kraichgau between the Rhine and the Neckar valleys. Except for the Ravensburg, there is only the single vineyard of Lerchenberg here, a site with no true personality of its own. For this reason Hagenbucher has rightly decided to dispense with vineyard designations. His unusual label is thus extremely easy to read. Well made from a technical viewpoint, his 1996s were not only modern in style but also easy to drink. With more depth of fruit, the 1997s are certainly the best wines that he has produced to date. Most readers will have had little or no experience with the Kraichgau, but things are changing for the better here.

1996 Grauer Burgunder
Kabinett trocken
9.25 DM, 11%, ♀ now **80**

1997 Riesling
trocken
7.50 DM/1.0 liter, 12.5%, ♀ now **82**

1996 Weißer Burgunder
Kabinett trocken
9 DM, 11.5%, ♀ now **82**

1996 Schwarzriesling
trocken
27 DM, 12.5%, ♀ till 2001 **84**

1996 Chardonnay
trocken
24 DM, 12.5%, ♀ now **84**

1997 Weißer Burgunder
Spätlese trocken
13.50 DM, 13.5%, ♀ till 2000 **84**

1997 Grauer Burgunder
Spätlese
13.25 DM, 13.5%, ♀ till 2000 **86**

——— Red wine ———

1996 Lemberger
trocken
24 DM, 12.5%, ♀ till 2000 **84**

WEINGUT THOMAS HAGENBUCHER
SULZFELD
BADEN
1996er
CHARDONNAY
»im Barrique gereift«
Gutsabfüllung:
Weingut Thomas Hagenbucher, Friedrichstr. 36, D-75056 Sulzfeld
Qualitätswein b.A. · A.P.Nr. 2958/10/97 · 12,5% vol. · 0,75 l

WEINGUT DR. HEGER

Owner: Joachim Heger
Vineyard manager: Jürgen Kühnle
Winemaker: Joachim Heger and Ulrich Hamm
79241 Ihringen, Bachenstraße 19
Tel. (0 76 68) 2 05, Fax 93 00
e-mail: WeingutDr.Heger@t-online.de
Directions: A 5 Frankfurt–Basel, exit Freiburg-Mitte, towards Breisach
Sales: Heger family
Opening hours: Mon.–Fri. 10 a.m. to noon and 1:30 p.m. to 5:30 p.m.
Sat. 10 a.m. to noon or by appointment

Vineyard area: 15 hectares
Annual production: 100,000 bottles
Top sites: Ihringer Winklerberg, Achkarrer Schloßberg
Soil types: Weathered volcanic soil, loess
Grape varieties: 24% each of Spätburgunder and Riesling, 19% Grauburgunder, 13% Weißburgunder, 8% Silvaner, 5% Chardonnay, 7% other varieties
Average yield: 50 hl/ha
Best vintages: 1995, 1996, 1997
Member: VDP, Deutsches Barrique Forum

Most wine lovers in Germany consider this to be the finest estate in Baden – and rightly so! The respected property was acquired in 1935 by country doctor Max Heger, who bit by bit pieced together the finest morsels of the Winklerberg vineyard. Today the major part of this outstanding site belongs to Joachim Heger, who took over the estate in 1992. Rarely in the life of a producer is it possible to bottle such a splendid collection of wines from a single vintage as Heger achieved in 1996. That need not, however, detract from the quality of his sumptuous 1997s, which were almost without peer in Baden. Even the simplest wines have character; the finest are inimitable. This extremely high standard applies to all the grape varieties, from Riesling and the Burgundian varieties through to the Muscat dessert wine. This estate stands head and shoulders above all other producers in Baden and belongs to an elite group of German wine producers. We expect even more from Joachim Heger in the years to come.

1997 Achkarrer Schloßberg
Riesling Spätlese trocken
24 DM, 13%, ♀ till 2002 **88**

1997 Ihringer Winklerberg
Grauer Burgunder Spätlese trocken
24 DM, 13.5%, ♀ till 2001 **88**

1997 Ihringer Winklerberg
Silvaner Spätlese trocken
24 DM, 12.5%, ♀ till 2002 **88**

1996 Ihringer Winklerberg
Weißer Burgunder Spätlese trocken
22.50 DM, 13%, ♀ till 2002 **88**

1997 Ihringer Winklerberg
Muskateller Auslese trocken ***
28 DM/0.375 liter, 14%, ♀ till 2007 **88**

1997 Achkarrer Schloßberg
Grauer Burgunder Spätlese trocken ***
35 DM, 14%, ♀ till 2000 **89**

1997 Achkarrer Schloßberg
Silvaner Spätlese trocken ***
28 DM, 13%, ♀ till 2003 **89**

1997 Ihringer Winklerberg
Chardonnay Spätlese trocken
35 DM, 13.3%, ♀ till 2002 **89**

1997 Ihringer Winklerberg
Riesling Spätlese trocken ***
28 DM, 13%, ♀ till 2003 **89**

1997 Ihringer Winklerberg
Weißer Burgunder Spätlese trocken
24 DM, 13.7%, ♀ till 2002 **89**

1996 Achkarrer Schloßberg
Silvaner Spätlese trocken ***
26 DM, 13%, ♀ till 2002 **89**

1996 Ihringer Winklerberg
Riesling Spätlese trocken ***
26 DM, 12.5%, ♀ till 2005 **89**

1996 Ihringer Winklerberg
Riesling Auslese
28 DM, 9%, ♀ till 2007 **89**

1996 Ihringer Winklerberg
Muskateller Spätlese trocken ***
26 DM, 12.5%, ♀ till 2003 **90**

1996 Ihringer Winklerberg
Weißer Burgunder Spätlese trocken ***
30 DM, 13%, ♀ till 2002 **90**

1997 Ihringer Winklerberg
Weißer Burgunder Spätlese trocken ***
33 DM, 13.5%, ♀ till 2003 **90**

1996 Ihringer Winklerberg
Grauer Burgunder Spätlese trocken
22.50 DM, 13%, ♀ till 2002 **90**

1997 Ihringer Winklerberg
Grauer Burgunder Spätlese trocken ***
33 DM, 13.5%, ♀ till 2002 **91**

1996 Ihringer Winklerberg
Grauer Burgunder Spätlese trocken ***
30 DM, 13%, ♀ till 2005 **91**

1996 Ihringer Winklerberg
Gewürztraminer Auslese
28 DM/0.375 liter, 10.5%, ♀ till 2002 **91**

1996 Achkarrer Schloßberg
Grauer Burgunder Spätlese trocken ***
30 DM, 13%, ♀ till 2004 **92**

1997 Ihringer Winklerberg
Riesling Beerenauslese
48 DM/0.375 liter, 9%, ♀ till 2007 **92**

1997 Ihringer Winklerberg
Muskateller Trockenbeerenauslese
110 DM/0.375 liter, 6%, ♀ till 2010 **95**

1996 Ihringer Winklerberg
Scheurebe Trockenbeerenauslese
68 DM/0.375 liter, ♀ till 2015 **95**

1996 Ihringer Winklerberg
Muskateller Trockenbeerenauslese
90 DM/0.375 liter, 8%, ♀ till 2015 **98**

——— Red wines ———

1996 Ihringer Winklerberg
Spätburgunder trocken "Mimus"
35 DM, 12.5%, ♀ till 2002 **88**

1995 Ihringer Winklerberg
Spätburgunder trocken "Mimus"
32.50 DM, 13%, ♀ till 2002 **88**

1996 Achkarrer Schloßberg
Cabernet Sauvignon trocken
30 DM, 13%, ♀ till 2005 **89**

1995 Ihringer Winklerberg
Spätburgunder trocken ***
45 DM, 13%, ♀ till 2005 **89**

1996 Ihringer Winklerberg
Spätburgunder trocken ***
50 DM, 13.5%, ♀ till 2003 **91**

JOACHIM HEGER

Owners: Silvia and Joachim Heger
Manager: Jürgen Kühnle
Winemakers: Walter Bibo, Ulrich Hamm
79241 Ihringen, Bachenstraße 19
Tel. (0 76 68) 2 05 und 78 33, Fax 93 00
e-mail: WeingutDr.Heger@t-online.de
Directions: A 5 Frankfurt–Basel, exit Freiburg-Mitte, towards Breisach
Sales: Silvia and Joachim Heger
Opening hours: Mon.–Fri. 10 a.m. to noon and 1:30 p.m. to 5 p.m.
Sat. 10 a.m. to noon or by appointment

Vineyard area: 19 hectares
Contracted growers: 16
Annual production: 150,000 bottles
Top sites: Munzinger Kapellenberg, Merdinger Bühl, Ihringer Fohrenberg
Soil types: Limestone bearing loess, weathered volcanic soil
Grape varieties: 55% Spätburgunder, 18% each of Weißer and Grauer Burgunder, 9% other varieties
Average yield: 70 hl/ha
Best vintages: 1995, 1996, 1997

As demand grew for the constantly improving wines from his father's estate, Joachim Heger often regretted that his wines were always sold out. In 1986 he thus decided to lease the vineyards of the former Count of Kageneck estate in the Tuniberg in order to produce fresh, fruity wines for everyday consumption. From these beginnings developed a kind of cooperative enterprise that now includes 16 contracted growers with about 19 hectares of fine vineyards. None of the labels, however, carry vineyard designations. Under the supervision of Walter Bibo and Heger's cellarmaster Ulrich Hamm the wines have developed a style reminiscent of the Dr. Heger estate. In the last three years the wines have improved significantly in quality, while the prices remain extremely reasonable for Baden. In fact, some producers would be tickled to be able to offer first label wines as good as Heger's second label.

1997 Grauer Burgunder
Kabinett trocken
13.50 DM, 13%, ♀ till 2000 **84**

1996 Weißer Burgunder
Kabinett trocken
12.75 DM, ♀ till 2000 **84**

1996 Grauer Burgunder
Kabinett trocken
12.75 DM, ♀ till 2000 **84**

1997 Grauer Burgunder
Spätlese trocken
23 DM, 14%, ♀ till 2001 **86**

1997 Weißer Burgunder
Spätlese trocken
23 DM, 12.5%, ♀ till 2000 **86**

——— Red wines ———

1996 Merdinger Bühl
Spätburgunder trocken
14.50 DM, 13%, ♀ till 2000 **82**

1996 Spätburgunder
trocken ***
26 DM, 13.5%, ♀ till 2002 **84**

1996 Spätburgunder
trocken
19 DM, 13%, ♀ till 2002 **86**

1997 Spätburgunder
trocken "Vitus"
19 DM, 13%, ♀ till 2003 **86**

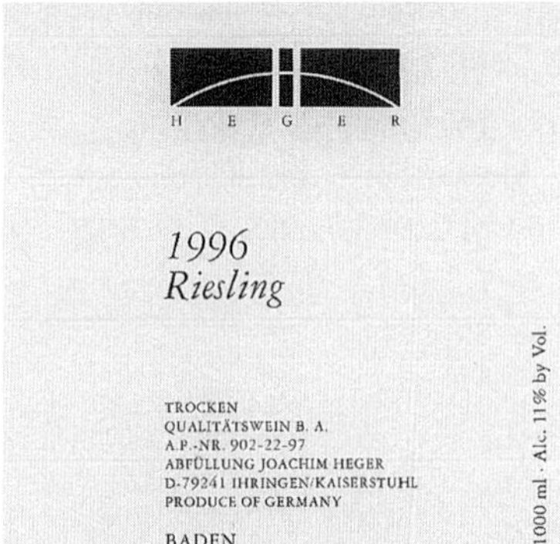

WEINGUT ERNST HEINEMANN & SOHN

Owner: Ernst Heinemann
Winemaker: Lothar Heinemann
79238 Ehrenkirchen-Scherzingen, Mengenerstraße 4
Tel. (0 76 64) 63 51, Fax 60 04 65
Directions: A 5 Frankfurt–Basel, exit Freiburg-Süd via Tiengen
Sales: Heinemann family
Opening hours: Mon.–Fri. 8 a.m. to noon and 1:30 p.m. to 6 p.m.
Sat. 8 a.m. to noon and 1 p.m. to 4 p.m.

Vineyard area: 13 hectares
Contracted growers: 20
Annual production: 100,000 bottles
Top site: Scherzinger Batzenberg
Soil types: Clay and loam, rich in limestone
Grape varieties: 40% Gutedel, 26% Spätburgunder, 10% each of Müller-Thurgau and Chardonnay, 7% Weißburgunder, 7% other varieties
Average yield: 65 hl/ha
Best vintages: 1995, 1996, 1997

Although they began to bottle their wines only after the war, the Heinemann family has owned this estate in the ancient wine village of Scherzingen south of Freiburg since 1556. Even today their wines are scarcely known outside the Markgräflerland; but there, word is out on the quality of their wines. In order to supply the demand for liter bottlings from the Gutedel, Müller-Thurgau and Spätburgunder varieties, the Müllers have to buy in fruit from about 20 small growers. After a rather modest showing in 1994, Heinemann produced a more convincing collection in 1995. He presented an appealing range of 1996s, all of which were thoroughly enjoyable to drink. The full-bodied 1997s are even better. This estate appears to be on the rise.

1997 Scherzinger Batzenberg
Grauer Burgunder Spätlese trocken
15.50 DM, 13%, ♀ now **82**

1997 Scherzinger Batzenberg
Gewürztraminer Spätlese trocken
15 DM/0.5 liter, 13.5%, ♀ till 2000 **82**

1996 Scherzinger Batzenberg
Gewürztraminer Spätlese
9.50 DM, 12.5%, ♀ till 2000 **82**

1996 Scherzinger Batzenberg
Chardonnay Kabinett trocken
18.50 DM, 12%, ♀ till 2000 **84**

1997 Scherzinger Batzenberg
Weißer Burgunder Spätlese trocken
14.50 DM, 13%, ♀ till 2000 **86**

1997 Scherzinger Batzenberg
Chardonnay Spätlese trocken
22 DM, 13%, ♀ till 2001 **86**

——— Red wines ———

1996 Scherzinger Batzenberg
Spätburgunder trocken
10 DM, 13%, ♀ till 2000 **80**

1997 Scherzinger Batzenberg
Spätburgunder Kabinett trocken
13 DM, 12.5%, ♀ till 2000 **82**

1996 Scherzinger Batzenberg
Spätburgunder trocken
14 DM, 13.5%, ♀ till 2002 **84**

1997 Scherzinger Batzenberg
Spätburgunder Spätlese trocken
18.50 DM, 13%, ♀ till 2001 **84**

Baden · 1993
Heinemann's
Grauer Burgunder
Spätlese Trocken
Scherzinger Batzenberg
Qualitätswein mit Prädikat
A. P. Nr. 218/03/94
13 % vol
0,75 l
ERZEUGERABFÜLLUNG ERNST HEINEMANN
D-79238 Scherzingen/Markgräflerland

WEINGUT ALBERT HEITLINGER

Owner: Albert Heitlinger and Company
Manager: Erhard Heitlinger
Technical Manager: Uwe Barnickel
Winemaker: Axel Rothermel
76684 Östringen-Tiefenbach, Am Mühlberg
Tel. (0 72 59) 9 11 20, Fax 91 12 99
Directions: 20 kilometers from Bruchsal
Sales: Ernst Bernhard Heitlinger
Opening hours: Mon.–Sun. 10 a.m. to 11 p.m. in the "Weinforum" restaurant

Vineyard area: 45 hectares
Annual production: 300,000 bottles
Top sites: Tiefenbacher Schellenbrunnen and Spiegelberg
Soil types: Stony clay, partly with loess overlay
Grape varieties: 20% Riesling, 25% Spätburgunder, 25% Grauburgunder, 8% Weißburgunder, 5% Lemberger, 17% other varieties
Average yield: 51 hl/ha
Best vintages: 1992, 1996, 1997
Member: VDP

Erhard Heitlinger, who took over this estate from his father in 1972, has never been lacking in ideas. For several years he issued his own newsletter, bottled individual wines with attractive names and created his own wine bar and restaurant "Besenkonsulat" as an additional outlet for his wines. After a considerable expansion of its vineyards, the estate added the corresponding cellar capacity in 1997. Since then a restaurant linked to modern lifestyles has opened in the "Weinforum," in which artists also display their works. In spite of the emphasis on packaging, pleasant wines were always produced at this estate. The 1997s, vinified in the newly remodelled cellars, show more fruit and depth than did the preceding vintages. Is more to come?

1996 Weißer Burgunder
trocken
9.75 DM, 11.5%, ♀ till 2000 **82**

1997 Riesling
Spätlese trocken
25 DM, 12.5%, ♀ till 2000 **84**

1996 Grauer Burgunder
Spätlese trocken
29 DM, 12.5%, ♀ till 2002 **84**

1997 Grauer Burgunder
Spätlese trocken "Grand Etage"
45 DM, 14%, ♀ till 2002 **84**

1997 Grauer Burgunder
Spätlese trocken
29 DM, 13.5%, ♀ till 2000 **86**

1996 Grauer Burgunder
Spätlese trocken "Grand Etage"
70 DM, 12.5%, ♀ 2003 **86**

——— Red wines ———

1994 Lemberger

1996 Lemberger
trocken
30 DM/0.5 liter, 12.5%, ♀ till 2000 **84**

1994 Lemberger
trocken
30 DM/0.5 liter, 12.5%, ♀ till 2005 **84**

WEINGUT REICHSGRAF UND MARQUIS ZU HOENSBROECH

Owner: Rüdiger Count and Marquess von und zu Hoensbroech
General Manager: Adrian Count Hoensbroech
Winemaker: Rüdiger Count Hoensbroech
74918 Angelbachtal-Michelfeld, Hermannsberg
Tel. (0 72 65) 91 10 34, Fax 91 10 35
e-mail: Hoendebroeck-Exklusivimport @t-online.de
Directions: A 6, exit Angelbachtal, 30 kilometers south of Heidelberg
Sales: Adrian Count Hoensbroech
Opening hours: Mon.–Fri. 9 a.m. to 6 p.m., Sat. 9 a.m. to 4 p.m.
Sun. by appointment
Worth seeing: Rüdiger Count Hoensbroech on his steed in the vineyard

Vineyard area: 17 hectares
Annual production: 120,000 bottles
Top sites: Michelfelder Himmelberg, Eichelberger Kapellenberg
Soil types: Loess and heavy red clay
Grape varieties: 35% Weißburgunder, 15% each of Riesling and Grauburgunder, 8% Spätburgunder, 27% other varieties
Average yield: 63 hl/ha
Best vintages: 1992, 1994, 1996
Member: VDP

Rüdiger Count Hoensbroech has waged a singlehanded campaign to put wines from the Kraichgau onto the lists of Germany's finest restaurants. Now his son Adrian has taken over part of the family business. The Weißburgunders have always represented the estate at its best and in some years – as the 1995 Spätlese handsomely demonstrated – are among the finest in all of Germany. The rest of the wines, including the liter bottlings, are always quite good, generally elegant and lively. That applies to the 1996s as well, even though they didn't quite reach the same heights of perfection as did previous vintages. The 1997s were, although simpler, similar in character. Some wine writers assert that this estate's wines lack true greatness. That may well be true, but we have always enjoyed drinking them.

1996 Michelfelder Himmelberg
Auxerrois Kabinett trocken
10.25 DM, 11.5%, 🍷 now **80**

1996 Michelfelder Himmelberg
Grauer Burgunder trocken
9.50 DM, 12%, 🍷 till 2000 **82**

1996 Michelfelder Himmelberg
Weißer Burgunder trocken
10 DM/1.0 liter, 11.5%, 🍷 now **82**

1997 Michelfelder Himmelberg
Chardonnay Spätlese trocken
19.15 DM, 13%, 🍷 till 2000 **82**

1997 Michelfelder Himmelberg
Riesling Spätlese trocken
16.80 DM, 12.5%, 🍷 till 2000 **82**

1997 Michelfelder Himmelberg
Weißer Burgunder Spätlese trocken
22.50 DM, 13%, 🍷 till 2000 **84**

1996 Michelfelder Himmelberg
Chardonnay Spätlese trocken
18 DM, 13%, 🍷 till 2000 **86**

1997 Michelfelder Himmelberg
Weißer Burgunder Spätlese
25.50 DM, 13%, 🍷 till 2001 **86**

1996 Michelfelder Himmelberg
Weißer Burgunder Spätlese trocken
22.50 DM, 13%, 🍷 till 2002 **88**

WEINGUT BERNHARD HUBER

Owner: Bernhard Huber
79364 Malterdingen,
Heimbacher Weg 19
Tel. (0 76 44) 12 00, Fax 82 22
Directions: A 5 Karlsruhe–Basel, exit Riegel
Sales: Bärbel and Bernhard Huber
Opening hours: By appointment
Worth seeing: House from the 16th century

Vineyard area: 15 hectares
Annual production: 100,000 bottles – includes 10,000 sparkling wine
Top sites: Hecklinger Schloßberg, Malterdinger Bienenberg
Soil types: Weathered fossil limestone
Grape varieties: 53% Spätburgunder, 15% Weißburgunder, 10% Chardonnay, 6% Grauburgunder, 16% other varieties
Average yield: 50 hl/ha
Best vintages: 1993, 1996, 1997
Member: VDP, Deutsches Barrique Forum

Bernhard Huber, who in 1987 was the first grower in Malterdingen to leave the local cooperative, is today one of Germany's most noteworthy red wine specialists. His wines, although often difficult to understand in their youth, belong to that small breed within Germany that mature exceedingly well. The spectacular showing of his Spätburgunder in the Burgundy tasting of the "Grand Jury Europeen" was ample proof of this fact. That his sumptuous wines now also display a distinct elegance has certainly contributed to his success. We were sufficiently impressed by Huber's 1995 Spätburgunder Reserve to award it the trophy as Red Wine of the Year in 1998. The 1996 is equally impressive. His dry 1996 Weißburgunder Spätlese also belongs to the best of the vintage. Although his 1997s were quite austere when first bottled, we expect them to evolve as have previous vintages. This performance has set Huber on a winning path and merits our congratulations!

1997 Hecklinger Schloßberg
Weißer Burgunder trocken
20 DM, 13%, 🍷 till 2000 **86**

1996 Malterdinger Bienenberg
Grauer Burgunder Spätlese trocken
16.50 DM, 13%, 🍷 till 2002 **86**

1997 Chardonnay
trocken
35 DM, 13.5%, 🍷 till 2002 **88**

1996 Malterdinger Bienenberg
Riesling Kabinett trocken
15 DM, 12%, 🍷 till 2000 **88**

1996 Malterdinger Bienenberg
Weißer Burgunder Spätlese trocken
19.50 DM, 13%, 🍷 till 2003 **91**

——— Red wines ———

1995 Spätburgunder
trocken
30 DM, 13%, 🍷 till 2002 **88**

1996 Spätburgunder
trocken "Alte Reben"
35 DM, 13%, 🍷 till 2003 **89**

1996 Spätburgunder
trocken "Reserve"
52 DM, 13%, 🍷 till 2006 **91**

1995 Spätburgunder
trocken "Reserve"
42 DM, 13%, 🍷 till 2003 **91**

Chardonnay
Trocken
Baden
1994 Qualitätswein A.P.Nr. 4721696 12,5%vol · 75 cl
ERZEUGERABFÜLLUNG
BERNHARD HUBER WEINGUT
D-79364 · MALTERDINGEN · bei RIEGEL

SCHLOSSGUT ISTEIN

Owner: County of Lörrach
Leased and managed by Albert Soder
79588 Istein, Im Innerdorf 23
Tel. (0 76 28) 12 84, Fax 86 32
Directions: A 5 Freiburg–Basel, exit Efringen-Kirchen
Sales: Albert and Anita Soder
Opening hours: Mon.–Fri. 9 a.m. to 5 p.m. or by appointment
Worth seeing: Chapel of Sankt Veits, Istein castle

Vineyard area: 10 hectares
Annual production: 65,000 bottles
Top site: Isteiner Kirchberg
Soil types: Weathered Jurassic limestone, loess and loam
Grape varieties: 35% Gutedel, 25% Spätburgunder, 10% each of Riesling and Weißburgunder, 5% each of Chardonnay and Grauburgunder, 10% other varieties
Average yield: 55 hl/ha
Best vintages: 1995, 1996, 1997
Member: VDP

Not far from Basel stands Schlossgut Istein, one of Germany's most southerly estates. As early as 1139 Pope Innocent II in Rome referred to the castle in documents. In the last ten years Albert Soder has managed to bring this once rundown property back to the limelight; today it is one of the leading wineries of the Markgräflerland. As Soder himself points out, his decision to market only wines that have been fermented to complete dryness is "rather uncompromising." Praiseworthy is the fact that he seldom boasts about himself or his wines; a rugged individualist, he feels more at home in the vineyard or the cellar. Soder's wines were always voluptuous, often too much so. Not everyone enjoys an Auslese with 16 percent alcohol! In spite of this, the whole range of wines in 1996 had a stylishness that one must ungrudgingly acknowledge. The 1997s are much better balanced, even spicy in character.

1997 Isteiner Kirchberg
Riesling Spätlese trocken
18.80 DM, 12.5%, ♀ till 2000 **84**

1997 Isteiner Kirchberg
Weißer Burgunder Spätlese trocken
18.50 DM, 13%, ♀ till 2000 **84**

1996 Isteiner Kirchberg
Riesling Spätlese trocken
18 DM, 12%, ♀ till 2002 **84**

1996 Isteiner Kirchberg
Chardonnay Spätlese trocken
26 DM, 13.5%, ♀ till 2000 **84**

1996 Isteiner Kirchberg
Gewürztraminer Spätlese trocken
20 DM, 13%, ♀ till 2002 **84**

1997 Isteiner Kirchberg
Chardonnay Spätlese trocken
28 DM, 13%, ♀ till 2001 **86**

——— Red wines ———

1996 Isteiner Kirchberg
Spätburgunder Kabinett trocken
17 DM, 12%, ♀ till 2001 **84**

1995 Isteiner Kirchberg
Spätburgunder Spätlese trocken
38 DM, 12.5%, ♀ till 2003 **86**

1995 Isteiner Kirchberg
Spätburgunder Auslese trocken
48 DM, 13.5%, ♀ till 2005 **88**

WEINGUT KARL H. JOHNER

Owners: Karl Heinz and Irene Johner
Winemakers: Karl Heinz and Patrick Johner
79235 Bischoffingen, Gartenstraße 20
Tel. (0 76 62) 60 41, Fax 83 80
Directions: A 5 Frankfurt–Basel, exit Riegel, towards Breisach and Vogtsburg
Sales: Irene Johner
Opening hours: Mon.–Fri. 2 p.m. to 5 p.m., Sat. 10 a.m. to noon and 2 p.m. to 4 p.m. or by appointment
Worth seeing: Round barrel room

Vineyard area: 16.5 hectares
Annual production: 100,000 bottles
Top site: Bischoffinger Steinbuck
Soil types: Weathered volcanic soil
Grape varieties: 30% Blauer Spätburgunder, 25% Grauburgunder, 18% Weißburgunder, 13% Rivaner, 5% Chardonnay, 3% Sauvignon Blanc, 6% other varieties
Average yield: 48 hl/ha
Best vintages: 1995, 1996, 1997
Member: Deutsches Barrique-Forum

No one's star has risen so swiftly in the past decade as that of Karl Heinz Johner, who was trained at Geisenheim and then helped foster winemaking skills in England. He is the only producer in Germany who ages all of his wines in small wooden barrels and markets them as simple "table wines" without vineyard designation. Necessity is the mother of invention; and given the 93 parcels of vines that this restless renegade manages in seven different vineyards, any other course of action would have been a nightmare. The result is that each wine is stamped with the mark of the winemaker rather than that of the vineyard. The 1996 whites showed luscious tropical aromas paired with a robust backbone of acidity. The outstanding 1996 Spätburgunder "SJ" was one of the best wines of the vintage. Don't miss them! Our first tasting of the slightly sweet 1997s was less convincing. Johner, however, believes that they are the best wines he has ever produced.

1996 Grauer Burgunder
Tafelwein trocken
22 DM, 12%, ♀ till 2000 **88**

1997 Weißer Burgunder & Chardonnay
Tafelwein
29 DM, 13.5%, ♀ till 2000 **88**

1996 Weißer Burgunder & Chardonnay
Tafelwein trocken
27.50 DM, ♀ till 2000 **89**

1996 Sauvignon Blanc
Tafelwein trocken
30 DM, ♀ till 2000 **89**

1996 Grauer Burgunder
Tafelwein trocken "SJ"
40 DM, ♀ till 2002 **89**

1996 Chardonnay
Tafelwein
45 DM, 13.5%, ♀ till 2003 **89**

1997 Grauer Burgunder
Tafelwein "SJ"
45 DM, 14%, ♀ till 2002 **89**

——— Red wines ———

1996 Blauer Spätburgunder
trocken
35 DM, 13.5%, ♀ till 2001 **86**

1995 Blauer Spätburgunder
trocken
27.50 DM, 13%, ♀ till 2000 **89**

1996 Blauer Spätburgunder
trocken "SJ"
65 DM, 13.5%, ♀ till 2003 **92**

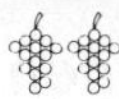

WEINGUT KALKBÖDELE

Owner: Mathis brothers
General Manager: Tobias Burtsche
79291 Merdingen, Enggasse 21
Tel. (0 76 68) 71 11 13, Fax 9 45 05
Directions: A 5 Karlsruhe–Basel, exit Freiburg-Mitte, towards Umkirch, via the Tuniberg
Sales: Tobias Burtsche
Opening hours: Mon.–Fri. 1 p.m. to 5 p.m., Sat. and Sun. by appointment
Worth seeing: Unusual barrel rooms

Vineyard area: 15 hectares
Annual production: 100,000 bottles
Top sites: Merdinger Bühl, Munzinger Kapellenberg
Soil types: Rocky limestone overlaid with loess
Grape varieties: 60% Spätburgunder, 15% Weißburgunder, 10% Grauburgunder, 7% Müller-Thurgau, 5% Riesling, 3% Gewürztraminer
Average yield: 58 hl/ha
Best vintages: 1993, 1995, 1996
Member: Deutsches Barrique Forum

Tobias Burtsche has not had an easy go since he took over the Mathis brothers' highly traditional estate in Merdingen. For years the winery, with its vineyards on the Tuniberg and Kaiserstuhl, has made a name for itself with Spätburgunder that are aged in French barrels. The red wines still receive most of the critical acclaim; but the white Burgundian varieties are gaining in stature. Step by step Burtsche has shown that he has his own precise idea of what makes good wine. The 1995s were the finest that we have ever tasted from this estate; the 1996s were of similar quality. The 1997s are somewhat lighter, but more elegant. Although many of these wines were quite closed in their youth, they nonetheless display unmistakable character.

1997 Merdinger Bühl
Weißer Burgunder Kabinett trocken
10.50 DM, 12%, ♀ now **82**

1996 Merdinger Bühl
Weißer Burgunder Spätlese trocken
14 DM, 13%, ♀ now **82**

1997 Munzinger Kapellenberg
Grauer Burgunder Spätlese trocken
15 DM, 13%, ♀ till 2000 **84**

1996 Merdinger Bühl
Weißer Burgunder Spätlese trocken "B"
20 DM, 13%, ♀ till 2000 **84**

1996 Munzinger Kapellenberg
Grauer Burgunder Spätlese trocken "B"
20 DM, 13%, ♀ till 2002 **84**

1997 Munzinger Kapellenberg
Gewürztraminer Spätlese trocken
11 DM/0.5 liter, 13.5%, ♀ till 2000 **86**

— Red wines —

1996 Merdinger Bühl
Spätburgunder Spätlese trocken "B"
30.30 DM, 13.5%, ♀ till 2001 **84**

1995 Merdinger Bühl
Spätburgunder Spätlese trocken "B"
30 DM, 13%, ♀ till 2000 **84**

FRANZ KELLER ERZEUGERGEMEINSCHAFT SCHWARZER ADLER

Owner: Franz Keller
Manager: Fritz Keller
Winemaker: Holger Koch
79235 Oberbergen, Badbergstraße 23
Tel. (0 76 62) 9 33 00, Fax 7 19
e-mail: franz-keller@t-online.de
Directions: A 5 Frankfurt–Basel, exit Riegel, towards Breisach
Sales: Werner Geiser
Opening hours: Mon.–Fri. 8 a.m. to 5 p.m., Sat. and Sun. 8 a.m. to noon or by appointment
Hotel and restaurant: "Zum Schwarzen Adler," closed on Wed. and Thur.
Worth seeing: The cellars that were bored into the side of the mountain

Vineyard area: 20 hectares owned by the estate
Contracted growers: 19 hectares
Number of adherents: 32
Annual production: 290,000 bottles
Top site: Oberbergener Bassgeige
Soil types: Loess over weathered basalt
Grape varieties: 30% Grauburgunder, 28% Spätburgunder, 15% Müller-Thurgau, 12% Weißburgunder, 8% Riesling, 7% other varieties
Average yield: 63 hl/ha
Best vintages: 1994, 1996, 1997

Franz Keller belongs to a small group of unique personalities within the German wine industry. As a dogged champion of completely dry wines he has encouraged many of his colleagues, albeit sometimes reluctantly, to follow his lead. Today, his son manages the estate. After a rather disappointing peformance in 1995, Fritz Keller produced much better wines in 1996. Forthright fruit and discreet use of oak were the dominant features of his better bottlings; but the simpler wines, such as the Rivaner, could and should have turned out better. Although it was not an easy vintage, the 1997s were produced with more foresight. This winery is certainly still not an overachiever, but the wines are improving in quality.

1996 Oberbergener Baßgeige
Riesling trocken
12.50 DM, 11.5%, 🍷 till 2000 — **82**

1997 Grauer Burgunder
Spätlese trocken "Alte Reben"
23 DM, 13.5%, 🍷 now — **84**

1996 Weißer Burgunder & Chardonnay
trocken "Selektion Franziskus"
24 DM, 12.5%, 🍷 till 2000 — **86**

1996 Oberbergener Baßgeige
Grauer Burgunder Spätlese trocken
18.50 DM, 13%, 🍷 till 2000 — **86**

1997 Oberbergener Pulverbuck
Weißer Burgunder Spätlese trocken "Classic"
19.50 DM, 13%, 🍷 till 2000 — **86**

1997 Grauer Burgunder
trocken "A"
48 DM, 13.5%, 🍷 till 2002 — **88**

1996 Chardonnay
Tafelwein trocken "S"
31 DM, 13%, 🍷 till 2002 — **89**

——— Red wine ———

1996 Spätburgunder
trocken "S"
26.50 DM, 13%, 🍷 till 2001 — **86**

WINZERGENOSSENSCHAFT KÖNIGSCHAFFHAUSEN

Manager: Edmund Schillinger
Winemaker: Helmut Staiblin
79346 Königschaffhausen,
Kiechlinsberger Straße 2
Tel. (0 76 42) 10 03, Fax 25 35
Directions: A 5 Frankfurt–Basel, exit Riegel, towards the Rhine
Sales: Harald Henninger and Karin Langenbacher
Opening hours: Mon.–Fri. 8 a.m. to noon and 1:30 p.m. to 5 p.m.
Sat. 9 a.m. to noon
Worth seeing: Old cellar for the barrels

Vineyard area: 165 hectares
Number of adherents: 360
Annual production: 1.23 million bottles
Top sites: Königschaffhauser Hasenberg and Steingrüble
Soil types: Loess and loam, partly over weathered volcanic soil
Grape varieties: 36% Müller-Thurgau, 33% Spätburgunder, 18% Grauburgunder, 7% Weißburgunder, 6% other varieties
Average yield: 70 hl/ha
Best vintages: 1995, 1996, 1997
Member: Deutsches Barrique Forum

For years Königschaffhausen has been at the top of its class among Baden's cooperatives. In the early 1970s sizeable investments were made here with a view to producing wines of better quality; today the growers are enjoying the fruits of this labor. Much of the explanation for the improved quality lies in lower yields, modern cellar equipment and the will to produce the finest wines possible. The 1995s were the best wines we have tasted from this cooperative for many years. In 1996 the growers again produced an astonishing range: juicy, lively, full of extract and all displaying good depth. Although well made, the 1997s are not quite as successful. Nonetheless, only a few private estates are able to make wines of similar quality. Moreover, even the dessert wines are often exemplary.

1997 Königschaffhauser Hasenberg
Weißer Burgunder Auslese trocken
48 DM, 13.5%, ♀ now **82**

1996 Königschaffhauser Hasenberg
Chardonnay Spätlese trocken
30 DM, 13%, ♀ now **84**

1996 Königschaffhauser Hasenberg
Grauer Burgunder Spätlese trocken
16 DM, 13%, ♀ now **86**

1995 Königschaffhauser Hasenberg
Ruländer Trockenbeerenauslese
46.50 DM/0.375 liter, ♀ till 2010 **94**

——— Red wines ———

1996 Königschaffhauser Steingrüble
Spätburgunder trocken "Regnum" **
24 DM, 13%, ♀ till 2000 **84**

1997 Königschaffhauser Steingrüble
Spätburgunder trocken "Selection"
17.50 DM, 12.5%, ♀ till 2002 **84**

1995 Königschaffhauser Steingrüble
Spätburgunder trocken **
28 DM, 13%, ♀ till 2000 **86**

1995 Königschaffhauser Hasenberg
Cabernet Sauvignon trocken
30 DM, 12.5%, ♀ till 2002 **86**

1997 Königschaffhauser Steingrüble
Spätburgunder Spätlese trocken
28.50 DM, 13%, ♀ till 2002 **88**

WEINGUT KONSTANZER

Owners: Horst and Petra Konstanzer
79241 Ihringen, Quellenstraße 22
Tel. (0 76 68) 55 37, Fax 50 97
Directions: A 5 Frankfurt–Basel, exit Freiburg-Mitte, towards Breisach
Opening hours: Mon.–Fri. 9 a.m. to 6 p.m., Sat. 9 a.m. to 4:30 p.m. or by appointment

Vineyard area: 6 hectares
Annual production: 40,000 bottles
Top site: Ihringer Winklerberg
Soil types: Weathered volcanic soil, loess
Grape varieties: 52% Spätburgunder, 20% Grauburgunder, 8% Silvaner, 7% Weißburgunder, 4% Müller-Thurgau, 3% each of Riesling, Muskateller and Chardonnay
Average yield: 63 hl/ha
Best vintages: 1995, 1996, 1997

This small estate on the southern end of the Kaiserstuhl was founded in 1983 by Horst and Petra Konstanzer with just a third of a hectare. Since 1989 the couple has worked full time running the property, which has now grown to six hectares. Half of their holdings are located in the magnificent Ihringer Winklerberg vineyard. Although we have been following the evolution of this estate for years, it was the 1995 vintage that first brought this estate out of the shadows. The wines were produced in a very traditional manner; and the lean, somewhat earthy style with its finely expressed varietal character has rightly found a loyal following. The 1996s were the best group of wines that this estate had ever produced, only to be trumped by succulently opulent 1997s. Expect to hear more from this estate in years to come!

1996 Ihringer Fohrenberg
Weißer Burgunder Spätlese trocken
14.50 DM, 13%, 🍷 now **82**

1997 Ihringer Winklerberg
Riesling Spätlese trocken
14.50 DM, 13.5%, 🍷 till 2001 **84**

1997 Ihringer Winklerberg
Silvaner Spätlese trocken
13.20 DM, 13%, 🍷 till 2000 **84**

1997 Ihringer Winklerberg
Grauer Burgunder Spätlese trocken
15.50 DM, 14%, 🍷 till 2000 **84**

1996 Ihringer Winklerberg
Chardonnay Spätlese trocken
20 DM, 13.5%, 🍷 now **84**

1997 Ihringer Winklerberg
Chardonnay Spätlese trocken
20.50 DM, 13.5%, 🍷 till 2000 **86**

——— Red wines ———

1996 Ihringer Winklerberg
Spätburgunder trocken
14.20 DM, 13.5%, 🍷 till 2000 **84**

1996 Ihringer Winklerberg
Spätburgunder Spätlese trocken
19.50 DM, 13.5%, 🍷 till 2000 **84**

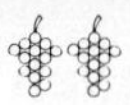

WEINGUT LÄMMLIN-SCHINDLER

Owner: Gerd Schindler
79418 Mauchen, Müllheimer Straße 4
Tel. (0 76 35) 4 40, Fax 4 36
Directions: A 5 Freiburg–Basel, exit Neuenburg, towards Schliengen
Opening hours: Mon.–Fri. 8:30 a.m. to noon and 2 p.m. to 6 p.m., Sat. 8:30 a.m. to noon and 2 p.m. to 4:30 p.m. or by appointment
Restaurant: "Zur Krone" in Mauchen, open from 11 a.m. to 11 p.m., except Mon. and Tue.
Specialties: Smoked sausage, oxtail with horseradish
History: The family has been making wine since the 12th century

Vineyard area: 19.4 hectares
Annual production: 130,000 bottles
Top sites: Mauchener Frauenberg, Mauchener Sonnenstück
Soil types: Weathered limestone, loess and loam
Grape varieties: 41% Spätburgunder, 23% Gutedel, 10% Weißburgunder, 8% Chardonnay, 5% Grauburgunder, 4% Müller-Thurgau, 9% other varieties
Average yield: 60 hl/ha
Best vintages: 1993, 1996, 1997
Member: BÖW

By joining the Federal Association of Organic Wine Growers in 1989 Gerd Schindler made an abrupt change to more ecologically sound production methods; since 1993 he has also displayed a similar approach to quality. Today his winery is one of the top producers in the Markgräflerland. Although his wines often seem a touch rustic in style, Gerd Schindler assembled a thoroughly respectable collection of wines from the 1996 vintage. The 1997s are more forthcoming in fruit and express a touch of finesse. They are probably the finest wines that he has ever produced. His wines are best enjoyed at the restaurant "Zur Krone" in Mauchen, which the Lämmlin family has run since 1862.

1997 Chardonnay
Kabinett trocken
15 DM, 13%, ♀ now — **84**

1997 Mauchener Frauenberg
Riesling Spätlese trocken
15.50 DM, 12.5%, ♀ till 2000 — **84**

1996 Mauchener Sonnenstück
Grauer Burgunder Spätlese trocken
16.50 DM, 13%, ♀ till 2000 — **84**

1997 Mauchener Sonnenstück
Weißer Burgunder Spätlese trocken
14.80 DM, 13%, ♀ till 2000 — **86**

1997 Chardonnay
Spätlese trocken
21.50 DM, 13%, ♀ till 2000 — **86**

1996 Chardonnay
Spätlese trocken
21.50 DM, 12.5%, ♀ till 2000 — **86**

——— Red wines ———

1996 Mauchener Sonnenstück
Spätburgunder Kabinett trocken
12.50 DM, 12.5%, ♀ till 2000 — **82**

1996 Mauchener Frauenberg
Spätburgunder Spätlese trocken "B"
27 DM, 13%, ♀ till 2000 — **82**

1995 Mauchener Sonnenstück
Spätburgunder trocken "B"
19.50 DM, 13%, ♀ till 2002 — **84**

WEINGUT ANDREAS LAIBLE

Owner: Andreas and Ingrid Laible
77770 Durbach, Am Bühl 6
Tel. (07 81) 4 12 38, Fax 3 83 39
Directions: A 5 Frankfurt–Basel, exit Appenweier or Offenburg, towards Durbach
Sales: Ingrid and Andreas Laible
Opening hours: Mon.–Fri. 8 a.m. to 6 p.m., Sat. 8 a.m. to 5 p.m. or by appointment
History: The estate has belonged to the family since 1672

Vineyard area: 6 hectares
Annual production: 28,000 bottles
Top sites: Durbacher Plauelrain
Soil types: Weathered granite
Grape varieties: 58% Riesling (Klingelberger), 15% Spätburgunder, 6% each of Traminer, Gewürztraminer and Scheurebe, 6% of Weißburgunder and Grauburgunder, 3% other varieties
Average yield: 53 hl/ha
Best vintages: 1993, 1994, 1996

As the Plauelrain vineyard in Durbach can only be cultivated manually, Andreas Laible has a backbreaking job. Further, he has shown himself to be a versatile craftsman. He built the house, courtyard and cellars himself, makes excellent schnapps from fruit grown in his orchard and even bakes his own bread in a hand-fired brick oven. Just as unique, and as full of character as Laible himself, are his wines. After an excellent showing in 1995, Laible repeated the performance in 1996 with an extremely appealing range of wines: there is not a poor wine in the lot! However, neither of the two vintages can quite match the sheer quality of the 1993s and 1994s. Poor weather in 1997 made the current vintage, however good the individual wines might be, his lightest since 1992. Nonetheless, no one else in the Ortenau can hold a candle to Laible; in Baden he retains his place among the elite.

1997 Durbacher Plauelrain
Grauer Burgunder Spätlese trocken
15 DM, 13%, ♀ till 2000 **86**

1997 Durbacher Plauelrain
Riesling Spätlese trocken – 31 –
18.20 DM, 12%, ♀ till 2002 **86**

1997 Durbacher Plauelrain
Riesling Auslese
22 DM, 11%, ♀ till 2003 **86**

1996 Durbacher Plauelrain
Riesling Spätlese trocken – 31 –
18 DM, 12%, ♀ till 2002 **88**

1997 Durbacher Plauelrain
Riesling Spätlese trocken “SL”
19.80 DM, 12%, ♀ till 2003 **88**

1997 Durbacher Plauelrain
Riesling Spätlese
18 DM, 10%, ♀ till 2005 **88**

1996 Durbacher Plauelrain
Gewürztraminer Spätlese
14.50 DM, 11%, ♀ till 2003 **88**

1997 Durbacher Plauelrain
Scheurebe Auslese
20 DM, 11%, ♀ till 2006 **89**

1996 Durbacher Plauelrain
Riesling Spätlese trocken “SL”
19.50 DM, 12%, ♀ till 2003 **90**

1996 Durbacher Plauelrain
Riesling Eiswein
42 DM/0.375 liter, 9%, ♀ till 2010 **91**

WEINGUT A.LAIBLE
BADEN
ORTENAU
1997er
DURBACHER PLAUELRAIN
Klingelberger (Riesling)
SPÄTLESE · TROCKEN
QUALITÄTSWEIN MIT PRÄDIKAT
A.P.NR. 514/31/98
12% VOL
0,75 LTR
ERZEUGERABFÜLLUNG
WEINGUT ANDREAS LAIBLE · D-7601 DURBACH AM BÜHL 6

WEINGUT HEINRICH MÄNNLE

Owner: Heinrich and Wilma Männle
Winemaker: Heinrich Männle
77770 Durbach, Sendelbach 16
Tel. (07 81) 4 11 01, Fax 44 01 05
Directions: A 5 Frankfurt–Basel, exit Appenweier or Offenburg, towards Durbach
Sales: Wilma Männle
Opening hours: Mon.–Sat. 8 a.m. to 6 p.m. or by appointment
History: The estate has belonged to the family since 1737
Worth seeing: Vaulted granite cellar and traditional house

Vineyard area: 5 hectares
Annual production: 38,000 bottles
Top sites: Durbacher Kochberg, Ölberg and Plauelrain
Soil types: Weathered granite
Grape varieties: 52% Spätburgunder, 10% Weißburgunder, 8% Riesling, 5% Grauburgunder, 25% other varieties
Average yield: 65 hl/ha
Best vintages: 1993, 1996, 1997

Founded in 1737, this estate is known in Baden primarily for its red wines. After two less successful vintages Heinrich Männle produced a stimulating collection in 1996. The whites were characterized by elegant fruitiness, delicate varietal expression and an appealing richness. Without a doubt, this was his best vintage since 1993. That the red wines from 1995, a year tainted by botrytis, are of only average quality is understandable. The 1996 Spätburgunders were much better. However, poor weather in 1997 made it impossible for Heinrich Männle to repeat this performance.

1997 Durbacher Kochberg
Grauer Burgunder Spätlese trocken
18.50 DM, 13%, ♀ till 2000 **84**

1997 Durbacher Kochberg
Scheurebe Spätlese
14.50 DM, 10%, ♀ till 2000 **84**

1996 Durbacher Kochberg
Müller-Thurgau Kabinett trocken
8 DM, 12%, ♀ till 2000 **86**

1996 Durbacher Kochberg
Weißer Burgunder Spätlese trocken
16.50 DM, 12%, ♀ till 2000 **86**

1996 Durbacher Ölberg
Gewürztraminer Spätlese
15.50 DM, 11.5%, ♀ till 2002 **88**

1996 Durbacher Kochberg
Grauer Burgunder Spätlese trocken
17 DM, 13%, ♀ till 2002 **89**

1996 Durbacher Kochberg
Scheurebe Spätlese
14 DM, 9.5%, ♀ till 2003 **89**

——— Red wines ———

1995 Durbacher Kochberg
Cabernet Sauvignon trocken
34.50 DM, 13%, ♀ till 2000 **84**

1996 Durbacher Kochberg
Spätburgunder trocken
43 DM, 13%, ♀ till 2001 **86**

WEINGUT EMIL MARGET

Owner: Marget family
General Manager: Reiner Marget
79379 Müllheim-Hügelheim, Schloßgartenstraße 4
Tel. (0 76 31) 23 54, Fax 17 24 65
Directions: A 5 Freiburg–Basel, exit Müllheim-Neuenburg
Sales: Mr. Marget and Ms. Klotz
Opening hours: Mon.–Fri. 8 a.m. to noon and 1:30 p.m. to 6 p.m.
Sat. 8 a.m. to noon and 2 p.m. to 5 p.m.
or by appointment
History: Owned by the family since 1771

Vineyard area: 7.5 hectares
Annual production: 55,000 bottles
Top sites: Hügelheimer Gottesacker, Höllberg and Schloßgarten
Soil types: Loess and loam
Grape varieties: 59% Gutedel, 11% each of Spätburgunder and Weißburgunder, 5% each of Silvaner and Nobling, 9% other varieties
Average yield: 55 hl/ha
Best vintages: 1995, 1996, 1997

Since 1771, when Friedrich Marget from Müllheim married into a family that had already been settled in Hügelheim for over 200 years, this estate has borne the name of Marget. The old property itself dates back to 1450. Emil Marget, after whom the estate is now named, placed greater emphasis on the wine business and in 1907 was the first in the Markgräflerland to bottle and market his own wines. As they were then, the wines are still matured in old casks in the vaulted cellars of the estate. Long known for its fully dry wines, the winery is particulary respected for its fresh and lively Gutedel. After less successful vintages in 1993 and 1994 Reiner Marget has bounced back. The 1995s were appealing, but are outshone by the 1996s and 1997s – all are bright and fruity, spicy and eminently drinkable.

1997 Hügelheimer Schloßgarten
Gutedel trocken "N"
8.50 DM, 10.5%, ♀ now **77**

1996 Hügelheimer Schloßgarten
Gutedel trocken "N"
8.25 DM, 10%, ♀ now **80**

1997 Hügelheimer Schloßgarten
Weißer Burgunder Kabinett trocken
12.75 DM, 12.5%, ♀ now **80**

1996 Hügelheimer Höllberg
Nobling Kabinett trocken
12.75 DM, 12%, ♀ now **80**

1996 Hügelheimer Gottesacker
Gutedel trocken
10 DM, 10.5%, ♀ now **82**

1996 Hügelheimer Schloßgarten
Weißer Burgunder Kabinett trocken
11.50 DM, 11%, ♀ now **82**

1997 Hügelheimer Schloßgarten
Gutedel Kabinett trocken "F"
10.45 DM, 10.5%, ♀ now **82**

1997 Hügelheimer Gottesacker
Grauer Burgunder Spätlese trocken
19.70 DM, 13%, ♀ now **82**

——— Red wine ———

1996 Hügelheimer Höllberg
Spätburgunder Kabinett trocken
14.50 DM, 11%, ♀ till 2000 **82**

WEINGUT MICHEL

Owners: Walter and Josef Michel
Winemaker: Josef Michel
79235 Achkarren, Winzerweg 24
Tel. (0 76 62) 4 29, Fax 7 63
Directions: A 5 Frankfurt–Basel, exit Riegel, towards the Rhine
Sales: Michel family
Opening hours: Mon.–Fri. 9 a.m. to 6 p.m. or by appointment

Vineyard area: 11 hectares
Annual production: 70,000 bottles
Top sites: Achkarrer Schloßberg and Castellberg
Soil types: Weathered volcanic soil, loess and loam
Grape varieties: 41% Spätburgunder, 26% Grauburgunder, 16% Weißburgunder, 12% Müller-Thurgau, 3% Silvaner, 2% Chardonnay
Average yield: 62 hl/ha
Best vintages: 1993, 1996, 1997

In 1983 Walter Michel and his wife, Margarete, former members of the local cooperative, set out on their own. From the beginning their son Josef has been responsible for the cellars. Blessed with vines in the outstanding Schloßberg vineyard in Achkarren, which are pruned short and picked by hand, the family was quickly able to make a name for themselves. They first attracted our attention with a pair of inspired 1993s. Nonetheless, we were astonished by the quality of the 1996s: each wine lovelier than the previous one. The 1997s are even better – lush, juicy and racy – and surely the finest wines that Josef has produced to date. This estate has what it takes to climb further up the ladder in Baden's hierarchy.

1997 Achkarrer Schloßberg
Chardonnay trocken
12 DM, 13%, ♀ till 2000 **84**

1997 Achkarrer Schloßberg
Weißer Burgunder Spätlese trocken
13.50 DM, 13.5%, ♀ till 2000 **86**

1996 Achkarrer Schloßberg
Grauer Burgunder Spätlese trocken ***
17 DM, 13.5%, ♀ till 2000 **86**

1996 Achkarrer Schloßberg
Weißer Burgunder Spätlese trocken ***
17 DM, 13.5%, ♀ till 2000 **86**

1996 Achkarrer Schloßberg
Chardonnay Spätlese trocken
17 DM, 13%, ♀ till 2000 **86**

1996 Achkarrer Schloßberg
Grauer Burgunder Spätlese trocken "B"
22 DM, 14%, ♀ till 2000 **86**

1997 Achkarrer Schloßberg
Weißer Burgunder Spätlese trocken ***
17 DM, 14%, ♀ till 2001 **88**

1997 Achkarrer Schloßberg
Grauer Burgunder Spätlese trocken ***
17 DM, 14%, ♀ till 2002 **88**

— Red wine —

1996 Achkarrer Schloßberg
Spätburgunder trocken
22 DM, 13%, ♀ till 2001 **86**

WEINGUT GEBRÜDER MÜLLER

Owner: Peter Bercher
Manager: Joachim Lang
79206 Breisach,
Richard-Müller-Straße 5
Tel. (0 76 67) 5 11, Fax 65 81
e-mail: weingut-mueller@netfit.de
Internet: www.netfit.de/weingut-mueller
Directions: A 5 Frankfurt–Basel, exit Bad Krozingen, towards Breisach
Sales: Joachim Lang, Ellen Bercher
Opening hours: Mon.–Fri. 10 a.m. to 5 p.m., Sat. 9 a.m. to 1 p.m. or by appointment

Vineyard area: 10 hectares
Annual production: 70,000 bottles
Top sites: Ihringer Winklerberg, Breisacher Eckartsberg
Soil types: Weathered volcanic soil, loess and rocks
Grape varieties: 45% Spätburgunder, 25% Weißburgunder, 11% Grauburgunder, 7% Riesling, 6% Silvaner, 6% other varieties
Average yield: 50 hl/ha
Best vintages: 1995, 1996, 1997
Member: Deutsches Barrique Forum

This estate was founded by Johann Baptist Hau, the first producer to make wines from the Kaiserstuhl known to a public outside Germany. Today the winery belongs to Peter Bercher, brother of the outstanding winemakers from Burkheim, Rainer and Eckhardt Bercher, who for many years were also responsible for the wines here. To give the estate its own identity Joachim Lang was hired in 1990 as winemaker and, at the same time, a new cellar was constructed. Over the past few years the estate has shown considerable consistency, especially with its red wines; but only since the 1995 vintage have the white wines been up to par. With the 1996 vintage, Bercher and Lang again produced an attractive range of wines. Even the two reds from 1995, which as a vintage was marred by problems, were well made. The 1997s are even better.

1996 Ihringer Winklerberg
Riesling Spätlese trocken
16 DM, 12%, ♀ till 2000 **84**

1997 Breisacher Eckartsberg
Grauer Burgunder Spätlese trocken
16.70 DM, 13.5%, ♀ till 2001 **86**

1996 Breisacher Eckartsberg
Weißer Burgunder Spätlese trocken
16.50 DM, 12.5%, ♀ till 2000 **86**

——— Red wines ———

1996 Ihringer Winklerberg
Cabernet Franc trocken
35 DM, 13%, ♀ till 2002 **86**

1996 Ihringer Winklerberg
Cabernet & Merlot trocken
35 DM, 13%, ♀ till 2002 **86**

1995 Ihringer Winklerberg
Cabernet & Merlot trocken
33 DM, 12.5%, ♀ till 2003 **86**

1996 Ihringer Winklerberg
Spätburgunder Spätlese trocken
25 DM, 13%, ♀ till 2001 **86**

1995 Ihringer Winklerberg
Spätburgunder Spätlese trocken
33 DM, 13%, ♀ till 2003 **86**

1996 Ihringer Winklerberg
Spätburgunder Spätlese trocken
35 DM, 13%, ♀ till 2003 **88**

WEIN- UND SEKTGUT NÄGELSFÖRST

Owner: Reinhard J. Strickler
Manager: Albert Mirbach
Winemaker: Martin Franzen
76534 Baden-Baden (Varnhalt), Nägelsförst 1
Tel. (0 72 21) 3 55 50, Fax 35 55 56
e-mail: gut.naegelsfoerst@t-online.de
Directions: A 5 Frankfurt–Basel, exit Baden-Baden
Sales: Albert Mirbach
Opening hours: Mon.–Fri. 9 a.m. to 6 p.m., Sat. 10 a.m. to 4 p.m. or by appointment

Vineyard area: 25 hectares
Annual production: 125,000 bottles
Top sites: Varnhalter Klosterbergfelsen, Neuweierer Mauerberg, Umweger Stich den Buben, Fremersberger Feigenwäldchen
Soil types: Weathered porphyry, granite and gneiss, red sandstone
Grape varieties: 48% Riesling, 19% Spätburgunder, 8% Müller-Thurgau, 6% each of Weißburgunder, Chardonnay and Bacchus, 3% Grauburgunder, 4% other varieties
Average yield: 40 hl/ha
Best vintages: 1995, 1996, 1997

Enthroned in the hills near the Yburg in the midst of the gorgeous landscape of the Black Forest, the Nägelsförst property overlooks the Rhine valley. It was once a Cistercian monastery, and Reinhard J. Strickler has invested enormous sums to reconstruct the estate, with its large dairy farm dating back to 1268. The wines have been improving year by year since 1994; and with the 1996 vintage the estate seemed to have made a breakthrough. The 1997s, however, were not nearly as good. The white Burgundian varieties often seemed somewhat broad and heavy. The experienced winemaker Martin Franzen, who was hired in the summer of 1998, should be able to put this estate back on the right track.

1996 Grauer Burgunder
Auslese "B"
45 DM, 14.5%, ♀ now **80**

1997 Neuweierer Mauerberg
Riesling Spätlese trocken
18.50 DM, 12.5%, ♀ till 2000 **82**

1997 Riesling
Spätlese trocken "RJS"
26.50 DM, 12.5%, ♀ till 2001 **82**

1996 Chardonnay
trocken "B"
27.50 DM, 12%, ♀ till 2000 **84**

1996 Riesling
Auslese "Selection RJS"
17.50 DM/0.375 liter, 12.5%, ♀ till 2002 **86**

1996 Riesling
Eiswein "Selection RJS"
110 DM/0.375 liter, 8.5%, ♀ till 2015 **95**

——— Red wines ———

1996 Spätburgunder
Spätlese trocken "Selection"
35 DM, 13.5%, ♀ till 2001 **84**

1996 Spätburgunder
trocken "B"
35 DM, 13%, ♀ till 2001 **86**

1996 Spätburgunder
Spätlese trocken "RJS"
45 DM, 13%, ♀ till 2002 **88**

WEINGUT SCHLOSS NEUWEIER

Owner: Gisela Joos
Manager: Holger Dütsch
Winemaker: Alexander Spinner
76534 Baden-Baden, Mauerbergstraße 21
Tel. (0 72 23) 9 66 70, Fax 6 08 64
Directions: A 5 Frankfurt–Basel, exit Bühl or Baden-Baden via Steinbach
Opening hours: Mon.–Fri. 9 a.m. to noon and 1 p.m. to 5 p.m.
Sat. 9 a.m. to 1 p.m.
Restaurant: In the castle, daily except Tuesday
Worth seeing: Terraced vineyard with stone walls, Neuweier Castle

Vineyard area: 10 hectares
Annual production: 65,000 bottles
Top sites: Neuweierer Schloßberg and Mauerberg
Soil types: Weathered granite and porphyry
Grape varieties: 85% Riesling, 12% Spätburgunder, 2% Weißburgunder, 1% Gewürztraminer
Average yield: 50 hl/ha
Best vintages: 1994, 1996, 1997

In 1992 Gisela Joos and her husband, Helmut, purchased the dilapidated Neuweier Castle. Since then they have lavished considerable sums on both the vineyards and the cellars; a distillery has also been built. The reconstruction of the castle, which has been restored to its former splendor, is also completed. Since the change of ownership, the steep single vineyard of Mauerberg, planted only with Riesling, has become the source of one of most elegant dry Rieslings in all of Baden. With the 1996 vintage Alexander Spinner produced wines that almost match the sheer quality of the lovely 1993s and 1994s. Even the modest "Qualitätswein" was a success. Given the difficult nature of the vintage, the 1997s are even better. No one in Baden, and only a few in Germany, can match the quality of these dry Rieslings.

1997 Neuweierer Mauerberg
Riesling Kabinett trocken
17 DM, 11.5%, ♀ till 2000 **84**

1996 Neuweierer Mauerberg
Riesling Kabinett trocken
17 DM, 11%, ♀ till 2000 **86**

1997 Neuweierer Schloßberg
Riesling Kabinett trocken "alte Reben"
18 DM, 11.5%, ♀ till 2000 **86**

1997 Neuweierer Mauerberg
Riesling Auslese halbtrocken
29.90 DM/0.5 liter, 14%, ♀ till 2002 **86**

1997 Neuweierer Mauerberg
Riesling Spätlese trocken
19.20 DM, 12%, ♀ till 2000 **88**

1996 Neuweierer Mauerberg
Riesling Spätlese trocken – 15 –
19 DM, 12%, ♀ till 2005 **88**

1996 Neuweierer Mauerberg
Riesling Spätlese trocken – 16 –
19 DM, 12%, ♀ till 2003 **88**

1996 Neuweierer Schloßberg
Riesling Kabinett trocken "Aus alten Reben"
18 DM, 11%, ♀ till 2005 **89**

1997 Neuweierer Schloßberg
Riesling Spätlese trocken "alte Reben"
21 DM, 12%, ♀ till 2002 **89**

1997 Neuweierer Mauerberg
Riesling Spätlese trocken "goldenes Loch"
25 DM, 12.5%, ♀ till 2002 **89**

WEINGUT SCHLOSS ORTENBERG

Owner: County of Ortenau, city of Offenburg
Manager: Winfried Köninger
Winemaker: Hans-Peter Rieflin
77799 Ortenberg, Am Sankt Andreas 1
Tel. (07 81) 9 34 30, Fax 93 43 20
Directions: A 5 Frankfurt–Basel, exit Offenburg, 3 kilometers on the B 33 towards Donaueschingen
Opening hours: Mon.–Fri. 8 a.m. to noon and 1 p.m. to 5 p.m.
Sat. 9 a.m. to 12:30 p.m.
History: Owned by the county since 1950
Worth seeing: Ortenberg castle

Vineyard area: 40 hectares
Annual production: 240,000 bottles
Top sites: Ortenberger Schloßberg and Andreasberg, Zeller Abtsberg
Soil types: Weathered primary rock
Grape varieties: 25% Riesling, 25% Spätburgunder, 20% Müller-Thurgau, 6% each of Grauburgunder, Weißburgunder, Chardonnay, Scheurebe and Sauvignon blanc
Average yield: 48 hl/ha
Best vintages: 1995, 1996, 1997

The merging of two communal wineries in 1997 created Baden's third largest estate. The county of Ortenau and the town of Offenburg joined forces and now market 40 hectares of wines with the label Schloss Ortenberg. The driving force behind this expansion was Winfried Köninger. He must now prove that he can manage a five-fold increase in vineyard size without compromising quality. The 1996 collection brought no definitive answer to this question. While the quality of the simplest wines lagged behind that of previous vintages, Köninger delivered some masterly dessert wines. Given the difficult nature of the vintage, 1997 was baptism by fire for Köninger; but he has now proven that this new estate can compete in the big leagues. The "S" was one of the finest dry Rieslings of the vintage and barrel samples of two red wines look very promising.

1997 Grauer Burgunder
Spätlese trocken
19.50 DM, 13.5%, ♀ till 2000 **84**

1997 Chardonnay
trocken
24.50 DM, 13.5%, ♀ till 2000 **86**

1996 Klingelberger (Riesling)
trocken "S"
19.50 DM, 11.5%, ♀ till 2002 **86**

1997 Riesling
Spätlese
15.50 DM, 10.5%, ♀ till 2003 **88**

1996 Scheurebe
Auslese
22.50 DM/0.5 liter, 11%, ♀ till 2006 **89**

1997 Riesling
trocken "S"
24.50 DM, 12.5%, ♀ till 2003 **91**

1996 Klingelberger (Riesling)
Eiswein
49 DM/0.375 liter, 9.5%, ♀ till 2010 **94**

1996 Scheurebe
Trockenbeerenauslese
65 DM/0.375 liter, 10%, ♀ till 2010 **94**

——— Red wine ———

1996 Spätburgunder
trocken
24.50 DM, 13%, ♀ till 2000 **86**

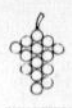

WINZERGENOSSENSCHAFT PFAFFENWEILER EG

Manager: Heinrich Stefan Männle
Winemaker: Roland Braun and Rolf Herbster
79292 Pfaffenweiler, Weinstraße 40
Tel. (0 76 64) 9 79 60, Fax 97 96 44
Directions: A 5 Frankfurt–Basel, exit Freiburg-Süd, B3 towards Bad Krozingen
Sales: Eric Schweigler
Opening hours: Mon.–Fri. 8 a.m. to 5 p.m., Sat. 9 a.m. to noon
History: Founded in 1952

Vineyard area: 108 hectares
Number of adherents: 268
Annual production: 830,000 bottles
Top sites: Pfaffenweiler Batzenberg and Oberdürrenberg
Soil types: Loam, loess with white limestone
Grape varieties: 31% Gutedel, 22% Spätburgunder, 20% Müller-Thurgau, 8% each of Weißer and Grauer Burgunder, 11% other varieties
Average yield: 71 hl/ha
Best vintages: 1996, 1997

Ten kilometers south of Freiburg lies the idyllic village of Pfaffenweiler, which was first documented as a wine producing area in the year 716. Until a couple of years ago the cooperative here was rarely mentioned; but since the arrival of Heinrich Stefan Männle, whose father runs the estate of that name in Durbach in the Ortenau, there has been an enormous change in quality. This has not happened without differences of opinion among the members, who were not accustomed to working in such an uncompromising fashion nor to taking risks, but the results speak for themselves. The 1996s and 1997s show what can be accomplished by a cooperative when the will is there. Long may it continue!

1997 Pfaffenweiler Oberdürrenberg
Grauer Burgunder Kabinett trocken
8.20 DM, 13%, ♀ now **82**

1997 Pfaffenweiler Oberdürrenberg
Gewürztraminer Spätlese trocken
14.90 DM, 14.5%, ♀ till 2000 **82**

1996 Pfaffenweiler Oberdürrenberg
Gewürztraminer Spätlese trocken
12 DM, 14%, ♀ now **82**

1997 Pfaffenweiler Oberdürrenberg
Grauer Burgunder Auslese trocken
19.90 DM, 15%, ♀ till 2000 **82**

1996 Pfaffenweiler Batzenberg
Scheurebe Kabinett
9.25 DM, 9.5%, ♀ now **82**

1997 Pfaffenweiler Oberdürrenberg
Ruländer Auslese
10.90 DM/0.5 liter, 10.5%, ♀ till 2000 **82**

1997 Pfaffenweiler Oberdürrenberg
Weißer Burgunder Spätlese trocken
16.90 DM, 14.5%, ♀ till 2000 **84**

1996 Pfaffenweiler Batzenberg
Gutedel Spätlese trocken "Primus"
12.50 DM, 12.5%, ♀ now **84**

1996 Pfaffenweiler Oberdürrenberg
Grauer Burgunder Spätlese trocken "Primus"
16.50 DM, 14%, ♀ now **84**

1996 Pfaffenweiler Oberdürrenberg
Ruländer Eiswein
99 DM/0.5 liter, 7.5%, ♀ till 2010 **91**

WEINGUT BURG RAVENSBURG

Owner: The family of Baron von Göler
Manager: Claus Burmeister
Winemaker: Karsten Rech
75056 Sulzfeld, Hauptstraße 44
Tel. (0 72 69) 9 14 10, Fax 91 41 40
Directions: A 5 Frankfurt–Basel, exit Bruchsal, B 293 towards Heilbronn
Sales: Claus Burmeister
Opening hours: Mon.–Fri. 8 a.m. to noon and 1 p.m. to 5 p.m.
Sat. 9 a.m. to noon
Restaurant: Burg Ravensburg, open daily except Monday
Specialties: Venison, local dishes
History: Vineyards first mentioned in 1249
Worth seeing: Ravensburg fortress and Amalienhof castle

Vineyard area: 22.7 hectares
Annual production: 140,000 bottles
Top sites: Burg Ravensburger Löchle, Husarenkappe and Dicker Franz
Soil types: Stony clay, heavy red clay
Grape varieties: 43% Riesling, 27% Schwarzriesling, 18% Lemberger, 12% other varieties
Average yield: 55 hl/ha
Best vintages: 1993, 1996, 1997
Member: VDP

In the early 12th century the fortress of Ravensburg was etablished on its present site. The three top vineyards, which are solely owned by this estate, are grouped together at the foot of the castle. With the 1996 vintage Claus Burmeister again produced an appealing collection of wines, without a doubt his finest since 1993. Healthy grapes were harvested at full maturity, resulting in over 90 percent of the production being declared as "Prädikatswein." Although the red wines lacked generosity of fruit, they were all, thanks to the soil, firm in their tannic structure and are likely to evolve satisfactorily. The new winemaker Karsten Rech has done an even better job with the difficult 1997 vintage. This old estate is showing new vigor!

1997 Burg Ravensburger Husarenkappe
Riesling Spätlese trocken
15.50 DM, 12.5%, ♀ now **80**

1997 Burg Ravensburger Löchle
Riesling Kabinett
10.90 DM, 10.5%, ♀ till 2000 **82**

1996 Burg Ravensburger Husarenkappe
Riesling Kabinett trocken
10 DM, 11%, ♀ now **84**

1997 Burg Ravensburger Löchle
Weißer Burgunder Spätlese trocken
15.50 DM, 12%, ♀ till 2000 **84**

1996 Burg Ravensburger Löchle
Riesling Eiswein
115 DM/0.375 liter, 10%, ♀ till 2010 **91**

——— Red wines ———

1996 Burg Ravensburger Löchle
Lemberger trocken
12.50 DM, 11.5%, ♀ till 2000 **82**

1997 Burg Ravensburger Löchle
Lemberger trocken
12.90 DM, 12.5%, ♀ till 2000 **84**

1995 Lemberger
Tafelwein trocken
23 DM/0.5 liter, 12.5%, ♀ till 2002 **84**

WEINGUT SALWEY

Owner: Wolf-Dietrich Salwey
79235 Oberrotweil, Hauptstraße 2
Tel. (0 76 62) 3 84, Fax 63 40
Directions: A 5 Frankfurt–Basel, exit Riegel, towards the Rhine, or, from the south, exit Bad Krozingen, towards Breisach
Opening hours: Mon.–Sat. 8 a.m. to 12:30 p.m. and 2 p.m. to 6 p.m.
History: Owned by the family since 1763

Vineyard area: 20 hectares
Annual production: 150,000 bottles
Top sites: Oberrotweiler Kirchberg and Eichberg, Glottertaler Eichberg
Soil types: Weathered volcanic soil, loess and weathered gneiss
Grape varieties: 42% Spätburgunder, 25% Grauburgunder, 8% each of Riesling and Silvaner, 8% Weißburgunder, 9% other varieties
Average yield: 55 hl/ha
Best vintages: 1995, 1996, 1997
Member: VDP, Deutsches Barrique Forum

Wolf-Dietrich Salwey has always been one of the most warm-hearted growers of the Kaiserstuhl. In spite of their intrinsic quality, his wines are made in a style as carefree and casual as Salwey himself. After the impeccable 1995s, Salwey produced an extremely good range of 1996s and 1997s. However, his whites from the two Burgundian varieties were outshone by their counterparts from Dr. Heger and Bercher; the reds can't lay claim to quite the same class as those from Johner or Huber. Further, Salwey's baroque style, with some wines registering as much as 15 percent alcohol, is often difficult to understand; and typical for this approach to winemaking in Baden, his wines need time to evolve. Be that as it may, the 1997s show more elegance than the 1996s; and, given the enormous investment he has made in his cellars, coming vintages may again place Salwey in the limelight. His schnapps, which he distills himself, are among the finest in Germany.

1997 Grauer Burgunder
Tafelwein trocken
26 DM, 12.5%, 🍷 till 2002 — **88**

1996 Oberrotweiler Kirchberg
Riesling Spätlese trocken ***
21 DM, 12.5%, 🍷 till 2002 — **88**

1996 Oberrotweiler Eichberg
Ruländer Spätlese trocken
32 DM, 15%, 🍷 till 2003 — **88**

1997 Oberrotweiler Eichberg
Ruländer Auslese ***
39 DM, 13.5%, 🍷 till 2002 — **88**

1997 Oberrotweiler Kirchberg
Silvaner Spätlese trocken ***
28 DM, 13.5%, 🍷 till 2002 — **89**

1997 Oberrotweiler Kirchberg
Weißer Burgunder Spätlese trocken ***
28 DM, 14%, 🍷 till 2002 — **89**

1996 Oberrotweiler Henkenberg
Grauer Burgunder Spätlese trocken
"Alte Reben"
28 DM, 14%, 🍷 till 2002 — **89**

1996 Oberrotweiler Kirchberg
Riesling Eiswein
Not yet for sale, 11.5%, 🍷 till 2004 — **94**

——— Red wine ———

1996 Oberrotweiler Kirchberg
Spätburgunder trocken "S"
34 DM, 12.5%, 🍷 till 2002 — **88**

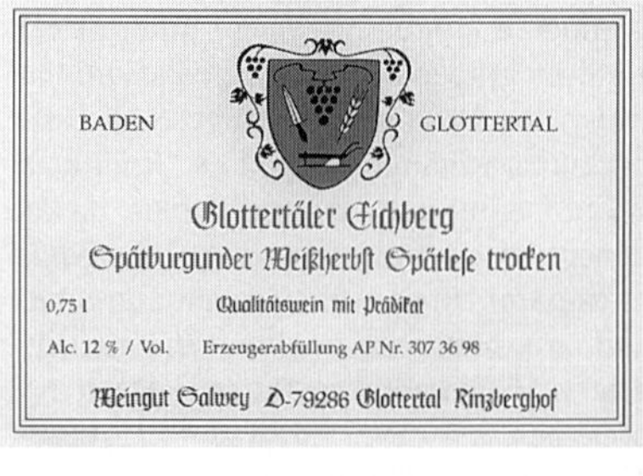

WINZERGENOSSENSCHAFT SASBACH AM KAISERSTUHL

Manager: Rolf Eberenz
Winemaker: Gerhard Staiblin
79361 Sasbach, Jechtinger Straße 26
Tel. (0 76 42) 9 03 10, Fax 90 31 50
Directions: A 5 Frankfurt–Basel, exit Riegel, towards the Rhine
Sales: Bertram Bohn
Opening hours: Mon.–Fri. 8 a.m. to noon and 1 p.m. to 4:30 p.m.
Sat. 9 a.m. to noon or by appointment
Worth seeing: Path through the vineyards of the Kaiserstuhl

Vineyard area: 101 hectares
Number of adherents: 324
Annual production: 770,000 bottles
Top sites: Sasbacher Rote Halde, Lützelberg, Scheibenbuck and Limburg
Soil types: Rocky weathered volcanic soil, partly with loess
Grape varieties: 45% Spätburgunder, 31% Müller-Thurgau, 11% Grauburgunder, 8% Weißburgunder, 5% other varieties
Average yield: 76 hl/ha
Best vintages: 1995, 1996, 1997
Member: Deutsches Barrique Forum

With more than 100 hectares of vineyards the Sasbach cooperative is one of the smallest in the Kaiserstuhl; but as far as quality is concerned, it can often be counted among the best. This may also be due to the fact that its more manageable size allows for better quality control. The growers of Sasbach have a natural potential for the production of both Weißburgunder and Spätburgunder, but it is their red wines that enjoy the greater reputation. After a modest showing in 1995, the cooperative made a slight recovery with the 1996 vintage. The white wines were decent enough, but no more than that; considering the vintage, the red wines pleasant, but nothing to write home to mother about. Although we have tasted only a few wines from the vintage, the 1997s do appear to be better.

1996 Sasbacher Limburg
Gewürztraminer Spätlese trocken
11.75 DM, 13%, ♀ now **80**

1997 Sasbacher Scheibenbuck
Weißer Burgunder Spätlese trocken
10.90 DM, 13%, ♀ now **82**

——— Red wines ———

1996 Sasbacher Lützelberg
Spätburgunder trocken
10.50 DM, 12.5%, ♀ till 2000 **80**

1996 Sasbacher Rote Halde
Spätburgunder Kabinett trocken
11 DM, 12%, ♀ now **80**

1997 Sasbacher Rote Halde
Spätburgunder Spätlese trocken
16.50 DM, 13.5%, ♀ now **80**

1996 Sasbacher Rote Halde
Spätburgunder Spätlese trocken
22.50 DM, 12.5%, ♀ now **80**

1996 Sasbacher Scheibenbuck
Spätburgunder Spätlese trocken "B"
34.90 DM, 13%, ♀ now **80**

1997 Sasbacher Lützelberg
Spätburgunder Auslese trocken
33.50 DM, 14%, ♀ till 2000 **84**

1995 Spätburgunder
Spätlese trocken "B"
39.75 DM, 12%, ♀ till 2000 **84**

WEINGUT HARTMUT SCHLUMBERGER

Owner: Hartmut Schlumberger
Winemaker: Ulrich Bernhart
79295 Laufen, Weinstraße 19
Tel. (0 76 34) 89 92, Fax 82 55
Directions: A 5 Frankfurt–Basel, exit Neuenburg, towards Müllheim and Sulzburg
Sales: Hella Schlumberger, Claudia Bernhart-Schlumberger
Opening hours: Mon.–Fri. 9 a.m. to noon and 2 p.m. to 6 p.m.
Sat. 9 a.m. to noon and 2 p.m. to 4 p.m.
History: The family has been producing wine since the 16th century

Vineyard area: 6.5 hectares
Annual production: 45,000 bottles
Top sites: Laufener Altenberg, Britzinger Sonnhohle
Soil types: Loess and loam
Grape varieties: 30% Gutedel, 25% Weißburgunder, 20% Spätburgunder, 6% Chardonnay, 5% each of Müller-Thurgau, Grauburgunder and Riesling, 4% other varieties
Average yield: 60 hl/ha
Best vintages: 1994, 1996, 1997

Since 1993 Schlumberger has been following the rules laid down by the organic vineyards association. His daughter, Claudia, has now concluded her studies at Geisenheim and since 1997 she and her husband Ulrich Bernhart, who hails from the Bernhart estate in the Palatinate, have taken a more active role in the estate. Together they have planted two further representatives of the Burgundian family of varieties, Auxerrois and Chardonnay, both of which have done well as "newcomers." The 1996 range of wines showed sufficient depth of fruit, but was marked by a robust and often steely acidity. Difficult to categorize, these wines will need time to develop. The 1997s have more substance and better balance. At present this estate is certainly one of the finest in the Markgräflerland.

1997 Riesling
Spätlese trocken
16.80 DM, 12.5%, 🍷 till 2001 **84**

1996 Auxerrois
Spätlese trocken
17.50 DM, 12.5%, 🍷 till 2000 **84**

1996 Chardonnay
trocken
22.50 DM, 12.5%, 🍷 till 2002 **86**

1997 Weißer Burgunder
Spätlese trocken
16 DM, 13.5%, 🍷 till 2001 **86**

1997 Auxerrois
Spätlese trocken
17.80 DM, 13%, 🍷 till 2002 **86**

1997 Chardonnay
Spätlese trocken
28.50 DM, 13.5%, 🍷 till 2002 **86**

1996 Grauer Burgunder
Spätlese trocken
17.50 DM, 13.5%, 🍷 till 2000 **86**

——— Red wines ———

1996 Spätburgunder
Spätlese trocken
38 DM, 13%, 🍷 till 2000 **84**

1995 Spätburgunder
trocken
38 DM, 13%, 🍷 till 2003 **86**

13% vol
0,75 l
GUTSABFÜLLUNG
H. SCHLUMBERGER
PRIVAT-WEINGUT
D-79295 LAUFEN
BADEN
MARKGRÄFLERLAND
1997
WEISSBURGUNDER SPÄTLESE
TROCKEN
QUALITÄTSWEIN MIT PRÄDIKAT
A.P.NR. 200-10-98 · Restzucker 5,3 g/l

WEINGUT SCHNEIDER

Owner: Claus Schneider
79576 Weil am Rhein,
Lörracher Straße 4
Tel. (0 76 21) 7 28 17, Fax 7 80 14
Directions: A 5 Frankfurt–Basel, exit Weil am Rhein
Sales: Susanne Hagin-Schneider
Opening hours: Mon. 2:30 p.m. to 6:30 p.m., Tue., Thur. and Fri. 9 a.m. to noon and 2:30 p.m. to 6:30 p.m. Wed. and Sat. 9 a.m. to noon or by appointment
History: The family has been making wine since 1425
Worth seeing: Vaulted cellar built in 1780

Vineyard area: 7.5 hectares
Annual production: 55,000 bottles
Top sites: Weiler Schlipf, Haltinger Stiege
Soil types: Loam with limestone content
Grape varieties: 34% Gutedel, 33% Spätburgunder, 13% Weißburgunder, 10% Grauburgunder, 10% other varieties
Average yield: 72 hl/ha
Best vintages: 1990, 1995, 1997

After completing his training as a wine technician in Weinsberg, Claus Schneider took over the family estate in 1982. Since then he has made major changes, especially in the cellar. With his wife, Susanne, who subsequently completed her studies in oenology at Geisenheim, he cultivates the Weiler Schlipf vineyard in the most southwesterly corner of Germany. This area is marked by an almost Mediterranean climate. The property has for years been among the leading estates of the Markgräflerland. Even if the 1996 wines didn't turn out splendidly, they were nonetheless a clear improvement on those of the previous vintage. The 1997s are marginally better. Admittedly, they are little more than straightforward, but are thoroughly attractive to quaff, especially the Spätburgunder sold in liter bottles. Perhaps this is why Schneider plans to expand his vineyard holdings.

1996 Weiler Schlipf
Chardonnay Spätlese trocken
19 DM, 12.5%, ♀ now **77**

1996 Weiler Schlipf
Weißer Burgunder Kabinett trocken
9.75 DM, 11.5%, ♀ now **80**

1997 Weiler Schlipf
Weißer Burgunder Spätlese trocken
14.80 DM, 13.5%, ♀ now **80**

1997 Weiler Schlipf
Grauer Burgunder Spätlese trocken
16.80 DM, 13.5%, ♀ now **80**

1996 Weiler Schlipf
Grauer Burgunder Spätlese trocken
18 DM, 13%, ♀ now **80**

1997 Haltinger Stiege
Gewürztraminer Spätlese trocken
12.80 DM, 13%, ♀ now **82**

——— Red wines ———

1995 Weiler Schlipf
Spätburgunder trocken
10 DM, 13%, ♀ now **77**

1996 Spätburgunder
trocken
9.75 DM/1.0 liter, 13%, ♀ now **80**

1996 Weiler Schlipf
Spätburgunder trocken
18.60 DM, 13.5%, ♀ till 2000 **84**

WEINGUT REINHOLD UND CORNELIA SCHNEIDER

Owners: Reinhold and Cornelia Schneider
Winemaker: Reinhold Schneider
79346 Endingen, Königschaffhauser Straße 2
Tel. (0 76 42) 52 78, Fax 20 91
Directions: A 5 Frankfurt–Basel, exit Riegel
Sales: Cornelia Schneider
Opening hours: Mon.–Fri. by appointment, Sat. 8 a.m. to 6 p.m.

Vineyard area: 8.8 hectares
Annual production: 42,000 bottles
Top sites: No single vineyard designations
Soil types: Loess, loam and weathered volcanic soil
Grape varieties: 34% Spätburgunder, 15% Müller-Thurgau, 11% Riesling, 15% Grauburgunder, 10% Weißburgunder, 10% Silvaner, 3% Muskateller, 2% Auxerrois
Average yield: 40 hl/ha
Best vintages: 1995, 1996, 1997
Member: VDP

First established as a winery in 1981, the estate of Reinhold Schneider and his wife, Cornelia, has always produced dry wines. At that time they also decided to pursue an organic form of viticulture. Sold without vineyard designations, their wines always offer good value for money. After somewhat disappointing results in 1994 and 1995 the Schneiders were back on their feet with a distinctly appealing collection of wines from the 1996 vintage. Both concentrated in aroma and typical of their varieties, they exhibited fine depth and forthright character. In spite of the difficult nature of the vintage, the 1997s are even better, displaying both opulent fruit and definite style. In particular, the often simple reds now show profile. It has been years since we have tasted such a convincing range from this estate.

1997 Riesling
Spätlese trocken ***
16 DM, 13%, ♀ till 2000 **84**

1996 Weißer Burgunder
Kabinett trocken
14 DM, 12%, ♀ till 2000 **86**

1997 Ruländer
Spätlese trocken "B"
18 DM, 15%, ♀ till 2001 **86**

1997 Weißer Burgunder
Spätlese trocken ***
18 DM, 14%, ♀ till 2002 **88**

1996 Weißer Burgunder
Spätlese trocken
18 DM, 13%, ♀ till 2002 **88**

1996 Ruländer
Spätlese trocken
18 DM, 13%, ♀ till 2003 **88**

1996 Ruländer
Spätlese trocken ***
22 DM, 13.5%, ♀ till 2002 **88**

——— Red wines ———

1996 Spätburgunder
trocken
18 DM, 13.5%, ♀ till 2000 **84**

1996 Spätburgunder
trocken ***
20 DM, 13%, ♀ till 2002 **88**

WEINGUT SEEGER

Owner: Helmut Seeger
Winemaker: Thomas Seeger
69181 Leimen, Rohrbacher Straße 101
Tel. (0 62 24) 7 21 78, Fax 7 83 63
Directions: A 5 Frankfurt–Basel, exit Heidelberg
Sales: Thomas Seeger
Opening hours: By appointment
Restaurant: "Jägerlust," open Tue. to Fri. from 6 p.m. to 11 p.m.
Specialities: Local fare
History: Restaurant since 1895

Vineyard area: 6.5 hectares
Annual production: 40,000 bottles
Top sites: Heidelberger Herrenberg, Leimener Herrenberg
Soil types: Loess and loam over limestone and red sandstone
Grape varieties: 20% Spätburgunder, 18% Riesling, 15% Weißburgunder, 12% Müller-Thurgau, 10% each of Portugieser, Grauburgunder and Lemberger, 5% Schwarzriesling
Average yield: 50 hl/ha
Best vintages: 1994, 1996, 1997
Member: Deutsches Barrique Forum

Although the Seeger family were first documented as growers in 1655, the name of this estate was seldom mentioned until recently. Thomas Seeger, who returned home in 1985 after a spell abroad, wants to change this. Since 1990 his wines have made great strides; but although Baden as a whole produced a number of wonderful wines in 1996, the whites here were less persuasive than in previous vintages. On the other hand, Seeger proved with the "lesser" vintage 1995 that he knows how to make red wines. Admittedly they were a touch tannic in their youth, but we are sure that they will develop well. In spite of improvements in the cellar, the 1997s still show more muscle than finesse.

1997 Weißer Burgunder
Spätlese trocken
23.50 DM, 13.5%, ♀ till 2000 **84**

1997 Grauer Burgunder
Spätlese trocken
23.50 DM, 13.5%, ♀ till 2001 **86**

1996 Grauer Burgunder
Spätlese trocken
22.50 DM, 13%, ♀ 2002 **86**

——— Red wines ———

1996 Heidelberger Herrenberg
Spätburgunder trocken "S"
34 DM, 13%, ♀ till 2001 **86**

1995 Lemberger
trocken
22.50 DM, 13%, ♀ till 2003 **86**

1995 "AnnA"
trocken
22.50 DM, 13%, ♀ till 2003 **88**

1996 Heidelberger Herrenberg
Spätburgunder trocken "R"
48 DM, 13.5%, ♀ till 2002 **88**

1995 Heidelberger Herrenberg
Spätburgunder trocken "S"
32 DM, 13%, ♀ till 2003 **89**

BADEN
WEINGUT SEEGER
1993
Weisser Burgunder
Heidelberger Herrenberg
Trocken
Qualitätswein mit Prädikat
Spätlese
13 %-Vol.
A.P.Nr. 620/7/94
75 cl
GUTSABFÜLLUNG SEKT- UND WEINGUT SEEGER
D-69181 LEIMEN/HEIDELBERG · BAD. BERGSTRASSE

STAATSWEINGUT FREIBURG UND BLANKENHORNSBERG

Owner: State of Baden-Württemberg
General Manager: Peter Wohlfahrt
Winemaker: Hans Breisacher and Werner Scheffelt
79100 Freiburg im Breisgau, Merzhauser Straße 119
Tel. (07 61) 4 01 65 44, Fax 4 01 65 70
Directions: A 5 Frankfurt–Basel, exit Freiburg/Breisgau
Sales: Michael Walker
Opening hours: Mon.–Fri. 8 a.m. to noon and 1 p.m. to 5 p.m.

Vineyard area: 35 hectares
Annual production: 300,000 bottles
Top sites: Blankenhornsberger Doktorgarten, Freiburger Schloßberg and Jesuitenschloß
Soil types: Weathered volcanic soil, loess and loam
Grape varieties: 20% Spätburgunder, 18% Riesling, 17% Müller-Thurgau, 16% Weißburgunder, 8% Grauburgunder, 21% other varieties
Average yield: 58 hl/ha
Best vintages: 1994, 1996, 1997

In 1997 the Freiburg and Blankenhornsberg wineries were merged to create this State Domaine. After the privatization of the vineyards in Durbach, Hecklingen and Müllheim, the production and marketing of the wines has been given a clear focus. The crown jewel of the estate will always be the Doktorgarten vineyard, which was sculpted and planted by Adolf Friedrich and Wilhelm Blankenhorn in 1842. In comparison, the wines from the Freiburg vineyards are second rank. Under the direction of Peter Wohlfahrt there has been a noticeable upturn in quality, which found its first true expression in the 1996 range. The 1997s were not quite as good, being marked more by body than elegance. There is enormous potential here, that has yet to be realized.

1997 Blankenhornsberger
Riesling Kabinett trocken
9.80 DM, 11.5%, ♀ now **80**

1997 Blankenhornsberger Doktorgarten
Weißer Burgunder Spätlese trocken
21.80 DM, 13.5%, ♀ till 2000 **82**

1996 Blankenhornsberger
Silvaner Spätlese trocken
11 DM, 13%, ♀ till 2000 **82**

1996 Freiburger Jesuitenschloß
Grauer Burgunder Spätlese trocken
10 DM, 12.5%, ♀ now **82**

1997 Blankenhornsberger Doktorgarten
Riesling Spätlese trocken
14.20 DM, 12.5%, ♀ till 2000 **84**

1997 Freiburger Schloßberg
Chardonnay Spätlese trocken
18 DM/0.5 liter, 14%, ♀ till 2001 **84**

1996 Blankenhornsberger
Riesling Spätlese trocken
13 DM, 11.5%, ♀ till 2000 **84**

1997 Blankenhornsberger Doktorgarten
Riesling Auslese
27 DM/0.5 liter, 13%, ♀ till 2001 **84**

1996 Blankenhornsberger Doktorgarten
Weißer Burgunder Spätlese trocken
16.25 DM, 13%, ♀ till 2000 **86**

1996 Blankenhornsberger
Riesling Spätlese
13 DM, 12%, ♀ till 2002 **86**

WEINGUT SCHLOSS STAUFENBERG

Owner: Max Markgraf von Baden
Leased and managed by Bernhard Ganter
77770 Durbach, Schloß Staufenberg 1
Tel. (07 81) 4 27 78, Fax 44 05 78
Directions: A 5 Frankfurt–Basel, exit Appenweier or Offenburg, follow the signs towards Durbach
Opening hours: Mon.–Fri. 10 a.m. to 5:30 p.m., Sat. 10 a.m. to 4 p.m.
Restaurant: Open from March to November, daily from 10 a.m. to 7 p.m.
Specialties: Local fare, "Schäufele," potato salad
History: The castle was built in the 12th century
Worth seeing: Fortress with its beautiful gardens and sun deck

Vineyard area: 26.5 hectares
Annual production: 154,000 bottles
Top site: Schloß Staufenberg
Soil types: Weathered granite
Grape varieties: 40% Riesling, 30% Spätburgunder, 10% Müller-Thurgau, 5% each of Traminer, Grauburgunder, Weißburgunder and Chardonnay
Average yield: 45 hl/ha
Best vintages: 1990, 1993, 1997

From the Staufenberg castle in a narrow valley above and behind Durbach there is a wonderful view onto this estate's vineyards, which attained their present size in 1832. In 1776 the former Margrave was already planting Riesling. Six years later a further 3500 vines were planted in the Klingelberg vineyard, which is why the name Klingelberger is registered as a synonym for Riesling in Baden. After the modest 1995s, the estate's 1996 collection marked a further eclipse in quality. Many of the wines were marked by a vegetal acidity and a slightly bitter aftertaste. The dry wines lacked weight; the dessert wines were artificial. The 1997s are marginally better, but certainly not up to our expectations. This once celebrated old estate still dreams of former glories.

1996 Durbacher Schloß Staufenberg
Riesling Kabinett trocken
10.50 DM, 9.5%, ♀ till 2000 **82**

1997 Durbacher Schloß Staufenberg
Riesling Spätlese trocken "SL"
15.50 DM, 11.5%, ♀ now **82**

1996 Durbacher Schloß Staufenberg
Klingelberger (Riesling) Kabinett
10.50 DM, 9.5%, ♀ till 2000 **82**

1996 Durbacher Schloß Staufenberg
Gewürztraminer Spätlese
14 DM, 11.5%, ♀ till 2000 **82**

1996 Durbacher Schloß Staufenberg
Klingelberger (Riesling) Auslese
20 DM/0.5 liter, 9.5%, ♀ till 2005 **86**

——— Red wines ———

1997 Durbacher Schloß Staufenberg
Spätburgunder Weißherbst Spätlese
15 DM, 12%, ♀ now **84**

1997 Durbacher Schloß Staufenberg
Spätburgunder Weißherbst Auslese
20 DM/0.5 liter, 10.5%, ♀ now **84**

1997 Durbacher Schloß Staufenberg
Spätburgunder Kabinett trocken
13.25 DM, 12%, ♀ till 2000 **82**

1997 Durbacher Schloß Staufenberg
Spätburgunder Spätlese "SL"
14 DM/0.5 liter, 13%, ♀ till 2001 **84**

WEINGUT STIGLER

Owner: Andreas Stigler
79241 Ihringen, Bachenstraße 29
Tel. (0 76 68) 2 97, Fax 9 41 20
Directions: A 5 Frankfurt–Basel, exit Teningen, towards Eichstetten
Sales: Regina Stigler
Opening hours: Mon.–Fri. 9 a.m. to noon and 2 p.m. to 6 p.m., Sat. 9 a.m. to noon and 2 p.m. to 4 p.m. or by appointment
History: Owned by the family since 1881

Vineyard area: 7.9 hectares
Annual production: 50,000 bottles
Top sites: Ihringer Winklerberg, Freiburger Schloßberg, Oberrotweiler Eichberg
Soil types: Rocky weathered volcanic and gneiss
Grape varieties: 36% Spätburgunder, 24% Riesling, 11% Weißburgunder, 9% each of Müller-Thurgau and Silvaner, 6% Grauburgunder, 5% Traminer
Average yield: 45 hl/ha
Best vintages: 1995, 1996, 1997
Member: VDP

This estate lies in the most southerly corner of the Kaiserstuhl and comprises six hectares of the celebrated Winklerberg vineyard. Long before it became fashionable, Rudolf Stigler made the majority of his wines dry in style. With the arrival of his son Andreas, who has pursued ingenious public relations work, this astutely managed business is well prepared for the future. Low yields mean that almost all the wines are harvested at "Prädikatswein" levels. Stigler usually delays delivering his wines for a year, even though this often means that some of them are sold out before they are released. The 1995 range was the best that this estate had produced since 1990. The 1996s were not quite as good, but Stigler bounced back in 1997 with a collection of wines that are the best that we have tasted since Andreas took the helm. The style remains somewhat old-fashioned and highly individual, but not without character.

1997 Ihringer Winklerberg
Riesling Kabinett trocken "F 2"
14.50 DM, 12%, ♀ till 2001 **84**

1997 Ihringer Winklerberg
Grauer Burgunder Spätlese trocken
18.90 DM, 13%, ♀ till 2000 **84**

1995 Ihringer Winklerberg
Weißer Burgunder Spätlese trocken
18.50 DM, 12%, ♀ till 2000 **84**

1995 Ihringer Winklerberg
Traminer Spätlese trocken
12.50 DM/0.375 liter, 15%, ♀ now **84**

1997 Ihringer Winklerberg
Riesling Spätlese trocken "F 36"
26 DM, 12.5%, ♀ till 2002 **86**

1997 Ihringer Winklerberg
Weißer Burgunder Spätlese trocken
18.90 DM, 13%, ♀ till 2001 **86**

1997 Ihringer Winklerberg
Silvaner Spätlese trocken
15.90 DM, 12.5%, ♀ till 2002 **88**

1997 Ihringer Winklerberg
Traminer Spätlese
19.50 DM, 13.5%, ♀ till 2007 **88**

1995 Ihringer Winklerberg
Riesling Trockenbeerenauslese
139 DM/0.375 liter, ♀ till 2010 **91**

TAUBERFRÄNKISCHE WINZERGENOSSENSCHAFT BECKSTEIN

Manager: Bernhard Stahl
Winemaker: Stefan Steffen
97922 Lauda-Königshofen, Weinstr. 30
Tel. (0 93 43) 50 00, Fax 52 77
Directions: A 81 Würzburg–Heilbronn, exit Tauberbischofsheim
Sales: Ms. Hönninger
Opening hours: Mon.–Fri. 8 a.m. to 6 p.m., Sat. 9 a.m. to 6 p.m.
Sun. 10 a.m. to 6 p.m.
From March to November only on Sat. 9 a.m. to 1 p.m.
History: Founded in 1894
Restaurant: Weinstuben Beckstein open from 10 a.m. to midnight, closed Wed.
Specialties: Vegetarian dishes

Vineyard area: 304 hectares
Number of adherents: 501
Annual production: 3 million bottles
Top sites: Becksteiner Kirchberg and Nonnenberg, Gerlachsheimer Herrenberg, Marbacher Frankenberg, Königshofer Turmberg
Soil types: Fossil limestone
Grape varieties: 50% Müller-Thurgau, 20% Schwarzriesling, 10% Kerner, 6% each of Bacchus and Silvaner, 2% each of Spätburgunder, Weißburgunder, Riesling as well as other varieties
Average yield: 72 hl/ha
Best vintages: 1990, 1993

The magic of the delightful Tauberfranken area captivates any wine enthusiast who visits this remote region along its so-called "Romantic Route." Here Müller-Thurgau reigns supreme. The members of the Tauberfranken cooperative farm over 300 hectares of the 800 contained within this erstwhile region of Franken, which today belongs to the state of Baden. The range of wines in 1995 was no match for those of the previous vintage; and those from 1996 are no more than enjoyable quaffing wines. All in all, the quality level here has left much to be desired for the last two years.

1996 Becksteiner Kirchberg
Silvaner trocken
6.50 DM, 10.5%, ♀ now **77**

1996 Marbacher Frankenberg
Bacchus trocken
7 DM, 10.5%, ♀ now **77**

1996 Müller-Thurgau
Kabinett trocken
10 DM, 10.5%, ♀ now **77**

1996 Becksteiner Kirchberg
Bacchus Auslese
22 DM, 13%, ♀ now **82**

1996 Becksteiner Kirchberg
Riesling Eiswein
52 DM/0.375 liter, 12%, ♀ till 2005 **86**

Red wines

1995 Becksteiner Kirchberg
Domina trocken
20 DM, 12%, ♀ now **77**

1996 Becksteiner Kirchberg
Schwarzriesling trocken
10 DM, 12%, ♀ now **80**

GRÄFLICH WOLFF METTERNICH'SCHES WEINGUT

Owners: G. and R. Hurrle
General Manager: Josef Rohrer
Winemaker: Franz Schwörer
77770 Durbach, Grohl 4
Tel. (07 81) 4 27 79, Fax 4 25 53
Directions: A 5 Frankfurt–Basel, exit Offenburg or Appenweier, towards Durbach
Opening hours: Mon.–Fri. 8 a.m. to noon and 1 p.m. to 5 p.m.
Sat. 9 a.m. to noon
History: Making wine since 1180
Worth seeing: The old cellar in the castle, the restored wooden presses

Vineyard area: 33 hectares
Annual production: 200,000 bottles
Top sites: Durbacher Schloß Grohl, Schloßberg, Plauelrain and Lahrer Herrentisch (sole owners)
Soil types: Weathered granite
Grape varieties: 32% Riesling, 30% Spätburgunder, 10% Weißburgunder, 8% Traminer, 7% Müller-Thurgau, 6% Grauburgunder, 5% Chardonnay, 2% other varieties
Average yield: 49 hl/ha
Best vintages: 1994, 1996, 1997

This old property in Durbach invariably produces expressive Rieslings that have traditionally been some of the finest of the Ortenau. For the last few years the quality level has not quite been up to expectations, even though its best wines in any given vintage remained above reproach. After the somewhat disappointing range in 1995, the 1996s were considerably better: fresh, fruity and rich in extract, a handful of them will age very well. The 1997s are, perhaps, even better. The new proprietors have renovated the old cellar, in which until 1926 the wines were crushed in seven old wooden presses. In one house they have even added accommodations for passing guests. If the wines were given similar care, this estate might again be one of the flagships of Baden.

1997 Durbacher Schloß Grohl
Grauer Burgunder Spätlese trocken
13.90 DM, 13.5%, ♀ now **82**

1997 Durbacher Schloß Grohl
Weißer Burgunder Spätlese trocken
15.65 DM, 13%, ♀ now **82**

1996 Durbacher Schloß Grohl
Grauer Burgunder Spätlese trocken
13.25 DM, 13%, ♀ now **84**

1996 Durbacher Schloßberg
Chardonnay Spätlese trocken
17.25 DM, 12%, ♀ now **84**

1997 Durbacher Plauelrain
Riesling Spätlese
15 DM, 10.5%, ♀ till 2001 **84**

1996 Durbacher Schloßberg
Klingelberger (Riesling) Spätlese
16.75 DM, 10%, ♀ till 2002 **84**

1997 Durbacher Schloß Grohl
Riesling Auslese
23 DM/0.5 liter, 9%, ♀ till 2003 **86**

1997 Durbacher Schloß Grohl
Scheurebe Auslese
19.70 DM/0.5 liter, 9%, ♀ till 2003 **88**

1996 Durbacher Schloß Grohl
Riesling Auslese
20 DM/0.5 liter, 9%, ♀ 2003 **89**

——— Red wine ———

1996 Durbacher Schloßberg
Spätburgunder trocken "B"
19.70 DM, 12%, ♀ now **84**

Silvaner's home sweet home

Franken is the home of Silvaner. Nowhere else in Germany does this grape variety achieve the same standing, nor the same quality. Müller-Thurgau may well boast that it accounts for almost half of Franken's total production, but the best wines of the region are produced from Silvaner, Riesling and, increasingly, Rieslaner.

The Franconian wine region stretches from Aschaffenburg to Haßfurt; but its heart lies on the banks of the River Main in and around the city of Würzburg, where the vines thrive on fossil limestone soils. Here, too, is the famous single vineyard site "Stein," which in former times provided not only the renown, but also the nickname for the whole of Franken's production: "Stein Wine."

Owing to its distinct continental climate, characterized by hot dry summers and cold winters, the best of the widely dispersed vineyards are planted on southerly slopes within the "Main triangle," where the river meanders in an enormous loop, as well as on the westerly slopes, with their soils of weathered clay, stone and slate, of the Steigerwald forest. But Franken is more than Würzburg and Iphofen. In the "Main square" in lower Franken the climatic conditions are milder; and in the Spessart area, with its ancient weathered soils and red sandstone, Pinot Noir, which can turn out splendidly in the hands of a vintner like Paul Fürst, is also grown.

The earliest written records of wine production in Franken date from 777. Five hundred years ago the total area under vine was ten times larger than it is today. The devastation caused by the Thirty Years' War, the toll of industrialization, taxes and the increase in beer consumption all helped to shrink the vineyard area to just 6,000 hectares. Slightly more than half of the total production is crushed by the region's seven cooperatives; but the days when their wines, packaged in the world-famous "Bocksbeutel" bottles, automatically fetched higher prices, are long gone. Even the best producers are no longer immune to international competition.

After two difficult years, the 1997 vintage offered the local vintners a chance to prove their mettle. A hard frost during the winter, hail in the spring and drought during the summer tested their nerves, but no one doubts today that it was the best vintage in Franken since 1994. The wines do not have the depth of fruit of a truly great vintage, but are generally well balanced. In particular, though, it was important to harvest based on acid rather than sugar levels. A goodly number of the dry Spätlese were crushed too late during the season. The resulting wines are alcoholic and bitter. Other than that, it was a relatively easy vintage to manage.

The 1996 vintage, however, required a lot of hard work from the growers who wanted to produce exceptional wines. After a belated budding there followed a prolonged flowering phase; and the weather remained cool and damp throughout the summer. Given such conditions, it was hard for the grapes to attain high sugar levels, much less complete physiological ripeness. Even when picked with higher must weights, the resulting wines seldom tasted like Spätlese or Auslese, which were, in any case, the exception. But after a string of vintages such as 1992, 1993 and 1994, which were high in alcohol, the abundance of somewhat lighter Kabinetts was a godsend for many producers.

The top estates were worried less about attaining higher must weights but rather, as Rowald Hepp of the Staatliche Hofkeller asserted, "about regulating the acidity." Through a carefully managed late harvest and prolonged aging in casks, artificial deacidification of the wines in the cellar could be avoided. Those who worked with skill, such as Karl M. Schmitt of the Schmitt's Kinder estate, produced wines that will age gracefully. Those growers, however, who picked early and deacidified, will not derive much pleasure from their wines – nor will the customer.

Among the elite producers in Franken we number Fürst, Schmitt's Kinder,

Wirsching and Juliusspital, in that order, followed closely by Ruck and Störrlein. Fürst, our current favorite, and Schmitt's Kinder have been by far the most consistent producers of late. On the other hand, the Juliusspital, after a couple of excellent vintages, now seems to be stumbling over its own feet. On an upward curve are such estates as Michael Fröhlich and Horst Sauer in Escherndorf as well as the Staatlicher Hofkeller in Würzburg and Fürst Castell in Castell, but we must await another first-rate vintage to see who is really capable of what.

Of the some 700 other wineries in Franken, numerous merit attention. An initiative known as "Der Müller," for Müller-Thurgau, has for example brought to the fore a group of young producers who have not only set themselves higher goals, but also want to polish the tarnished reputation of that grape varietal. The Knoll estate "am Stein" in Würzburg is the leading member of this association. This year we were also surprised by the wines of Arnold in Iphofen and Dr. Heigel in Zeil.

Rating scale for the estates

Highest rating: These producers belong to the world's finest.

Excellent estates: These producers are among Germany's best.

Very good producers, known for their consistently high quality.

Good estates, offering better than average quality.

Reliable producers that offer well-made standard quality.

The leading estates of Franken

Weingut Rudolf Fürst, Bürgstadt

Weingut Juliusspital, Würzburg

Weingut Schmitt's Kinder, Randersacker

Weingut Hans Wirsching, Iphofen

Fürstlich Castellsches Domänenamt, Castell

Weingut Michael Fröhlich, Escherndorf

Weingut Johann Ruck, Iphofen

Weingut Horst Sauer, Escherndorf

Staatlicher Hofkeller, Würzburg

Weingut Josef Störrlein, Randersacker

Weingut Bickel-Stumpf, Frickenhausen

Weingut Waldemar Braun, Nordheim

Weingut Bürgerspital zum Heiligen Geist, Würzburg

Weingut Glaser-Himmelstoß, Nordheim

Weingut Fürst Löwenstein, Kreuzwertheim

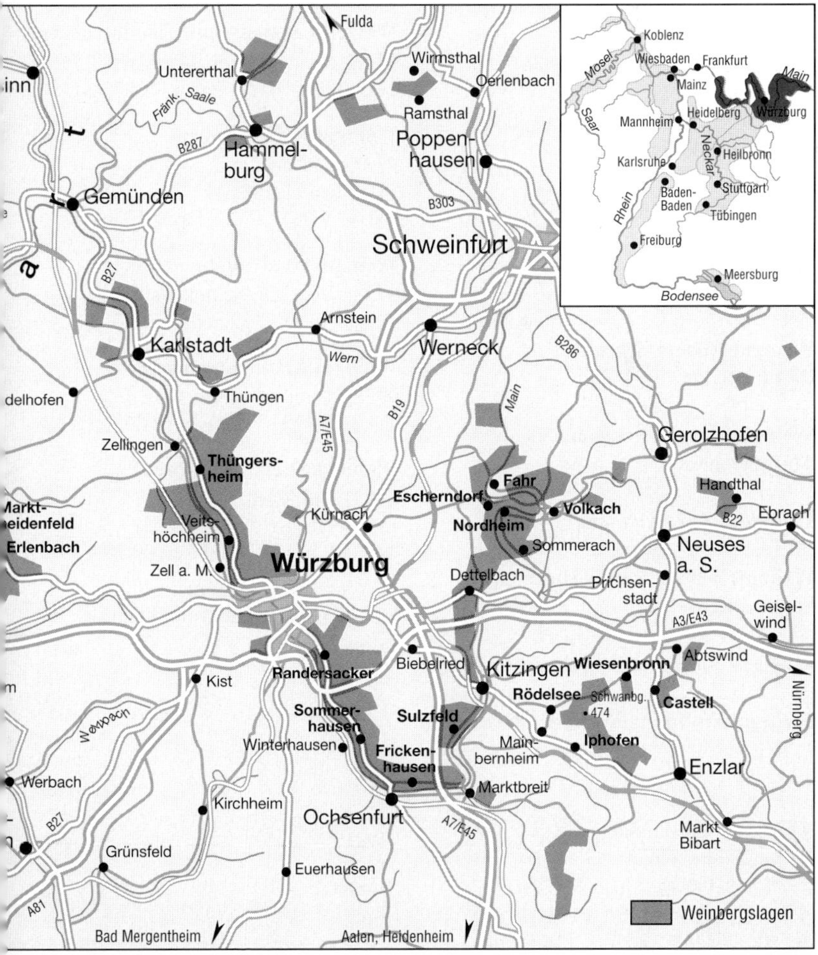

Weingut "Am Lump," Escherndorf

Weingut Gerhard Roth, Wiesenbronn

Weinbau Egon Schäffer, Escherndorf bei Volkach

Weingut Zehnthof, Sulzfeld

Weingut Helmut Christ, Nordheim

Weingut Josef Deppisch, Erlenbach bei Marktheidenfeld

Weingut Martin Göbel, Randersacker

Weingut Franz Kirch, Fahr bei Volkach

Weingut Ernst Popp, Iphofen

Weingut Richard Schmitt, Randersacker

Weingut Robert Schmitt, Randersacker

Weingut Gregor Schwab, Thüngersheim

Weingut "Zur Schwane," Volkach

Weingut Schloß Sommerhausen, Sommerhausen

Weingut am Stein, Würzburg

Weingut Wolfgang Weltner, Rödelsee

🍇🍇🍇🍇🍇 : Outstanding
🍇🍇🍇🍇 : Excellent
🍇🍇🍇 : Good
🍇🍇 : Average
🍇 : Poor

Other notable producers

Winzerhof Johann Arnold
97346 Iphofen, Lange Gasse 26/28
Tel. (0 92 32) 8 98 33, Fax 8 98 34

Städtisches Weingut Erlenbach
63906 Erlenbach, Klingenberger Straße 29
Tel. (0 93 72) 7 04 61, Fax 7 04 10

Weingut Dr. Heigel
97475 Zeil am Main, Haßfurter Straße 12
Tel. (0 95 24) 31 10, Fax 31 09

Weingut Höfler
63755 Michelbach, Albstädter Straße 1
Tel. (0 60 23) 54 95, Fax 3 14 17

Winzergenossenschaft Randersacker
97236 Randersacker, Maingasse 33
Tel. (09 31) 70 56 50, Fax 70 73 31

Weingut Rainer Sauer
97332 Escherndorf,
Bocksbeutelstraße 15
Tel. (0 93 81) 25 27, Fax 7 13 40

Weingut Graf von Schönborn
97332 Volkach, Schloß Hallburg
Tel. (0 93 81) 24 15, Fax 37 80

Weingut Artur Steinmann
97286 Sommerhausen, Plan 4
Tel. (0 93 33) 2 50, Fax 18 55

Weingut Stich "Im Löwen"
63927 Bürgstadt,
Freudenberger Straße 73
Tel. (0 93 71) 57 05, Fax 8 09 73

Vintage chart for Franken

vintage	quality	drink
1997	🍇🍇🍇🍇	till 2001
1996	🍇🍇🍇	till 2000
1995	🍇🍇	now
1994	🍇🍇🍇🍇	now
1993	🍇🍇🍇🍇	till 2000
1992	🍇🍇🍇🍇	now
1991	🍇🍇	now
1990	🍇🍇🍇🍇🍇	now
1989	🍇🍇🍇	now
1988	🍇🍇🍇🍇	now

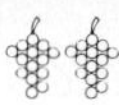

WEINGUT BICKEL-STUMPF

Owner: Reimund and Carmen Stumpf
97252 Frickenhausen, Kirchgasse 5
Tel. (0 93 31) 28 47, Fax 71 76
Directions: A 3 Würzburg–Nürnberg, exit Randersacker, via B 13, 17 kilometers along the Main
Sales: Carmen Stumpf
Opening hours: Mon.–Sat. 8 a.m. to 6 p.m. or by appointment
Restaurant: "Zur Weinkönigin" open from 11 a.m. to 11 p.m. except Wednesday
Specialties: Regional fare

Vineyard area: 7.8 hectares
Annual production: 65,000 bottles
Top sites: Frickenhäuser Kapellenberg, Thüngersheimer Johannisberg
Soil types: Fossil limestone, colored sandstone
Grape varieties: 32% Silvaner, 20% Müller-Thurgau, 11% Riesling, 9% Portugieser, 5% Spätburgunder, 4% Rieslaner, 19% other varieties
Average yield: 60 hl/ha
Best vintages: 1992, 1993, 1994
Member: VDP

Located in an idyllic spot between the river and the vineyards, the charming medieval village of Frickenhausen is blessed with southern slopes and abundant sunshine. In the shadow of the old church Reimund Stumpf, a native of Thüngersheim, and his wife, Carmen, often produce attractive wines that nonetheless receive little recognition outside Franken. Though he made excellent wines in 1992 and 1993, we were less impressed by the early releases of the 1994s; however, they evolved relatively well. After the appealing 1995s Reimund Stumpf again presented a rather rustic range of 1996s. Although we expected more from the vintage, the 1997s were noticeably better. Now that his cellars have been newly appointed, Strumpf believes that future vintages should be even more impressive.

1996 Frickenhäuser Markgraf Babenberg
Bacchus Kabinett trocken
9 DM, 12%, 🍷 now **80**

1996
Scheurebe
8 DM, 11%, 🍷 till 2000 **80**

1995 Frickenhäuser Kapellenberg
Rieslaner Spätlese
30 DM, 12.5%, 🍷 till 2000 **80**

1997 Frickenhäuser Kapellenberg
Silvaner Kabinett trocken
11.50 DM, 12.5%, 🍷 till 2001 **82**

1997 Frickenhäuser Kapellenberg
Riesling Kabinett trocken
14.50 DM, 12.5%, 🍷 till 2001 **82**

1997 Thüngersheimer Scharlachberg
Kerner Kabinett
9.80 DM, 11.5%, 🍷 till 2000 **82**

1997 Frickenhäuser Kapellenberg
Silvaner Spätlese trocken
15.50 DM, 13%, 🍷 till 2003 **84**

1997 Scheurebe
Spätlese
15 DM, 12%, 🍷 till 2004 **86**

1997
BICKEL
STUMPF
THÜNGERSHEIMER
JOHANNISBERG
KABINETT
MÜLLER-THURGAU TROCKEN
Qualitätswein mit Prädikat
A. P. Nr. 3055-003-98
11,5%vol. 0,75 l
FRANKEN
GUTSABFÜLLUNG
Weingut Bickel-Stumpf
97252 Frickenhausen/Main

WEINGUT WALDEMAR BRAUN

Owner: Waldemar Braun
97334 Nordheim, Langgasse 10
Tel. (0 93 81) 90 61, Fax 7 11 79
Directions: A 3 Würzburg–Nürnberg, exit Wiesentheid, via Volkach
Sales: Heidi Braun
Opening hours: By appointment

Vineyard area: 6.5 hectares
Annual production: 40,000 bottles
Top sites: Nordheimer Vögelein and Kreuzberg
Soil types: Fossil limestone beneath a layer of wind-blown sand
Grape varieties: 35% Müller-Thurgau, 20% Silvaner, 10% Bacchus, 8% Riesling, 6% Domina, 5% Rieslaner, 4% Spätburgunder, 12% other varieties
Average yield: 78,5 hl/ha
Best vintages: 1992, 1994, 1997

In 1985 Waldemar Braun fulfilled his dream of owning his own estate. As a member of an ecologically oriented study group known as "Naturnaher Weinbau," his principal focus lies in the production of wines fermented to dryness that reflect the specific character of the grape variety, vineyard site and vintage. As this rising star remarks, he is "trying to bring ecology and economics into harmony." The liter bottlings are often well made, fresh and crisp; and the red wines are growing in stature. However, the overall production in 1995 and 1996 cannot compare with the truly appealing collections made in 1992 and 1994. After these two rather weak performances cast a shadow on his reputation, Braun bounced back with very attractive 1997s. In particular the Silvaners show much better. He also believes that his wines, "streaked with acidity and rich in extract, will develop well."

1997 Nordheimer Vögelein
Weißer Burgunder Kabinett trocken
11.50 DM, 12%, ♀ till 2000 **82**

1997 Sommeracher Katzenkopf
Silvaner trocken
8 DM, 11.5%, ♀ till 2001 **82**

1997 Nordheimer Vögelein
Silvaner Kabinett trocken
10 DM, 12%, ♀ till 2001 **84**

1997 Sommeracher Rosenberg
Scheurebe Kabinett
11 DM, 11.5%, ♀ till 2002 **84**

1997 Nordheimer Vögelein
Riesling trocken
9 DM, 10.5%, ♀ till 2002 **84**

1997 Nordheimer Vögelein
Rieslaner Kabinett trocken
10 DM, 12%, ♀ till 2002 **86**

1997 Nordheimer Vögelein
Kerner Spätlese
14 DM, 13.5%, ♀ till 2003 **86**

1997 Nordheimer Vögelein
Rieslaner Spätlese
17 DM, 12.5%, ♀ till 2003 **86**

1997 Nordheimer Vögelein
Silvaner Spätlese trocken
14 DM, 14%, ♀ till 2003 **88**

WEINGUT in D-97334 Nordheim – Tel. 09381/9061
Waldemar
Braun
14,0% vol
1997
SILVANER
0,75 l
trocken
Nordheimer Vögelein
SPÄTLESE
Qualitätswein mit Prädikat
Gutsabfüllung
A. P. Nr. 4864-015-98
FRANKEN

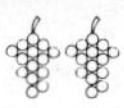

WEINGUT BÜRGERSPITAL ZUM HEILIGEN GEIST

Owner: Charitable trust
General Manager: Rudolf Fries
Winemaker: Robert Braungardt, Lothar Dausacker
97070 Würzburg, Theaterstraße 19
Tel. (09 31) 3 50 30, Fax 3 50 34 44
Directions: In the center of Würzburg
Sales: Reinhard Sauer, Heinrich Bauer
Opening hours: Mon.–Fri. 9 a.m. to 6 p.m., Sat. 9 a.m. to 3 p.m. in the wine shop
Restaurant: "Bürgerspital Weinstuben," open from 9 a.m. to midnight, except Tue.
History: Charitable trust from 1319 for poor and aged citizens
Worth seeing: Hospital church, baroque courtyards, vaulted cellars

Vineyard area: 120 hectares
Annual production: 900,000 bottles
Top sites: Würzburger Stein, Stein-Harfe, Abtsleite and Innere Leiste, Randersackerer Pfülben and Teufelskeller
Soil types: Weathered fossil limestone
Grape varieties: 32% Riesling, 21% Silvaner, 17% Müller-Thurgau, 5% Grauburgunder, 4% each of Weißburgunder and Spätburgunder, 17% other varieties
Average yield: 63 hl/ha
Best vintages: 1988, 1990, 1993
Member: VDP

Although some wine connoisseurs maintain that the Bürgerspital is still one of the finest wineries of Franken, in the past few years this establishment has seldom done justice to its reputation. The principal building of the ancient foundation is picturesque, and the splendidly furnished cellars are exquisite. Yet since 1990 outstanding wines have been the exception rather than the rule. This is equally true of the modest 1996s and only marginally better 1997s, although some of the wines will perhaps need more bottle age to evolve.

1996 Würzburger Stein
Riesling Kabinett trocken
16.25 DM, 10.5%, ♀ now **80**

1997 Randersackerer Teufelskeller
Riesling Spätlese trocken
19 DM, 13.5%, ♀ till 2000 **80**

1996 Würzburger Stein-Harfe
Silvaner Kabinett "feinherb"
16.25 DM, 10%, ♀ now **82**

1996 Würzburger Stein
Riesling Kabinett "feinherb"
16.25 DM, 10%, ♀ till 2000 **82**

1997 Würzburger Pfaffenberg
Müller-Thurgau Spätlese
15.60 DM, 11%, ♀ till 2001 **84**

1997 Würzburger Stein
Riesling Spätlese
21 DM, 13%, ♀ till 2002 **84**

1996 Würzburger Pfaffenberg
Müller-Thurgau Auslese
32.25 DM, 13%, ♀ till 2005 **88**

1997 Randersackerer Pfülben
Rieslaner Beerenauslese
80 DM, 12.5%, ♀ till 2004 **89**

1997 Würzburger Stein
Riesling Trockenbeerenauslese
250 DM, 12%, ♀ till 2006 **91**

FÜRSTLICH CASTELLSCHES DOMÄNEAMT

Owner: Ferdinand Erbgraf zu Castell
Manager: Karl-Heinz Rebitzer
Vineyard manager: Peter Hemberger
Winemaker: Christian Frieß and Reinhard Firnbach
97335 Castell, Schloßplatz 5
Tel. (0 93 25) 6 01 70, Fax 6 01 85
Directions: A 3 Würzburg–Nürnberg, exit Wiesentheid, following the B 286
Sales: Frank Dietrich
Opening hours: Mon.–Fri. 7:30 a.m. to noon and 1 p.m. to 5 p.m.
Sat. 10 a.m. to 4 p.m.
Restaurant: "Weinstall," open from 11 a.m. to 11 p.m.
Specialties: Regional fare
History: Producing wine since the 13th century
Worth seeing: Vaulted cellars, lovely paths in the gardens of the castle

Vineyard area: 65 hectares
Annual production: 400,000 bottles
Top sites: Casteller Schloßberg, Hohnart, Kirchberg, Kugelspiel, Bausch
Soil types: Gypsum with stony clay
Grape varieties: 34% Silvaner, 29% Müller-Thurgau, 6% each of Riesling and Domina, 5% each of Rieslaner and Bacchus, 15% other varieties
Average yield: 50 hl/ha
Best vintages: 1990, 1993, 1997
Member: VDP, Naturland

This estate is a jewel of an agricultural enterprise that has been in the possession of the same family since the 12th century. In the principality's archives is stored the first written reference to Silvaner's existence as a grape variety. The large vineyard area, which stretches from the forested Steigerwald to the plains of the Main, is run on strict organic principles. Indeed, the property is the largest organic wine estate in Germany. Since 1996 it has been run by Count Ferdinand, heir to his father's title. Following the reorganization and classification of the vineyards, the near future will see further investments in the cellars. 1996 was a light year here, as in most of Franken, but left us with the impression that this estate was on its way back to its former greatness. The fine 1997s confirmed that hypothesis. We particularly enjoyed the excellent dry Silvaner Spätlese from the Schloßberg.

1997 Casteller Hohnart
Silvaner Kabinett trocken
14.30 DM, 12.5%, 🍷 till 2002 **86**

1997 Casteller Bausch
Traminer Spätlese
21 DM, 12.5%, 🍷 till 2004 **86**

1995 Casteller Kugelspiel
Rieslaner Beerenauslese
48 DM/0.375 liter, 11%, 🍷 till 2008 **86**

1997 Casteller Schloßberg
Silvaner Spätlese trocken
36 DM, 13%, 🍷 till 2003 **88**

1997 Casteller Schloßberg
Riesling Spätlese
22.50 DM, 12%, 🍷 till 2003 **88**

1997 Casteller Kugelspiel
Rieslaner Spätlese
22.50 DM, 13%, 🍷 till 2007 **91**

1996 Casteller Kugelspiel
Silvaner Eiswein
68 DM/0.375 liter, 11%, 🍷 till 2012 **91**

1997 Casteller Kugelspiel
Silvaner Eiswein
85 DM/0.375 liter, 11.5%, 🍷 till 2007 **95**

WEINGUT HELMUT CHRIST

Owner: Helmut Christ
97334 Nordheim, Volkacher Straße 6
Tel. (0 93 81) 28 06, Fax 66 40
Directions: A 3 Würzburg–Nürnberg, exit Volkach, via Schwarzach and Sommerach
Sales: Angelika Christ
Opening hours: Mon.–Sat. 10 a.m. to noon and 1 p.m. to 6 p.m.
Worth seeing: Baroque courtyard

Vineyard area: 8.3 hectares
Annual production: 55,000 bottles
Top sites: Volkacher Ratsherr, Nordheimer Vögelein, Dettelbacher Berg Rondell
Soil types: Fossil limestone, sandy loam
Grape varieties: 29% Müller-Thurgau, 24% Silvaner, 16% Kerner, 12% red varieties, 6% Gewürztraminer, 5% each of Riesling and Bacchus, 3% other varieties
Average yield: 62 hl/ha
Best vintages: 1988, 1990, 1993
Member: Bioland

After Helmut Christ handled the difficult 1995 vintage with success, 1996 was not a great challenge for him. In spite of the threatening weather during the autumn, he postponed the harvest in order to prolong the ripening period of the grapes. This past year, however, drought from early August until the harvest severely limited the potential quality of the vintage. For over twenty years now Christ has been gathering experience in organic winemaking. Moreover, his work in the cellar has improved steadily. Given the nature of the vintage, his range of wines from 1996 turned out well. The 1997s, however, should have been better.

1997 Volkacher Ratsherr
Riesling Kabinett
13 DM, 12.5%, 🍷 till 2000 **77**

1996 Dettelbacher Berg Rondell
Müller-Thurgau Kabinett trocken
10 DM, 11.5%, 🍷 now **80**

1996 Stammheimer Eselsberg
Bacchus Kabinett trocken
10.50 DM/1.0 liter, 11.5%, 🍷 now **80**

1996 Dettelbacher Berg Rondell
Müller-Thurgau Spätlese trocken
14 DM, 13%, 🍷 now **80**

1997 Stammheimer Eselsberg
Bacchus Spätlese
13 DM, 12.5%, 🍷 till 2001 **80**

1997 Nordheimer Vögelein
Kerner Spätlese
13 DM, 13%, 🍷 till 2001 **80**

1996 Nordheimer Vögelein
Müller-Thurgau Kabinett trocken
10 DM, 11.5%, 🍷 now **82**

1996 Nordheimer Vögelein
Traminer Spätlese trocken
16 DM, 12.5%, 🍷 till 2000 **82**

1997 Nordheimer Vögelein
Rieslaner Spätlese
17 DM, 13.5%, 🍷 till 2002 **84**

FRANKEN
Weingut
Helmut Christ
1996
Volkacher Kirchberg
SILVANER
11,5 % vol
trocken
1 l
Qualitätswein
A.P.Nr. 4294-003-97
Gutsabfüllung
Bioland®
ÖKOLOGISCHER LANDBAU
WEIN AUS ÖKOLOGISCH ERZEUGTEN TRAUBEN
DE 002 Ökokontrollstelle
Helmut Christ D-97334 Nordheim/Main Volkacher Str. 6

WEINGUT JOSEF DEPPISCH

Owner: Theo and Johannes Deppisch
Manager: Johannes Deppisch
Winemaker: Günter Schubert
97837 Erlenbach bei Marktheidenfeld, An der Röthe 2
Tel. (0 93 91) 9 82 70, Fax 51 58
e-mail: info@deppisch.com
Directions: A 3 Frankfurt–Würzburg, exit Marktheidenfeld, follow the B 8
Sales: Anja and Johannes Deppisch, Robert Göbel
Opening hours: Mon.–Fri. 7 a.m. to 5 p.m., Sat. and Sun. 8 a.m. to noon in Hotel Anker
Restaurant: In Hotel Anker, open from 6 p.m. to 1 a.m., except Tue.
Specialties: Venison, "Blaue Zipfel," regional fare

Vineyard area: 15 hectares
Annual production: 150,000 bottles
Top sites: Marktheidenfelder Kreuzberg, Erlenbacher Krähenschnabel, Homburger Kallmuth
Soil types: Fossil limestone, often reddish in hue
Grape varieties: 37% Müller-Thurgau, 35% Silvaner, 11% Riesling, 7% Bacchus, 3% each of Spätburgunder and Grauburgunder, 4% other varieties
Average yield: 60 hl/ha
Best vintages: 1992, 1994, 1997

Since Johannes Deppisch returned home in 1988, this estate has grown in size and in importance. Father and son own excellent vineyards and are especially proud of their 400-year-old vaulted cellars, which are filled with old casks. These are located beneath the family's hotel in the old part of town, where they have operated a restaurant since the 17th century. After a rather mediocre range of wines in 1995 and 1996, the 1997s brought a noticeable improvement. Nonetheless, this estate has potential that is not being fully exploited.

1997 Homburger Kallmuth
Silvaner Kabinett trocken
14 DM, 11%, ♀ till 2000 **80**

1996 Dertinger Mandelberg
Kerner
10 DM, 10.5%, ♀ now **80**

1995 Homburger Kallmuth
Silvaner Kabinett trocken
13.50 DM, 11%, ♀ till 2000 **82**

1997 Marktheidenfelder Kreuzberg
Silvaner Spätlese trocken
22 DM, 12.5%, ♀ till 2001 **82**

1997 Marktheidenfelder Kreuzberg
Rieslaner Spätlese
22 DM, 13.5%, ♀ till 2003 **86**

——— Red wines ———

1994 Erlenbacher Krähenschnabel
Spätburgunder trocken
25 DM, 12%, ♀ now **82**

1995 Erlenbacher Krähenschnabel
Dornfelder trocken
16.50 DM, 12%, ♀ till 2000 **82**

1996 Erlenbacher Krähenschnabel
Spätburgunder trocken
26.50 DM, 13%, ♀ till 2000 **84**

WEINGUT MICHAEL FRÖHLICH

Owner: Michael Fröhlich
97332 Escherndorf,
Bocksbeutelstraße 41
Tel. (0 93 81) 28 47, Fax 7 13 60
Directions: A 7 Würzburg–Kassel, exit Würzburg-Estenfeld, follow the road towards Volkach
Opening hours: Mon.–Sat. 8 a.m. to 6 p.m., Sun. by appointment

Vineyard area: 10 hectares
Annual production: 85,000 bottles
Top sites: Escherndorfer Lump and Fürstenberg
Soil types: Fossil limestone
Grape varieties: 25% Müller-Thurgau, 20% Silvaner, 10% Riesling, 20% red wine varieties, 25% other varieties
Average yield: 75 hl/ha
Best vintages: 1993, 1996
Member: VDP

One cannot really say any longer that Michael Fröhlich is unknown. Yet he is still paid little attention beyond the borders of Franken. He has now closed the estate's nursery, where he became an expert on new cultivars, in order to focus his efforts on making wines from the classical grape varieties. In 1996 he submitted only a few bottlings, all of which were very fine for the vintage, including a wine that was arguably the best Riesling from Franken. Critics of his style have long maintained that his wines lack refinement. They were given solid evidence for their case in 1997, which proved to be somewhat disappointing for the vintage. Fröhlich's wines have never been sparkling gems; rather they are solidly handcrafted products with hard-headed individuality.

1996 Escherndorfer Lump
Silvaner Kabinett trocken
10.50 DM, 10.5%, ♀ now **84**

1997 Escherndorfer Lump
Rieslaner Spätlese trocken
17.50 DM, 13.5%, ♀ till 2002 **84**

1997 Escherndorfer Lump
Riesling Spätlese halbtrocken
17.50 DM, 11.5%, ♀ till 2002 **84**

1996 Untereisenheimer Sonnenberg
Muskateller Kabinett trocken
9.50 DM, 10.5%, ♀ now **86**

1995 Escherndorfer Lump
Riesling Kabinett trocken
12 DM, 11.5%, ♀ now **86**

1996 Escherndorfer Lump
Riesling Spätlese
19 DM, 12%, ♀ till 2000 **86**

1997 Untereisenheimer Sonnenberg
Muskateller Spätlese
15 DM, 12%, ♀ till 2004 **88**

1995 Escherndorfer Lump
Rieslaner Spätlese
17.50 DM, 11.5%, ♀ till 2003 **88**

WEINGUT RUDOLF FÜRST

Owner: Paul Fürst
63927 Bürgstadt, Hohenlindenweg 46
Tel. (0 93 71) 86 42, Fax 6 92 30
e-mail:
weingut.rudolf.fuerst@t-online.de
Directions: A 3 Frankfurt–Würzburg, exit Stockstadt or Wertheim, towards Miltenberg
Sales: Monika Fürst
Opening hours: Mon.–Fri. 9 a.m. to noon and 2 p.m. to 6 p.m.
Sat. 9 a.m. to 3 p.m.
History: The family has been making wine since 1638

Vineyard area: 14.2 hectares
Annual production: 95,000 bottles
Top site: Bürgstadter Centgrafenberg
Soil types: Red sandstone beneath layers of loam and clay
Grape varieties: 40% Spätburgunder, 22% Silvaner, 16% Riesling, 7% each of Frühburgunder and Müller-Thurgau, 8% other varieties
Average yield: 56 hl/ha
Best vintages: 1993, 1994, 1997
Member: VDP,
Deutsches Barrique Forum

Paul Fürst never harvested Riesling as late as he did in 1996: from the 4th to 11th of November. 1995 was also an extremely difficult year for an estate that is particularly well known for its red wines. Only a third of the grapes could be selected for use, a prerequisite for making untainted red wines in that vintage. After three difficult years Fürst presented a beautiful collection of 1997s. Certainly one of the finest vintners in Franken, he showed his peers what was possible from this highly touted but often only marginally successful vintage. After a glance at the beautiful cellar, the visitor can enjoy a wonderful view of the Main valley and the village of Miltenberg from the terrace of the winery set in the middle of the steep, south-facing Centgrafenberg vineyard. Fürst also makes fine sparkling wine and distills exquisite fruit schnapps. Above all, those made from sloe and from wild sour cherries merit special attention.

1996 Bürgstadter Centgrafenberg
Rieslaner Auslese
26 DM/0.375 liter, 10%, 🍷 till 2003 **86**

1996 Bürgstadter Centgrafenberg
Weißer Burgunder trocken
28 DM, 12%, 🍷 till 2006 **88**

1997 Volkacher Karthäuser
Silvaner Spätlese trocken
22 DM, 12.5%, 🍷 till 2005 **89**

1997 Bürgstadter Centgrafenberg
Riesling Spätlese trocken
25 DM, 12%, 🍷 till 2004 **89**

1997 Bürgstadter Centgrafenberg
Weißer Burgunder Spätlese trocken
34 DM, 13%, 🍷 till 2004 **89**

1997 Volkacher Karthäuser
Silvaner Spätlese
27 DM, 12.5%, 🍷 till 2006 **89**

1996 Bürgstadter Centgrafenberg
Rieslaner Beerenauslese
78 DM/0.375 liter, 10%, 🍷 till 2006 **91**

1997 Bürgstadter Centgrafenberg
Rieslaner Auslese
26 DM/0.375 liter, 10%, 🍷 till 2010 **92**

——— Red wines ———

1996 Bürgstadter Centgrafenberg
Frühburgunder trocken
33 DM, 13%, 🍷 till 2004 **88**

1997 Bürgstadter Centgrafenberg
Spätburgunder trocken
16.50 DM, 12.5%, 🍷 till 2005 **89**

Weingut Rudolf Fürst, D-63927 Bürgstadt
Qualitätswein, A.P.Nr. 1095-021-97
FÜRST
1996
Weißer Burgunder
Franken
trocken · 750 ml · alc 12,0% by vol.
Bürgstadter Centgrafenberg · Gutsabfüllung

WEINGUT GLASER-HIMMELSTOSS

Owner: Wolfgang and Monika Glaser
Winemaker: Wolfgang Glaser
97334 Nordheim, Langgasse 7
Tel. (0 93 81) 46 02, Fax 64 02
Directions: A 3 Würzburg–Nürnberg, exit Kitzingen via Schwarzach
Opening hours: Mon.–Fri. 9 a.m. to 6 p.m., except Tue.
Sat. and Sun. 10 a.m. to 4 p.m.
Restaurant: "Himmelstoss," Bamberger Straße 3, Dettelbach, Tel. (0 93 24) 47 76 or 23 05, open from 11:30 a.m. to midnight, except Mon. and Tue.
Specialties: Excellent regional fare

Vineyard area: 11 hectares
Annual production: 100,000 bottles
Top sites: Dettelbacher Berg Rondell, Sommeracher Katzenkopf, Nordheimer Vögelein
Soil types: Fossil limestone, sand, clay and loam
Grape varieties: 30% Müller-Thurgau, 20% Silvaner, 10% each of Bacchus and Kerner, 6% each of Scheurebe and Spätburgunder, 5% each of Riesling and Schwarzriesling, 8% other varieties
Average yield: 78 hl/ha
Best vintages: 1994, 1996, 1997
Member: VDP

Wolfgang and Monika Glaser, whose maiden name was Himmelstoss, united the wine estates of their parents Siegfried Glaser and Hans Himmelstoss. Since 1997 the estate, which is run strictly along organic lines, has been renamed Glaser-Himmelstoss. The 1996s, albeit not inspired throughout the range, were well-bodied and intriguingly tart in their fruit. The 1997s are the finest wines that we have ever tasted from this estate. Selective harvesting, as well as the reorganization of the fermentation procedures, are clearly beginning to pay off. The young couple's clientele has already caught wind of this development. Glaser now regrets that he can scarcely satisfy demand.

1996 Nordheimer Kreuzberg
Bacchus Kabinett
9.50 DM, 10%, ♀ now **82**

1996 Dettelbacher Berg Rondell
Müller-Thurgau Spätlese
18 DM, 13%, ♀ now **82**

1997 Dettelbacher Berg Rondell
Riesling Kabinett trocken
13.50 DM, 11.5%, ♀ till 2002 **84**

1997 Obervolkacher Landsknecht
Müller-Thurgau Spätlese trocken
15 DM, 13%, ♀ till 2001 **84**

1997 Nordheimer Vögelein
Rieslaner Kabinett trocken
14 DM, 12%, ♀ till 2003 **86**

1997 Grauer Burgunder
Spätlese
19 DM, 12.5%, ♀ till 2003 **86**

1997 Nordheimer Vögelein
Traminer Auslese
22 DM/0.5 liter, 12.5%, ♀ till 2006 **89**

——— Red wine ———

1997 Dettelbacher Berg Rondell
Spätburgunder trocken
14.50 DM, 12.5%, ♀ till 2002 **84**

WEINGUT MARTIN GÖBEL

Owner: Hubert Göbel
97236 Randersacker, Friedhofstraße 9
Tel. (09 31) 70 93 80, Fax 70 93 80
Directions: A 3 Würzburg–Nürnberg, exit Randersacker
Sales: Rosemarie Göbel
Opening hours: Mon.–Sat. 8 a.m. to 7 p.m., Sun. by appointment

Vineyard area: 6 hectares
Annual production: 65,000 bottles
Top sites: Randersackerer Pfülben, Marsberg, Teufelskeller and Sonnenstuhl
Soil types: Fossil limestone
Grape varieties: 31% each of Silvaner and Müller-Thurgau, 4% each of Kerner, Spätburgunder and Frühburgunder, 3% each of Rieslaner, Weißburgunder, Gewürztraminer and Domina, 14% other varieties
Average yield: 69 hl/ha
Best vintages: 1992, 1993, 1994
Member: VDP

When one meets the shy Hubert Göbel one would never suspect that he belongs to the ranks of Franken's best-known winemakers. Nor would such a thought enter one's head after a visit to the quaint, old-fashioned cellars. Nevertheless, there is no doubt that some of the finest sweet Rieslaners of the region once emerged, and sometimes still do, from this nondescript property opposite the cemetery. Everything here is done by hand, in the vineyard as well as in the cellar. There is no lack of dedication, but the unassuming Göbel is more a craftsman than an artist. That is perhaps why, with the exception of the sweet wines, he rarely produces anything of real stature. 1996 was far from an easy year for anyone, yet we were again disappointed by his lackluster range of wines. Although the vintage was excellent, the 1997s are no better. This estate is definitely underperforming at present.

1997 Randersackerer Pfülben
Müller-Thurgau Spätlese trocken
14 DM, 12.5%, ♀ till 2001 **77**

1996 Randersackerer Teufelskeller
Scheurebe Kabinett trocken
10 DM, 10%, ♀ now **80**

1996 Randersackerer Marsberg
Traminer Kabinett trocken
12.50 DM, 11.5%, ♀ now **80**

1997 Randersackerer Marsberg
Frühburgunder Auslese trocken
22 DM/0.5 liter, 14.5%, ♀ till 2001 **80**

1996 Randersackerer Pfülben
Rieslaner Spätlese
17 DM, 12%, ♀ till 2000 **82**

1997 Randersackerer Pfülben
Rieslaner Auslese
20 DM/0.5 liter, 13.5%, ♀ till 2001 **82**

1996 Randersackerer Marsberg
Albalonga Auslese
30 DM, 13.5%, ♀ till 2002 **82**

1997 Randersackerer Pfülben
Silvaner Eiswein
95 DM/0.5 liter, 8.7%, ♀ till 2008 **92**

WEINGUT JULIUSSPITAL

Owner: Juliusspital Foundation
General Manager: Horst Kolesch
Winemaker: Friedrich Franz and Benedikt Then
97070 Würzburg, Klinikstraße 1
Tel. (09 31) 3 93 14 00, Fax 3 93 14 14
e-mail: info@juliusspital.de
Directions: In the center of Würzburg, between the convention grounds and the train station
Sales: Wolfgang Apel, Kordula Geier
Opening hours: Mon.–Thur. 7:30 a.m. to 4:30 p.m., Fri. 7:30 a.m. to noon
Cellar door sales: Weineck Julius Echter, Koellikerstraße 1–2, Mon.–Fri. 9 a.m. to 6 p.m., Sat. 9 a.m. to 1 p.m.
Restaurant: Weinstuben Juliusspital, open from 11 a.m. to midnight, except Wed.
Specialties: Regional fare
History: Founded in 1576 by the Bishop Julius Echter von Mespelbrunn
Worth seeing: Baroque palace, garden pavilions and vaulted cellars

Vineyard area: 127 hectares
Annual production: 1 million bottles
Top sites: Würzburger Stein, Iphöfer Julius-Echter-Berg, Randersackerer Pfülben, Rödelseer Küchenmeister
Soil types: Fossil limestone, loam with humus, and gypsum with stony clay
Grape varieties: 35% Silvaner, 20% Müller-Thurgau, 18% Riesling, 5% Spätburgunder, 4% Kerner, 18% other varieties
Average yield: 60 hl/ha
Best vintages: 1990, 1993, 1994
Member: VDP

Given the reputation of this property, the lackluster range of wines from Juliusspital in 1996 was a disappointment. We searched in vain for persuasive wines and found instead numerous poor ones. Some had been deacidified, others were slightly tart and even bitter. Moreover, in comparison with the other leading estates of the region, the whole range was uninspired. It wasn't easy, given the size of this estate, to master such a difficult vintage, but even the wines from the excellent vintage 1997 were often overblown, lacking elegance and finesse. We can definitely no longer justify our old view of Juliusspital as Franken's most outstanding estate.

1996 Würzburger Stein
Riesling Kabinett trocken
17.25 DM, 11%, ♀ till 2000 **84**

1997 Würzburger Stein
Riesling Spätlese trocken
24.40 DM, 12.5%, ♀ till 2002 **84**

1996 Volkacher Karthäuser
Weißer Burgunder Spätlese trocken
24.25 DM, 12.5%, ♀ till 2000 **84**

1997 Randersackerer Pfülben
Riesling Spätlese trocken
24.40 DM, 12.5%, ♀ till 2003 **86**

1996 Iphöfer Julius-Echter-Berg
Rieslaner Spätlese
25.50 DM, 11%, ♀ till 2003 **86**

1997 Würzburger Stein
Silvaner Beerenauslese
104 DM/0.375 liter, 12%, ♀ till 2005 **88**

1997 Randersackerer Pfülben
Rieslaner Auslese
34.80 DM, 12.5%, ♀ till 2005 **89**

1997 Würzburger Stein
Riesling Beerenauslese
104 DM/0.375 liter, 13%, ♀ till 2007 **89**

WEINGUT FRANZ KIRCH

Owner: Franz Kirch
Winemaker: Matthias Kirch
97332 Fahr bei Volkach,
Mönchbergstraße 11
Tel. (0 93 81) 8 08 70, Fax 80 87 22
Directions: A 3 Würzburg–Nürnberg, exit Wiesentheid, via Volkach
Sales: Margarete Kirch
Opening hours: Mon.–Fri. 9 a.m. to noon and 1 p.m. to 7 p.m., Sat. 9 a.m. to 5 p.m., Sun. by appointment

Vineyard area: 9 hectares
Annual production: 90,000 bottles
Top site: Volkacher Ratsherr
Soil types: Weathered fossil limestone
Grape varieties: 24% Müller-Thurgau, 22% Silvaner, 12% Riesling, 9% Kerner, 8% Spätburgunder, 6% Schwarzriesling, 5% each of Weißburgunder, Bacchus and Scheurebe, 4% Rieslaner
Average yield: 84 hl/ha
Best vintages: 1993, 1994, 1996

The old Franconian cellar of this estate was laid out to offer passing wine lovers the opportunity to taste the predominately dry wines of this otherwise unknown property in a relaxing atmosphere. Matthias Kirch, who is responsible for the vast improvements at this estate, also makes the wines of father-in-law Gebhard Kram in Nordheim. In addition, he operates as a shipper in a nearby, highly modern cellar that caters exclusively to wholesale customers. After the rather disappointing 1995 vintage, his estate put its best foot forward with the 1996s. With Johann Ruck he produced one of the year's most agreeable collections. He delicately handled the otherwise tart style of the vintage in order not to have to deacidify. There were no great wines among them, but they were all fresh and appealing. Although easy to drink, his 1997s thus came as a disappointment.

1997 Volkacher Kirchberg
Scheurebe Kabinett
13 DM, 11%, ♀ till 2000 **80**

1997 Volkacher Ratsherr
Weißer Burgunder Kabinett trocken
11 DM, 12%, ♀ till 2001 **82**

1996 Volkacher Ratsherr
Riesling Kabinett trocken
12 DM, 10.5%, ♀ now **82**

1996 Volkacher Ratsherr
Weißer Burgunder Kabinett trocken
12 DM, 11%, ♀ now **82**

1996 Volkacher Ratsherr
Riesling Kabinett
12 DM, 9.5%, ♀ till 2000 **84**

1996 Volkacher Ratsherr
Rieslaner Kabinett
12 DM, 12%, ♀ till 2000 **84**

1996 Volkacher Ratsherr
Weißer Burgunder Eiswein
60 DM/0.375 liter, 14%, ♀ till 2010 **91**

——— Red wines ———

1996 Volkacher Ratsherr
Spätburgunder trocken – 1 –
13 DM, 12.5%, ♀ till 2002 **80**

1996 Volkacher Ratsherr
Spätburgunder trocken – 33 –
13 DM, 12.5%, ♀ till 2002 **82**

WEINGUT FÜRST LÖWENSTEIN

Owner: Alois Konstantin Fürst zu Löwenstein-Wertheim-Rosenberg
General Manager: Robert Haller
97892 Kreuzwertheim, Rathausgasse 5
Tel. (0 93 42) 9 23 50, Fax 92 35 50
e-mail: fuerst.loewenstein@loewenstein.de
Internet: www.loewenstein.de
Directions: A 3 Würzburg–Frankfurt, exit Wertheim or Marktheidenfeld
Sales: Ms. Baunach
Opening hours: Mon.–Fri. 7:30 a.m. to noon and 1 p.m. to 5 p.m.
Sat. 9 a.m. to noon
Worth seeing: Newly renovated Renaissance palace

Vineyard area: 26.5 hectares
Annual production: 200,000 bottles
Top sites: Homburger Kallmuth, Bürgstadter Centgrafenberg, Reicholzheimer Satzenberg
Soil types: Fossil limestone, red sandstone
Grape varieties: 34% Silvaner, 19% Spätburgunder, 17% Müller-Thurgau, 10% Riesling, 8% Bacchus, 6% Kerner, 4% Weißburgunder, 2% other varieties
Average yield: 60 hl/ha
Best vintages: 1993, 1994, 1995
Member: VDP

In the almost Alpine setting of Kallmuth in Homburg, one of the few vineyards that has remained unaltered since the previous century, there is enormous potential for quality wines. In recent years the Löwenstein princes rarely made the most of it; but since the ambitious Robert Haller has taken control, there has been a clear improvement. In 1996 Haller managed to extract the best fruit from a small crop, and the wines must be counted among the finest of the vintage, including the best liter bottling of the region. The 1997s are even better. The two dry Silvaner Spätlese are as good as anything that we have tasted here in quite a while. The wines are gaining in spiciness and character. It may not be that long before the estate can again be considered among the top wineries of Franken.

1996 Homburger Kallmuth
Silvaner trocken
10 DM/1.0 liter, 11%, 🍷 now **82**

1996 Lengfurter Alter Berg
Silvaner trocken
12 DM, 11%, 🍷 now **82**

1997 Homburger Kallmuth
Silvaner Kabinett trocken
14 DM, 11.5%, 🍷 till 2000 **82**

1996 Homburger Kallmuth
Silvaner trocken
14 DM, 11.5%, 🍷 till 2000 **84**

1996 Homburger Kallmuth
Riesling trocken
14 DM, 11.5%, 🍷 till 2000 **84**

1997 Lengfurter Alter Berg
Silvaner Kabinett trocken
13 DM, 12%, 🍷 till 2000 **84**

1997 Reicholzheimer Satzenberg
Weißer Burgunder Spätlese trocken
19 DM, 12%, 🍷 till 2000 **84**

1997 Homburger Kallmuth
Silvaner Spätlese trocken
20 DM, 12%, 🍷 till 2002 **86**

1997 Homburger Kallmuth
Silvaner Spätlese trocken "Asphodill"
25 DM, 12.5%, 🍷 till 2003 **88**

WEINGUT "AM LUMP"

Owner: Paul Sauer
Manager and winemaker: Albrecht Sauer
97332 Escherndorf, Bocksbeutelstraße 60
Tel. (0 93 81) 90 35, Fax 61 35
Directions: A 3 Würzburg–Nürnberg, exit Kitzingen-Schwarzach, towards Dettelbach, via Neuses a.B.
Sales: Margarete and Paul, Anne and Albrecht Sauer
Opening hours: Mon.–Sat. 8 a.m. to 7 p.m., Sun. 10 a.m. to 3 p.m.

Vineyard area: 10.5 hectares
Annual production: 85,000 bottles
Top sites: Escherndorfer Lump and Fürstenberg
Soil types: Fossil limestone, loess and loam
Grape varieties: 26% Silvaner, 21% Riesling, 20% Müller-Thurgau, 8% Spätburgunder, 7% Schwarzriesling, 5% Scheurebe, 4% each of Weißburgunder and Bacchus, 3% Rieslaner, 2% Kerner
Average yield: 75 hl/ha
Best vintages: 1993, 1996, 1997

Although this property has been in the family for generations, it was only in 1976 that Paul Sauer first settled in the idyllic landscape at the foot of the steep Escherndorfer Lump vineyard with a panoramic view over a bend in the River Main – and the wines produced from this vineyard are the village's finest. Together with his son Albrecht, Sauer is clearly setting the estate on an upward swing. We tasted a pleasing range of wines from the 1996 vintage. All were attractive, with the acidity well integrated. We were nonetheless hardly prepared for the metamorphosis in 1997. This is the finest range of wines that we have ever tasted from this estate and one of best in Franken from the vintage.

1997 Escherndorfer Lump
Silvaner Kabinett trocken
8.90 DM, 11%, 🍷 till 2000 **80**

1997 Escherndorfer Lump
Riesling Kabinett trocken
10 DM, 11.5%, 🍷 till 2000 **80**

1996 Escherndorfer Lump
Riesling Kabinett trocken
10.50 DM, 🍷 till 2000 **80**

1997 Escherndorfer Lump
Weißer Burgunder Spätlese
13.50 DM, 12.5%, 🍷 till 2002 **84**

1996 Escherndorfer Fürstenberg
Müller-Thurgau Spätlese
11.50 DM, 🍷 till 2000 **84**

1997 Escherndorfer Lump
Riesling Spätlese trocken
14 DM, 12%, 🍷 till 2003 **88**

1997 Escherndorfer Lump
Silvaner Spätlese
12.50 DM, 11.5%, 🍷 till 2003 **88**

1997 Escherndorfer Lump
Riesling Auslese
24 DM, 12%, 🍷 till 2008 **88**

1997 Escherndorfer Lump
Rieslaner Auslese
22 DM, 12.5%, 🍷 till 2006 **89**

1996 Escherndorfer Lump
Riesling Eiswein
16.50 DM/0.375 liter, 🍷 till 2013 **91**

WEINGUT AM LUMP
0,75 L
12,0 % vol
1997er
Escherndorfer Lump
Riesling
Auslese
Gutsabfüllung
Qualitätswein mit Prädikat
A. P. Nr. 4173-021-98
PAUL SAUER · D-97332 ESCHERNDORF/MAIN
FRANKEN

WEINGUT ERNST POPP

Owner: Michael Popp
Winemaker: Mr. Giel
97343 Iphofen, Rödelseer Straße 14
Tel. (0 93 23) 33 71, Fax 57 81
Directions: A 7 exit Marktbreit, A 3 exit Rüdenhausen
Sales: Maria Popp
Opening hours: Mon.–Sat. 8 a.m. to 6 p.m., Sun. 10 a.m. to noon
Worth seeing: Old cellar

Vineyard area: 34 hectares
Number of adherents: 27
Annual production: 300,000 bottles
Top sites: Iphöfer Julius-Echter-Berg, Kalb and Kronsberg, Rödelseer Küchenmeister and Schwanleite
Soil types: Gypsum with stony clay
Grape varieties: 51% Silvaner, 18% Müller-Thurgau, 10% Riesling, 3% each of Kerner and Scheurebe, 15% other varieties
Average yield: 70 hl/ha
Best vintages: 1994, 1995, 1996

This estate has been in Iphofen since 1878. Today Michael Popp vinifies the crop from 17 hectares of vines which belong to 27 small growers alongside that of his own vineyards. As a rule, fermentation takes place in temperature-controlled stainless steel tanks, but he also has the possibility to stock the young wines in casks, which is often of great importance. For years the wines from this estate were seldom particularly impressive. Yet beginning with the 1994 vintage we discerned a slight increase in quality. In 1995 Popp finally presented a genuinely attractive collection of wines. Given the difficult conditions in 1996, he again made wines of decent quality. The 1997s, however, are a disappointment. Quo vadis?

1997 Iphöfer Julius-Echter-Berg
Riesling Kabinett trocken
14.50 DM, 12%, 🍷 till 2000 **80**

1996 Iphöfer Kronsberg
Silvaner Kabinett trocken
12.50 DM, 11%, 🍷 now **80**

1996 Iphöfer Kalb
Silvaner Kabinett trocken
13 DM, 10.5%, 🍷 now **80**

1996 Iphöfer Julius-Echter-Berg
Riesling Kabinett trocken
14 DM, 10.5%, 🍷 now **80**

1997 Rödelseer Schwanleite
Weißer Burgunder Spätlese trocken
18.50 DM, 13%, 🍷 till 2000 **80**

1997 Iphöfer Kronsberg
Scheurebe Kabinett
12.30 DM, 11%, 🍷 till 2001 **80**

1996 Iphöfer Julius-Echter-Berg
Silvaner Kabinett trocken
12.50 DM, 11%, 🍷 now **82**

1996 Rödelseer Schwanleite
Weißer Burgunder Kabinett trocken
12.80 DM, 11.5%, 🍷 now **82**

1996 Iphöfer Burgweg
Bacchus Kabinett
13 DM, 11%, 🍷 now **82**

1997 Iphöfer Kronsberg
Bacchus Spätlese
15 DM, 12.5%, 🍷 till 2001 **82**

WEINGUT GERHARD ROTH

Owner: Gerhard Roth
97355 Wiesenbronn, Büttnergasse 11
Tel. (0 93 25) 3 73, Fax 5 28
Directions: A 3 Würzburg–Nürnberg, exit Schweinfurt Süd/Wiesentheid
Opening hours: Mon.–Sat. 9 a.m. to 11 a.m. and 1 p.m. to 5 p.m.

Vineyard area: 11 hectares
Annual production: 90,000 bottles
Top site: Wiesenbronner Geißberg
Soil types: Stony clay
Grape varieties: 30% Silvaner, 15% Müller-Thurgau, 10% each of Spätburgunder and Portugieser, 8% Lemberger, 6% each of Schwarzriesling and Domina, 5% each of Riesling and Kerner, 5% other varieties
Average yield: 68 hl/ha
Best vintages: 1993, 1994, 1996
Member: Naturland

Among the organic estates in Germany, Gerhard Roth is often extolled as an example; but he doesn't think of himself as a "green" warrior. Ever since he stopped using certain sprays in 1974, it has been essentially a matter of health – for himself and for the vineyard. His image has also been enhanced by the fact that, compared to other Franken estates, he produces a high proportion of red wines, some 40 percent. These are Roth's passion. In 1996 Roth also presented a pleasant collection of white wines. The varietal specificity was well defined and the acidity extremely well integrated. The 1997s, on the other hand, were at best innocuous. Given the quality of the vintage, this was certainly a dissatisfying performance for Roth.

1997 Wiesenbronner Wachhügel
Müller-Thurgau Spätlese trocken
13 DM, 13%, ♀ till 2002 **82**

1997 Wiesenbronner Geißberg
Rieslaner Kabinett
10 DM, 11%, ♀ till 2000 **82**

1997 Wiesenbronner Geißberg
Scheurebe Kabinett trocken
11 DM, 12%, ♀ till 2003 **84**

1997 Wiesenbronner Geißberg
Kerner Spätlese
13 DM, 12%, ♀ till 2004 **84**

1996 Wiesenbronner Geißberg
Rieslaner Spätlese
18 DM, 11%, ♀ till 2002 **84**

1997 Wiesenbronner Wachhügel
Müller-Thurgau Auslese
20 DM/0.5 liter, 13%, ♀ till 2004 **84**

1996 Wiesenbronner Wachhügel
Bacchus Beerenauslese
80 DM, 11.5%, ♀ till 2010 **89**

——— Red wine ———

1995 Wiesenbronner Geißberg
Lemberger trocken
21.50 DM, 12.5%, ♀ till 2002 **84**

WEINGUT JOHANN RUCK

Owner: Johann Ruck
97346 Iphofen, Marktplatz 19
Tel. (0 93 23) 33 16, Fax 50 35
Directions: A 3 Würzburg–Nürnberg, exit Kitzingen or Schweinfurt-Wiesentheid
Sales: Birgit Ruck
Opening hours: Mon.–Sat. 9 a.m. to noon and 1 p.m. to 6 p.m.
Sun. 10 a.m. to noon

Vineyard area: 11 hectares
Annual production: 80,000 bottles
Top sites: Iphöfer Julius-Echter-Berg, Kronsberg and Kalb, Rödelseer Schwanleite
Soil types: Heavy stony clay, gypsum with stony clay and red sandstone
Grape varieties: 40% Silvaner, 20% Müller-Thurgau, 10% each of Riesling and Grauburgunder, 5% each of Scheurebe and Kerner, 4% Spätburgunder, 6% other varieties
Average yield: 60 hl/ha
Best vintages: 1993, 1996
Member: VDP

Johann Ruck is convinced that only by vinifying in stainless steel tanks and bottling early can he enable his dry wines to taste as "natural as possible." He advocates and pursues ecologically sound viticulture, planting green cover and employing restrained pruning practices; he uses pesticides only when necessary. These measures are reflected in his wines: there is nothing forced or artificial about them. In an otherwise poor vintage Ruck gave an exemplary performance in 1996. His wines were clean, lively, lean and thoroughly drinkable. He clarified the must before fermentation, which took place at cool temperatures. With such reductive vinification, he often retains plenty of carbon dioxide in the wine, which confers even more liveliness on them. The 1997 vintage was certainly not of the same caliber. His best wines came from new cultivars.

1996 Rödelseer Schwanleite
Weißer Burgunder Kabinett trocken
18 DM, 11%, ♀ now **82**

1997 Iphöfer Julius-Echter-Berg
Riesling Kabinett trocken
16.50 DM, 11.5%, ♀ till 2001 **84**

1996 Iphöfer Julius-Echter-Berg
Silvaner Kabinett trocken
16.50 DM, 11%, ♀ now **84**

1996 Iphöfer Kronsberg
Bacchus Kabinett trocken
14 DM, 12%, ♀ now **84**

1996 Iphöfer Kronsberg
Müller-Thurgau Kabinett trocken
12 DM, 12%, ♀ now **84**

1997 Rödelseer Schwanleite
Grauer Burgunder Spätlese trocken
28 DM, 13.5%, ♀ till 2002 **84**

1997 Iphöfer Julius-Echter-Berg
Scheurebe Spätlese trocken
17.50 DM, 13%, ♀ till 2004 **86**

1997 Iphöfer Julius-Echter-Berg
Rieslaner Spätlese
21 DM, 13%, ♀ till 2002 **86**

1997 Iphöfer Kalb
Huxelrebe Auslese
32 DM, 10.5%, ♀ till 2008 **92**

WEINGUT HORST SAUER

Owner: Horst Sauer
97332 Escherndorf,
Bocksbeutelstraße 14
Tel. (0 93 81) 43 64, Fax 68 43
Directions: A 3 Würzburg–Nürnberg, exit Wiesentheid, via Volkach; A 7 Kassel–Würzburg, exit Estenfeld, towards Volkach
Sales: Magdalena Sauer
Opening hours: Mon.–Fri. 9 a.m. to 6 p.m., Sat. 10 a.m. to 6 p.m.
Sun. 10 a.m. to noon or by appointment

Vineyard area: 9.4 hectares
Annual production: 76,500 bottles
Top sites: Escherndorfer Lump and Fürstenberg
Soil types: Fossil limestone, stony clay, loess and loam
Grape varieties: 34% Müller-Thurgau, 27% Silvaner, 11% Bacchus, 10% Riesling, 7% Kerner, 6% red wine varieties, 5% other varieties
Average yield: 81 hl/ha
Best vintages: 1993, 1996, 1997

Horst Sauer has always worked in harmony with nature, conscious that the roots of high quality are to be found in the vineyard. In the cellar his major concern is that each wine should conserve its natural qualities through gentle vinification practices. Ever since he left the local cooperative in 1977, Sauer has had a particular affection for the steep Lump vineyard. His goal is, as is that of his colleagues Egon Schäffer and Michael Fröhlich, to restore this site to its former glories. That he has succeeded was proven by his fine range from the 1995 vintage, which stunned our palates by means of lively fruit, varietal typicity and balanced acidity. His 1996s showed the hand of an equally inspired vintner. The 1997s are even better. This estate definitely has the "right stuff." Even the dry wines are improving in quality!

1997 Escherndorfer Lump
Silvaner Kabinett trocken
11.50 DM, 11.5%, ♀ till 2001 **84**

1997 Escherndorfer Lump
Riesling Kabinett trocken
12 DM, 12%, ♀ till 2002 **84**

1996 Escherndorfer Lump
Riesling Spätlese
18 DM, 11%, ♀ now **84**

1996 Escherndorfer Fürstenberg
Bacchus Spätlese
12 DM, 11%, ♀ now **86**

1997 Escherndorfer Lump
Silvaner Spätlese trocken
15 DM, 13%, ♀ till 2004 **88**

1997 Escherndorfer Lump
Riesling Spätlese
18 DM, 12%, ♀ till 2005 **89**

1997 Escherndorfer Lump
Riesling Auslese
28 DM/0.5 liter, 10.5%, ♀ till 2008 **91**

1997 Escherndorfer Lump
Silvaner Eiswein
78 DM/0.375 liter, 10.5%, ♀ till 2010 **92**

1997 Escherndorfer
Silvaner Trockenbeerenauslese
55 DM/0.375 liter, 10%, ♀ till 2008 **92**

1997 Escherndorfer Lump
Riesling Beerenauslese
38 DM/0.375 liter, 9%, ♀ till 2012 **94**

WEINBAU EGON SCHÄFFER

Owner: Egon Schäffer
97332 Escherndorf bei Volkach,
Astheimer Straße 17
Tel. (0 93 81) 93 50, Fax 48 34
Directions: A 3 Würzburg–Nürnberg, exit Wiesentheid, via Volkach; A 7 Kassel–Würzburg, exit Estenfeld, towards Volkach
Opening hours: Mon.–Sat. 8 a.m. to 7 p.m., by appointment

Vineyard area: 3.1 hectares
Annual production: 25,000 bottles
Top sites: Escherndorfer Lump and Fürstenberg
Soil types: Fossil limestone
Grape varieties: 44% Silvaner, 36% Müller-Thurgau, 15% Riesling, 5% Bacchus
Average yield: 63 hl/ha
Best vintages: 1990, 1993, 1994
Member: VDP

Egon Schäffer took over this small estate in Escherndorf from his father, Hermann, in 1988. Within a short period he set the estate on a path to success. After seeing the quaint old cellar, it becomes obvious even to the most naive consumer that one can produce outstanding wines without costly equipment. After the first-rate 1993s and 1994s, the 1995s were certainly less successful. In comparison with those of his esteemed colleagues, the 1996s were rustic and lacking in depth. The 1997s are even less attractive. What has happened? Egon Schäffer still belongs among the ranks of the good Franken producers; but his position among the elite can no longer be maintained on the basis of the last two vintages.

1997 Untereisenheimer Sonnenberg
Müller-Thurgau Kabinett trocken
9.80 DM/1.0 liter, 12%, ♀ till 2000 **80**

1997 Escherndorfer Fürstenberg
Silvaner Kabinett trocken
12 DM, ♀ till 2000 **80**

1996 Untereisenheimer Sonnenberg
Silvaner trocken
9 DM, 11.5%, ♀ now **82**

1996 Escherndorfer Lump
Silvaner Kabinett trocken
13.50 DM, 11%, ♀ now **82**

1996 Escherndorfer Lump
Riesling Kabinett trocken “Stahltank”
14 DM, 10.5%, ♀ now **82**

1997 Escherndorfer Lump
Silvaner Kabinett 2
13 DM, ♀ till 2000 **82**

1996 Escherndorfer Lump
Riesling Kabinett trocken “Holzfaß”
14.50 DM, 10.5%, ♀ now **84**

1997 Escherndorfer Lump
Riesling Spätlese trocken
19 DM, ♀ till 2001 **84**

1997 Escherndorfer Lump
Riesling Kabinett
13.50 DM, ♀ till 2000 **84**

1997 Escherndorfer Fürstenberg
Müller-Thurgau Kabinett
9.20 DM, 12.5%, ♀ till 2001 **86**

WEINGUT SCHMITT'S KINDER

Owner: Karl Martin Schmitt
97236 Randersacker, Am Sonnenstuhl
Tel. (09 31) 7 05 91 97, Fax 7 05 91 98
e-mail:
schmitts-kinder-weingut@t-online.de
Directions: A 3 Würzburg–Nürnberg, exit Randersacker near Würzburg
Sales: Renate Schmitt
Opening hours: Mon.–Fri. 8 a.m. to 6 p.m., Sat. 9 a.m. to 5 p.m. or by appointment
History: The family has been producing wine since 1710

Vineyard area: 13.8 hectares
Annual production: 120,000 bottles
Top sites: Randersackerer Pfülben, Sonnenstuhl, Marsberg and Teufelskeller
Soil types: Weathered fossil limestone
Grape varieties: 26% Silvaner, 25% Müller-Thurgau, 14% Bacchus, 10% Riesling, 5% each of Kerner and Scheurebe, 3% each of Rieslaner and Domina, 9% other varieties
Average yield: 66 hl/ha
Best vintages: 1993, 1994, 1997
Member: VDP

Karl Schmitt is one of the most unassuming vintners in Franken. Nonetheless, innate talent and hard work have brought him to the forefront in the region. Although neither 1995 nor 1996 was an easy vintage, there was not a single poor wine produced at this estate; and the range was among the few with sufficient extract, combined with an elegant balance in sweetness and acidity, to ensure that the wines will mature well. In their youth they were difficult to fathom, but they have matured gracefully. The 1997s put the estate back in the spotlight. Even the dry wines are a pleasure to drink. This estate must certainly be counted among the finest in Franken.

1996 Randersackerer Ewig Leben
Müller-Thurgau Kabinett trocken
9.50 DM, 11.5%, ♀ now **84**

1996 Randersackerer Marsberg
Silvaner Kabinett
12 DM, 10%, ♀ now **84**

1996 Randersackerer Sonnenstuhl
Rieslaner Kabinett
16 DM, 10%, ♀ till 2000 **84**

1997 Randersackerer Pfülben
Riesling Kabinett
14 DM, 10.5%, ♀ till 2002 **86**

1997 Randersackerer Sonnenstuhl
Silvaner Spätlese trocken
17 DM, 12.5%, ♀ till 2002 **88**

1997 Randersackerer Marsberg
Silvaner Spätlese trocken
18.60 DM, 13%, ♀ till 2003 **88**

1997 Randersackerer Pfülben
Riesling Spätlese
23 DM, 12.5%, ♀ till 2006 **89**

1997 Randersackerer Pfülben
Riesling Auslese
45 DM, 12%, ♀ till 2007 **91**

1997 Randersackerer Sonnenstuhl
Rieslaner Auslese
42 DM, 12%, ♀ till 2004 **91**

1997 Randersackerer Sonnenstuhl
Rieslaner Beerenauslese
36 DM/0.375 liter, 13%, ♀ till 2008 **92**

WEINGUT RICHARD SCHMITT

Owner: Richard Schmitt
Winemaker: Bernhard Schmitt
97236 Randersacker, Friedenstraße 3
Tel. (09 31) 70 82 17, Fax 70 60 00
Directions: A 3 Würzburg–Nürnberg, exit Randersacker near Würzburg
Opening hours: Mon.–Sat. 8 a.m. to 6 p.m., Sun. by appointment

Vineyard area: 11 hectares
Annual production: 80,000 bottles
Top sites: Randersackerer Pfülben, Sonnenstuhl, Teufelskeller and Marsberg
Soil types: Fossil limestone, clay, loam and sand
Grape varieties: 45% Silvaner, 35% Müller-Thurgau, 10% Riesling, 4% Kerner, 6% other varieties
Average yield: 67 hl/ha
Best vintages: 1992, 1993, 1994
Member: VDP

Bernhard Schmitt, who now shoulders the responsibility for his family's estate, does not have it easy trying to market yet another Schmitt winery in Randersacker. In terms of quality, however, he often has no reason to feel superfluous. This fact was confirmed by his appealing range from the 1996 vintage. There were no great wines in the lot, for they all turned out rather light, yet at the same time they were well balanced and enjoyable to drink. On the other hand, the 1997s were a shot in the dark, ranging between rustic bitterness and overblown alcohol levels. If this estate were more consistent we would certainly give it higher marks.

1996 Randersackerer Sonnenstuhl
Silvaner Kabinett trocken
4.50 DM/0.25 liter, 10%, ♀ now **77**

1997 Randersackerer Teufelskeller
Riesling Kabinett
9.50 DM/0.5 liter, 12%, ♀ till 2000 **77**

1996 Randersackerer Teufelskeller
Müller-Thurgau Kabinett
8.50 DM, 10%, ♀ now **77**

1996 Randersackerer Pfülben
Riesling Kabinett trocken
11 DM, 10%, ♀ till 2000 **80**

1997 Randersackerer Pfülben
Traminer Spätlese
18.50 DM, 13%, ♀ till 2001 **80**

1997 Randersackerer Pfülben
Rieslaner Spätlese
18.50 DM, 14%, ♀ till 2002 **80**

1996 Randersackerer Pfülben
Traminer Kabinett
12 DM, 10.5%, ♀ till 2000 **82**

1996 Randersackerer Teufelskeller
Bacchus Kabinett
9.50 DM, 11.5%, ♀ till 2000 **82**

1996 Randersackerer Pfülben
Rieslaner Spätlese
19.50 DM, 12%, ♀ till 2002 **84**

WEINGUT ROBERT SCHMITT

Owner: Bruno Schmitt
97236 Randersacker, Maingasse 13
Tel. (09 31) 70 83 51, Fax 70 83 52
Directions: A 3 Würzburg–Nümberg, exit Randersacker near Würzburg
Opening hours: Mon.–Sat. 8 a.m. to 6 p.m. or by appointment
History: The family has been making wine since 1676
Worth seeing: Estate building, more than 400 years old

Vineyard area: 7.5 hectares
Annual production: 50,000 bottles
Top sites: Randersackerer Pfülben and Sonnenstuhl, Würzburger Abtsleite
Soil types: Fossil limestone
Grape varieties: 26% Müller-Thurgau, 25% Silvaner, 20% Kerner, 15% Riesling, 14% other varieties
Average yield: 50 hl/ha
Best vintages: 1990, 1992, 1994
Member: VDP

As a champion of unchaptalized wines, and following in the footsteps of his uncle Robert, Bruno Schmitt makes wines that are seldom enjoyable when young. That was certainly true of the rather modest range of wines from the 1996 vintage. In comparison with the disappointing 1995s, he made positive changes in his vinification technics: all of the wines were thus more refined in their aromas and less alcoholic. Nonetheless, a grassy, almost bitter acidity combined with malty fruit flavors marred our pleasure in drinking them. The 1997s are even less enjoyable. We're now a far cry from the 1979s or 1983s, when this estate was at the head of its class. The winery seems to be moving further and further from its once dominant position in Franken. That's a shame; but young Bruno Schmitt has yet to earn his spurs.

1997 Randersackerer Sonnenstuhl
Silvaner Spätlese trocken
16 DM, 12.5%, ♀ till 2000 **77**

1997 Randersackerer Sonnenstuhl
Riesling Spätlese trocken
17 DM, 12.5%, ♀ till 2000 **77**

1997
Spätlese
17 DM, 12.5%, ♀ till 2000 **77**

1996 Randersackerer Sonnenstuhl
Silvaner Kabinett trocken
12 DM, 11%, ♀ now **80**

1997 Randersackerer Pfülben
Riesling Spätlese trocken
19 DM, 12.5%, ♀ till 2001 **80**

1997 Randersackerer Sonnenstuhl
Rieslaner Auslese
15 DM/0.375 liter, 13.5%, ♀ till 2002 **80**

1996 Randersackerer Sonnenstuhl
Müller-Thurgau Spätlese trocken
14 DM, 12.5%, ♀ till 2000 **82**

1996 Randersackerer Sonnenstuhl
Rieslaner Spätlese trocken
18 DM, 13.5%, ♀ till 2000 **84**

1997 Randersackerer Sonnenstuhl
Rieslaner Beerenauslese
35 DM/0.375 liter, 12.5%, ♀ till 2005 **88**

WEINGUT GREGOR SCHWAB

Owner: Thomas Schwab
97291 Thüngersheim, Bühlstraße 17
Tel. (0 93 64) 8 91 83, Fax 8 91 84
e-mail: schwab-weingut@t-online.de
Directions: B 27 Würzburg–Fulda, exit Thüngersheim, towards Karlstadt
Sales: Andrea Schwab
Opening hours: Mon.–Fri. 8 a.m. to 6 p.m., Sat. and Sun. by appointment

Vineyard area: 9.9 hectares
Annual production: 80,000 bottles
Top sites: Thüngersheimer Johannisberg and Scharlachberg
Soil types: Weathered fossil limestone
Grape varieties: 37% Müller-Thurgau, 14% each of Riesling and Silvaner, 11% Bacchus, 10% Kerner, 5% Spätburgunder, 9% other varieties
Average yield: 70 hl/ha
Best vintages: 1990, 1993, 1997
Member: VDP

In 1990 Thomas Schwab took over the family's estate from his father, Gregor. Their property lies on the edge of the village of Thüngersheim, some 15 kilometers north of Würzburg. The label displays the village's coat of arms featuring the archangel Michael. In recent years the younger Schwab has made efforts to obtain recognition for the winery beyond Franken itself. However, the range of the rather light and old-fashioned 1995s left much to be desired. Nor were the 1996s a revelation. The 1997s, on the other hand, are the best wines that the estate has produced since 1993. This is not the pinnacle of Franken's production, but certainly good wines for everyday drinking.

1997 Thüngersheimer Scharlachberg
Müller-Thurgau Kabinett trocken
7.50 DM/1.0 liter, 11.5%, ♀ till 2000 **80**

1996 Thüngersheimer Johannisberg
Silvaner Kabinett trocken
8.50 DM, 11%, ♀ now **80**

1997 Thüngersheimer Johannisberg
Silvaner Spätlese trocken
13 DM, 12%, ♀ till 2001 **80**

1997 Thüngersheimer Johannisberg
Riesling Kabinett trocken
9 DM, 11.5%, ♀ till 2001 **82**

1997 Thüngersheimer Johannisberg
Müller-Thurgau Spätlese trocken
11 DM, 12%, ♀ till 2001 **82**

1997 Thüngersheimer Johannisberg
Silvaner Auslese
10 DM/0.25 liter, 12%, ♀ till 2002 **82**

1997 Thüngersheimer Johannisberg
Silvaner Spätlese
13 DM, 12%, ♀ till 2003 **84**

1997 Thüngersheimer Johannisberg
Kerner Auslese
18 DM, 11.5%, ♀ till 2004 **86**

1996 Thüngersheimer Johannisberg
Silvaner Eiswein
28 DM/0.25 liter, 12%, ♀ till 2005 **86**

WEINGUT "ZUR SCHWANE"

Owner: Eva Pfaff-Düker and Ralph Düker
Winemaker: Stefan Ott and Eva Pfaff-Düker
97332 Volkach, Hauptstraße 12
Tel. (0 93 81) 80 66 61, Fax 80 66 66
e-mail: schwane-romantik.de
Directions: A 3 Würzburg–Nürnberg, exit Kitzingen, towards Volkach
Sales: Eva Pfaff-Düker and Ralph Düker
Opening hours: Mon.–Sun. 7 a.m. to 10 p.m.
Restaurant: "Zur Schwane," open from noon to 2 p.m. and 6 p.m. to 9:30 p.m., except Mon.
Specialties: Regional fare
History: Oldest original restaurant in Franken

> Vineyard area: 11 hectares
> Annual production: 80,000 bottles
> Top sites: Volkacher Ratsherr, Escherndorfer Lump, Iphöfer Kalb
> Soil types: Fossil limestone, gypsum with stony clay
> Grape varieties: 34% Silvaner, 28% Riesling, 17% Müller-Thurgau, 12% Kerner, 9% other varieties
> Average yield: 67 hl/ha
> Best vintages: 1993, 1996
> Member: VDP

This estate's insignia can be traced back to the Schwan family, who acquired the property on a bend in the River Main in 1404. In 1935 Josef Pfaff II acquired the inn, which is now a member of the small but quality-minded "Romantik Hotels." Since 1994 the winery has also been a member of the VDP. The wines, which once were marketed by a wholesale operation, are now produced only from specific vineyards. After three increasingly better vintages, 1995 was a disappointment. In 1996 Eva Pfaff-Düker and Ralph Düker took over the winery from their parents. Their first collection was far from spectacular. The 1997s, however, show that they have learned their lesson. We particularly enjoyed the Rieslaner Spätlese.

1996 Obereisenheimer Höll
Silvaner trocken
9.50 DM, 10.5%, ♀ now **77**

1997 Volkacher Ratsherr
Riesling Kabinett trocken
16.10 DM, 11%, ♀ till 2000 **77**

1997 Obervolkacher Landsknecht
Müller-Thurgau Kabinett
9 DM, 11.5%, ♀ till 2000 **77**

1997 Escherndorfer Lump
Riesling Kabinett trocken
16.90 DM, 12%, ♀ till 2001 **80**

1996 Volkacher Ratsherr
Bacchus Kabinett
9.25 DM, 10.5%, ♀ now **80**

1996 Volkacher Karthäuser
Müller-Thurgau Spätlese
13 DM, 12.5%, ♀ now **80**

1997 Escherndorfer Lump
Scheurebe Kabinett
13.90 DM, 10.5%, ♀ till 2002 **82**

1997 Volkacher Ratsherr
Rieslaner Spätlese
22 DM, 11.5%, ♀ till 2003 **86**

WEINGUT SCHLOSS SOMMERHAUSEN

Owner: Johann Kaspar Steinmann family
General Manager: Martin Steinmann
Winemaker: Heinrich Gutbrod
97286 Sommerhausen, Ochsenfurter Straße 17–19
Tel. (0 93 33) 2 60, Fax 14 88
Directions: A 3 Würzburg–Nürnberg, exit Randersacker near Würzburg
Sales: Gerd Wenzel
Opening hours: Mon.–Fri. 7:30 a.m. to 7 p.m., Sat. 9 a.m. to noon
Sun. by appointment in the castle, Tel. (0 93 33) 2 08
Worth seeing: The castle Schloß Sommerhausen

Vineyard area: 20 hectares
Annual production: 160,000 bottles
Top sites: Sommerhäuser Steinbach and Reifenstein, Randersackerer Sonnenstuhl
Soil types: Fossil limestone, stony clay
Grape varieties: 21% Silvaner, 16% Riesling, 8% Müller-Thurgau, 7% each of Bacchus and Dornfelder, 5% each of Auxerrois, Weißer Burgunder, Grauer Burgunder and Chardonnay, 21% other varieties
Average yield: 70 hl/ha
Best vintages: 1993, 1994, 1996
Member: VDP

Founded in the 15th century, Schloß Sommerhausen has belonged to the family Steinmann since 1968. The finest vineyards of the estate were already managed by the same family over three generations ago. In 1954 Steinmann founded a nursery that today is the Germany's largest provider of vines and clonal material. The wines produced here are generally dry in style and have been consistent in quality over the years. In 1993 and 1994 Heinrich Gutbrod and Martin Steinmann outdid themselves. After a disappointing 1995 vintage, the 1996s turned out well: spicy fruit with a well-balanced acidity. The 1997 dry wines are disappointing again, the sweet wines very good.

1996 Eibelstadter Kapellenberg
Weißer Burgunder Kabinett trocken
13 DM, 11%, 🍷 now **80**

1997 Eibelstadter Kapellenberg
Grauer Burgunder Spätlese trocken
18.50 DM, 13%, 🍷 till 2000 **80**

1996 Chardonnay
Kabinett trocken
13 DM, 11.5%, 🍷 now **82**

1997 Sommerhäuser Steinbach
Riesling Spätlese trocken
18.50 DM, 13%, 🍷 till 2002 **82**

1996 Sommerhäuser Ölspiel
Silvaner Kabinett halbtrocken
12.50 DM, 🍷 now **82**

1996 Randersackerer Sonnenstuhl
Silvaner Kabinett trocken
12.50 DM, 11%, 🍷 now **84**

1997 Sommerhäuser Steinbach
Gewürztraminer Eiswein
85 DM/0.375 liter, 12.5%, 🍷 till 2004 **91**

1997 Sommerhäuser Steinbach
Rieslaner Spätlese
22 DM, 10.5%, 🍷 till 2007 **92**

1997 Sommerhäuser Reifenstein
Scheurebe Eiswein
150 DM/0.375 liter, 10%, 🍷 till 2008 **92**

1997 Sommerhäuser Steinbach
Rieslaner Trockenbeerenauslese
105 DM/0.375 liter, 10%, 🍷 till 2010 **92**

STAATLICHER HOFKELLER

Owner: State of Bavaria
General Manager: Dr. Rowald Hepp
Winemaker: Helmut Brönner and Heinz Gößwein
97070 Würzburg, Residenzplatz 3
Tel. (09 31) 3 05 09 21, Fax 3 05 09 33
Directions: The Hofkeller is located in the center of Würzburg
Sales: Siegbert Henkelmann and Marcus Wicher
Opening hours: Mon.–Fri. 8:30 a.m. to 5:30 p.m., Sat. 8:30 to noon
Restaurants: Both in the fortress Marienberg and at the residence, open daily, except Mon.
Specialties: Local fare
History: Hofkeller since 1128
Worth seeing: The baroque palace of the residence, cellar

Vineyard area: 150 hectares
Annual production: 850,000 bottles
Top sites: Würzburger Stein and Innere Leiste, Randersackerer Pfülben and Lämmerberg
Soil types: Fossil limestone, gypsum with clay, slate and red sandstone
Grape varieties: 23% Riesling, 20% Müller-Thurgau, 18% Silvaner, 7% Rieslaner, 6% Kerner, 5% Spätburgunder, 21% other varieties
Average yield: 61 hl/ha
Best vintages: 1995, 1996, 1997
Member: VDP

The State of Bavaria now manages the former estates of the prince bishop and archdukes of Franken. Since 1952 the provinicial institute for winemaking and horticulture has also formed part of this operation. Under the direction of Rowald Hepp the estate has improved its quality over the past three years. The 1996s were one of the best ranges of Franken wines of the vintage. The 1997 set a new quality level for the estate. Thanks to their aging in casks the wines have acquired greater harmony. The classical grape varieties are now often among the best wines of any given vintage.

1997 Würzburger Stein
Riesling Kabinett trocken
17.50 DM, 12%, ♀ till 2001 **86**

1997 Würzburger Stein
Silvaner Spätlese trocken
28.50 DM, 12%, ♀ till 2002 **86**

1996 Würzburger Stein
Silvaner Spätlese trocken
28 DM, 12.5%, ♀ till 2000 **86**

1997 Würzburger Innere Leiste
Riesling Spätlese trocken
21.50 DM, 12.5%, ♀ till 2004 **88**

1997 Würzburger Stein
Riesling Spätlese trocken
22.70 DM, 12.5%, ♀ till 2005 **88**

1997 Würzburger Stein
Rieslaner Auslese
38.50 DM, 12%, ♀ till 2006 **89**

1996 Würzburger Innere Leiste
Riesling Beerenauslese
90 DM/0.375 liter, 10%, ♀ till 2006 **89**

1997 Randersackerer Marsberg
Rieslaner Spätlese
19.80 DM, 11%, ♀ till 2008 **91**

1996 Würzburger Stein
Riesling Eiswein
140 DM/0.375 liter, 9%, ♀ till 2013 **92**

1997 Würzburger Stein
Riesling Trockenbeerenauslese
160 DM/0.375 liter, 7.5%, ♀ till 2012 **98**

WEINGUT AM STEIN

Owner: Ludwig Knoll
97070 Würzburg,
Mittlerer Steinbergweg 5
Tel. (09 31) 2 58 08, Fax 2 58 80
Directions: The estate is located in Würzburg in the midst of the famous Stein vineyard
Sales: Sandra Knoll
Opening hours: Mon.–Fri. 9 a.m. to 1 p.m. and 2 p.m. to 6 p.m.
Sun. 10 a.m. to 2 p.m.
Restaurant: "Knollstube," open from 4 p.m. to midnight, except Mon.

Vineyard area: 12 hectares
Annual production: 90,000 bottles
Top sites: Stettener Stein, Würzburger Innere Leiste and Stein, Randersackerer Marsberg, Thüngersheimer Scharlachberg
Soil types: Fossil limestone
Grape varieties: 25% Silvaner, 22% Müller-Thurgau, 16% Riesling, 12% Spätburgunder, 9% Grauburgunder, 6% Weißburgunder, 10% other varieties
Average yield: 60 hl/ha
Best vintages: 1993, 1994, 1996

After graduating in winemaking from Geisenheim in 1991, Ludwig Knoll and his wife, Sandra, have been managing his family's winery in the celebrated Würzburger Stein vineyard. As he admits, "the 1996 vintage didn't offer us the best fruit." Nonetheless, with his range of lean, fresh, and fruity wines, this ambitious young grower proved that he made good use of his time at university. All of the wines had distinct personality and well-balanced acidity without any of the bitterness that characterizes the vintage. The 1997s are even better. In particular the simple wines are well made. It is well worth visiting Ludwig Knoll in his tasting room, which he calls his "wine workshop." Afterwards you can dine on local fare in their restaurant. This is certainly one of our pleasant discoveries in Franken these past years.

1997 Silvaner
Kabinett trocken
9.50 DM, 11.5%, ♀ till 2000 **80**

1996 Stettener Stein
Grauer Burgunder trocken
13 DM, 11.5%, ♀ now **82**

1996 Würzburger Stein
Silvaner Kabinett trocken
12 DM, 11%, ♀ now **82**

1997 Würzburger Innere Leiste
Riesling Spätlese trocken
18 DM, 12.5%, ♀ till 2001 **82**

1997 Würzburger Innere Leiste
Riesling Kabinett
13 DM, 11.5%, ♀ till 2002 **84**

1997 Stettener Stein
Grauer Burgunder Spätlese
18 DM, 13%, ♀ till 2001 **84**

1997 Stettener Stein
Riesling Auslese
20 DM/0.375 liter, 13%, ♀ till 2004 **84**

1997 Stettener Stein
Silvaner Eiswein
55 DM/0.375 liter, 13%, ♀ till 2002 **84**

1997 Müller-Thurgau
trocken "Frank&Frei"
9.50 DM, 11.5%, ♀ till 2001 **84**

WEINGUT JOSEF STÖRRLEIN

Owner: Armin Störrlein
97236 Randersacker, Schulstraße 14
Tel. (09 31) 70 82 81, Fax 70 11 55
Directions: A 3 Würzburg–Nürnberg, exit Randersacker near Würzburg
Sales: Ruth Störrlein
Opening hours: Mon.–Sat. 8 a.m. to 7 p.m., Sun. by appointment

Vineyard area: 7,5 hectares
Annual production: 65,000 bottles
Top sites: Randersackerer Marsberg, Sonnenstuhl and Dabug
Soil types: Fossil limestone
Grape varieties: 25% each of Müller-Thurgau and Silvaner,
10% Riesling, 8% Schwarzriesling,
6% each of Spätburgunder, Domina and Bacchus, 5% each of Kerner and Scheurebe, 4% Weißburgunder
Average yield: 75 hl/ha
Best vintages: 1988, 1993, 1994
Member: VDP

Armin Störrlein, who founded this estate from scratch in 1970, describes his philosophy simply: quality originates in the vineyard. His white wines are fermented in stainless steel tanks, aged in large casks and bottled as late as possible so as to obtain classic varietal typicity. This applies especially to the Silvaner, his darling. Störrlein occasionally even ages his wines in small barrels, which are – including the reds – often among the most appealing in Franken. Because Störrlein is such an excellent craftsman, we thought the 1996 vintage was an uncharacteristic disappointment. The wines were well balanced and quite drinkable, but lacked clarity of style. The 1997s were again not up to his standard. We expect more from this estate.

1997 Randersackerer Ewig Leben
Silvaner Kabinett trocken
9.50 DM, 11.5%, 🍷 till 2000 **80**

1997 Randersackerer Marsberg
Riesling Kabinett trocken
14 DM, 11.5%, 🍷 till 2000 **80**

1996 Randersackerer Sonnenstuhl
Silvaner Kabinett trocken
10 DM, 11.5%, 🍷 now **82**

1996 Randersackerer Dabug
Bacchus Kabinett
11.50 DM, 12%, 🍷 now **82**

1996 Randersackerer Sonnenstuhl
Riesling trocken
10.50 DM, 10.5%, 🍷 now **84**

1997 Randersackerer Sonnenstuhl
Silvaner Spätlese trocken
15.50 DM, 12.5%, 🍷 till 2002 **86**

1997 Randersackerer Sonnenstuhl
Riesling Spätlese trocken
17 DM, 12%, 🍷 till 2002 **86**

1997 Randersackerer
Weißer Burgunder Spätlese
26 DM, 13%, 🍷 till 2004 **88**

——— Red wine ———

1997 Randersackerer
Domina Spätlese trocken
20 DM, 12.5%, 🍷 till 2004 **86**

WEINGUT WOLFGANG WELTNER

Owner: Wolfgang Weltner
97348 Rödelsee,
Wiesenbronner Straße 17
Tel. (0 93 23) 36 46, Fax 38 46
Directions: A 3 Würzburg–Nürnberg, exit Kitzingen or Schweinfurt-Wiesentheid
Sales: Renate Weltner
Opening hours: Mon.–Sat. 8 a.m. to 6 p.m., Sun. by appointment
History: The family has been producing wine since 1553

Vineyard area: 6 hectares
Annual production: 45,000 bottles
Top sites: Rödelseer Küchenmeister and Schwanleite
Soil types: Gypsum with stony clay and loam
Grape varieties: 41% Silvaner, 22% Müller-Thurgau, 8% Scheurebe, 6% each of Riesling, Kerner, Bacchus and Domina, 5% Gewürztraminer
Average yield: 55 hl/ha
Best vintages: 1992, 1993, 1997
Member: VDP

To Wolfgang Weltner's regret, this estate's excellent vineyards near the Rödelsee are still overshadowed by those of their better known neighbors in Iphofen. The family has been involved in various aspects of the wine business for generations and can boast of owning the finest estate in Rödelsee, even if the wines from the many recent vintages have not always been much more than satisfactory. We tasted only a handful of the 1996s, but they were thoroughly pleasant. In 1997 Weltner produced his finest collection since 1993. This winery has again shown itself to be more than dependable, without yet being able to make claims to greater glory.

1996 Rödelseer Küchenmeister
Silvaner Kabinett trocken
9 DM/1.0 liter, ♀ now **80**

1997 Müller-Thurgau
Kabinett trocken
8.50 DM, 11.5%, ♀ till 2000 **82**

1996 Müller-Thurgau
Kabinett trocken
8.50 DM, ♀ now **82**

1997 Rödelseer Küchenmeister
Silvaner Kabinett trocken
9 DM, 12%, ♀ till 2000 **84**

1997 Rödelseer Küchenmeister
Müller-Thurgau Spätlese trocken
12 DM, 13%, ♀ till 2001 **84**

1997 Rödelseer Küchenmeister
Silvaner Spätlese trocken
14 DM, 13.5%, ♀ till 2002 **86**

1997 Rödelseer Küchenmeister
Riesling Spätlese trocken
18 DM, 13%, ♀ till 2003 **86**

1997 Rödelseer Küchenmeister
Traminer Spätlese trocken
17 DM, 13%, ♀ till 2004 **86**

WEINGUT HANS WIRSCHING

Owner: Dr. Heinrich Wirsching
Winemaker: Werner Probst
97343 Iphofen, Ludwigstraße 16
Tel. (0 93 23) 8 73 30, Fax 87 33 90
e-mail: Wirsching@t-online.de
Directions: A 3 Würzburg–Nürnberg, exit Kitzingen or Schweinfurt-Wiesentheid
Sales: Armin Huth and Dr. Uwe Matheus
Opening hours: Mon.–Sat. 8 a.m. to 6 p.m., Sun. 9:30 a.m. to 12:30 p.m.
History: In the family since 1630
Worth seeing: Old estate with vaulted cellar

Vineyard area: 69 hectares
Annual production: 450,000 bottles
Top sites: Iphöfer Julius-Echter-Berg, Kalb and Kronsberg
Soil types: Gypsum with stony clay beneath an overlay of sandstone
Grape varieties: 38% Silvaner, 18% Riesling, 12% Müller-Thurgau, 8% Scheurebe, 6% Weißburgunder, 5% Portugieser, 4% Kerner, 9% other varieties
Average yield: 49 hl/ha
Best vintages: 1993, 1994, 1997
Member: VDP

This old family estate is one of the largest in private hands in Germany. Dr. Heinrich Wirsching, who is as prudent as he is likeable, was very satisfied with the 1995s – an extremely appealing collection of delicate Kabinett wines from what he calls a "normal harvest." The wines from the 1996 vintage, however, were a poor performance for such a leading estate. The 1997s were much better, but still a far cry from what we expect from such an intelligent producer. This estate was once the finest in Franken. Today it is being outperformed by younger winemakers.

1996 Iphöfer Julius-Echter-Berg
Silvaner Kabinett trocken
16 DM, 10.5%, ♀ till 2000 — **84**

1997 Iphöfer Julius-Echter-Berg
Riesling Kabinett trocken
16.80 DM, 11%, ♀ till 2002 — **86**

1997 Iphöfer Julius-Echter-Berg
Silvaner Spätlese trocken
24 DM, 13%, ♀ till 2001 — **86**

1997 Iphöfer Julius-Echter-Berg
Riesling Spätlese trocken "S"
28 DM, 13.5%, ♀ till 2002 — **86**

1997 Iphöfer Kronsberg
Scheurebe Spätlese trocken "S"
19 DM, 13%, ♀ till 2003 — **86**

1996 Iphöfer Kronsberg
Weißer Burgunder Auslese
35 DM, 11%, ♀ till 2003 — **86**

1997 Iphöfer Kronsberg
Riesling Spätlese trocken
23 DM, 12.5%, ♀ till 2004 — **88**

1997 Iphöfer Julius-Echter-Berg
Silvaner Spätlese trocken "S"
28 DM, 14%, ♀ till 2003 — **88**

1997 Iphöfer Kronsberg
Riesling Spätlese "S"
28 DM, 12%, ♀ till 2005 — **88**

1997 Iphöfer Kalb
Traminer Spätlese
24 DM, 12.5%, ♀ till 2008 — **89**

WEINGUT ZEHNTHOF

Owner: Luckert family
General Manager: Wolfgang Luckert
Winemaker: Ulrich Luckert
97320 Sulzfeld, Kettengasse 3–5
Tel. (0 93 21) 2 37 78, Fax 50 77
Directions: A 3 Würzburg–Nürnberg, exit Biebelried or Kitzingen
Sales: Wolfgang Luckert
Opening hours: Mon.–Sat. 8 a.m. to 6 p.m.
Worth seeing: The narrow cellars

Vineyard area: 12 hectares
Annual production: 100,000 bottles
Top sites: Sulzfelder Cyriakusberg and Maustal
Soil types: Fossil limestone
Grape varieties: 35% Silvaner, 25% Müller-Thurgau, 10% each of Riesling and Weißburgunder, 5% Kerner, 2% each of Spätburgunder, Domina, Rieslaner and Gewürztraminer, 7% other varieties
Average yield: 69 hl/ha
Best vintages: 1992, 1994, 1997
Member: VDP

The name of this family estate is derived from the "Zehntkeller" – a tithe barn belonging to the former prince bishops, which the Luckerts acquired in the late 1970s. Silvaner and Müller-Thurgau are the principal varieties grown here, but the estate has also made a name for itself with its Weißburgunder, which is partially aged in small oak barrels. Fermentation takes place in temperature-controlled stainless steel tanks and the aging continues, for the most part, in large old casks. Luckert did a surprising job in 1996, putting his best foot forward in a difficult vintage. Although the Silvaners could have been better, the 1997s are a cut above the 1996s. This estate appears to be back on the right track.

1997 Sulzfelder Maustal
Silvaner Spätlese trocken
16 DM, 12.5%, ♀ till 2001 **82**

1996 Sulzfelder Cyriakusberg
Silvaner trocken
8 DM, 11%, ♀ now **84**

1996 Sulzfelder Cyriakusberg
Riesling trocken
9 DM, 11%, ♀ till 2000 **84**

1996 Sulzfelder Cyriakusberg
Silvaner Kabinett trocken
10.50 DM, 11%, ♀ now **84**

1996 Sulzfelder Maustal
Riesling Kabinett trocken
13 DM, 10.5%, ♀ now **84**

1997 Sulzfelder Cyriakusberg
Weißer Burgunder Spätlese trocken
20 DM, 13.5%, ♀ till 2002 **84**

1997 Sulzfelder Cyriakusberg
Riesling Spätlese trocken
22 DM, 12.5%, ♀ till 2002 **84**

1997 Sulzfelder Cyriakusberg
Kerner Spätlese
14 DM, 13.5%, ♀ till 2003 **86**

1997 Sulzfelder Maustal
Rieslaner Spätlese
20 DM, 12%, ♀ till 2003 **88**

1997 Sulzfelder Maustal
Rieslaner Auslese
25 DM/0.5 liter, 11%, ♀ till 2005 **91**

A one-man show

Until Sachsen and Saale-Unstrut became a part of modern Germany after reunification, the Hessische Bergstraße had been the smallest of the German wine growing regions for over two decades. This little area with its mere 450 hectares of vines stretching from Darmstadt to Heppenheim was only created in 1971 after Baden incorporated its "Bergstraße" – or hilly route – into the official vineyards of Baden. The Rheingau, however, expressed no interest in adding the Hessische Bergstraße to its portfolio – indeed, their wines are thoroughly different – and so a separate growing region was formed.

From time immemorial the region between Heidelberg and Darmstadt east of the Rhine has been lavishly endowed with sunshine. When frost still extends its icy grip elsewhere, almonds already blossom along the western ridges of the Odenwald forest. It should thus come as no surprise that the slow-ripening Riesling varietal covers over half the total area under vine. Müller-Thurgau and Silvaner are also widely planted, but the Burgundian varieties are gaining ground.

The growers here have few problems selling their wines, which should surprise no one familiar with the outstanding State Winery in Bensheim, the leading estate of the region. In fact, they are almost a one-man show. The 1996s and 1997s were again of excellent quality, a tribute to the long tenure of Heinrich Hillenbrand. The majority of the other vineyards are cultivated by hobby growers, most of whose wines are consumed within the region by locals and their guests. And they come in droves! The Hessische Bergstraße is understandably popular not only with tourists but also, on weekends, with inhabitants of the Rhine and Main regions. Few of these visitors, however, will be familiar with the "Odenwälder Weininsel," 50 hectares of isolated vineyards located north-east of Bensheim, which also forms part of the region.

Rating scale for the estates

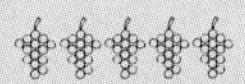

Highest rating: These producers belong to the world's finest.

Excellent estates: These producers are among Germany's best.

Very good producers, known for their consistently high quality.

Good estates, offering better than average quality.

Reliable producers that offer well-made standard quality.

The leading estates of the Hessische Bergstraße

🍇🍇🍇🍇

Staatsweingut Bergstraße, Bensheim

🍇🍇

Weingut Simon-Bürkle, Zwingenberg

Weingut der Stadt Bensheim

🍇

Bergsträßer Winzer eG, Heppenheim

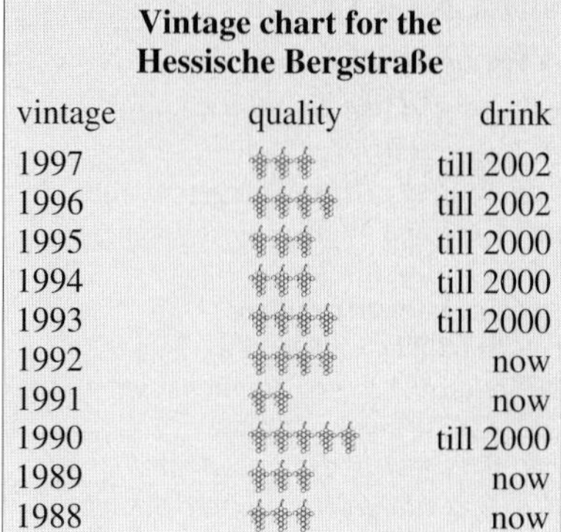

Vintage chart for the Hessische Bergstraße

vintage	quality	drink
1997	🍇🍇🍇	till 2002
1996	🍇🍇🍇🍇	till 2002
1995	🍇🍇🍇	till 2000
1994	🍇🍇🍇	till 2000
1993	🍇🍇🍇🍇	till 2000
1992	🍇🍇🍇🍇	now
1991	🍇🍇	now
1990	🍇🍇🍇🍇🍇	till 2000
1989	🍇🍇🍇	now
1988	🍇🍇🍇	now

🍇🍇🍇🍇🍇 : Outstanding
🍇🍇🍇🍇 : Excellent
🍇🍇🍇 : Good
🍇🍇 : Average
🍇 : Poor

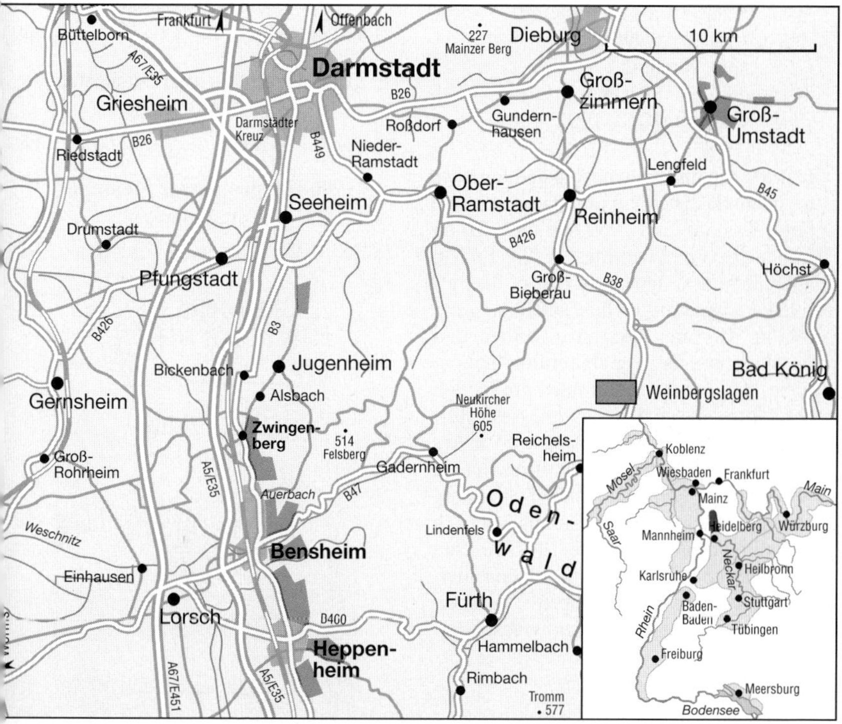

Other notable producer

Weingut Volker Dingeldey
64625 Bensheim-Gronau
Tel. (0 62 51) 3 98 16, Fax 3 98 16

BERGSTRÄSSER WINZER EG

Owner: 530 cooperative members
Manager: Otto Guthier
Winemakers: Hans-Jürgen Weber and Gerhard Weiß
64646 Heppenheim, Darmstädter Straße 56
Tel. (0 62 52) 7 30 16, Fax 7 74 92
Directions: A 5, exit Heppenheim, towards the center of town, then left towards Dannstadt and after two kilometers again to the left
Opening hours: Mon.–Fri. 8 a.m. to 6:30 p.m., Sat. 8:30 a.m. to 4 p.m. Sun. 10. a.m. to 3 p.m.
Restaurant: "Winzerkeller"

> Vineyard area: 269 hectares
> Annual production: 2 million bottles
> Top sites: Heppenheimer Stemmler and Steinkopf, Bensheimer Kalkgasse
> Soil types: Loess and loam, weathered granite and red sandstone
> Grape varieties: 58% Riesling, 12% Müller-Thurgau, 9% Grauburgunder, 6% Silvaner, 15% other varieties
> Average yield: 80 hl/ha
> Best vintages: 1990, 1993, 1994

In 1904 the first growers banded together to form the Starkenburger cooperative, but it was not until 1960 that they settled into their current facilities. Today the 530 adherents farm more than half of the cultivated vineyards in this small growing region. The members have at their disposal storage for over six million liters of wine. Given the enormous production here, it is unusual that they release dessert wines at Trockenbeerenauslese levels almost every year. The 1996 Riesling ice wines from Heppenheimer Schloßberg and Stemmler were fine examples of such exceptional products. The 1997s are not nearly as good; and there is still considerable work to be done to improve the average quality of the remaining wines.

1996 Heppenheimer Stemmler
Weißer Burgunder trocken
8.20 DM, 11%, ♀ now **80**

1996 Grauer Burgunder
Kabinett trocken
7.90 DM, 11%, ♀ now **80**

1996 Heppenheimer Guldenzoll
Riesling Spätlese halbtrocken
10.30 DM, 10.5%, ♀ now **80**

1997 Heppenheimer Maiberg
Riesling Spätlese
9.40 DM, 10%, ♀ till 2001 **80**

1997 Heppenheimer Stemmler
Grauer Burgunder Spätlese trocken
11.70 DM, 12.5%, ♀ till 2001 **82**

1997 Heppenheimer Eckweg
Riesling Kabinett halbtrocken
7.70 DM, 10.5%, ♀ till 2002 **82**

1997 Bensheimer Paulus
Gewürztraminer Spätlese
13.90 DM, 10%, ♀ till 2004 **84**

1997 Heppenheimer Stemmler
Riesling Eiswein
65 DM/0.375 liter, 7%, ♀ till 2005 **88**

1996 Heppenheimer Stemmler
Riesling Eiswein
75 DM/0.375 liter, 6%, ♀ till 2010 **95**

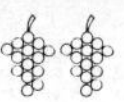

WEINGUT SIMON-BÜRKLE

Owners: Kurt Simon and Wilfried Bürkle
Winemaker: Kurt Simon
64673 Zwingenberg, Wiesenpromenade 13
Tel. (0 62 51) 7 64 46, Fax 78 86 41
Directions: A 5 Walldorf–Frankfurt, exit Zwingenberg
Sales: Dagmar Simon and Sigrid Bürkle
Opening hours: Mon.–Fri. 9 a.m. to noon and 3 p.m. to 6 p.m.
Sat. 9 a.m. to 1 p.m.
Wine pub: In the old village of Zwingenberg, Am Obertor 6, open daily from 5 p.m. to 1 a.m., except Thur.
Sun. and holidays 11 a.m. to 1 a.m.
Specialties: Local fare

Vineyard area: 10 hectares
Annual production: 50,000 bottles
Top sites: Zwingenberger Alte Burg and Steingeröll, Auerbacher Fürstenlager and Höllberg
Soil types: Very deep loess and loam over weathered granite
Grape varieties: 42% Riesling, 21% Burgundian varieties, 16% red wine varieties, 21% other varieties
Average yield: 50 hl/ha
Best vintages: 1992, 1993, 1995

After studying winemaking together at the Weinsberg college in Württemberg, Kurt Simon and Wilfried Bürkle founded this estate in Zwingenberg in 1991. In 1993 they opened a wine bar, and their own asparagus business now completes the range. Because the yields here are very low, it is no surprise that even the liter bottlings can be astonishing. Across the board the 1995s were very reliable, which is more than we can say about the disparate quality of the 1996s. Kurt Simon bounced back with a much more successful collection in 1997. Not only was the dry Riesling Spätlese quite attractive, even the rosé and red wines were notably better.

1996 Zwingenberger Steingeröll
Silvaner trocken
8.70 DM, 11%, ♀ now **82**

1995 Zwingenberger Alte Burg
Riesling Spätlese trocken
12.80 DM, 11.5%, ♀ till 2000 **82**

1996 Zwingenberger Alte Burg
Riesling Kabinett trocken
9.40 DM, 11%, ♀ till 2000 **84**

1997 Zwingenberger Steingeröll
Riesling Spätlese halbtrocken
13.20 DM, 12%, ♀ till 2001 **84**

1997 Zwingenberger Steingeröll
Silvaner trocken
8.50 DM, 12%, ♀ till 2001 **84**

1997 Zwingenberger Steingeröll
Riesling Spätlese trocken
13.20 DM, 12%, ♀ till 2003 **86**

——— Red wines ———

1996 Zwingenberger Alte Burg
Spätburgunder trocken
17.80 DM, 12.5%, ♀ till 2000 **82**

1996 Auerbacher Fürstenlager
Dunkelfelder trocken
17.80 DM, 12.5%, ♀ till 2004 **86**

STAATSWEINGUT BERGSTRASSE

Owner: State of Hesse
Manager: Heinrich Hillenbrand
Winemaker: Volker Hörr
64625 Bensheim, Grieselstraße 34–36
Tel. (0 62 51) 31 07, Fax 6 57 06
Directions: A 5, exit Bensheim, towards Lindenfels
Sales: Mr. Hillenbrand, Ms. Stanzel
Opening hours: Mon.–Thur. 7:30 a.m. to noon and 1:30 p.m. to 5 p.m. Fri. to 6 p.m., Sat. 9 a.m. to noon
History: Founded in 1904 by the Archduke of Hessen-Darmstadt
Worth seeing: Vaulted cellars, new Vinothek

Vineyard area: 36 hectares
Annual production: 240,000 bottles
Top sites: Heppenheimer Centgericht (sole owners) and Steinkopf, Schönberger Herrnwingert (sole owners), Bensheimer Kalkgasse and Streichling
Soil types: Very deep loess and loam, red sandstone, weathered gravel
Grape varieties: 73% Riesling, 9.5% Weißburgunder, 6.5% Grauburgunder, 5% Spätburgunder, 6% other varieties
Average yield: 57 hl/ha
Best vintages: 1990, 1993, 1996
Member: VDP

The State Domaine is tucked away in the old village of Bensheim. As the estate's gifted manager, Heinrich Hillenbrand, casually remarks: "Pearls lie hidden; you have to seek them out." In 1972 the first ice wine was harvested from the Heppenheimer Centgericht vineyard and this feat has been repeated every year since 1977. The winery has built its excellent reputation principally on its Rieslings, but its Weißburgunder and Grauburgunder can also be of high quality. The 1996 range from Auslese upwards was of exceptional distinction. The 1997s were quite good, but no match for the previous vintage. If Hillenbrand could increase the general quality of the standard wines, this estate could be one of the finest in Germany.

1996 Schönberger Herrnwingert
Weißer Burgunder Kabinett trocken
10.20 DM, 11.5%, ♀ till 2001 **88**

1997 Heppenheimer Steinkopf
Riesling Spätlese trocken
14.10 DM, 11.5%, ♀ till 2003 **88**

1997 Heppenheimer Centgericht
Riesling Spätlese
15 DM, 11%, ♀ till 2005 **89**

1997 Heppenheimer Centgericht
Riesling Spätlese halbtrocken
15 DM, 11.5%, ♀ till 2005 **91**

1997 Heppenheimer Centgericht
Ruländer Auslese
Not yet for sale, 8.5%, ♀ till 2006 **94**

1996 Heppenheimer Centgericht
Riesling Auslese
35 DM, 8%, ♀ till 2010 **95**

1996 Heppenheimer Centgericht
Spätburgunder Weißherbst Eiswein
Not yet for sale, 6%, ♀ till 2008 **96**

1996 Heppenheimer Centgericht
Riesling Eiswein
Not yet for sale, 6.5%, ♀ till 2015 **98**

1996 Heppenheimer Centgericht
Spätburgunder Weißherbst Eiswein
Not yet for sale, 7%, ♀ till 2010 **98**

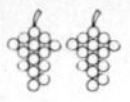

WEINGUT DER STADT BENSHEIM

Owner: City of Bensheim
General Manager: Axel Seiberth
Winemaker: Volker Dingeldey
64625 Bensheim, Darmstädter Straße 6
Tel. (0 62 51) 1 42 69, Fax 6 49 70
Directions: On the B 3
Sales: Axel Seiberth
Opening hours: Mon.–Fri. 8 a.m. to 4:30 p.m., Sat. 10 a.m. to noon
Restaurant: “Kirchberghäuschen,” open Tue. to Sun. from 11 a.m. to 9 p.m.
Specialties: Smoked trout

Vineyard area: 13 hectares
Annual production: 100,000 bottles
Top sites: Bensheimer Kalkgasse and Kirchberg, Auerbacher Fürstenlager
Soil types: Rocky weathered limestone, loess-loam
Grape varieties: 60% Riesling, 14% Rotberger, 6% Dornfelder, 4% each of Müller-Thurgau, Grauburgunder and Weißburgunder, 2% each of Chardonnay, Gewürztraminer, Scheurebe and Spätburgunder
Average yield: 63 hl/ha
Best vintages: 1994, 1995, 1996

Winemaking has a long history in Bensheim. As long ago as 1504 the town already employed its own cooper, a fact that is well documented in old papers in their archives. The jewel in the crown of the town’s wine estate is the well-known Kalkgasse vineyard, which derives its name from the weathered limestone in its soil. Yields are kept within limits, which is apparent in the depth of the wines. The 1996 vintage followed in the footsteps of the equally successful 1995 range. The 1997s are a tad better. Even the dry Riesling sold in liter bottles is well made. This winery remains the second-best producer in the region.

1996 Bensheimer Kalkgasse
Weißer Burgunder trocken
10 DM, 11.5%, 🍷 till 2000 **84**

1997 Bensheimer Kirchberg
Riesling Kabinett halbtrocken
10.50 DM, 11%, 🍷 till 2003 **84**

1996 Bensheimer Kalkgasse
Grauer Burgunder trocken
12 DM, 12%, 🍷 till 2000 **86**

1997 Bensheimer Kalkgasse
Riesling Kabinett trocken
10.50 DM, 12%, 🍷 till 2002 **86**

1996 Bensheimer Kirchberg
Riesling Spätlese trocken
12.50 DM, 12%, 🍷 till 2001 **86**

1997 Bensheimer Kirchberg
Riesling Spätlese trocken
12.50 DM, 12%, 🍷 till 2004 **88**

1996 Bensheimer Kirchberg
Riesling Kabinett
10.50 DM, 10%, 🍷 till 2001 **88**

1997 Bensheimer Kalkgasse
Riesling Spätlese
12.50 DM, 9%, 🍷 till 2004 **88**

1997 Bensheimer Kirchberg
Riesling Beerenauslese
52 DM/0.5 liter, 7%, 🍷 till 2005 **88**

Hessische Bergstraße
1995
BENSHEIMER
KALKGASSE
Weißer Burgunder
trocken
Qualitätswein
Amtliche Prüfnummer
50 012 006 96
Erzeugerabfüllung
Weingut der Stadt Bensheim
D-64625 Bensheim 1
11,5%vol
75 cl

Mittelrhein

Outstanding Riesling from the romantic Rhine valley

Nowhere else in Germany is such a wide selection of racy Rieslings at such modest prices to be found as in the Mittelrhein. A considerable proportion of these often underrated wines are consumed by many tourists attracted by the charm of the idyllic Rhine valley and its ruined castles; but few of them appreciate what they are drinking.

Even in mediocre vintages the growers of the Mittelrhein enjoy numerous advantages. Their vineyards, which are almost all steep and terraced, are blessed with more than sufficient sunshine, protected from strong winds and the watery expanse of the Rhine river regulates the temperatures. These natural conditions ensure a good average quality for the wines produced. With sufficient extract and structure, the Rieslings – which occupy three-quarters of the vineyard area – are sometimes reminiscent of those from the Rheingau; but like the wines from the Saar, they are often marked by a vivacious acidity tweaked with minerals. For that reason, they were long the source of excellent base wines for the sparkling industry.

There are 111 single vineyards lining both sides of the Rhine over a distance of 100 kilometers. On the left bank of the Rhine the vines stretch from the Nahe estuary to Koblenz, on the right bank as far north as the hills of the Siebengebirge. Around Leutesdorf in the lower Mittelrhein the loess soils are heavy. On the other hand, the slate cliffs near Boppard, where the finest sweeter styles of Riesling emerge, are interspersed with pumice. In Bacharach and Steeg, where the soils are pure Devon slate, the vines traditionally produce the best dry wines of the region.

The vineyard area along the picturesque Mittelrhein is receding from year to year. At the turn of the century, there were 2000 hectares planted; by 1980, there were less than half that number. By the end of this century only 600 hectares will remain cultivated. Many of the outstanding vineyards, which are too steep to negotiate for all but the foolhardy, now lie fallow.

"We could drink all of our 1996s ourselves," declared Peter Jost of the leading Hahnenhof estate, "so good is the vintage and so small the quantity harvested." Although the wines from Bacharach were classic in style, the best wines from the 1996 vintage were to be found in Boppard and Spay, where the Rieslings showed more extract and depth. In general, the 1996s are more closed than those of the preceding vintages and will certainly require more time to develop. The 1997s, on the other hand, are almost as good, but promise to be readily accessible. The wines from Bacharach have the upper hand in this vintage. Unfortunately, the yields were even more limited than in 1996, which has led to strict allocations.

The Hahnenhof estate still stands alone at the top of the some 370 producers within the region, not the least because of the often breathtaking quality of its noble late harvest Rieslings. But in recent years the number of pretenders to Jost's throne has risen. August Perll was once the sole rising star, but he has now been seconded by the talented Florian Weingart and Heinrich Müller. Toni Lorenz and Walter Perll may also soon be joining their ranks.

Vintage chart for the Mittelrhein

vintage	quality	drink
1997	🍇🍇🍇	till 2003
1996	🍇🍇🍇🍇	till 2005
1995	🍇🍇🍇	till 2003
1994	🍇🍇🍇🍇	till 2007
1993	🍇🍇🍇🍇🍇	till 2010
1992	🍇🍇🍇🍇	now
1991	🍇🍇🍇	now
1990	🍇🍇🍇🍇	till 2005
1989	🍇🍇🍇🍇🍇	till 2000
1988	🍇🍇🍇	now

🍇🍇🍇🍇🍇 : Outstanding
🍇🍇🍇🍇 : Excellent
🍇🍇🍇 : Good
🍇🍇 : Average
🍇 : Poor

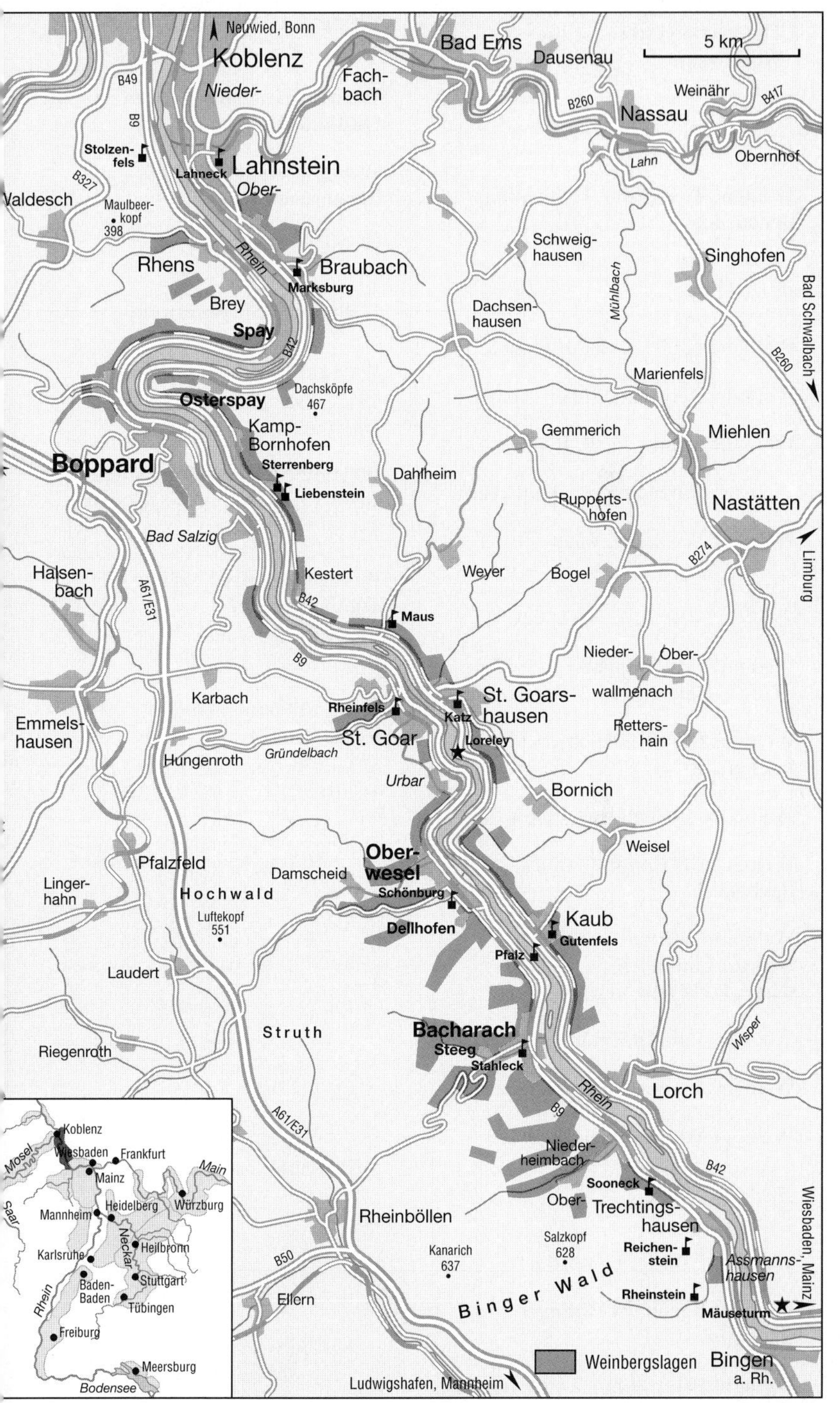
Neuwied, Bonn
Koblenz
Nieder-
Fach-
bach
Bad Ems
Dausenau
5 km
Weinähr
B260
B417
Nassau
Obernhof
Lahn
B49
B9
Stolzen-
fels
Lahneck
Lahnstein
Ober-
B327
Valdesch
Maulbeer-
kopf
398
Schweig-
hausen
Singhofen
Rhens
Rhein
Braubach
Marksburg
Mühlbach
Bad Schwalbach
Brey
Dachsen-
hausen
Spay
B42
B260
Marienfels
Dachsköpfe
467
Osterspay
Kamp-
Bornhofen
Gemmerich
Miehlen
Boppard
Sterrenberg
Liebenstein
Dahlheim
Rupperts-
hofen
Nastätten
Bad Salzig
B274
Limburg
Halsen-
bach
Kestert
Weyer
Bogel
A61/E31
B42
Maus
B9
Nieder-
Ober-
wallmenach
Karbach
St. Goars-
hausen
Rheinfels
Katz
Emmels-
hausen
St. Goar
Loreley
Retters-
hain
Hungenroth
Gründelbach
Urbar
Bornich
Pfalzfeld
Ober-
wesel
Weisel
Linger-
hahn
Damscheid
Hochwald
Schönburg
Luftekopf
551
Dellhofen
Kaub
Gutenfels
Pfalz
Laudert
Struth
Bacharach
Steeg
Stahleck
Wisper
Riegenroth
Rhein
Lorch
B9
Koblenz
Mosel
Wiesbaden
Frankfurt
Main
Mainz
A61/E31
Nieder-
heimbach
B42
Saar
Mannheim
Heidelberg
Würzburg
Sooneck
Ober-
Trechtings-
hausen
Wiesbaden, Mainz
Neckar
Heilbronn
Rheinböllen
Karlsruhe
Salzkopf
628
Reichen-
stein
Kanarich
637
Assmanns-
hausen
B50
Baden-
Baden
Stuttgart
Rhein
Tübingen
Ellern
Binger Wald
Rheinstein
Mäuseturm
Freiburg
Meersburg
Bodensee
Weinbergslagen
Bingen
a. Rh.
Ludwigshafen, Mannheim

The leading estates of the Mittelrhein

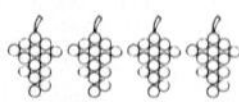

Weingut Toni Jost – Hahnenhof, Bacharach

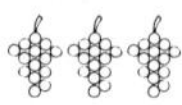

Weingut Toni Lorenz, Boppard

Weingut Heinrich Müller, Spay

Weingut August Perll, Boppard

Weingut Ratzenberger, Bacharach

Weingut Weingart, Spay

Weingut Fritz Bastian "Zum Grünen Baum," Bacharach

Weingut Karl Heidrich, Bacharach

Weinhaus Heilig Grab, Boppard

Weingut Dr. Randolf Kauer, Bacharach

Wein und Sektgut Goswin Lambrich, Oberwesel-Dellhofen

Weingut Lanius-Knab, Oberwesel

Weingut Mades, Bacharach-Steeg

Weingut Walter Perll, Boppard

Weingut Breisig, Leutesdorf

Weingut Bernhard Didinger, Osterspai

Weingut Peter Hohn, Leutesdorf

Weingut Albert Lambrich, Oberwesel-Dellhofen

Weingut Hermann Ockenfels, Leutesdorf

Weingut Bernhard Praß, Bacharach-Steeg

Weingut Volk, Spay

Other notable producers

Weingut Lieschied-Rollauer
55422 Bacharach, Blücherstraße 88
Tel. (0 67 43) 10 48

Weingut Mathias Mohr Söhne
56599 Leutesdorf, Krautsgasse 16
Tel. (0 26 31) 7 21 11, Fax 7 57 31

Weingut Manfred Müller – Tomberger Hof
53639 Königswinter
Tel. (0 22 23) 2 29 20

Weingut Sonnenhang – Heinz Uwe Fetz
55348 Dorscheid bei Kaub
Tel. (0 67 74) 15 48, Fax 82 19

Rating scale for the estates

Highest rating: These producers belong to the world's finest.

Excellent estates: These producers are among Germany's best.

Very good producers, known for their consistently high quality.

Good estates, offering better than average quality.

Reliable producers that offer well-made standard quality.

WEINGUT FRITZ BASTIAN "ZUM GRÜNEN BAUM"

Owner: Friedrich Bastian
55422 Bacharach, Oberstraße 63
Tel. (0 67 43) 12 08, Fax 28 37
Directions: A 61 Koblenz–Bingen, exit Rheinböllen, towards Bacharach
Sales: Doris Bastian
Opening hours: By appointment
Restaurant: "Zum grünen Baum," open from 1 p.m. to midnight, except Thur.
Specialties: Homemade wurst
History: Founded in 1697

Vineyard area: 5.8 hectares
Annual production: 30,000 bottles
Top sites: Bacharacher Posten, Wolfshöhle and Insel Heyles'en Werth
Soil types: Blue slate, weathered clay
Grape varieties: 80% Riesling, 10% Scheurebe, 5% Spätburgunder, 5% Portugieser
Average yield: 35 hl/ha
Best vintages: 1992, 1996, 1997
Member: VDP

This winery has been bottling its own production since 1903. Since 1989 Fritz Bastian has been assisted by his son Friedrich, who has managed the estate since 1993. The winery – and historic wine bar "Zum grünen Baum" – has always produced very pert Rieslings with pronounced acidity, which in their youth often remind one of wines from the Saar. The estate is the sole owner of the Insel Heyles'en Werth vineyard on an island in the Rhine river. Here, on sandy loess soils, the Rieslings develop a character of their own. In 1996 Fritz Bastian produced highly individual wines: reductive in style, yeasty and smoky in aroma. Quite closed in their youth, they have developed well. The 1997s are somewhat more accessible, but their robust acidic structure still means that they will be less attractive to drink in their youth.

1996 Bacharacher Insel Heyles'en Werth
Riesling halbtrocken
8.50 DM, 10%, ♀ till 2000 **82**

1996 Bacharacher
Riesling halbtrocken
9 DM, 9.5%, ♀ till 2000 **82**

1997 Bacharacher Insel Heyles'en Werth
Riesling Spätlese halbtrocken
14.50 DM, 11.5%, ♀ till 2001 **82**

1997 Bacharacher Insel Heyles'en Werth
Riesling Kabinett
10 DM, 8.5%, ♀ till 2000 **82**

1997 Riesling
Spätlese halbtrocken
13.50 DM, 11%, ♀ till 2001 **84**

1996 Bacharacher Insel Heyles'en Werth
Riesling Kabinett
10 DM, 8%, ♀ till 2000 **84**

1997 Bacharacher Posten
Riesling Spätlese trocken
15 DM, 12%, ♀ till 2000 **86**

1997 Bacharacher Posten
Riesling Spätlese
15.30 DM, 10.5%, ♀ till 2003 **86**

1996 Bacharacher Posten
Riesling Spätlese
14 DM, 9%, ♀ till 2003 **88**

BASTIAN
BACHARACH
Mittelrhein
1993er
Bacharacher Insel Heyles´en Werth
Riesling Kabinett
halbtrocken
9,5 % vol. - AP-Nr. 1 698 006 08 94 - 0,75 l
Weingut Fritz Bastian - D-55422 Bacharach/Rhein
Qualitätswein mit Prädikat - Gutsabfüllung - Product of Germany

WEINGUT BREISIG

Owner: Richard Breisig
56599 Leutesdorf, Hauptstraße 83
Tel. (0 26 31) 7 37 23
Directions: A 3 Köln–Frankfurt, exit Neuwied
Opening hours: By appointment

> Vineyard area: 1.5 hectares
> Annual production: 12,000 bottles
> Top sites: Leutesdorfer Forstberg and Gartenlay
> Soil types: Slate and clay
> Grape varieties: 85% Riesling, 10% Kerner, 5% Optima
> Average yield: 65 hl/ha
> Best vintages: 1995, 1996, 1997

It is reassuring to see that numerous small growers in the Mittelrhein are now taking their profession seriously. Since he owns no more than a hectare and a half of vineyards, from which it is impossible to make a prosperous living, Breisig remains modest – all the more surprising when you compare his high standards and low prices. He practices severe pruning, costly leaf pulling and the thinning of surplus grapes. As a consequence, the yields are kept fairly low. His work in the cellar is also undertaken with care, which allows a wide variety of aromas to develop in the wines. Nonetheless, a livelier acidity would fare well in some of the wines. As long as his father, Richard, born in 1934, remains so hale and hearty, son Hans-Günter need not consider giving up his job at the agricultural chamber of commerce in Bad Kreuznach to follow in his father's footsteps. Breisig's 1996s were certainly as good as the fruity wines from the 1995 vintage. The 1997s, however, are a bit less successful. As in previous vintages, the ostensibly simpler Hochgewächse were better than the Spätlese.

1997 Leutesdorfer Forstberg
Riesling Spätlese trocken
7.80 DM, 10.5%, 🍷 now **80**

1997 Leutesdorfer Gartenlay
Riesling Spätlese halbtrocken
8.50 DM, 11%, 🍷 till 2000 **80**

1996 Leutesdorfer Forstberg
Riesling Spätlese trocken
9 DM, 11%, 🍷 now **82**

1997 Leutesdorfer Gartenlay
Riesling Kabinett halbtrocken
7.20 DM, 10%, 🍷 till 2000 **82**

1996 Leutesdorfer Gartenlay
Riesling Auslese halbtrocken
11.50 DM, 12%, 🍷 till 2000 **82**

1996 Leutesdorfer Gartenlay
Riesling Spätlese
9.50 DM, 9%, 🍷 till 2000 **82**

1997 Leutesdorfer Gartenlay
Riesling Hochgewächs
7.20 DM, 9%, 🍷 till 2000 **82**

1997 Leutesdorf Forstberg
Riesling Hochgewächs halbtrocken
7 DM, 11%, 🍷 till 2000 **82**

1997 Leutesdorfer Gartenlay
Riesling Hochgewächs trocken
7 DM, 12%, 🍷 till 2000 **82**

1996 Leutesdorfer Gartenlay
Riesling Hochgewächs
7 DM, 8.5%, 🍷 till 2000 **84**

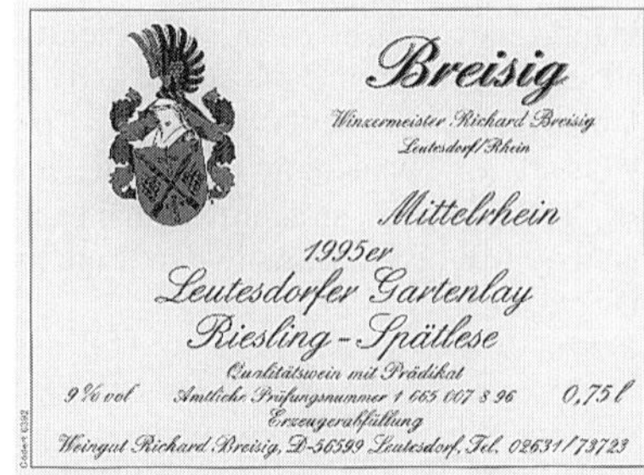

WEINGUT BERNHARD DIDINGER

Owner: Jens Didinger
Winemaker: Jens Didinger
56340 Osterspai, Rheinuferstraße 13
Tel. (0 26 27) 5 12 und 19 04
Directions: A 61 Koblenz–Bingen, exit Boppard
Sales: Didinger family
Opening hours: By appointment
Restaurant: "Bopparder Hamm," open from 3 p.m., except Wed.

Vineyard area: 2.5 hectares
Annual production: 27,500 bottles
Top site: Bopparder Hamm Feuerlay
Soil types: Weathered slate
Grape varieties: 80% Riesling, 7% Kerner, 7% Spätburgunder, 6% Dornfelder
Average yield: 80 hl/ha
Best vintages: 1995, 1996, 1997

Only after the vineyards were reorganized, did viticulture become the main focus of this small estate. Since Bernhard Didinger had no children, he convinced his nephew to join the family business in 1993. After accepting, Jens extended his knowledge about wine with Fritz Allendorf in the Rheingau as well as at the college in Bad Kreuznach. In 1997 he not only leased the winery from his uncle but also produced the best wines of his career: crisp, clean and fruity. Part of the vineyard is pruned for low yields, another part provides the quaffing wine for the adjoining wine bar. This is a reliable address for daily drinking at affordable prices.

1997 Bopparder Hamm Feuerlay
Riesling Hochgewächs halbtrocken
6.50 DM, 11.5%, ♀ till 2000 **80**

1997 Bopparder Hamm Feuerlay
Riesling Spätlese trocken
8 DM, 12%, ♀ till 2000 **82**

1997 Bopparder Hamm Feuerlay
Riesling Kabinett halbtrocken
7 DM, 11%, ♀ till 2000 **82**

1996 Bopparder Hamm Feuerlay
Riesling Spätlese halbtrocken
8 DM, 11.5%, ♀ now **82**

1996 Bopparder Hamm Feuerlay
Riesling Kabinett
7 DM, 9%, ♀ till 2000 **82**

1997 Bopparder Hamm Feuerlay
Kerner Spätlese lieblich
8.50 DM, 9.5%, ♀ till 2000 **82**

1997 Bopparder Hamm Feuerlay
Riesling Spätlese halbtrocken
8 DM, 11.5%, ♀ till 2002 **84**

1997 Bopparder Hamm Fässerlay
Riesling Kabinett
7 DM, 9%, ♀ till 2001 **84**

1996 Bopparder Hamm Feuerlay
Riesling Spätlese
8 DM, 10%, ♀ till 2002 **84**

1997 Bopparder Hamm Feuerlay
Riesling Auslese
11 DM, 9%, ♀ till 2003 **86**

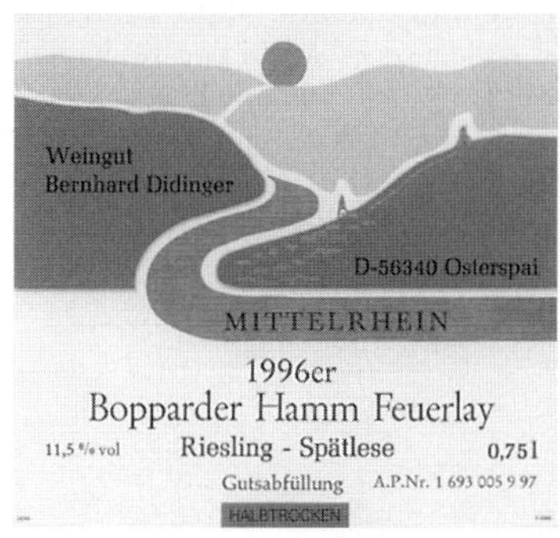

WEINGUT KARL HEIDRICH

Owner: Markus Heidrich
55422 Bacharach, Oberstraße 16–18
Tel. (0 67 43) 9 30 60, Fax 9 30 61
Directions: A 61 Koblenz–Bingen, exit Rheinböllen, towards Bacharach
Sales: Susanne and Markus Heidrich
Opening hours: Mon.–Sun. 11 a.m. to 11 p.m.
Restaurant: "Zum Weinkrug," open from 11 a.m. to 11 p.m., except Wed.
Specialties: Sauerkraut soup, "Spundekäs," suckling pig
History: Owned by the family since 1505

Vineyard area: 4.5 hectares
Annual production: 27,000 bottles
Top sites: Bacharacher Posten and Wolfshöhle
Soil types: Weathered slate
Grape varieties: 75% Riesling, 10% Müller-Thurgau, 6% Silvaner, 7% Spätburgunder, 2% other varieties
Average yield: 54 hl/ha
Best vintages: 1995, 1996, 1997

The name Heidrich is not uncommon in Bacharach. Karl Heidrich is known for his wine bar "Zum Weinkrug," founded at the turn of the century, and his namesake Rolf runs his own bar "Zum Rebstock." As far as quality is concerned, Karl is undoubtedly the better of the two winemakers. Since 1992 he has won admiration from his clientele for his organic approach in the vineyard; yet only since 1995 has one really begun to talk about his Rieslings. His red wines, however, are still of little interest. 1996 brought the best collection of wines that we had ever tasted from this estate, only to be topped by the 1997s. With these two vintages Heidrich has worked his way into the forefront of the Mittelrhein.

1996 Bacharacher Wolfshöhle
Riesling Kabinett halbtrocken
10 DM, 9.5%, ♀ now **82**

1996 Bacharacher Posten
Riesling Spätlese trocken
12.50 DM, 12%, ♀ till 2000 **84**

1997 Bacharacher Posten
Riesling Spätlese
13.50 DM, 9.5%, ♀ till 2000 **84**

1997 Bacharacher Wolfshöhle
Riesling Spätlese trocken
13.50 DM, 12%, ♀ till 2001 **86**

1997 Bacharacher Posten
Riesling Spätlese halbtrocken
13.50 DM, 11%, ♀ till 2002 **86**

1997 Bacharacher Posten
Riesling Auslese
19.50 DM/0.5 liter, 9%, ♀ till 2005 **86**

1996 Bacharacher Posten
Riesling Spätlese halbtrocken
12.50 DM, 10.5%, ♀ till 2000 **88**

WEINHAUS HEILIG GRAB

Owner: Rudolf Schoeneberger
56154 Boppard, Zelkesgasse 12
Tel. (0 67 42) 23 71, Fax 8 12 20
e-mail: weinhausheiliggrab@t-online.de
Directions: A 61 Koblenz–Bingen, exit Boppard
Sales: Rudolf and Susanne Schoeneberger
Opening hours: Mon.–Sun. 3 p.m. to midnight or by appointment
Wine bar: Open from 3 p.m. to midnight, except Tue.
Worth seeing: Wine garden under the old chestnut trees

Vineyard area: 2.7 hectares
Annual production: 30,000 bottles
Top sites: Bopparder Hamm Feuerlay, Mandelstein and Fässerlay
Soil types: Weathered slate with a loess component
Grape varieties: 90% Riesling, 5% Kerner, 5% Spätburgunder
Average yield: 80 hl/ha
Best vintages: 1995, 1996, 1997

The pub with the strange name of "Heilig Grab" – or "Holy Grave" – is the oldest wine bar in Boppard and has been owned for over two centuries by the Schoeneberger family. There, beneath old chestnut trees in a quiet alley within the village, we first tasted these wines, all of which come from the finest sites in Boppard. Often reticent in their youth, they are generally forthright in style; and even if they sometimes lacked a touch of freshness and vivacity, the Rieslings produced by Rudolf Schoeneberger were always made in a well-crafted fashion. The 1996s reflect the conditions nature offered in that vintage. Yields of 50 hectoliters per hectare signal one of the smallest harvests of the last 20 years; and the quality of the wines is on par with those of the previous vintage. The 1997s are the finest wines that we have ever tasted from this estate. Even the simple liter bottlings for the bar are pleasant to drink. It is a shame, however, that Schoeneberger does not concentrate more effort on the fruitier style of Spätlese and Auslese.

1997 Bopparder Hamm
Riesling halbtrocken
DM, 10.5%, ♀ till 2000 **80**

1996 Bopparder Hamm Mandelstein
Riesling halbtrocken Hochgewächs
7 DM, 11%, ♀ now **82**

1997 Bopparder Hamm Feuerlay
Kerner Spätlese
10 DM, 10.5%, ♀ till 2000 **82**

1997 Bopparder Hamm Fässerlay
Riesling Hochgewächs halbtrocken
7 DM, 10.5%, ♀ till 2000 **82**

1996 Bopparder Hamm Feuerlay
Riesling Auslese trocken
15 DM, 13%, ♀ now **84**

1997 Bopparder Hamm Feuerlay
Riesling Spätlese
10 DM, 9%, ♀ 2002 **84**

1997 Bopparder Hamm Elfenlay
Riesling Hochgewächs trocken
7 DM, 11%, ♀ till 2001 **84**

1997 Bopparder Hamm Feuerlay
Riesling Spätlese trocken
9 DM, 11%, ♀ till 2001 **86**

1997 Bopparder Hamm Mandelstein
Riesling Spätlese halbtrocken
9 DM, 10.5%, ♀ till 2002 **86**

WEINGUT PETER HOHN

Owner: Peter Hohn
56599 Leutesdorf,
In der Gartenlay 50
Tel. (0 26 31) 7 18 17, Fax 7 22 09
Directions: B 42 Koblenz–Bonn, seven kilometers north of Neuwied
Sales: Annette and Peter Hohn
Opening hours: By appointment
History: Owned by the family since 1638

Vineyard area: 3.4 hectares
Annual production: 30,000 bottles
Top sites: Leutesdorfer Rosenberg, Gartenlay and Forstberg
Soil types: Weathered slate
Grape varieties: 80% Riesling, 10% Müller-Thurgau, 8% Kerner, 2% other varieties
Average yield: 68 hl/ha
Best vintages: 1995, 1996, 1997

This small property lies just outside of Leutesdorf in the middle of the vineyards. Peter Hohn, who joined the family business after extensive training and a year spent working in the United States, took over the estate from his father in 1991. Together with his wife, Annette, he represents the family's profession in the 12th generation. His goal is to conserve the varietal character of each wine through gentle treatment. The wines are certainly well made and typical of their varietal; nonetheless an old fashioned style, characterized by the casks in which the wines are aged, marks the collection. For that reason the off-dry and sweeter wines, which show more fruit, invariably taste better than the dry Rieslings. As did most of his colleagues, Peter Hohn suffered a small harvest in 1996. In terms of quality though, the wines were on par with those made in 1993 and 1994. The 1997s are better. However, we are somewhat surprised that the Spätlese are hardly better than the simple wines.

1996 Riesling
halbtrocken "Loreley"
8 DM, 10%, 🍷 now **80**

1996 Leutesdorfer Gartenlay
Riesling Spätlese
12 DM, 8.5%, 🍷 now **80**

1997 Leutesdorfer Forstberg
Riesling Hochgewächs trocken
7.50 DM, 11%, 🍷 now **80**

1997 Leutesdorfer Forstberg
Riesling Spätlese trocken
10.10 DM, 11.5%, 🍷 till 2000 **82**

1996 Leutesdorfer Forstberg
Riesling Spätlese trocken
9.25 DM, 11%, 🍷 now **82**

1997 Riesling
halbtrocken "Loreley"
8.60 DM, 10%, 🍷 till 2000 **82**

1996 Leutesdorfer Rosenberg
Riesling und Kerner Spätlese halbtrocken
10 DM, 10.5%, 🍷 now **82**

1997 Leutesdorfer Rosenberg
Riesling Spätlese halbtrocken
10.60 DM, 11%, 🍷 till 2002 **84**

1997 Leutesdorfer Rosenberg
Kerner Spätlese
11.60 DM, 10.5%, 🍷 till 2001 **84**

WEINGUT TONI JOST – HAHNENHOF

Owner: Peter Jost
55422 Bacharach am Rhein, Oberstraße 14
Tel. (0 67 43) 12 16, Fax 10 76
Directions: A 61 Koblenz–Bingen, exit Rheinböllen
Sales: Linde Jost
Opening hours: By appointment
Worth seeing: Old German tasting room in the beautiful village of Bacharach

Vineyard area: 8.5 hectares
Annual production: 55,000 bottles
Top sites: Bacharacher Hahn and Wolfshöhle
Soil types: Weathered Devon slate
Grape varieties: 85% Riesling, 15% Spätburgunder
Average yield: 50 hl/ha
Best vintages: 1994, 1995, 1996
Member: VDP

The "Hahnenhof" takes its name from the outstanding vineyard Bacharacher Hahn, which lies along the Rhine with a sublime southeasterly exposure. It has belonged to the Jost family for five generations. Its dark rocky slate retains the sun's heat; the intensity of its rays are magnified further by their reflection from the river. The vineyard has produced excellent wines for many years, but they are only now beginning to receive merited recognition. The 1995 range from Peter Jost was excellent, even though it lacked the dessert wines that have made the estate famous. In 1996 the crop was extremely small. The wines were perhaps less unctuous than those from the previous vintage, but they were top notch across the range. Albeit a touch less successful, the 1997s were the finest produced in the Mittelrhein. Jost remains the unchallenged leader here and, for the moment, stands well above his peers.

1997 Bacharacher Hahn
Riesling Kabinett
12.80 DM, 9%, ♀ till 2002 **88**

1997 Bacharacher Hahn
Riesling Spätlese trocken
19.80 DM, 11.5%, ♀ till 2002 **89**

1996 Bacharacher Hahn
Riesling Spätlese
20 DM, 8%, ♀ till 2003 **89**

1997 Bacharacher Hahn
Riesling Auslese
26 DM/0.5 liter, 9%, ♀ till 2004 **89**

1997 Bacharacher Hahn
Riesling Spätlese trocken ***
26 DM, 12%, ♀ till 2003 **91**

1997 Bacharacher Hahn
Riesling Spätlese
19.80 DM, 9%, ♀ till 2005 **91**

1996 Bacharacher Hahn
Riesling Auslese
32.50 DM, 7.5%, ♀ till 2008 **94**

1996 Bacharacher Hahn
Riesling Beerenauslese
150 DM/0.375 liter, 7%, ♀ till 2010 **94**

1996 Bacharacher Hahn
Riesling Trockenbeerenauslese
210 DM/0.375 liter, 6%, ♀ till 2008 **96**

WEINGUT DR. RANDOLF KAUER

Owner: Martina and Randolf Kauer
Winemaker: Dr. Randolf Kauer
55422 Bacharach, Mainzer Straße 21
Tel. (0 67 43) 22 72, Fax 9 36 61
Directions: A 61 Koblenz–Bingen, exit Rheinböllen, towards Bacharach
Sales: Martina Kauer
Opening hours: By appointment

Vineyard area: 2 hectares
Annual production: 10,000 bottles
Top sites: Bacharacher Kloster Fürstental and Wolfshöhle, Urbarer Beulsberg
Soil types: Weathered clay-slate
Grape varieties: 100% Riesling
Average yield: 38 hl/ha
Best vintages: 1994, 1995
Member: Ecovin

The amiable Randolf Kauer founded this property in 1989 as his small contribution to the preservation of the wine industry along the Mittelrhein. In 1996 he was able to acquire the former Wasum cellars and thus unite his residence and workplace under one roof. In these cool vaulted cellars he has installed fermentation equipment and casks. Dr. Kauer manages his vineyards on federally approved organic principles, favors fermentation with indigenous yeasts and doesn't fine his wines. Whoever treasures crystalline, tart Rieslings is well served here, for the dry wines show a tight structure which is seldom found at other estates. We have often asked ourselves what such a capable winemaker might achieve with noble late harvest grapes? Kauer actually wanted to produce a Spätlese in 1996, but wild boars had feasted on the grapes before he could harvest them. But the fact that such wines are absent from his range doesn't detract from his overall performance. Nonetheless, neither the 1996s nor the 1997s show the richness of previous vintages.

1997 Urbarer Beulsberg
Riesling trocken
8.90 DM, 11.5%, ♀ till 2000 **80**

1997 Bacharacher Wolfshöhle
Riesling Kabinett trocken
10.80 DM, 11.5%, ♀ till 2000 **82**

1997 Bacharacher Kloster Fürstental
Riesling Kabinett halbtrocken
11.40 DM, 10%, ♀ till 2001 **82**

1996 Bacharacher Kloster Fürstental
Riesling Kabinett trocken
10.25 DM, 9.5%, ♀ now **84**

1997 Bacharacher Kloster Fürstental
Riesling Spätlese halbtrocken
15.50 DM, 11.5%, ♀ till 2002 **84**

1996 Urbarer Beulsberg
Riesling trocken
9 DM, 10%, ♀ till 2000 **86**

1996 Bacharacher Kloster Fürstental
Riesling halbtrocken
9 DM, 10.5%, ♀ till 2000 **86**

1996 Bacharacher Wolfshöhle
Riesling Kabinett halbtrocken
11 DM, 9.5%, ♀ till 2002 **86**

WEINGUT ALBERT LAMBRICH

Owner: Albert Lambrich
55430 Oberwesel-Dellhofen, Rheinhöhenstraße 15
Tel. (0 67 44) 82 76, Fax (0 67 43) 94 90 01
Directions: A 61 Koblenz–Bingen, exit Laudert, towards Oberwesel
Sales: Lambrich family
Opening hours: By appointment
Restaurant: “Dellhofener Winzerstube,” open Fri. from 6 p.m., Sat. from 4 p.m. Sun. from 3 p.m.
Specialties: Homemade potato salad

Vineyard area: 3 hectares
Annual production: 30,000 bottles
Top sites: Oberweseler Römerkrug
Soil types: Weathered slate
Grape varieties: 70% Riesling, 12% Müller-Thurgau, 10% Spätburgunder, 8% other varieties
Average yield: 60 hl/ha
Best vintages: 1993, 1996, 1997

After completing his training in oenology at Bad Kreuznach, Albert Lambrich returned home to his family's estate in Oberwesel. Although he at first leased the property from his father, the 31-year-old Albert took over the estate in 1996. For most consumers in Germany this estate is still completely unknown. We first discovered its wines in 1995 and found them tasty. The 1996s were even better, and the 1997s the best wines that we have tasted to date. Admittedly there are still some very simple Rieslings in the lot, which often taste rather old fashioned, yet they all remain appealing. Lambrich's style reflects an individualistic blend of traditional and modern thoughts on vinification. With only three hectares of vines, production is small. So Albert Lambrich's wife also runs a four-hectare estate in Niederheimbach, which is home to a wine bar.

1996 Oberweseler Schloß Schönburg
Riesling trocken Hochgewächs
6 DM, 10.5%, ♀ now **75**

1997 Oberweseler Römerkrug
Riesling Spätlese trocken
9.20 DM, 12%, ♀ now **80**

1996 Oberweseler Römerkrug
Riesling halbtrocken Hochgewächs
6 DM, 10%, ♀ now **80**

1996 Oberweseler Römerkrug
Riesling Spätlese trocken
9 DM, 10.5%, ♀ now **82**

1997 Oberweseler Römerkrug
Riesling Spätlese halbtrocken
9 DM, 10.5%, ♀ till 2000 **82**

1996 Oberweseler Römerkrug
Riesling Spätlese
9 DM, 8%, ♀ now **84**

1996 Oberweseler Römerkrug
Riesling Auslese
13 DM, 7.5%, ♀ till 2002 **84**

1997 Oberweseler Römerkrug
Riesling Spätlese
9 DM, 8%, ♀ till 2002 **86**

1997 Oberweseler Römerkrug
Riesling Auslese
13 DM, 8%, ♀ till 2003 **86**

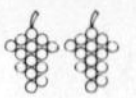

WEIN- UND SEKTGUT GOSWIN LAMBRICH

Owner: Gerhard Lambrich
55430 Oberwesel-Dellhofen,
Auf der Kripp 3
Tel. (0 67 44) 80 66, Fax 80 03
Directions: A 61 Koblenz–Bingen, exit Laudert/Oberwesel
Sales: Lambrich family
Opening hours: By appointment
Restaurant: March to December, Fri. to Sun., open from 3 p.m. to 11 p.m.
Specialties: Products from their own farm

Vineyard area: 6.8 hectares
Annual production: 30,000 bottles
Top sites: Oberweseler Oelsberg, Sankt Martinsberg, Bernstein and Römerkrug
Soil types: Weathered slate
Grape varieties: 77% Riesling, 8% Spätburgunder, 8% Kerner, 7% Weißburgunder
Average yield: 61 hl/ha
Best vintages: 1993, 1994, 1997

Gerhard Lambrich began selling his wines by the bottle in 1975. Before that the production was sold in bulk. Since then his 0.8 hectares of vines have grown to almost seven hectares. Admittedly there are still cows housed in the stalls, and Lambrich also farms over 20 hectares of fields, yet dry Riesling now stands at the center of his enterprise. The self-taught Lambrich quickly grasped what most matters: "One has to know who is making the finest wines and say to oneself, that's where I'm headed." He is still a ways from the top of the pack, but after two rather poor performances Lambrich has produced an attractive range of 1997s. Lambrich now favors a longer period of aging on the lees and is planning to install stainless steel fermentation tanks for the next vintage. Little by little he appears to be charting a better course for the future.

1996 Oberweseler Oelsberg
Riesling Spätlese
11.75 DM, 9%, ♀ now **82**

1997 Oberweseler Bernstein
Riesling Hochgewächs halbtrocken
7.10 DM, 11.5%, ♀ till 2000 **82**

1997 Oberweseler St. Martinsberg
Weißer Burgunder Spätlese trocken
11.70 DM, 12.5%, ♀ till 2000 **84**

1997 Oberweseler St. Martinsberg
Riesling Spätlese halbtrocken
10.50 DM, 11%, ♀ till 2001 **84**

1997 Oberweseler Oelsberg
Riesling Spätlese
11.60 DM, 9.5%, ♀ till 2002 **84**

1997 Oberweseler St. Martinsberg
Riesling Auslese trocken
14 DM, 12.5%, ♀ till 2001 **86**

1997 Oberweseler St. Martinsberg
Riesling Auslese halbtrocken
14 DM, 12%, ♀ till 2003 **86**

1997 Oberweseler Oelsberg
Riesling Auslese
14.40 DM, 8.5%, ♀ till 2004 **88**

1996 Dellhofener Sankt Wernerberg
Riesling Eiswein
148.50 DM/0.5 liter, ♀ till 2006 **88**

1997 Oberweseler Römerkrug
Riesling Eiswein
148 DM/0.5 liter, 10.5%, ♀ till 2007 **89**

WEINGUT LANIUS-KNAB

Owner: Jörg Lanius
55430 Oberwesel, Mainzer Straße 38
Tel. (0 67 44) 81 04, Fax 15 37
Directions: A 61 Koblenz–Bingen, exit Laudert/Oberwesel
Sales: Anne and Jörg Lanius
Opening hours: Mon.–Fri. by appointment, Sat. 8 a.m. to 5 p.m.
Worth seeing: Jugendstil house with two-storied vaulted cellars

Vineyard area: 5.7 hectares
Annual production: 30,000 bottles
Top sites: Engehöller Bernstein and Goldemund
Soil types: Weathered slate and grey slate
Grape varieties: 85% Riesling, 10% Spätburgunder, 5% Müller-Thurgau
Average yield: 50 hl/ha
Best vintages: 1995, 1996, 1997
Member: VDP

The vineyards of this estate in Oberwesel lie in the Engehöll valley and are among the steepest sites on the Mittelrhein. It is well worth a detour just to visit the historic buildings and the two-storied vaulted cellars. In the previous five vintages the property, which has been in the hands of the family for over two centuries, has evolved dramatically. Jörg Lanius now devotes himself to quasi-organic winemaking. Always subdued in aroma, his Rieslings, which are fermented in stainless steel and matured in traditional oak casks, often showcase a distinct acidic structure, so that a slight touch of residual sugar stands them well. The noble late harvest Rieslings have also gained in stature, as the excellent 1996s demonstrated. The 1997s were not of the same ilk. If that level of quality were more consistent, Jörg Lanius might well evolve into one of the more respected vintners of the region.

1997 Engehöller Bernstein
Riesling Spätlese trocken
14 DM, 11%, ♀ till 2000 **82**

1997 Engehöller Bernstein
Riesling Spätlese halbtrocken
14 DM, 10.5%, ♀ till 2001 **82**

1996 Engehöller Goldemund
Riesling Kabinett
9.50 DM, 8%, ♀ till 2000 **82**

1997 Engehöller Goldemund
Riesling Spätlese
14 DM, 9%, ♀ till 2002 **86**

1996 Engehöller Bernstein
Riesling Spätlese
12.50 DM, 9.5%, ♀ till 2004 **86**

1997 Engehöller Bernstein
Riesling Auslese
26 DM, 8%, ♀ till 2003 **86**

1996 Engehöller Bernstein
Riesling Auslese
21.75 DM/0.5 liter, 7.5%, ♀ till 2006 **88**

1997 Engehöller Bernstein
Riesling Beerenauslese
65 DM/0.375 liter, 6%, ♀ till 2007 **88**

1996 Engehöller Bernstein
Riesling Beerenauslese
62 DM/0.375 liter, 7%, ♀ till 2012 **92**

1996 Engehöller Goldemund
Riesling Eiswein
120 DM/0.25 liter, 6.5%, ♀ till 2016 **95**

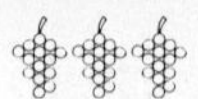

WEINGUT TONI LORENZ

Owner: Toni Lorenz
Winemaker: Joachim Lorenz
56154 Boppard, Ablaßgasse 4
Tel. (0 67 42) 35 11, Fax 10 90 63
Directions: A 61 Koblenz–Bingen, exit Boppard
Sales: Lorenz family
Opening hours: Mon.–Fri. 8 a.m. to 7:30 p.m., Sat. 8 a.m. to 6 p.m. or by appointment
Worth seeing: 400-year-old vaulted cask cellar in the form of a cross

Vineyard area: 3.5 hectares
Annual production: 25,000 bottles
Top sites: Bopparder Hamm Feuerlay, Mandelstein and Fässerlay
Soil types: Weathered slate
Grape varieties: 82% Riesling, 10% Spätburgunder, 8% other varieties
Average yield: 85 hl/ha
Best vintages: 1995, 1996, 1997

Since Joachim Lorenz – born in 1964 – began working at his family's estate in the early 1990s, the quality has improved throughout the range. He trained in oenology at the Kreuznach college and profits as well from the experience he gains as a taster for the state. Happily describing his style as "fresh, fruity and lively," he nonetheless does not produce simple wines. With their unusually high acidities, precise fruit and traditional style, they make few concessions to today's distrust of wines with strong character. This is a complicated style that one rarely encounters these days. But drinking his lovely 1996s proves that such wines can provide real pleasure. They are well marked by their slate soils and are certainly as good as the brilliant 1995s; the Spätlese are again the most inspired wines of the vintage. The 1997s are perhaps not quite as good, but Lorenz is still on his way to the head of the pack in the Mittelrhein.

1996 Bopparder Hamm Fässerlay
Riesling trocken Hochgewächs
6.50 DM, 10%, ♀ now **82**

1997 Bopparder Hamm Fässerlay
Riesling Hochgewächs halbtrocken
6.80 DM, 6.8%, ♀ till 2000 **82**

1996 Bopparder Hamm Feuerlay
Riesling Spätlese trocken
9 DM, 11.5%, ♀ till 2000 **86**

1997 Bopparder Hamm Feuerlay
Riesling Spätlese halbtrocken
9 DM, 10.5%, ♀ till 2002 **86**

1997 Bopparder Hamm Feuerlay
Riesling Auslese
17 DM/0.5 liter, 9.5%, ♀ till 2003 **88**

1997 Bopparder Hamm Feuerlay
Kerner Auslese
17 DM/0.5 liter, 9%, ♀ till 2002 **88**

1996 Bopparder Hamm Mandelstein
Riesling Auslese
14 DM, 9%, ♀ till 2005 **88**

1996 Bopparder Hamm Feuerlay
Riesling Spätlese
9 DM, 8.5%, ♀ till 2005 **89**

1996 Bopparder Hamm Fässerlay
Riesling Spätlese halbtrocken
9 DM, 10%, ♀ till 2002 **90**

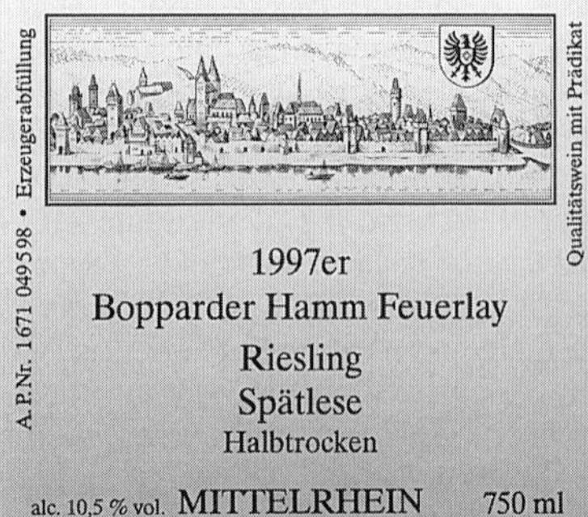

Toni Lorenz
A.P.Nr. 1671 049598 • Erzeugerabfüllung
Qualitätswein mit Prädikat
1997er
Bopparder Hamm Feuerlay
Riesling
Spätlese
Halbtrocken
alc. 10,5 % vol. MITTELRHEIN 750 ml
Weingut Toni Lorenz • D-56154 Boppard • Ablassgasse 4

WEINGUT MADES

Owner: Helmut Mades
55422 Bacharach-Steeg,
Borbachstraße 35–36
Tel. (0 67 43) 14 49, Fax 31 24
Directions: A 61 Koblenz–Bingen, exit Rheinböllen
Sales: Mades family
Opening hours: Mon.–Sun. all day
By appointment
Restaurant: Open from March to late October, Fri., Sat. and Sun. evening
Specialties: Riesling soup, "Hinkelsdreck"
History: Owned by family since 1663
Worth seeing: The family's house from the 16th century

Vineyard area: 2.5 hectares
Annual production: 16,000 bottles
Top sites: Bacharacher Posten and Wolfshöhle, Steeger Sankt Jost
Soil types: Weathered Devon slate
Grape varieties: 100% Riesling
Average yield: 43 hl/ha
Best vintages: 1995, 1996, 1997
Member: VDP

Besides his small estate on the Mittelrhein, Helmut Mades – whose family boasts three centuries of winemaking tradition – also manages the property of his wife in Wallertheim in Rheinhessen. In Steeg, Riesling is trump, producing attractive wines on a regular basis. After an appealing range of wines in 1994 and excellent 1995s, we found both the 1996s and 1997s somewhat disappointing. The wines were not as crisp and refreshing as earlier vintages, and were even in some cases rustic. These two vintages were certainly not as easy in Bacharach and Steeg as in Boppard, but the sparkling clarity of fruit from the previous years was lacking. Be that as it may, when his Spätlese are good, they are very pleasant to drink.

1997 Bacharacher Wolfshöhle
Riesling Kabinett
10.20 DM, 8.5%, ♀ till 2000 **82**

1997 Bacharacher Wolfshöhle
Riesling Spätlese trocken
14.20 DM, 11%, ♀ till 2000 **84**

1996 Steeger Sankt Jost
Riesling Kabinett halbtrocken
9.50 DM, 9%, ♀ now **84**

1997 Bacharacher Posten
Riesling Spätlese halbtrocken
14.20 DM, 10.5%, ♀ till 2001 **84**

1996 Bacharacher Posten
Riesling Spätlese halbtrocken
13 DM, 9.5%, ♀ till 2000 **84**

1996 Bacharacher Wolfshöhle
Riesling Kabinett
10 DM, ♀ till 2000 **84**

1996 Bacharacher Wolfshöhle
Riesling Spätlese
13 DM, 8%, ♀ till 2002 **86**

1996 Bacharacher Posten
Riesling Auslese
24 DM, 7.5%, ♀ till 2003 **86**

WEINGUT HEINRICH MÜLLER

Owners: Heinrich and Matthias Müller
56322 Spay, Mainzer Straße 45
Tel. (0 26 28) 87 41, Fax 33 63
Directions: A 61 Koblenz–Bingen, exit Boppard
Sales: Hilde and Marianne Müller
Opening hours: Mon.–Sat. all day
Sun. 10 a.m. to 6 p.m.

Vineyard area: 6 hectares
Annual production: 55,000 bottles
Top sites: Bopparder Hamm Feuerlay, Mandelstein, Engelstein and Ohlenberg
Soil types: Weathered Devon slate
Grape varieties: 80% Riesling, 8% Spätburgunder, 8% Grauburgunder, 4% Kerner
Average yield: 69 hl/ha
Best vintages: 1995, 1996, 1997

The Müller family can trace their heritage as wine producers back some 300 years. At one time they farmed a wide variety of products, but nowadays there are only grapes in their steep vineyard sites. Although the estate began to bottle its own wines in the early 1920s, it is only in recent years that has it drawn much attention to itself. Matthias Müller, born in 1963, recently joined his father Heinrich and has quickly put what he learned during his studies at the college in Bad Kreuznach to good use. In 1994 father and son produced a refreshing range of wines. The 1995 Rieslings were awash in elegant fruit: dense, well focused and deliciously attractive. The 1996s were of similar pedigree. The Riesling Spätlese from the Feuerlay vineyard was one of the top wines of the vintage. Given the difficult vintage, the 1997s are also first rate. This is an estate to follow.

1997 Bopparder Hamm Ohlenberg
Riesling Spätlese trocken
9.50 DM, 12.5%, ♀ till 2002 **88**

1997 Bopparder Hamm Feuerlay
Riesling Spätlese halbtrocken
9 DM, 10%, ♀ till 2003 **88**

1997 Bopparder Hamm Engelstein
Riesling Spätlese
9.50 DM, 9%, ♀ till 2003 **88**

1997 Bopparder Hamm Ohlenberg
Riesling Spätlese
11.50 DM, 8.5%, ♀ till 2005 **89**

1996 Bopparder Hamm Mandelstein
Riesling Auslese
14 DM, 9.5%, ♀ till 2006 **89**

1997 Bopparder Hamm Feuerlay
Riesling Auslese
38 DM/0.5 liter, 8%, ♀ till 2007 **91**

1996 Bopparder Hamm Engelstein
Riesling Auslese
16 DM/0.5 liter, 9.5%, ♀ till 2008 **91**

1996 Bopparder Hamm Feuerlay
Riesling Beerenauslese
40 DM/0.5 liter, 9.5%, ♀ till 2010 **91**

1996 Bopparder Hamm Feuerlay
Riesling Spätlese
10 DM, 9.5%, ♀ till 2006 **91**

WEINGUT HERMANN OCKENFELS

Owner: Hermann Ockenfels
56599 Leutesdorf, Oelbergstraße 3
Tel. (0 26 31) 7 25 93
Directions: A 3 Köln–Frankfurt, exit Neuwied
Opening hours: By appointment

Vineyard area: 1.3 hectares
Annual production: 15,000 bottles
Top sites: Leutesdorfer Rosenberg, Gartenlay and Forstberg
Soil types: Weathered slate
Grape varieties: 80% Riesling, 4% each of Müller-Thurgau, Kerner, Portugieser, Dornfelder and Regent
Average yield: 90 hl/ha
Best vintages: 1995, 1996, 1997

Although he did his apprenticeship in the vineyard, for many years Hermann Ockenfels ran a butcher's shop with its own abattoir. With his weekend wine-making hobby he nonetheless won numerous prizes. Little by little the estate grew and shortly before his sixtieth birthday Ockenfels gave up the butcher's trade in order to devote himself to his real calling. The rooms of the old butcher's shop are now used by his daughter for her pottery studio. They sell their products jointly, which makes for an unusual combination. Ockenfels is happy holding wine tastings in his "Bacchus Lounge," which he enlivens with hearty dishes from his own kitchen. Admittedly the dry wines still leave something to be desired, but the fruitier styles can be charming. Typical of the region, in 1997 he produced a dozen wines on the three acres he calls his own.

1997 Leutesdorfer Forstberg
Riesling Kabinett halbtrocken
8 DM, 10.5%, ♀ till 2000 **82**

1996 Leutesdorfer Rosenberg
Riesling Spätlese
9.25 DM, 8.5%, ♀ now **84**

1996 Leutesdorfer Gartenlay
Riesling Spätlese
9.75 DM, 8.5%, ♀ now **84**

1997 Leutesdorfer Gartenlay
Riesling Hochgewächs halbtrocken – 1 –
6.60 DM, 11%, ♀ till 2001 **84**

1997 Leutesdorfer Rosenberg
Riesling Hochgewächs trocken
6.80 DM, 11.5%, ♀ till 2000 **84**

1997 Leutesdorfer Rosenberg
Riesling Spätlese
9 DM, 10%, ♀ till 2003 **86**

1996 Leutesdorfer Rosenberg
Riesling Auslese
14 DM, 9%, ♀ till 2000 **86**

1997 Leutesdorfer Gartenlay
Riesling Spätlese "feinherb" – 5 –
10 DM, 10.5%, ♀ till 2002 **86**

1997 Leutesdorfer Gartenlay
Riesling Spätlese "feinherb" – 6 –
8.60 DM, 10.5%, ♀ till 2001 **86**

WEINGUT AUGUST PERLL

Owners: August and Thomas Perll
Winemaker: Thomas Perll
56154 Boppard, Oberstraße 81
Tel. (0 67 42) 39 06, Fax 8 17 26
Directions: A 61 Koblenz–Bingen, exit Buchholz, towards Boppard
Sales: Christa and Petra Perll
Opening hours: Mon.–Fri. 8 a.m. to noon and 3 p.m. to 6 p.m., Sat. 9 a.m. to 2 p.m. or by appointment
Worth seeing: Old vaulted cellar

Vineyard area: 6.5 hectares
Annual production: 70,000 bottles
Top sites: Bopparder Hamm Mandelstein, Feuerlay, Ohlenberg and Fässerlay
Soil types: Weathered Devon slate
Grape varieties: 80% Riesling, 7% Kerner, 7% Spätburgunder, 6% other varieties
Average yield: 85 hl/ha
Best vintages: 1995, 1996, 1997

The first name of August has a long tradition in the Perll family. For five generations the property has been run by a Perll bearing that name. Now young Thomas Perll is preparing to take over the family's estate, which traces its origins back to the year 1606, when the original buildings were constructed. The rich soils, intensive work in the vineyards and a late harvest often result in wines with high degrees of ripeness that are sold at extremely reasonable prices: the annual production is divided equally between dry, off-dry and fruitier styles. The attractive 1994 range set a new tone at the property. The splendid 1995s continued that development. The 1996s and 1997s were perhaps a touch less luscious, but nonetheless still attain a similarly high standard of quality. Along with Heinrich Müller and Florian Weingart, this is one of the few up and coming estates within reach of frontrunner Toni Jost.

1997 Bopparder Hamm Feuerlay
Riesling Spätlese halbtrocken
9.50 DM, 10.5%, ♀ till 2002 **86**

1997 Bopparder Hamm Fässerlay
Riesling Spätlese trocken
9.50 DM, 12.5%, ♀ till 2002 **88**

1997 Bopparder Hamm Ohlenberg
Riesling Kabinett
7.50 DM, 9%, ♀ till 2002 **88**

1996 Bopparder Hamm Feuerlay
Riesling Spätlese halbtrocken
10 DM, 11.5%, ♀ till 2002 **89**

1996 Bopparder Hamm Mandelstein
Riesling Spätlese
10 DM, 9%, ♀ till 2003 **89**

1997 Bopparder Hamm Mandelstein
Riesling Spätlese – 6 –
9.50 DM, 8.5%, ♀ till 2003 **89**

1996 Bopparder Hamm Mandelstein
Riesling Auslese
17 DM, 8.5%, ♀ till 2006 **91**

1997 Bopparder Hamm Feuerlay
Riesling Eiswein
40 DM/0.375 liter, 10.5%, ♀ till 2007 **91**

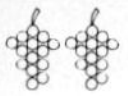

WEINGUT WALTER PERLL

Owner: Walter Perll
56154 Boppard, Ablaßgasse 11
Tel. (0 67 42) 36 71, Fax 30 23
Directions: A 61 Koblenz–Bingen, exit Boppard
Sales: Doris Perll
Opening hours: Mon.–Fri. 9 a.m. to noon and 2 p.m. to 6 p.m., Sat. 9 a.m. to 4 p.m., Sun. 10 a.m. to noon or by appointment

Vineyard area: 5.4 hectares
Annual production: 50,000 bottles
Top sites: Bopparder Hamm Mandelstein, Feuerlay, Ohlenberg and Fässerlay
Soil types: Weathered Devon slate
Grape varieties: 83% Riesling, 10% Spätburgunder, 7% other varieties
Average yield: 70 hl/ha
Best vintages: 1993, 1995, 1996

Walter Perll, whose family has made its home in Boppard since 1675, pursues a policy of reductive winemaking – emphasizing gentle treatment and an early racking of the wines so as to retain their fresh fruit. His preference for fully ripe grapes, which are seldom vinified to complete dryness, is something he shares with his brother August. In 1973 the brothers divided the parental estate between them; but further purchases and leasing contracts have led to an expansion of both estates since that time. They both offer wines at extremely reasonable prices that can fairly be described – in the best sense of the term – as old fashioned, ranging in quality from good to very good. Although Walter Perll was rewarded with a federal gold medal in 1992, his brother August has had the edge in quality for the past two vintages. But Walter remains on his heels. His 1996 Rieslings were juicy, mouthwatering and much more elegant than his 1995s. The 1997s are not quite as successful, but do show character in a somewhat difficult vintage.

1997 Bopparder Hamm Feuerlay
Riesling Spätlese halbtrocken
8.50 DM, 11%, 🍷 till 2000 **82**

1996 Bopparder Hamm Feuerlay
Riesling Spätlese halbtrocken
8.50 DM, 11.5%, 🍷 till 2000 **82**

1996 Bopparder Hamm Ohlenberg
Riesling Spätlese trocken
8.50 DM, 12%, 🍷 now **84**

1997 Bopparder Hamm Ohlenberg
Riesling Spätlese
8.50 DM, 9%, 🍷 till 2002 **84**

1997 Bopparder Hamm Mandelstein
Riesling Spätlese
8.50 DM, 9.5%, 🍷 till 2003 **86**

1996 Bopparder Hamm Ohlenberg
Riesling Spätlese
8.50 DM, 9%, 🍷 till 2002 **86**

1997 Bopparder Hamm Mandelstein
Riesling Auslese
13 DM, 9.5%, 🍷 till 2004 **86**

1996 Bopparder Hamm Mandelstein
Riesling Spätlese
9 DM, 10%, 🍷 till 2003 **88**

1996 Bopparder Hamm Feuerlay
Riesling Spätlese
9 DM, 8.5%, 🍷 till 2003 **88**

1996 Bopparder Hamm Mandelstein
Riesling Auslese
13 DM, 9%, 🍷 till 2006 **89**

WEINGUT BERNHARD PRASS

Owner: Bernhard Praß
55422 Bacharach-Steeg, Blücherstraße 132
Tel. (0 67 43) 15 85, Fax 32 60
Directions: A 61 Koblenz–Bingen, exit Rheinböllen
Opening hours: Mon.–Fri. 6 p.m. to 9 p.m., Sat. and Sun. 9 a.m. to 8 p.m.

Vineyard area: 1.5 hectares
Annual production: 15,000 bottles
Top sites: Bacharacher Wolfshöhle, Steeger Sankt Jost
Soil types: Weathered Devon slate and grey slate
Grape varieties: 60% Riesling, 20% Weißburgunder, 15% Spätburgunder, 5% Dornfelder
Average yield: 70 hl/ha
Best vintages: 1992, 1993, 1997

Bernhard Prass is convinced that the Rieslings from the Mittelrhein, with their hearty acidic structures, are particularly well suited to being vinified as "Hochgewächs," an upscale version of the traditional "Qualitätswein." Perhaps that is why these wines, especially those in an off-dry style, are frequently his best. The demand for them is so strong that he now bottles almost his entire Riesling production at this quality level. On the downside, this policy means that he rarely produces Spätlese or Auslese. With his limited acreage he has little room to maneuver anyway; but if he wants to increase the reputation of his estate he will have to offer his clientele not only more variety but also wines of greater depth and style. The 1996s were charming, yet lacked any great finesse. The 1997s are also pleasant, a respectable range of wines at fair prices.

1997 Bacharacher Schloß Stahleck
Riesling
6.50 DM, 10.5%, ♀ now **80**

1997 Riesling
Hochgewächs halbtrocken
7 DM, 10.5%, ♀ now **80**

1997 Riesling
Hochgewächs trocken
7 DM, 11%, ♀ now **80**

1996 Bacharacher
Riesling halbtrocken Hochgewächs
7 DM, 10.5%, ♀ till 2000 **82**

1997 Steeger
Riesling Kabinett halbtrocken
8 DM, 10%, ♀ now **82**

1996 Steeger Sankt Jost
Riesling Hochgewächs
7 DM, 10%, ♀ till 2000 **82**

1997 Steeger St. Jost
Riesling Spätlese
9.50 DM, 9%, ♀ till 2000 **82**

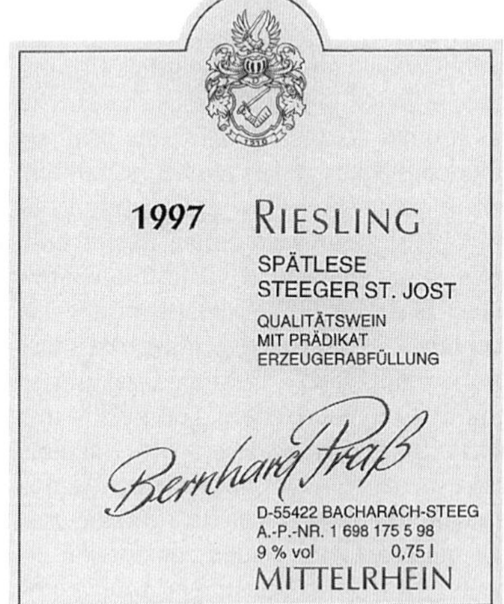

WEINGUT RATZENBERGER

Owner: Ratzenberger family
General Manager: Jochen Ratzenberger
55422 Bacharach, Blücherstraße 167
Tel. (0 67 43) 13 37, Fax 28 42
Directions: A 61 Koblenz–Bingen, exit Rheinböllen, towards Bacharach
Sales: Jochen Ratzenberger
Opening hours: Mon.–Sat. 9 a.m. to 5 p.m., Sun. 10 a.m. to 3 p.m. or by appointment
Worth seeing: Large vaulted cellar

Vineyard area: 8 hectares
Annual production: 50,000 bottles
Top sites: Steeger Sankt Jost, Bacharacher Posten and Wolfshöhle
Soil types: Weathered Devon slate
Grape varieties: 74% Riesling, 15% Spätburgunder, 8% Müller-Thurgau, 3% other varieties
Average yield: 50 hl/ha
Best vintages: 1993, 1994, 1997
Member: VDP

Over the past 20 years Jochen Ratzenberger has transformed this estate into one of the most renowned in Steeg. In addition, he is also one of the few producers on the Mittelrhein who in recent years has ventured to increase his vineyard holdings. His Rieslings once tended to be tart and dry, but Ratzenberger now produces elegant and polished noble late harvest wines as well. The high quality of the 1993 vintage was a perfect example of this development; the 1994s followed suit. The 1995s, on the other hand, were somewhat disappointing. The 1996s were not much better. The 1997s are only marginally more successful, but they are at least more traditional in style. We sometimes have the impression that, rather than let nature take her course, this estate is trying too hard to make finer wines.

1996 Bacharacher Posten
Riesling Spätlese halbtrocken
15.75 DM, 10%, ♀ till 2002 **84**

1997 Bacharacher Wolfshöhle
Riesling Spätlese
16.40 DM, 8.5%, ♀ till 2002 **86**

1996 Bacharacher Wolfshöhle
Riesling Spätlese
16.50 DM, 7.5%, ♀ till 2003 **86**

1997 Steeger Sankt Jost
Riesling Auslese
28 DM/0.5 liter, 9%, ♀ till 2003 **86**

1997 Bacharacher Wolfshöhle
Riesling Auslese
28 DM/0.5 liter, 8%, ♀ till 2005 **88**

1996 Bacharacher Posten
Riesling Auslese
24 DM/0.5 liter, 8%, ♀ till 2005 **88**

1996 Steeger Sankt Jost
Riesling Beerenauslese
99 DM/0.375 liter, 7%, ♀ till 2010 **89**

1997 Bacharacher Kloster Fürstental
Riesling Eiswein
100 DM/0.375 liter, 8%, ♀ till 2007 **91**

1997 Bacharacher Kloster Fürstental
Riesling Trockenbeerenauslese
195 DM/0.375 liter, 7%, ♀ till 2010 **92**

WEINGUT VOLK

Owner: Jürgen Volk
56322 Spay, Koblenzer Straße 6
Tel. (0 26 28) 82 90, Fax 98 74 16
e-mail: Weingut.Volk@t-online.de
Directions: A 61 Koblenz–Bingen, exit Boppard
Sales: Heidi Volk
Opening hours: By appointment

Vineyard area: 2.5 hectares
Annual production: 25,000 bottles
Top sites: Bopparder Hamm Ohlenberg and Weingrube
Soil types: Weathered grey slate
Grape varieties: 82% Riesling, 8% Spätburgunder, 5% Müller-Thurgau, 5% Kerner
Average yield: 85 hl/ha
Best vintages: 1995, 1996, 1997

Although this estate has been growing grapes since the 19th century, it has only slowly made wine the principal focus of its business. Hermann Volk was the first to make wine production his main occupation; and in 1995 Jürgen and Heidi Volk, both qualified oenologists, took over the estate. Since the cellar was built in 1969 both the vineyard size and the number of faithful clients have grown steadily; and in 1992 the family was awarded one of the federal government's highest prizes. The wines have always had plenty of substance; but they often lacked vivacity and the aromas were not always well defined. Nonetheless, the Volks have shown – especially with their fruity Auslese – that they know how to produce attractive wines. Given their modest prices, this may well turn out to be an estate to follow.

1997 Bopparder Hamm Weingrube
Riesling Hochgewächs trocken
6.20 DM, 11.5%, ♀ now **77**

1996 Bopparder Hamm Weingrube
Riesling halbtrocken Hochgewächs
6 DM, 11%, ♀ till 2000 **80**

1997 Bopparder Hamm Ohlenberg
Riesling Kabinett halbtrocken
6.70 DM, 10%, ♀ now **80**

1997 Bopparder Hamm Ohlenberg
Riesling Spätlese trocken
8 DM, 12%, ♀ now **82**

1996 Bopparder Hamm Ohlenberg
Riesling Auslese trocken
13 DM, 12%, ♀ till 2000 **82**

1997 Bopparder Hamm Weingrube
Riesling Hochgewächs halbtrocken
6.20 DM, 11%, ♀ till 2000 **82**

1997 Bopparder Hamm Weingrube
Kerner Auslese
12 DM, 10.5%, ♀ till 2001 **84**

1996 Bopparder Hamm Ohlenberg
Riesling Auslese
13 DM, 9.5%, ♀ till 2006 **88**

WEINGUT WEINGART

Owner: Florian Weingart and family
Manager: Florian Weingart
56322 Spay, Mainzer Straße 32
Tel. (0 26 28) 87 35, Fax 28 35
e-mail: Weingart-wein.spay@t-online.de
Directions: A 61 Koblenz–Bingen, exit Boppard, towards Spay
Sales: Helga and Ulrike Weingart
Opening hours: By appointment
Restaurant: Sat. open from 3 p.m. Sun. and holidays from 10 a.m. Closed from Christmas until early February

Vineyard area: 6.1 hectares
Annual production: 80,000 bottles
Top sites: Bopparder Hamm Ohlenberg, Feuerlay, Engelstein and Mandelstein
Soil types: Weathered slate
Grape varieties: 90% Riesling, 3% Müller-Thurgau, 3% Grauburgunder, 4% experimental varieties
Average yield: 78 hl/ha
Best vintages: 1995, 1996, 1997

In 1997 Adolf Weingart turned his estate over to his son Florian, who had been working at the family's property since 1994. As demand for their wines exceeds supply, the Weingarts purchase grapes from their neighbors. Most of the Rieslings produced here are off-dry or sweet, perfectly balancing the racy acidity so prevalent in the Mittelrhein. The 1996s, the first vintage to bear only Florian's signature, were the best wines we have ever tasted from this estate: expressive, luscious and simply delicious. Given the difficult nature of the vintage, the 1997s are perhaps even better. Florian Weingart is clearly staking out higher ground. Many here believe that he has the stuff to give Toni Jost a run for his money.

1997 Bopparder Hamm Feuerlay
Riesling Auslese halbtrocken
13 DM, 12.5%, ♀ till 2003 **86**

1997 Bopparder Hamm Feuerlay
Riesling Spätlese halbtrocken
9 DM, 10.5%, ♀ till 2002 **88**

1996 Bopparder Hamm Engelstein
Riesling Spätlese trocken
8.50 DM, 11%, ♀ till 2000 **89**

1997 Bopparder Hamm Ohlenberg
Riesling Auslese trocken
12 DM, 12.5%, ♀ till 2003 **89**

1997 Bopparder Hamm Ohlenberg
Riesling Spätlese
9 DM, 9%, ♀ till 2003 **89**

1996 Bopparder Hamm Ohlenberg
Riesling Spätlese
8.50 DM, 10%, ♀ till 2006 **89**

1997 Bopparder Hamm Feuerlay
Riesling Auslese
16 DM, 9%, ♀ till 2005 **89**

1996 Bopparder Hamm Feuerlay
Riesling Spätlese halbtrocken
8.50 DM, 11%, ♀ till 2003 **91**

1997 Bopparder Hamm Feuerlay
Riesling Auslese *
16 DM, 7.5%, ♀ till 2007 **91**

1996 Bopparder Hamm Feuerlay
Riesling Auslese
12 DM, 10%, ♀ till 2007 **91**

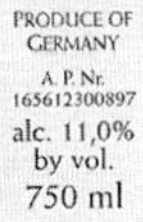

Mosel-Saar-Ruwer

The King of Riesling

Long before the first growths in Bordeaux were established, the Mosel had already set the benchmark in terms of quality for racy, elegantly fruity Rieslings. At the end of the last century the Rieslings from the most reputable estates in

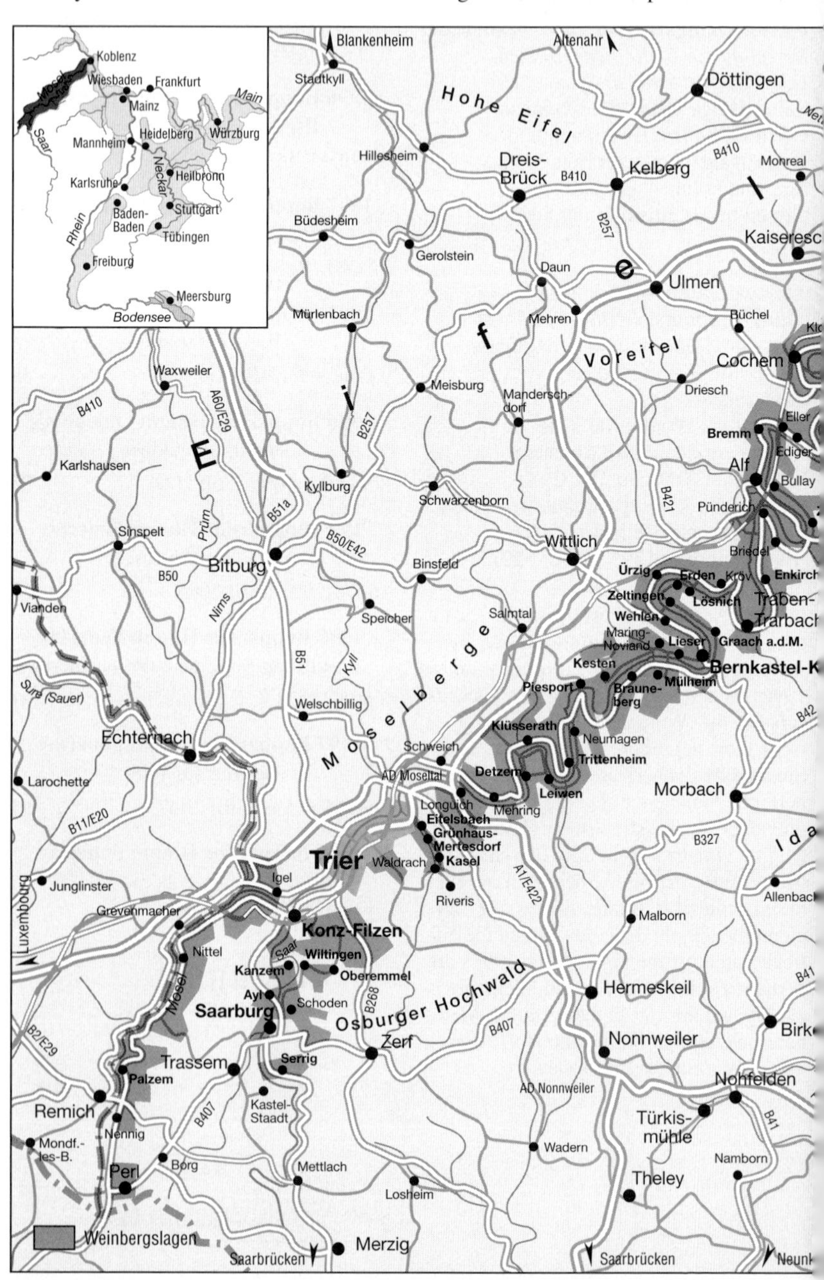

Bernkastel and Wehlen were the most expensive wines in the world. Even today, it is impossible to find such full-flavored yet stylish Rieslings anywhere else in the world. The pure fruit of the Mosel and the piquant spice of its tributaries, the Saar and Ruwer, are inimitable. From the light Kabinetts to the harmonious Spätlese and succulent Auslese to the heights of the noble sweet Beerenauslese, Trockenbeerenauslese and pungent ice wines, this region has at its disposal an unbelievably multi-faceted potential.

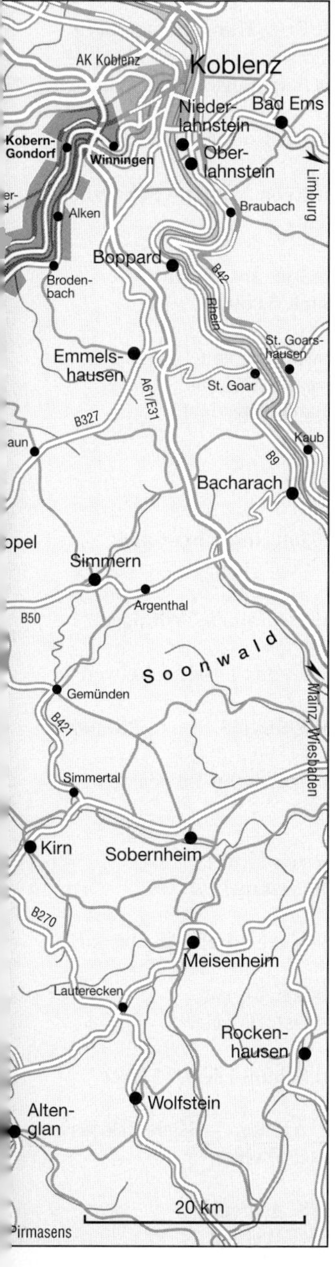

As exquisite as the sweet wines may be, only a handful of estates are capable of producing good dry Rieslings. Understanding how to shape the natural attributes of the Mosel – low alcohol content and high acidity – into a delicious symbiosis is the key to success; and all too few estates have truly understood this "marriage" to be their mission statement. Further, even many off-dry Rieslings – this was a problem in 1996 – are so marked by acidity that they provide only a moderately pleasurable drinking experience. This is no plea for sweet wines from the Mosel; on the contrary, we often feel that many producers are becoming far too generous with residual sugar.

Nowhere else in the Germany do brilliance and poverty lie so inextricably entwined as on the Mosel, Saar and Ruwer. On the one hand, the region's stars – Fritz Haag, Egon Müller, Joh. Jos. Prüm and Schubert – achieve record prices at the local auction in Trier. More than a thousand marks for a single bottle of a young wine is not a rare occurrence! Some 25 other vintners are also doing very well; Christoph Tyrell, Ernst Loosen, Willi Schaefer and Johannes Selbach even have their own fan clubs. Markus Molitor seems intent on making his mark as well. On the other hand, the number of dissatisfied growers – there are over 4,000 of them today – has steadily increased. For many, cultivating a small parcel of vines and selling the wine in bulk ekes out, at best, only a very modest living. Applying for the generous German unemployment benefits remains a serious financial alternative. Who wants to spend their days in the vertiginously steep slate slopes above the river for nothing other than the beauty of the scenery? Fortunately, numerous young growers such as Clemens Busch, Gerd Haart, Claudia Loch, Martin Müllen and Hans Resch have not abandoned hope.

The fact is, though, that far too much wine is produced on the Mosel. Yields of more than 100 hectoliters per hectare – even if they were considerably lower in 1997 – are not unusual. Further, far too little is produced in the best sites; and who in South Dakota would know the difference between the stunning Wehlener Sonnenuhr and the fictional Himmlisches Kanonenrohr? Even worse, half of the region is planted with varieties other than Riesling – Müller-Thurgau, Elbling and various new hybrids, to name but a few. But in Japan most consumers believe that a Kröver Nacktarsch or a Black Tower are synonyms for fine Riesling, even if there is no mention of Riesling on the label. Where was Ralph Nader when Germany needed him?

Even the top estates sometimes make it difficult for one to retain one's perspective. Numerous producers market a succession of wines under exactly the same label, for they bottle one cask at a time. It is thus important to keep an eye on the small print on the label, but who can truly keep track of the lot numbers? There is also a tradition among certain estates to distinguish outstanding Auslese by the use of gold capsules or obscure numbers. Others, today, dress their best wines with as many as five stars on the label. This small but brilliant world is becoming more and more confusing. The only solution is to trust your palate. Or ours. For in spite of the inherent problems in this region, Riesling from the Mosel is a "must" for every wine lover!

The leading estates of Mosel-Saar-Ruwer

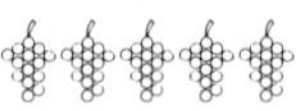

Weingut Fritz Haag, Brauneberg

Weingut Karthäuserhof, Eitelsbach

Weingut Dr. Loosen, Bernkastel

Weingut Egon Müller – Scharzhof, Wiltingen

Weingut Joh. Jos. Prüm, Bernkastel-Wehlen

Gutsverwaltung von Schubert – Grünhaus, Grünhaus-Mertesdorf

Weingut Joh. Jos. Christoffel Erben, Ürzig

Weingut Le Gallais, Wiltingen

Weingut Grans-Fassian, Leiwen

Weingut Reinhold Haart, Piesport

Weingut Heymann-Löwenstein, Winningen

Weingut von Hövel, Konz-Oberemmel

Weingut Karlsmühle, Mertesdorf

Weingut Reichsgraf von Kesselstatt, Trier

Weingut Schloß Lieser, Lieser

Weingut Molitor – Haus Klosterberg, Bernkastel-Wehlen

Weingut S. A. Prüm, Bernkastel-Wehlen

Weingut Sankt Urbans-Hof, Leiwen

Weingut Willi Schaefer, Graach

Weingut Selbach-Oster, Zeltingen

Weingut Forstmeister Geltz – Zilliken, Saarburg

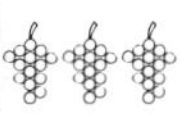

Weingut Erben von Beulwitz, Mertesdorf

Bischöfliche Weingüter, Trier

Weingut Clüsserath-Weiler, Trittenheim

Weingut Reinhold Franzen, Bremm

Weingut Willi Haag, Brauneberg

Weingut Albert Kallfelz, Zell-Merl/Mosel

Weingut Kees-Kieren, Graach

Weingut Heribert Kerpen, Bernkastel-Wehlen

Weingut Reinhard und Beate Knebel, Winningen

Weingut Peter Lauer Weinhaus Ayler Kupp, Ayl

Weingut Carl Loewen, Leiwen

Weingut Meulenhof, Erden

Weingut Milz – Laurentiushof, Trittenheim

Weingut Dr. Pauly-Bergweiler, Bernkastel-Kues

Weingut Max Ferd. Richter, Mülheim

Weingut Josef Rosch, Leiwen

Weingut Schloß Saarstein, Serrig

Weingut Studert-Prüm – Maximinhof, Bernkastel-Wehlen

Weingut Wwe. Dr. H. Thanisch – Erben Thanisch, Bernkastel-Kues,

Weingut Dr. Heinz Wagner, Saarburg

Gutsverwaltung Geheimrat J. Wegeler Erben, Bernkastel-Kues

Weingut Dr. F. Weins-Prüm, Bernkastel-Wehlen

Weingut Ernst Clüsserath, Trittenheim

Weingut Erben Stephan Ehlen, Lösnich

Weingut Franz-Josef Eifel, Trittenheim

Rating scale for the estates

Highest rating: These producers belong to the world's finest.

Excellent estates: These producers are among Germany's best.

Very good producers, known for their consistently high quality.

Good estates, offering better than average quality.

Reliable producers that offer well-made standard quality.

Weingut Robert Eymael – Mönchhof, Ürzig

Weingut Kurt Hain, Piesport

Weingut Freiherr von Heddesdorff, Winningen

Weingut Carl August Immich – Batterieberg, Enkirch

Weingut Kirsten, Klüsserath

Weingut Lehnert-Veit, Piesport

Weingut Alfred Merkelbach Geschw. Albertz-Erben, Ürzig

Weingut von Othegraven, Kanzem

Weingut Paulinshof, Kesten

Weingut Piedmont, Konz-Filzen

Weingut Johann Peter Reinert, Kanzem

Weingut Reuscher-Haart, Piesport

Weingut Edmund Reverchon, Konz-Filzen

Vintage chart for the Mosel-Saar-Ruwer

vintage	quality	drink
1997	♣♣♣♣	till 2005
1996	♣♣♣♣	till 2006
1995	♣♣♣♣	till 2006
1994	♣♣♣♣♣	till 2005
1993	♣♣♣♣	till 2004
1992	♣♣♣♣	now
1991	♣♣♣	now
1990	♣♣♣♣♣	till 2004
1989	♣♣♣♣	till 2000
1988	♣♣♣♣	now

♣♣♣♣♣ : Outstanding
♣♣♣♣ : Excellent
♣♣♣ : Good
♣♣ : Average
♣ : Poor

Weingut Heinz Schmitt, Leiwen

Weingut Peter Terges, Trier

Weingut Wwe. Dr. H. Thanisch – Erben Müller-Burggraef, Bernkastel-Kues

Weingut Weller-Lehnert, Piesport

Stiftung Friedrich-Wilhelm-Gymnasium, Trier

Winzergenossenschaft Kasel, Kasel

Weingut Walter Rauen, Detzem

Weingut Freiherr von Schleinitz, Kobern-Gondorf

Schloß Thorn, Schloß Thorn

Other notable producers

Weingut Altenhofen
54441 Ayl, Zuckerberg 2
Tel. (0 65 81) 39 27

Weingut Bastgen & Vogel
54518 Kesten, Moselstraße 1
Tel. (0 65 35) 71 42, Fax 15 79

Weingut Clemens Busch
56862 Pünderich, Im Wingert 39
Tel. (0 65 42) 2 21 80, Fax 16 25

Weingut Clüsserath-Eifel
54349 Trittenheim, Moselweinstraße 39
Tel. (0 65 07) 9 90 00, Fax 9 90 02

Weingut Johannes Fuchs
56829 Pommern, Zehnthofstraße 6
Tel. (0 26 72) 70 03, Fax 10 01

Weingut Leo Fuchs
56829 Pommern, Hauptstraße 3
Tel. (0 26 72) 13 26, Fax 13 36

Weingut Joh. Haart
54498 Piesport,
Sankt-Michael-Straße 47
Tel. (0 65 07) 29 55, Fax 61 55

Weingut Heinrichshof
Karl-Heinz Griebeler
54492 Zeltingen-Rachtig,
Chur-Kölner-Straße 23
Tel. (0 65 32) 31 51, Fax 31 51

Weinhof Herrenberg
Claudia Loch
54441 Schoden, Hauptstraße 80
Tel. (0 65 81) 12 58, Fax 12 58

Weingut Herrenberg
Bert Simon
54455 Serrig, Römerstraße 63
Tel. (0 65 81) 22 08, Fax 22 42

Weingut Jordan & Jordan
54459 Wiltingen, Dehenstraße 2
Tel. (0 65 01) 1 65 10, Fax 1 31 06

Weingut Kanzlerhof
54340 Pölich, Hauptstraße 23
Tel. (0 65 07) 31 93, Fax 31 93

Weingut Chr. Karp-Schreiber
54472 Brauneberg, Moselweinstraße 186
Tel. (0 65 34) 2 36, Fax 7 90

Weingut Sybille Kuntz
54470 Lieser, Moselstraße 25
Tel. (0 65 31) 9 10 00, Fax 9 10 01

Weingut Christa Lenhardt
54346 Mehring, Wiesenflurweg 4
Tel. (0 65 02) 72 98, Fax 72 03

Weingut Lubentiushof
56332 Niederfell, Kehrstraße 16
Tel. (0 26 07) 81 35, Fax 84 25

Weingut Martin Müllen
56841 Traben-Trarbach, Schwanenstraße 8
Tel. (0 65 41) 94 70, Fax 94 70

Weingut Norwig-Schreiber
54472 Burgen, Am Frohnbach 1
Tel. (0 65 34) 7 63, Fax 7 63

Weingut Franz-Josef Regnery
54340 Klüsserath, Mittelstraße 39
Tel. (0 65 07) 46 36, Fax 30 53

Weingut Winfried Reh
54340 Schleich, Weierbachstraße 12
Tel. (0 65 07) 9 91 10, Fax 9 91 11

Weingut Hans Resch
54459 Wiltingen, Kirchstraße 29
Tel. (0 65 01) 1 64 50, Fax 1 45 86

Weingut Heinrich Schmitges
☞ *See below, page 244*

Weingut Erben Hubert Schmitges
54492 Erden, Hauptstraße 79
Tel. (0 65 32) 22 33

Weingut Carl Schmitt-Wagner
54340 Longuich, Mühlenstraße 3
Tel. (0 65 02) 24 37, Fax 99 44 30

Weingut Alfons Stoffel
54340 Leiwen, Maximinstraße 15
Tel. (0 65 07) 33 12, Fax 46 51

Wein- und Sektgut Thielen
56856 Zell-Merl, Im Stephansberg
Tel. (0 65 42) 2 17 45, Fax 2 17 45

WEINGUT ERBEN VON BEULWITZ

Owner and manager: Herbert Weis
Winemaker: Stefan Rauen
54318 Mertesdorf,
Eitelsbacher Straße 4
Tel. (06 51) 9 56 10, Fax 9 56 11 50
Directions: A 48, exit Kenn–Ruwertal, in the direction of Mertesdorf
Opening hours: By appointment
Restaurant: "Vinum"
Open daily from 10 a.m. to 10 p.m.
Specialties: Terrine of smoked Ruwer trout

Vineyard area: 3.4 hectares
Annual production: 28,000 bottles
Top sites: Kaseler Nies'chen, Kehrnagel and Hitzlay
Soil types: Weathered slate
Grape varieties: 100% Riesling
Average yield: 58 hl/ha
Best vintages: 1994, 1995, 1997
Member: Bernkasteler Ring

Tradition counts for a great deal among the von Beulwitz heirs. They can boast that they won an award at the Paris world fair in 1867, yet the present owner, Herbert Weis, who acquired the estate in Kasel from the Fumetti family in 1982 and subsequently merged it with his own property in Mertesdorf, need not look to the past. The 1995 wines were so outstanding that they catapulted him into the ranks of the top five estates in the Ruwer valley. The dry 1996 wines couldn't match those of the previous vintage, but the Auslese were once again top notch; and the 1997s are sensational! Weis gives the credit for his success to the vineyards, where Riesling vines planted on their own roots still survive. In addition he continues to cultivate in the traditional fashion on individual stakes; low yields complete the picture. A quaint little hotel and restaurant are attached to the estate.

1996 Kaseler Nies'chen
Riesling Spätlese – 6 –
16.50 DM, 8.5%, ♀ till 2002 **84**

1997 Kaseler Nies'chen
Riesling Kabinett halbtrocken
9.80 DM, 10%, ♀ till 2001 **86**

1997 Kaseler Nies'chen
Riesling Spätlese trocken
19.40 DM, 11%, ♀ till 2003 **88**

1996 Kaseler Nies'chen
Riesling Spätlese – 7 –
12.50 DM, 7.5%, ♀ till 2003 **88**

1997 Kaseler Nies'chen
Riesling Kabinett
9.80 DM, 8%, ♀ till 2005 **89**

1997 Kaseler Nies'chen
Riesling Spätlese
14.50 DM, 8%, ♀ till 2005 **91**

1996 Kaseler Nies'chen
Riesling Auslese – 9 –
25 DM, 7.5%, ♀ till 2008 **91**

1997 Kaseler Nies'chen
Riesling Auslese – 10 –
28.50 DM, 8%, ♀ till 2006 **92**

1997 Kaseler Nies'chen
Riesling Auslese – 11 –
53.35 DM, 8%, ♀ till 2008 **94**

1996 Kaseler Nies'chen
Riesling Eiswein
130 DM/0.5 liter, 9%, ♀ 2000 till 2010 **94**

BISCHÖFLICHE WEINGÜTER

Owner: Bischöfliches Priesterseminar and Konvikt, Hohe Domkirche Trier
Director: Wolfgang Richter
Winemaker: Johannes Becker
54290 Trier, Gervasiusstraße 1
Tel. (06 51) 4 34 41, Fax 4 02 53
e-mail: Bischoefliche.Weingueter. Trier@t-online.de
Directions: In the center of Trier
Sales: Erwin Engel
Opening hours: Mon.–Fri. 9 a.m. to 5 p.m.
Worth seeing: 400-year-old vaulted cellars

Vineyard area: 97 hectares
Annual production: 650,000 bottles
Top sites: Scharzhofberger, Erdener Prälat, Ürziger Würzgarten, Kaseler Nies'chen
Soil types: Devon slate and grey slate
Grape varieties: 98% Riesling, 2% Spätburgunder
Average yield: 60 hl/ha
Best vintages: 1994, 1995, 1997

This estate owns excellent vineyards in the Mosel, Saar and Ruwer valleys. In the legendary Scharzhofberg vineyard alone the estate is blessed with six hectares. It came to its present form through the amalgamation of three once independent ecclesiastical properties: the Hohe Domkirche, the Bischöfliche Priesterseminar and the Bischöfliche Konvikt. The list of its top sites is almost endless, as are the passages through the extended cask cellar that lies beneath the old Roman city of Trier. The cellarmaster uses a bicycle to speed up his travels underground. Despite its size, this estate has again been producing racy, elegantly fruity Rieslings for several years now; the 1995 vintage was a fine confirmation of this fact. Although the ice wine from the Nies'chen vineyard was one of the finest wines of the year, the 1996s were not quite as good as the wines from previous vintages. The collection of 1997s has put the estate back on the quality map in Trier!

1996 Ayler Kupp
Riesling Auslese trocken
20 DM, 11%, ♀ till 2002 **86**

1996 Dhron Hofberger
Riesling Spätlese halbtrocken
12.70 DM, 9.5%, ♀ till 2001 **86**

1996 Scharzhofberger
Riesling Kabinett
12 DM, 8.5%, ♀ till 2003 **86**

1996 Wiltinger Kupp
Riesling Spätlese
12.70 DM, 8%, ♀ till 2004 **86**

1997 Scharzhofberger
Riesling Auslese trocken
25 DM, 12.5%, ♀ till 2004 **88**

1997 Kaseler Nies'chen
Riesling Spätlese
14 DM, 8.5%, ♀ till 2005 **88**

1996 Dhron Hofberger
Riesling Auslese
20 DM, 7%, ♀ till 2005 **89**

1997 Eitelsbacher Marienholz
Riesling Auslese Goldkapsel
24 DM/0.5 liter, 7.5%, ♀ till 2008 **91**

1997 Kanzemer Altenberg
Riesling Auslese Goldkapsel
28 DM/0.5 liter, 7.5%, ♀ till 2007 **91**

1996 Kaseler Nies'chen
Riesling Eiswein
100 DM/0.375 liter, ♀ till 2010 **94**

WEINGUT JOH. JOS. CHRISTOFFEL ERBEN

Owner: Hans Leo Christoffel
54539 Ürzig, Schanzstraße 2
Tel. (0 65 32) 21 76, Fax 14 71
Directions: Via the B 53
Sales: Hilde and Hans Leo Christoffel
Opening hours: By appointment
History: Owned by the family for 400 years
Worth seeing: Traditional German house, which is a historic monument

Vineyard area: 2.2 hectares
Annual production: 20,000 bottles
Top sites: Erdener Treppchen, Ürziger Würzgarten
Soil types: Weathered Devon slate, with reddish bands
Grape varieties: 100% Riesling
Average yield: 80 hl/ha
Best vintages: 1995, 1996, 1997
Member: VDP

The vineyards of Hans Leo Christoffel and his family are small but of extremely high quality. Planted only with Riesling vines, most are still on their own roots and all trained in the traditional fashion on individual stakes in the celebrated steep slate vineyards of Erdener Treppchen and Ürziger Würzgarten. Thanks to rigorously selective harvesting, gentle pressing and cautious aging of the wines in old wooden casks, Christoffel strives to produce racy Rieslings that are typical of their vintage – and succeeds marvelously! He is particularly proud of his top dry wines, and in good vintages they can be remarkable. However, the true potential of his vineyards is more clearly shown in the delicately fruity, noble late harvest Rieslings. In his top vineyard, the Ürziger Würzgarten, Christoffel sometimes differentiates between no fewer than five Auslese, which he labels with stars to distinguish them. The excellent 1996 and stunning 1997 ranges confirm the success story of this estate and reinforce its standing among the top producers of the region.

1996 Erdener Treppchen
Riesling Kabinett
12.50 DM, 7.5%, ♀ till 2003 **88**

1997 Ürziger Würzgarten
Riesling Kabinett
12.40 DM, 7.5%, ♀ till 2005 **88**

1997 Ürziger Würzgarten
Riesling Spätlese
15.20 DM, 8%, ♀ till 2006 **91**

1996 Ürziger Würzgarten
Riesling Spätlese
15.50 DM, 7.5%, ♀ till 2005 **92**

1996 Ürziger Würzgarten
Riesling Auslese **
30 DM, 7.5%, ♀ till 2006 **94**

1997 Ürziger Würzgarten
Riesling Auslese ***
48 DM, 8%, ♀ till 2010 **94**

1997 Ürziger Würzgarten
Riesling Auslese Goldkapsel
130.15 DM, 8.5%, ♀ till 2012 **94**

1997 Ürziger Würzgarten
Riesling Beerenauslese
Not yet for sale, 7.5%, ♀ till 2009 **94**

1997 Ürziger Würzgarten
Riesling Eiswein
120 DM/0.375 liter, 7.5%, ♀ till 2015 **96**

WEINGUT ERNST CLÜSSERATH

Owner: Ernst Clüsserath
54349 Trittenheim, Moselweinstr. 67
Tel. (0 65 07) 26 07, Fax 66 07
Directions: A 1 from the north, exit Salmtal, A 1 from the south, exit Mehring
Sales: Ernst Clüsserath
Opening hours: By appointment
Hotel: Bed and breakfast

Vineyard area: 2.7 hectares
Annual production: 25,000 bottles
Top sites: Trittenheimer Apotheke and Altärchen
Soil types: Rocky weathered slate
Grape varieties: 93% Riesling, 5% Müller-Thurgau, 2% Kerner
Average yield: 70 hl/ha
Best vintages: 1990, 1994, 1995
Member: Bernkasteler Ring

This estate is one of those small family properties on the middle stretch of the Mosel that often do not receive much attention but that nonetheless continue to produce wines of above average quality. Ernst Clüsserath has been responsible for the cellar since 1982 and in 1991 took over full control of the business. Since then he has garnered much critical acclaim: from the top German prize and an accolade from the International Wine Challenge to the Decanter Award, he now has numerous certificates to hang on his walls. As was the case in 1994, we found the sweeter 1995 Rieslings most convincing. Astonishingly, in 1996 he changed his emphasis to off-dry styles, which most consumers will still find more than dry enough. In 1997 the range is more evenly mixed. Be that as it may, the Auslese from the Apotheke is the highlight of the vintage.

1997 Trittenheimer Apotheke
Riesling Spätlese trocken
14 DM, 11.5%, ♀ till 2001 **82**

1996 Trittenheimer Apotheke
Riesling Spätlese trocken
13 DM, 11.5%, ♀ till 2001 **84**

1996 Trittenheimer Altärchen
Riesling Kabinett halbtrocken
9.10 DM, 9.5%, ♀ till 2002 **84**

1997 Trittenheimer Altärchen
Riesling Kabinett halbtrocken
9.30 DM, 10%, ♀ till 2002 **84**

1997 Trittenheimer Apotheke
Riesling Spätlese halbtrocken
14 DM, 11.5%, ♀ till 2002 **84**

1996 Trittenheimer Apotheke
Riesling Spätlese halbtrocken
13 DM, 10.5%, ♀ till 2002 **86**

1996 Trittenheimer Apotheke
Riesling Spätlese
13 DM, 9.5%, ♀ till 2005 **86**

1997 Trittenheimer Apotheke
Riesling Spätlese
14 DM, 9%, ♀ till 2004 **86**

1996 Trittenheimer Apotheke
Riesling Auslese halbtrocken
23 DM, 11.5%, ♀ till 2004 **89**

1997 Trittenheimer Apotheke
Riesling Auslese
21 DM, 8.5%, ♀ till 2008 **89**

WEINGUT CLÜSSERATH-WEILER

Owner: Helmut and Hilde Clüsserath
Winemaker: Helmut Clüsserath
54349 Trittenheim,
Haus an der Brücke
Tel. (0 65 07) 50 11, Fax 56 05
Directions: A 1 from the north, exit Salmtal, A 1 from the south, exit Mehring
Sales: Hilde Clüsserath
Opening hours: By appointment
Guest house: View onto the Mosel and the vineyards
Worth seeing: Vaulted cellars from the turn of the century

Vineyard area: 4.2 hectares
Annual production: 35,000 bottles
Top sites: Trittenheimer Apotheke and Altärchen
Soil types: Slate
Grape varieties: 100% Riesling
Average yield: 75 hl/ha
Best vintages: 1995, 1996, 1997

Helmut Clüsserath has won numerous awards for his wines in recent years. That comes as little surprise, since his family has always placed quality at the top of its list of priorities. At the turn of the century his grandfather belonged to the pioneers who began selling their wines in bottle; it was also he who constructed the attractive vaulted cellars, in which the wines still age in oak casks for up to two years before bottling. The average age of the vines is about 25 years. Two thirds of the wines are made in either a dry or an off-dry style, and in varying degrees of quality, depending on the vintage. Whereas the dry 1995 range showed a perfectly brilliant character, the 1996s resembled the zesty 1994 collection. The 1997s are well balanced across the board and reflect well the estate's true capabilities.

1996 Trittenheimer Apotheke
Riesling Spätlese – 10 –
16 DM, 8%, ♀ till 2003 **86**

1996 Mehringer Zellerberg
Riesling Auslese halbtrocken
24 DM, 12%, ♀ till 2003 **89**

1996 Trittenheimer Apotheke
Riesling Spätlese ** – 4 –
20 DM, 8.5%, ♀ till 2005 **89**

1997 Trittenheimer Apotheke
Riesling Spätlese * – 24 –
18 DM, 8.5%, ♀ till 2005 **89**

1997 Trittenheimer Apotheke
Riesling Spätlese ** – 15 –
20 DM, 9%, ♀ till 2006 **89**

1997 Trittenheimer Apotheke
Riesling Auslese – 18 –
30 DM, 8%, ♀ till 2008 **91**

1996 Trittenheimer Apotheke
Riesling Auslese ** – 18 –
35 DM/0.5 liter, 8%, ♀ till 2008 **92**

1997 Trittenheimer Apotheke
Riesling Auslese ** – 26 –
40 DM/0.5 liter, 8%, ♀ till 2008 **92**

1997 Trittenheimer Apotheke
Riesling Beerenauslese – 26 –
70 DM/0.375 liter, 8.5%, ♀ till 2009 **94**

WEINGUT ERBEN STEPHAN EHLEN

Owner: Stephan Ehlen
54492 Lösnich, Hauptstraße 21
Tel. (0 65 32) 23 88
Directions: A 48, exit Wittlich, in the direction of Zeltingen, left after the bridge, after five kilometers opposite the fountain
Sales: Stephan Ehlen
Opening hours: By appointment
History: Owned by the family since 1648
Worth seeing: Vaulted cellars

Vineyard area: 2.2 hectares
Annual production: 20,000 bottles
Top sites: Erdener Treppchen, Lösnicher Försterlay, Erdener Bußlay
Soil types: Slate, sandy loam
Grape varieties: 75% Riesling, 15% Kerner, 10% Müller-Thurgau
Average yield: 75 hl/ha
Best vintages: 1994, 1995, 1997
Member: Bernkasteler Ring

The slate house, which the owner's grandfather built in 1889, adorns to this day the traditional label of this estate; the property, however, has been in the family's hands for over three centuries. Be that as it may, its performance has never been of such high caliber as over the past ten years. Year in and year out the experienced Stephan Ehlen produces a fine range of wines, whose strength lies in the fruitier, sweeter styles. Most of the vines are trained on individual stakes and have an average age of 45 years! Ehlen has also reduced the yields in the past few years. The 1996 collection, although good, didn't quite match the quality of the two previous vintages. The 1997s are similar, good but without the complexity of the finer estates.

1997 Riesling
Hochgewächs
7.50 DM, 9.5%, ♀ till 2003 **82**

1996 Erdener Treppchen
Riesling Kabinett
8.25 DM, 8.5%, ♀ till 2001 **86**

1997 Erdener Treppchen
Riesling Kabinett
8.50 DM, 7.5%, ♀ till 2004 **86**

1996 Lösnicher Försterlay
Riesling Spätlese
11 DM, 8%, ♀ till 2003 **86**

1996 Erdener Treppchen
Riesling Spätlese
12.50 DM, 8%, ♀ till 2003 **86**

1997 Erdener Treppchen
Riesling Spätlese
12 DM, 8.5%, ♀ till 2005 **86**

1997 Lösnicher Försterlay
Riesling Auslese
20 DM, 8%, ♀ till 2005 **88**

1996 Erdener Treppchen
Riesling Auslese – 6 –
20 DM, 8%, ♀ till 2006 **89**

1997 Erdener Treppchen
Riesling Auslese
34.80 DM, 8%, ♀ till 2007 **89**

1996 Erdener Treppchen
Riesling Auslese
32 DM, 8%, ♀ till 2006 **91**

WEINGUT FRANZ-JOSEF EIFEL

Owner: Franz-Josef Eifel
54349 Trittenheim,
Engelbert-Schue-Weg 2
Tel. (0 65 07) 7 00 09, Fax 70 14 40
Directions: A 1, exit Salmtal, or A 62, exit Mehring
Sales: Franz-Josef and Sabine Eifel
Opening hours: By appointment

Vineyard area: 4 hectares
Annual production: 25,000 bottles
Top sites: Trittenheimer Apotheke, Neumagener Rosengärtchen
Soil types: Slate, gravel, sand
Grape varieties: 80% Riesling, 13% Müller-Thurgau, 7% Kerner
Average yield: 71 hl/ha
Best vintages: 1995, 1996, 1997

Wines from this small estate in Trittenheim are unmistakable: on the label the property's owner Franz-Josef Eifel vouches for the quality of each bottle's contents with his own fingerprint. Although it certainly grabs the limelight, his spirited signature implies a healthy self-confidence, which is well founded. Since 1993 the yields have been kept within limits; and quality has increased. The trio of vintages from 1993 to 1995 moved from strength to strength. The 1996 range carries this development a step further; and although the Auslese is not quite as spicy, the 1997s are on the whole even a touch better. Moreover, selective harvesting – with up to three pickings in each vineyard – has enhanced the quality of the wines even further. With about 20 percent of the production still being sold off in casks, only the best wines of each vintage find their way into bottles, most of which are sold to a loyal following of private customers.

1996 Trittenheimer Altärchen
Riesling Kabinett halbtrocken
10.50 DM, 10%, ♀ till 2001 **84**

1997 Trittenheimer Apotheke
Riesling Spätlese trocken
18 DM, 12%, ♀ till 2004 **86**

1997 Neumagener Rosengärtchen
Riesling Spätlese halbtrocken
16 DM, 11%, ♀ till 2005 **86**

1996 Trittenheimer Altärchen
Riesling Spätlese
15 DM, 8.5%, ♀ till 2004 **86**

1996 Trittenheimer Apotheke
Riesling Spätlese
16 DM, 8.5%, ♀ till 2003 **88**

1997 Trittenheimer Altärchen
Riesling Spätlese
16 DM, 8%, ♀ till 2004 **88**

1997 Trittenheimer Apotheke
Riesling Spätlese
18 DM, 8.5%, ♀ till 2006 **89**

1997 Trittenheimer Apotheke
Riesling Auslese
Not yet for sale, 8.5%, ♀ till 2007 **89**

1996 Trittenheimer Apotheke
Riesling Auslese
Not yet for sale, 7.5%, ♀ till 2005 **92**

WEINGUT ROBERT EYMAEL – MÖNCHHOF

Owner: Robert Eymael
General Manager: Robert Eymael, Volker Besch
Winemaker: Robert Eymael
54539 Ürzig, Mönchhof
Tel. (0 65 32) 9 31 64, Fax 9 31 66
Directions: A 48 Koblenz–Trier, exit Wittlich, in the direction of Traben-Trarbach
Sales: Robert Eymael, Volker Besch
Opening hours: Mon.–Fri. 9 a.m. to 8 p.m., Sat. and Sun. 11 a.m. to 8 p.m.
History: Winery based in Mönchhof since 1177, when it was owned by Cistercian monks. Since 1803 the property of the Eymael family
Worth seeing: Medieval vaulted cellars; the main buildings are a historic monument

Vineyard area: 10 hectares
Annual production: 60,000 bottles
Top sites: Ürziger Würzgarten, Erdener Treppchen and Prälat
Soil types: Devon slate, loam with slate and red sandstone
Grape varieties: 100% Riesling
Average yield: 60 hl/ha
Best vintages: 1996, 1997
Member: VDP

As the location of the television series "Moselbrück" this estate experienced its last moment of glory. Within a few months both Robert Eymael and his wife died. Despite these unexpected difficulties Robert Eymael Jr. decided to revive the family estate and has now taken sole charge of the strategy of the property; and the quality of the wines is being restored. The 1996 range staged a significant comeback and fostered dreams of further improvements to come. The 1997s have brought some of these to life. Demand for the better wines has even encouraged Eymael to lease another ten acres of vineyards in the finest neighboring sites, including a choice parcel in the Erdener Prälat.

1996 Ürziger Würzgarten
Riesling Kabinett
12.80 DM, 8.5%, ♀ till 2003 **82**

1996 Ürziger Würzgarten
Riesling Spätlese
16.50 DM, 8%, ♀ till 2004 **84**

1997 Ürziger Würzgarten
Riesling Spätlese
16.80 DM, 7.5%, ♀ till 2004 **86**

1997 Erdener Treppchen
Riesling Spätlese
19.80 DM, 7.5%, ♀ till 2004 **86**

1997 Ürziger Würzgarten
Riesling Auslese
32.50 DM, 7.5%, ♀ till 2005 **86**

1997 Ürziger Würzgarten
Riesling Auslese Goldkapsel
45 DM/0.375 liter, 7.5%, ♀ till 2003 **86**

1996 Ürziger Würzgarten
Riesling Auslese
28.50 DM, 7.5%, ♀ till 2005 **88**

1997 Erdener Prälat
Riesling Auslese
32.50 DM, 7.5%, ♀ till 2008 **89**

1996 Erdener Prälat
Riesling Auslese
94 DM/0.375 liter, 7.5%, ♀ till 2008 **91**

1996 Ürziger Würzgarten
Riesling Auslese lange Goldkapsel
146 DM/0.375 liter, 7.5%, ♀ till 2009 **92**

WEINGUT REINHOLD FRANZEN

Owner: Ulrich Franzen
56814 Bremm, Gartenstraße 14
Tel. (0 26 75) 4 12, Fax 16 55
Directions: From Koblenz, Bremm lies 50 kilometers upstream between Cochem and Zell
Sales: Iris and Ulrich Franzen
Opening hours: By appointment

Vineyard area: 4.2 hectares
Annual production: 40,000 bottles
Top sites: Bremmer Calmont, Neefer Frauenberg
Soil types: Devon slate, sandy loam
Grape varieties: 70% Riesling, 13% Weißburgunder, 7% Elbling, 5% Spätburgunder, 5% other varieties
Average yield: 70 hl/ha
Best vintages: 1994, 1996, 1997
Member: Bernkasteler Ring

Ulrich Franzen boasts that he owns the "steepest vineyard in Europe," namely the Bremmer Calmont. Certainly this young grower obtains his finest Rieslings from these terraced slate soils; yet he also produces quite remarkable wines from the Neefer Frauenberg. Franzen rounds out his range with Weißburgunder and Spätburgunder as well as Elbling, which thrive on loamy soils and thus seldom have the distinction of the Rieslings. Long ago he renounced the "light little Mosel wines supported with a dash of sweetness." Instead, he has focused his attention on the production of concentrated dry wines. For years he did without indications of quality levels such as Spätlese or Auslese and marketed his finest wines using golden capsules. This has only added to the confusion, for in the last two years "Prädikatsweine" with discreet levels of residual sugar have resurfaced. In quality the solid 1996 range was similar to that of the preceding vintage. The excellent 1997s set a new frame of reference for the estate!

1996 Bremmer Calmont
Riesling trocken
15 DM, 11.5%, ♀ till 2001 **86**

1996 Bremmer Calmont
Riesling trocken Goldkapsel
25 DM, 12%, ♀ till 2001 **86**

1996 Neefer Frauenberg
Riesling Spätlese
25 DM, 11%, ♀ till 2002 **86**

1997 Neefer Frauenberg
Riesling trocken
13.50 DM, 11.5%, ♀ till 2002 **86**

1997 Bremmer Calmont
Riesling trocken Goldkapsel
25 DM, 12%, ♀ till 2004 **88**

1997 Bremmer Calmont
Riesling trocken
15 DM, 12%, ♀ till 2004 **89**

1997 Neefer Frauenberg
Riesling trocken Goldkapsel
25 DM, 13%, ♀ till 2005 **89**

1997 Neefer Frauenberg
Riesling Auslese halbtrocken
38.30 DM, 12%, ♀ till 2006 **90**

1997 Bremmer Calmont
Riesling Auslese
38 DM, 9%, ♀ till 2005 **91**

STIFTUNG FRIEDRICH-WILHELM-GYMNASIUM

Owner: A public trust fund
Director: Helmut Kranich
Winemaker: Günter Welter
54290 Trier, Weberbach 75
Tel. (06 51) 97 83 00, Fax 4 54 80
Directions: In the center of Trier, opposite the basilica
Sales: Ms. Schiff, Ms. Hasenstab
Opening hours: Mon.–Fri. 9 a.m. to 5:45 p.m., Sat. 9 a.m. to 1:30 p.m.
History: Founded in 1561 to support gifted children without means
Worth seeing: Old vaulted cellars

Vineyard area: 28 hectares
Annual production: 250,000 bottles
Top sites: Graacher Himmelreich and Domprobst, Zeltinger Sonnenuhr, Trittenheimer Apotheke, Neumagener Rosengärtchen, Mehringer Blattenberg
Soil types: Blue Devon slate, and slate ranging from sand to clay in content
Grape varieties: 90% Riesling, 10% Müller-Thurgau
Average yield: 75 hl/ha
Best vintages: 1993, 1994, 1996

The principal holdings of this estate lie on the Saar, but it also manages outstanding sites on the Mosel in Graach, Zeltingen and Trittenheim. Helmut Kranich, who is now the director, was in charge of the estate of Freiherr Langwerth von Simmern in the Rheingau for over a decade before coming here. This estate values tradition, both in the vineyard and in the cellar; however, it is also open to the latest technological developments. Hand picking is a matter of course, as is the aging of the wines in oak casks. The 1996 range was of thoroughly reliable quality; the dry wines were perceptibly superior to those of the previous vintage. The 1997s, on the other hand, are little more than pleasant.

1997 Trittenheimer Apotheke
Riesling Kabinett
11 DM, 7.5%, ♀ till 2002 **80**

1997 Bernkasteler Badstube
Riesling halbtrocken
8.80 DM, 11.5%, ♀ till 2002 **80**

1997 Graacher Himmelreich
Riesling Kabinett
11 DM, 8%, ♀ till 2003 **82**

1996 Bernkasteler Badstube
Riesling halbtrocken
8 DM, 10.5%, ♀ now **84**

1997 Neumagener Rosengärtchen
Riesling Spätlese
14.70 DM, 8%, ♀ till 2003 **84**

1997 Graacher Himmelreich
Riesling Auslese
20.50 DM, 8.5%, ♀ till 2005 **84**

1996 Trittenheimer Apotheke
Riesling Kabinett
10.60 DM, 8%, ♀ till 2001 **86**

1997 Zeltinger Sonnenuhr
Riesling Spätlese
14.70 DM, 7.5%, ♀ till 2005 **86**

1996 Graacher Himmelreich
Riesling Spätlese
15.40 DM, 8%, ♀ till 2003 **86**

1996 Mehringer Blattenberg
Riesling Auslese
19.70 DM, 8%, ♀ till 2005 **89**

WEINGUT LE GALLAIS

Owner: Gerald Villanova
General Manager: Egon Müller
Winemaker: Horst Frank
54459 Wiltingen,
Gutsverwaltung Scharzhof
Tel. (0 65 01) 1 72 32, Fax 15 02 63
Directions: From Trier via Konz, follow the direction to Wiltingen-Oberemmel
Opening hours: Tasting by appointment
Worth seeing: Scharzhof and park

Vineyard area: 4 hectares
Annual production: 20,000 bottles
Top site: Wiltinger Braune Kupp (sole owners)
Soil types: Weathered slate
Grape varieties: 100% Riesling
Average yield: 45 hl/ha
Best vintages: 1994, 1996, 1997
Member: VDP

Egon Müller's Scharzhof numbers among the most celebrated wine estates in Germany, if not the world. Since the 1950s the Müllers have also leased the Le Gallais estate in Kanzem, where they produce splendid wines in the steep Wiltinger Braune Kupp vineyard. Since the recent purchase of two hectares from the Vereinigten Hospitien this site is in the sole possession of Le Gallais. Compared with the Scharzhofberg, the Braune Kupp is somewhat lower in altitude and the average temperatures a touch higher. Moreover the soil is heavier, due to the higher loam content. For this reason the wines can, in certain vintages, be superior in both fruit and body to those of the Scharzhofberg. Not surprisingly, the noble late harvest wines produced here are often among the most interesting from the whole region. The magnificent 1994s offered eloquent evidence of this fact. The 1995 range didn't quite match these standards, but the 1996s again approached such quality. And the 1997s are first rate! A lovely Spätlese and an extremely elegant Gold Capsule Auslese are the proof. In lesser years the estate often sells off the bulk of its wines to wholesalers.

1996 Wiltinger Braune Kupp
Riesling Kabinett
20 DM, 8%, ♀ till 2001 **86**

1997 Wiltinger Braune Kupp
Riesling Kabinett
43 DM, 8%, ♀ till 2003 **88**

1997 Wiltinger Braune Kupp
Riesling Spätlese
38 DM, 8.5%, ♀ till 2005 **89**

1996 Wiltinger Braune Kupp
Riesling Spätlese – 15 –
28 DM, 7.5%, ♀ till 2003 **89**

1997 Wiltinger Braune Kupp
Riesling Spätlese
91 DM, 8%, ♀ till 2006 **91**

1996 Wiltinger Braune Kupp
Riesling Spätlese – 11 –
32 DM, 8.5%, ♀ till 2004 **91**

1997 Wiltinger Braune Kupp
Riesling Auslese
77 DM, 7.5%, ♀ till 2010 **94**

1996 Wiltinger Braune Kupp
Riesling Auslese Goldkapsel – 18 –
194 DM, 8%, ♀ till 2008 **94**

1997 Wiltinger Braune Kupp
Riesling Auslese Goldkapsel
267 DM, 7%, ♀ till 2012 **95**

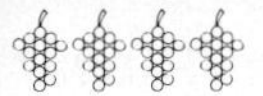

WEINGUT GRANS-FASSIAN

Owner: Gerhard Grans
54340 Leiwen, Römerstraße 28
Tel. (0 65 07) 31 70, Fax 81 67
Directions: A 48 Koblenz–Trier, exit Schweich, in the direction of Leiwen
Sales: Gerhard and Doris Grans
Opening hours: By appointment
Restaurant: "Landgasthof Grans-Fassian," Moselpromenade 4, 54349 Trittenheim, Tel. (0 65 07) 20 33, Fax 70 10 92, closed Monday
History: Owned by the family since 1624

Vineyard area: 8.4 hectares
Annual production: 65,000 bottles
Top sites: Trittenheimer Apotheke, Leiwener Laurentiuslay, Piesporter Goldtröpfchen
Soil types: Devon slate
Grape varieties: 89% Riesling, 6% Weißburgunder, 5% other varieties
Average yield: 68 hl/ha
Best vintages: 1993, 1995, 1996

When in the mid-1980s the young growers of Leiwen resolved to draw attention to the quality potential of their village, Gerhard Grans was at the forefront of the movement. He continually produces Rieslings with fine polish and robust acidity. The dry wines, which make up about half of the production, are impressive in their body and structure, even though they often taste somewhat angular and roughly hewn. The 1996 range was above such criticism, but the 1997s are across the board, in spite of the high standard, not quite as successful. Grans makes a humorous joke with the "Cuvée 9": the large numeral on the label refers to the low alcoholic content of this delicious summer wine. Recently he and his wife opened a wine bar in the house belonging to her parents along the river promenade in Trittenheim. The dining rooms have been renovated and Roland Preussler, the brother-in-law of the two-star chef Hans-Stefan Steinheuer, now prepares excellent local fare for his guests.

1997 Trittenheimer Altärchen
Riesling Kabinett
13.50 DM, 8.5%, ♀ till 2003 **86**

1996 Trittenheimer Apotheke
Riesling Spätlese
21 DM, 8%, ♀ till 2005 **89**

1997 Piesporter Goldtröpfchen
Riesling Spätlese
23 DM, 8.5%, ♀ till 2008 **91**

1997 Trittenheimer Apotheke
Riesling Spätlese – 12 –
25 DM, 9%, ♀ till 2007 **91**

1997 Trittenheimer Apotheke
Riesling Auslese – 11 –
29 DM, 8%, ♀ till 2008 **91**

1997 Trittenheimer Apotheke
Riesling Auslese Goldkapsel
60 DM, 8%, ♀ till 2007 **91**

1997 Trittenheimer Apotheke
Riesling Beerenauslese
150 DM/0.375 liter, 8.5%, ♀ till 2006 **91**

1996 Piesporter Goldtröpfchen
Riesling Auslese
29 DM, 8%, ♀ till 2007 **92**

1996 Trittenheimer Apotheke
Riesling Auslese Goldkapsel – 11 –
69 DM, 7.5%, ♀ till 2012 **94**

1996 Riesling
Eiswein Goldkapsel
230 DM/0.375 liter, 6.5%, ♀ till 2010 **95**

WEINGUT
GRANS-FASSIAN
1995
RIESLING
ALC. 10,0% VOL
750 ML
MOSEL-SAAR-RUWER

WEINGUT FRITZ HAAG

Owner: Wilhelm Haag
54472 Brauneberg,
Dusemonder Straße 44
Tel. (0 65 34) 4 10, Fax 13 47
Directions: A 48 Koblenz–Trier, exit Salmtal, in the direction of Bernkastel-Mülheim, B 53 to Brauneberg
Sales: Ilse Haag
Opening hours: By appointment
History: Owned by the family since 1605

Vineyard area: 7 hectares
Annual production: 65,000 bottles
Top sites: Brauneberger Juffer and Juffer-Sonnenuhr
Soil types: Slate
Grape varieties: 100% Riesling
Average yield: 68 hl/ha
Best vintages: 1993, 1994, 1997
Member: VDP

Few winemakers in the Mosel Valley pursue their profession with the dedication shown by Wilhelm Haag. That we named him Winemaker of the Year in 1994 was hardly accidental; he has worked hard for years to build his current reputation. The raw materials were developed by this man – famous for his ferocious handshake – through steady acquisitions of chosen parcels in the top vineyards of Brauneberg. But what is most impressive about Wilhelm Haag is the consistent high quality of his wines, from the basic dry Rieslings sold in liter bottles to the stunning noble late harvest wines, which fetch mind-boggling prices at the auctions held by the "Großer Ring" each autumn in Trier. Year after year his Rieslings are among the best to be found not only on the Mosel but anywhere in Germany. The 1995 range did not quite attain the ethereal heights of the splendid wines made in 1993 and 1994; nor were the 1996 Auslese quite as brilliant. Nonetheless, the two collections were very good for the respective vintages, reaching the quality levels expected from this estate. The 1997s are again brilliant, Riesling at its finest!

1997 Brauneberger Juffer-Sonnenuhr
Riesling Spätlese – 7 –
20 DM, 7.5%, ♀ till 2007 **94**

1997 Brauneberger Juffer-Sonnenuhr
Riesling Spätlese – 14 –
59 DM, 7%, ♀ till 2008 **94**

1996 Brauneberger Juffer-Sonnenuhr
Riesling Auslese Goldkapsel – 9 –
58 DM, 7%, ♀ till 2008 **94**

1997 Brauneberger Juffer-Sonnenuhr
Riesling Auslese lange Goldkapsel – 16 –
355 DM, 7%, ♀ till 2015 **94**

1997 Brauneberger Juffer-Sonnenuhr
Riesling Auslese Goldkapsel – 9 –
58 DM, 7%, ♀ till 2012 **95**

1997 Brauneberger Juffer-Sonnenuhr
Riesling Auslese Goldkapsel – 15 –
58 DM, 7.5%, ♀ till 2012 **95**

1996 Brauneberger Juffer-Sonnenuhr
Riesling Auslese Goldkapsel – 12 –
130 DM, 7%, ♀ till 2010 **95**

1996 Brauneberger Juffer-Sonnenuhr
Riesling Auslese lange Goldkapsel
258 DM, 7%, ♀ till 2012 **95**

1997 Brauneberger Juffer-Sonnenuhr
Riesling Beerenauslese
220 DM, 7%, ♀ till 2018 **95**

1997 Brauneberger Juffer-Sonnenuhr
Riesling Auslese Goldkapsel – 13 –
184 DM, 7%, ♀ till 2015 **96**

WEINGUT WILLI HAAG

Owner: Marcus Haag
54472 Brauneberg,
Moselweinstraße 173
Tel. (0 65 34) 4 50, Fax 6 89
Directions: A 48 Koblenz–Trier, exit Salmtal, in the direction of Bernkastel-Mülheim, B 53 to Brauneberg
Sales: Marcus and Inge Haag
Opening hours: By appointment
History: Estate in family ownership for 400 years

Vineyard area: 3.5 hectares
Annual production: 30,000 bottles
Top sites: Brauneberger Juffer-Sonnenuhr and Juffer
Soil types: Devon slate
Grape varieties: 100% Riesling
Average yield: 65 hl/ha
Best vintages: 1994, 1995, 1997
Member: VDP

In the early 1960s the Ferdinand Haag estate was divided between his sons Fritz and Willi. In 1994, after years of mediocrity, this estate emerged from the shadow of its perhaps overly dominant neighbor, Fritz Haag. The 1992 and 1993 vintages had already hinted at this development, but the true potential of this estate began to jell only in the following vintage. We were all the more astonished that the 1995 collection, albeit from an inferior vintage, was even better. While the 1996 wines weren't quite able to sustain this level of quality, they were nonetheless quite pleasant. The 1997s, if not dazzling, are nonetheless finer and again show this estate from its better side. The majority are made in a fruity sweetish style, destined for the export market.

1996 Brauneberger Juffer
Riesling Spätlese
10.50 DM, 8.5%, ♀ till 2003 **86**

1996 Brauneberger Juffer-Sonnenuhr
Riesling Spätlese
12.70 DM, 8.5%, ♀ till 2003 **86**

1997 Brauneberger Juffer-Sonnenuhr
Riesling Auslese – 11 –
18 DM, 8.5%, ♀ till 2005 **88**

1996 Brauneberger Juffer
Riesling Auslese
17 DM, 8.5%, ♀ till 2005 **88**

1996 Brauneberger Juffer-Sonnenuhr
Riesling Auslese
19.80 DM, 8.5%, ♀ till 2005 **88**

1996 Brauneberger Juffer
Riesling Auslese lange Goldkapsel
98 DM, 8.5%, ♀ till 2003 **88**

1997 Brauneberger Juffer-Sonnenuhr
Riesling Auslese – 10 –
18 DM, 9.5%, ♀ till 2006 **89**

1997 Brauneberger Juffer-Sonnenuhr
Riesling Auslese lange Goldkapsel – 13 –
62.15 DM/0.375 liter, 9%, ♀ till 2007 **89**

1997 Brauneberger Juffer-Sonnenuhr
Riesling Beerenauslese
Not yet for sale, 8.5%, ♀ till 2008 **91**

WEINGUT REINHOLD HAART

Owner: Theo Haart
54498 Piesport, Ausoniusufer 18
Tel. (0 65 07) 20 15, Fax 59 09
Directions: A 48 Koblenz–Trier, exit Salmtal, then down towards the Mosel valley
Sales: Theo and Edith Haart
Opening hours: By appointment
History: Estate has been owned by the family since 1337

Vineyard area: 6.7 hectares
Annual production: 55,000 bottles
Top sites: Piesporter Goldtröpfchen and Domherr
Soil types: Weathered clay and slate
Grape varieties: 100% Riesling
Average yield: 60 hl/ha
Best vintages: 1993, 1994, 1996
Member: VDP

The Haarts are by far the most well-established family of winemakers in Piesport; their cellar lies at the foot of the legendary Piesporter Goldtröpfchen vineyard. Current owner Theo Haart has more than doubled his vineyard holdings over the past decade by purchasing and leasing additional parcels of land. Today he owns a total of three hectares in the Goldtröpfchen. The 1996 range was perfect proof of the potential residing in these steep slate vineyards – and they highlighted both more elegance and balance than their predecessors at the same point in their development. The 1997s are again fine, but certainly not as impressive as either the 1996s or 1994s. Theo Haart continues to sell three fourths of his production abroad, with Japan taking an important share of each year's crop. The remainder of his wines are allocated to specialist merchants and private customers. Unfortunately, very little is sold to German restaurants. The neck label, with its characteristic Mickey Mouse ears harking back to a tradition from the first half of this century, was revived in 1988.

1997 Piesporter Goldtröpfchen
Riesling Kabinett
14 DM, 8.5%, 🍷 till 2005 **89**

1997 Piesporter Goldtröpfchen
Riesling Spätlese
22 DM, 8.5%, 🍷 till 2007 **89**

1996 Piesporter Goldtröpfchen
Riesling Kabinett
13.50 DM, 8.5%, 🍷 till 2005 **91**

1997 Wintricher Ohligsberg
Riesling Spätlese
20 DM, 8%, 🍷 till 2006 **91**

1996 Wintricher Ohligsberg
Riesling Spätlese
20 DM, 8%, 🍷 till 2006 **91**

1997 Piesporter Goldtröpfchen
Riesling Auslese
38 DM, 8.5%, 🍷 till 2008 **91**

1996 Piesporter Goldtröpfchen
Riesling Auslese – 8 –
38 DM, 7.5%, 🍷 till 2008 **92**

1996 Piesporter Goldtröpfchen
Riesling Spätlese
22 DM, 7.5%, 🍷 till 2006 **93**

1996 Piesporter Goldtröpfchen
Riesling Auslese – 11 –
60 DM, 7.5%, 🍷 till 2008 **95**

1996 Piesporter Goldtröpfchen
Riesling Beerenauslese
90 DM/0.375 liter, 7.5%, 🍷 till 2012 **96**

WEINGUT KURT HAIN

Owner: Gernot Hain
54498 Piesport, Am Domhof 5
Tel. (0 65 07) 24 42, Fax 68 79
Directions: A 48 Koblenz–Trier, exit Salmtal, in the direction of Klausen-Piesport, to the Mosel bridge
Opening hours: Mon.–Sat. 8 a.m. to 8 p.m.
Hotel and Weinhaus: "Piesporter Goldtröpfchen," open Mon.–Sun. from noon to 9 p.m.
Specialties: Regional fare
History: Estate owned by family since 1600
Worth seeing: 200-year-old vaulted cellars

Vineyard area: 4.8 hectares
Annual production: 35,000 bottles
Top sites: Piesporter Domherr and Goldtröpfchen, Neumagener Rosengärtchen, Dhron Hofberger
Soil types: Clay-slate, partially weathered
Grape varieties: 80% Riesling, 5% each of Weißburgunder, Spätburgunder, Bacchus and Müller-Thurgau
Average yield: 75 hl/ha
Best vintages: 1995, 1996, 1997

When Gernot Hain took over this estate in 1988 he was able to build upon the solid reputation of his ancestors. Not only had his father extended the hotel and winery, but he had also put the estate on new footing by acquiring some of the best vineyards in Piesport, thus laying the foundations for the current quality. In the damp vaulted cellars Gernot Hain oversees a distinctly reductive style of winemaking, which highlights the character of Piesporter's leading sites. He was initially advised by Reinhold Haart, yet his wines are not mere copies of his neighbor's successful example. Although the 1996s maintained the estate's image of quality, we were surprised that the Auslese often lacked polish. That problem has been solved with the 1997s, which are the finest wines that we have ever tasted from this up and coming producer.

1997 Piesporter Goldtröpfchen
Riesling Kabinett
8.50 DM, 8%, ♀ till 2003 **86**

1996 Piesporter Goldtröpfchen
Riesling Kabinett
8.20 DM, 8%, ♀ till 2002 **86**

1996 Piesporter Goldtröpfchen
Riesling Spätlese – 13 –
12 DM, 8%, ♀ till 2003 **86**

1996 Piesporter Goldtröpfchen
Riesling Auslese
17 DM/0.5 liter, 8%, ♀ till 2004 **86**

1996 Piesporter Goldtröpfchen
Riesling Auslese – 17 –
16 DM/0.5 liter, 8%, ♀ till 2005 **86**

1997 Piesporter Goldtröpfchen
Riesling Spätlese – 14 –
12.50 DM, 8.5%, ♀ till 2004 **88**

1997 Piesporter Goldtröpfchen
Riesling Spätlese – 12 –
11.50 DM, 8%, ♀ till 2004 **88**

1997 Piesporter Goldtröpfchen
Riesling Auslese
19 DM/0.5 liter, 9%, ♀ till 2005 **89**

1997 Piesporter Domherr
Riesling Auslese
21 DM, 8%, ♀ till 2006 **89**

1997 Piesporter Goldtröpfchen
Riesling Beerenauslese
34 DM/0.5 liter, 9.5%, ♀ till 2006 **89**

WEINGUT FREIHERR VON HEDDESDORFF

Owner: Andreas von Canal
56333 Winningen, Moselufer 1
Tel. (0 26 06) 96 20 33, Fax 96 20 34
e-mail:
WeingutvonHeddesdorff@t-online.de
Directions: From Koblenz via B 416, A61, exit Koblenz-Metternich
Sales: Andreas von Canal
Opening hours: Mon.–Fri. 9 a.m. to 6 p.m., on weekends by appointment
Worth seeing: 1000-year-old mansion on three floors, crenelated tower on the east corner

Vineyard area: 4 hectares
Annual production: 35,000 bottles
Top sites: Winninger Uhlen, Röttgen and Brückstück
Soil types: Slate
Grape varieties: 100% Riesling
Average yield: 60 hl/ha
Best vintages: 1995, 1996, 1997

The pedigreee of the Heddesdorff family stretches back to the time of the Crusades. Since 1424 the estate has been in the hands of the family, which until 1920 was largely a farming business. Andreas von Canal is yet another of those growers in Winningen – part of the "Deutsches Eck" at the confluence of the Mosel and Rhine rivers – who has pursued the path of quality. The prerequisites are, of course, owning the best vineyard sites and maintaining low yields. The estate is well represented in two top sites: Winninger Röttgen and Uhlen. And by means of natural farming practices von Canal strives to extract the best from his vines. Late harvesting, prolonged aging on the lees and early bottling are routine practices in the cellar, enabling him to retain both fruit and freshness in his wines. The 1996s and 1997s brought a new dimension of quality to the fore and confirm our judgment of this property as one of the best in Winningen.

1996 Winninger Hamm
Riesling halbtrocken
7 DM, 11%, ♀ till 2000 **84**

1997 Winninger Uhlen
Riesling Kabinett halbtrocken
8.50 DM, 9.5%, ♀ till 2003 **84**

1996 Winninger Hamm
Riesling Kabinett halbtrocken
8 DM, 9%, ♀ now **84**

1997 Winninger Röttgen
Riesling Spätlese halbtrocken
11 DM, 9.5%, ♀ till 2003 **84**

1997 Winninger Uhlen
Riesling trocken
8 DM, 12%, ♀ till 2002 **84**

1997 Winninger Röttgen
Riesling Spätlese
11 DM, 9%, ♀ till 2004 **86**

1996 Winninger Röttgen
Riesling Spätlese
11 DM, 9.5%, ♀ till 2003 **88**

1996 Winninger Brückstück
Riesling Auslese
16.50 DM/0.5 liter, 9%, ♀ till 2004 **88**

1997 Winninger Röttgen
Riesling Auslese
17 DM/0.5 liter, 8.5%, ♀ till 2007 **89**

Freiherr von Heddesdorff
RIESLING
1995er
Winninger Brückstück
Auslese
Gutsabfüllung · A. P.-Nr. 1 658 020 10 96 · Qualitätswein mit Prädikat
Mosel-Saar-Ruwer · 500 ml · Alc. 10.0 % by vol.
Weingut Freiherr von Heddesdorff · D-56333 Winningen

WEINGUT HEYMANN-LÖWENSTEIN

Owner: Reinhard Löwenstein
56333 Winningen, Bahnhofstraße 10
Tel. (0 26 06) 19 19, Fax 19 09
e-mail: heymann-loewenstein@msn.com
Directions: A 61, exit Koblenz-Metternich, in the direction of Winningen, main road to train tracks, left into Bahnhofstraße
Opening hours: Mon.–Fri. by appointment, Sat. 10 a.m. to 4 p.m.
Worth seeing: Art Nouveau winery, terraced vineyards with dry stone walls

Vineyard area: 6 hectares
Annual production: 45,000 bottles
Top sites: Winninger Uhlen and Röttgen
Soil types: Weathered slate
Grape varieties: 96% Riesling, 2% each of Müller-Thurgau and Weißburgunder
Average yield: 53 hl/ha
Best vintages: 1995, 1996, 1997
Member: VDP

Whoever phones the Heymann-Löwenstein estate need not feel slighted to find that the boss isn't around, for even the answering machine shows sparkling wit and originality. Further, no grower in Germany writes more intelligently about his wines than Reinhard Löwenstein, who is also one of the most persuasive champions of dry Mosel Rieslings. But this is just the cheerful marketing side of "Master" Löwenstein, who in the past few years has undergone an astonishing transformation from rebel to traditionalist. He used to ferment Beerenauslese to total dryness, but now professes the classical credo of the winemaker's craft. In 1994 he produced two outstanding Trockenbeerenauslese; and the top flight 1995s achieved new heights. The dry 1996s are of immaculate quality; the Trockenbeerenauslese close to perfection. The 1997s are even better! Further congratulations are also in order as this estate was the first in the "Deutsches Eck" to be admitted to the VDP.

1997 Winninger Uhlen
Riesling trocken
25 DM, 12%, ♀ till 2002 **88**

1996 Winninger Uhlen
Riesling trocken
25 DM, 12%, ♀ till 2003 **89**

1997 Riesling
trocken "Schieferterrassen"
14.50 DM, 11.5%, ♀ till 2003 **89**

1996 Winninger Röttgen
Riesling trocken
19.50 DM, 12%, ♀ till 2002 **90**

1997 Riesling
Auslese "Von blauem Schiefer"
27 DM, 9%, ♀ till 2010 **92**

1997 Winniger Röttgen
Riesling Auslese
32 DM, 8%, ♀ till 2012 **94**

1997 Winninger Uhlen
Riesling Auslese lange Goldkapsel
142 DM, 8%, ♀ till 2012 **95**

1997 Winninger Röttgen
Riesling Beerenauslese
150 DM/0.375 liter, 7.5%, ♀ till 2020 **96**

1996 Winninger Uhlen
Riesling Trockenbeerenauslese
430 DM/0.5 liter, 6.5%, ♀ 2002 till 2012 **96**

WEINGUT VON HÖVEL

Owner: Eberhard von Kunow
Winemaker: Hermann Jäger
54329 Konz-Oberemmel,
Agritiusstraße 56
Tel. (0 65 01) 1 53 84, Fax 1 84 98
Directions: B 51 towards Konz, in Konz follow signs to Oberemmel
Sales: Eberhard von Kunow
Opening hours: By appointment
History: Monastic quarters of the St. Maximin Abbey, since 1803 owned by the family
Worth seeing: Old monastic buildings, cellars from the 12th century

Vineyard area: 9 hectares
Annual production: 40,000 bottles
Top sites: Oberemmeler Hütte (sole owners), Scharzhofberger
Soil types: Devon slate
Grape varieties: 100% Riesling
Average yield: 48 hl/ha
Best vintages: 1994, 1995, 1997
Member: VDP

Eberhard von Kunow, the invariably good humored proprietor of this highly traditional estate, owns almost three hectares of the celebrated Scharzhofberg vineyard; however, his best wines often come from the five hectares in the Oberemmeler Hütte, of which he is the sole proprietor. In view of the delicate structure and lively acidity of his Rieslings, it is understandable that von Kunow ferments only a minority of his production to complete dryness. Nonetheless, his dry Weißburgunder is almost always appealing. In top years such as 1989, 1990 and 1995 von Kunow succeeds in producing excellent ice wines and Beerenauslese, which are regularly among the best of the region. The quality of the 1996 range was no match for those of the two preceding vintages, but the 1997s are again quite successful.

1997 Scharzhofberger
Riesling Kabinett halbtrocken
13.50 DM, 10%, ♀ till 2002 **84**

1996
Riesling
10.50 DM, 8.5%, ♀ till 2001 **86**

1997 Oberemmeler Hütte
Riesling Kabinett
13.50 DM, 8.5%, ♀ till 2004 **88**

1996 Oberemmeler Hütte
Riesling Kabinett
13 DM, 7.5%, ♀ till 2002 **88**

1996 Scharzhofberger
Riesling Kabinett
13 DM, 7.5%, ♀ till 2002 **88**

1997 Oberemmeler Hütte
Riesling Spätlese
16 DM, 7.5%, ♀ till 2006 **89**

1997 Oberemmeler Hütte
Riesling Spätlese
31.95 DM, 7%, ♀ till 2006 **89**

1997 Oberemmeler Hütte
Riesling Auslese
24 DM, 7.5%, ♀ till 2006 **91**

1997 Oberemmeler Hütte
Riesling Auslese Goldkapsel
36 DM/0.375 liter, 8%, ♀ till 2008 **92**

1997 Oberemmeler Hütte
Riesling Auslese Goldkapsel
60.35 DM/0.375 liter, 8%, ♀ till 2008 **92**

WEINGUT CARL AUGUST IMMICH – BATTERIEBERG

Owners: Gert and Sabine Basten
General manager: Sabine Basten
Winemaker: Uwe Jostock
56850 Enkirch, Im Alten Tal 2
Tel. (0 65 41) 8 30 50, Fax 83 05 16
Directions: A 48 Koblenz–Trier, exit Wittlich, in the direction of Traben-Trarbach
Sales: Sabine Basten
Opening hours: Mon.–Fri. 10 a.m. to noon and 2 p.m. to 5 p.m. , Sat. by appointment
Worth seeing: Medieval buildings, 1000-year-old cellars, bases of Roman columns in the old cask cellar

Vineyard area: 4.3 hectares
Annual production: 23,000 bottles
Top sites: Enkircher Batterieberg and Steffensberg
Soil types: Blue Devon slate
Grape varieties: 100% Riesling
Average yield: 45 hl/ha
Best vintages: 1995, 1996, 1997

The Immichs founded this estate in Enkirch in 1425. From the long line of family members, history will remember Georg-Heinrich Immich, who in the 19th century assaulted the slate massif of the present day Batterieberg vineyard with countless explosive charges in order to plant vines upon it. In 1989 Sabine and Gert Basten acquired this old estate. The new proprietors have invested considerable sums in renovating and restructuring the cellars. During this time there was also a radical departure from the conservative style of earlier years. Today all the wines are fermented at low temperatures in stainless steel tanks; only a few are left to evolve further for a few months in casks. The wines from the 1995 vintage were at that time the best that we had ever tasted from the Bastens' era, but the 1996s made it clear that the new owners were not content to rest on those laurels. The 1997s promise even finer things to come. This estate is on the right path!

1997 Enkircher Batterieberg
Riesling Spätlese trocken
17.80 DM, 12%, 🍷 till 2003 **84**

1997 Enkircher Batterieberg
Riesling Spätlese trocken **
19 DM, 12.5%, 🍷 till 2004 **86**

1997 Enkircher Batterieberg
Riesling Spätlese halbtrocken
17.80 DM, 11%, 🍷 till 2004 **86**

1996 Riesling
Kabinett
10.50 DM, 9%, 🍷 till 2001 **86**

1996 Enkircher Batterieberg
Riesling Spätlese
18.50 DM, 8%, 🍷 till 2002 **88**

1996 Enkircher Batterieberg
Riesling Auslese
28 DM, 7.5%, 🍷 till 2004 **89**

1997 Enkircher Steffensberg
Riesling Eiswein
69 DM/0.375 liter, 6.5%, 🍷 till 2010 **89**

1997 Enkircher Batterieberg
Riesling Spätlese
22 DM, 8%, 🍷 till 2008 **91**

1997 Enkircher Batterieberg
Riesling Auslese ***
38 DM/0.5 liter, 8%, 🍷 till 2010 **92**

1997 Enkircher Batterieberg
Riesling Beerenauslese
90 DM/0.375 liter, 7%, 🍷 till 2008 **92**

WEINGUT ALBERT KALLFELZ

Owner and director: Albert Kallfelz
Winemakers: Albert Kallfelz and Rüdiger Nilles
56856 Zell-Merl/Mosel, Hauptstraße 60–62
Tel. (0 65 42) 9 38 80, Fax 93 88 50
Directions: A 61, exit Rheinböllen, via Simmern to Zell-Merl
Sales: Ms. Kallfelz, Ms. Martiny and Albert Kallfelz Jr.
Opening hours: Mon.–Fri. 8 a.m. to 8 p.m., Sat. 9 a.m. to 2 p.m.
History: Wine estate since 1450

> Vineyard area: 27.5 hectares
> Annual production: 230,000 bottles
> Top sites: Merler Adler, Stephansberg, Königslay-Terrassen and Fettgarten
> Soil types: Slate, loam and loess
> Grape varieties: 84% Riesling, 9% Weißburgunder and 7% Müller-Thurgau
> Average yield: 85 hl/ha
> Best vintages: 1995, 1996, 1997

This is one of those successful family estates on the Mosel which are all too seldom mentioned in the press. Albert Kallfelz, however, has quite a bit to show for himself: over the last decade his wines have won a plethora of awards both at the provincial and at the federal level. Kallfelz is careful to keep his yields low; in 1996, for example, he produced only about 65 hectoliters per hectare. Kallfelz's booklet "Wine, People, Nature" contains useful information about his winemaking practices. He is sarcastic about wine politics and openly expresses his criticisms of the German wine laws. Only the wines from his top vineyards are released with a vineyard designation. The 1996s, like those from the previous vintage, were all well made, with the dry wines proving even more convincing than in earlier years. The 1997s are even better. This estate is on the rise.

1997 Merler Adler
Riesling Spätlese trocken
16.70 DM, 11%, ♀ till 2004 — **86**

1996 Merler Königslay-Terrassen
Riesling Spätlese
19.50 DM, 10%, ♀ till 2003 — **86**

1997 Merler Fettgarten
Riesling Spätlese trocken
16.50 DM/0.5 liter, 11%, ♀ till 2005 — **88**

1997 Merler Königslay-Terrassen
Riesling Spätlese halbtrocken
16.50 DM/0.5 liter, 11%, ♀ till 2006 — **88**

1997 Merler Stephansberg
Riesling Spätlese trocken
12.80 DM, 11%, ♀ till 2004 — **89**

1997 Merler Stephansberg
Riesling Spätlese halbtrocken
16.20 DM, 11%, ♀ till 2004 — **89**

1996 Merler Adler
Auslese
28 DM/0.375 liter, 9.5%, ♀ till 2006 — **89**

1997 Merler Königslay-Terrassen
Riesling Auslese halbtrocken
19 DM/0.5 liter, 12%, ♀ till 2006 — **90**

1997 Merler Stephansberg
Riesling Auslese – 50 –
26.50 DM/0.5 liter, 9%, ♀ till 2007 — **91**

WEINGUT KARLSMÜHLE

Owner: Peter Geiben
54318 Mertesdorf, Im Mühlengrund 1
Tel. (06 51) 51 24, Fax 5 20 16
Internet:
http://www.intrinet.de/karlsmuehle
Directions: A 48 Koblenz–Trier, exit Kenn-Ruwertal, in the direction of Mertesdorf, between Mertesdorf and Kasel
Opening hours: Mon.–Fri. 8 a.m. to 10 p.m., Sat. and Sun. 9 a.m. to 8 p.m. or by appointment
Restaurant: Daily from noon to midnight, except Mon.
Specialties: Trout in Riesling
Worth seeing: 600-year-old stone mill

Vineyard area: 12 hectares
Annual production: 65,000 bottles
Top sites: Lorenzhöfer Felslay and Mäuerchen, Kaseler Nies'chen and Kehrnagel
Soil types: Clay and slate
Grape varieties: 90% Riesling, 3% Spätburgunder, 2% each of Müller-Thurgau, Weißburgunder and Kerner, 1% Elbling
Average yield: 50 hl/ha
Best vintages: 1994, 1995, 1997

Since the time of Napoleon, the Geiben family has been making wine in the Ruwer valley. The core of their holdings are in the Lorenzhöfer Mäuerchen and Felslay vineyards, both of which are owned exclusively by the family. The unassuming Peter Geiben produces not only fine dry Riesling but has also mastered the art of the off-dry and sweeter styles. In 1994 Geiben raised the quality potential of his business by acquiring several top sites in Kasel from the former Patheiger estate, which he continues to market under a different label. Overall Geiben's 1996s didn't quite match the quality level of the very successful trio of vintages 1993, 1994 and 1995, but he bounced back with lovely 1997s, which he considers to be some of the finest wines that he has ever produced. Who are we to disagree?

1997 Lorenzhöfer
Riesling Kabinett halbtrocken
11 DM, 9.5%, ♀ till 2003 **86**

1997 Kaseler Nies'chen
Riesling Spätlese
22 DM, 10%, ♀ till 2006 **86**

1997 Lorenzhöfer
Riesling Auslese trocken
18.50 DM, 11%, ♀ till 2002 **88**

1996 Lorenzhöfer Mäuerchen
Riesling Kabinett
10.50 DM, 7.5%, ♀ till 2002 **88**

1996 Lorenzhöfer Felslay
Riesling Spätlese
18.50 DM, 8%, ♀ till 2004 **89**

1997 Kaseler Kehrnagel
Riesling Spätlese halbtrocken Patheiger
16.50 DM, 10.5%, ♀ till 2004 **91**

1996 Kaseler Nies'chen
Riesling Eiswein
64 DM/0.375 liter, 7%, ♀ till 2009 **91**

1997 Kaseler Kehrnagel
Riesling Auslese Patheiger
30 DM, 7.5%, ♀ till 2010 **92**

1997 Lorenzhöfer
Riesling Auslese lange Goldkapsel
49.50 DM, 7.5%, ♀ till 2010 **94**

WEINGUT KARTHÄUSERHOF

Owner: Christoph Tyrell
Winemaker: Ludwig Breiling
54292 Eitelsbach, Karthäuserhof
Tel. (06 51) 51 21, Fax 5 35 57
Directions: A 48, exit Kenn, in Ruwer on Brunnenplatz in the direction of Eitelsbach
Sales: Christoph and Graciela Tyrell
Opening hours: Mon.–Fri. 8 a.m. to 5 p.m. or by appointment
History: Prince Balduin of Luxemburg presented the estate to the Carthusian monks in 1335
Worth seeing: 13th-century water tower, historic tasting room with Delft tiles

Vineyard area: 19 hectares
Annual production: 150,000 bottles
Top site: Eitelsbacher Karthäuserhofberg
Soil types: Weathered Devon slate
Grape varieties: 94% Riesling, 6% Weißburgunder
Average yield: 55 hl/ha
Best vintages: 1994, 1995, 1997
Member: VDP

It is admirable to see how Graciela and Christoph Tyrell have, within a decade, restored this property to its place in the top ranks not only of the region but in all of Germany. Thanks to the amalgamation of the dispersed sites of Stirn, Kronenberg, Orthsberg and Sang into a single vineyard – owned exclusively by the estate and now known simply as the Eitelsbacher Karthäuserhofberg, it is much easier for Christoph Tyrell to explore numerous new possibilities through selective harvesting. The property, which is surrounded by a beautiful stand of old trees, has also been completely renovated. Apart from its finely balanced noble late harvest wines, Tyrell also produces dry wines that are often among the finest of the whole region. Not surprisingly, these are to be found on many of Germany's finest restaurant wine lists. The 1996 range, however good it was, did not quite attain the quality level of the excellent 1995 vintage. The 1997s, on the other hand, are the finest that Christoph Tyrell has produced since he took over the estate in 1986.

1997 Eitelsbacher Karthäuserhofberg
Riesling Kabinett
16 DM, 10%, ♀ till 2004 **88**

1997 Eitelsbacher Karthäuserhofberg
Riesling Spätlese
21 DM, 9.5%, ♀ till 2005 **89**

1997 Eitelsbacher Karthäuserhofberg
Riesling Auslese trocken Selection
39 DM, 12.5%, ♀ till 2006 **91**

1996 Eitelsbacher Karthäuserhofberg
Riesling Spätlese
18 DM, 7.5%, ♀ till 2005 **91**

1996 Eitelsbacher Karthäuserhofberg
Riesling Auslese – 34 –
41 DM, 7.5%, ♀ till 2008 **92**

1997 Eitelsbacher Karthäuserhofberg
Riesling Auslese – 18 –
47 DM, 9%, ♀ till 2008 **94**

1997 Eitelsbacher Karthäuserhofberg
Riesling Auslese – 34 –
62.10 DM, 8%, ♀ till 2008 **94**

1997 Eitelsbacher Karthäuserhofberg
Riesling Auslese Goldkapsel – 35 –
200 DM, 8%, ♀ till 2010 **95**

1996 Eitelsbacher Karthäuserhofberg
Riesling Eiswein
Not yet for sale, 7%, ♀ till 2012 **95**

1997 Eitelsbacher Karthäuserhofberg
Riesling Beerenauslese
Not yet for sale, 7%, ♀ till 2012 **95**

WINZERGENOSSENSCHAFT KASEL

Chairman: Ludwig Scherf
Winemaker: Ludwig Scherf
54317 Kasel, Schulstraße 1
Tel. (06 51) 5 21 17
Directions: A 48 Koblenz–Trier, exit Hermeskeil, on the B 52 to the exit Mertesdorf-Kasel
Sales: Ludwig Scherf
Opening hours: By appointment
History: Founded in 1934

Vineyard area: 3.6 hectares
Adherents: 16 members
Annual production: 20,000 bottles
Top sites: Kaseler Nies'chen, Kehrnagel and Herrenberg
Soil types: Weathered Devon slate
Grape varieties: 95% Riesling, 2% each of Müller-Thurgau and Kerner, 1% Optima
Average yield: 80 hl/ha
Best vintages: 1993, 1994

This is one of the smallest and certainly most appealing cooperatives in Germany. Its 16 members all pursue other professions during the day and tend their vineyards in the evening or on the weekend. Only Ludwig Scherf, who combines the roles of chairman and cellarmaster, is involved with the wine business during the day as the manager of Deinhard's vineyards in Kasel. In 1934 the four founding members of the cooperative purchased the cellars in Kasel from the Prüms of Wehlen, which continue to be used to make the wines. Once there were twice as many members as today, but the siblings often had no desire to carry on in their father's footsteps and sold their vineyards. The future of the union is thus far from secured; nor is the present altogether rosy. The 1995s were somewhat disappointing. However, the vintage 1996 did bring a slight improvement in quality. The 1997s are similar. The growers, though, are capable of infinitely more.

1997 Kaseler Kehrnagel
Riesling halbtrocken Hochgewächs
7.50 DM, 10.5%, ♀ till 2001 **77**

1996 Kaseler Nies'chen
Riesling Kabinett
7.50 DM, 8%, ♀ till 2001 **80**

1997 Kaseler Herrenberg
Riesling Kabinett
7.80 DM, 8%, ♀ till 2002 **82**

1996 Kaseler Herrenberg
Riesling trocken
7 DM, 9%, ♀ till 2000 **84**

1997 Kaseler Nies'chen
Riesling Spätlese
9.80 DM, 7.5%, ♀ till 2003 **84**

1997 Kaseler Kehrnagel
Riesling Auslese
15 DM, 8%, ♀ till 2005 **84**

1997 Mertesdorfer Herrenberg
Riesling Auslese
14.50 DM, 7%, ♀ till 2004 **84**

1996 Kaseler Nies'chen
Riesling Spätlese
9.80 DM, 8%, ♀ till 2001 **86**

1996 Riesling
Auslese
12 DM/0.5 liter, 8.5%, ♀ till 2003 **86**

1996 Riesling
Eiswein
60 DM/0.375 liter, 7%, ♀ till 2008 **92**

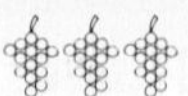

WEINGUT KEES-KIEREN

Owners: Ernst-Josef and Werner Kees
54470 Graach, Hauptstraße 22
Tel. (0 65 31) 34 28, Fax 15 93
Directions: A 48, exit Wittlich, in the direction of Bernkastel-Kues
Sales: Ernst-Josef Kees
Opening hours: Mon.–Fri. 9 a.m. to 7 p.m., Sat. 10 a.m. to 6 p.m. or by appointment
Restaurant: On Pentecost and just after Trinity Sunday from 11 a.m. to midnight
Specialties: "Gräwes," Riesling soup
History: Family business since 1648
Worth seeing: Vaulted cellars of 1826

Vineyard area: 4.5 hectares
Annual production: 40,000 bottles
Top sites: Graacher Domprobst and Himmelreich
Soil types: Devon slate
Grape varieties: 90% Riesling, 5% Kerner, 3% Müller-Thurgau and 2% Spätburgunder
Average yield: 70 hl/ha
Best vintages: 1994, 1995, 1997
Member: Bernkasteler Ring

In recent years this venerable estate in Graach has received numerous awards. Among others it shared with superstar Weil from the Rheingau the top prize from the "Pro Riesling" association. Ernst-Josef and Werner Kees attribute their success to the vineyards. In the autumn the grapes are picked in successive flights according to their ripeness levels. The goal of their vinification is to produce fresh, light Rieslings enlivened by racy acidity. The dry wines are often favored by those who like crisp Rieslings, but the strength of the estate clearly lies in the off-dry and delicately sweet wines. Such specialties result from partial fermentation to retain the natural residual sugars of the grapes. Our favorite wines from the last two vintages are the 1997 Graacher Himmelreich Kabinett and the 1996 Erdener Treppchen Spätlese, solid quality at fair prices.

1997 Kinheimer Rosenberg
Riesling halbtrocken Hochgewächs
8.50 DM, 11%, ♀ till 2002 **84**

1996 Graacher Domprobst
Riesling Spätlese halbtrocken
12.50 DM, 10%, ♀ till 2002 **86**

1997 Graacher Domprobst
Riesling Auslese ***
77.70 DM, 8.5%, ♀ till 2003 **86**

1997 Graacher Domprobst
Riesling Spätlese trocken
13 DM, 10.5%, ♀ till 2003 **88**

1997 Graacher Himmelreich
Riesling Kabinett
10 DM, 8%, ♀ till 2005 **88**

1997 Graacher Himmelreich
Riesling Hochgewächs
8.50 DM, 9.5%, ♀ till 2004 **88**

1997 Graacher Domprobst
Riesling Spätlese feinherb
16.25 DM, 9.5%, ♀ till 2003 **88**

1996 Graacher Himmelreich
Riesling Kabinett
9.50 DM, 8.5%, ♀ till 2004 **89**

1996 Erdener Treppchen
Riesling Spätlese *
17.60 DM, 8.5%, ♀ till 2006 **89**

WEINGUT HERIBERT KERPEN

Owner: Martin Kerpen
54470 Bernkastel-Wehlen, Uferallee 6
Tel. (0 65 31) 68 68, Fax 34 64
Directions: A 48 Koblenz–Trier, exit Wittlich, in the direction of Bernkastel-Kues, in village center close to riverbank
Opening hours: Mon.–Fri. 8 a.m. to 6 p.m., Sat., Sun., holidays and evenings by appointment
History: Winery now in its eighth generation
Worth seeing: Art Nouveau house along the banks of the Mosel, old basket press

Vineyard area: 5 hectares
Annual production: 40,000 bottles
Top sites: Wehlener Sonnenuhr, Graacher Domprobst and Himmelreich, Bernkasteler Bratenhöfchen
Soil types: Devon slate
Grape varieties: 100% Riesling
Average yield: 65 hl/ha
Best vintages: 1992, 1994, 1995
Member: Bernkasteler Ring

Alongside the various Prüm estates, the winery of Heribert Kerpen must be numbered among the finest producers in Wehlen. His vineyards in Wehlen, Bernkastel and Graach are a guaranty for success. In the early 1970s the family had already begun vinifying dry and off-dry wines, while continually improving the fruitier styles. Hanne Kerpen, who for years ran the estate while pursuing her profession as a schoolteacher, has now turned over the management of the business to her son Martin. He has concentrated his efforts on further improving the dry and off-dry wines. The 1994 Wehlener Sonnenuhr Auslese trocken won the "Feinschmecker" prize as Germany's best dry Riesling of that vintage. Be that as it may, we still rate the elegantly fruity Rieslings of the estate, which sadly account for only about half of the production, as their most brilliant wines. The last two vintages, although nice, were not as fine as the excellent 1994s and 1995s.

1997 Wehlener Sonnenuhr
Riesling Kabinett
10.90 DM, 8.5%, ♀ till 2003 **86**

1996 Wehlener Sonnenuhr
Riesling Kabinett
10.50 DM, 8.5%, ♀ till 2002 **86**

1997 Wehlener Sonnenuhr
Riesling Beerenauslese
65 DM/0.375 liter, 8%, ♀ till 2003 **86**

1997 Wehlener Sonnenuhr
Riesling Spätlese *
17.50 DM, 8%, ♀ till 2006 **89**

1996 Wehlener Sonnenuhr
Riesling Spätlese *
17.50 DM, 8.5%, ♀ till 2003 **89**

1996 Wehlener Sonnenuhr
Riesling Auslese ***
37 DM/0.375 liter, 8.5%, ♀ till 2003 **89**

1997 Wehlener Sonnenuhr
Riesling Auslese *
23 DM, 8%, ♀ till 2008 **91**

1996 Wehlener Sonnenuhr
Riesling Beerenauslese *
59 DM/0.375 liter, 8%, ♀ till 2006 **91**

1997 Wehlener Sonnenuhr
Riesling Auslese **
35 DM, 8%, ♀ till 2008 **92**

WEINGUT REICHSGRAF VON KESSELSTATT

Owner: Günther Reh family
Manager: Annegret Reh-Gartner, Roland Birr
Winemaker: Bernward Keiper
54290 Trier, Liebfrauenstraße 9–10
Tel. (06 51) 7 51 01, Fax 7 33 16
e-mail: vinonet.com@kesselstatt.htm
Directions: Via A 602 in direction of Trier, in the inner city opposite the cathedral
Sales: Annegret Reh-Gartner, Roland Birr
Opening hours: By appointment
Restaurant: Daily from 11:30 a.m. to midnight
Specialties: Regional cooking
History: In 1377 Friedrich von Kesselstatt was appointed director of the winery
Worth seeing: Palais Kesselstatt, built in 1745

Vineyard area: 57 hectares
Annual production: 400,000 bottles
Top sites: Josephshöfer (sole owners), Wehlener Sonnenuhr, Bernkasteler Doctor, Piesporter Goldtröpfchen and Domherr, Scharzhofberger, Kaseler Nies'chen
Soil types: Weathered Devon slate mingled with various other soils
Grape varieties: 100% Riesling
Average yield: 51 hl/ha
Best vintages: 1990, 1993, 1995

Since the Reh family purchased this estate in 1978 much has changed. The property was originally expanded to exploit its brilliant reputation, but more recently the estate has reduced their vineyard holdings in order to concentrate only on quality Riesling from the finest sites. Vinification in the beautifully modernized Schloß Marienlay cellars, which were renovated in 1988, has done much in this regard. The 1996s and 1997s were perhaps not quite as good as the three previous vintages, but the estate certainly has the vineyards, the cellars and the desire to be one of the best producers of the region. They know what they want to be doing and are on the right road. Keep an eye on the developments here!

1997 Scharzhofberger
Riesling Kabinett
17 DM, 8%, ♀ till 2004 **88**

1996 Piesporter Goldtröpfchen
Riesling Spätlese
20.50 DM, 7.5%, ♀ till 2004 **88**

1996 Josephshöfer
Riesling Spätlese
23 DM, 7.5%, ♀ till 2004 **88**

1997 Bernkasteler Doctor
Riesling Auslese
36 DM/0.375 liter, 8%, ♀ till 2004 **88**

1997 Scharzhofberger
Riesling Spätlese
22 DM, 8.5%, ♀ till 2006 **89**

1997 Josephshöfer
Riesling Auslese
20 DM/0.375 liter, 7.5%, ♀ till 2005 **89**

1997 Kaseler Nies'chen
Riesling Spätlese
21 DM, 8%, ♀ till 2006 **91**

1997 Scharzhofberger
Riesling Auslese
32 DM, 8%, ♀ till 2008 **91**

1996 Scharzhofberger
Riesling Beerenauslese
83 DM/0.375 liter, ♀ till 2006 **91**

1996 Scharzhofberger
Riesling Eiswein
123 DM/0.375 liter, 7.5%, ♀ till 2010 **92**

WEINGUT KIRSTEN

Owner: Bernhard Kirsten
54340 Klüsserath, Krainstraße 5
Tel. (0 65 07) 9 91 15, Fax 9 91 13
Directions: A 48, exit Salmtal
Sales: Bernhard Kirsten
Opening hours: By appointment

Vineyard area: 5.5 hectares
Annual production: 40,000 bottles
Top sites: Klüsserather Bruderschaft, Trittenheimer Apotheke
Soil types: Weathered slate
Grape varieties: 90% Riesling, 5% each of Kerner and Weißburgunder
Average yield: 50 hl/ha
Best vintages: 1994, 1995, 1997

The lion's share of this property's holdings lie just outside their back door: 4.5 hectares in the famous Klüsserather Bruderschaft vineyards. In the 1960s Bernhard Kirsten became the fourth generation of his family to manage this estate. The first thing he did was to reduce yields. "Great wine is made outdoors" is his motto, and he delves to bring the conditions offered by mother nature into harmony with his work in the cellars. Nonetheless, he embraces modern winemaking research on whole-cluster pressing and must oxidation. Apart from that, everything here is done traditionally. The Rieslings are vinified reductively in steel tanks and only a small quantity aged in casks. Most of the production is dry or off-dry, but the sweeter styles are often the finest. The 1996 range was comparable in quality to that of the previous vintage. The 1997s are perhaps a touch better. The quality curve of Kirsten's estate is certainly moving in the right direction.

1997 Klüsserather Bruderschaft
Riesling Spätlese trocken Herzstück
16 DM, 12.5%, ♀ till 2001 **82**

1996 Klüsserather Bruderschaft
Riesling Spätlese trocken
16 DM, 12%, ♀ till 2000 **84**

1997 Klüsserather Bruderschaft
Riesling Spätlese halbtrocken Herzstück
16 DM, 11.5%, ♀ till 2002 **84**

1997 Klüsserather Bruderschaft
Riesling halbtrocken
12 DM, 11%, ♀ till 2003 **84**

1996 Klüsserather Bruderschaft
Riesling Auslese
22 DM/0.5 liter, 8.5%, ♀ till 2005 **86**

1996 Klüsserather Bruderschaft
Riesling Spätlese
15 DM, 8.5%, ♀ till 2003 **88**

1997 Klüsserather Bruderschaft
Silvaner Spätlese Herzstück
16 DM, 9%, ♀ till 2006 **88**

1997 Klüsserather Bruderschaft
Riesling Auslese
22 DM/0.5 liter, 8.5%, ♀ till 2005 **88**

1996 Riesling
Auslese
22 DM/0.5 liter, 8.5%, ♀ till 2006 **89**

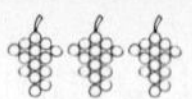

WEINGUT REINHARD UND BEATE KNEBEL

Owners: Reinhard and Beate Knebel
Winemaker: Reinhard Knebel
56333 Winningen,
August-Horch-Straße 24
Tel. (0 26 06) 26 31, Fax 25 69
e-mail:
riesling-Knebel@abo.rhein-zeitung.de
Directions: A 61, exit Koblenz-Metternich, in the direction of Winningen
Opening hours: By appointment

Vineyard area: 5 hectares
Annual production: 40,000 bottles
Top sites: Winninger Uhlen, Röttgen and Brückstück
Soil types: Weathered slate, blue slate
Grape varieties: 93% Riesling, 4% Weißburgunder, 3% Kerner
Average yield: 65 hl/ha
Best vintages: 1994, 1995, 1996
Member: Bernkasteler Ring

After completing his studies in oenology at Weinsberg, Reinhard Knebel returned to his family's estate in Winningen. In 1990 the property was divided among various branches of the family. Reinhard and his wife, Beate, took their share of 2.7 hectares, which they have expanded to five. In that same year they were also among the winners of the prizes awarded by "Pro Riesling." For many it was a surprise to see that a winery from the Lower Mosel could hold its own with the more famous growths of the Middle Mosel, Saar and Ruwer. Be that as it may, their character remains distinctly different. Admission to the "Bernkasteler Ring" was an additional compliment for the estate. The 1996 and 1997s ranges throw the Knebels into new spotlights: their wines are splendid. With the estate of Reinhard Löwenstein this is without doubt one of the top producers of the Lower Mosel.

1996 Winninger Uhlen
Riesling Auslese trocken
26 DM, 12%, ♀ till 2002 **88**

1997 Winninger Brückstück
Riesling Spätlese halbtrocken
11.50 DM, 10.5%, ♀ till 2004 **88**

1997 Winninger Röttgen
Riesling Spätlese
12 DM, 9%, ♀ till 2006 **88**

1997 Winninger Röttgen
Riesling Auslese
38 DM/0.5 liter, 9%, ♀ till 2008 **89**

1996 Winninger Röttgen
Riesling Auslese
43 DM/0.5 liter, 8%, ♀ till 2006 **91**

1996 Winninger Brückstück
Riesling Eiswein
Not yet for sale, 8%, ♀ till 2009 **94**

1997 Winninger Röttgen
Riesling Beerenauslese
60 DM/0.375 liter, 7.5%, ♀ till 2008 **94**

1997 Winninger
Riesling Trockenbeerenauslese
Not yet for sale, 6%, ♀ till 2010 **96**

1996 Winninger Uhlen
Riesling Trockenbeerenauslese
Not yet for sale, 6%, ♀ till 2010 **96**

RIESLING
1992er WINNINGER RÖTTGEN SPÄTLESE
QUALITÄTSWEIN MIT PRÄDIKAT ERZEUGERABFÜLLUNG
0.75 l MOSEL SAAR RUWER 8.0 % vol
WEINGUT REINHARD UND BEATE KNEBEL AUGUST-HORCH-STR. 24
D-5406 WINNINGEN/MOSEL A.P.NR. 1658 069 1193

WEINGUT PETER LAUER WEINHAUS AYLER KUPP

Owners: Julia and Peter Lauer
54441 Ayl, Trierer Straße 49
Tel. (0 65 81) 30 31, Fax 23 44
Directions: From Trier via B 51 to Ayl, from Saarbrücken: A 61 to Merzig, via B 51 to Mettlach, Saarburg and Ayl
Sales: Julia and Peter Lauer
Opening hours: Tue.–Fri. noon to 2 p.m. and 6 p.m. to 10 p.m.
Sat. noon to 10 p.m. or by appointment
Restaurant: Weinhaus "Zur Ayler Kupp," open Tue.–Fri. from noon to 2 p.m. and 6 p.m. to 10 p.m., Sat. from noon to 2 p.m. and 6 p.m. to 10 p.m.
Sun. from noon, Mon. closed
Specialties: Liver pâté, potato soup, fish soup, Riesling aspic

Vineyard area: 3.8 hectares
Annual production: 35,000 bottles
Top site: Ayler Kupp
Soil types: Light weathered slate
Grape varieties: 100% Riesling
Average yield: 77 hl/ha
Best vintages: 1994, 1995, 1997

This is a very typical family estate from the Saar. From the environmentally conscious cultivation of the steep vineyards in Ayl and Schoden, through the handling of the grapes and their vinification, up to the marketing of the wines, all operations are undertaken by the family. Peter Lauer has his own ideas about how his wines should taste: "Racy acidity, rounded off with a touch of fruity sweetness." He ferments the must with their indigenous yeasts and ages the young wine for at least six months in casks, so that the acidity integrates itself in a natural fashion. The 1996 range was marked by such an assertive acidity that it will definitely require further aging to convey full enjoyment. The well-balanced 1997s are more easily accessible. Lauer continues to bottle almost every cask separately, and this is documented with a number on the label. Most of his wines are sold to passing customers; the rest is consumed at his wine bar, "Zur Ayler Kupp."

1996 Ayler Kupp
Riesling Kabinett halbtrocken – 19 –
13.50 DM, 9.5%, 🍷 till 2000 **84**

1996 Ayler Kupp
Riesling Kabinett – 12 –
13.50 DM, 10%, 🍷 till 2000 **84**

1997 Ayler Kupp
Riesling Kabinett trocken – 2 –
12.50 DM, 10%, 🍷 till 2002 **86**

1997 Ayler Kupp
Riesling Kabinett halbtrocken – 1 –
11.50 DM, 9%, 🍷 till 2004 **86**

1997 Ayler Kupp
Riesling Spätlese trocken – 9 –
16 DM, 10%, 🍷 till 2004 **88**

1997 Ayler Kupp
Riesling Spätlese halbtrocken – 5 –
15 DM, 10%, 🍷 till 2005 **88**

1996 Ayler Kupp
Riesling Spätlese – 11 –
16 DM, 7.5%, 🍷 till 2004 **88**

1997 Ayler Kupp
Riesling Spätlese – 3 –
16 DM, 8%, 🍷 till 2008 **89**

1997 Ayler Kupp
Riesling Spätlese – 4 –
15 DM, 8.5%, 🍷 till 2007 **89**

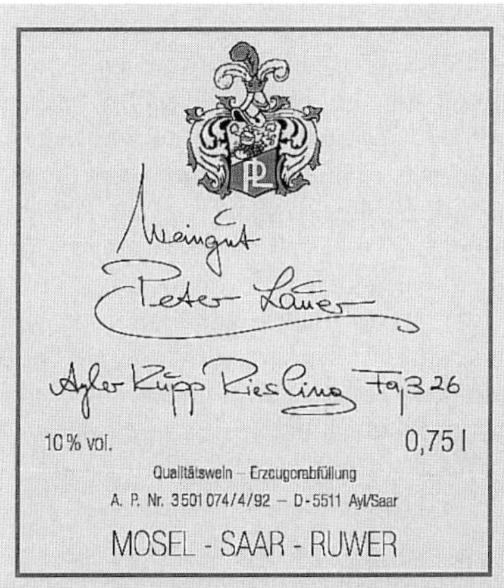

WEINGUT LEHNERT-VEIT

Owner: Erich Lehnert
54498 Piesport, In der Dur 10
Tel. (0 65 07) 21 23, Fax 71 45
Directions: A 48, exit Salmtal-Piesport
Sales: Ingrid and Erich Lehnert
Opening hours: Mon.–Fri. 9 a.m. to 8 p.m., Sat. 10 a.m. to 8 p.m.
Restaurant: 11 a.m. to 11 p.m.
Specialties: Regional cooking in a Mediterranean garden
Worth seeing: 4th-century Roman cellar, old cross belonging to the family

Vineyard area: 5.3 hectares
Annual production: 40,000 bottles
Top sites: Piesporter Goldtröpfchen, Falkenberg and Treppchen
Soil types: Weathered slate with clay
Grape varieties: 70% Riesling, 20% Müller-Thurgau, 3% Spätburgunder, 2% Kerner and 5% other varieties
Average yield: 86 hl/ha
Best vintages: 1992, 1994, 1995
Member: Bernkasteler Ring

This up and coming estate in Piesport first attracted our attention with the astonishingly fine 1992s. The bulk of its holdings are found in the Piesporter Treppchen vineyard, where the family owns 2.6 hectares. In its flatter sections Erich Lehnert also cultivates Kerner and Müller-Thurgau, from which he makes wines characterized by distinct varietal typicity. The vines planted in the Goldtröpfchen and Falkenberg sites, on the other hand, are all Riesling. The once higher proportion of wines sold in bulk to wholesalers continues to diminish, while ever greater quantities are required by the estate's wine bar. The 1996 and 1997 ranges offer the same dependable quality as did the 1995s; the dry wines are even improving in quality. The once high yields are being gradually reduced through rigorous pruning and leaf-thinning.

1997 Piesporter Falkenberg
Riesling Kabinett halbtrocken
8.90 DM, 9.5%, ♀ till 2001 **82**

1997 Piesporter Goldtröpfchen
Riesling Spätlese halbtrocken
11.80 DM, 10.5%, ♀ till 2002 **82**

1996 Piesporter Falkenberg
Riesling Kabinett halbtrocken
9.20 DM, 10%, ♀ till 2001 **84**

1997 Piesporter Goldtröpfchen
Riesling Spätlese *
11.80 DM, 9.5%, ♀ till 2002 **84**

1996 Piesporter Goldtröpfchen
Riesling Spätlese trocken
11.60 DM, 11.5%, ♀ till 2000 **86**

1996 Piesporter Goldtröpfchen
Riesling Spätlese halbtrocken
11 DM, 10.5%, ♀ till 2002 **86**

1996 Piesporter Goldtröpfchen
Riesling Spätlese – 11 –
11 DM, 8.5%, ♀ till 2004 **86**

1997 Piesporter Goldtröpfchen
Riesling Spätlese
14.50 DM, 8%, ♀ till 2004 **88**

1996 Piesporter Goldtröpfchen
Riesling Spätlese – 12 –
19.80 DM, 8.5%, ♀ till 2004 **88**

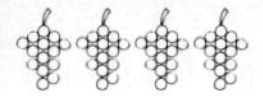

WEINGUT SCHLOSS LIESER

Owner: Thomas Haag
54470 Lieser, Am Markt 1
Tel. (0 65 31) 64 31, Fax 10 68
Directions: A 48, exit Wittlich-Salmtal, in the direction of Mülheim-Lieser, left side of the river
Sales: Thomas Haag
Opening hours: By appointment
History: Estate formerly the property of the Baron von Schorlemer

Vineyard area: 6.6 hectares
Annual production: 40,000 bottles
Top sites: Lieser Niederberg Helden, Süssenberg, Schloßberg, Graacher Domprobst, Himmelreich
Soil types: Weathered slate
Grape varieties: 100% Riesling
Average yield: 45 hl/ha
Best vintages: 1994, 1995, 1997

Until the real estate broker Wolfgang Reichel imbued it with new life, the cellars and vineyards of the once renowned Schorlemer estate in Lieser were in a seriously depressed condition. Reichel engaged as his director Thomas Haag, the eldest son of Wilhelm Haag, certainly one of the most talented young winemakers of the region. Thomas set to work with both enthusiasm and the knowledge he had acquired both at the University in Geisenheim and at the family estate in Brauneberg. His debut in 1992 created not only a stir but was also commercially successful. The 1993 vintage brought the first major breakthrough; the outstanding 1994s provided a perfect encore. The 1995s were of a similar quality, from the Kabinett up to the finest Auslese. The 1996 and 1997 ranges were both better as late harvest Rieslings, the dry wines being marked by crisp acidity. Thomas Haag recently purchased the estate, which will now give him the opportunity to pursue his quality goals as he sees fit. Look for even finer wines in the future.

1997 Riesling
Kabinett
11 DM, 9.5%, ♀ till 2004 **86**

1997 Lieser Niederberg Helden
Riesling Spätlese
14.80 DM, 9%, ♀ till 2006 **88**

1996 Riesling
Kabinett
11 DM, 8.5%, ♀ till 2004 **89**

1997 Lieser Niederberg Helden
Riesling Auslese
19.50 DM, 8.5%, ♀ till 2007 **89**

1997 Lieser Niederberg Helden
Riesling Auslese *** – 11 –
27 DM/0.375 liter, 7.5%, ♀ till 2008 **92**

1996 Lieser Niederberg Helden
Riesling Auslese ***
27.50 DM/0.375 liter, 8%, ♀ till 2008 **94**

1997 Lieser Niederberg Helden
Riesling Auslese *** – 10 –
27 DM/0.375 liter, 7.5%, ♀ till 2008 **95**

1997 Lieser Niederberg Helden
Riesling Beerenauslese
70 DM/0.375 liter, 7.5%, ♀ till 2010 **95**

1996 Lieser Niederberg Helden
Riesling Beerenauslese
70 DM/0.375 liter, 7%, ♀ till 2010 **95**

WEINGUT CARL LOEWEN

Owner: Karl Josef Loewen
54340 Leiwen, Matthiasstraße 30
Tel. (0 65 07) 30 94, Fax 80 23 32
Directions: A 48, exit Schweich, in the direction of Leiwen, village center
Sales: Edith and Karl Josef Loewen
Opening hours: Mon.–Fri. by appointment, Sat. 1 p.m. to 4 p.m.
History: Wine estate since 1803

Vineyard area: 6.2 hectares
Annual production: 45,000 bottles
Top site: Leiwener Laurentiuslay and Klostergarten, Thörnicher Ritsch, Detzemer Maximiner Klosterlay
Soil types: Devon and light weathered slate
Grape varieties: 98% Riesling, 2% Müller-Thurgau
Average yield: 71 hl/ha
Best vintages: 1993, 1994, 1995

Thanks to the secularization about 200 years ago the ancestors of Karl Josef Loewen acquired the Detzemer Maximiner Klosterlay. In 1982 Karl Josef Loewen himself bought vines in the extremely steep Laurentiuslay, which is the most outstanding vineyard of Leiwen. Ten years after laying out the site, the vines have begun to show their full capacity. Loewen does not try to force quality by very severe pruning; rather his goal is to attain small-berried, healthy grapes using normal pruning practices. He is convinced that small berries impart incomparably richer and more elegantly fruity aromas. His ideal of a fine Riesling is a powerfully expressive wine with lean body and considerable length. Loewen's wines first drew our attention with the fine 1992 range. This was followed by the even better 1993s, which was his best vintage to date; but the 1994s and 1995s were also quite good. The 1996s, on the other hand, left a bit to be desired. The 1997s are better, but not as successful as the trio of earlier vintages.

1996 Leiwener Klostergarten
Riesling Kabinett halbtrocken
7.80 DM, 9%, ♀ till 2001 **86**

1996 Detzemer Maximiner Klosterlay
Riesling Spätlese halbtrocken
12 DM, 9.5%, ♀ till 2001 **86**

1996 Leiwener Klostergarten
Riesling
7.30 DM, 10.5%, ♀ now **86**

1996 Leiwener Laurentiuslay
Riesling Spätlese
14 DM, 8.5%, ♀ till 2003 **86**

1996 Thörnicher Ritsch
Riesling Spätlese
15 DM, 8.5%, ♀ till 2003 **86**

1997 Detzemer Maximiner Klosterlay
Riesling Auslese
24 DM/0.5 liter, 8%, ♀ till 2006 **86**

1997 Leiwener Laurentiuslay
Riesling Spätlese – 11 –
15 DM, 8.5%, ♀ till 2006 **88**

1997 Thörnicher Ritsch
Riesling Auslese
26 DM/0.5 liter, 8%, ♀ till 2006 **88**

1997 Leiwener Laurentiuslay
Riesling Auslese
29 DM/0.5 liter, 8.5%, ♀ till 2006 **88**

1996 Leiwener Klostergarten
Riesling Eiswein
115 DM/0.375 liter, 9.5%, ♀ till 2009 **94**

WEINGUT DR. LOOSEN

Owner: Ernst F. Loosen
Winemaker: Bernhard Schug
54470 Bernkastel, St. Johannishof
Tel. (0 65 31) 34 26, Fax 42 48
e-mail: dr.loosen@t-online.de
Directions: A 48 Koblenz–Trier, exit Wittlich, follow B 53 one kilometer to the outskirts of Bernkastel
Sales: Ernst F. Loosen
Opening hours: Mon.–Fri. 8 a.m. to 5 p.m., by appointment

Vineyard area: 10 hectares
Annual production: 70,000 bottles
Top sites: Bernkasteler Lay, Erdener Treppchen and Prälat, Wehlener Sonnenuhr, Ürziger Würzgarten
Soil types: Devon slate and red layered soils
Grape varieties: 97% Riesling, 3% Müller-Thurgau
Average yield: 55 hl/ha
Best vintages: 1995, 1996, 1997
Member: VDP

For years Ernie Loosen's wines were better known in export markets than in Germany itself; even today more than half of his production is sold abroad. Interest in the domestic market was first awakened when his 1989 dry Riesling was named Riesling of the Year by *Feinschmecker* magazine. Loosen's cellarmaster Bernhard Schug explains the philosophy of his young boss: "slow fermentation, natural yeasts, no fining and minimal movement of the wine." The 1993 vintage catapulted Ernst Loosen into the elite ranks of Mosel producers. In the following year many of his wines appeared to be maturing quickly, yet their overall quality was undeniable. The 1995 range lay midway between the preceding two vintages: the wines had plenty of depth and body, and shone with their crisp acidity. The 1996s were of similar structure. The 1997 vintage brought a new dimension of quality to Loosen's work. Never before have his Auslese, Beerenauslese and Trockenbeerenauslese been so stunning, with the Beerenauslese from the Erdener Treppchen being the finest wine produced in Germany from that vintage!

1997 Wehlener Sonnenuhr
Riesling Kabinett
14.50 DM, 8.5%, ♀ till 2003 **88**

1996 Erdener Treppchen
Riesling Kabinett
14.90 DM, ♀ till 2002 **88**

1997 Erdener Treppchen
Riesling Spätlese
20.80 DM, 8.5%, ♀ till 2005 **88**

1996 Wehlener Sonnenuhr
Riesling Kabinett
14.50 DM, 8%, ♀ till 2002 **89**

1996 Wehlener Sonnenuhr
Riesling Spätlese
20 DM, 7.5%, ♀ till 2005 **89**

1996 Erdener Treppchen
Riesling Spätlese
20.80 DM, 7.5%, ♀ till 2005 **89**

1996 Ürziger Würzgarten
Riesling Spätlese
20.80 DM, 7%, ♀ till 2008 **91**

1996 Ürziger Würzgarten
Riesling Auslese
30 DM, 7.5%, ♀ till 2007 **91**

1997 Ürziger Würzgarten
Riesling Spätlese
55.60 DM, 7.5%, ♀ till 2008 **92**

1996 Ürziger Würzgarten
Riesling Spätlese
47 DM, 8%, ♀ till 2008 **92**

1997 Wehlener Sonnenuhr
Riesling Auslese
33 DM, 8.5%, ♀ till 2006 **92**

1997 Ürziger Würzgarten
Riesling Auslese
42.90 DM, 7%, ♀ till 2008 **92**

1997 Erdener Prälat
Riesling Auslese – 34 –
47.90 DM, 7%, 🍷 till 2008 **92**

1996 Wehlener Sonnenuhr
Riesling Auslese
30 DM, 7.5%, 🍷 till 2008 **92**

1997 Erdener Prälat
Riesling Auslese Goldkapsel – 22 –
72.50 DM, 7%, 🍷 till 2012 **92**

1996 Erdener Prälat
Riesling Auslese
47.90 DM, 7.5%, 🍷 till 2008 **94**

1996 Ürziger Würzgarten
Riesling Auslese Goldkapsel
43 DM, 7%, 🍷 till 2008 **95**

1996 Erdener Prälat
Riesling Auslese Goldkapsel
72.50 DM, 7.5%, 🍷 till 2012 **95**

1996 Erdener Treppchen
Riesling Beerenauslese
200 DM, 6.5%, 🍷 till 2010 **95**

1997 Erdener Prälat
Riesling Auslese lange Goldkapsel – 36 –
385 DM/0.375 liter, 7%, 🍷 till 2015 **96**

1997 Ürziger Würzgarten
Riesling Trockenbeerenauslese
Not yet for sale, 7%, 🍷 till 2015 **96**

1997 Erdener Treppchen
Riesling Beerenauslese
360 DM, 6.5%, 🍷 till 2015 **98**

WEINGUT ALFRED MERKELBACH GESCHW. ALBERTZ-ERBEN

Owners: Alfred and Rolf Merkelbach
54539 Ürzig, Brunnenstraße 11
Tel. (0 65 32) 45 22, Fax 28 89
Directions: Via B 53 to Ürzig
Sales: Alfred Merkelbach
Opening hours: Mon.–Fri. 8 a.m. to 7 p.m., Sat. 10 a.m. to 6 p.m.
By appointment

Vineyard area: 1.9 hectares
Annual production: 17,000 bottles
Top sites: Ürziger Würzgarten, Erdener Treppchen, Kinheimer Rosenberg
Soil types: Slate
Grape varieties: 100% Riesling
Average yield: 92 hl/ha
Best vintages: 1994, 1996, 1997
Member: Bernkasteler Ring

While glancing behind the scenes at this small estate in Ürzig one has roughly the same impression as is given by the very conventional, almost kitschy label. One easily imagines that time has stood still here since the late 1960s. The Merkelbach brothers, whose winery lies in a side street not far from the river, do in fact have high regard for traditional practices. No grape variety other than Riesling has any place in their vineyards. The two bachelors cultivate 1.2 hectares in the celebrated Ürziger Würzgarten site. Each plant is trained on individual stakes and the vines have an average age of 40 years. Until the early 1990s the vineyards were often overcropped; only in recent years have lower yields become part of the ritual. Even though they lacked subtlety, the 1996 vintage brought a batch of reliable wines. The 1997s are significantly better, certainly the finest collection that we have tasted from this estate in recent years.

1996 Ürziger Würzgarten
Riesling Spätlese – 6 –
9.50 DM, 8.5%, ♀ till 2003 **84**

1996 Erdener Treppchen
Riesling Spätlese – 9 –
10.80 DM, 8.5%, ♀ till 2003 **84**

1996 Ürziger Würzgarten
Riesling Spätlese – 13 –
12 DM, 9%, ♀ till 2003 **84**

1997 Erdener Treppchen
Riesling Spätlese – 4 –
9.30 DM, 8.5%, ♀ till 2003 **86**

1997 Ürziger Würzgarten
Riesling Spätlese – 24 –
9.50 DM, 8%, ♀ till 2004 **86**

1996 Ürziger Würzgarten
Riesling Auslese – 12 –
14 DM, 8.5%, ♀ till 2005 **86**

1996 Ürziger Würzgarten
Riesling Auslese – 11 –
32 DM, 8.5%, ♀ till 2004 **86**

1997 Ürziger Würzgarten
Riesling Spätlese – 20 –
11 DM, 8.5%, ♀ till 2006 **88**

1997 Ürziger Würzgarten
Riesling Auslese – 17 –
15 DM, 9%, ♀ till 2008 **91**

1997 Ürziger Würzgarten
Riesling Auslese – 16 –
18 DM, 9%, ♀ till 2008 **91**

WEINGUT MEULENHOF

Owner: Stefan Justen
Winemaker: Stefan Justen
54492 Erden, Zur Kapelle 8
Tel. (0 65 32) 22 67, Fax 15 52
Directions: A 48 Koblenz–Trier, exit Wittlich, in the direction of Bernkastel-Kues, in Zeltingen left to Erden
Opening hours: By appointment
Worth seeing: Roman cellar in the Erdener Treppchen

Vineyard area: 4.3 hectares
Annual production: 30,000 bottles
Top sites: Erdener Prälat and Treppchen, Wehlener Sonnenuhr
Soil types: Weathered slate
Grape varieties: 75% Riesling, 15% Müller-Thurgau, 10% Kerner
Average yield: 84 hl/ha
Best vintages: 1994, 1995, 1997
Member: Bernkasteler Ring

Born in 1959, Stefan Justen is yet another of those young growers from the Middle Mosel who is not satisfied producing ordinary wines. Since 1982 he has been responsible for the vinification at his parents' winery; in 1990 he took full charge at the estate. Justen is not content with only selective harvesting; he sometimes harvests vine by vine! He strives to make Rieslings that are lacily fruity in style, yet his wines often appear full-bodied, even massive, with a tendency to retain residual sugar. For this reason they generally demand patience. The 1994s impressed us with their exuberant character and led to accrued recognition for the estate. The 1995 range was of comparable quality and indicated that Justen had set his sights even higher. The 1996 range, however, did not reach the standard he had set for himself; the 1997s are much closer to the mark.

1996 Erdener Treppchen
Riesling Spätlese – 7 –
10.80 DM, 8%, ♀ till 2003 **86**

1996 Erdener Prälat
Riesling Auslese – 16 –
20 DM/0.5 liter, 8.5%, ♀ till 2003 **86**

1996 Erdener Treppchen
Riesling Spätlese – 12 –
15 DM, 8.5%, ♀ till 2003 **88**

1997 Wehlener Sonnenuhr
Riesling Auslese
18 DM, 8.5%, ♀ till 2004 **88**

1997 Erdener Treppchen
Riesling Spätlese – 19 –
12 DM/1.0 liter, 8.5%, ♀ till 2006 **89**

1997 Erdener Treppchen
Riesling Auslese – 20 –
25 DM, 8.5%, ♀ till 2007 **89**

1996 Erdener Treppchen
Riesling Auslese – 11 –
34.50 DM, 8.5%, ♀ till 2003 **89**

1997 Erdener Prälat
Riesling Auslese
25 DM/0.5 liter, 8.5%, ♀ till 2008 **91**

1996 Erdener Bußlay
Riesling Eiswein
70 DM/0.375 liter, 8.5%, ♀ till 2007 **91**

WEINGUT MILZ – LAURENTIUSHOF

Owner: Karl-Josef and Markus Milz
Manager and Winemaker:
Thomas Hermes
54349 Trittenheim, Moselstraße 7–9
Tel. (0 65 07) 23 00, Fax 56 50
Directions: A 48, exit Schweich, in the direction of Trittenheim
Sales: Bettina and Markus Milz
Opening hours: Mon.–Fri. 8 a.m. to 5 p.m., by appointment
History: Wine estate belonging to the family since 1520
Worth seeing: Cellar from 1680

Vineyard area: 6.9 hectares
Annual production: 65,000 bottles
Top sites: Trittenheimer Leiterchen (sole owners), Felsenkopf (sole owners), Altärchen and Apotheke
Soil types: Weathered slate
Grape varieties: 100% Riesling
Average yield: 64 hl/ha
Best vintages: 1994, 1995, 1996
Member: VDP

The Milz family have run this estate for almost 500 years. Land that was once owned by the Knights von Warsberg and the Counts von Hunolstein now belongs to their estate. The family is especially proud of the three weathered slate vineyards of which they are sole proprietors: the Trittenheimer Leiterchen and Felsenkopf as well as the Neumagener Nußwingert. The Milz family also own property in the Trittenheimer Altärchen and Apotheke. By placing priority on environmentally conscious practices in the vineyards and imposing limits on their yields, they have notably improved the quality of the wines in recent vintages. The aging of the wines still takes place exclusively in traditional oak casks; and the sweeter styles are made by arresting fermentation to retain the natural grape sugars. Both the 1996 and 1997 ranges were highlighted by the fruity Spätlese and Auslese styles, which were quite good for the respective vintages; the dry wines are still less convincing.

1996 Trittenheimer Felsenkopf
Riesling Kabinett
12.20 DM, 7.5%, ♀ till 2002 — **88**

1997 Trittenheimer Apotheke
Riesling Auslese
33.50 DM/0.5 liter, 7.5%, ♀ till 2006 — **88**

1997 Trittenheimer Leiterchen
Riesling Spätlese
13.70 DM, 7.5%, ♀ till 2008 — **89**

1997 Trittenheimer Felsenkopf
Riesling Spätlese
13.70 DM, 7%, ♀ till 2006 — **89**

1996 Trittenheimer Leiterchen
Riesling Spätlese
13.50 DM, 7.5%, ♀ till 2005 — **89**

1997 Trittenheimer Leiterchen
Riesling Auslese Goldkapsel
55 DM/0.5 liter, 7.5%, ♀ till 2008 — **89**

1997 Neumagener Nußwingert
Riesling Spätlese
13.70 DM, 7%, ♀ till 2007 — **91**

1996 Neumagener Nußwingert
Riesling Spätlese
25 DM, 8%, ♀ till 2006 — **91**

1996 Trittenheimer Leiterchen
Riesling Auslese
48 DM/0.5 liter, 8%, ♀ till 2007 — **91**

WEINGUT MOLITOR – HAUS KLOSTERBERG

Owner: Markus Molitor
54470 Bernkastel-Wehlen,
Klosterberg (Post: 54492 Zeltingen)
Tel. (0 65 31) 39 39, Fax (0 65 32) 42 25
Directions: A 48, exit Wittlich, in the direction of Zeltingen
Sales: Molitor family
Opening hours: Mon.–Fri. 8 a.m. to 8 p.m., Sat. and Sun. 10 a.m. to 8 p.m.
Worth seeing: Old vaulted cellars built from slate in the cliffs

Vineyard area: 20 hectares
Annual production: 150,000 bottles
Top sites: Zeltinger Sonnenuhr and Schloßberg, Wehlener Sonnenuhr, Graacher Domprobst
Soil types: Blue Devon slate, weathered slate
Grape varieties: 92% Riesling, 5% Weißburgunder, 3% Spätburgunder
Average yield: 56 hl/ha
Best vintages: 1995, 1996, 1997
Member: Bernkasteler Ring

Since he took over from his father in 1984 Markus Molitor has doubled the size of his vineyard holdings and now has more than enough vines to produce the noble late harvest rarities that are his specialty. Young Molitor generally mobilizes his forces in the Zeltinger Sonnenuhr site. And few play for such high stakes in autumn; he often prolongs the harvest until December. The rewards of such risks are often a lovely bouquet of Auslese and other delights. After an assault by hail ruined a substantial portion of his crop in 1996, Markus Molitor had an enormous challenge to overcome, but the results merited our respect. In June of 1997 Molitor married Verena Klüsserath, a grower's daughter from Piesport. As a belated wedding gift he brought her a brilliant array of 1997 Rieslings, sparkling diamonds on a golden ring. We tasted over two dozen wines from the vintage and found each one better than the last. A stunning performance!

1997 Graacher Himmelreich
Riesling Auslese halbtrocken
19.50 DM, 11%, ♀ till 2004 **89**

1996 Wehlener Sonnenuhr
Riesling Kabinett
12 DM, 8%, ♀ till 2003 **89**

1997 Zeltinger Sonnenuhr
Riesling Auslese halbtrocken
21.50 DM, 10.5%, ♀ till 2004 **89**

1997 Bernkasteler Graben
Riesling Spätlese
18 DM, 8%, ♀ till 2008 **91**

1997 Zeltinger Sonnenuhr
Riesling Spätlese – 30 –
18.50 DM, 7.5%, ♀ till 2008 **91**

1996 Zeltinger Sonnenuhr
Riesling Auslese ***
126 DM, 8%, ♀ till 2008 **92**

1997 Zeltinger Sonnenuhr
Riesling Auslese
23.20 DM, 7.5%, ♀ till 2008 **94**

1997 Zeltinger Sonnenuhr
Riesling Auslese ***
73 DM/0.375 liter, 10.5%, ♀ till 2012 **95**

1997 Zeltinger Sonnenuhr
Riesling Beerenauslese
Not yet for sale, 8.5%, ♀ till 2015 **95**

1996 Zeltinger Sonnenuhr
Riesling Trockenbeerenauslese *
Not yet for sale, 7%, ♀ till 2012 **96**

WEINGUT EGON MÜLLER – SCHARZHOF

Owner: Egon Müller
Winemaker: Horst Frank
54459 Wiltingen, Scharzhof
Tel. (0 65 01) 1 72 32, Fax (06 50) 15 02 63
Directions: From Trier via Konz in the direction of Wiltingen–Oberemmel
Tasting: By appointment
History: Owned by the family since 1797
Worth seeing: Manor house, courtyard and park

Vineyard area: 8 hectares
Annual production: 50,000 bottles
Top site: Scharzhofberg
Soil types: Well-drained weathered slate
Grape varieties: 98% Riesling, 2% other varieties
Average yield: 45 hl/ha
Best vintages: 1994, 1995, 1997
Member: VDP

The Müllers are understandably proud to own seven hectares in the finest parcels of the celebrated Scharzhofberg vineyard. There they can make full use of their enormous resources, a prerequisite for anyone seeking to be better than average. The fabulous Auslese, extraordinary ice wines and breathtaking Trockenbeerenauslese regularly demonstrate that no one in Germany can surpass the Müllers in these categories. For such wines they fetch – year in and year out – record prices at the traditional auctions organized by the "Großer Ring" in Trier, most recently 4,700 Marks for the 1990 Trockenbeerenauslese. The bulk of the wines are exported, of late increasingly to Japan. The incredibly complex 1996 and 1997 Auslese "Goldkapsel" were both exceptional wines from the respective vintages; the fantastic 1996 ice wine and breathtaking 1997 Trockenbeerenauslese even better. It was no surprise that we raised our glasses to the Seigneurs of Scharzhof last year in awarding them the title "Winemaker of the Year 1998."

1996 Scharzhofberger
Riesling Kabinett – 7 –
24 DM, 7.5%, ♀ till 2002 **89**

1997 Scharzhofberger
Riesling Spätlese – 14 –
45 DM, 8%, ♀ till 2006 **91**

1996 Scharzhofberger
Riesling Spätlese
62 DM, 8%, ♀ till 2005 **91**

1997 Scharzhofberger
Riesling Spätlese – 19 –
103 DM, 8%, ♀ till 2008 **94**

1997 Scharzhofberger
Riesling Auslese – 26 –
75 DM, 7.5%, ♀ till 2012 **95**

1997 Scharzhofberger
Riesling Auslese – 21 –
178 DM, 7.5%, ♀ till 2012 **95**

1997 Scharzhofberger
Riesling Auslese Goldkapsel
533 DM, 7%, ♀ till 2015 **96**

1996 Scharzhofberger
Riesling Auslese Goldkapsel
390 DM, 7.5%, ♀ till 2012 **96**

1996 Scharzhofberger
Riesling Eiswein
Not yet for sale, 6.5%, ♀ 2000 till 2015 **98**

1997 Scharzhofberger
Riesling Trockenbeerenauslese
Not yet for sale, 7%, ♀ till 2020 **98**

WEINGUT VON OTHEGRAVEN

Owner: Dr. Heidi Kegel
Winemaker: Heinz Nehrbass
54441 Kanzem, Weinstraße 1
Tel. (0 65 01) 15 00 42, Fax 1 88 79
e-mail: v.othegraven@novalis.net
Directions: From Trier via Konz to Kanzem on the right side of the river Saar
Sales: Dr. Heidi Kegel and Heinz Nehrbass
Opening hours: Mon.–Fri. 8 a.m. to 5 p.m. or by appointment
History: Privately owned estate since 16th century
Worth seeing: Lovely park with old trees

Vineyard area: 7 hectares
Annual production: 22,000 bottles
Top site: Kanzemer Altenberg
Soil types: Slate, Devon slate
Grape varieties: 100% Riesling
Average yield: 47 hl/ha
Best vintages: 1993, 1996, 1997
Member: VDP

This property at the foot of the Kanzemer Berg – one of the top sites in the Saar valley – is again on its way to becoming one of the leading estates of the region, as it was until the mid-1970s. We well remember the wonderful 1971 Auslese and 1975 Spätlese, which were among the finest wines of those vintages. Then, plantings of new varieties led to wines that tasted, at best, broad and dull. Recently things have again changed for the better: Riesling has returned to the vineyards. The 1994 vintage built upon the initial success of the 1993s, but the 1995s were again not up to standard. The 1996 range, however, was clearly of superior quality, with the elegantly fruity Spätlese and Auslese suggesting that this estate would soon be back on track. The lovely 1997s confirmed our expectations. It has been a long time since we tasted such a succulent Auslese from this estate; even the dry wines were appealing. But the best may be yet to come!

1997 Kanzemer Altenberg
Riesling Kabinett halbtrocken
12.50 DM, 11.5%, ♀ till 2001 **84**

1996 Kanzemer Altenberg
Riesling Spätlese – 10 –
13.30 DM, 8%, ♀ till 2001 **84**

1997 Riesling
trocken "Maximus"
14.50 DM, 11%, ♀ till 2000 **84**

1996 Kanzemer Altenberg
Riesling Spätlese – 7 –
18 DM, 8.5%, ♀ till 2002 **86**

1997 Kanzemer Altenberg
Riesling trocken
23.50 DM, 12%, ♀ till 2001 **86**

1997 Kanzemer Altenberg
Riesling Spätlese
29.70 DM, 8.5%, ♀ till 2002 **88**

1996 Kanzemer Altenberg
Riesling Spätlese – 13 –
27 DM, 7.5%, ♀ till 2004 **88**

1996 Kanzemer Altenberg
Riesling Auslese Goldkapsel
66 DM, 8.5%, ♀ till 2005 **88**

1997 Kanzemer Altenberg
Riesling Beerenauslese
110 DM/0.375 liter, 11%, ♀ till 2007 **91**

1997 Kanzemer Altenberg
Riesling Auslese
47.30 DM, 7.5%, ♀ till 2007 **92**

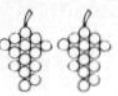

WEINGUT PAULINSHOF

Owner: Klaus Jüngling
Winemaker: Klaus Jüngling
54518 Kesten, Paulinsstraße 14
Tel. (0 65 35) 5 44, Fax 12 67
Directions: A 48/1, exit Wittlich or Salmtal
Sales: Klaus and Christa Jüngling
Opening hours: Mon.–Fri. 8 a.m. to 6 p.m., Sat. 9 a.m. to 5 p.m. or by appointment
History: First mentioned in documents in 936
Worth seeing: Former foundation of the Saint Paulin church in Trier, buildings and cellar from 1716 and 1770

Vineyard area: 7.5 hectares
Annual production: 75,000 bottles
Top sites: Brauneberger Kammer (sole owners), Juffer-Sonnenuhr and Juffer, Kestener Paulins-Hofberger
Soil types: Weathered slate
Grape varieties: 90% Riesling, 8% Müller-Thurgau, 2% Kerner
Average yield: 75 hl/ha
Best vintages: 1995, 1996, 1997
Member: Bernkasteler Ring

This estate in the idyllic old "Stiftshof" has been managed since 1969 by the Jüngling family. The original two hectares of vines have been expanded to almost eight, most recently with parcels in Brauneberg that belonged to the old Bergweiler estate. The Jünglings strive for a fresh style of Riesling with the right balance of fruit and acidity. The best wines are sold in tall stylish bottles bearing the coat of arms of the Saint Paulin church. Klaus Jüngling – who is also an ardent collector of old cars – outdid himself in 1996; this was without doubt his best range of the decade. From the dry wines to the excellent Auslese his Rieslings were all first-rate. If not of the same class, the 1997s are nonetheless quite good. If this trend continues, we will certainly hear more from this producer in the future.

1997 Kestener Paulins-Hofberger
Riesling Kabinett halbtrocken
13.50 DM, 10.5%, ♀ till 2003 **84**

1996 Brauneberger Juffer
Riesling Kabinett
11.80 DM, 7%, ♀ till 2003 **86**

1996 Brauneberger Kammer
Riesling Auslese trocken
25 DM, 12%, ♀ till 2002 **88**

1997 Brauneberger Kammer
Riesling Auslese halbtrocken
24 DM, 12%, ♀ till 2004 **88**

1997 Kestener Paulinsberg
Riesling Spätlese
17 DM, 8%, ♀ till 2005 **88**

1997 Brauneberger Juffer-Sonnenuhr
Riesling Auslese
22 DM, 9%, ♀ till 2006 **88**

1996 Kestener Paulinsberg
Riesling Spätlese
17 DM, 7.5%, ♀ till 2005 **89**

1997 Brauneberger Kammer
Riesling Auslese
28 DM, 9.5%, ♀ till 2007 **89**

1996 Brauneberger Kammer
Riesling Auslese halbtrocken
58 DM, 11%, ♀ till 2003 **91**

1996 Brauneberger Juffer-Sonnenuhr
Riesling Auslese
22 DM, 8%, ♀ till 2008 **91**

WEINGUT DR. PAULY-BERGWEILER

Owner: Dr. Peter Pauly
Manager and winemaker: Edmund Licht
54470 Bernkastel-Kues, Gestade 15
Tel. (0 65 31) 30 02, Fax 72 01
Directions: Via B 53 and the motorway through the Eifel, exit Bernkastel-Kues
Sales: Pauly family and Monika Schmitt
Opening hours: Mon.–Sat. 10 a.m. to 6 p.m., Sun by appointment
Worth seeing: Imposing estate mansion with small chapel, large vaulted cellars and baroque hall

Vineyard area: 14 hectares
Annual production: 130,000 bottles
Top sites: Bernkasteler Lay, Alte Badstube am Doctorberg, Wehlener Sonnenuhr, Graacher Himmelreich and Domprobst
Soil types: Weathered slate
Grape varieties: 90% Riesling, 5% Müller-Thurgau, 5% Spätburgunder
Average yield: 61 hl/ha
Best vintages: 1992, 1995, 1996
Member: Bernkasteler Ring

Issuing from four old families, Dr. Peter Pauly owns vineyards in the very finest sites in the Middle Mosel that provide him with an exceptional basis for his business. Thanks to his marriage to Helga Berres, the property also manages the Peter Nicolay estate, whose wines are marketed separately; from time to time they can be superb, as was the case again with the sumptuous 1996 Ürziger Würzgarten Trockenbeerenauslese with its aromas of exotic fruits. With his convincing range of 1995s Dr. Pauly won our admiration anew; his late harvested 1996s more than lived up to our heightened expectations. Although the dry wines were less successful, the 1997s as a whole are of similar quality. Interestingly enough though, the Spätlese are finer than the Auslese.

1997 Erdener Prälat
Riesling Auslese
40.60 DM, 10.5%, ♀ till 2004 **86**

1997 Ürziger Würzgarten
Riesling Auslese
24.50 DM, 9%, ♀ till 2005 **88**

1996 Bernkasteler Lay
Riesling Auslese
25 DM, 7.5%, ♀ till 2004 **88**

1997 Bernkasteler Badstube
Riesling Spätlese
19.50 DM, 8.5%, ♀ till 2006 **89**

1997 Bernkasteler Alte Badstube am Doctorberg
Riesling Spätlese
22 DM, 8.5%, ♀ till 2008 **91**

1996 Bernkasteler Alte Badstube am Doctorberg
Riesling Auslese
39 DM, 8%, ♀ till 2005 **91**

1997 Bernkasteler Alte Badstube am Doctorberg
Riesling Trockenbeerenauslese
Not yet for sale, 9.5%, ♀ till 2005 **92**

1996 Graacher Himmelreich
Riesling Eiswein
120 DM, 7.5%, ♀ till 2008 **94**

1996 Bernkasteler Lay
Riesling Eiswein
125 DM, 7%, ♀ till 2008 **95**

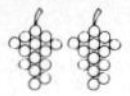

WEINGUT PIEDMONT

Owners: Claus and Monika Piedmont
Winemaker: Albert Permesang
54329 Konz-Filzen, Saartal 1
Tel. (0 65 01) 9 90 09, Fax 9 90 03
Directions: From Trier to Konz, on the right side of the river three kilometers upstream
Opening hours: Mon.–Fri. 9 a.m. to 7 p.m., Sat. 10 a.m. to 7 p.m.
Worth seeing: Estate buildings from the Maximin monastery of 1698, owned by the family since 1881

Vineyard area: 6 hectares
Annual production: 50,000 bottles
Top sites: Filzener Pulchen and Urbelt
Soil types: Devon slate
Grape varieties: 90% Riesling, 10% Weißburgunder
Average yield: 60 hl/ha
Best vintages: 1995, 1996, 1997
Member: VDP

Claus Piedmont has done something that many other wineries would do well to emulate: he has reduced his range to about six wines per year. His price list is thus both understandable and consumer friendly. He also shrewdly markets his "light" Mosel wines to appeal to modern young wine lovers conscious of their health. After a weak run in the 1980s, Piedmont's wines have clearly improved in quality since 1993 and once again embody the traditional fresh style of Saar Riesling. His cellarmaster achieves the wines' youthful character through an extremely reductive winemaking process in oak casks; and so that none of the freshness is lost, they are bottled early in March, preserving aromas reminiscent of grapefruit and flint. Athough some 20 percent of the wines are vinified dry, the strength of the range lies in the off-dry and delicately fruity Rieslings.

1997 Filzener Pulchen
Riesling Kabinett halbtrocken
9.80 DM, 9.5%, ♀ till 2000 **84**

1997 Filzener Urbelt
Riesling Kabinett trocken
9.80 DM, 9.5%, ♀ till 2002 **86**

1996 Filzener Pulchen
Riesling Kabinett halbtrocken
9.80 DM, 9%, ♀ till 2001 **86**

1996 Filzener Pulchen
Riesling Spätlese
13.80 DM, 8%, ♀ till 2003 **86**

1996 Filzener Pulchen
Riesling Auslese
23 DM, 8%, ♀ till 2002 **86**

1997 Filzener Pulchen
Riesling Spätlese
13.90 DM, 8%, ♀ till 2002 **88**

1997 Filzener Pulchen
Riesling Auslese
23.20 DM, 7.5%, ♀ till 2004 **88**

1997 Filzener Pulchen
Riesling
9.80 DM, 8.5%, ♀ till 2003 **88**

1996 Filzener Pulchen
Riesling Auslese Goldkapsel
50 DM, 8%, ♀ till 2005 **91**

WEINGUT JOH. JOS. PRÜM

Owners: Dr. Manfred and Wolfgang Prüm
General Manager: Dr. Manfred Prüm
54470 Bernkastel-Wehlen, Uferallee 19
Tel. (0 65 31) 30 91, Fax 60 71
Directions: From Bernkastel-Kues follow the left riverbank until Wehlen, in village center right to the Uferallee
Opening hours: By appointment
History: Founded in 1911 after the division of the original Prüm estate
Worth seeing: The elegant manor house on the banks of the Moselle

Vineyard area: 14 hectares
Annual production: 120,000 bottles
Top sites: Wehlener Sonnenuhr, Graacher Himmelreich, Zeltinger Sonnenuhr, Bernkasteler Badstube
Soil types: Slate
Grape varieties: 100% Riesling
Average yield: 63 hl/ha
Best vintages: 1994, 1995, 1997
Member: VDP

This estate is, without doubt, one of the most exceptional producers in Germany. Well over half of the vines are planted in the finest parcels of the exceptional vineyards of Wehlener Sonnenuhr and Graacher Himmelreich, where in great vintages Dr. Manfred Prüm regularly harvests his noble late harvest wines. Through minimal manipulation he normally retains both a dose of natural carbon dioxide and residual sugar in these astonishingly long-lived wines. When asked for details on his vinification process, the usually talkative head of the house prefers to remain silent; the cellars are, as they always have been, barred to visitors. The entire range from the 1996 vintage was of convincing quality. The top wine was the Auslese "Goldkapsel" from the Wehlener Sonnenuhr; however, Dr. Prüm also produced an ice wine that he has no wish to show until "it is ready." The 1997s are even finer, including the elegant Spätlese – 34 – that we consider to be the finest of its class from that vintage.

1996 Graacher Himmelreich
Riesling Kabinett
16 DM, 8.5%, ♀ till 2004 **89**

1997 Wehlener Sonnenuhr
Riesling Spätlese – 22 –
26 DM, 7.5%, ♀ till 2008 **94**

1997 Wehlener Sonnenuhr
Riesling Spätlese – 34 –
47 DM, 7%, ♀ till 2008 **94**

1997 Wehlener Sonnenuhr
Riesling Auslese – 26 –
35 DM, 7.5%, ♀ till 2010 **94**

1996 Zeltinger Sonnenuhr
Riesling Auslese
27 DM, 7.5%, ♀ till 2006 **94**

1996 Wehlener Sonnenuhr
Riesling Auslese
32 DM, 8%, ♀ till 2008 **94**

1997 Wehlener Sonnenuhr
Riesling Auslese Goldkapsel – 29 –
128 DM, 8%, ♀ till 2008 **94**

1996 Wehlener Sonnenuhr
Riesling Auslese Goldkapsel
125 DM, 8.5%, ♀ till 2008 **94**

1997 Wehlener Sonnenuhr
Riesling Auslese – 35 –
70 DM, 7.5%, ♀ till 2012 **95**

1997 Wehlener Sonnenuhr
Riesling Auslese lange Goldkapsel
465 DM, 7.5%, ♀ till 2012 **95**

WEINGUT S. A. PRÜM

Owner: Raimund Prüm
General Manager: Gerd Faber
Winemaker: Raimund Prüm
54470 Bernkastel-Wehlen,
Uferallee 25-26
Tel. (0 65 31) 31 10, Fax 85 55
e-mail: s.a.pruem@t-online.de
Directions: A 48, exit Wittlich, in the direction of Bernkastel
Opening hours: Mon.–Sat. 10 a.m. to 6 p.m., Sun. by appointment

Vineyard area: 10.5 hectares
Annual production: 100,000 bottles
Top sites: Wehlener Sonnenuhr, Bernkasteler Lay and Graben, Graacher Himmelreich and Domprobst
Soil types: Devon slate
Grape varieties: 85% Riesling, 15% Weißburgunder
Average yield: 56 hl/ha
Best vintages: 1995, 1996, 1997
Member: VDP

The purchase by Dr. Renate Willkomm has been good for this estate. Raimund Prüm, who continues to manage the business, can now concentrate all his efforts on winemaking – and the wines since 1993 have shown undeniable character. The 1996 and 1997 ranges were astonishingly good. From the liter bottlings, through the Kabinett to the delicately fruity Spätlese and Auslese, everything was first rate. Our favorite wines this year were the elegant Wehlener Sonnenuhr Spätlese and the exuberantly fruity Graacher Himmelreich Auslese. The vines average 45 years of age; as a consequence the yields are low and the extracts high. In the new cellars the quality should continue to rise. The traditional label is now used only for the finest wines of each vintage from the top sites. The remaining Rieslings are sold without vineyard designation using a simplified label.

1996 Riesling
Kabinett halbtrocken
14 DM, 9%, ♀ till 2004 **88**

1997 Wehlener Sonnenuhr
Riesling Spätlese halbtrocken
26 DM, 10%, ♀ till 2005 **89**

1996 Wehlener Sonnenuhr
Riesling Spätlese halbtrocken
26 DM, 10%, ♀ till 2003 **89**

1996 Wehlener Sonnenuhr
Riesling Kabinett
17 DM, 8%, ♀ till 2004 **89**

1997 Wehlener Sonnenuhr
Riesling Spätlese
26 DM, 7%, ♀ till 2006 **91**

1997 Bernkasteler Graben
Riesling Spätlese
23.50 DM, 7.5%, ♀ till 2006 **91**

1996 Wehlener Sonnenuhr
Riesling Spätlese
26 DM, 7.5%, ♀ till 2006 **91**

1997 Wehlener Sonnenuhr
Riesling Auslese – 30 –
38.50 DM, 8%, ♀ till 2008 **92**

1996 Wehlener Sonnenuhr
Riesling Auslese – 22 –
45 DM, 8%, ♀ till 2007 **92**

1997 Graacher Himmelreich
Riesling Auslese
30 DM/0.5 liter, 7.5%, ♀ till 2010 **94**

WEINGUT WALTER RAUEN

Owners: Walter and Irmtrud Rauen
Winemaker: Stefan Rauen
54340 Detzem, Im Würzgarten
Tel. (0 65 07) 32 78, Fax 83 72
Directions: A 48, exit Salmtal, A 1, exit Mehring. The winery lies in the middle of the vineyards above Detzem
Opening hours: By appointment

Vineyard area: 8.1 hectares
Annual production: 49,000 bottles
Top sites: Detzemer Maximiner Klosterlay and Würzgarten
Soil types: Weathered slate, sandy gravel
Grape varieties: 65% Riesling, 15% Müller-Thurgau, 8% Spätburgunder, 7% Weißburgunder, 5% other varieties
Average yield: 83 hl/ha
Best vintages: 1995, 1996, 1997

When Walter Rauen relocated his business in the 1960s to the outskirts of the village, he chose as his new address "Im Würzgarten" after the vineyard in which he had built his winery. In the early 1970s he was then elected mayor of the village, which he remains to this day. Of late a younger generation is gradually taking over more responsibility in the winery. His son Stefan, after completing his studies in Würzburg, is now overseeing the winemaking and surprised us with his lively 1996 Rieslings. The 1997s are eminently better. If this trend continues, we will certainly hear more from this estate in the years to come.

1997 Detzemer Würzgarten
Riesling Kabinett trocken
7.50 DM, 10%, ♀ till 2001 **82**

1997 Detzemer Würzgarten
Riesling Kabinett halbtrocken
7.50 DM, 10%, ♀ till 2001 **82**

1997 Detzemer Maximiner Klosterlay
Riesling Spätlese halbtrocken
9.50 DM, 10%, ♀ till 2002 **82**

1996 Trittenheimer Altärchen
Riesling Auslese
18 DM/0.375 liter, 9%, ♀ till 2005 **82**

1996 Detzemer Maximiner Klosterlay
Riesling Spätlese
9 DM, 9%, ♀ till 2003 **84**

1997 Weißer Burgunder
Auslese trocken
15 DM, 12.5%, ♀ till 2003 **86**

1996 Detzemer Maximiner Klosterlay
Riesling Beerenauslese
40 DM/0.375 liter, 9.5%, ♀ till 2005 **86**

1997 Detzemer Maximiner Klosterlay
Riesling Spätlese
9.50 DM, 9%, ♀ till 2005 **88**

1997 Trittenheimer Altärchen
Riesling Auslese
18 DM, 9%, ♀ till 2006 **89**

1997 Detzemer Würzgarten
Riesling Eiswein
70 DM/0.375 liter, 10%, ♀ till 2007 **92**

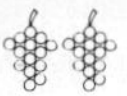

WEINGUT JOHANN PETER REINERT

Owner: Johann Peter Reinert
54441 Kanzem, Alter Weg 7a
Tel. (0 65 01) 1 32 77, Fax 15 00 68
Directions: From Trier via B 51 to Konz, third Konz exit towards Kanzem
Sales: Annetrud and J. P. Reinert
Opening hours: By appointment
History: Owned by the family since 1813

Vineyard area: 3.8 hectares
Annual production: 20,000 bottles
Top sites: Ayler Kupp, Kanzemer Sonnenberg, Wiltinger Schlangengraben
Soil types: Slate
Grape varieties: 70% Riesling, 8% Elbling, 6% Weißburgunder, 5% each of Rivaner and Ortega, 6% other varieties
Average yield: 53 hl/ha
Best vintages: 1990, 1994, 1995
Member: Bernkasteler Ring

As an estate that retains close contact to nature, Johann Peter Reinert plants his vines wide apart so that light and sunshine can reach the grapes and leaves; and the herbs flowering between the rows of vines are a welcome sight. Within only a few short years Reinert has moved his estate to the forefront in Kanzem. Although he is not endowed with vineyards in the village's top site, the Altenberg, he nevertheless belongs to the small group of the finest growers from the Saar, a fact that was driven home by the excellent 1994 and 1995 vintages. Without being disappointments, neither the 1996 nor 1997 ranges quite attain the quality level of those two previous vintages. Be that as it may, the Auslese still remain lively and elegant. Although he has won a number of prizes at the auctions organized by the Bernkasteler Ring, the majority of his wines are reasonably priced, which must surely please his clientele.

1996 Wawerner Ritterpfad
Riesling Kabinett halbtrocken
7.60 DM, 8%, ♀ now **84**

1997 Wiltinger Schlangengraben
Riesling Spätlese halbtrocken
9.60 DM, 10.5%, ♀ till 2002 **84**

1997 Wiltinger Klosterberg
Riesling Auslese halbtrocken
25.50 DM, 11.5%, ♀ till 2003 **84**

1996 Wiltinger Schlangengraben
Riesling
7 DM, 9%, ♀ now **84**

1997 Kanzemer Sonnenberg
Riesling Kabinett
8.40 DM, 8%, ♀ till 2004 **84**

1996 Ayler Kupp
Riesling Kabinett
8 DM, 8%, ♀ till 2000 **84**

1997 Ayler Kupp
Riesling Spätlese
13.80 DM, 7.5%, ♀ till 2005 **84**

1996 Wiltinger Schlangengraben
Riesling Kabinett
7.80 DM, 8%, ♀ till 2000 **86**

1997 Ayler Kupp
Riesling Auslese
34.50 DM, 8%, ♀ till 2006 **88**

1996 Wiltinger Schlangengraben
Riesling Auslese
38 DM, 8.5%, ♀ till 2004 **89**

WEINGUT REUSCHER-HAART

Owner: Franz-Hugo Schwang
54498 Piesport,
Sankt-Michael-Straße 20–22
Tel. (0 65 07) 24 92, Fax 56 74
Directions: A 1/48, exit Salmtal, onto the B 53 to Piesport
Opening hours: By appointment
History: Wine estate owned by the family since 1337

Vineyard area: 4.3 hectares
Annual production: 25,000 bottles
Top sites: Piesporter Goldtröpfchen, Domherr and Falkenberg
Soil types: Slate
Grape varieties: 90% Riesling, 10% Müller-Thurgau
Average yield: 54 hl/ha
Best vintages: 1992, 1994, 1997

This small winery owns numerous parcels in the best vineyard sites of Piesport, which have been completely replanted in the past few years. Franz-Hugo Schwang took this opportunity to change the trellising of the vineyards from the customary individual stake method to wires. As a result the number of vines per hectare has been reduced, yet the plants have more leaf exposure, which should lead to an improvement in quality. During this time the average yields have plummeted. In 1996 they were down to 58 hectoliters per hetare; in 1997 to 47. We were pleasantly surprised by the 1992s, which the 1994s equalled in quality. The last three vintages have all also been quite pleasant, with 1997 taking the prize as the best of the trio. The lovely Kabinett – 6 – is a steal for less than ten Marks. Like many other estates in Piesport, Reuscher-Haart sell the lion's share of their wines abroad.

1997 Piesporter Goldtröpfchen
Riesling Kabinett – 7 –
10.50 DM, 8%, ♀ till 2001 **84**

1997 Piesporter Goldtröpfchen
Riesling Spätlese – 11 –
14 DM, 9%, ♀ till 2003 **84**

1996 Piesporter Goldtröpfchen
Riesling Kabinett
9.50 DM, 8.5%, ♀ till 2001 **86**

1997 Piesporter Goldtröpfchen
Riesling Spätlese – 9 –
14.20 DM, 8.5%, ♀ till 2003 **86**

1997 Piesporter Goldtröpfchen
Riesling Spätlese – 10 –
14.60 DM, 8%, ♀ till 2003 **86**

1996 Piesporter Goldtröpfchen
Riesling Spätlese – 9 –
12 DM, 8%, ♀ till 2001 **86**

1996 Piesporter Goldtröpfchen
Riesling Spätlese – 8 –
12 DM, 8.5%, ♀ till 2002 **88**

1997 Piesporter Goldtröpfchen
Riesling Kabinett – 6 –
9.60 DM, 7.5%, ♀ till 2004 **89**

1996 Piesporter Goldtröpfchen
Riesling Spätlese – 10 –
14 DM, 8%, ♀ till 2004 **89**

1997 Piesporter Goldtröpfchen
Riesling Auslese
21 DM/0.5 liter, 8.5%, ♀ till 2006 **89**

WEINGUT EDMUND REVERCHON

Owner: Eddie Reverchon
General Manager: Jens Reverchon
Manager: Christoph Händle
Winemaker: Karl-Heinz Alt
54329 Konz-Filzen, Saartalstraße 2–3
Tel. (0 65 01) 1 69 09 and 1 73 19, Fax 1 82 41
Directions: B 51 from Trier via Konz, about three kilometers from Konz along the Saar in a southerly direction
Sales: Andrea Reverchon
Opening hours: Mon.–Fri. 8 a.m. to 5 p.m. or by appointment
Restaurant: Open Fri. from 6 p.m., Sat., Sun. and on holidays from 3 p.m.
Specialties: "Gerupfter," baked cheese
Worth seeing: Mansion is a protected monument, with park and vaulted cellar

Vineyard area: 18 hectares
Annual production: 100,000 bottles
Top sites: Filzener Herrenberg (sole owners), Steinberg und Urbelt, Wiltinger Gottesfuß
Soil types: Devon slate
Grape varieties: 92% Riesling, 2% Weißburgunder, 1% Chardonnay, 5% other varieties
Average yield: 65 hl/ha
Best vintages: 1994, 1995, 1997
Member: Bernkasteler Ring

Although we still prefer the fruitier Rieslings, Eddie Reverchon has long been a specialist in hearty dry and off-dry wines, which now account for about two-thirds of his production. Long before it became fashionable, Reverchon was marketing these wines in designer bottles. Since 1979 he has even been using an individual bottle for his dry wines from the Herrenberg and Steinberg vineyards. After the rather irregular quality of the 1980s, this estate has recovered and, since the 1993 vintage, consistently produced reliable wines. Although the 1996s didn't quite reach the level of quality of the preceding vintages, the 1997s were again very successful. This estate is still heading in an upward spiral.

1996 Konzer Karthäuser Klosterberg
Riesling Spätlese halbtrocken
17 DM, 9.5%, ♀ till 2001 **84**

1997 Wiltinger Gottesfuß
Riesling Kabinett
20.55 DM, 8%, ♀ till 2003 **84**

1997 Filzener Herrenberg
Riesling trocken
14.50 DM, 11.5%, ♀ till 2002 **84**

1997 Filzener Herrenberg
Riesling Spätlese halbtrocken
17 DM, 10%, ♀ till 2002 **86**

1996 Kanzemer Altenberg
Riesling Kabinett
14.70 DM, 8%, ♀ till 2000 **86**

1997 Wiltinger Gottesfuß
Riesling Spätlese
29 DM, 7.5%, ♀ till 2005 **86**

1997 Filzener Herrenberg
Riesling Spätlese
17 DM, 7%, ♀ till 2004 **88**

1997 Wiltinger Gottesfuß
Riesling Auslese
47.55 DM, 7.5%, ♀ till 2005 **89**

1997 Filzener Herrenberg
Riesling Auslese
25 DM, 11.5%, ♀ till 2007 **89**

1996 Filzener Herrenberg
Riesling Eiswein
90 DM/0.375 liter, 9%, ♀ till 2008 **91**

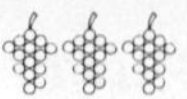

WEINGUT MAX FERD. RICHTER

Owners: Ökonomierat Horst Richter and Dr. Dirk Richter
General manager: Werner Franz
Winemaker: Walter Hauth
54486 Mülheim, Hauptstraße 37/85
Tel. (0 65 34) 7 04 and 93 30 03, Fax 12 11
e-mail: m.f.richter@t-online.de
Directions: A 48, exit Salmtal, in the direction of Mülheim
Sales: Dr. Dirk Richter and Anneliese Hauth
Opening hours: Mon.–Fri. 9 a.m. to 6 p.m., Sat. 9 a.m. to 1 p.m. or by appointment
History: Owned by the family since 1680
Worth seeing: Baroque estate house, French garden, cask cellar from 1880

Vineyard area: 14.3 hectares
Annual production: 120,000 bottles
Top sites: Brauneberger Juffer and Juffer-Sonnenuhr, Graacher Domprobst
Soil types: Weathered clay-slate
Grape varieties: 90% Riesling, 10% other varieties
Average yield: 65 hl/ha
Best vintages: 1993, 1995, 1997

This winery traces its origins to a trading enterprise founded in 1680 and boasts the most extensive cask cellar in the Middle Mosel. The estate owns excellent vineyards in Graach, Wehlen and Mülheim as well as Brauneberg, which helps explain the fact that it is well established in the export market. Before World War II large quantities of the estate's wines were dispatched to eastern Europe. Even today two-thirds of the off-dry and late harvested wines are exported, mostly to Japan. In view of the hail damage, it is not surprising that the 1996s were not as successful as the 1995s. It was thus all the more astonishing that the Brauneberger Juffer-Sonnenuhr Trockenbeerenauslese should be one of the finest wines of the year! While the 1997 vintage brought few wines of this level, the average quality was much better.

1997 Brauneberger Juffer
Riesling Kabinett
12 DM, 8.5%, ♀ till 2003 **84**

1996 Brauneberger Juffer
Riesling Kabinett
11.65 DM, 8%, ♀ till 2002 **84**

1997 Brauneberger Juffer-Sonnenuhr
Riesling Spätlese
16 DM, 8%, ♀ till 2005 **88**

1996 Brauneberger Juffer-Sonnenuhr
Riesling Spätlese
15.50 DM, 7.5%, ♀ till 2004 **88**

1996 Graacher Domprobst
Riesling Spätlese
16 DM, 8%, ♀ till 2004 **88**

1997 Wehlener Sonnenuhr
Riesling Spätlese
16 DM, 7.5%, ♀ till 2006 **89**

1997 Graacher Himmelreich
Riesling Auslese
20 DM, 8%, ♀ till 2007 **89**

1997 Wehlener Sonnenuhr
Riesling Auslese
28 DM, 8%, ♀ till 2008 **91**

1996 Graacher Domprobst
Riesling Beerenauslese
77 DM/0.375 liter, 8.5%, ♀ till 2008 **92**

1996 Brauneberger Juffer-Sonnenuhr
Riesling Trockenbeerenauslese
151 DM/0.375 liter, 8.5%, ♀ till 2013 **96**

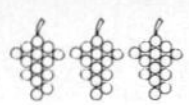

WEINGUT JOSEF ROSCH

Owner: Werner Rosch
54340 Leiwen, Mühlenstraße 8
Tel. (0 65 07) 42 30, Fax 82 87
Directions: A 48 Koblenz–Trier, exit Salmtal, A1, exit Mehring
Opening hours: By appointment

Vineyard area: 4.5 hectares
Annual production: 45,000 bottles
Top sites: Leiwener Laurentiuslay, Trittenheimer Apotheke and Altärchen
Soil types: Slate
Grape varieties: 97% Riesling, 3% other varieties
Average yield: 70 hl/ha
Best vintages: 1993, 1994, 1995

One of the founding generation of the young growers in Leiwen, Werner Rosch first staked his claim to wider recognition in 1988 when his dry Spätlese from the Laurentiuslay vineyard took second place in a blind tasting organized by the magazine *Capital*, well ahead of many more prominent estates. His wines from the early 1990s were even more successful, so that Rosch has now been able to obtain nationwide acclaim for his production. The first-rate range from the 1995 vintage – above all the Auslese and the ice wine from the Klostergarten – added new dimensions to his repertoire. However, neither the 1996s nor 1997s have been at the same quality level. Given our expectations, the latter vintage was even disappointing. Although private customers buy the majority of his wines, dry Rieslings – which constitute about half of the total production – often turn up on the wine lists of fine restaurants. This is attributable to the fact that Rosch is just as much a promoter of his wines as he is of himself. To date little of his wine has been exported.

1997 Leiwener Klostergarten
Riesling Kabinett
10 DM, 8%, ♀ till 2004 **84**

1997 Leiwener Klostergarten
Riesling halbtrocken
8.60 DM, 10.5%, ♀ till 2003 **84**

1997 Trittenheimer Apotheke
Riesling Auslese ***
45 DM/0.5 liter, 9%, ♀ till 2006 **86**

1997 Trittenheimer Apotheke
Riesling Spätlese
18 DM, 9%, ♀ till 2006 **88**

1997 Leiwener Klostergarten
Riesling Auslese **
26 DM/0.5 liter, 9%, ♀ till 2006 **88**

1996 Leiwener Klostergarten
Riesling Kabinett
9.80 DM, 8%, ♀ till 2003 **89**

1996 Dhron Hofberger
Riesling Spätlese
14.50 DM, 8.5%, ♀ till 2004 **89**

1996 Trittenheimer Apotheke
Riesling Auslese
22 DM, 9%, ♀ 1999 till 2005 **91**

1996 Leiwener Klostergarten
Riesling Eiswein
69 DM, 8%, ♀ 2001 till 2008 **92**

WEINGUT JOSEF ROSCH
D-54340 LEIWEN/MOSEL
WEINGUT JOSEF ROSCH
RIESLING
AUSLESE
1996
Trittenheimer Apotheke
GUTSABFÜLLUNG
Qualitätswein mit Prädikat - A. P. Nr. 3 529 153 8 97 - Produce of Germany
9,0% vol MOSEL-SAAR-RUWER 0,5 l

WEINGUT SCHLOSS SAARSTEIN

Owner: Christian Ebert
54455 Serrig
Tel. (0 65 81) 23 24, Fax 65 23
Directions: B 51 Trier–Saarburg–Serrig
Sales: Andrea Ebert
Opening hours: By appointment
Worth seeing: Chateau built at the turn of the century

Vineyard area: 11 hectares
Annual production: 60,000 bottles
Top site: Serriger Schloss Saarsteiner
Soil types: Weathered slate
Grape varieties: 97% Riesling, 2% Weißburgunder, 1% other varieties
Average yield: 45 hl/ha
Best vintages: 1994, 1995, 1997
Member: VDP

In 1956 Dieter Ebert bought this turn-of-the-century mansion along with the Serriger Schloss Saarstein vineyard. After completing his studies in oenology at Geisenheim, his son Christian entered the business in 1986. Since then the estate has literally blossomed. In his endeavor Christian is now ably supported by his wife, Andrea, who is as charming as she is capable. This is hardly surprising, since she was raised on the Wirsching estate in Franken. All of the work in the vineyard is quite conventional; in the cellar Christian Ebert operates according to the motto "as little as possible, as much as is necessary." The wines are fermented in casks. The dry and off-dry Rieslings – which are always quite racy – are marketed with a simpler green and yellow label; the elegant and fruitier classic wines are sold under the traditional Saarstein label. The 1996s were perhaps a touch below the usual standard, but it was a difficult year for the Saar. Ebert bounced back with a stunning collection of 1997s, which are certainly the finest wines that he has produced in some time.

1997 Serriger Schloss Saarsteiner
Riesling Spätlese halbtrocken
19.50 DM, 11%, ♀ till 2003 **88**

1997 Serriger Schloss Saarsteiner
Riesling Kabinett
12.50 DM, 8.5%, ♀ till 2005 **88**

1996 Serriger Schloss Saarsteiner
Riesling Kabinett
12 DM, 8%, ♀ till 2001 **88**

1996 Serriger Schloss Saarsteiner
Riesling Spätlese
18.50 DM, 8%, ♀ till 2003 **89**

1997 Serriger Schloss Saarsteiner
Riesling Spätlese
19 DM, 8%, ♀ till 2006 **91**

1997 Serriger Schloss Saarsteiner
Riesling Auslese Goldkapsel
59 DM/0.375 liter, 10%, ♀ till 2006 **91**

1996 Serriger Schloss Saarsteiner
Riesling Auslese Goldkapsel
Not yet for sale, 9%, ♀ till 2005 **91**

1997 Serriger Schloss Saarsteiner
Riesling Auslese
29 DM, 8%, ♀ till 2008 **92**

1997 Serriger Schloss Saarsteiner
Riesling Auslese lange Goldkapsel
108 DM/0.375 liter, 8%, ♀ till 2010 **95**

1997 Serriger Schloss Saarsteiner
Riesling Beerenauslese
Not yet for sale, 7.5%, ♀ till 2010 **95**

WEINGUT SANKT URBANS-HOF

Owner: Hermann Weis
General Manager: Nik Weis
Winemaker: Rudolf Hoffmann
54340 Leiwen, Urbanusstraße 16
Tel. (0 65 07) 9 37 70, Fax 93 77 30
e-mail: st.urbanshof@t-online.de
Directions: A 48, exit Salmtal, in the direction of Hetzerath-Bekond; A 1, exit Mehring, in the direction of Büdlicher Brück
Sales: Nik Weis and Rudolf Hoffmann
Opening hours: Mon.–Fri. 9 a.m. to 6 p.m., Sat. and Sun. 9 a.m. to 8 p.m. Evenings by appointment
Restaurant: "Landhaus St. Urban," open Thur.–Mon. from noon to 2 p.m. and 6 p.m. to 10 p.m.
Closed Tue. and Wed. until 6 p.m.
Specialties: Excellent regional cooking
Worth seeing: Old mill bakery

Vineyard area: 35 hectares
Annual production: 350,000 bottles
Top sites: Leiwener Laurentiuslay, Piesporter Goldtröpfchen, Ockfener Bockstein, Wiltinger Schlangengraben
Soil types: Devon slate
Grape varieties: 90% Riesling, 5% Müller-Thurgau, 5% other varieties
Average yield: 60 hl/ha
Best vintages: 1993, 1994, 1996

This estate, founded just after World War II by Nicolaus Weis, has enjoyed dynamic development in the past decade. Hermann Weis, patron of the young growers of Leiwen, has virtually doubled the estate's vineyard holdings by making purchases in the Saar. For the past few years his son Nik has managed the estate, often excelling with his impressive dry Rieslings from the Laurentiuslay. Although the 1996s will perhaps not be remembered as our favorites, the 1997s are again right on the mark. Although Weis recently purchased a parcel of vines within the Piesporter Goldtröpfchen, he is keen to reduce his overall holdings.

1997 Leiwener Laurentiuslay
Riesling Spätlese trocken
19 DM, 11%, ♀ till 2003 **88**

1996 Ockfener Bockstein
Riesling Kabinett
13 DM, 8%, ♀ till 2000 **89**

1997 Piesporter Goldtröpfchen
Riesling Spätlese
21 DM, 7.5%, ♀ till 2007 **91**

1997 Ockfener Bockstein
Riesling Auslese – 4 –
50 DM, 8.5%, ♀ till 2007 **91**

1997 Wiltinger Schlangengraben
Riesling Spätlese
30 DM, 8%, ♀ till 2008 **92**

1996 Piesporter Goldtröpfchen
Riesling Spätlese
21 DM, 8%, ♀ till 2005 **92**

1997 Ockfener Bockstein
Riesling Auslese – 12 –
70 DM, 8%, ♀ till 2008 **92**

1996 Wiltinger Schlangengraben
Riesling Auslese
70 DM, 8.5%, ♀ till 2007 **92**

1996 Leiwener Klostergarten
Riesling Eiswein
80 DM, 6%, ♀ till 2012 **94**

WEINGUT WILLI SCHAEFER

Owner: Willi Schaefer
54470 Graach, Hauptstraße 130
Tel. (0 65 31) 80 41, Fax 14 14
Directions: A 48, exit Wittlich, in the direction of Bernkastel-Kues
Sales: Schaefer family
Opening hours: Mon.–Fri. 9 a.m. to noon and 2 p.m. to 6 p.m.
Sat. 10 a.m. to noon
Sun. by appointment
History: Estate owned by the family since 1590

Vineyard area: 2.6 hectares
Annual production: 26,000 bottles
Top sites: Graacher Domprobst and Himmelreich
Soil types: Devon slate
Grape varieties: 100% Riesling
Average yield: 68 hl/ha
Best vintages: 1993, 1995, 1997
Member: VDP

Of all the growers in Graach, Willi Schaefer makes by far the best wine. His success is based on two hectares of choicest parcels in the outstanding vineyards of Himmelreich and Domprobst in Graach as well as a smaller site in the Wehlener Sonnenuhr. Since the early 1990s Schaefer has been on a roll; and the quality of his wines has improved from year to year. The 1995 range was the climax of a string of excellent vintages and earned him the title of "Rising Star" in that year's edition of this guide. The 1996s, albeit very good, didn't quite match this standard; but the Kabinetts were of exceptional quality nonetheless, and remained good value for money. The 1997s are again first-rate, with the Domprobst Spätlese and Auslese numbering among the finest wines of the vintage. Now that son Christoff has begun his studies at Geisenheim, father Willi is giving thought to a cautious expansion of the estate – "to no more than five hectares." His faithful clients relish the prospect. For nobody's wines are harder to find, nor more worth the search, than Schaefer's.

1997 Graacher Himmelreich
Riesling Kabinett
11.50 DM, 7.5%, ♀ till 2006 **89**

1996 Graacher Himmelreich
Riesling Kabinett
10.50 DM, 7.5%, ♀ till 2006 **89**

1997 Graacher Domprobst
Riesling Spätlese
19 DM, 8.5%, ♀ till 2007 **91**

1996 Graacher Domprobst
Riesling Spätlese – 4 –
17.50 DM, 7.5%, ♀ till 2007 **91**

1997 Graacher Domprobst
Riesling Spätlese
47.30 DM, 8%, ♀ till 2008 **92**

1997 Graacher Domprobst
Riesling Auslese
60 DM, 9%, ♀ till 2010 **94**

1996 Graacher Domprobst
Riesling Auslese Goldkapsel
130 DM, 9%, ♀ till 2008 **94**

1997 Graacher Domprobst
Riesling Beerenauslese
160 DM, 9.5%, ♀ till 2012 **95**

1997 Graacher Domprobst
Riesling Beerenauslese
Not yet for sale, 9.5%, ♀ till 2010 **95**

1997 Graacher Domprobst
Riesling Auslese
189 DM, 8.5%, ♀ till 2010 **96**

WEINGUT FREIHERR VON SCHLEINITZ

Owner: Konrad Hähn
56330 Kobern-Gondorf, Kirchstraße 17
Tel. (0 26 07) 97 20 20, Fax 97 20 22
e-mail: WeingutvonSchleinitz@t-online.de
Internet: http://www.vinonet.com/schleinitz.htm
Directions: A 61, exit Dieblich or Plaidt, A 48, exit Kobern
Opening hours: Mon.–Fri. 8 a.m. to 5 p.m., Sat. 8 a.m. to 1 p.m. or by appointment
Restaurant: Open daily from 4 p.m. Sun. from 10 a.m., except Tue.

Vineyard area: 7 hectares
Annual production: 50,000 bottles
Top sites: Koberner Weißenberg and Uhlen
Soil types: Slate with layers of reddish-hued soil
Grape varieties: 97% Riesling, 3% Spätburgunder
Average yield: 62 hl/ha
Best vintages: 1993, 1995, 1996

Konrad Hähn runs this winery near Koblenz just as his forefathers did. All the vineyards are so steep that costly manual labor is required to cultivate them. The owner favors natural farming practices, including the use of organic manure. In the cellar all measures – including the use of cultivated yeasts – serve the cause of a gentle vinification. Hähn has exchanged the traditional wooden casks for steel tanks and produces fresh, fruity Rieslings by bottling early. In recent years he has also steadily increased the proportion of dry wines so that today dry, off-dry and sweetish Rieslings each account for one third of total production. Over half of this is sold directly to private customers. Over the past decade this estate has had a succession of good vintages. The 1994 range was somewhat weaker, but the 1995s and 1996s brought a return to the familiar, dependable level of quality. The 1997s are even a touch better.

1997 Koberner Weißenberg
Riesling trocken
7.90 DM, 11.5%, ♀ till 2000 **77**

1996 Koberner Uhlen
Riesling trocken
9.50 DM, 11%, ♀ now **80**

1996 Koberner Uhlen
Riesling halbtrocken
10 DM, 10.5%, ♀ till 2000 **80**

1997 Koberner Uhlen
Riesling halbtrocken
10 DM, 11.5%, ♀ till 2002 **82**

1997 Koberner Uhlen
Riesling trocken
10 DM, 12%, ♀ till 2002 **82**

1997 Koberner Uhlen
Riesling Auslese trocken
19 DM, 11.5%, ♀ till 2002 **84**

1996 Koberner Weißenberg
Riesling Spätlese halbtrocken
12.50 DM, 10%, ♀ till 2001 **84**

1997 Koberner Weißenberg
Riesling Spätlese
12.50 DM, 9.5%, ♀ till 2004 **84**

1997 Koberner Weißenberg
Riesling Spätlese trocken
12.50 DM, 11%, ♀ till 2002 **86**

WEINGUT HEINRICH SCHMITGES

Owner: Andreas Schmitges
54492 Erden, Im Unterdorf 12
Tel. (0 65 32) 27 43, Fax 39 34
Directions: A 48 Koblenz–Trier, exit Zeltingen, five kilometers in the direction of Traben-Trarbach, in the village center
Sales: Waltraud Schmitges
Opening hours: Mon.–Fri. 6 p.m. to 8 p.m., Sat. 3 p.m. to 6 p.m. or by appointment

Vineyard area: 4.5 hectares
Annual production: 55,000 bottles
Top sites: Erdener Treppchen and Prälat, Wehlener Sonnenuhr
Soil types: Slate
Grape varieties: 85% Riesling, 15% Müller-Thurgau,
Average yield: 80 hl/ha
Best vintages: 1994, 1995, 1996

Andreas and Waltraud Schmitges have considerably polished the image of this estate since they took it over in 1990. This occurred through distinct marketing practices and intensive customer service. But that is only the glitter on the surface; the wine quality has improved as well. The family is endowed with vineyards in the most renowned parcels of Erden and Wehlen, which provide the fundamentals for each wine's quality. Since 1991 the must has been fermented in stainless steel tanks; thereafter the wines age for three to four months in wooden casks. We were again pleasantly surprised by the quality of the latest vintage. The 1996s are full of character, from the simple dry Rivaner to the sweetest Auslese. And incidentally, Andreas Schmitges is one of the few to have refrained from the confusing use of stars to indicate different levels of quality for his Spätlese and Auslese.

1996 Riesling
trocken
9.50 DM, 11%, ♀ till 2000 **84**

1996 Erdener Treppchen
Riesling Kabinett trocken
11 DM, 10%, ♀ till 2000 **84**

1997
Riesling
9.50 DM, 10%, ♀ till 2001 **84**

1996 Wehlener Sonnenuhr
Riesling Spätlese halbtrocken
15 DM, 10.5%, ♀ till 2002 **86**

1997 Erdener Treppchen
Riesling Kabinett
11 DM, 8.5%, ♀ till 2003 **86**

1996 Erdener Treppchen
Riesling Spätlese trocken
14.50 DM, 11%, ♀ till 2002 **88**

1996 Erdener Treppchen
Riesling Kabinett
10.50 DM, 8.5%, ♀ till 2004 **88**

1996 Erdener Treppchen
Riesling Auslese
15 DM/0.375 liter, 7.5%, ♀ till 2006 **89**

1996 Erdener Prälat
Riesling Auslese
Not yet for sale, 7.5%, ♀ till 2008 **91**

SCHMITGES
WEINBAU SEIT MDCCXLIV
1996
Erdener Treppchen
Riesling Spätlese
Trocken
GUTSABFÜLLUNG · WEINGUT HEINRICH SCHMITGES · D - 54492 ERDEN
QUALITÄTSWEIN MIT PRÄDIKAT · PRODUCE OF GERMANY · A. P. NR. 2582071997
alc 11%byVol *Mosel-Saar-Ruwer* e 750 ml

WEINGUT HEINZ SCHMITT

Owner: Heinz Schmitt
54340 Leiwen, Stephanusstraße 4
Tel. (0 65 07) 42 76, Fax 81 61
e-mail:
weingut-heinz-schmitt@t-online.de
Directions: A 48 Koblenz–Trier, exit Salmtal; A 1 Saarbrücken–Trier, exit Mehring
Sales: Silvi and Heinz Schmitt, Götz Drewitz
Opening hours: By appointment

Vineyard area: 9 hectares
Annual production: 87,000 bottles
Top sites: Schweicher Annaberg, Longuicher Maximiner Herrenberg, Trittenheimer Altärchen
Soil types: Slate and weathered slate, red slate with red sandstone and grey slate
Grape varieties: 86% Riesling, 7% Weißburgunder, 6% Müller-Thurgau, 1% Kerner
Average yield: 73 hl/ha
Best vintages: 1994, 1996, 1997

When Heinz Schmitt took over this property in 1983 he didn't rush to make changes. He joined forces with the other young growers of Leiwen and devoted himself to his further training. He repeatedly visited model wineries in California and made an intensive study of modern winemaking methods. Schmitt now opts for careful handling in the cellar, including slow fermentations. Given his attachment to California, it is no wonder that his range is dominated by wines made in a dry and off-dry style. The dry Rieslings, however, are often somewhat hearty in style. The 1995s were hardly up to the standard of the very successful 1994 vintage, but the 1996s brought an improvement, which was partially accounted for by the low yields of 58 hectoliters per hectare. The 1997s were even better, certainly the finest collection of wines that we have ever tasted from this estate. If this continues, we may well write the same thing about the 1998s.

1997 Schweicher Annaberg
Riesling Spätlese trocken
16 DM, 12%, ♀ till 2003 **86**

1997 Longuicher Maximiner Herrenberg
Riesling Kabinett halbtrocken
14 DM, 10%, ♀ till 2004 **86**

1996 Longuicher Maximiner Herrenberg
Riesling Auslese halbtrocken
22 DM, 11%, ♀ till 2004 **86**

1997 Longuicher Maximiner Herrenberg
Riesling Spätlese
16 DM, 8%, ♀ till 2004 **86**

1997 Riesling
trocken
9 DM, 11.5%, ♀ till 2002 **86**

1997 Köwericher Laurentiuslay
Riesling Spätlese
16 DM, 10%, ♀ till 2004 **88**

1997 Klüsserather Bruderschaft
Riesling Auslese “S”
30 DM, 9.5%, ♀ till 2006 **89**

1997 Mehringer Blattenberg
Riesling Auslese “S”
27 DM, 8.5%, ♀ till 2006 **91**

1997 Mehringer Blattenberg
Riesling Beerenauslese
80 DM/0.375 liter, 9.5%, ♀ till 2008 **91**

GUTSVERWALTUNG VON SCHUBERT – GRÜNHAUS

Owner: Dr. Carl-Ferdinand von Schubert
Manager and winemaker: Alfons Heinrich
54318 Grünhaus-Mertesdorf
Tel. (06 51) 51 11, Fax 5 21 22
Directions: A 48, exit Kenn/Trier-Ruwer, after two kilometers left into the Ruwertal
Sales: Dr. Carl-Ferdinand von Schubert
Opening hours: Mon.–Fri. 8:15 a.m. to noon and 1 p.m. to 4:45 p.m.
Sat. 9 a.m. to noon, by appointment
History: First documented in 966 as part of St. Maximin Abbey, owned by the Schubert family since 1882
Worth seeing: Ensemble of mansion and stables in Gothic style with surrounding wall

Vineyard area: 34 hectares
Annual production: 200,000 bottles
Top sites: Maximin Grünhäuser Abtsberg and Herrenberg
Soil types: Blue Devon slate
Grape varieties: 97% Riesling, 2% Müller-Thurgau, 1% Kerner
Average yield: 45 hl/ha
Best vintages: 1993, 1995, 1997

Under the direction of Dr. Carl-Ferdinand von Schubert this estate has evolved into one of the most sought-after producers of dry Rieslings in Germany, a style that today accounts for some two thirds of total sales. One can buy these bottles – with their ununsual Jugendstil label – without tasting the content; it will invariably be an extremely delicate wine. In finer vintages the elegantly spiced, noble late harvest wines often represent the epitome of what Riesling can achieve in Germany. The impressive 1996 range, crowned by a marvelous ice wine from the Abtsberg, confirmed the enduring standards of this estate that we named "Winemaker of the Year" in 1995. The graceful 1997 Abtsberg Kabinett and succulent Spätlese are perfect examples of what this style of Riesling is all about.

1996 Maximin Grünhäuser Abtsberg
Riesling Kabinett
18 DM, 10%, ♀ till 2004 **89**

1997 Maximin Grünhäuser Abtsberg
Riesling Kabinett
22 DM, 8%, ♀ till 2006 **91**

1997 Maximin Grünhäuser Herrenberg
Riesling Spätlese
24 DM, 8%, ♀ till 2007 **91**

1996 Maximin Grünhäuser Abtsberg
Riesling Spätlese
23 DM, 7.5%, ♀ till 2006 **91**

1996 Maximin Grünhäuser Abtsberg
Riesling Auslese
35 DM, 7%, ♀ till 2008 **92**

1996 Maximin Grünhäuser Abtsberg
Riesling Auslese – 55 –
50 DM, 7.5%, ♀ till 2008 **92**

1997 Maximin Grünhäuser Abtsberg
Riesling Spätlese
25 DM, 8%, ♀ till 2010 **94**

1997 Maximin Grünhäuser Abtsberg
Riesling Auslese – 57 –
67 DM, 8.5%, ♀ till 2010 **94**

1997 Maximin Grünhäuser Herrenberg
Riesling Auslese – 89 –
56 DM, 7.5%, ♀ till 2010 **94**

1996 Maximin Grünhäuser Abtsberg
Riesling Eiswein – 135 –
340 DM, 7%, ♀ till 2012 **96**

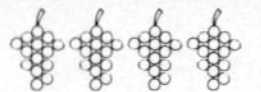

WEINGUT SELBACH-OSTER

Owners: Hans and Johannes Selbach
Winemakers: Klaus-Rainer Schäfer and Hans Selbach
54492 Zeltingen, Uferallee 23
Tel. (0 65 32) 20 81, Fax 40 14
e-mail: selbach.zeltingen@t-online.de
Internet: www.vinonet.com/selbach.htm
Directions: A 48, exit Wittlich, over the Mosel bridge to Zeltingen
Sales: Selbach family
Opening hours: By appointment
History: Owned by the family since 1661

Vineyard area: 10.6 hectares
Annual production: 85,000 bottles
Top sites: Zeltinger Sonnenuhr, Wehlener Sonnenuhr, Graacher Domprobst
Soil types: Stony slate, partly with loam
Grape varieties: 100% Riesling
Average yield: 68 hl/ha
Best vintages: 1992, 1995, 1996

Johannes Selbach has been running this estate in Zeltingen with his father, Hans, since 1989. Since then both the estate and the family's wine merchant business have seen a significant upturn in their fortunes. The Selbach are owners of choicest parcels in the steep sites of Zeltingen, Wehlen, Graach and Bernkastel, which are all planted with very old Riesling vines on their own roots. A heavy hailstorm in late July 1996 wrecked a large proportion of the still ripening fruit; the result was an extremely small crop, with production less than half of that expected from a normal vintage. The remarkable wines at the top quality levels proved that the arduous battle to produce great wines was worth the fight! Although the vineyard still suffers the scars of the hailstorm, the 1997s are very finely balanced. The three Sonnenuhr Spätlese are all delicious.

1997 Wehlener Sonnenuhr
Riesling Kabinett
12.50 DM, 8.5%, ♀ till 2004 **89**

1996 Wehlener Sonnenuhr
Riesling Spätlese *
19.50 DM, 8%, ♀ till 2005 **89**

1997 Zeltinger Sonnenuhr
Riesling Spätlese – 23 –
18 DM, 8%, ♀ till 2007 **91**

1997 Zeltinger Sonnenuhr
Riesling Spätlese * – 2 –
20 DM, 7.5%, ♀ till 2007 **91**

1997 Zeltinger Sonnenuhr
Riesling Auslese **
39.50 DM, 8.5%, ♀ till 2006 **92**

1996 Zeltinger Sonnenuhr
Riesling Auslese *
36 DM, 7.5%, ♀ till 2006 **92**

1996 Zelinger Sonnenuhr
Riesling Auslese ***
75 DM, 8%, ♀ till 2006 **94**

1996 Bernkasteler Badstube
Riesling Eiswein
115 DM/0.375 liter, 9%, ♀ till 2010 **95**

1997 Riesling
Beerenauslese Goldkapsel
91 DM/0.375 liter, 9%, ♀ till 2014 **95**

1996 Zeltinger Sonnenuhr
Riesling Trockenbeerenauslese
220 DM/0.375 liter, 7%, ♀ till 2014 **96**

WEINGUT STUDERT-PRÜM – MAXIMINHOF

Owners: Stephan and Gerhard Studert
54470 Bernkastel-Wehlen, Hauptstraße 150
Tel. (0 65 31) 24 87, Fax 39 20
Directions: From Bernkastel follow the left side of the Mosel to Wehlen
Opening hours: Mon.–Fri. 8 a.m. to 7 p.m., Sat. 10 a.m. to 4 p.m. Sun. by appointment
History: First mentioned in 1256 by St. Maximin Abbey. Owned by the Studert family for 12 generations
Worth seeing: The Maximinhof of the former St. Maximin Abbey

Vineyard area: 5 hectares
Annual production: 40,000 bottles
Top sites: Wehlener Sonnenuhr, Graacher Himmelreich and Domprobst
Soil types: Devon slate
Grape varieties: 95% Riesling, 5% Müller-Thurgau
Average yield: 53 hl/ha
Best vintages: 1994, 1995, 1997
Member: VDP

In Wehlen there are a number of wineries named after the Prüm family and all date back to the time some 80 years ago when the property of Sebastian Aloys Prüm was divided among his six children. The name Studert-Prüm derives from the marriage of Stephan Studert senior to a daughter of Peter Prüm's. At the time of the secularization of the church's properties in 1805 the Studert family had acquired the Maximinhof; today the winery manages five hectares of noteworthy vineyards in Wehlen, Graach and Bernkastel. The present owners are the brothers Stephan Jr. and Gerhard Studert. Since 1990 they have produced a string of successful vintages, culminating in the excellent 1994s and 1995s. Although far from disappointing, as the two Auslese attest, the 1996 range was not quite up to par. Although the 1997 Kabinett and Spätlese are again considerably better, the noble late harvest Rieslings were not up to the estate's standards.

1997 Wehlener Sonnenuhr
Riesling Spätlese
13 DM, 8%, ♀ till 2004 **86**

1996 Wehlener Sonnenuhr
Riesling Spätlese
13 DM, 8%, ♀ till 2004 **86**

1997 Wehlener Sonnenuhr
Riesling Kabinett
10 DM, 7.5%, ♀ till 2005 **88**

1997 Wehlener Sonnenuhr
Riesling Spätlese **
15 DM, 8%, ♀ till 2006 **89**

1997 Wehlener Sonnenuhr
Riesling Auslese ***
25 DM/0.375 liter, 9%, ♀ till 2006 **89**

1996 Wehlener Sonnenuhr
Riesling Auslese – 9 –
16 DM, 7.5%, ♀ till 2006 **89**

1996 Wehlener Sonnenuhr
Riesling Auslese – 10 –
20 DM/0.375 liter, 8.5%, ♀ till 2006 **89**

1997 Wehlener Sonnenuhr
Riesling Eiswein
100 DM/0.375 liter, 8%, ♀ till 2006 **89**

1997 Wehlener Sonnenuhr
Riesling Beerenauslese
55 DM/0.375 liter, 9.5%, ♀ till 2006 **89**

1997 Wehlener Sonnenuhr
Riesling Auslese **
19 DM, 8.5%, ♀ till 2008 **91**

WEINGUT PETER TERGES

Owner: Peter Terges
54295 Trier, Olewiger Straße 145
Tel. (06 51) 3 10 96, Fax 30 96 71
Directions: A 48, exit Trier-Olewig
Opening hours: By appointment

Vineyard area: 5 hectares
Annual production: 40,000 bottles
Top sites: Trierer Burgberg, Deutschherrenberg and Jesuitenwingert
Soil types: Slate and Devon slate
Grape varieties: 70% Riesling, 15% Weißburgunder, 10% Müller-Thurgau, 5% Kerner
Average yield: 92 hl/ha
Best vintages: 1990, 1993, 1995

Peter Terges is ambitious; he wants to be one of the best producers of the region. Although his vineyards are not entirely of the highest quality and his yields at the upper end of the acceptable, he has produced a range of notable wines in the past few years. Still, he is a long way from his goal. In order to develop further, Terges regularly tastes the wines of his distinguished colleagues. As he himself observes, the 1994 vintage was rather disappointing; on the other hand he was justifiably proud of his 1995s. The majority of his wines – of which some 70 percent are sold to private customers – are made in a sweetish style, which is clearly where his strength lies. He has also specialized in producing ice wines, but again his 1996s were not up to par. He himself describes it as the "best of the weak." The 1997s – although no ice wine was produced – are notably better, but still not as fine as his 1993s and 1995s.

1997 Trierer Burgberg
Riesling Kabinett
8 DM, 8%, 🍷 till 2000 **84**

1996 Trierer Burgberg
Riesling Auslese
24.50 DM, 🍷 till 2003 **84**

1997 Trierer Burgberg
Riesling Spätlese
12.50 DM, 7.5%, 🍷 till 2002 **86**

1997 Trierer Deutschherrenberg
Riesling Spätlese
13.50 DM, 7.5%, 🍷 till 2002 **86**

1997 Trierer Burgberg
Riesling Auslese
22 DM, 8%, 🍷 till 2003 **86**

1996 Trierer Deutschherrenberg
Riesling Auslese
26.50 DM, 🍷 till 2003 **86**

1996 Trierer Jesuitenwingert
Riesling Eiswein
40 DM/0.375 liter, 🍷 till 2000 **86**

1996 Trierer Burgberg
Riesling Eiswein
50 DM/0.375 liter, 🍷 till 2000 **86**

1997 Trierer Deutschherrenberg
Riesling Auslese
18 DM, 7.5%, 🍷 till 2003 **88**

1996 Trierer Deutschherrenberg
Riesling Eiswein
60 DM/0.375 liter, 🍷 till 2002 **89**

WEINGUT WWE. DR. H. THANISCH – ERBEN THANISCH

Owner: Sofia Thanisch-Spier
Winemaker: Olaf Kaufmann
54470 Bernkastel-Kues, Saarallee 31
Tel. (0 65 31) 22 82, Fax 22 26
Directions: A 48, exit Wittlich, in Bernkastel-Kues on the left bank of the Mosel in the Kues district
Opening hours: Mon.–Fri. by appointment
History: Wine estate owned by the family since 1636, in female ownership for the fourth generation
Worth seeing: Cellar under the Doctor vineyard, estate mansion

Vineyard area: 6 hectares
Annual production: 50,000 bottles
Top sites: Bernkasteler Doctor, Lay and Badstube, Brauneberger Juffer-Sonnenuhr
Soil types: Weathered Devon slate
Grape varieties: 100% Riesling
Average yield: 70 hl/ha
Best vintages: 1990, 1994, 1995
Member: VDP

This traditional estate is located in a handsome stone house on the banks of the Mosel. Since Dr. Thanisch's granddaughter took over there has been a noticeable improvement in quality. Until a few years ago the wines here were invariably made in a sweeter style for export. Since that now almost forgotten period when the dollar was weak, and demand abroad slack, the wines have also been enjoying considerable success on the German market, albeit in dry and off-dry styles. The inexorable return of this estate to the ranks of the leading properties on the Mosel began with the 1988 vintage. Since then excellent wines have been made every year. The loss of cellarmaster Norbert Breit to the rival Wegeler estate caused a surprising drop in quality in 1993, which was largely compensated for by the fine 1994s. The 1995 vintage was even better! The modest 1996s and 1997s are certainly not of the same level.

1996 Bernkasteler Badstube
Riesling Kabinett
13 DM, 8%, ♀ till 2002 **84**

1997 Bernkasteler Doctor
Riesling Spätlese trocken
38 DM, 11%, ♀ till 2002 **86**

1996 Bernkasteler Doctor
Riesling Kabinett
28 DM, 8%, ♀ till 2002 **86**

1996 Bernkasteler Badstube
Riesling Spätlese
45 DM, 8%, ♀ till 2004 **86**

1997 Bernkasteler Badstube
Riesling Auslese trocken
23 DM, 11.5%, ♀ till 2003 **88**

1997 Bernkasteler Badstube
Riesling Kabinett
13 DM, 8%, ♀ till 2004 **88**

1997 Brauneberger Juffer-Sonnenuhr
Riesling Kabinett
13 DM, 8%, ♀ till 2004 **88**

1997 Bernkasteler Doctor
Riesling Spätlese
56.80 DM, 8%, ♀ till 2006 **89**

1996 Bernkasteler Doctor
Riesling Auslese
65 DM/0.375 liter, 8.5%, ♀ till 2006 **91**

1996 Bernkasteler Doctor
Riesling Auslese lange Goldkapsel
132 DM/0.375 liter, 8.5%, ♀ till 2006 **95**

WEINGUT WWE. DR. H. THANISCH – ERBEN MÜLLER-BURGGRAEF

Owner: Ms. Müller-Burggraef
Director: Barbara Rundquist-Müller
Manager: Andreas Bauer
Winemaker: Hans Leiendecker
54470 Bernkastel-Kues, Saarallee 24
Tel. (0 65 31) 75 70, Fax 79 10
Directions: A 48, exit Wittlich, in Bernkastel-Kues follow the left bank of the Mosel to the Kues district
Sales: Mr. Leiendecker and Mr. Bauer
Opening hours: Mon.–Fri. 8 a.m. to 5 p.m., Sat. and Sun. 8 a.m. to 3 p.m. or by appointment
History: Wine estate owned by the family since 1636, in female hands for the fourth generation
Worth seeing: Cellar under the Doctor vineyard, wine treasury

Vineyard area: 6.5 hectares
Annual production: 45,000 bottles
Top sites: Bernkasteler Doctor, Badstube and Lay, Wehlener Sonnenuhr, Graacher Himmelreich, Brauneberger Juffer-Sonnenuhr
Soil types: Weathered clay-slate
Grape varieties: 97% Riesling, 3% Dornfelder
Average yield: 60 hl/ha
Best vintages: 1993, 1994, 1996

Until recently this property was managed as a unified estate with that of Erben Thanisch under the name of Dr. Thanisch. Differing opinions about how the estate should be run led to its division in 1988, at which time the vineyards were divided between the Thanisch and Müller-Burggraef heirs. Although the name Müller-Burggraef is portrayed in large gold letters at the top of the label, the similarity between the two Thanisch labels remains a major problem for unwitting consumers. The 1996s here were reminiscent of the fine vintages in both 1993 and 1994. The 1997s are not quite as successful. Nonetheless, it is becoming difficult to speak of this estate as the second fiddle among the two Thanisch properties.

1996 Bernkasteler Badstube
Riesling Kabinett
9 DM, 7.5%, ♀ till 2001 **84**

1997 Bernkasteler Graben
Riesling Spätlese
15 DM, 8%, ♀ till 2001 **84**

1997 Wehlener Sonnenuhr
Riesling Kabinett
12 DM, 8%, ♀ till 2004 **86**

1996 Bernkasteler Graben
Riesling Spätlese
13.50 DM, 8%, ♀ till 2004 **86**

1996 Bernkasteler Doctor
Riesling Kabinett
24 DM, 8.8%, ♀ till 2003 **88**

1996 Bernkasteler Doctor
Riesling Spätlese
28 DM, 10.5%, ♀ till 2004 **88**

1996 Lieser Niederberg Helden
Riesling Auslese
16 DM, 9%, ♀ till 2006 **88**

1997 Bernkasteler Doctor
Riesling Auslese lange Goldkapsel
50 DM/0.375 liter, 9%, ♀ till 2002 **88**

1997 Bernkasteler Doctor
Riesling Auslese
55 DM, 8.5%, ♀ till 2008 **89**

1996 Bernkasteler Doctor
Riesling Beerenauslese
80 DM, 9.5%, ♀ till 2008 **94**

SCHLOSS THORN

Owner: Dr. Baron von Hobe-Gelting
Winemaker: Andreas Schneider
54439 Schloss Thorn, Palzem
Tel. (0 65 83) 4 33, Fax 14 33
e-mail: weingut@schloss-thorn.com
Internet: http://www.schloss-thorn.com
Directions: Along B 419, between Nennig and Palzem
Sales: Ms. Niederweis
Opening hours: Mon.–Fri. 9 a.m. to 11 a.m. or by appointment
History: Located in the remains of a Roman tower, which kept watch over the Mosel. Owned by the family since 1534
Worth seeing: Castle, old wooden press

Vineyard area: 18.35 hectares
Annual production: 130,000 bottles
Top site: Schloss Thorn
Soil types: Fossil limestone
Grape varieties: 30% Riesling, 30% white Elbling, 22% Müller-Thurgau, 15% red Elbling, 3% Schwarzriesling
Average yield: 73 hl/ha
Best vintages: 1993, 1994, 1996

When in 1974 Georg Baron von Hobe-Gelting inherited this estate from his father, Bertram, the 28-year-old young man assumed a heavy burden. The castle, which had been badly damaged during World War II, had to be restored in a protracted and costly fashion. In order to limit the yields of the generally highly productive and often belittled Elbling variety on the fossil limestone soils of his estate, von Hobe chose low-bearing rootstock. That alone makes him one of the most serious producers of this grape variety in the whole of Germany. Since by law white wines should have no hint of pink in their color, von Hobe markets the red Elbling as a rosé. The baron has had this and other problems with the wine bureaucrats. And because the state boundary between the Rheinland-Pfalz and the Saarland bisects both his castle and his vineyards, he has to deal with not only two provincial administrations but also two different wine authorities.

1997 Müller-Thurgau
Spätlese halbtrocken
12 DM, 10.5%, ♀ till 2001 **80**

1996 Elbling
trocken
6.40 DM, 10%, ♀ now **82**

1996 Riesling
Kabinett halbtrocken
9.90 DM, 8.5%, ♀ now **82**

1997 Elbling
Auslese halbtrocken
24 DM, 10%, ♀ till 2002 **82**

1997 Elbling
Kabinett
9.40 DM, 8%, ♀ till 2001 **82**

1996 Riesling
Kabinett
9.90 DM, 7.5%, ♀ till 2000 **84**

1997 Elbling
Spätlese
12.20 DM, 8.5%, ♀ till 2203 **84**

1997 Riesling
Spätlese
15.50 DM, 8.5%, ♀ till 2003 **84**

1997 Elbling
Auslese – 103 –
30 DM/0.375 liter, 9%, ♀ till 2001 **84**

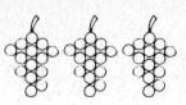

WEINGUT DR. HEINZ WAGNER

Owner: Heinz Wagner
54439 Saarburg, Bahnhofstraße 3
Tel. (0 65 81) 24 57, Fax 60 93
Directions: Near the railway station in Saarburg
Sales: Heinz and Ulrike Wagner
Opening hours: By appointment
History: Founded in 1880 as the first sparkling-wine merchant in the Saar
Worth seeing: Largest vaulted cellar in the Saar

> Vineyard area: 9 hectares
> Annual production: 60,000 bottles
> Top sites: Saarburger Rausch, Kupp and Antoniusbrunnen, Ockfener Bockstein
> Soil types: Very deep slate
> Grape varieties: 100% Riesling
> Average yield: 75 hl/ha
> Best vintages: 1994, 1995, 1997
> Member: VDP

Heinz Wagner owns vines in the choicest parcels of the steepest vineyards in Saarburg, Ockfen and Ayl, where he regularly produces some of the best dry wines of the Saar. These are laced by the slate soils and age exceptionally well thanks to their minerally toned freshness. But like many of his colleagues in the Saar valley the rather shy Wagner displays his finest skills by making Spätlese and Auslese. In these wines he pairs the crisp acidity of the Riesling grape with lushly sweet fruit in a masterly fashion to create veritable masterpieces; and he can look back on a long string of fine vintages over the past two decades. The 1996 range was less convincing than that of any of the three preceding vintages, but the 1997s are again very successful, confirming Wagner's reputation as one of the most serious producers from the valley. His dry and off-dry wines are bottled with a plain white label; the fruitier wines, which more often found abroad, are dressed with an old-fashioned label bearing a red heraldic seal.

1996 Ockfener Bockstein
Riesling
10 DM, 8%, ♀ till 2002 **84**

1997 Ockfener Bockstein
Riesling
11 DM, 8%, ♀ till 2003 **84**

1996 Saarburger Rausch
Riesling Kabinett
12 DM, 8%, ♀ till 2002 **86**

1996 Ockfener Bockstein
Riesling Kabinett
12 DM, 8%, ♀ till 2004 **86**

1996 Ockfener Bockstein
Riesling Spätlese
18 DM, 8%, ♀ till 2003 **86**

1996 Ayler Kupp
Riesling Spätlese
27 DM, 8%, ♀ till 2004 **88**

1997 Ockfener Bockstein
Riesling Spätlese
25.40 DM, 7.5%, ♀ till 2006 **89**

1997 Ockfener Bockstein
Riesling Auslese Goldkapsel
55 DM, 7.5%, ♀ till 2006 **91**

1997 Saarburger Rausch
Riesling Auslese Goldkapsel – 21 –
55 DM/0.375 liter, 7.5%, ♀ till 2010 **92**

1997 Saarburger Rausch
Riesling Auslese Goldkapsel – 20 –
74 DM, 7.5%, ♀ till 2010 **94**

GUTSVERWALTUNG GEHEIMRAT J. WEGELER ERBEN

Owner: Wegeler family
General Manager: Norbert Breit
54470 Bernkastel-Kues, Martertal 2
Tel. (0 65 31) 24 93, Fax 87 23
Directions: From Bernkastel via the Mosel bridge, left at the station
Sales: Norbert Breit
Opening hours: By appointment
History: In 1890 the first vineyards were acquired and the mansion constructed
Worth seeing: Wine cellar in the Doctor vineyard

Vineyard area: 19 hectares
Annual production: 140,000 bottles
Top sites: Bernkasteler Doctor, Wehlener Sonnenuhr
Soil types: Weathered slate
Grape varieties: 96% Riesling, 4% other varieties
Average yield: 60 hl/ha
Best vintages: 1993, 1995, 1997

For many years the lion's share of this estate's sweeter wines were exported. Over the last decade, under the direction of Norbert Holderrieth, the Rieslings have become ever drier in style. In some years, such as 1996 or 1997, they are even able to produce excellent dry Spätlese from the Bernkasteler Doctor vineyard. Five years ago the Wegelers invested heavily in a stainless steel cellar and hired Norbert Breit as their new cellarmaster. This set the estate on course for a more promising future. The 1993 vintage brought the first fruits. To date 1995 was the finest vintage under Breit's management, although the 1997s are almost as good. The 1996s were not quite of the same standard. The estate has just sold about half of its vineyards, principally those in Wehlen and in the Ruwer valley, in order to focus on their finer sites.

1997 Graacher Himmelreich
Riesling Kabinett halbtrocken
13.80 DM, 10%, ♀ 2003 **86**

1996 Bernkasteler Graben
Riesling Spätlese
18 DM, 9%, ♀ till 2003 **86**

1997 Wehlener Sonnenuhr
Riesling Spätlese trocken
22 DM, 10.5%, ♀ till 2004 **88**

1997 Wehlener Sonnenuhr
Riesling Spätlese
22 DM, 9.5%, ♀ till 2006 **88**

1996 Bernkasteler Doctor
Riesling Spätlese trocken
45 DM, 10.5%, ♀ till 2003 **89**

1996 Wehlener Sonnenuhr
Riesling Spätlese
22 DM, 8.5%, ♀ till 2004 **89**

1997 Bernkasteler Doctor
Riesling Spätlese
45 DM, 9%, ♀ till 2008 **91**

1997 Wehlener Sonnenuhr
Riesling Auslese
50 DM, 8.5%, ♀ till 2010 **91**

1997 Bernkasteler Doctor
Riesling Auslese
70 DM, 8.5%, ♀ till 2010 **94**

1996 Kaseler Nies'chen
Riesling Eiswein
65 DM/0.5 liter, 9%, ♀ till 2008 **94**

WEINGUT DR. F. WEINS-PRÜM

Owner: Bert Selbach
Manager and winemaker: Bert Selbach
54470 Bernkastel-Wehlen, Uferallee 20
Tel. (0 65 31) 22 70, Fax 31 81
Directions: From Bernkastel follow the left bank of the Mosel, in the village center of Wehlen right to the Uferallee
Opening hours: By appointment
Worth seeing: Old cross-shaped vaulted cellar

Vineyard area: 4 hectares
Annual production: 40,000 bottles
Top sites: Wehlener Sonnenuhr, Ürziger Würzgarten, Erdener Prälat, Graacher Himmelreich and Domprobst
Soil types: Slate
Grape varieties: 100% Riesling
Average yield: 67 hl/ha
Best vintages: 1994, 1995, 1997
Member: VDP

In 1924 Dr. Weins-Prüm erected his estate buildings above a cross-shaped vaulted cellar. It is located along a row of mansions on the banks of the Mosel in Wehlen belonging to the many branches of the Prüm family. The present owner of the estate, Bert Selbach, lives there today. He is also the proprietor of fine parcels of vines in Erden, Ürzig, Wehlen and Graach. The quality of production here has been improving rapidly over the past few years. The 1994s, 1995s and 1997s were all exemplary; only the 1996 range was perhaps not quite of that same caliber. Although the Auslese from the Erdener Prälat vineyard was excellent, the Spätlese, however good they may have been, were less exciting than those from the other vintages. Demand from private customers in Germany is definitely increasing, but about half of the production is still exported. Also increasing is the proportion of the wine made in the sweeter fruity style, which is without doubt the strength of this estate.

1997 Wehlener Sonnenuhr
Riesling Kabinett
11.30 DM, 8%, ♀ till 2004 **86**

1996 Graacher Domprobst
Riesling Kabinett
10.90 DM, 8.5%, ♀ till 2002 **86**

1997 Graacher Domprobst
Riesling Spätlese
14.10 DM, 7.5%, ♀ till 2005 **88**

1997 Erdener Prälat
Riesling Spätlese
15.80 DM, 8%, ♀ till 2008 **89**

1996 Ürziger Würzgarten
Riesling Spätlese
13.70 DM, 7.5%, ♀ till 2004 **89**

1996 Wehlener Sonnenuhr
Riesling Spätlese
14 DM, 8%, ♀ till 2005 **89**

1997 Erdener Prälat
Riesling Auslese
31 DM, 8%, ♀ till 2008 **89**

1997 Wehlener Sonnenuhr
Riesling Spätlese
14.30 DM, 8%, ♀ till 2007 **91**

1997 Wehlener Sonnenuhr
Riesling Auslese
24.50 DM, 8%, ♀ till 2008 **91**

1996 Erdener Prälat
Riesling Auslese
28 DM, 7.5%, ♀ till 2008 **94**

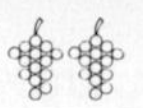

WEINGUT WELLER-LEHNERT

Owner: Petra Matheus
Winemaker: Jörg Matheus
54498 Piesport,
St.-Michael-Straße 27–29
Tel. (0 65 07) 24 98, Fax 67 66
Directions: A 1, exit Salmtal;
A 48 Koblenz–Trier, exit Salmtal,
down into the Mosel valley
Opening hours: By appointment
History: Wine estate in family ownership for eight generations

Vineyard area: 6 hectares
Annual production: 35,000 bottles
Top sites: Piesporter Goldtröpfchen, Domherr and Treppchen, Dhron Hofberger
Soil types: Weathered slate
Grape varieties: 92% Riesling, 4% Müller-Thurgau, 4% Weißburgunder
Average yield: 64 hl/ha
Best vintages: 1995, 1996, 1997
Member: Bernkasteler Ring

This is another of those rapidly improving properties in Piesport. Petra Matheus took over the estate in 1991, initially leasing it from her father, who has since died. Her husband, Jörg Matheus, who studied winemaking at Geisenheim, joined her in 1992. They have since built new winery facilities with offices, a tasting room and five guest rooms. They have also founded a distillery, where Jörg Matheus produces appealing fine and marc. Although the export side of the business is still flourishing – about 40 percent of the production goes abroad – Jörg and Petra Matheus now want to devote more of their time to their private customers. The young owners realize that yields must be kept in check, which was not the case before 1992. In 1994 the yields were a sensible 64 hectoliters per hectare, in 1995 only 61 and in 1997 a mere 58. The fine 1996 and 1997 ranges more than merit the confidence that we have placed in this estate in recent years.

1996 Piesporter Treppchen
Riesling Kabinett
8 DM, 8.5%, 🍷 till 2000 **84**

1996 Piesporter Goldtröpfchen
Riesling Kabinett
8.80 DM, 9%, 🍷 till 2001 **84**

1996 Piesporter Goldtröpfchen
Riesling Spätlese – 11 –
22.50 DM, 8%, 🍷 till 2002 **86**

1997 Piesporter Domherr
Riesling Auslese trocken
29.50 DM/0.5 liter, 13%, 🍷 till 2003 **88**

1997 Piesporter Goldtröpfchen
Riesling Spätlese
21.50 DM, 9%, 🍷 till 2005 **88**

1996 Piesporter Goldtröpfchen
Riesling Spätlese – 7 –
12.50 DM, 8%, 🍷 till 2004 **88**

1997 Piesporter Goldtröpfchen
Riesling Auslese – 6 –
29.50 DM, 9%, 🍷 till 2006 **89**

1997 Piesporter Goldtröpfchen
Riesling Auslese – 8 –
30 DM/0.375 liter, 10%, 🍷 till 2005 **89**

1996 Piesporter Goldtröpfchen
Riesling Auslese ** – 8 –
18 DM, 8%, 🍷 till 2006 **89**

1997 Piesporter Goldtröpfchen
Riesling Auslese – 7 –
24.50 DM/0.5 liter, 9.5%, 🍷 till 2008 **91**

WELLER-LEHNERT
PIESPORTER DOMHERR
RIESLING - AUSLESE
TROCKEN
1993
Gutsabfüllung WEINGUT Weller-Lehnert D-54498 Piesport
MOSEL-SAAR-RUWER

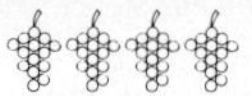

WEINGUT FORSTMEISTER GELTZ – ZILLIKEN

Owner: Hans-Joachim Zilliken
Winemaker: Hans-Joachim Zilliken
54439 Saarburg, Heckingstraße 20
Tel. (0 65 81) 24 56, Fax 67 63
Directions: B 51 from Trier via the Saar bridge, after the tunnel take first street on the right
Opening hours: By appointment
History: Ferdinand Geltz was royal Prussian director of the local forests
Worth seeing: Deep vaulted cellar

Vineyard area: 10 hectares
Annual production: 50,000 bottles
Top sites: Saarburger Rausch, Ockfener Bockstein
Soil types: Devon slate
Grape varieties: 100% Riesling
Average yield: 50 hl/ha
Best vintages: 1993, 1995, 1997
Member: VDP

Hans-Joachim Zilliken is no braggart. Instead he belongs to the ranks of his more reserved countrymen who are often – undeservedly – lost in the shadows of those growers celebrated as superstars. Nonetheless, he is – without any doubt – one of the finest producers from the Saar. The 1994, and above all the 1995 and 1997 vintages, are reminiscent of the excellent 1983s, which first brought him to our attention. When young, his dry wines once seemed edgy and sharp; today they are often somewhat more supple but are still by no means the showpieces of the estate. That role is left to the sweeter Prädikat wines, which make up about two thirds of his production, for they almost always show both concentration and elegance. The best wines usually come from the Saarburger Rausch vineyard, where Zilliken owns five hectares. Whenever possible, he produces an ice wine there. After a merely good performance in 1996, Zilliken has produced a fine array of Spätlese and Auslese in 1997 that exemplify his style at its best.

1997 Saarburger Rausch
Riesling Kabinett
15 DM, 8%, ♀ till 2004 **86**

1996 Ockfener Bockstein
Riesling Kabinett – 5 –
13.50 DM, 7.5%, ♀ till 2002 **86**

1997 Saarburger Rausch
Riesling Spätlese – 8 –
34.30 DM, 8%, ♀ till 2007 **88**

1996 Saarburger Rausch
Riesling Spätlese – 3 –
18 DM, 7.5%, ♀ till 2005 **88**

1997 Saarburger Rausch
Riesling Auslese – 5 –
55.60 DM, 7.5%, ♀ till 2008 **91**

1996 Saarburger Rausch
Riesling Auslese Goldkapsel
118 DM, 8%, ♀ till 2007 **91**

1997 Saarburger Rausch
Riesling Auslese Goldkapsel – 4 –
71 DM/0.375 liter, 7.5%, ♀ till 2008 **92**

1997 Saarburger Rausch
Riesling Auslese lange Goldkapsel – 3 –
129 DM/0.375 liter, 7.5%, ♀ till 2010 **92**

1997 Saarburger Rausch
Riesling Beerenauslese
Not yet for sale, 7%, ♀ till 2008 **94**

1997 Saarburger Rausch
Riesling Eiswein
Not yet for sale, 7%, ♀ till 2008 **95**

Stepping out of the Rheingau's shadow

Although the Nahe has established its reputation among wine writers, for many consumers this wine-growing district is still relatively unknown. Hugh Johnson writes, for instance, that it is "the origin of one of the best white wines of the world," but even in nearby Frankfurt the wines are seldom given sufficient attention. With 4,600 hectares of vineyards, it is half again as large as the Rheingau, of which it was once a part. Indeed, earlier in this century Rieslings from the Nahe were sold as Rhine wines. An official decree in the 1930s then established the Nahe as an independent wine-growing region. The current boundaries, however, were established by law only in 1971.

The multiplicity of soil types on the Nahe is enormous: between Monzingen and Traisen porphyry, melaphyre and red sandstone predominate, in Bad Kreuznach loess and loam, on the lower Nahe clay, quartz and slate. The highly productive Müller-Thurgau was for years the most widely planted grape varietal on the whole of the Nahe. Since the early 1980s, Riesling has taken over that role. Now planted on about a third of the total area under vine, this noble grape has brought the Nahe to new horizons; but wines from the Burgundian family – Grauburgunder, Weißburgunder and Spätburgunder – have equal importance in terms of quality.

A reform in 1993 simplified things on the Nahe. Whereas in earlier times the vineyards were officially divided between the regions of Schloßböckelheim and Kreuznach, today there is just the Nahe valley. The authorities in other regions would do well to imitate this decision in order to impede nondescript wines from being labeled using the names of celebrated villages such as Johannisberg, Bernkastel or Nierstein.

Further, the proposed vineyard classification will bring added clarity to the region. From 1997 onwards, member es-

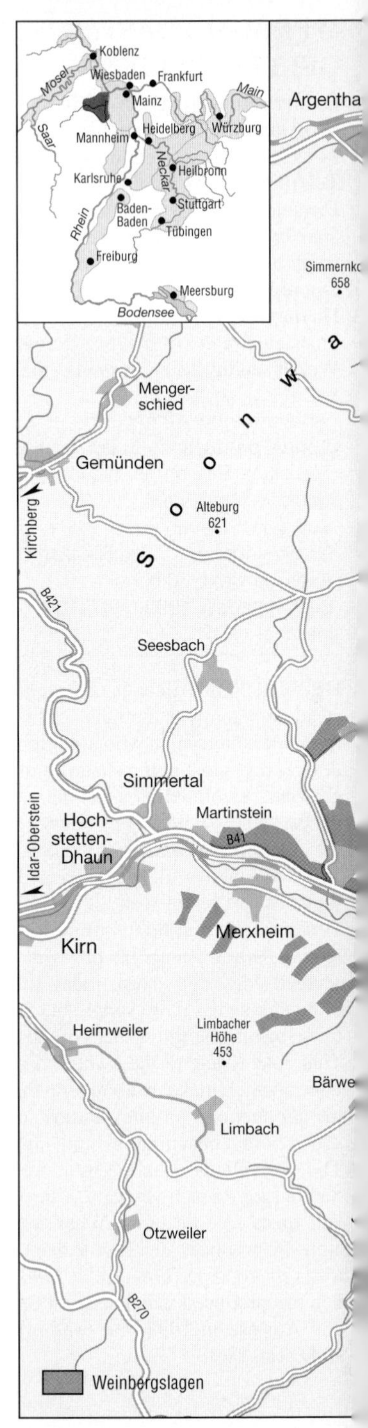

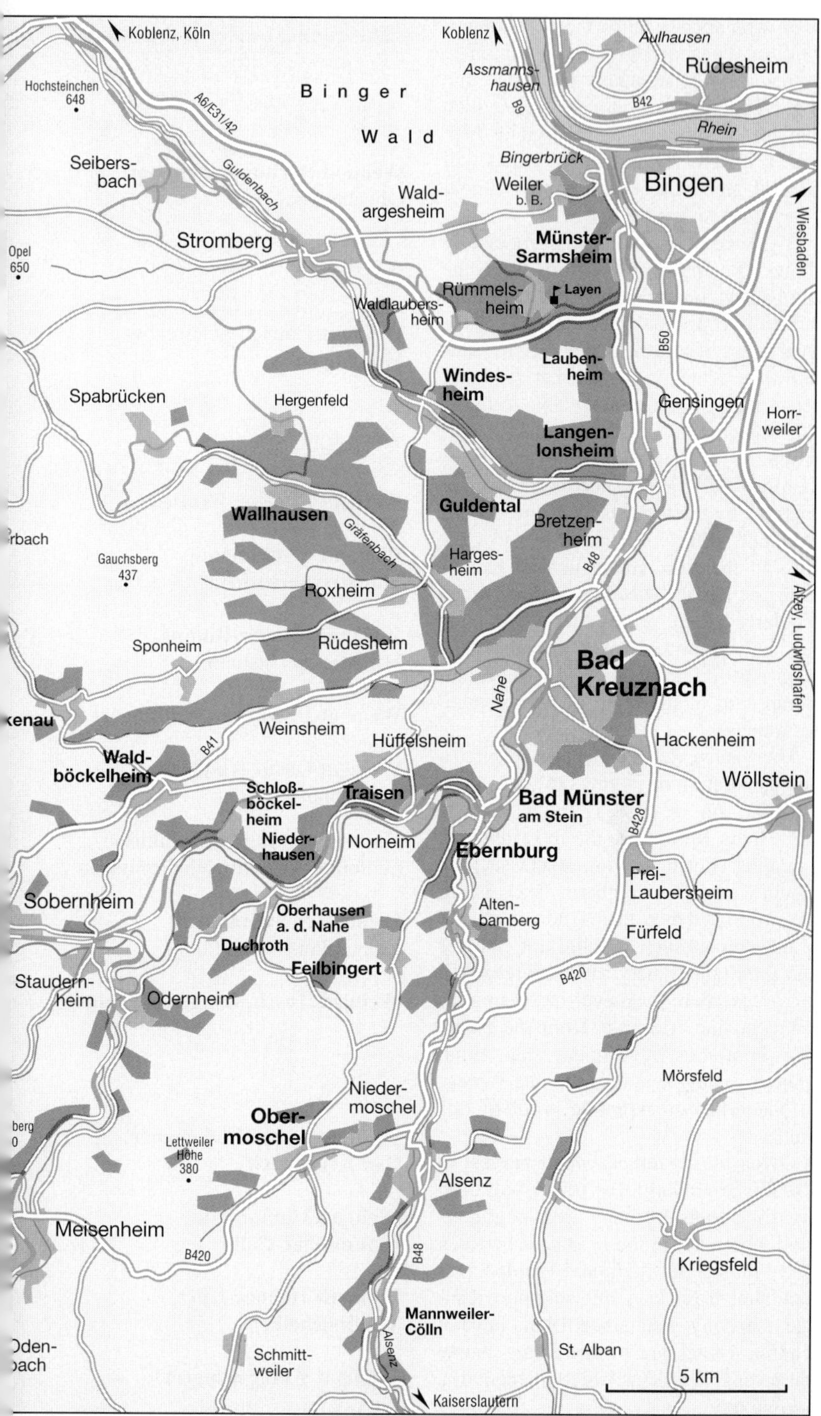

Koblenz, Köln
Koblenz
Aulhausen
Rüdesheim
Hochsteinchen
648
B i n g e r
W a l d
Assmannshausen
B9
B42
Rhein
A6/E31/42
Seibersbach
Guldenbach
Bingerbrück
Weiler b. B.
Bingen
Waldargesheim
Wiesbaden
Stromberg
Münster-Sarmsheim
Opel
650
Rümmelsheim
Layen
Waldlaubersheim
B50
Laubenheim
Windesheim
Spabrücken
Hergenfeld
Gensingen
Horrweiler
Langenlonsheim
Guldental
Wallhausen
Gräfenbach
Bretzenheim
Gauchsberg
437
Hargesheim
B48
Roxheim
Alzey, Ludwigshafen
Sponheim
Rüdesheim
Bad Kreuznach
Nahe
Weinsheim
Hüffelsheim
Hackenheim
B41
Wald-böckelheim
Wöllstein
Schloß-böckelheim
Traisen
Bad Münster am Stein
B428
Nieder-hausen
Norheim
Ebernburg
Sobernheim
Frei-Laubersheim
Oberhausen a. d. Nahe
Alten-bamberg
Duchroth
Fürfeld
Feilbingert
Staudernheim
Odernheim
B420
Mörsfeld
Nieder-moschel
Ober-moschel
Lettweiler Höhe
380
Alsenz
Meisenheim
B420
B48
Kriegsfeld
Mannweiler-Cölln
Schmitt-weiler
Alsenz
St. Alban
5 km
Kaiserslautern

tates will specify only their best vineyards on the labels of their Rieslings. The grapes must be manually harvested, the sugar content considerably higher than that specified by law and the yields kept low. Logically, all remaining wines will be sold merely as estate wines without vineyard designations.

A glance at the vintage chart clearly shows that the growers from the Nahe can hardly complain about weather conditions over the past decade. They have used a run of excellent vintages to position their wines in the market at higher prices than they were once able to fetch. The self-confidence of numerous smaller producers – and there are over 800 of them – is built on the success achieved at auctions by the top estates of the region: Dönnhoff, Emrich-Schönleber and Crusius. In the Römerhalle in Bad Kreuznach late harvest Rieslings and ice wines regularly attain prices that were once seen only at the auctions in Kloster Eberbach and Trier. Be that as it may, the trump card of the region remains value for money.

The positive development has inspired a new generation of vintners to focus their attention on quality. Helmut Mathern and Stefan Rumpf are the most obvious examples, but numerous others such as Göttelmann, Schweinhardt and Tesch have followed their lead. And the success of newcomers such as Joh. Bapt. Schäfer and the State Winery in Bad Kreuznach prove that there is an ever-increasing interest in fine Rieslings from the Nahe. The enormous investment that Erich Maurer has made in the old State Winery in Niederhausen is ample proof of this fact.

Given the extremely small harvest in 1997, it is unlikely that prices will drop any time soon. In many areas of the region, above all in the heartland between Bad Münster am Stein and Waldböckelheim, late frosts have inflicted more damage than any year since 1956. Several leading estates are in dire straits, some harvesting as little as twenty percent of a normal crop.

The leading estates of the Nahe

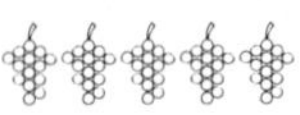

Weingut Hermann Dönnhoff, Oberhausen

Weingut Emrich-Schönleber, Monzingen

Weingut Crusius, Traisen

Weingut Göttelmann, Münster-Sarmsheim

Weingut Kruger-Rumpf, Münster-Sarmsheim

Weingut Lötzbeyer, Feilbingert

Weingut Oskar Mathern, Niederhausen

Gutsverwaltung Niederhausen-Schloßböckelheim, Niederhausen

Weingut Schweinhardt, Langenlonsheim

Weingut Tesch, Langenlonsheim

Weingut Anton Finkenauer, Bad Kreuznach

Weingut Hahnmühle, Mannweiler-Cölln

Weingut Hehner-Kiltz, Waldböckelheim

Weingut Königswingert, Guldental

Weingut Korrell – Johanneshof, Bad Kreuznach-Bosenheim

Weingut Prinz zu Salm-Dalberg, Wallhausen

Weingut Schäfer-Fröhlich, Bockenau

Weingut Schmidt, Obermoschel

Weingut Jakob Schneider, Niederhausen

Weingut Wilhelm Sitzius, Langenlonsheim

Weingut Paul Anheuser, Bad Kreuznach

Weingut Carl Finkenauer, Bad Kreuznach

Weingut Jung, Ebernburg

Weingut Lindenhof, Windesheim

Weingut Reichsgraf von Plettenberg, Bad Kreuznach

Weingut Rapp, Bad Münster am Stein-Ebernburg

Weingut Michael Schäfer, Burg Layen

Weingut Karl von der Weiden, Langenlonsheim

Note: One of the authors of this guide is Armin Diel, owner of Schlossgut Diel in Burg Layen. His estate has not been rated here.

Rating scale for the estates

Highest rating: These producers belong to the world's finest.

Excellent estates: These producers are among Germany's best.

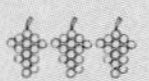

Very good producers, known for their consistently high quality.

Good estates, offering better than average quality.

Reliable producers that offer well-made standard quality.

Other notable producers

Wein- und Sektgut Karl-Kurt Bamberger
55566 Meddersheim, Römerstraße 10
Tel. (0 67 51) 26 24, Fax 21 41

Wein- und Sektgut Großmann
67821 Oberndorf, Hauptstraße 9
Tel. (0 63 62) 34 97, Fax 41 46

Weingut Helmut Hexamer
55566 Meddersheim, Sobernheimer Straße 3
Tel. (0 67 51) 22 69, Fax 9 47 07

Weingut Klostermühle
55571 Odernheim, Am Disibodenberg
Tel. (0 67 55) 3 19, Fax 3 20

Weingut Meinhard
☞ *See below, page 281*

Weingut Sascha Montigny
55452 Laubenheim, Weidenpfad 46
Tel. (0 67 04) 14 68, Fax 16 02

Weingut Alfred Porr
55585 Duchroth, Schloßstraße 1
Tel. (0 67 55) 2 07

Weingut Joh. Bapt. Schäfer
55452 Burg Layen,
Burg Layen 8
Tel. (0 67 21) 4 35 52, Fax 4 78 41

Weingut Erich Schauß & Sohn
55569 Monzingen,
Römerstraße 5 & 12
Tel. (0 67 51) 28 82, Fax 68 60

Staatsweingut Bad Kreuznach
55545 Bad Kreuznach,
Rüdesheimer Straße 68
Tel. (06 71) 82 02 51, Fax 82 02 94

Weingut Steitz
67811 Dielkirchen-Steingruben,
Alsenzstraße 7
Tel. (0 63 61) 10 62, Fax 88 25

Weingut Weinmann
55585 Duchroth,
Naheweinstraße 70
Tel. (0 67 55) 27 51, Fax 18 73

Weingut im Zwölberich
55450 Langenlonsheim,
Schützenstraße 14
Tel. (0 67 04) 92 00, Fax 9 20 40

Vintage chart for the Nahe

vintage	quality	drink
1997	🍇🍇🍇🍇	till 2004
1996	🍇🍇🍇🍇	till 2005
1995	🍇🍇🍇🍇	till 2005
1994	🍇🍇🍇🍇	till 2004
1993	🍇🍇🍇🍇🍇	till 2004
1992	🍇🍇🍇🍇	till 2000
1991	🍇🍇🍇	now
1990	🍇🍇🍇🍇🍇	till 2005
1989	🍇🍇🍇🍇	till 2000
1988	🍇🍇🍇	now

🍇🍇🍇🍇🍇 : Outstanding
🍇🍇🍇🍇 : Excellent
🍇🍇🍇 : Good
🍇🍇 : Average
🍇 : Poor

WEINGUT PAUL ANHEUSER

Owner: Peter Anheuser
55545 Bad Kreuznach,
Stromberger Straße 15–19
Tel. (06 71) 2 87 48, Fax 4 25 71
Directions: B 41, exit Kreuznach-Nord, after 1.5 kilometers first street on the right
Sales: Dorothee Anheuser
Opening hours: Mon.–Fri. 8 a.m. to 5 p.m., Sat. 9 a.m. to noon or by appointment
History: Winery owned by the family since 1627, now in its 13th generation
Worth seeing: Vaulted cellars

Vineyard area: 63 hectares
Annual production: 500,000 bottles
Top sites: Kreuznacher Brückes, Kahlenberg and Krötenpfuhl, Schloßböckelheimer Kupfergrube, Königsfels and Felsenberg
Soil types: Loam, gravel, porphyry, weathered slate
Grape varieties: 71% Riesling, 11% Burgundian varieties, 7% Kerner, 11% other varieties
Average yield: 64 hl/ha
Best vintages: 1989, 1990, 1993
Member: VDP

Peter Anheuser is a very busy man: he is both a deputy in the local parliament and president of the regional wine association, to name but two of his official offices. It is thus not surprising that he has handed over the day-to-day management of his estate – by far the largest on the Nahe – to his hard-working wife, Dorothee. The estate's vineyards are scattered over 30 kilometers from Bad Kreuznach to Monzingen. The choicest parcels are to be found in Bad Kreuznach itself and in Schloßböckelheim, but the estate also owns fine sites in Niederhausen, Altenbamberg and Roxheim. Up to two-thirds of the wines are made in a dry style. Unfortunately, the 1996 and 1997 ranges, like their predecessors, highlight the fact that this estate is not living up to its full potential.

1997 Kreuznacher Krötenpfuhl
Riesling Spätlese halbtrocken
13.50 DM, 12%, ♀ till 2000 **80**

1997 Kreuznacher Kahlenberg
Riesling Spätlese
13.50 DM, 8.5%, ♀ till 2001 **80**

1997 Kreuznacher Hinkelstein
Riesling halbtrocken
8.50 DM/1.0 liter, 10.5%, ♀ till 2000 **80**

1996 Kreuznacher Krötenpfuhl
Riesling Spätlese halbtrocken
12 DM, 10%, ♀ now **82**

1996 Schloßböckelheimer Felsenberg
Riesling
8.50 DM, ♀ now **82**

1997 Schloßböckelheimer Felsenberg
Riesling Spätlese
14 DM, 8%, ♀ till 2002 **84**

1996 Kreuznacher Kahlenberg
Riesling Spätlese
12 DM, 8.5%, ♀ till 2001 **84**

1997 Kreuznacher Krötenpfuhl
Riesling Auslese
21.50 DM, 10%, ♀ till 2002 **84**

1996 Niederhäuser Pfingstweide
Riesling Kabinett
9 DM, 8%, ♀ till 2001 **86**

1996 Kreuznacher Brückes
Riesling Auslese
27 DM, ♀ till 2001 **86**

WEINGUT CRUSIUS

Owner: Dr. Peter Crusius
55595 Traisen, Hauptstraße 2
Tel. (06 71) 3 39 53, Fax 2 82 19
Directions: A 61, exit Bad Kreuznach, along the B 41 in the direction of Kirn, exit Bad Münster
Opening hours: Mon.–Sat. 9 a.m. to 5 p.m., by appointment
History: Family has been farming grapes in Traisen since 1586
Worth seeing: Unique vineyard called "Traiser Bastei" beneath the cliffs of the Rotenfels, vaulted cellars

Vineyard area: 12.5 hectares
Annual production: 80,000 bottles
Top sites: Traiser Bastei and Rotenfels, Schloßböckelheimer Felsenberg, Niederhäuser Felsensteyer, Norheimer Kirschheck
Soil types: Volcanic and weathered slate, gravelly loam
Grape varieties: 75% Riesling, 13% Burgunder varietals, 10% Müller-Thurgau, 2% Silvaner
Average yield: 59 hl/ha
Best vintages: 1989, 1995, 1996
Member: VDP

Although this estate owns top sites such as the Niederhäuser Felsensteyer, the core of its holdings lie in or near Traisen. The jewel in their crown is undoubtedly the small parcel in the Traiser Bastei where, at the foot of exceptionally steep cliffs, wines of most remarkable character flourish. Yields here are low and the average age of the vines high, both prerequisites for outstanding quality. Today Dr. Peter Crusius continues the life work of his father, Hans, who in the 1960s and 1970s raised this estate to its place as first among equals among the finest properties of the Nahe. After a brief lapse in quality, the 1995s again set new standards; the 1996s continued this positive trend. Severe frosts in 1997, however, limited not only the yields but also set this estate back a step on its uphill battle to rejoin the very top vineyards on the Nahe.

1997 Traiser
Riesling Kabinett halbtrocken
11.90 DM, 10%, ♀ till 2002 **84**

1997 Schloßböckelheimer Felsenberg
Riesling Spätlese halbtrocken
15.70 DM, 11.5%, ♀ till 2003 **86**

1996 Traiser Rotenfels
Riesling Kabinett trocken
10.30 DM, 10%, ♀ till 2000 **88**

1997 Traiser Rotenfels
Riesling Spätlese trocken
15 DM, 12%, ♀ till 2002 **88**

1997 Niederhäuser Felsensteyer
Riesling Spätlese
14.90 DM, 10.5%, ♀ till 2003 **88**

1996 Traiser Bastei
Riesling Spätlese
15 DM, 9.5%, ♀ till 2001 **88**

1996 Schloßböckelheimer Felsenberg
Riesling Spätlese trocken
14.30 DM, 11%, ♀ till 2003 **89**

1996 Schloßböckelheimer Felsenberg
Riesling Spätlese halbtrocken
14.50 DM, 11%, ♀ till 2000 **89**

1996 Schloßböckelheimer Felsenberg
Riesling Auslese
23 DM, 7.5%, ♀ till 2004 **91**

1997 Traiser Rotenfels
Riesling Auslese Goldkapsel
73 DM/0.5 liter, ♀ till 2006 **91**

SCHLOSSGUT DIEL

Owner: Armin Diel
Winemaker: Christoph J. Friedrich
55452 Burg Layen
Tel. (0 67 21) 9 69 50, Fax 4 50 47
Directions: Autobahn 61, exit Dorsheim, 500 meters to Burg Layen
Sales: Bernd Benz
Opening hours: Mon.–Thur. 8 a.m. to 5 p.m., Fri. 8 a.m. to 2 p.m.
Tastings by appointment
History: Burg Layen dates from the 12th century and has been owned by the Diel family since 1802
Worth seeing: Ruins of Burg Layen, artistically appointed winery, historic vaulted cellars

Vineyard area: 15 hectares
Annual production: 90,000 bottles
Top sites: Dorsheimer Goldloch, Pittermännchen and Burgberg
Soil types: Gravelly loam with slate
Grape varieties: 70% Riesling, 30% Burgundian varieties
Average yield: 45 hl/ha
Best vintages: 1993, 1995, 1996
Member: VDP, Deutsches Barrique Forum

Since Armin Diel – who is now chairman of the Nahe chapter of the VDP – took over this property from his father in 1987 it has experienced a swift rise in both quality and reputation. After acquiring almost two hectares of vineyard from the State Domaine, his estate is now the largest landowner in the top sites of Dorsheim: Goldloch, Pittermännchen and Burgberg. The yields are kept low and the vinification of the Rieslings is carefully nurtured in both traditional wooden casks and steel tanks; the Burgundian varieties are aged in small oak barrels. Two-thirds of the wines are still made in the dry style for which the estate is well-known, but since 1995 the fruitier Spätlese and Auslese have become considerably more elegant and refined. The noble late harvest wines often reach extraordinary prices at auctions. As Armin Diel is co-author of this guide we have refrained from rating either his estate or the individual wines.

1997 Diel de Diel
trocken
16.80 DM, 12%, 🍷 till 2001

1997 Grauer Burgunder
trocken Barrique
32 DM, 13.5%, 🍷 till 2005

1997 Cuvée Victor
trocken Barrique
48 DM, 14%, 🍷 till 2006

1997 Dorsheimer Burgberg
Riesling Kabinett
19.50 DM, 8%, 🍷 till 2004

1997 Dorsheimer Goldloch
Riesling Spätlese
28 DM, 7.5%, 🍷 till 2006

1997 Dorsheimer Pittermännchen
Riesling Auslese
48 DM, 7.5%, 🍷 till 2010

1996 Riesling
Auslese Goldkapsel
61 DM, 7%, 🍷 till 2008

1996 Riesling
Eiswein
130 DM/0.375 liter, 7%, 🍷 till 2010

WEINGUT HERMANN DÖNNHOFF

Owner: Helmut Dönnhoff
55585 Oberhausen, Bahnhofstraße 11
Tel. (0 67 55) 2 63, Fax 10 67
Directions: A 61, exit Bad Kreuznach along the B 41 to Bad Münster, via Norheim and Niederhausen to Oberhausen
Opening hours: By appointment
History: Winery owned by the family since 1750
Worth seeing: Wonderful view of the celebrated vineyards of Niederhausen and Schloßböckelheim

Vineyard area: 12.5 hectares
Annual production: 80,000 bottles
Top sites: Niederhäuser Hermannshöhle, Oberhäuser Brücke, Schloßböckelheimer Felsenberg and Kupfergrube, Norheimer Kirschheck and Dellchen
Soil types: Grey slate, porphyry and weathered volcanic soil
Grape varieties: 75% Riesling, 25% Weißburgunder and Grauburgunder
Average yield: 48 hl/ha
Best vintages: 1993, 1995, 1997
Member: VDP

Helmut Dönnhoff is not a man to brag about his achievements; but listen to him carefully and you will soon realize that behind every minute detail stands a vast reserve of experience and love of wine. He is very traditional in his outlook and hence an expert in the classical vinification of Riesling in oak casks; and as far as vineyards are concerned, only the best is good enough for Dönnhoff. Recently he enlarged his holdings: in Norheim he purchased parcels in the top sites of Kirschheck and Dellchen, and in Schloßböckelheim he has acquired part of the legendary Kupfergrube. He has now also joined the ranks of castle owners. Within the Schloßböckelheimer Felsenberg vineyard is a small chateau that he will soon renovate as a tasting room in arguably the most picturesque location in the Nahe valley. It is a worthy setting for his wines, which are not only the finest of the valley but often as stunning as the best produced on the Mosel and Rhine – a fact that the graceful 1997s amply document. Our choice of Helmut Dönnhoff as Winemaker of the Year will come as no surprise to anyone who has ever tasted his wines.

1996 Oberhäuser Leistenberg
Riesling Kabinett
12.50 DM, 9%, ♀ till 2004 **88**

1997 Grauer Burgunder
Spätlese trocken
24 DM, 12.5%, ♀ till 2003 **89**

1997 Norheimer Dellchen
Riesling Spätlese trocken
27 DM, 11.5%, ♀ till 2004 **89**

1996 Niederhäuser Hermannshöhle
Riesling Spätlese trocken
21 DM, 11.5%, ♀ till 2003 **89**

1996 Norheimer Dellchen
Riesling Kabinett
14.50 DM, 9%, ♀ till 2005 **89**

1997 Norheimer Kirschheck
Riesling Spätlese
19.50 DM, 9%, ♀ till 2005 **89**

1997 Schloßböckelheimer Kupfergrube
Riesling Spätlese
22 DM, 9%, ♀ till 2005 **89**

1996 Norheimer Kirschheck
Riesling Spätlese
18.50 DM, 8%, ♀ till 2005 **89**

1997 Weißer Burgunder
Spätlese trocken
30 DM, 13.5%, ♀ till 2004 **90**

1997 Oberhäuser Brücke
Riesling Spätlese
24 DM, 9%, ♀ till 2005 **91**

1996 Schloßböckelheimer Kupfergrube
Riesling Spätlese
20 DM, 9%, ♀ till 2005 **91**

1996 Niederhäuser Hermannshöhle
Riesling Spätlese – 14 –
21 DM, 8.5%, 🍷 till 2006 **91**

1996 Niederhäuser Hermannshöhle
Riesling Spätlese – 19 –
34.50 DM, 8.5%, 🍷 till 2006 **91**

1997 Niederhäuser Hermannshöhle
Riesling Spätlese
25 DM, 9%, 🍷 till 2006 **92**

1996 Oberhäuser Brücke
Riesling Auslese
58 DM, 8.5%, 🍷 till 2008 **92**

1997 Niederhäuser Hermannshöhle
Riesling Auslese
48 DM, 8.5%, 🍷 till 2008 **94**

1996 Niederhäuser Hermannshöhle
Riesling Auslese
88.50 DM, 8.5%, 🍷 till 2008 **94**

1997 Oberhäuser Brücke
Riesling Eiswein
Not yet for sale, 8%, 🍷 till 2015 **96**

1997 Oberhäuser Brücke
Riesling Auslese "Goldkapsel"
101 DM, 8.5%, 🍷 till 2010 **96**

1996 Oberhäuser Brücke
Riesling Eiswein – 26 –
95 DM, 7.5%, 🍷 till 2010 **96**

1996 Oberhäuser Brücke
Riesling Eiswein – 27 –
95 DM, 7.5%, 🍷 till 2010 **98**

1996 Oberhäuser Brücke
Riesling Eiswein – 28 –
530 DM, 7%, 🍷 till 2015 **99**

DÖNNHOFF
Niederhäuser Hermannshöhle
Riesling Spätlese
1997
ERZEUGERABFÜLLUNG
WEINGUT HERMANN DÖNNHOFF · D-55585 OBERHAUSEN/NAHE
QUALITÄTSWEIN MIT PRÄDIKAT · A. P. Nr. 7753010000598
PRODUCE OF GERMANY
alc.
9.0% vol.
NAHE
750 ml e

WEINGUT EMRICH-SCHÖNLEBER

Owners: Hannelore and Werner Schönleber
55569 Monzingen, Naheweinstraße 10a
Tel. (0 67 51) 27 33, Fax 48 64
e-mail: weingut@schoenleber.de
Directions: From B 41 turn off to the center of the village, Soonwaldstraße
Opening hours: Mon.–Fri. 8 a.m. to noon and 1 p.m. to 6 p.m.
Sat. 8 a.m. to noon and 1 p.m. to 4 p.m.
By appointment
History: Owned by the family for over 250 years

Vineyard area: 13.8 hectares
Annual production: 110,000 bottles
Top sites: Monzinger Halenberg and Frühlingsplätzchen
Soil types: A blend of quartz, slate and basalt
Grape varieties: 76% Riesling, 7% Grauburgunder, 5% each of Kerner, Müller-Thurgau and Bacchus, 2% Weißburgunder
Average yield: 68 hl/ha
Best vintages: 1992, 1993, 1994
Member: VDP

Werner Schönleber maintains a stronghold of top quality wines in the far western region of the Nahe. Already at the age of 19 he won the federal prize for oenology. Since then, and building on the achievements established in his father's time, he has steadily honed his skills, devoting his attention in equal measure to both vineyards and vinification. The quality of the 1992, 1993 and 1994 vintages catapulted his estate into the forefront of the region. The 1995 range was perhaps not quite up to this high standard; and the 1996s – with the exception of the ice wine from the Frühlingsplätzchen – were very good but less stunning than the wines produced earlier in the decade. Nor are the 1997s, however good they might be, as mouthwatering as the trio of earlier vintages. Nonetheless, this estate must be reckoned as one of the key players of the Nahe.

1996 Monzinger Halenberg
Riesling Spätlese trocken
27 DM, 12%, 🍷 till 2000 **88**

1997 Monzinger Frühlingsplätzchen
Riesling Kabinett halbtrocken
11.50 DM, 10%, 🍷 till 2003 **88**

1996 Monzinger Frühlingsplätzchen
Riesling Kabinett halbtrocken
11 DM, 10%, 🍷 till 2001 **88**

1997 Monzinger Frühlingsplätzchen
Riesling Kabinett
11 DM, 9%, 🍷 till 2004 **88**

1997 Monzinger Halenberg
Riesling Spätlese halbtrocken
16 DM, 11%, 🍷 till 2004 **89**

1997 Monzinger Halenberg
Riesling Spätlese
22 DM, 9.5%, 🍷 till 2004 **89**

1996 Monzinger Frühlingsplätzchen
Riesling Spätlese
23 DM, 9%, 🍷 till 2004 **89**

1996 Monzinger Frühlingsplätzchen
Riesling Auslese *** Goldkapsel
49.50 DM/0.375 liter, 9%, 🍷 till 2006 **91**

1997 Monzinger Halenberg
Riesling Auslese ***
33 DM/0.5 liter, 9.5%, 🍷 till 2007 **92**

1996 Monzinger Frühlingsplätzchen
Riesling Eiswein
79 DM/0.375 liter, 8.5%, 🍷 till 2015 **95**

Weingut Emrich-Schönleber
Nahe
1997
Monzinger Halenberg
Riesling Spätlese trocken
Qualitätswein mit Prädikat
alc 12% vol 750 ml
D-55569 Monzingen an der Nahe

WEINGUT ANTON FINKENAUER

Owner: Hans-Anton Finkenauer
Winemaker: Hans-Anton Finkenauer
55543 Bad Kreuznach, Rheingrafenstraße 15
Tel. (06 71) 6 22 30, Fax 6 22 10
Directions: A 61, exit Bad Kreuznach, in the direction of Bad Münster, in the spa district
Sales: Finkenauer family
Opening hours: Mon.–Fri. 8:30 a.m. to 6:30 p.m., weekends by appointment
History: Owned for over 250 years by the family

Vineyard area: 8 hectares
Annual production: 60,000 bottles
Top sites: Kreuznacher Kahlenberg and Brückes
Soil types: Weathered red sandstone, sandy loam
Grape varieties: 63% Riesling, 16% Müller-Thurgau, 5% each of Scheurebe and Grauburgunder, 4% Spätburgunder, 7% other varieties
Average yield: 75 hl/ha
Best vintages: 1992, 1994, 1997

In the first quarter of this century Anton and Carl Finkenauer ran their family's estate jointly; in 1925 the brothers went their separate ways, splitting the vineyards between themselves. Since then there have been two properties bearing the Finkenauer name and both are to be found not far from the center of Bad Kreuznach near the entrance to the spa. While Carl Finkenauer and his descendants enlarged their estate to a considerable degree, the Anton Finkenauer estate has remained to this day a small family business. Thanks to their ability to keep costs down, the prices of Anton Finkenauer's wines remain low, generally ensuring excellent value for money. The 1995 range wasn't quite up to the quality of the previous vintages, and the modest 1996s were again somewhat disappointing, but the 1997s brought this estate back into the spotlight.

1996 Kreuznacher Rosenberg
Riesling halbtrocken
5.50 DM, 10.5%, ♀ now **84**

1997 Kreuznacher Osterhöll
Kerner Auslese halbtrocken
13.50 DM, 13%, ♀ till 2003 **84**

1996 Kreuznacher Tilgesbrunnen
Scheurebe
4.80 DM, 9.5%, ♀ till 2000 **84**

1997 Kreuznacher Rosenberg
Riesling Spätlese trocken
8.50 DM, 12.5%, ♀ till 2002 **86**

1997 Kreuznacher Forst
Grauer Burgunder Auslese trocken
12.80 DM, 13.5%, ♀ till 2002 **86**

1997 Kreuznacher Osterhöll
Riesling Kabinett halbtrocken
6.80 DM, 10.5%, ♀ till 2003 **86**

1997 Kreuznacher Hinkelstein
Riesling Spätlese halbtrocken
8.30 DM, 10.5%, ♀ till 2002 **86**

1997 Kreuznacher Brückes
Riesling Spätlese halbtrocken
8.50 DM, 11%, ♀ till 2003 **86**

1997 Kreuznacher Hinkelstein
Riesling Spätlese
8.50 DM, 9.5%, ♀ till 2004 **86**

1997 Kreuznacher Kahlenberg
Riesling Auslese *
14 DM, 8%, ♀ till 2005 **88**

QUALITÄTSWEIN MIT PRÄDIKAT
A. P. Nr. 7 710 034 12 98
NAHE
1997er
Kreuznacher Osterhöll
Riesling Kabinett
HALBTROCKEN
alc. 10,5% vol.
GUTSABFÜLLUNG
0,75 l
Weingut Anton Finkenauer, D-55543 Bad Kreuznach

WEINGUT CARL FINKENAUER

Owner: The Bayer, Nicolay, Schmitt, Steitz and Trummert-Finkenauer families
Manager: Karl-Heinz Schmitt, Hans-Georg Trummert-Finkenauer
Winemaker: Karl-Heinz Schmitt
55543 Bad Kreuznach, Salinenstraße 60
Tel. (06 71) 2 87 71, Fax 3 52 65
Directions: A 61, exit Bad Kreuznach, in the direction of Bad Münster, before the turnoff for the spa district on the right
Opening hours: Mon.–Fri. 8 a.m. to 5 p.m., Sat. and Sun. by appointment
History: Owned by the family for over 170 years
Worth seeing: Vaulted cellars with over 100 oak casks

Vineyard area: 30 hectares
Annual production: 190,000 bottles
Top sites: Roxheimer Mühlenberg, Kreuznacher Brückes
Soil types: Weathered red sandstone, loess and loam
Grape varieties: 54% Riesling, 7% Scheurebe, 6% Weißburgunder, 5% each of Silvaner, Müller-Thurgau and Spätburgunder, 4% Grauburgunder, 14% other varieties
Average yield: 54 hl/ha
Best vintages: 1990, 1992, 1994

For years the wines from the Carl Finkenauer estate have featured prominently in fine restaurants; and as two-thirds of the production is sold to German restaurants, it is no surprise that the majority of the wines are made in a dry style. Alongside Riesling, the Burgundian varieties also play an important role. Unfortunately the quality here has been on a roller-coaster ride over the past decade. With the 1994 range it seemed as if the estate were on its way up again, but the 1995s were as flat and dull as the 1996s were acidic and coarse. The 1997s are only marginally better. To remedy this problem the estate has taken on new shareholders.

1997 Kreuznacher Gutenthal
Riesling Spätlese
13.80 DM, 10%, 🍷 till 2001 **80**

1997 Chardonnay
trocken
11.50 DM, 11.5%, 🍷 till 2000 **80**

1997 Kreuznacher Krötenpfuhl
Riesling Kabinett trocken
10.50 DM, 11%, 🍷 till 2001 **82**

1996 Kreuznacher Hinkelstein
Weißer Burgunder Kabinett trocken
9.50 DM, 10.5%, 🍷 now **82**

1996 Kreuznacher Narrenkappe
Grauer Burgunder Kabinett trocken
9.50 DM, 10.5%, 🍷 now **82**

1997 Weißer Burgunder
Spätlese trocken
13.50 DM, 11.5%, 🍷 2000 **82**

1996 Kreuznacher Gutenthal
Riesling Spätlese
12.50 DM, 10.5%, 🍷 till 2000 **84**

1997 Kreuznacher St. Martin
Riesling Auslese
22.50 DM, 9.5%, 🍷 till 2002 **84**

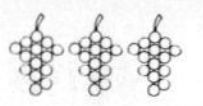

WEINGUT GÖTTELMANN

Owners: Ruth Göttelmann-Blessing, Götz Blessing
55424 Münster-Sarmsheim, Rheinstraße 77
Tel. (0 67 21) 4 37 75, Fax 4 26 05
Directions: A 61, exit Dorsheim, in the direction of Münster-Sarmsheim
Sales: Blessing family
Opening hours: Mon.–Sun. 10 a.m. to 9 p.m., by appointment
Restaurant: Open from March to September, 6 p.m. to midnight, except Mon. and Tue.
Specialties: Regional dishes

Vineyard area: 9.5 hectares
Annual production: 60,000 bottles
Top sites: Münsterer Dautenpflänzer, Pittersberg and Rheinberg
Soil types: Weathered slate, loess and loam
Grape varieties: 56% Riesling, 9% Silvaner, 15% Burgundian varieties, 10% red varieties, 6% Chardonnay, 4% other varieties
Average yield: 66 hl/ha
Best vintages: 1995, 1996, 1997

This property has always been well-endowed in top sites within Münster; and with both the Pittersberg and Dautenpflänzer vineyards planted with Riesling, the stage was set for what followed. After both Götz Blessing and his wife, Ruth Göttelmann, had trained at Geisenheim, they drew our attention with a persuasive 1993 range. The equally good 1994s established their reputation for consistent quality, which was confirmed by the 1995s and 1996s. The top wine of that year was the excellent Münsterer Rheinberg Spätlese. The 1997s are not only better, they set new standards of quality for this up and coming estate. Few producers in Germany offer such fine wine for so little money.

1996 Sarmsheimer Liebehöll
Riesling Kabinett
7 DM, 8%, ♀ now **86**

1997 Münsterer
Chardonnay Spätlese trocken
9.80 DM, 12%, ♀ till 2004 **88**

1997 Münsterer Dautenpflänzer
Riesling Spätlese halbtrocken
9.80 DM, 11%, ♀ till 2004 **88**

1997 Münsterer Dautenpflänzer
Riesling Spätlese
9.50 DM, 9%, ♀ till 2004 **89**

1996 Münsterer Rheinberg
Riesling Spätlese
9.80 DM, 8.5%, ♀ till 2002 **89**

1997 Münsterer Rheinberg
Riesling Spätlese
9.50 DM, 8%, ♀ till 2005 **91**

1997 Münsterer Dautenpflänzer
Riesling Spätlese
10.30 DM, 7.5%, ♀ till 2006 **91**

1997 Münsterer Rheinberg
Riesling Auslese – 13 –
16.50 DM, 8%, ♀ till 2006 **91**

1997 Münsterer Rheinberg
Riesling Auslese – 10 –
28 DM, 9%, ♀ till 2008 **92**

WEINGUT HAHNMÜHLE

Owners: Peter and Martina Linxweiler
67822 Mannweiler-Cölln,
Alsenzstraße 25
Tel. (0 63 62) 99 30 99, Fax 44 66
Directions: A 61, exit Gau-Bickelheim, via B 420 and B 48 in the direction of Kaiserslautern, at the village end left over railway and bridge
Opening hours: Mon.–Fri. 8 a.m. to 7 p.m., Sat. 8 a.m. to 5 p.m.
History: The mill dates from the 13th century and has been owned by the family since 1898

Vineyard area: 8.8 hectares
Annual production: 45,000 bottles
Top sites: Oberndorfer Beutelstein, Alsenzer Elkersberg
Soil types: Weathered sandstone and slate
Grape varieties: 57% Riesling, 11% Gewürztraminer, 10% Silvaner, 9% Weißburgunder, 7% Spätburgunder, 3% each of Portugieser and Chardonnay
Average yield: 40 hl/ha
Best vintages: 1995, 1996, 1997
Member: Quintessenz

Off the beaten track of the River Nahe, in the wild and romantic Alsenz valley, Martina and Peter Linxweiler have long devoted themselves to producing wines of quality. Organic viticulture practiced on meager soils ensures that yields are kept low. Selective manual harvesting and the aging of the young wines in casks are the choices here. The family's main vineyard is the steep Oberndorfer Beutelstein, where the young vines are gradually beginning to bear fruit. A traditional wine known as "Alisencia" comes from the Alsenzer Elkersberg vineyard. The Linxweilers are beginning to find their own style: generally vinified dry, the wines are lightly yeasty in aroma and fresh on the palate; fortunately they have also become better balanced in their acidic structure. The 1996 Chardonnay turned out well and, in spite of severe frost, the whole of the 1997 range is even better.

1997 Cöllner Rosenberg
Riesling Spätlese halbtrocken
14.50 DM, 12%, ♀ till 2002 **86**

1997 Cöllner Rosenberg
Riesling and Traminer Auslese halbtrocken
22.50 DM/0.5 liter, 12.5%, ♀ till 2004 **86**

1997 Oberndorfer Beutelstein
Traminer Auslese halbtrocken
24.50 DM, 13%, ♀ till 2005 **86**

1997 Oberndorfer Beutelstein
Riesling Auslese
24.50 DM/0.5 liter, 13%, ♀ till 2005 **86**

1996 Cöllner Rosenberg
Riesling Eiswein
49 DM/0.375 liter, 15%, ♀ till 2004 **86**

1997 Riesling
trocken "Alisencia"
9.80 DM, 12%, ♀ till 2002 **86**

1996 Oberndorfer Beutelstein
Chardonnay Spätlese trocken
24.50 DM, 12%, ♀ till 2001 **88**

1997 Oberndorfer Beutelstein
Chardonnay Auslese trocken
28 DM, 13%, ♀ till 2002 **88**

Hahnmühle
1996
RIESLING
TROCKEN
„ALISENCIA"
QUALITÄTSWEIN
NAHE
GUTSABFÜLLUNG A. P. NR. 7 786 010 16 97
WEINGUT HAHNMÜHLE, P. + M. LINXWEILER
D-67822 MANNWEILER-CÖLLN
DE-029-Öko Kontrollstelle
0,75 l
11,0 % vol

WEINGUT HEHNER-KILTZ

Owners: Georg and Helmut Hehner
General manager: Walter Hehner, Mario Emrich
Winemaker: Georg Hehner
55596 Waldböckelheim, Hauptstraße 4
Tel. (0 67 58) 79 18, Fax 86 20
Directions: Via A 60 or 61, B 41 between Bad Kreuznach and Idar-Oberstein
Sales: Georg Hehner
Opening hours: Mon.–Sun. 8 a.m. to 8 p.m.
Restaurant: Weinhaus Hehner, open year-round
Specialties: Regional cooking

> Vineyard area: 21 hectares
> Annual production: 180,000 bottles
> Top sites: Schloßböckelheimer Kupfergrube, Felsenberg and Königsfels, Meddersheimer Rheingrafenberg
> Soil types: Volcanic, gravelly sandy loam
> Grape varieties: 60% Riesling, 8% Müller-Thurgau, 6% each of Spätburgunder and Kerner, 3% Silvaner, 17% other varieties
> Average yield: 44 hl/ha
> Best vintages: 1992, 1993, 1994

One cannot say that the Hehner brothers are of a timorous disposition nor that they shrink from taking risks. Over the past decade an attractive hotel has been built around their popular wine bar. Moreover, the small estate of their parents was expanded in the 1980s to an impressive 11 hectares; leasing an additional 10 from the Beck estate in Meddersheim in 1995 led to a short-term tripling of their annual production. We were uncertain as to whether such an expansion could be handled successfully. The 1996 vintage brought a clear answer: seldom had we tasted such a disappointing range of wines. The simple wines were sold inexpensively under the Beck estate label without specific vineyard names, but that did little to improve the top end of the flight. Severe frost in 1997 prevented the brothers from proving their mettle. The judgment is still out.

1997 Meddersheimer Rheingrafenberg
Riesling Spätlese halbtrocken
11.50 DM, 11%, 🍷 till 2001 **82**

1997 Meddersheimer Rheingrafenberg
Weißer Burgunder Auslese
16.50 DM, 12.5%, 🍷 till 2001 **82**

1997 Schloßböckelheimer Felsenberg
Riesling Kabinett trocken
9.50 DM, 10.5%, 🍷 till 2002 **84**

1996 Schloßböckelheimer Königsfels
Riesling halbtrocken
8 DM, 10%, 🍷 till 2000 **84**

1996 Monzinger Halenberg
Riesling halbtrocken
8.50 DM, 10%, 🍷 now **84**

1996 Schloßböckelheimer Königsfels
Riesling
8 DM, 10.5%, 🍷 till 2000 **84**

1997 Schloßböckelheimer Königsfels
Riesling Spätlese trocken
13.50 DM, 11%, 🍷 till 2003 **86**

1997 Grauer Burgunder
Auslese
16.50 DM, 12%, 🍷 till 2003 **86**

Hehner-Kiltz
NAHE
1997
SCHLOSSBÖCKELHEIMER
KÖNIGSFELS
RIESLING
SPÄTLESE trocken
QUALITÄTSWEIN MIT PRÄDIKAT
A. P. Nr. 7 777 023 15 98
GUTSABFÜLLUNG
WEINGUT HEHNER-KILTZ · D-55596 WALDBÖCKELHEIM
750 ml alc. 11.0% by vol.

WEINGUT JUNG

Owners: Eckard and Karl-Otto Jung
Winemakers: Karl-Otto and Eckard Jung
55583 Ebernburg, Burgstraße 8
Tel. (0 67 08) 66 00 93, Fax 66 00 94
Directions: Via A 61 to Bad Kreuznach, B 48 in the direction of Bad Münster am Stein-Ebernburg
Sales: Karl-Otto Jung
Opening hours: Mon.–Sat. 8 a.m. to 6 p.m. or by appointment
Restaurant: Mid-June to end of August, open from 5 p.m. to 11 p.m., except Sat. and Sun.
Worth seeing: Collection of rarities from 1893 onwards, idyllic flower-filled courtyard

Vineyard area: 9.6 hectares
Annual production: 45,000 bottles
Top sites: Bad Münsterer Felseneck, Norheimer Dellchen, Altenbamberger Rotenberg and Ebernburger Erzgrube
Soil types: Weathered slate, weathered porphyry
Grape varieties: 60% Riesling, 15% Müller-Thurgau, 5% each of Kerner, Dornfelder and Portugieser, 4% each of Silvaner and Grauburgunder, 2% Gewürztraminer
Average yield: 47 hl/ha
Best vintages: 1993, 1994, 1996

Eckard and Karl-Otto Jung belong to an incorrigible band of vintners who torment themselves by cultivating steep vineyards – and there are more than enough of these at this highly traditional estate. The Bad Münsterer Felseneck, which they own exclusively, is a case in point: one of the top sites in the Nahe, it's situated at the foot of the Rotenfels cliff and enjoys an exceptional microclimate. Here they regularly harvest Spätlese and Auslese. And the celebrated Norheimer Dellchen, too, belongs to the finest sites of the Nahe. Karl-Otto Jung, the cellarmaster, specializes in sweet Rieslings, which account for about half of the estate's offerings. We particularly liked the 1996 Spätlese from the Erzgrube vineyard, but even the two dry Spätlese from Dellchen and Felseneck were well-balanced. Unfortunately, this trend was short-lived. The 1997s are disappointing.

1997 Altenbamberger Rotenberg
Riesling Spätlese halbtrocken
12.30 DM, 9.5%, ♀ till 2001 **80**

1997 Bad Münsterer Felseneck
Riesling Spätlese
11.80 DM, 8.5%, ♀ till 2002 **80**

1997 Norheimer Dellchen
Riesling Spätlese
12.20 DM, 9.5%, ♀ till 2002 **80**

1996 Altenbamberger Rotenberg
Riesling Kabinett halbtrocken
8.80 DM, 8%, ♀ now **82**

1997 Bad Münsterer Felseneck
Riesling Spätlese halbtrocken
11.80 DM, 9.5%, ♀ till 2002 **82**

1996 Norheimer Dellchen
Riesling Spätlese trocken
12.60 DM, 10%, ♀ till 2000 **84**

1997 Bad Münsterer Felseneck
Riesling Auslese
20 DM, 9%, ♀ till 2003 **84**

1996 Bad Münsterer Felseneck
Riesling Spätlese trocken
12.30 DM, 10%, ♀ till 2000 **86**

1996 Ebernburger Erzgrube
Riesling Spätlese
11.70 DM, 9%, ♀ till 2001 **88**

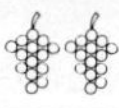

WEINGUT KÖNIGSWINGERT

Owner: Linus Zimmermann
Winemaker: Gregor Zimmermann
55452 Guldental, Naheweinstraße 44
Tel. (0 67 07) 87 65, Fax 82 13
Directions: A 61, exit Windesheim, via Windesheim to Guldental
Opening hours: Mon.–Fri. 8 a.m. to 8 p.m., Sat. 8 a.m. to 3 p.m. or by appointment
History: Owned by the family for almost 140 years
Worth seeing: Old vaulted cellars with carved casks

Vineyard area: 12 hectares
Annual production: 85,000 bottles
Top sites: Bretzenheimer Pastorei, Guldentaler Hipperich and Sonnenberg
Soil types: Gravelly loam, with reddish slate
Grape varieties: 22% Riesling, 19% Müller-Thurgau, 14% Silvaner, 8% Scheurebe, 5% Spätburgunder, 4% each of Kerner, Grau- and Weißburgunder, 20% other varieties
Average yield: 74 hl/ha
Best vintages: 1994, 1995, 1997

Guldental is now once again home to a talented young grower eager to make more than merely simple wines from the indisputable potential of this valley's vineyards. Gregor Zimmermann's wines are fruit driven, but at the same time elegant and appetizing. It's little wonder, since he trained at the estate of the outstanding winemaker Helmut Dönnhoff – and one can readily taste the influence! The wines are rich and full in body, yet graceful in their aftertaste. Zimmerman has lowered the yields to 75 hectoliters per hectare. Unfortunately, Riesling constitutes only a quarter of the holdings, but all of the wines are of consistent quality. We particularly enjoyed the 1996 Bretzenheimer Pastorei Spätlese and 1997 Guldentaler Hipperich Auslese. This is a paradise for bargain hunters!

1997 Guldentaler Hipperich
Grauer Burgunder Spätlese trocken
11.50 DM, 12.5%, 🍷 till 2000 **84**

1997 Guldentaler Hipperich
Riesling Spätlese trocken
11 DM, 11.5%, 🍷 till 2000 **86**

1997 Guldentaler Hipperich
Riesling Spätlese halbtrocken
11 DM, 11%, 🍷 till 2002 **86**

1996 Guldentaler Hipperich
Riesling Spätlese halbtrocken
10.50 DM, 11.5%, 🍷 till 2001 **86**

1997 Riesling
halbtrocken
7 DM, 11%, 🍷 till 2001 **86**

1997 Guldentaler Hipperich
Riesling Spätlese
9.90 DM, 9.5%, 🍷 till 2004 **88**

1996 Bretzenheimer Pastorei
Riesling Spätlese
9.90 DM, 10%, 🍷 till 2002 **88**

1996 Guldentaler Hipperich
Riesling Auslese
15 DM, 9%, 🍷 till 2005 **88**

1997 Guldentaler Hipperich
Riesling Auslese
18 DM, 8.5%, 🍷 till 2006 **91**

WEINGUT
KÖNIGSWINGERT
1996
GULDENTALER HIPPERICH
RIESLING AUSLESE
QUALITÄTSWEIN MIT PRÄDIKAT
9,0% vol GUTSABFÜLLUNG e0,75 l
NAHE
LINUS ZIMMERMANN · D-6531 GULDENTAL/NAHE

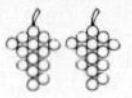

WEINGUT KORRELL – JOHANNESHOF

Owners: Wilfried and Martin Korrell
55545 Bad Kreuznach-Bosenheim, Parkstraße 4
Tel. (06 71) 6 36 30, Fax 7 19 54
Directions: A 61, exit Bad Kreuznach, take the main road to the first traffic light, then left to Bosenheim
Opening hours: Mon.–Fri. 8 a.m. to 6 p.m., Sat. 9 a.m. to 1 p.m. or by appointment
History: Winery established 1760, family coat of arms since 1483

Vineyard area: 17.6 hectares
Annual production: 140,000 bottles
Top site: Kreuznacher Paradies
Soil types: Clay with fossil limestone, gravel with a proportion of clay, loess and loam
Grape varieties: 25% Riesling, 10% each of Müller-Thurgau, Spätburgunder, Portugieser and Grauburgunder, 8% Dornfelder, 6% Weißburgunder, 4% Chardonnay and 17% other varieties
Average yield: 75 hl/ha
Best vintages: 1993,1996, 1997

With much hard work and a touch of luck the Korrells have developed this estate – which until the legal reorganization of 1971 was part of Rheinhessen – into one of the most successful family wineries of the Nahe. Their enterprise takes many forms: the neighboring wine bar was long run independently, but has now been leased; just a few meters from the estate they restored an old farmhouse in the late 1980s, creating a bed and breakfast as well as rooms for special events; their daughters, Astrid and Sonja, run a wine shop in the spa district of Bad Kreuznach. There are similar shops in Cologne and Steinfurt. Wilfried Korrell, their father, is particularly proud of his son Martin. After studying in the Ahr region and later in Australia he joined the family business in 1995. Not surprisingly, the last two vintages have been particularly successful.

1996 Kreuznacher Tilgesbrunnen
Weißer Burgunder halbtrocken
8.90 DM, 10.5%, ♀ till 2000 **84**

1997 Kreuznacher Paradies
Riesling Kabinett halbtrocken
7.90 DM, 10%, ♀ till 2001 **84**

1996 Kreuznacher Hirtenhain
Riesling Spätlese halbtrocken
9.80 DM, 10%, ♀ till 2001 **84**

1997 Kreuznacher St. Martin
Riesling Auslese halbtrocken
15.80 DM, 11%, ♀ till 2002 **84**

1997 Kreuznacher Rosenberg
Chardonnay trocken
9.90 DM, 12.5%, ♀ till 2001 **84**

1997 Weißer Burgunder
trocken Selection "Johannes K"
17.80 DM, 12%, ♀ till 2002 **84**

1997 Kreuznacher St. Martin
Riesling Spätlese
11.50 DM, 9%, ♀ till 2004 **86**

1997 Kreuznacher St. Martin
Riesling Auslese
15.80 DM, 8%, ♀ till 2006 **89**

1996 Kreuznacher Hirtenhain
Riesling Eiswein
49.80 DM/0.5 liter, 8%, ♀ till 2008 **92**

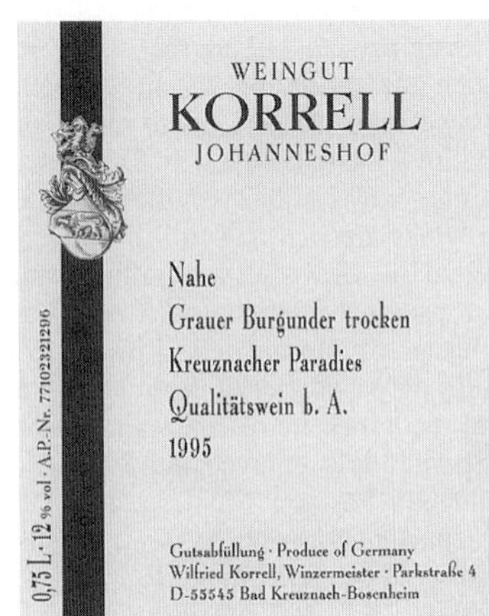

WEINGUT KRUGER-RUMPF

Owners: Stefan and Cornelia Rumpf
55424 Münster-Sarmsheim, Rheinstraße 47
Tel. (0 67 21) 4 38 59, Fax 4 18 82
Directions: A 61, exit Dorsheim, B 48 in the direction of Bingen, main street of Münster-Sarmsheim
Opening hours: Mon.–Sat. 9 a.m. to 7 p.m. and Sun. 4 p.m. to 8 p.m.
Wine bar and restaurant: 4 p.m. to 11 p.m., except Mon.
Specialties: Good homemade cooking
Worth seeing: Historic house, idyllic courtyard with old paving

Vineyard area: 16 hectares
Annual production: 110,000 bottles
Top sites: Münsterer Dautenpflänzer and Pittersberg, Dorsheimer Goldloch and Burgberg
Soil types: Slate and volcanic soil
Grape varieties: 65% Riesling, 10% each of Silvaner and Weißburgunder, 5% each of Chardonnay, Grauburgunder and Spätburgunder
Average yield: 63 hl/ha
Best vintages: 1992, 1994, 1996
Member: VDP

This estate has traditionally been one of the most reliable addresses in the Nahe valley. Top vineyards in Münster-Sarmsheim and Dorsheim planted with old vines ensure that Rumpf harvests ripe grapes, which he generally vinifies as full-bodied dry wines. Although Riesling dominates, the Burgundian varieties are being given an increasing share of the total production. Moreover, the old Silvaner vines also yield surprising wines. The quality of the 1994 range led us to believe that Stefan Rumpf had set himself new goals; unfortunately, the 1995 range did not confirm that impression. The 1996s, however, were clearly of superior quality, certainly the finest wines of Stefan Rumpf's career. His investments in the winery are now beginning to pay off; and even if the 1997s were not quite as good, if his performance remains at this level his estate will soon be one of the top producers of the region.

1997 Münsterer Pittersberg
Riesling Spätlese trocken Silberkapsel
16.50 DM, 11.5%, ♀ till 2003 **88**

1997 Münsterer Dautenpflänzer
Riesling Spätlese
16.50 DM, 10.5%, ♀ till 2005 **88**

1997 Weißer Burgunder
trocken Silberkapsel
15 DM, 12.5%, ♀ till 2003 **88**

1996 Münsterer Pittersberg
Riesling Spätlese
15 DM, 10%, ♀ till 2004 **89**

1996 Münsterer Dautenpflänzer
Riesling Spätlese
16 DM, 10%, ♀ till 2006 **89**

1997 Münsterer Dautenpflänzer
Riesling Auslese
80 DM/0.375 liter, 9%, ♀ till 2006 **89**

1996 Münsterer Dautenpflänzer
Riesling Auslese
28 DM, 10%, ♀ till 2008 **89**

1996 Münsterer Pittersberg
Riesling Auslese Goldkapsel
54 DM, 10.5%, ♀ till 2008 **89**

1997 Münsterer Dautenpflänzer
Riesling Spätlese halbtrocken
15 DM, 11.5%, ♀ till 2005 **90**

1996 Münsterer Pittersberg
Riesling Eiswein
61 DM/0.375 liter, 8%, ♀ till 2010 **94**

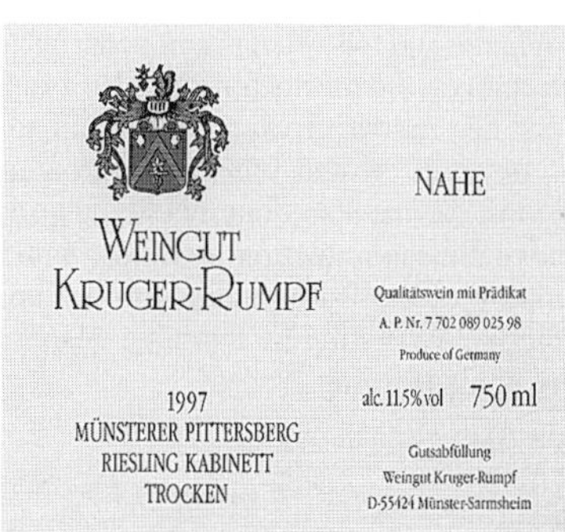

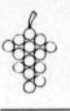

WEINGUT LINDENHOF

Owner: Herbert Reimann
Winemaker: Martin Reimann
55452 Windesheim, Lindenhof
Tel. (0 67 07) 3 30, Fax 83 10
Directions: A 61, exit Windesheim, in the village follow main road in the direction of Bad Kreuznach, last street on left
Opening hours: Mon.–Fri. 8 a.m. to 6 p.m., Sat. 9 a.m. to 4 p.m.

Vineyard area: 6.7 hectares
Annual production: 45,000 bottles
Top sites: Schweppenhäuser Steyerberg, Windesheimer Rosenberg and Römerberg
Soil types: Slate, sandy loam, reddish slate
Grape varieties: 32% Riesling, 18% each of Spätburgunder and Weißburgunder, 8% each of Kerner and Scheurebe, 16% other varieties
Average yield: 54 hl/ha
Best vintages: 1994, 1996, 1997

It was a fanfare for a new red wine star of the Nahe: two of Martin Reimann's 1994 Spätburgunders showed well in our final tasting of that year's best reds. This led to such a run on his Spätburgunder that not only are his 1995s now sold out, but his 1996s and 1997s as well. The 1996 whites were also attractive, although not as good as the reds, but the 1997s are quite the opposite: Never have we tasted such well-balanced whites from this estate. The sparkling wines, too, belong to the upper ranks. For years Reimann has maintained contact with the wine college in Beaune and has often organized trips to Burgundy – the mecca for Pinot Noir fans – for his fellow growers. But Reimann has not only visited other wine-growing regions, he has also done his homework. Above all, the reduction in yields, bunch thinning of the Burgundian varieties and selective harvesting by hand have been a part of his learning process.

1996 Weißer Burgunder
trocken Selection
10.50 DM, 11.5%, ♀ till 2000 **84**

1997 Riesling
Spätlese trocken
9.80 DM, 11.5%, ♀ till 2001 **84**

1996 Riesling
halbtrocken
8.20 DM, 11%, ♀ till 2000 **84**

1997 Weißer Burgunder
Spätlese trocken *Barrique*
15 DM, 13%, ♀ till 2002 **86**

1997 Riesling
Spätlese
10.50 DM, 9%, ♀ till 2002 **86**

1997 Riesling
Spätlese Selection
14 DM, 9%, ♀ till 2005 **88**

——— Red wine ———

1997 Spätburgunder
trocken *Barrique*
18 DM, 13%, ♀ till 2002 **84**

WEINGUT LINDENHOF
HERBERT REIMANN
D-55452 WINDESHEIM
TELEFON 06707.330
1 9 9 4
SPÄTBURGUNDER
QUALITÄTSWEIN TROCKEN
NAHE GUTSABFÜLLUNG
13% VOL A.P.-NR. 7 782 086 596 75 CL
LINDENHOF

WEINGUT LÖTZBEYER

Owner: Adolf Lötzbeyer
67824 Feilbingert, Kirchstraße 6
Tel. (0 67 08) 22 87, Fax 46 67
Directions: A 61, exit Bad Kreuznach, B 48 to Bad Münster am Stein-Ebernburg, in the direction of Obermoschel
Opening hours: Mon.–Fri. 9 a.m. to 6 p.m., Sat. and Sun. 10 a.m. to 1 p.m. By appointment
History: Founded 1880

Vineyard area: 6.2 hectares
Annual production: 50,000 bottles
Top sites: Norheimer Dellchen, Niederhäuser Rosenberg
Soil types: Volcanic soils and basalt
Grape varieties: 53% Riesling, 13% Müller-Thurgau, 10% each of Bacchus and Scheurebe, 4% Portugieser, 10 % other varieties
Average yield: 47 hl/ha
Best vintages: 1993, 1994, 1995

Although on the far edge of the Nahe and essentially unknown in Germany, Adolf Lötzbeyer quickly moved into the spotlight in the United States after Robert Parker praised his wines in *The Wine Advocate*. In terms of value for money, the high proportion of exported wines is also easily explained. When it comes to the succulently sweet wines we often concur with that critic's assessment. However, the dry wines are much less successful, which is why he seldom submits them for tasting. And after our sideswipe at the jazzy blue bottle, he replied disarmingly: "Our customers are crazy about the packaging!" Be that as it may, the 1996s and 1997s were again of good quality and secure for this estate a place among the best properties from the Nahe.

1997 Feilbingerter Königsgarten
Riesling Spätlese
10.50 DM, 9%, ♀ till 2004 **88**

1997 Niederhäuser Stollenberg
Riesling Auslese
14 DM, 8%, ♀ till 2005 **89**

1997 Norheimer Dellchen
Riesling Auslese
16.80 DM, 8.5%, ♀ till 2005 **89**

1996 Feilbingerter Königsgarten
Riesling Eiswein – 13 –
35 DM/0.375 liter, 8%, ♀ till 2006 **89**

1996 Feilbingerter Königsgarten
Riesling Eiswein – 15 –
59 DM/0.375 liter, 7%, ♀ till 2007 **91**

1996 Feilbingerter Königsgarten
Scheurebe Eiswein
58 DM/0.375 liter, 7.5%, ♀ till 2010 **94**

1997 Feilbingerter Königsgarten
Riesling Eiswein
45 DM/0.375 liter, 7.5%, ♀ till 2010 **95**

WEINGUT OSKAR MATHERN

Owner: Helmut Mathern
55585 Niederhausen, Winzerstraße 7
Tel. (0 67 58) 67 14, Fax 81 09
Directions: Via Bad Kreuznach–Bad Münster–Norheim–Niederhausen
Opening hours: By appointment
Worth seeing: In 1981 given the "Golden Grape" as the loveliest wine grower's house in the Nahe region

Vineyard area: 9 hectares
Annual production: 90,000 bottles
Top sites: Niederhäuser Rosenberg, Kertz and Rosenheck, Norheimer Dellchen and Kirschheck
Soil types: Porphyry and slate
Grape varieties: 80% Riesling, 9% Müller-Thurgau, 3% each of Kerner and Dornfelder, 5% other varieties
Average yield: 77 hl/ha
Best vintages: 1995, 1996, 1997

When it comes to raking in medals, the estate of Oskar Mathern in Niederhausen has always been in the forefront: it has won numerous prizes at both provincial and federal levels over the past two decades. Even if one regards these awards with some skepticism, the consumer nonetheless always fares very well at this estate. The 1992 range, however, was the first to awaken our professional interest and the 1993s were also of good quality. The high point of Helmut Mathern's career to date was the excellent 1995 vintage, which earned him the title of "Discovery of the Year." The 1996 range followed in the footsteps of this successful vintage, only to be outshone by the excellent 1997s. With this effort Mathern has earned his place among the elite estates from the Nahe. A tip in passing: bargain hunters should cover their needs with sufficient quantities of the 1996s as the frost that descended in April of 1997 greatly reduced that year's crop.

1996 Niederhäuser Kertz
Riesling Spätlese
9.50 DM, 9%, ♀ till 2003 **89**

1997 Niederhäuser Rosenberg
Riesling Spätlese trocken
10 DM, 12.5%, ♀ till 2003 **91**

1997 Niederhäuser Rosenheck
Riesling Spätlese halbtrocken
10 DM, 11.5%, ♀ till 2004 **91**

1997 Niederhäuser Rosenheck
Riesling Spätlese
10 DM, 10.5%, ♀ till 2004 **91**

1996 Norheimer Dellchen
Riesling Spätlese
10 DM, 9%, ♀ till 2004 **91**

1996 Norheimer Dellchen
Riesling Auslese
18 DM, 10%, ♀ till 2005 **91**

1997 Niederhäuser Rosenberg
Riesling Auslese "Henning"
16 DM/0.5 liter, 10.5%, ♀ till 2008 **91**

1997 Norheimer Dellchen
Riesling Auslese "Luisa"
16 DM/0.5 liter, 11%, ♀ till 2007 **91**

1997 Niederhäuser Kertz
Riesling Spätlese
10 DM, 10%, ♀ till 2005 **92**

WEINGUT MEINHARD

Owner: Steffen Meinhard
Winemaker: Steffen Meinhard
55545 Bad Kreuznach-Winzenheim, Kirchstrasse 13
Tel. (06 71) 4 30 30, Fax 4 30 06
Directions: A 61, exit Windesheim, after four kilometers left, in the center of Winzenheim
Opening hours: Mon.–Sat. 8 a.m. to 6 p.m. or by appointment
Restaurant: Open Thur. and Fri. from 7 p.m., Sat. from 6 p.m. and Sun. from 5 p.m.
Specialties: Regional cooking

Vineyard area: 7 hectares
Annual production: 40,000 bottles
Top sites: Winzenheimer Rosenheck, Bretzenheimer Pastorei
Soil types: Loam with gravel and loess
Grape varieties: 27% Riesling, 14% Weißburgunder, 12% Grauburgunder, 9% each of Spätburgunder and Silvaner, 6% each of Portugieser and Kerner, 17% other varieties
Average yield: 80 hl/ha
Best vintages: 1992, 1994, 1996

This is another of those young growers from the Nahe who is producing notable wines. Steffen Meinhard, who has been running the family estate since 1990, has chosen to specialize in Riesling and the Burgundian varieties; and as the soils around Bad Kreuznach are particularly well suited to this aim, he even plans to increase the proportion of Weißburgunder, Grauburgunder and Spätburgunder. His policy of aging these wines in small oak barrels will also be cautiously expanded. The whole family is deployed in the estate's activities at the winery dinners in spring and autumn. A wine bar opened in the spring of 1998. We remain somewhat dubious about the packaging of the "Select" range, which is the name given to the somewhat better wines that the estate produces. Should sweet Riesling be marketed in a green Bordeaux bottle?

1997 Bretzenheimer Pastorei
Riesling Spätlese trocken
10 DM, 12%, ♀ till 2000 **80**

1996 Kreuznacher St. Martin
Grauer Burgunder Spätlese trocken
14.50 DM, 12.5%, ♀ now **84**

1996 Bretzenheimer Pastorei
Riesling Spätlese
12.50 DM, 10%, ♀ till 2002 **84**

1996 Winzenheimer Honigberg
Weißer Burgunder Spätlese trocken
14.50 DM, 12.5%, ♀ till 2000 **86**

——— Red wines ———

1997 Bretzenheimer Hofgut
Portugieser trocken "Select"
11.50 DM, 12%, ♀ now **80**

1996 Bretzenheimer Hofgut
Portugieser trocken
11.50 DM, 12.5%, ♀ till 2000 **82**

1996 Bretzenheimer Hofgut
Portugieser trocken *Barrique*
11.50 DM, 13%, ♀ till 2000 **84**

1997 Bretzenheimer Pastorei
Spätburgunder trocken
9.50 DM, 13%, ♀ till 2000 **84**

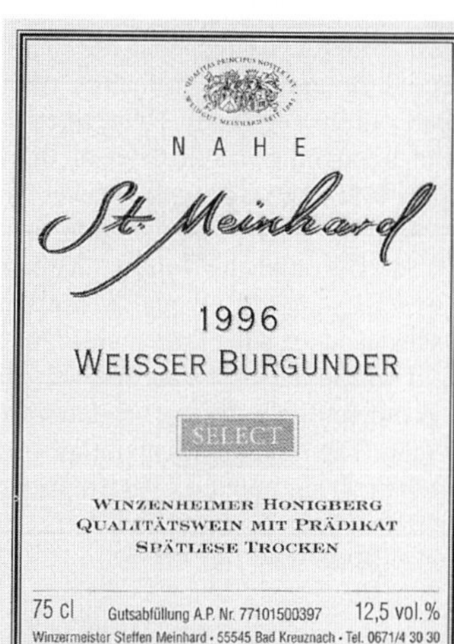

GUTSVERWALTUNG NIEDERHAUSEN-SCHLOSSBÖCKELHEIM

Owner: Erich Maurer family
Director: Kurt Gabelmann
Manager: Hartmut Günther
Winemaker: Kurt Gabelmann
55585 Niederhausen
Tel. (0 67 58) 9 25 00, Fax 92 50 19
Directions: Bad Kreuznach–Norheim, beyond Niederhausen turn right
Sales: Inge Schroeder, Werner Bumke
Opening hours: Mon.–Fri. 8 a.m. to 4:30 p.m., 1st Sat. in month 10 a.m. to 4 p.m.
History: Founded by the Prussian state as a model wine estate in 1902
Worth seeing: Art Nouveau buildings in the middle of the vineyards

Vineyard area: 34 hectares
Annual production: 200,000 bottles
Top sites: Niederhäuser Hermannsberg (sole owners) and Hermannshöhle, Schloßböckelheimer Kupfergrube and Felsenberg
Soil types: Volcanic soil, grey slate
Grape varieties: 95% Riesling, 5% other varieties
Average yield: 53 hl/ha
Best vintages: 1990, 1994, 1997
Member: VDP

For years the Domaine – as the estate was known – had at its disposal the greatest potential of excellent vineyards of any property in the region. In 1994, after a renewed financial consolidation of the estate, the best vineyards in the Lower Nahe were sold in order to concentrate on the finest sites around the winery. Although the overall standard of quality remained at a serious level, the estate was no longer what it was in the 1960s and 1970s, when it was indisputably the top producer from the Nahe. The last couple of vintages were again better, but now all eyes are focused on what – after privatization – the new owner will do with this estate.

1997 Altenbamberger Rotenberg
Riesling Kabinett
12.90 DM, 9.5%, ♀ till 2006 **88**

1997 Altenbamberger Rotenberg
Riesling Spätlese halbtrocken
18.40 DM, 10.5%, ♀ till 2004 **89**

1997 Schloßböckelheimer Kupfergrube
Riesling Spätlese
19.80 DM, 9%, ♀ till 2005 **89**

1997 Altenbamberger Rotenberg
Riesling Spätlese
18.40 DM, 9.5%, ♀ till 2006 **89**

1996 Niederhäuser Kertz
Riesling Spätlese
15.40 DM, 9%, ♀ till 2003 **89**

1996 Schloßböckelheimer Kupfergrube
Riesling Auslese
30 DM, 6.5%, ♀ till 2005 **89**

1997 Schloßböckelheimer Kupfergrube
Riesling Auslese
28.60 DM, 9%, ♀ 2006 **91**

1996 Niederhäuser Hermannshöhle
Riesling Beerenauslese
65 DM/0.375 liter, 8%, ♀ till 2010 **92**

1996 Niederhäuser Hermannsberg
Riesling Eiswein
99 DM/0.375 liter, 8.5%, ♀ till 2010 **96**

Staatliche Weinbaudomäne
Niederhausen-
Schloßböckelheim
D-55585 Oberhausen/Nahe
NAHE
1994er
Niederhäuser Steinberg
Riesling Auslese
Gutsabfüllung
L-A. P. Nr. 7 750 053 008 95
Qualitätswein mit Prädikat
alc. 10.0% by vol. · e 750 ml
Produce of Germany

WEINGUT REICHSGRAF VON PLETTENBERG

Owners: Counts Egbert and Franz von Plettenberg
Winemaker: Walter Eschborn
55545 Bad Kreuznach, Winzenheimer Straße
Tel. (06 71) 22 51, Fax 4 52 26
Directions: B 41, exit Kreuznach-Nord
Sales: Egbert Count von Plettenberg
Opening hours: Mon.–Fri. 9 a.m. to 4 p.m. or by appointment
History: Owned in the 19th century by a noted family of industrialists, the Puricellis, and since 1912 by the Plettenberg family

Vineyard area: 41 hectares
Annual production: 350,000 bottles
Top sites: Kreuznacher Brückes and Kahlenberg, Winzenheimer Rosenheck, Bretzenheimer Pastorei
Soil types: Loam and volcanic soils
Grape varieties: 67% Riesling, 20% Weißburgunder, 5% Müller-Thurgau, 4% each of Spätburgunder and Portugieser
Average yield: 61 hl/ha
Best vintages: 1993, 1994, 1997

The Counts von Plettenberg have extensive vineyard holdings in the Nahe, stretching from Bretzenheim via Bad Kreuznach almost as far as Roxheim. The excellent but remoter vineyards in Schloßböckelheim were recently traded to Helmut Dönnhoff in exchange for parcels he owned in Kreuznach. Until the 1960s this estate was among the leading properties in the Nahe valley; thereafter followed a period when quality was inconsistent. The property began showing signs of improvement with the 1993 vintage, which were repeated the following year. The 1995s, however, were not up to par and the 1996s among the weakest wines of the decade. With a range of well made 1997s the estate has resurfaced. The new winemaker's job is now to provide continuity of style.

1996 Roxheimer Höllenpfad
Riesling Spätlese halbtrocken
16.90 DM, 11%, ♀ now **80**

1997 Winzenheimer Berg
Grauer Burgunder Spätlese halbtrocken
19.80 DM, 11.5%, ♀ till 2002 **82**

1996 Kreuznacher Brückes
Riesling Spätlese
15.40 DM, 9%, ♀ till 2001 **82**

1997 Kreuznacher Hinkelstein
Weißer Burgunder Spätlese trocken
16.50 DM, 13%, ♀ till 2001 **84**

1997 Winzenheimer Berg
Chardonnay Spätlese trocken
19.80 DM, 11.5%, ♀ till 2001 **84**

1997 Kreuznacher Mönchberg
Riesling Spätlese
16.50 DM, 10.5%, ♀ till 2003 **86**

1997 Kreuznacher Kahlenberg
Riesling Auslese
23.50 DM, 8.5%, ♀ till 2005 **88**

1997 Winzenheimer Rosenheck
Riesling Auslese
23.50 DM, 8.5%, ♀ till 2004 **88**

1996 Kreuznacher Brückes
Riesling Auslese
23.80 DM, 7.5%, ♀ till 2002 **88**

Schloss Plettenberg®
1997
Winzenheimer Rosenheck
Riesling Auslese Nahe
Qualitätswein mit Prädikat
L-A.P.Nr. 7 710 069 0 16 98
8,5%vol 750ml
Art. Nr. 24260-2
Produce of Germany · Erzeugerabfüllung
Weingut Reichsgraf von Plettenberg
D-55545 Bad Kreuznach

WEINGUT RAPP

Owner: Walter Rapp
Winemaker: Walter Rapp
55583 Bad Münster a. St.-Ebernburg, Schloßgartenstraße 100
Tel. (0 67 08) 23 12, Fax 30 74
Directions: Via Bad Kreuznach to Ebernburg, at village exit (Schloßgartenstraße) take the entrance to the Ebernburg
Opening hours: Mon.–Fri. 8 a.m. to 8 p.m., Sat. and Sun. 8 a.m. to 6 p.m.

Vineyard area: 7 hectares
Annual production: 55,000 bottles
Top sites: Ebernburger Schloßberg, Erzgrube and Stephansberg, Altenbamberger Rotenberg
Soil types: Porphyry, slate, sandstone
Grape varieties: 55% Riesling, 16% Müller-Thurgau, 8% Scheurebe, 6% Grauburgunder, 5% each of Silvaner, Kerner and Spätburgunder
Average yield: 60 hl/ha
Best vintages: 1993, 1995, 1997

The Rapps are one of those families from the Nahe that still maintain their struggle with steep vineyard sites and thereby make an invaluable contribution to the preservation of the landscape. The lively Rieslings from the vineyards in Ebernburg and Altenbamberg are almost always a pleasure to drink. The 1996s, however, were marked by high acidities and definitely not as good as those from the previous year. Son Walter Rapp, who did his apprenticeship at the State Domaine in Niederhausen and then attended the wine college in Kreuznach, has now taken complete command of the estate. Perhaps as a result the 1997s are more successful. For the past twenty-five years the estate has maintained a guest house for private customers, which allows them to keep close contact with the winery; not surprisingly, 80 percent of the wines are sold directly to this clientele. And as was always the case, a considerable proportion of the production is vinified as sparkling wine.

1996 Ebernburger Feuerberg
Grauer Burgunder Spätlese trocken
9 DM, 12%, ♀ now **80**

1997 Ebernburger Luisengarten
Riesling Spätlese trocken
9 DM, 11%, ♀ till 2000 **82**

1997 Ebernburger
Riesling Spätlese trocken
8.60 DM, 11%, ♀ till 2001 **82**

1996 Ebernburger Köhler Köpfchen
Riesling halbtrocken
6.80 DM, 10.5%, ♀ now **82**

1997 Ebernburger Stephansberg
Riesling Kabinett halbtrocken
7.50 DM, 10%, ♀ till 2001 **82**

1997 Altenbamberger Rotenberg
Riesling Spätlese trocken
9 DM, 11%, ♀ till 2001 **84**

1996 Altenbamberger Rotenberg
Riesling halbtrocken
7.80 DM, 10.5%, ♀ now **84**

1997 Ebernburger Stephansberg
Riesling Auslese halbtrocken
12.50 DM, 11%, ♀ till 2002 **84**

1997 Ebernburger Feuerberg
Grauer Burgunder Auslese halbtrocken
12.50 DM, 12.5%, ♀ till 2002 **86**

WEINGUT PRINZ ZU SALM-DALBERG

Owner: Michael Prinz zu Salm-Salm
General Manager: Harald Eckes
55595 Wallhausen, Schloßstraße 3
Tel. (0 67 06) 94 44 11, Fax 94 44 24
e-mail: salm.dalberg@salm-salm.de
Directions: A 61, exit Waldlaubersheim, after three kilometers right at traffic light, at village end left over the bridge
Sales: Christiane Schöning
Opening hours: Mon.–Fri. 8 a.m. to noon and 1 p.m. to 5 p.m.
Sat. and Sun. by appointment
History: First mentioned in 1200, Germany's oldest estate to be owned continuously by the same family
Worth seeing: Schloß Wallhausen and the ruins of the Dalburg castle

Vineyard area: 11.5 hectares
Annual production: 70,000 bottles
Top sites: Wallhäuser Johannisberg and Felseneck, Roxheimer Berg
Soil types: Reddish slate
Grape varieties: 60% Riesling, 15% Spätburgunder, 4% Silvaner, 8% Müller-Thurgau, 5% each of Kerner and Scheurebe, 3% Grauburgunder
Average yield: 42 hl/ha
Best vintages: 1992, 1993, 1997
Member: VDP, Naturland

As the president of the VDP, Prince Michael Salm is known to all, but he also frequents the circles of the organic producers. In 1989 his estate adopted the practices of organic viticulture; in 1995 it was officially certified. Prince Salm is well endowed in his village's top vineyard, the Wallhäuser Johannisberg, as well as in the celebrated Roxheimer Berg, and only these sites are ever mentioned on the label. The Rieslings are often marked by an assertive acidity, which can seem excessive in fully dry wines from more difficult vintages; on the other hand, this acidity provides a welcome balance for the fruitier, late harvest wines. The 1996 range was similar to that of 1995, but did not match the quality of the finer vintages of the early 1990s. The estate's 1997s are considerably more attractive.

1997 Wallhäuser Felseneck
Riesling Spätlese halbtrocken
18.50 DM, 11%, ♀ till 2002 **86**

1996 Roxheimer Berg
Riesling
9.80 DM, 9.5%, ♀ till 2001 **86**

1997 Riesling
Kabinett
12 DM, 9%, ♀ till 2002 **86**

1996 Wallhäuser Johannisberg
Riesling Spätlese
18.50 DM, 8%, ♀ till 2002 **86**

1997 Wallhäuser Felseneck
Riesling Spätlese
18.50 DM, 9%, ♀ till 2005 **88**

1997 Wallhäuser Felseneck
Riesling Auslese
35 DM, 8.5%, ♀ till 2007 **88**

1997 Riesling
Eiswein Goldkapsel
150 DM/0.375 liter, 7.5%, ♀ till 2005 **89**

——— Red wine ———

1997 Schloß Wallhausen
Spätburgunder Auslese trocken *Barrique*
65 DM, 12.5%, ♀ till 2004 **86**

WEINGUT MICHAEL SCHÄFER

Owners: Alfred and Karl-Heinz Schäfer
55452 Burg Layen, Hauptstraße 15
Tel. (0 67 21) 4 30 97, Fax 4 20 31
Directions: A 61, exit Dorsheim
Opening hours: Mon.–Fri. 8 a.m. to 7 p.m. or by appointment
History: Owned by the family for more than 250 years
Worth seeing: Old courthouse in the center of Burg Layen

Vineyard area: 14 hectares
Annual production: 95,000 bottles
Top sites: Dorsheimer Pittermännchen, Burg Layer Schloßberg
Soil types: Slate, gravelly loam
Grape varieties: 42% Riesling, 14% Kerner, 8% Silvaner, 7% each of Scheurebe and Weißburgunder, 6% red varieties, 16% other varieties
Average yield: 68 hl/ha
Best vintages: 1992, 1993, 1997

Twenty years ago the Schäfers moved their family's wine business to a location in the vineyards on the outskirts of Burg Layen near Waldlaubersheim. As the negociant side of their operation dwindled to almost nothing, the winery began focusing their attention on estate bottlings. Alfred Schäfer is a specialist in the more fruity styles, which are generally exported, but wine merchants in Germany also buy a significant proportion of his production. In the 1970s and 1980s the estate made its mark with wines from new grape varieties, but today Riesling and Weißburgunder yield the best results. Although Alfred and Karl-Heinz Schäfer trumpeted new ambitions in the early 1990s, the quality of the 1994 and 1995 vintages was certainly not up to our heightened expectations. Nor were the rather acidic 1996s – which were partially made by whole-cluster pressing – as good as other vintages from the early 1990s. The 1997s are marginally better, but still a far cry from what this estate is capable of producing.

1996 Burg Layer Schloßberg
Riesling trocken
8.90 DM, 11%, 🍷 now **80**

1996 Burg Layer Schloßberg
Riesling halbtrocken
8.90 DM, 11%, 🍷 now **80**

1997 Burg Layer Schloßberg
Riesling halbtrocken
8.90 DM, 10.5%, 🍷 till 2001 **80**

1997 Burg Layer Schloßberg
Riesling trocken
8.90 DM, 11%, 🍷 till 2000 **80**

1997 Burg Layer Schloßkapelle
Weißer Burgunder Kabinett trocken
8.90 DM, 12%, 🍷 till 2000 **82**

1997 Burg Layer Johannisberg
Scheurebe Kabinett
8.20 DM/0.5 liter, 8.5%, 🍷 till 2004 **82**

1996 Laubenheimer Vogelsang
Riesling Spätlese
12 DM, 7.5%, 🍷 till 2000 **82**

1996 Burg Layer Schloßberg
Riesling Spätlese
13 DM, 7%, 🍷 till 2000 **84**

1996 Burg Layer Johannisberg
Scheurebe Spätlese
10.50 DM, 7.5%, 🍷 till 2001 **84**

1997 Dorsheimer Pittermännchen
Riesling
10.80 DM, 7.5%, 🍷 till 2003 **84**

WEINGUT SCHÄFER-FRÖHLICH

Owners: Hans and Karin Fröhlich
Winemakers: Tim and Karin Fröhlich
55595 Bockenau, Schulstraße 6
Tel. (0 67 58) 65 21, Fax 87 94
Directions: B 41, exit Waldböckelheim, right towards Bockenau
Sales: Hans Fröhlich
Opening hours: Mon.–Fri. 9 a.m. to 8 p.m., Sat. 10 a.m. to 1 p.m. or by appointment
History: Wine estate owned by the family since 1800

Vineyard area: 9.5 hectares
Annual production: 70,000 bottles
Top sites: Schloßböckelheimer Felsenberg, Bockenauer Stromberg and Felseneck
Soil types: Volcanic soils, weathered porphyry
Grape varieties: 47% Riesling, 16% Weißburgunder, 10% Spätburgunder, 8% Kerner, 7% Bacchus, 6% each of Grauburgunder and Gewürztraminer
Average yield: 55 hl/ha
Best vintages: 1995, 1996, 1997

Along with four other growers Hans Fröhlich and his family have kept wine production alive in Bockenau, a side valley of the Nahe. In the past few years he has made substantial investments – certainly not the least because of the urgings of son Tim, who graduated from college with a degree in oenology and now manages the cellars with his mother. Expansion has taken place in the vineyards as well. Not long ago the family acquired two hectares of Riesling as well as a parcel in the excellent Schloßböckelheimer Felsenberg site. The excellent 1996s were the best that we had ever tasted from this estate, only to be outdone by the 1997s! All wines show a distinctive mineral character and crisp acidity, but are nonetheless fully ripe in their fruit. Without doubt, the 1996 ice wine was one of the best from that vintage. The Pinot Noir was equally surprising and even the sparkling wine merits mention.

1997 Bockenauer Stromberg
Weißer Burgunder trocken
8.50 DM, 12%, ♀ till 2001 **84**

1997 Bockenauer Felseneck
Riesling Spätlese trocken
12 DM, 11%, ♀ till 2002 **86**

1997 Bockenauer Felseneck
Riesling Spätlese halbtrocken
12 DM, 11%, ♀ till 2002 **86**

1997 Bockenauer Felseneck
Riesling halbtrocken
9 DM, 11%, ♀ till 2002 **86**

1997 Bockenauer Felseneck
Riesling Spätlese
12.80 DM, 9%, ♀ till 2004 **88**

1997 Bockenauer Felseneck
Riesling
9 DM, 11%, ♀ till 2003 **88**

1996 Riesling
Eiswein
75 DM/0.375 liter, 7%, ♀ till 2012 **92**

——— Red wine ———

1996 Spätburgunder
trocken *Barrique*
20 DM, 13%, ♀ till 2004 **89**

WEINGUT
SCHÄFER-FRÖHLICH
NAHE
1995
BOCKENAUER
FELSENECK
Riesling
TROCKEN
Qualitätswein
GUTSABFÜLLUNG
WEINGUT SCHÄFER-FRÖHLICH · D-55595 BOCKENAU/NAHE
11,5% vol „L" A.P.Nr. 7 713 041 4 96 0,75 l

WEINGUT SCHMIDT

Owners: Herbert and Andreas Schmidt
Winemaker: Andreas Schmidt
67823 Obermoschel, Luitpoldstr. 24
Tel. (0 63 62) 12 65, Fax 41 45
Directions: A 61, exit Gau-Bickelheim, via B 420
Sales: Schmidt family
Opening hours: Mon.–Sat. 8 a.m. to 8 p.m. or by appointment

Vineyard area: 19 hectares
Annual production: 250,000 bottles
Top sites: Obermoscheler Silberberg and Schloßberg, Norheimer Dellchen
Soil types: Slate, volcanic soil
Grape varieties: 59% Riesling, 12% Müller-Thurgau, 11% Silvaner, 7% red varieties, 5% Kerner, 3% Grauburgunder, 3% other varieties
Average yield: 55 hl/ha
Best vintages: 1989, 1992, 1994

This winery is the largest in the Alsenz valley, a small part of the growing region of the Nahe that lies south of the river. Herbert and Andreas Schmidt manage 16 hectares of vineyards and purchase grapes from a few other growers on a contract basis as well in order to supply the demand. What they value most in their vineyards – many of which are steep sites that are very difficult to cultivate – is the high humus content of the soil. The harvest is often late, ending only in November, which assures grapes with the highest possible ripeness. In the cellar the Schmidts believe in reductive winemaking in order to keep the wines fresh and lively. The 1994 range showed a marked increase in quality. Although there were fewer wines at the higher Prädikat levels, the 1995s and 1996s were of roughly the same quality. Given the frost damage last year, the 1997s were a mixed bag: the dry wines were disappointing, the late harvest wines quite successful.

1997 Obermoscheler Silberberg
Riesling Kabinett halbtrocken
10.90 DM, 10.5%, ♀ till 2001 **82**

1996 Obermoscheler Schloßberg
Riesling trocken
8.50 DM, 11%, ♀ till 2000 **84**

1996 Obermoscheler Silberberg
Riesling trocken
8.50 DM, 11%, ♀ now **84**

1996 Obermoscheler Schloßberg
Riesling halbtrocken
8.50 DM, 11%, ♀ now **84**

1996 Obermoscheler Silberberg
Riesling Kabinett halbtrocken
9.50 DM, 9%, ♀ till 2000 **84**

1996 Obermoscheler Silberberg
Riesling Kabinett
9.50 DM, 8%, ♀ till 2001 **86**

1997 Obermoscheler Silberberg
Riesling Spätlese
13.20 DM, 8%, ♀ till 2004 **86**

1997 Obermoscheler Schloßberg
Riesling Auslese
18.80 DM, 9%, ♀ till 2004 **88**

WEINGUT JAKOB SCHNEIDER

Owner: Jakob Schneider
55585 Niederhausen, Winzerstraße 15
Tel. (0 67 58) 9 35 33, Fax 9 35 35
Directions: From Bad Kreuznach via Bad Münster and Norheim to Niederhausen, right to village center
Opening hours: Mon.–Sun. 8 a.m. to 7 p.m.
Worth seeing: Vaulted cellars with wooden casks, and a courtyard with stables

Vineyard area: 10 hectares
Annual production: 50,000 bottles
Top sites: Niederhäuser Hermannshöhle and Rosenheck, Norheimer Dellchen and Kirschheck
Soil types: Volcanic soils, slate
Grape varieties: 90% Riesling, 10% other varieties
Average yield: 58 hl/ha
Best vintages: 1995, 1996, 1997

With two hectares, the estate of Jakob Schneider is the largest proprietor within the Niederhäuser Hermannshöhle, one of the legendary vineyards of the Nahe. Jakobs father, Hans Schneider, never tires of pointing out that the tax authorities assessed this site as the top vineyard in the region. Along with Schneider it was the State Domaine that made the Hermannshöhle famous. By harvesting late in order to attain higher levels of ripeness, the estate does its best to increase quality. The conservatively made Rieslings are then vinified in large casks and portray a classic Nahe style that is seldom encountered these days. In the early 1990s we had the impression that the natural potential of Schneider's vineyards was not fully realized. The 1994 vintage signalled a slight turnaround in quality that was followed by a similar performance in 1995. Although not as persuasive, the 1996s and 1997s were again of comparable quality. Jakob Schneider now plans to install stainless steel tanks to give his Rieslings more vibrant fruit.

1997 Niederhäuser Felsensteyer
Riesling Spätlese halbtrocken
8.50 DM, 11%, ♀ till 2003 **84**

1997 Norheimer Dellchen
Riesling Spätlese
8.80 DM, 9%, ♀ till 2003 **84**

1997 Niederhäuser Klamm
Riesling Spätlese
8.80 DM, 9%, ♀ till 2003 **84**

1996 Niederhäuser Hermannshöhle
Riesling Spätlese trocken
8.80 DM, 11%, ♀ till 2000 **86**

1997 Niederhäuser Hermannshöhle
Riesling Spätlese
9 DM, 9%, ♀ till 2004 **86**

1997 Norheimer Kirschheck
Riesling Spätlese
9 DM, 10%, ♀ till 2004 **86**

1996 Norheimer Kirschheck
Riesling Spätlese
8.70 DM, 9%, ♀ till 2001 **86**

1996 Norheimer Dellchen
Riesling Spätlese
8.80 DM, 9%, ♀ till 2002 **86**

1997 Niederhäuser Hermannshöhle
Riesling
7.30 DM, 9.5%, ♀ till 2003 **86**

Anno 1575
NAHE NAHE
1997er
Niederhäuser Hermannshöhle
Riesling Spätlese trocken
Qualitätswein mit Prädikat
A. P. Nr. 7 750 052 3 98
alc. 11,5% vol. GUTSABFÜLLUNG 750 ml
WEINGUT JAKOB SCHNEIDER
D - 55585 NIEDERHAUSEN - Telefon 0 67 58 / 9 35 33

WEINGUT BÜRGERMEISTER WILLI SCHWEINHARDT NACHF.

Owners: Wilhelm and Axel Schweinhardt
Manager: Wilhelm Schweinhardt
Winemaker: Axel Schweinhardt
55450 Langenlonsheim, Heddesheimer Straße 1
Tel. (0 67 04) 9 31 00, Fax 93 10 50
e-mail: Weingut.Schweinhardt@t-online.de
Directions: A 61 from north: exit Dorsheim, A 61 from south: exit Bad Kreuznach/Langenlonsheim
Opening hours: Mon.–Fri. 9 a.m. to 6 p.m., Sat. 10 a.m. to noon
Sun. by appointment
Worth seeing: Distillery, courtyard from the last century

Vineyard area: 36.5 hectares
Annual production: 300,000 bottles
Top sites: Langenlonsheimer Rothenberg, Löhrer Berg and Königsschild
Soil types: Weathered red sandstone, gravel, and loess
Grape varieties: 35% Riesling, 13% Gau- and Weißburgunder, 17% red wine, 35% other varieties
Average yield: 59 hl/ha
Best vintages: 1990, 1994, 1997

With over 35 hectares of vineyards this estate is one of the largest properties of the Nahe. One striking feature of their holdings is the high average age of the vines, which naturally lowers yields and thus promotes higher quality. In order to produce wines that are fresh and lively, Wilhelm Schweinhardt and his son Axel place great value on working cleanly and swiftly. The quality of the 1996s was comparable to that of the previous vintage, but certainly not as fine as that of the 1994s. The 1997s represent a new dimension in quality for the pair, the finest range that we have tasted from this estate to date!

1997 Langenlonsheimer Rothenberg
Riesling Spätlese
11.50 DM, 9%, 🍷 till 2004 **86**

1997 Langenlonsheimer Löhrer Berg
Grauer Burgunder Spätlese trocken
9.90 DM, 13%, 🍷 till 2002 **88**

1997 Langenlonsheimer Königsschild
Riesling Spätlese trocken
10.60 DM, 11.5%, 🍷 till 2002 **88**

1997 Langenlonsheimer Löhrer Berg
Weißer Burgunder Spätlese trocken
13.50 DM, 13%, 🍷 till 2002 **88**

1997 Langenlonsheimer Rothenberg
Riesling Spätlese halbtrocken
10.40 DM, 11%, 🍷 till 2002 **88**

1996 Langenlonsheimer Rothenberg
Riesling Spätlese halbtrocken
9.80 DM, 10.5%, 🍷 till 2001 **88**

1997 Langenlonsheimer Löhrer Berg
Riesling Auslese
18.50 DM, 9%, 🍷 till 2005 **88**

1997 Langenlonsheimer Bergborn
Chardonnay Auslese trocken
28 DM, 13%, 🍷 till 2005 **90**

1997 Guldentaler Rosenteich
Grauer Burgunder Auslese trocken
17.50 DM, 13.5%, 🍷 till 2002 **91**

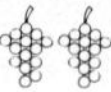

WEINGUT WILHELM SITZIUS

Owners: Sonja and Wilhelm Sitzius
Winemaker: Wilhelm Sitzius
55450 Langenlonsheim, Naheweinstraße 87
Tel. (0 67 04) 13 09, Fax 27 81
Directions: A 61, exit Dorsheim, via Laubenheim to Langenlonsheim
Opening hours: Mon.–Fri. 10 a.m. to 7 p.m., Sat. 10 a.m. to 4 p.m. Sun. by appointment
History: Wine estate now owned by the tenth generation

Vineyard area: 12 hectares
Annual production: 90,000 bottles
Top sites: Niederhäuser Hermannshöhle, Langenlonsheimer Königsschild and Rothenberg
Soil types: Volcanic soil, slate, gravelly loam
Grape varieties: 45% Riesling, 12% Spätburgunder, 10% Kerner, 8% Portugieser, 7.5% each of Grauburgunder and Weißburgunder, 5% each of Müller-Thurgau and Silvaner
Average yield: 59 hl/ha
Best vintages: 1993, 1995, 1997

This estate in Langenlonsheim owns classic sites in the lower as well as the middle stretches of the Nahe. Sitzius cultivates a share of the best vineyards in Langenlonsheim, is well represented in Oberhausen in the Kieselberg and Leistenberg vineyards and even owns a small parcel of the exceptional Niederhäuser Hermannshöhle. In his cellar Wilhelm Sitzius seeks to preserve the individual character of both vineyard and grape variety, hoping to optimize each wine's quality by bottling at exactly the right moment. The 1996 range was of sound quality and, in this respect, comparable to that of the 1995s. However, alongside the better wines there were too many black sheep, a fact that somewhat tarnished our overall impression of this estate. The average quality of the 1997s was much higher.

1997 Guldentaler Rosenteich
Weißer Burgunder Spätlese trocken
10.60 DM, 13%, ♀ till 2002 **84**

1996 Langenlonsheimer Steinchen
Grauer Burgunder Spätlese trocken
12 DM, 11.5%, ♀ now **84**

1996 Langenlonsheimer Lauerweg
Riesling Spätlese trocken
10.70 DM, 11%, ♀ till 2000 **86**

1997 Langenlonsheimer Königsschild
Riesling Spätlese
9.20 DM, 9.5%, ♀ till 2003 **86**

1996 Langenlonsheimer Löhrer Berg
Riesling Spätlese
9.20 DM, 9.5%, ♀ till 2001 **86**

1997 Langenlonsheimer Rothenberg
Riesling Spätlese trocken
9.40 DM, 12.5%, ♀ till 2004 **89**

1997 Langenlonsheimer Lauerweg
Riesling Auslese
21.50 DM, 8%, ♀ till 2007 **91**

——— Red wine ———

1996 Langenlonsheimer St. Antoniusweg
Spätburgunder Auslese trocken
34 DM, 14.5%, ♀ till 2005 **89**

WEINGUT TESCH

Owner: Hartmut Tesch
Manager: Hartmut Tesch and Dr. Martin Tesch
55450 Langenlonsheim, Naheweinstraße 99
Tel. (0 67 04) 9 30 40, Fax 93 04 15
Directions: A 61, exit Dorsheim, in the direction of Langenlonsheim
Opening hours: Mon.–Fri. 9 a.m. to 6 p.m. or by appointment
History: Owned by the family since 1723

Vineyard area: 19.4 hectares
Annual production: 150,000 bottles
Top sites: Laubenheimer Karthäuser, Krone and St. Remigiusberg, Langenlonsheimer Königsschild and Löhrer Berg
Soil types: Red cliffs, loam with gravel, loamy clay, weathered sandstone
Grape varieties: 75% Riesling, 8% each of Weißburgunder and Spätburgunder, 6% Silvaner, 3% other varieties
Average yield: 73 hl/ha
Best vintages: 1993, 1996, 1997
Member: VDP

Hartmut Tesch is the tenth generation of his family to run this estate, which now owns 19 hectares of vineyard in and around Langenlonsheim. His son Martin, who studied microbiology, will one day take over the management of the estate from his father. During vinification Tesch insists on utmost cleanliness. The majority of the wines are made in a reductive fashion in stainless steel tanks and some carbon dioxide always remains in the wines at bottling to insure that they stay fresh and lively. What is unusual at this estate is that almost all of them go through malolactic fermentation, which gives them an unusual style with stable acidities. The red grapes are always vinified as rosé wines. After a run of rather ordinary vintages, we were delighted to taste the fine 1996s. The 1997s are even finer. This estate appears to be on the rise.

1997 Grauer Burgunder
Spätlese trocken
15 DM, 12.5%, ♀ till 2003 **88**

1997 Riesling
halbtrocken
9 DM, 10.5%, ♀ till 2003 **88**

1997 Laubenheimer St. Remigiusberg
Riesling Spätlese trocken
16.80 DM, 12.5%, ♀ till 2004 **89**

1997 Langenlonsheimer Königsschild
Riesling Auslese trocken Goldkapsel
21.50 DM, 12.5%, ♀ till 2004 **89**

1997 Langenlonsheimer Königsschild
Riesling Spätlese halbtrocken
14.50 DM, 11%, ♀ till 2005 **89**

1997 Laubenheimer Karthäuser
Riesling Spätlese
14.80 DM, 9.5%, ♀ till 2006 **91**

1997 Langenlonsheimer Königsschild
Riesling Auslese
28 DM, 8%, ♀ till 2008 **91**

1996 Laubenheimer Karthäuser
Riesling Auslese
31 DM, 8%, ♀ till 2006 **91**

1997 Laubenheimer Karthäuser
Riesling Beerenauslese
80 DM/0.375 liter, 8.5%, ♀ till 2006 **91**

1997 Langenlonsheimer Löhrer Berg
Riesling Eiswein
90 DM/0.375 liter, 9.5%, ♀ till 2010 **94**

WEINGUT KARL VON DER WEIDEN

Owner: Karl-Heinz von der Weiden
Winemaker: Karl-Heinz von der Weiden
55450 Langenlonsheim, Naheweinstraße 66
Tel. (0 67 04) 15 27, Fax 3 58 43
e-mail: vdw.lalo@net-art.de
Directions: A 61, exit Dorsheim, via Laubenheim to Langenlonsheim
Opening hours: Mon.–Fri. 9 a.m. to 8 p.m., Sat. and Sun. by appointment
Restaurant: Open Sept. to Nov., Fri.–Sun. from 5 p.m. to midnight
Specialties: Homemade sausage and meat
History: Von der Weiden family first mentioned in 1652

Vineyard area: 5.8 hectares
Annual production: 43,000 bottles
Top sites: Langenlonsheimer Königsschild and Rothenberg
Soil types: Quartz and heavy chalky loam
Grape varieties: 35% Riesling, 15% each of Silvaner and Weißburgunder, 9% each of Kerner and Scheurebe, 5% Müller-Thurgau, 12% other varieties
Average yield: 51.5 hl/ha
Best vintages: 1991, 1994, 1995

Until 1973 Karl von der Weiden sold his production wholesale in cask. Since then he has gradually begun to bottle his own wines; and under the influence of his son Karl-Heinz the proportion of dry wines has risen to almost half. In recent years the estate has faired well principally because of its Weißburgunder and Grauburgunder. Since 1996 the estate has marketed most of its wines – in particular the Rieslings – with individual vineyard designations; the name of the "Großlage" Sonnenborn is now used only sparingly. The Riesling Spätlese and Auslese from the top Langenlonsheim vineyards of Königsschild and Rothenberg have been the most successful wines from the last two vintages. The dry wines have been little more than acceptable.

1997 Langenlonsheimer Bergborn
Weißer Burgunder Spätlese trocken
11.50 DM, 12%, 🍷 till 2000 **80**

1996 Langenlonsheimer Bergborn
Silvaner Spätlese halbtrocken
8.75 DM, 10%, 🍷 now **80**

1997 Langenlonsheimer Bergborn
Silvaner Spätlese halbtrocken
8.75 DM, 10.5%, 🍷 till 2000 **82**

1997 Langenlonsheimer Lauerweg
Riesling Kabinett
8.50 DM, 9.5%, 🍷 till 2002 **82**

1996 Langenlonsheimer Rothenberg
Riesling Spätlese
9.75 DM, 8%, 🍷 till 2002 **82**

1997 Langenlonsheimer Rothenberg
Riesling Auslese
19 DM, 8.5%, 🍷 till 2002 **82**

1997 Langenlonsheimer Königsschild
Riesling Spätlese halbtrocken
10 DM, 11%, 🍷 till 2002 **84**

1996 Langenlonsheimer Königsschild
Riesling Spätlese
9.50 DM, 8.5%, 🍷 till 2004 **84**

1997 Lagenlonsheimer Königsschild
Riesling Auslese
19 DM, 8%, 🍷 till 2004 **88**

Rising from the ashes

The Palatinate, or "Pfalz" in German, stretches from the edge of the Rheinhessen near Worms in the north to the French border in the south. The small band of vineyards covers almost 24,000 hectares, strung out along some 80 kilometers between the Rhine valley floor and the Pfalz forest, a narrow strip only 7 kilometers in width. Much of that would perhaps better be used for potatoes; but in a region where almonds and figs ripen annually, grapes too enjoy favorable growing conditions, as the Romans knew some 2000 years ago.

Most of the vines lie sheltered from the wind on the eastern slopes of the Haardt mountains, where sufficient rainfall ensures a mild climate. The soils show great diversity – ranging from loess and weathered red sandstone to fossil limestone, heavy chalky loam, granite, rocky porphyry, slate and clay – and this is reflected in the character of the wines. Whereas the Rieslings from the northern Pfalz are aromatic, well-structured and lively, the Burgundian varieties from the Südliche Weinstraße, or Southern Wine Route, are more reminiscent of the lush full-bodied wines of Alsace.

In the Mittelhaardt, Riesling calls the tune; and with 21 percent of all vineyards in the Pfalz, it has now relegated Müller-Thurgau to second place in the charts. In the southern Pfalz, Grauburgunder, Weißburgunder and increasingly Chardonnay are the favored varieties. Among the reds, Portugieser is the leading grape by volume; but, like the popular Dornfelder, is rarely the source of ambitious wines. The high-quality Spätburgunder variety represents a mere two percent of the total vineyard area, but generally produces the finest reds of the region; some growers are also experimenting with Cabernet Sauvignon.

Frost, hail and drought made 1997 a difficult vintage for the average estate in the Palatinate, but the top estates were nonetheless able to turn out excellent wines. Harvesting ripe grapes was not a problem, as much of the crop was brought in at Kabinett levels, but the Spätlese and Auslese often posess neither the necessary depth of fruit nor the acidic structure to support their weight. It was, however, an exciting vintage for Muskateller and Gewürztraminer.

The 1996 vintage, on the other hand, has turned out rather better in the Pfalz than many had thought possible last September, but it was important to delay the harvest until the grapes were physiologically ripe. Quality-conscious producers thus began picking Riesling only in mid-October; some waited until early November. The Bürklin-Wolf estate even harvested one of its most inspiring dry Spätlese on December, 8!

With average yields of 94 hectoliters per hectare in 1996, the Pfalz once again had the largest crop in Germany. The share crushed as simple "Qualitätswein" was substantial, much as was the case in 1991 or 1987. However, the large proportion of Spätlese and Auslese is more reminiscent of 1992 or 1989. Hansjörg Rebholz even sees "parallels with the great 1990 vintage." However, the vintage was not as straightforward as many claimed. The village of Forst, for example, had an easier time of it than did that of Deidesheim, where, as Frank John of the von Buhl estate reported, it was necessary to send pickers through the vineyards ten times in order to obtain a decent Kabinett. Steffen Christmann in Gimmeldingen also regards 1996 as "a very good but not great year." That is, however, too modest, for it would be hard to produce finer dry Rieslings than those bottled by the best estates in 1996.

The Rieslings from the Mittelhaardt north of Neustadt have always been the gems of the region. The names of villages such as Forst, Deidesheim, Ruppertsberg, Wachenheim, Ungstein and Kallstadt have always set wine lovers' pulses racing. Not long ago the names of the leading estates of Bürklin-Wolf, von Buhl and Bassermann-Jordan had a similar effect.

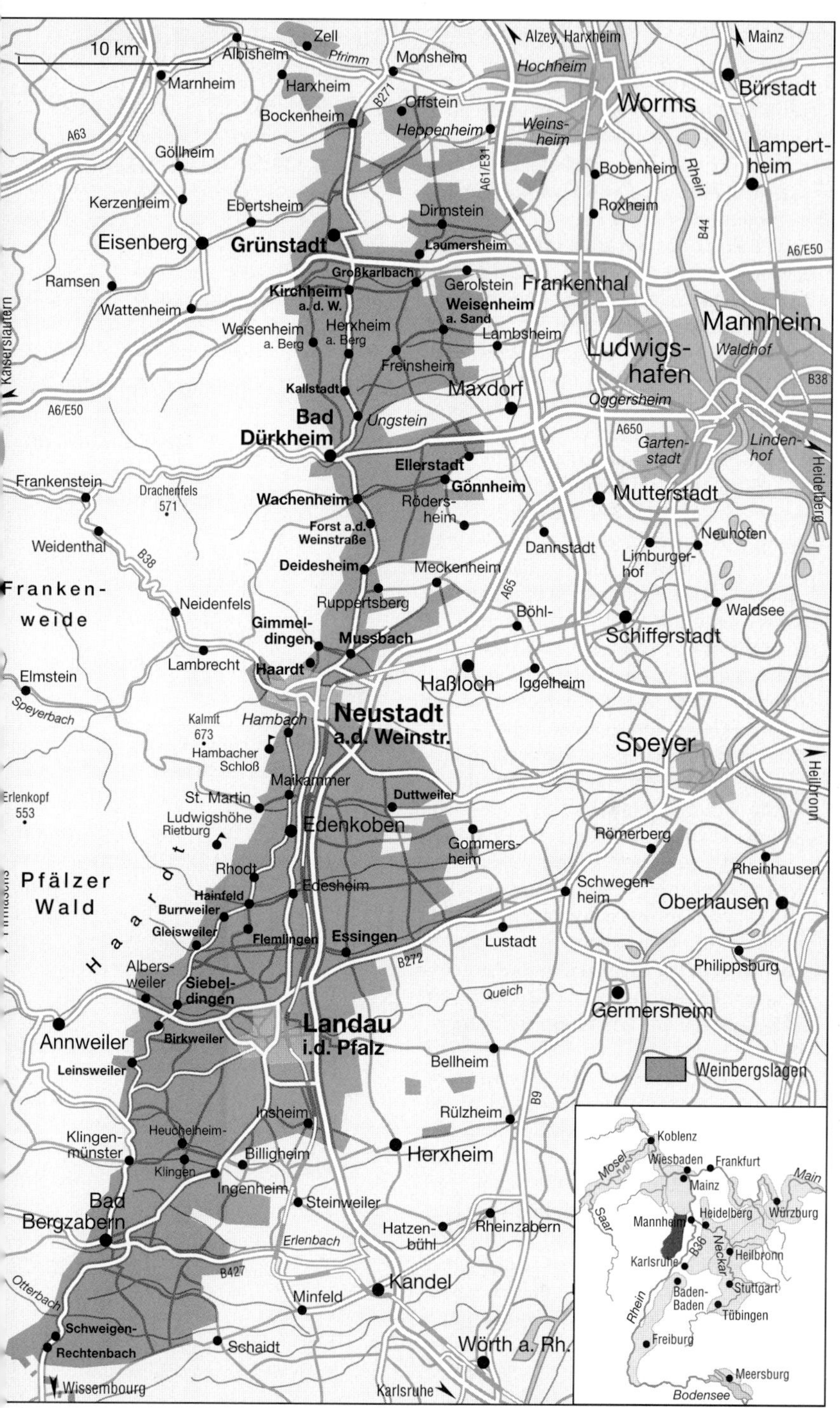
10 km
Alzey, Harxheim
Mainz
Worms
Bürstadt
Lampertheim
Mannheim
Ludwigshafen
Frankenthal
Grünstadt
Eisenberg
Bad Dürkheim
Neustadt a.d. Weinstr.
Speyer
Landau i.d. Pfalz
Germersheim
Herxheim
Kandel
Wörth a. Rh.
Bad Bergzabern
Annweiler
Pfälzer Wald
Frankenweide
Haardt
Weinbergslagen
Koblenz
Wiesbaden
Frankfurt
Mainz
Mannheim
Heidelberg
Würzburg
Karlsruhe
Heilbronn
Stuttgart
Baden-Baden
Tübingen
Freiburg
Meersburg
Bodensee
Rhein
Neckar
Mosel
Saar
Main

After a brief eclipse, these three estates are again beginning to shine and have inaugurated a renaissance in the region. Bürklin-Wolf in Wachenheim presented such a breathtaking range of wines in both 1996 and 1997 that it now belongs, alongside Müller-Catoir, to the very first rank of producers from the Pfalz.

The Reichsrat von Buhl estate, with its late harvest Rieslings, has moved closer to the frontrunners; and the estate of Bassermann-Jordan, now under the direction of Ulrich Mell, is again showing real class. Georg Mosbacher in Forst, and increasingly Christmann in Gimmeldingen, have also worked their way up to the top ranks within the region. The highly individualistic wines of the Koehler-Ruprecht estate in Kallstadt, although difficult to comprehend in their youth, also belong to this group. Further, after replanting his vineyard, Karl Fuhrmann in Pfeffingen is slowly returning to his previous form.

In recent years there have also been distinct changes in the southern Pfalz. The Rebholz estate in Siebeldingen has long been not only the guiding light of this subregion but also one of the best producers in the whole of the Pfalz; but Karl-Heinz Wehrheim in Birkweiler has been gaining overall in stature, in 1996 and 1997. The wines of Messmer in Burrweiler and Becker in Schweigen, on the other hand, have been less consistent than in the past, so that today these two properties are hardly better than their ambitious colleagues Siegrist in Leinsweiler, Bernhart in Schweigen and Münzberg in Godramstein.

Equally exciting are the myriad new talents, often from marginal areas of the region, springing up each year among the over 1,700 producers in the Pfalz. But Knipser in Laumersheim, the regions finest red wine estate, and Bergdolt in Duttweiler have long ceased to be insiders' tips; and in 1996 the surprises came rather from the more renowned villages, where we found the established estates of Kurt Darting in Bad Dürkheim, Müller in Forst and Weegmüller in Haardt doing extremely well.

The leading estates of the Pfalz

Weingut Müller-Catoir, Haardt

Weingut Dr. Bürklin-Wolf, Wachenheim

Weingut Christmann, Gimmeldingen

Weingut Koehler-Ruprecht, Kallstadt

Weingut Georg Mosbacher, Forst

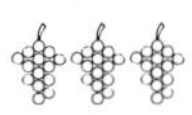

Weingut Geheimer Rat Dr. von Bassermann-Jordan, Deidesheim

Weingut Friedrich Becker, Schweigen-Rechtenbach

Rating scale for the estates

Highest rating: These producers belong to the world's finest.

Excellent estates: These producers are among Germany's best.

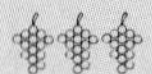

Very good producers, known for their consistently high quality.

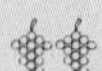

Good estates, offering better than average quality.

Reliable producers that offer well-made standard quality.

Weingut Bergdolt, Duttweiler

Weingut Josef Biffar, Deidesheim

Weingut Reichsrat von Buhl, Deidesheim

Weingut Kurt Darting, Bad Dürkheim

Weingut Dr. Deinhard, Deidesheim

Weingut Knipser, Laumersheim

Weingut Lucashof – Pfarrweingut, Forst

Weingut Herbert Meßmer, Burrweiler

Weingut Münzberg, Landau-Godramstein

Weingut Pfeffingen – Fuhrmann-Eymael, Bad Dürkheim

Weingut Ökonomierat Rebholz, Siebeldingen

Weingut Karl Schaefer, Bad Dürkheim

Weingut Dr. Wehrheim, Birkweiler

Weingut Weegmüller, Neustadt-Haardt

Weingüter Geheimrat J. Wegeler Erben – Gutshaus Deidesheim, Deidesheim

Weingut Weik, Neustadt-Mußbach

Weingut Werlé Erben, Forst

Weingut Wilhelmshof, Siebeldingen

Weingut J. L. Wolf, Wachenheim

Weingut Bernhart, Schweigen

Weingut Eymann, Gönnheim

Weingut Fitz-Ritter, Bad Dürkheim

Weingut Eugen Müller, Forst

Weingut Herbert Müller Erben, Neustadt-Haardt

Weinhof Scheu, Schweigen-Rechtenbach

Weingut Siegrist, Leinsweiler

Weingut Peter Argus, Gleisweiler

Weingut Winfried Frey & Söhne, Essingen

Weingut Karl-Heinz Gaul, Grünstadt-Sausenheim

Weingut Bernd Grimm, Schweigen

Weingut Georg Henninger IV., Kallstadt

Weingut Jülg, Schweigen-Rechtenbach

Weingut Julius Ferdinand Kimich, Deidesheim

Weingut Gerhard Klein, Hainfeld

Weingut Johannes Kleinmann, Birkweiler

Weingut Leiningerhof, Kirchheim

Weingut Theo Minges, Flemlingen

Weingut Neckerauer, Weisenheim am Sand

Weingut Georg Siben Erben, Deidesheim

Other notable producers

Weingut Acham-Magin
67147 Forst, Weinstraße 67
Tel. (0 63 26) 3 15, Fax 62 32

Weingut Gerhard Beck
76889 Schweigen, Pauliner Straße 5
Tel. (0 63 42) 5 35, Fax 74 48

Forster Winzerverein
67147 Forst, Weinstraße 57
Tel. (0 63 26) 3 06, Fax 13 91

Weingut Wolfgang Geißler
67435 Duttweiler, Burggarten 7
Tel. (0 63 27) 27 70, Fax 15 46

Weingut Herbert Giessen Erben
67142 Deidesheim, Weinstraße 3
Tel. (0 63 26) 3 91, Fax 3 91

Weingut Ernst Karst
67098 Bad Dürkheim,
In den Almen 15
Tel. (0 63 22) 28 62, Fax 6 59 65

Weingut Philipp Kuhn
67229 Laumersheim,
Großkarlbacher Straße 20
Tel. (0 62 38) 6 56, Fax 46 02

Weingut Lergenmüller
☞ *See below, page 323*

Weingut Lingenfelder
☞ *See below, page 324*

Weingut Heinrich Meyer
76889 Klingenmünster, Im Stift 10
Tel. (0 63 49) 74 46, Fax 57 52

Weingut Motzenbäcker
67152 Ruppertsberg, Weinstraße 1
Tel. (0 63 26) 77 33, Fax 41 79

Weingut Mugler
67435 Neustadt, Peter-Koch-Straße 50
Tel. (0 63 21) 6 60 62, Fax 6 86 09

Weingut Petri
67273 Herxheim am Berg, Weinstraße 43
Tel. (0 63 53) 23 45, Fax 41 81

Weingut Egon Schmitt
67098 Bad Dürkheim, Am Neuberg 6
Tel. (0 63 22) 58 30, Fax 6 88 99

Weingut Schumacher
67273 Herxheim am Berg, Hauptstraße 40
Tel. (0 63 53) 9 35 90, Fax 93 59 22

Weingut Peter Stolleis – Carl-Theodor-Hof
67435 Gimmeldingen, Kurpfalzstraße 99
Tel. (0 63 21) 6 60 71, Fax 6 03 48

Weingut Tiemann
67146 Deidesheim, Marktplatz 1
Tel. (0 63 26) 77 04, Fax 63 43

Winzergenossenschaft Vier Jahreszeiten
67098 Bad Dürkheim, Limburgstraße 8
Tel. (0 63 22) 6 80 11, Fax 82 40

Weingut Heinrich Vollmer
☞ *See below, page 340*

Weingut Jürgen Wilker
76889 Oberhofen, Hauptstraße 30
Tel. (0 63 43) 22 02, Fax 43 79

Vintage chart for the Pfalz

vintage	quality	drink
1997	⚘⚘⚘⚘	till 2002
1996	⚘⚘⚘⚘⚘	till 2003
1995	⚘⚘⚘	now
1994	⚘⚘⚘⚘	now
1993	⚘⚘⚘⚘	now
1992	⚘⚘⚘⚘	now
1991	⚘⚘⚘	now
1990	⚘⚘⚘⚘⚘	till 2000
1989	⚘⚘⚘	now
1988	⚘⚘⚘⚘	now

⚘⚘⚘⚘⚘ : Outstanding
⚘⚘⚘⚘ : Excellent
⚘⚘⚘ : Good
⚘⚘ : Average
⚘ : Poor

WEINGUT PETER ARGUS

Owner: Peter Argus
76835 Gleisweiler, Hauptstraße 23
Tel. (0 63 45) 91 94 24, Fax 91 94 25
e-mail: Argus.Weingut@t-online.de
Directions: A 65, exit Edenkoben, follow the wine route south to Gleisweiler
Sales: Peter and Eva Argus
Opening hours: Mon.–Fri. by appointment, Sat. 2 p.m. to 5 p.m.
Sun. 10 a.m. to noon
Worth seeing: Vaulted cellars from 1610

Vineyard area: 7 hectares
Annual production: 60,000 bottles
Top site: Gleisweiler Hölle
Soil types: Loamy sand and limestone
Grape varieties: 41% Riesling, 11% Grauburgunder, 9% each of Kerner and Müller-Thurgau, 7% Weißburgunder, 6% each of Spätburgunder and Portugieser, 11% other varieties
Average yield: 85 hl/ha
Best vintages: 1993, 1994, 1997

Although the Argus family of Gleisweiler raised crops and cattle, they now concentrate their efforts on farming grapes and making wine near the southern border of the Pfalz. Peter Argus, who took over the estate in 1994, has been involved in the business for years. Working in the shadow of the better-known estates of the Mittelhaardt, this winery regularly produces well-made wines at extremely reasonable prices. After the appealing 1993 range and the surprisingly good 1994s, the 1995s suffered from bad weather throughout the growing season. Unfortunately the 1996s were also of mediocre quality, lacking expression across the board. The 1997s speak with a better accent. Further investments in the cellar are now planned, which should improve the quality for the years to come.

1996 Gleisweiler Hölle
Weißer Burgunder Spätlese trocken
9.50 DM, 12%, ♀ now **80**

1996 Frankweiler Kalkgrube
Grauer Burgunder Spätlese trocken
9 DM, 13%, ♀ now **80**

1997 Gleisweiler Hölle
Riesling Spätlese trocken
9 DM, 12%, ♀ till 2000 **82**

1997 Böchinger Rosenkranz
Weißer Burgunder Spätlese trocken
9 DM, 13%, ♀ now **82**

1997 Frankweiler Kalkgrube
Grauer Burgunder Spätlese trocken
9 DM, 13%, ♀ till 2000 **84**

1997 Frankweiler Kalkgrube
Grauer Burgunder Spätlese trocken
17 DM, 13.5%, ♀ till 2000 **86**

——— Red wines ———

1997 Spätburgunder
trocken
6.50 DM, 12.5%, ♀ now **80**

1996 Frankweiler Kalkgrube
Spätburgunder Spätlese trocken
17 DM, 12%, ♀ till 2000 **84**

WEINGUT GEHEIMER RAT DR. VON BASSERMANN-JORDAN

Owners: Margrit and Gabriele von Bassermann-Jordan
General Manager: Gunther Hauck
Winemaker: Ulrich Mell
67142 Deidesheim, Kirchgasse 10
Tel. (0 63 26) 60 06, Fax 60 08
Directions: On the wine route between Neustadt and Bad Dürkheim
Sales: Astrid Müllers
Opening hours: Mon.–Fri. 8 a.m. to noon and 1 p.m. to 6 p.m., Sat. 10 a.m. to 3 p.m.
History: Owned by the family since 1718
Worth seeing: Ancient vaulted cellars

Vineyard area: 42 hectares
Annual production: 350,000 bottles
Top sites: Deidesheimer Grainhübel and Hohenmorgen, Forster Kirchenstück and Ungeheuer
Soil types: Weathered red sandstone with porphyry, loess, sandy loam and weathered stony basalt
Grape varieties: 100% Riesling
Average yield: 60 hl/ha
Best vintages: 1996, 1997
Member: VDP

Dr. Ludwig von Bassermann-Jordan, the son of the famous wine historian, established the reputation of this estate abroad; and for decades it was one of the most reliable sources of fine wine in the Pfalz. The property itself, with its stylish cellars and furnishings, was always first class; yet for years the estate's star has not shone as brightly as it once did. Nonetheless, since 1994 the estate has been making a slow comeback. The responsibility now rests on the shoulders of the new cellar-master Ulrich Mell to complete the turn-around. As he officially took over the technical direction of the estate only in early 1997, he was not wholly responsible for the 1996s, yet the fruity wines of that vintage were already very promising. As the 1997s were the first wines to bear his full signature, he pulled all the stops. This is the most promising vintage that we have tasted from this estate in years!

1996 Forster Jesuitengarten
Riesling Kabinett
12 DM, 11%, ♀ till 2002 **86**

1997 Forster Freundstück
Riesling Spätlese trocken
19.50 DM, 12.5%, ♀ till 2002 **88**

1996 Forster Kirchenstück
Riesling Spätlese
22 DM, 9.5%, ♀ till 2003 **88**

1996 Forster Jesuitengarten
Riesling Auslese
25 DM, 10.5%, ♀ till 2003 **88**

1997 Forster Jesuitengarten
Riesling Spätlese trocken
21 DM, 12.5%, ♀ till 2002 **89**

1997 Forster Kirchenstück
Riesling Spätlese
23 DM, 11%, ♀ till 2003 **89**

1997 Ruppertsberger Reiterpfad
Riesling Auslese
35 DM, 11%, ♀ till 2004 **89**

1996 Forster Jesuitengarten
Riesling Spätlese
21 DM, 8.5%, ♀ till 2005 **92**

1996 Forster Ungeheuer
Riesling Eiswein
100 DM/0.375 liter, 9%, ♀ till 2010 **94**

1997 Ruppertsberger Reiterpfad
Riesling Trockenbeerenauslese
155 DM/0.375 liter, 8.5%, ♀ till 2015 **96**

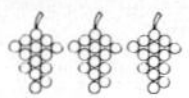

WEINGUT FRIEDRICH BECKER

Owner: Friedrich Becker
General Manager: Rolf Charlier
Winemaker: Stefan Dorst
76889 Schweigen-Rechtenbach, Hauptstraße 29
Tel. (0 63 42) 2 90, Fax 61 48
Directions: A 65, exit Landau-Süd, in the direction of Weißenburg in Alsace
Sales: Heidrun Becker
Opening hours: Mon.–Fri. by appointment, Sat. 9 a.m. to noon and 2 p.m. to 5 p.m.
Worth seeing: The estate's distillery

Vineyard area: 13.4 hectares
Annual production: 90,000 bottles
Top site: Schweigener Sonnenberg
Soil types: Loess, clay, heavy chalky loam
Grape varieties: 60% Burgundian varieties, 22% Riesling, 18% other varieties, including Silvaner, Gewürztraminer, Kerner and Müller-Thurgau
Average yield: 87 hl/ha
Best vintages: 1993, 1994, 1997

In just twenty years Friedrich Becker has erected his house and home, acquired a loyal private clientele and gained the recognition of wine writers and wine lovers for his barrel-matured red wines. Today, the fact that his best vineyards lie on the other side of the border in Alsace is no more than a curiosity. As a matter of principle Becker vinifies all of his wines in the style he most enjoys himself, namely dry. In 1995 this uncompromising winemaker presented a very nice range of wines; the 1996 whites, on the other hand, were of a different ilk. Many were light and, moreover, tweaked by acidity; nor was the 1995 Spätburgunder, for which he is known, a star. The 1997 whites look much better. Not only are the white wines more palatable, the 1996 Spätburgunder Reserve is the finest red wine that this estate has ever made.

1997 Schweigener Sonnenberg
Grauer Burgunder Kabinett trocken
8.80 DM, 11.5%, ♀ now **82**

1997 Schweigener Sonnenberg
Grauer Burgunder Spätlese
14.50 DM, 12.5%, ♀ now **82**

1997 Schweigener Sonnenberg
Weißer Burgunder Kabinett trocken
9 DM, 11%, ♀ now **84**

1997 Schweigener Sonnenberg
Silvaner Spätlese trocken
15.80 DM, 12.5%, ♀ now **84**

1997 Schweigener Sonnenberg
Riesling Spätlese trocken
17 DM, 12%, ♀ till 2000 **84**

1996 Schweigener Sonnenberg
Riesling Spätlese
16.50 DM, 11%, ♀ till 2002 **84**

1997 Schweigener Sonnenberg
Gewürztraminer Spätlese
15.80 DM, 12.5%, ♀ till 2001 **86**

— Red wines —

1996 Spätburgunder
Tafelwein trocken
38 DM, 13.5%, ♀ till 2001 **86**

1996 Spätburgunder
Tafelwein trocken "Reserve"
65 DM, 14.5%, ♀ till 2003 **91**

WEINGUT BERGDOLT

Owners: Rainer and Günther Bergdolt
Winemaker: Rainer Bergdolt
67435 Duttweiler,
Klostergut Sankt Lamprecht
Tel. (0 63 27) 50 27, Fax 17 84
Directions: A 65, exit Neustadt-Süd
Opening hours: Mon.–Fri. 8 a.m. to noon and 1 p.m. to 6 p.m.
Sat. 9 a.m. to 5 p.m.
History: Former estate of the St. Lamprecht monastery

Vineyard area: 19 hectares
Annual production: 145,000 bottles
Top sites: Kirrweiler Mandelberg, Duttweiler Kalkberg
Soil types: Loess and sandy loam
Grape varieties: 35% Weißburgunder, 32% Riesling, 8% each of Chardonnay and Spätburgunder, 6% each of Silvaner and Kerner, 5% Dornfelder
Average yield: 69 hl/ha
Best vintages: 1995, 1996, 1997
Member: VDP, Deutsches Barrique Forum

Rainer and Günther Bergdolt are the eighth generation of their family to run the former ecclesiastical estate of Saint Lamprecht. For years they have drawn attention to themselves with wines matured in small oak barrels. Grown on the very deep soils of Kirrweil, such Weißburgunders often resemble a Meursault; and these wines remain the estate's showpieces. Compared to such quality, the Rieslings are often poor cousins. After the two outstanding vintages of 1992 and 1993, the 1994s were less attractive. In both 1995 and 1996 the Burgundian varieties shone, confirming again our assumption that this estate belongs to the top producers in the Pfalz. The 1997s are, across the board, even more reliable, yet without the individual highlights of the previous two vintages.

1996 Kirrweiler Mandelberg
Weißer Burgunder Kabinett trocken
10.50 DM, 12%, ♀ now **84**

1996 Duttweiler Kreuzberg
Riesling Spätlese trocken
13.50 DM, 11.5%, ♀ till 2000 **84**

1996 Kirrweiler Mandelberg
Weißer Burgunder Spätlese trocken – 7 –
15 DM, 13%, ♀ now **86**

1997 Kirrweiler Mandelberg
Weißer Burgunder Spätlese trocken – 10 –
16 DM, 13.5%, ♀ till 2000 **86**

1997 Weißer Burgunder
Spätlese trocken
20.50 DM, 13.5%, ♀ till 2002 **88**

1997 Chardonnay
Spätlese trocken
20.50 DM, 13%, ♀ till 2001 **88**

1996 Weißer Burgunder
Spätlese trocken – 29 –
20.50 DM, 13%, ♀ till 2002 **88**

1997 Kirrweiler Mandelberg
Weißer Burgunder Spätlese trocken – 14 –
19.50 DM, 13%, ♀ till 2002 **88**

1996 Chardonnay
Spätlese trocken
19.50 DM, 13%, ♀ till 2000 **90**

——— Red wine ———

1996 Duttweiler Kalkberg
Spätburgunder Spätlese trocken
32 DM, 13%, ♀ till 2002 **88**

WEINGUT BERNHART

Owner: Willi Bernhart
Winemaker: Gerd Bernhart
76889 Schweigen, Hauptstraße 8
Tel. (0 63 42) 72 02, Fax 63 96
Directions: A 65, exit Landau-Süd, in the direction of Weißenburg
Sales: Wilma Bernhart
Opening hours: Fri. and Sat. 9 a.m. to 6 p.m. or by appointment

> Vineyard area: 12.5 hectares
> Annual production: 65,000 bottles
> Top site: Schweigener Sonnenberg
> Soil types: Loess, loam, sand, clay and chalk
> Grape varieties: 17% Spätburgunder, 15% each of Riesling and Weißburgunder, 10% each of Grauburgunder and Portugieser, 8% Gewürztraminer, 5% each of Müller-Thurgau, Chardonnay and Silvaner, 10% other varieties
> Average yield: 66 hl/ha
> Best vintages: 1994, 1996, 1997

This estate was founded in 1900 with the purchase of vineyards in Weißenburg, which lies just across the German border in Alsace. Until 1960 these sites were cultivated as a hobby and the grapes were sold to the local cooperative. In those days the Bernharts produced one cask from the best grapes of each vintage for their own requirements. In 1972 Willi Bernhart bottled all of his wine for the first time. Today he, his wife, Wilma, and son Gerd run an estate of some 12 hectares in Schweigen and Weißenburg. The white wines, which are vinified in a reductive and fruity style, have always been appealing; but the estate, as before, continues to receive the most critical acclaim for its barrel-aged Spätburgunder. 1996 was no exception. Nonetheless, 1997 was an extremely good white vintage for the family. Seldom have we tasted such a well-made collection of wines from this estate!

1997 Schweigener Sonnenberg
Weißer Burgunder Kabinett trocken
8.20 DM, 12.5%, 🍷 till 2000 — **84**

1996 Schweigener Sonnenberg
Riesling Kabinett trocken
8 DM, 11%, 🍷 till 2000 — **84**

1997 Schweigener Sonnenberg
Grauer Burgunder Spätlese trocken
12.50 DM, 13%, 🍷 till 2000 — **84**

1996 Schweigener Sonnenberg
Gewürztraminer Spätlese trocken
12 DM, 13%, 🍷 now — **84**

1996 Schweigener Sonnenberg
Chardonnay Spätlese trocken
24 DM, 13%, 🍷 now — **86**

1997 Schweigener Sonnenberg
Weißer Burgunder Spätlese trocken
12.50 DM, 12.5%, 🍷 till 2001 — **88**

——— Red wines ———

1995 Schweigener Sonnenberg
Spätburgunder trocken
23 DM, 13%, 🍷 now — **84**

1996 Schweigener Sonnenberg
Spätburgunder Auslese trocken
"Selektion"
35 DM, 14%, 🍷 till 2003 — **89**

WEINGUT JOSEF BIFFAR

Owner: Gerhard Biffar
Manager: Dirk Roth
67146 Deidesheim,
Niederkirchener Straße 13
Tel. (0 63 26) 50 28, Fax 76 97
Directions: A 650 towards Bad Dürkheim, then follow signs to Deidesheim
Sales: Lilli Biffar-Hirschbil
Opening hours: Mon.–Fri. 10 a.m. to noon and 1 p.m. to 5 p.m., Sat. 10 a.m. to 12:30 p.m. and 1:30 p.m. to 4 p.m. By appointment
History: The family came here from Lyon in 1723
Worth seeing: Beautiful courtyard, which is a historic monument, and the deep vaulted cellars

Vineyard area: 12.5 hectares
Annual production: 85,000 bottles
Top sites: Deidesheimer Grainhübel, Kalkofen and Kieselberg, Ruppertsberger Reiterpfad, Wachenheimer Goldbächel and Gerümpel
Soil types: Weathered red sandstone with loess, clay and basalt or limestone
Grape varieties: 80% Riesling, 15% Weißburgunder, 2% Spätburgunder, 3% Dornfelder and Sauvignon Blanc
Average yield: 60 hl/ha
Best vintages: 1993, 1994, 1996
Member: VDP

In the autumn of 1996 Dirk Roth took over from Ulrich Mell as cellarmaster at this estate. As a newcomer he will need time to become acquainted with the individual style of the estate and to chart his own course. Though 1996 could scarcely compare with some of the outstanding vintages of the early 1990s, the range was respectable. Still, many of the wines seemed simple, perhaps even rustic in character, and often a touch acidic. The 1997s are even more disappointing. The wines are all pleasant, but far from the head of the class. Further, this year's bottlings often retain excessive amounts of carbon dioxide. Once a jewel of the Pfalz, this estate must now work hard to stay apace of developments in the region.

1997 Deidesheimer Kieselberg
Riesling Spätlese trocken
20.90 DM, 13%, 🍷 till 2000 **84**

1997 Wachenheimer Gerümpel
Riesling Kabinett trocken
14.50 DM, 12%, 🍷 till 2000 **86**

1996 Deidesheimer Grainhübel
Riesling Spätlese trocken
23 DM, 12.5%, 🍷 till 2000 **86**

1996 Wachenheimer Goldbächel
Riesling Spätlese
20.75 DM, 10.5%, 🍷 till 2002 **86**

1997 Wachenheimer Gerümpel
Riesling Spätlese halbtrocken
28.90 DM, 12%, 🍷 till 2002 **88**

1997 Deidesheimer Herrgottsacker
Riesling Spätlese
19.95 DM, 11.5%, 🍷 till 2003 **88**

1997 Deidesheimer Kieselberg
Riesling Auslese
26.70 DM, 11.5%, 🍷 till 2004 **88**

1996 Deidesheimer Kieselberg
Riesling Auslese
26.50 DM, 10%, 🍷 till 2005 **88**

1997 Wachenheimer Altenburg
Riesling Spätlese
23.20 DM, 11.5%, 🍷 till 2003 **89**

1996 Deidesheimer Mäushöhle
Riesling Eiswein
92 DM, 10.5%, 🍷 till 2010 **92**

WEINGUT JOSEF BIFFAR

1996
DEIDESHEIMER HERRGOTTSACKER
RIESLING KABINETT HALBTROCKEN
GUTSABFÜLLUNG JOSEF BIFFAR D-67146 DEIDESHEIM a. d. WEINSTRASSE
QUALITÄTSWEIN MIT PRÄDIKAT · A.P.Nr. 5 106 026 018 97 · PRODUCE OF GERMANY
alc. 11% vol PFALZ 750 ml e

WEINGUT DR. BÜRKLIN-WOLF

Owners: Bettina Bürklin-von Guradze, Christian von Guradze
General Manager: Bruno Sebastian
Winemaker: Fritz Knorr
67157 Wachenheim, Weinstraße 65
Tel. (0 63 22) 9 53 30, Fax 95 33 30
e-mail: buerklin-wolf@t-online.de
Directions: In the Mittelhaardt between Neustadt und Bad Dürkheim
Sales: Klaus Bauer
Opening hours: Mon.–Fri. 8 a.m. to noon and 1 p.m. to 6 p.m., Sat. and Sun. 11 a.m. to 4 p.m.
Restaurant: Gasthaus "Zur Kanne" in Deidesheim, 11 a.m. to midnight
History: Founded in 1597
Worth seeing: Courtyard, vaulted cellars

Vineyard area: 95 hectares
Annual production: 600,000 bottles
Top sites: Forster Jesuitengarten and Ungeheuer, Wachenheimer Rechbächel and Gerümpel, Ruppertsberger Reiterpfad and Nußbien
Soil types: Limestone, basalt, loam, yellow and reddish sandstone
Grape varieties: 80% Riesling, 13% red varieties, 7% other varieties
Average yield: 61 hl/ha
Best vintages: 1995, 1996, 1997
Member: VDP

With the outstanding 1996 vintage this highly traditional estate moved to the top of its class in the Pfalz. Together with Christmann and Müller-Catoir, Bürklin-Wolf must now be counted among the trio of superlative estates in the Pfalz. This is a remarkable performance for a producer that cultivates almost 100 hectares of vineyards. Today, even the quality of the liter bottlings is appealing. By harvesting extremely late – on December 8 they were still picking grapes for 1996 dry wines – the estate staked everything on chance and won. No one in Germany produced such a stunning range of dry wines in 1996. The 1997s are of similar pedigree. This estate is without doubt the king of dry Riesling in Germany.

1996 Wachenheimer Gerümpel
Riesling Spätlese halbtrocken
19 DM, 12%, ♀ till 2000 **89**

1996 Ruppertsberger Gaisböhl
Riesling Spätlese trocken
31 DM, 13%, ♀ till 2002 **90**

1997 Forster Kirchenstück
Riesling Spätlese trocken
"Erstes Gewächs"
40 DM, 13%, ♀ till 2007 **91**

1997 Forster Jesuitengarten
Riesling Spätlese trocken
"Erstes Gewächs"
38 DM, 13%, ♀ till 2004 **91**

1997 Forster Ungeheuer
Riesling Spätlese trocken
"Erstes Gewächs"
36 DM, 13%, ♀ till 2003 **91**

1996 Forster Ungeheuer
Riesling Spätlese trocken
31 DM, 13%, ♀ till 2003 **91**

1996 Forster Pechstein
Riesling Spätlese trocken
31 DM, 13%, ♀ till 2002 **92**

1996 Forster Kirchenstück
Riesling Spätlese trocken
35 DM, 13%, ♀ till 2005 **92**

1996 Wachenheimer Gerümpel
Riesling Eiswein
150 DM/0.375 liter, 8.5%, ♀ till 2015 **96**

WEINGUT REICHSRAT VON BUHL

Owner: Reichsfreiherr Georg Enoch von und zu Gutenberg
Leased by the Reichsrat von Buhl GmbH
Managing Director: Stefan Weber
Winemaker: Frank John
67146 Deidesheim, Weinstraße 16
Tel. (0 63 26) 9 65 00, Fax 96 50 24
Directions: A 61 towards Bad Dürkheim, exit Deidesheim
Sales: Bernhard Wolff and Nicole Rebehn
Opening hours: Mon.–Fri. 8 a.m. to 6 p.m., Sat. and Sun. 10 a.m. to 5 p.m.
Worth seeing: The whole property is a historic monument

Vineyard area: 50 hectares
Annual production: 350,000 bottles
Top sites: Forster Kirchenstück, Ungeheuer, Jesuitengarten, Freundstück and Pechstein, Deidesheimer Herrgottsacker and Mäushöhle
Soil types: Sandy loam, weathered limestone and basalt
Grape varieties: 88% Riesling, 4% Spätburgunder, 8% other varieties
Average yield: 60 hl/ha
Best vintages: 1994, 1996, 1997
Member: VDP

Since 1989 enormous sums have been lavished on this venerable estate, which now boasts a fairy-tale cellar. With these tools winemaker Frank John has gradually been able to exploit the full potential of this estate's magnificent vineyard. With the excellent 1994s and fine 1995s this property began its qualitative ascent. In 1996 it presented a breathtaking array of noble late harvest specialities. They were the reward for scrupulous attention to detail throughout the autumn, when harvesters went into certain vineyards as many as ten times. The dry 1996 Rieslings, which appeared soft despite their racy acidity, were also good, but not as imposing as the botrytis nectar. Although the late harvest wines were not quite as stunning, the same is true of the 1997 vintage. Few producers in the Pfalz produce such fine sweet wine.

1997 Deidesheimer Mäushöhle
Riesling Spätlese halbtrocken
16.50 DM, 12.5%, ♀ till 2001 **86**

1997 Ruppertsberger Reiterpfad
Riesling Spätlese trocken "Classic"
19.80 DM, 13.5%, ♀ till 2002 **88**

1996 Ruppertsberger Reiterpfad
Riesling Kabinett trocken "Classic"
14 DM, 11.5%, ♀ till 2000 **89**

1996 Forster Pechstein
Riesling Spätlese halbtrocken
16 DM, 11.5%, ♀ till 2003 **89**

1997 Forster Jesuitengarten
Riesling Spätlese
17.50 DM, 9%, ♀ till 2003 **89**

1997 Forster Ungeheuer
Riesling Auslese
28.50 DM, 9.5%, ♀ till 2007 **92**

1996 Forster Ungeheuer
Riesling Auslese "Classic"
20 DM/0.375 liter, 9.5%, ♀ till 2006 **94**

1997 Forster Ungeheuer
Riesling Beerenauslese
65 DM/0.375 liter, 8.5%, ♀ till 2012 **94**

1996 Forster Jesuitengarten
Riesling Eiswein
82 DM, 8%, ♀ till 2010 **95**

1996 Forster Ungeheuer
Riesling Trockenbeerenauslese
165 DM/0.375 liter, 7.5%, ♀ till 2006 **98**

WEINGUT CHRISTMANN

Owners: Karl-Friedrich and Steffen Christmann
General Manager: Günter Braun
67435 Gimmeldingen,
Peter-Koch-Staße 43
Tel. (0 63 21) 6 60 39, Fax 6 87 62
Directions: A 65, exit Neustadt-Lambrecht, follow directions to Gimmeldingen
Sales: Gisela Christmann
Opening hours: Mon.–Fri. 9 a.m. to 11:30 a.m. and 2 p.m. to 6 p.m.
Sat. 8 a.m. to noon or by appointment
Restaurant: "Meerspinnkeller," 5 p.m. to 10 p.m., except Mon. and Tue.
Worth seeing: Vaulted cellars from 1575

> Vineyard area: 12.9 hectares
> Annual production: 100,000 bottles
> Top sites: Ruppertsberger Reiterpfad and Nußbien, Königsbacher Idig and Ölberg, Gimmeldinger Mandelgarten
> Soil types: Loam, clay, sand, heavy chalky loam, weathered red sandstone
> Grape varieties: 61% Riesling, 13% Spätburgunder, 8% Weiß-burgunder, 7% Grauburgunder, 11% other varieties
> Average yield: 53 hl/ha
> Best vintages: 1995, 1996, 1997
> Member: VDP

The success of the Christmann family is easy to explain, yet very laborious to implement: selective manual harvesting, no mechanical pumping of either grapes or must, whole-cluster pressing. The 1994s and 1995s were the best wines that we had ever tasted from this estate and set new standards for their chosen quality. Even though the owners themselves did not regard the vintage as particularly good, the 1996s were again first-rate. The quality of the dry and off-dry styles has risen from year to year. 1997 was again a difficult vintage, but father and son did almost everything right. Even the late harvest Rieslings were excellent. These two have the right stuff!

1997 Ruppertsberger Reiterpfad
Riesling Spätlese trocken
"Erstes Gewächs"
24 DM, 13%, ♀ till 2002 **89**

1996 Ruppertsberger Linsenbusch
Riesling Spätlese halbtrocken
18.50 DM, 12.5%, ♀ till 2002 **89**

1996 Königsbacher Idig
Riesling Spätlese
24 DM, 12%, ♀ till 2006 **89**

1996 Ruppertsberger Reiterpfad
Riesling Spätlese trocken
24 DM, 13.5%, ♀ till 2003 **90**

1997 Deidesheimer Hohenmorgen
Riesling Spätlese trocken
"Erstes Gewächs"
32 DM, 13%, ♀ till 2005 **90**

1996 Königsbacher Idig
Riesling Spätlese trocken
26 DM, 12.5%, ♀ till 2005 **91**

1997 Königsbacher Idig
Riesling Auslese
38 DM, 11.5%, ♀ till 2005 **92**

1997 Deidesheimer Hohenmorgen
Riesling Beerenauslese
65 DM/0.375 liter, 9.5%, ♀ till 2010 **94**

1997 Ruppertsberger Reiterpfad
Riesling Trockenbeerenauslese
125 DM/0.375 liter, 8%, ♀ till 2015 **95**

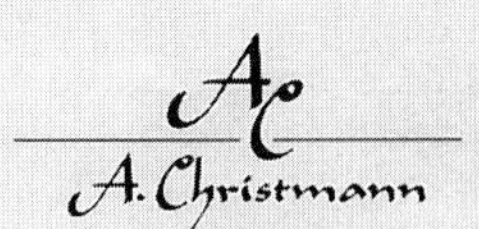

1995
Ruppertsberger Reiterpfad
Riesling Spätlese Trocken

Pfalz
Gutsabfüllung - Qualitätswein mit Prädikat
Weingut A. Christmann, D-67435 Gimmeldingen/Pfalz
A. P. Nr. 5 173 021 012 96
750 ml
12% vol

WEINGUT KURT DARTING

Owner: Kurt and Helmut Darting
Winemaker: Helmut Darting
67098 Bad Dürkheim, Am Falltor 2
Tel. (0 63 22) 29 83, Fax 6 23 03
e-mail:
weingut.kurt.darting@t-online.de
Directions: Via A 61 and then A 650
Sales: Darting family
Opening hours: Mon.–Sat. 8 a.m. to noon and 1 p.m. to 6 p.m.
Sun. by appointment

Vineyard area: 16 hectares
Annual production: 150,000 bottles
Top sites: Dürkheimer Michelsberg, Spielberg and Hochbenn, Ungsteiner Herrenberg
Soil types: Heavy chalky loam, sandy gravel, loess and loam
Grape varieties: 44% Riesling, 8% Weißburgunder, 6% Rieslaner, 5% Scheurebe, 4% each of Portugieser, Muskateller and Ortega, 3% each of Chardonnay and Spätburgunder, 19% other varieties
Average yield: 62 hl/ha
Best vintages: 1992, 1994, 1996

Helmut Darting learned his craft at the Müller-Catoir estate. With each passing year his own wines have become both more aromatic and substantial. Darting also devotes ever more attention to dry styles, which now constitute half of his production. Nonetheless, the elegant Auslese and noble Beerenauslese remain the showpieces of his estate. In 1990 and 1992 Darting had established standards for high quality. With his 1996s he has not only done justice to the vintage, but surpassed our expectations. Perhaps it had something to do with his new temperature-controlled tanks, which allowed him better management of the fermentations. In any case, the wines have depth, fruit and spice that we had not previously tasted. And given the attractive quality of even the liter bottlings, it was clear to see that this estate was on a roll. The 1997s were, although pleasant, not quite as good.

1997 Dürkheimer Michelsberg
Riesling Spätlese trocken
10.50 DM, 12.5%, 🍷 till 2000 — **84**

1997 Dürkheimer Spielberg
Riesling Kabinett trocken
8 DM, 11.5%, 🍷 now — **86**

1997 Ungsteiner Herrenberg
Riesling Spätlese halbtrocken
9.50 DM, 12%, 🍷 till 2002 — **86**

1996 Dürkheimer Fronhof
Riesling Spätlese halbtrocken
9 DM, 12%, 🍷 now — **86**

1997 Dürkheimer Fronhof
Riesling Kabinett
7 DM, 9.5%, 🍷 till 2001 — **86**

1996 Dürkheimer Spielberg
Riesling Spätlese
9 DM, 10%, 🍷 till 2000 — **88**

1997 Ungsteiner Herrenberg
Riesling Auslese
16 DM, 10%, 🍷 till 2003 — **88**

1996 Dürkheimer Herrenberg
Riesling Auslese
15 DM, 9.5%, 🍷 till 2000 — **89**

1996 Dürkheimer Fronhof
Scheurebe Trockenbeerenauslese
42 DM/0.5 liter, 7.5%, 🍷 till 2010 — **91**

Pfalz
1996
Wachenheimer
Mandelgarten
Kerner Kabinett
halbtrocken
A.P.Nr. 5 180 346 008 97
Qualitätswein mit Prädikat
Gutsabfüllung
11,5 % vol
1 Liter
WEINGUT
KURT DARTING
D-67098 BAD DÜRKHEIM/WEINSTRASSE

WEINGUT DR. DEINHARD

Owner: Hoch family
Manager: Heinz Bauer
Winemaker: Ludwig Molitor
67146 Deidesheim, Weinstraße 10
Tel. (0 63 26) 2 21, Fax 79 20
Directions: Between Neustadt and Dürkheim on the wine route
Sales: Heinz Bauer
Opening hours: Mon.–Fri. 8 a.m. to 5:30 p.m., Sat. 9:30 a.m. to 5 p.m. or by appointment
Worth seeing: The estate's red and yellow sandstone buildings

> Vineyard area: 26.5 hectares
> Annual production: 195,000 bottles
> Top sites: Deidesheimer Kalkofen, Grainhübel, Leinhöhle, Kieselberg and Mäushöhle, Ruppertsberger Reiterpfad, Nußbien and Spieß, Forster Jesuitengarten and Ungeheuer
> Soil types: Red sandstone, loess and loam, clay and sand, tertiary limestone, basalt and gravel
> Grape varieties: 85% Riesling, 15% other varieties
> Average yield: 67 hl/ha
> Best vintages: 1992, 1994, 1996
> Member: VDP

Founded in 1849 by Friedrich Deinhard of the Koblenz sparkling-wine dynasty, this estate owns 42 hectares of excellent vineyards. Since 1973, however, the estate has restricted itself to 26 hectares; the rest is leased to the Wegeler family. After a rather mediocre performance in 1993, Heinz Bauer returned to form with the excellent 1994s, which were reminiscent of the wines from the great vintages of 1990 and 1992. After a slight drop in quality in 1995, the 1996s were again first rate. The Rieslings were all tight in structure, with the dry wines being lively and reductive in the best sense of the term. The superb ice wine from the Reiterpfad vineyard in Ruppertsberg, however, was the top wine of the vintage for this venerable estate. The 1997s were well-made, but not nearly so good.

1997 Deidesheimer Grainhübel
Riesling Spätlese trocken
14.50 DM, 12.5%, ♀ till 2000 **84**

1997 Forster Jesuitengarten
Riesling Spätlese trocken
14.50 DM, 12.5%, ♀ till 2000 **84**

1996 Deidesheimer Mäushöhle
Riesling Kabinett halbtrocken
9 DM, 10.5%, ♀ till 2000 **84**

1996 Deidesheimer Herrgottsacker
Riesling Spätlese halbtrocken
12.50 DM, 11.5%, ♀ till 2000 **84**

1997 Ruppertsberger Linsenbusch
Weißer Burgunder Spätlese
14.70 DM, 12.5%, ♀ now **84**

1997 Ruppertsberger Reiterpfad
Gewürztraminer Kabinett
9.30 DM, 11.5%, ♀ till 2000 **86**

1997 Deidesheimer Grainhübel
Riesling Auslese
23 DM, 11.5%, ♀ till 2003 **86**

1996 Forster Jesuitengarten
Riesling Spätlese trocken
14.50 DM, 12.5%, ♀ till 2002 **88**

1996 Deidesheimer Grainhübel
Riesling Beerenauslese
50 DM/0.375 liter, 11%, ♀ till 2010 **92**

1996 Ruppertsberger Reiterpfad
Riesling Eiswein
70 DM, 8.5%, ♀ till 2016 **96**

WEINGUT EYMANN

Owner: Rainer Eymann
67161 Gönnheim, Ludwigstraße 35
Tel. (0 63 22) 28 08, Fax 6 87 92
e-mail: Weingut.Eymann@t-online.de
Directions: From the A 61, exit "Kreuz Ludwigshafen," via A 650 in the direction of Bad Dürkheim, exit Gönnheim
Sales: Ingeborg Wagner-Eymann
Opening hours: Mon.–Fri. 8 a.m. to noon and 1 p.m. to 6 p.m.
Sat. 10 a.m. to 7 p.m.
Restaurant: Open from 5 p.m. to midnight, except Sun., Mon. and Tue.

Vineyard area: 16 hectares
Annual production: 120,000 bottles
Top site: Gönnheimer Sonnenberg
Soil types: Loess and gravelly sand
Grape varieties: 33% Riesling, 12% Spätburgunder, 11% Portugieser, 10% Grauburgunder, 8% Gewürztraminer, 6% Weißburgunder, 20% other varieties
Average yield: 63 hl/ha
Best vintages: 1992, 1996, 1997
Member: Quintessenz

In 1350 the Eymann family was mentioned in a leased property called "Toreye." The winery itself, however, has been known outside of the Pfalz only for the past couple of years. Although we tasted a representative collection of wines from 1995, Rainer Eymann himself stated that it was "a poor vintage for us." The 1996s, on the other hand, showed what this ambitious young grower is capable of producing. Honest and tightly structured, each wine exudes its pure varietal character. We particularly liked the robustly fresh Riesling and the Grauburgunder "Toreye." Our first encounter with Eymann's tannic red wines provided less pleasure. The 1997s were better. In particular, the late harvest Gewürztraminer and Muskateller are first class. We expect to hear even more from this estate in the years to come.

1997 Gönnheimer Sonnenberg
Chardonnay Spätlese trocken
12.10 DM, 13%, 🍷 now **82**

1997 Gönnheimer Sonnenberg
Grauer Burgunder Spätlese trocken
12.10 DM, 13.5%, 🍷 till 2000 **84**

1997 Gönnheimer Sonnenberg
Weißer Burgunder Spätlese trocken
12.10 DM, 13.5%, 🍷 till 2000 **84**

1996 Gönnheimer Sonnenberg
Riesling Spätlese trocken
12 DM, 12%, 🍷 now **84**

1996 Gönnheimer Sonnenberg
Grauer Burgunder Spätlese trocken
12.50 DM, 11.5%, 🍷 now **84**

1997 Gönnheimer Sonnenberg
Riesling Spätlese halbtrocken
12.10 DM, 11.5%, 🍷 till 2000 **84**

1997 Gönnheimer Sonnenberg
Riesling Spätlese
12.10 DM, 11%, 🍷 till 2001 **84**

1997 Gönnheimer Martinshöhe
Gewürztraminer Auslese "Toreye"
16.20 DM/0.5 liter, 12%, 🍷 till 2003 **88**

1997 Gönnheimer Sonnenberg
Gelber Muskateller Auslese "Toreye"
16.20 DM/0.5 liter, 13%, 🍷 till 2003 **88**

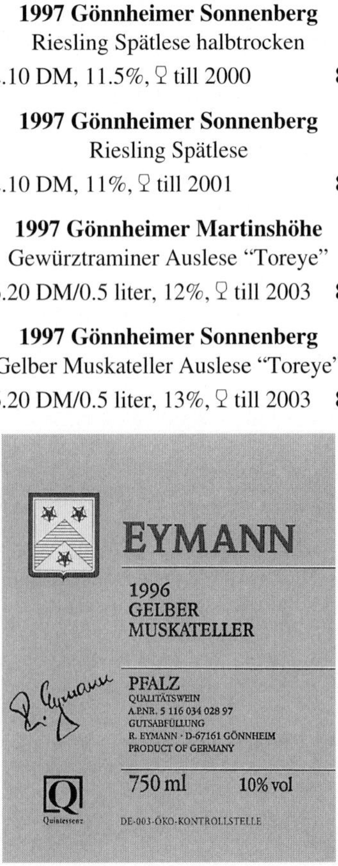

WEINGUT FITZ-RITTER

Owner: Konrad M. Fitz
General Manager: Karlheinz Bender
Winemaker: Rolf Hanewald
67098 Bad Dürkheim,
Weinstraße Nord 51
Tel. (0 63 22) 53 89, Fax 6 60 05
e-mail: weingut@compuserve.com
Directions: From A 61, exit "Kreuz Ludwigshafen," via A 650, in the direction of Bad Dürkheim
Sales: Roland Hauck
Opening hours: Mon.–Fri. 8 a.m. to noon and 1 p.m. to 6 p.m., Sat. 9 a.m. to 1 p.m. or by appointment
History: Owned by the family since 1785
Worth seeing: The most beautiful gardens on the German wine route

> Vineyard area: 20 hectares
> Annual production: 150,000 bottles
> Top sites: Ungsteiner Herrenberg, Dürkheimer Michelsberg, Spielberg, Abtsfronhof and Hochbenn
> Soil types: Sandy loam, partly containing limestone
> Grape varieties: 65% Riesling, 6% Spätburgunder, 5% Gewürztraminer, 4% Chardonnay, 20% other varieties
> Average yield: 71 hl/ha
> Best vintages: 1994, 1996, 1997
> Member: VDP

This picturesque, half-timbered house was once one of the Pfalz's most celebrated inns. Thanks to the beautifully laid-out gardens, it was in earlier times a favorite meeting place for well-off couples. The wines are still aged in the sandstone vaulted cellars, both in casks and increasingly in stainless steel tanks. The Rieslings are made in an ever more modern and individualistic style. After the appealing 1994s, the overall quality of the 1995s left a bit to be desired. The 1996s, however, were the best range that we had ever tasted from this estate. The 1997s maintain this standard.

1997 Dürkheimer Spielberg
Chardonnay Spätlese trocken
14.50 DM, 12.5%, 🍷 till 2000 **84**

1997 Dürkheimer Abtsfronhof
Riesling Spätlese trocken
12 DM, 12.5%, 🍷 till 2000 **84**

1997 Dürkheimer Abtsfronhof
Gewürztraminer Spätlese
14 DM, 11%, 🍷 till 2001 **84**

1996 Dürkheimer Abtsfronhof
Riesling Spätlese trocken
11.50 DM, 12.5%, 🍷 till 2000 **86**

1997 Ungsteiner Herrenberg
Riesling Spätlese
12 DM, 11.5%, 🍷 till 2003 **86**

1996 Dürkheimer Nonnengarten
Gewürztraminer Spätlese
11.50 DM, 10.5%, 🍷 till 2000 **86**

1996 Ungsteiner Herrenberg
Riesling Spätlese
11.50 DM, 11%, 🍷 till 2002 **88**

1997 Dürkheimer Hochbenn
Riesling Eiswein
65 DM/0.5 liter, 10.5%, 🍷 till 2007 **88**

1996 Wachenheimer Mandelgarten
Huxelrebe Beerenauslese
60 DM, 10.5%, 🍷 till 2006 **89**

1996 Dürkheimer Hochbenn
Riesling Eiswein
65 DM/0.5 liter, 10%, 🍷 till 2012 **91**

WEINGUT WINFRIED FREY & SÖHNE

Owner: Winfried, Ursula, Jürgen and Peter Frey
Winemaker: Jürgen Frey
76879 Essingen, Spanierstraße 1/2
Tel. (0 63 47) 82 24, Fax 72 90
Directions: Southern wine route near Landau
Sales: Ursula Frey
Opening hours: Mon.–Fri. 8 a.m. to 6 p.m., Sat. 8 a.m. to noon
Sun. by appointment
Worth seeing: Small wine museum

Vineyard area: 10 hectares
Annual production: 80,000 bottles
Top sites: Essinger Rossberg, Sonnenberg and Osterberg
Soil types: Loess and sandy loam
Grape varieties: 35% Riesling, 15% Grauburgunder, 10% each of Weißburgunder, Portugieser and Dornfelder, 5% each of Gewürztraminer, Kerner, Spätburgunder and Sankt Laurent
Average yield: 60 hl/ha
Best vintages: 1994, 1996, 1997

Winfried Frey's estate vineyards are certainly not located in a particularly esteemed corner of the Pfalz. Indeed, this area is better known as farmland. Nonetheless, Frey has been able to establish his reputation as a specialist for noble late harvest wines from a broad range of grape varieties. He now plans to use the period of vineyard reorganization, which will continue until 2003, in order to concentrate on more classical styles of wine. The sweet wines, which can be absolutely stunning, remain his best. The dry styles, which account for half of his production, are respectable, but rarely exciting. Since 1995 son Jürgen Frey has been responsible for the vinification.

1997 Ortega
Spätlese
9 DM, 9.5%, ♀ till now **80**

1996 Huxelrebe
Spätlese
8.50 DM, 10%, ♀ now **80**

1997 Scheurebe
Spätlese
12 DM, 8%, ♀ now **82**

1997 Chardonnay & Riesling
Eiswein
95 DM/0.375 liter, 7%, ♀ till 2010 **88**

1996 Riesling
Eiswein
60 DM/0.375 liter, 7%, ♀ till 2010 **88**

1997 Chardonnay
Beerenauslese
75 DM/0.375 liter, 9.5%, ♀ till 2007 **88**

1995 Chardonnay
Beerenauslese
50 DM/0.375 liter, 11%, ♀ till 2006 **88**

1996 Riesling
Beerenauslese
45 DM, 8%, ♀ till 2010 **88**

——— Red wine ———

1996 Dunkelfelder and Dornfelder
trocken
9.50 DM, 12%, ♀ now **80**

WEINGUT KARL-HEINZ GAUL

Owner: Karl-Heinz Gaul
67269 Grünstadt-Sausenheim, Bärenbrunnenstraße 15
Tel. (0 63 59) 8 45 69, Fax 8 74 98
Directions: A 6 Mannheim–Saarbrücken, exit Grünstadt
Sales: Rosemarie Gaul
Opening hours: Mon.–Fri. 8 a.m. to 6 p.m., Sat. 9 a.m. to 3 p.m.

Vineyard area: 9.75 hectares
Annual production: 80,000 bottles
Top sites: Sausenheimer Honigsack, Asselheimer Sankt Stephan
Soil types: Heavy, very chalky loam with sandy gravel and loam
Grape varieties: 44% Riesling, 8% each of Portugieser and Spätburgunder, 6% each of Weißburgunder, Schwarzriesling, Silvaner, St. Laurent and Huxelrebe, 10% other varieties
Average yield: 81 hl/ha
Best vintages: 1993, 1996, 1997

This property was created in 1993 through the division of the parental estate, which has existed for generations. In the tasting room, set among the vineyards, one can watch the sun set over 80-year-old oleander bushes, which bloom in twelve colors. After an excellent start, the vintages 1994 and 1995 were somewhat less than convincing. With the 1996 range, this estate again put its best foot forward. The 1997s are perhaps not quite as good, but the firm acidity characteristic of the vintage helped Karl-Heinz Gaul to produce a delightful Riesling Spätlese and an Auslese. An interesting discovery!

1997 Sausenheimer Hütt
Riesling Auslese trocken
14 DM, 14%, ♀ now **80**

1997 Sausenheimer Höllenpfad
Riesling Spätlese halbtrocken
9.50 DM, 12%, ♀ till 2001 **80**

1996 Sausenheimer Honigsack
Riesling Spätlese halbtrocken
9 DM, 11%, ♀ now **80**

1997 Sausenheimer Hütt
Riesling Spätlese trocken
9.80 DM, 12%, ♀ till 2001 **82**

1996 Sausenheimer Hütt
Riesling Spätlese trocken
9.50 DM, 12%, ♀ now **82**

1996 Sausenheimer Hütt
Riesling Spätlese halbtrocken
9.50 DM, 11.5%, ♀ now **82**

1996 Sausenheimer Honigsack
Riesling Spätlese
9 DM, 9.5%, ♀ now **82**

1997 Sausenheimer Hütt
Riesling Auslese
13.50 DM/0.5 liter, 9%, ♀ till 2006 **89**

1996 Sausenheimer Hütt
Riesling Eiswein
38 DM/0.375 liter, 9.5%, ♀ till 2010 **91**

Weingut
GAUL
Pfalz
RIESLING
Spätlese halbtrocken
1996er Sausenheimer Honigsack
Qualitätswein mit Prädikat
A.P.Nr. 5120021 1397
Erzeugerabfüllung
11%vol
Weingut Karl-Heinz Gaul
0,75l
D-67269 Grünstadt-Sausenheim
Bärenbrunnenstraße 15 · Telefon 0 63 59 / 8 45 69

WEINGUT BERND GRIMM

Owners: Christine and Bernd Grimm
76889 Schweigen, Bergstraße 4
Tel. (0 63 42) 91 90 45, Fax 91 90 46
Directions: A 65, exit Landau Süd in the direction of Weißenburg
Sales: Christine Grimm
Opening hours: Fri. 1 p.m. to 6 p.m. Sat. 8 a.m. to 6 p.m., Sun. 10 a.m. to noon or by appointment

Vineyard area: 7.5 hectares
Annual production: 70,000 bottles
Top site: Schweigener Sonnenberg
Soil types: Heavy chalky loam, loess and loam with sand and layers of clay
Grape varieties: 19% Riesling, 15% Weißburgunder, 13% Dornfelder, 11% Müller-Thurgau, 7% Spätburgunder, 6% Chardonnay, 5% each of Silvaner, Grauburgunder and Portugieser, 14% other varieties
Average yield: 86 hl/ha
Best vintages: 1993, 1996, 1997

Like many of his colleagues, Bernd Grimm once delivered his grapes to the local cooperative. Since 1971 he has managed, without any serious difficulty, to market his entire production in bottles. The estate is best known for its well-made Chardonnay, but the Grauburgunder is also often most appealing. In 1997 it was certainly his finest wine. If Grimm would reduce his yields, his other wines – which often lack expression – would show greater stature. Nevertheless, this estate is a perfect example of a phenomenon often encountered in the Pfalz, namely that respectable small producers are able to release decent wines for everyday consumption at modest prices. The Grimm family also grow fruit for brandy distillation on their own premises.

1997 Schweigener Sonnenberg
Riesling trocken
6 DM/1.0 liter, 11.5%, 🍷 now **75**

1997 Schweigener Sonnenberg
Riesling Kabinett trocken
8.50 DM, 11%, 🍷 now **77**

1997 Schweigener Sonnenberg
Weißer Burgunder Kabinett trocken
7.50 DM, 11.5%, 🍷 now **80**

1996 Schweigener Sonnenberg
Grauer Burgunder Kabinett trocken
7.50 DM, 11%, 🍷 now **80**

1996 Schweigener Sonnenberg
Gewürztraminer Spätlese
9.50 DM, 12%, 🍷 now **80**

1997 Schweigener Sonnenberg
Riesling Hochgewächs trocken
7.50 DM, 11.5%, 🍷 now **80**

1996 Schweigener Sonnenberg
Grauer Burgunder Spätlese trocken
15 DM, 13%, 🍷 now **82**

1997 Schweigener Sonnenberg
Chardonnay Spätlese trocken
13 DM, 13%, 🍷 till 2000 **84**

1996 Schweigener Sonnenberg
Chardonnay Spätlese trocken
12 DM, 13%, 🍷 now **84**

1997 Schweigener Sonnenberg
Grauer Burgunder Spätlese trocken
15 DM, 13%, 🍷 till 2001 **88**

WEINGUT GEORG HENNINGER IV.

Owner: Walter Henninger
General Manager: Ulrich Meyer
Winemaker: Jan Kux
67169 Kallstadt, Weinstraße 93
Tel. (0 63 22) 22 77, Fax 6 28 61
Directions: A 6, exit Grünstadt, in the direction of Bad Dürkheim
Sales: Walter Henninger
Opening hours: Tue.–Sun. 11 a.m. to 8 p.m., tastings by appointment
Restaurant: "Weinhaus Henninger," closed Mon.
Specialties: Good local cooking
History: Wine estate since 1615
Worth seeing: Old half-timbered house

Vineyard area: 4.5 hectares
Annual production: 35,000 bottles
Top sites: Kallstadter Annaberg, Saumagen and Steinacker, Leistadter Kalkofen
Soil types: Weathered sandstone, limestone debris, loess and loam
Grape varieties: 51% Riesling, 11% each of Spätburgunder and Müller-Thurgau, 8% Weißburgunder, 7% Chardonnay, 4% Grauburgunder, 8% other varieties
Average yield: 68 hl/ha
Best vintages: 1990, 1993, 1994
Member: VDP

The old manor of this estate is located in the heart of Kallstadt. It's a beautiful half-timbered house that is now a country restaurant offering good cooking in a hospitable atmosphere at reasonable prices. The wines are produced across the street in the cellars of the Koehler-Ruprecht estate. As Walter Henninger abhors residual sugar the wines are, for the most part, vinified dry and bottled early. Consequently, they often need time to develop. The few younger wines that we have tasted from this estate were less convincing than the 1993s and 1994s; the last truly successful vintage was 1990.

1996 Herxheimer Honigsack
Weißer Burgunder Kabinett trocken
13 DM, 11.5%, ♀ now **80**

1996 Kallstadter
Riesling
9.50 DM/1.0 liter, 10.5%, ♀ now **80**

1997 Kallstadter Annaberg
Riesling Kabinett trocken
12.50 DM, 11.5%, ♀ till 2000 **82**

1996 Leistadter Kalkofen
Riesling Kabinett trocken
12.50 DM, 11%, ♀ now **82**

1997 Kallstadter Annaberg
Chardonnay Spätlese trocken
18 DM, 12%, ♀ now **82**

1996 Kallstadter Annaberg
Weißer Burgunder Spätlese trocken
20 DM, 13.5%, ♀ now **82**

1996 Kallstadter Steinacker
Grauer Burgunder Spätlese trocken
20 DM, 13.5%, ♀ till 2000 **84**

1997 Kallstadter Saumagen
Riesling Spätlese trocken
16 DM, 12.5%, ♀ till 2001 **84**

1996 Kallstadter Saumagen
Riesling Spätlese halbtrocken
18 DM, 11%, ♀ till 2000 **84**

WEINGUT JÜLG

Owner: Werner Jülg
Manager: Andreas Eck
76889 Schweigen-Rechtenbach, Hauptstraße 1
Tel. (0 63 42) 91 90 90, Fax 91 90 91
Directions: A 65, exit Landau-Süd, in the direction of Weißenburg
Opening hours: Mon.–Fri. by appointment, Sat. and Sun. 10 a.m. to 6 p.m.
Restaurant: 11 a.m. to 10 p.m., except Thur. and Fri.

Vineyard area: 15.5 hectares
Annual production: 100,000 bottles
Top site: Schweigener Sonnenberg
Soil types: Heavy chalky loam, clay, loess
Grape varieties: 25% Riesling, 15% each of Weißburgunder, Spätburgunder and Müller-Thurgau, 10% each of Grauburgunder and Chardonnay, 10% other varieties
Average yield: 62 hl/ha
Best vintages: 1994, 1996, 1997

In the mid-1980s Peter and Werner Jülg took over this estate from their parents and got it into shape. Their wines have always been intensely aromatic and are now among the most appealing of the southern Pfalz. They show distinct character and are often essentially Alsatian in style. Their current relations with that neighboring region are not only that part of their vineyards lie in Alsace; Peter Jülg has married an Alsatian and taken over the estate of her parents in Seebach. After a rather bland 1995 vintage, Werner Jülg produced a much finer array of 1996s that had astonishing freshness and acidity for the southern Pfalz, and the clean varietal character of each wine was well defined. Although the barrel-aged 1997s are quite pleasant, the general quality of the vintage suffered due to hail in June. Nonetheless, if the winery's performance continues at this standard we will certainly hear more from the Jülg brothers in the future.

1997 Schweigener Sonnenberg
Weißer Burgunder Spätlese trocken
12 DM, 13%, ♀ now **80**

1996 Schweigener Sonnenberg
Grauer Burgunder Spätlese trocken
9.50 DM, 12.7%, ♀ now **82**

1997 Schweigener Sonnenberg
Chardonnay Spätlese
17 DM/0.5 liter, 13.5%, ♀ till 2001 **82**

1996 Schweigener Sonnenberg
Riesling Kabinett trocken
8.25 DM, 11.5%, ♀ now **84**

1997 Schweigener Sonnenberg
Weißer Burgunder Spätlese trocken
21 DM, 13.5%, ♀ till 2000 **84**

1996 Schweigener Sonnenberg
Weißer Burgunder Spätlese trocken
9.50 DM, 12.5%, ♀ now **84**

1997 Schweigener Sonnenberg
Grauer Burgunder Spätlese trocken
22 DM, 13%, ♀ till 2001 **86**

——— Red wines ———

1996 Schweigener Sonnenberg
Dornfelder trocken
17.50 DM, 13%, ♀ till 2000 **80**

1996 Schweigener Sonnenberg
Spätburgunder Spätlese trocken
26 DM, 13.5%, ♀ now **80**

1996 Schweigener Sonnenberg
Cabernet Sauvignon Spätlese trocken
27 DM, 13.5%, ♀ till 2001 **82**

WEINGUT JULIUS FERDINAND KIMICH

Owner: Franz Arnold
67142 Deidesheim, Weinstraße 54
Tel. (0 63 26) 3 42, Fax 98 04 14
Directions: On the wine route between Neustadt and Bad Dürkheim
Sales: Arnold family
Opening hours: Mon.–Sat. 8 a.m. to 6 p.m., Sun. 10 a.m. to noon and 2 p.m. to 5 p.m.

Vineyard area: 9 hectares
Annual production: 70.000 bottles
Top sites: Deidesheimer Grainhübel and Kalkofen, Forster Ungeheuer and Pechstein, Ruppertsberger Reiterpfad and Nußbien
Soil types: Sandy loam
Grape varieties: 77% Riesling, 8% Müller-Thurgau, 6% Weiß- and Grauburgunder, 3% Spätburgunder, 2% Gewürztraminer, 4% other varieties
Average yield: 68 hl/ha
Best vintages: 1990, 1993, 1996
Member: VDP

This estate was founded in 1758 by an Alsatian cooper. Today it is run in the sixth generation by Franz Arnold and his son. They continue the estate's tradition of aging most of their wines in old oak casks, but the once solid Rieslings of this classical style have lost much of their flair in recent vintages: the 1994 range left plenty to be desired; the 1995s were downright disappointing. We were pleased to note a slight improvement with the 1996 vintage, but the 1997s are again little more than ordinary. Admittedly, many of the wines are still simple in character, but they are at least not nearly as rustic as they were before.

1996 Deidesheimer Leinhöhle
Riesling Kabinett trocken
8.75 DM, 12%, ♀ now **80**

1996 Ruppertsberger Reiterpfad
Gewürztraminer Spätlese trocken
14 DM, 13.5%, ♀ now **80**

1997 Deidesheimer Paradiesgarten
Riesling Kabinett halbtrocken
8.20 DM, 11%, ♀ now **80**

1996 Ruppertsberger Reiterpfad
Riesling Kabinett halbtrocken
7.75 DM, 11%, ♀ now **80**

1996 Deidesheimer Kalkofen
Riesling Spätlese halbtrocken
11.50 DM, 11.5%, ♀ now **80**

1997 Forster Pechstein
Riesling Kabinett trocken
8.80 DM, 11.5%, ♀ now **82**

1997 Deidesheimer Nonnenstück
Weißer Burgunder Spätlese trocken
12 DM, 12.5%, ♀ now **82**

1996 Deidesheimer Kieselberg
Riesling Spätlese trocken
13 DM, 12.5%, ♀ now **82**

1996 Ruppertsberger Reiterpfad
Riesling Spätlese halbtrocken
11 DM, 11.5%, ♀ till 2000 **82**

1996 Deidesheimer Grainhübel
Riesling Auslese trocken
18 DM, 13%, ♀ till 2000 **84**

WEINGUT GERHARD KLEIN

Owners: Sieglinde and Gerhard Klein
Winemaker: Thomas Fischer
76835 Hainfeld, Weinstraße 38
Tel. (0 63 23) 27 13, Fax 8 13 43
Directions: From A 65 via B 10, from Landau take the Edesheim direction
Sales: Sieglinde Klein
Opening hours: Mon.–Fri. 8 a.m. to 6 p.m., Sat. 9 a.m. to 5 p.m.

Vineyard area: 13 hectares
Annual production: 200,000 bottles
Top site: Hainfelder Letten
Soil types: Heavy loam
Grape varieties: 20% each of Riesling and Spätburgunder, 15% Weißburgunder, 10% each of Grauburgunder and Müller-Thurgau, 8% each of Gewürztraminer and Kerner, 9% other varieties
Average yield: 89 hl/ha
Best vintages: 1990, 1993, 1996

The Klein estate in Hainfeld is further evidence that a number of the largely unknown estates of the southern Pfalz deserve greater recognition. Gerhard Klein, born in 1953, conceives of his estate as an ambassador of the south, where Mother Nature exudes her happiest expression; where almonds, figs, lemons and sweet chestnuts flourish, there must be room for wine as well. After a rather modest range in 1995, the estate made a comeback in 1996 with a number of ambitious wines. Three of the 1997s are also attractive, but the general quality of the vintage is clearly inferior to that of 1996. Cellarmaster Thomas Fischer cultivates a classic Pfalz, almost Alsatian, style; and all of his wines are well made. But in some cases the "simpler" wines are better than the Spätlese; and the Auslese are often a touch heavy.

1997 Edesheimer Rosengarten
Kerner Spätlese
7.50 DM, 9.5%, ♀ till 2000 **80**

1996 Hainfelder Letten
Gewürztraminer Kabinett trocken
7.50 DM, 12%, ♀ now **82**

1996 Hainfelder Letten
Weißer Burgunder Spätlese trocken
9 DM, 12%, ♀ now **82**

1996 Hainfelder Letten
Weißer Burgunder Auslese halbtrocken
15 DM, 14%, ♀ till 2000 **82**

1996 Hainfelder Letten
Muskateller Spätlese
9.50 DM/0.5 liter, 10%, ♀ till 2000 **82**

1997 Hainfelder Letten
Gewürztraminer Kabinett trocken
7.80 DM, 12%, ♀ now **84**

1996 Edelsheimer Rosengarten
Kerner Spätlese
7.50 DM, 9%, ♀ till 2002 **84**

1996 Hainfelder Letten
Gewürztraminer Auslese
11 DM/0.5 liter, 11.5%, ♀ till 2002 **84**

1997 Hainfelder Letten
Muskateller Spätlese
9.50 DM, 10.5%, ♀ till 2003 **88**

WEINGUT JOHANNES KLEINMANN

Owner: Karl-Heinz Kleinmann
76831 Birkweiler, Hauptstraße 17
Tel. (0 63 45) 35 47, Fax 77 77
Directions: A 65 via B 10, near Landau-Nord
Sales: Hannelore Kleinmann
Opening hous: Mon.–Fri. 8 a.m. to 6 p.m., Sat. 9 a.m. to 4 p.m.

Vineyard area: 10 hectares
Annual production: 85,000 bottles
Top sites: Birkweiler Kastanienbusch, Mandelberg and Rosenberg
Soil types: Red sandstone, weathered porphyry, heavy chalky loam, stony clay
Grape varieties: 20% each of Riesling, Weißburgunder and Sankt Laurent, 15% each of Grauburgunder and Müller-Thurgau, 7% Spätburgunder, 3% other varieties
Average yield: 67 hl/ha
Best vintages: 1994, 1995, 1997

The Kleinmann family founded their cooperage business in 1733 in an attractive house in Birkweiler. Already at the turn of the century the estate had begun to market its wines in bottles rather than casks. Karl-Heinz Kleinmann took over the property from his parents in 1980. In addition to harvesting his own 10 hectares of vineyards, Kleinmann also buys the crops from ten of his neighbors. Over the years this estate has belonged to that small group of producers in the southern Pfalz that merited attention; and its wines often appear on merchants' lists and in restaurants. After an impeccable range from the difficult 1995 vintage, the rather simple 1996s were at best modest, and a robust, sometimes bitter acidity masked their fruit. The opulent 1997s have swung to the other extreme, with often high alcoholic levels diminishing our drinking pleasure.

1997 Birkweiler Mandelberg
Grauer Burgunder Auslese trocken
19.50 DM/0.5 liter, 15.5%, ♀ now **80**

1997 Birkweiler Rosenberg
Weißer Burgunder Spätlese trocken
12.50 DM, 13.5%, ♀ now **82**

1996 Birkweiler Mandelberg
Grauer Burgunder Spätlese trocken
13 DM, 12.5%, ♀ now **82**

1996 Birkweiler Mandelberg
Gewürztraminer Spätlese trocken
14 DM, 13%, ♀ now **82**

1996 Birkweiler Kastanienbusch
Riesling Spätlese trocken
12.50 DM, 12%, ♀ till 2000 **82**

1997 Birkweiler Kastanienbusch
Riesling Spätlese halbtrocken
15 DM, 12%, ♀ till 2000 **82**

——— Red wines ———

1996 Birkweiler Rosenberg
Dornfelder trocken
18.50 DM, 12.5%, ♀ till 2000 **84**

1996 Birkweiler Kastanienbusch
Spätburgunder Spätlese trocken
24 DM, 12.5%, ♀ till 2001 **84**

WEINGUT KNIPSER

Owners: Werner and Volker Knipser
67229 Laumersheim, Johannishof
Tel. (0 62 38) 7 42 and 24 12, Fax 43 77
Directions: A 6 Mannheim–Saarbrücken, exit Grünstadt
Opening hours: Mon.–Fri. 8 a.m. to 6 p.m., Sat. 9 a.m. to 5 p.m. or by appointment

Vineyard area: 20 hectares
Annual production: 120,000 bottles
Top sites: Laumersheimer Mandelberg and Kirschgarten, Großkarlbacher Burgweg and Osterberg
Soil types: Sandy loam, partly with gravel, on a limestone subsoil
Grape varieties: 27% Spätburgunder, 23% Riesling, 10% Scheurebe, 9% Portugieser, 7% Sankt Laurent, 5% each of Weißburgunder, Ehrenfelser and Dornfelder, 9% other varieties
Average yield: 75 hl/ha
Best vintages: 1993, 1996, 1997
Member: VDP, Deutsches Barrique Forum

This estate has been located in Laumersheim since 1877, but it was only after Werner Knipser began to pioneer the use of small oak barrels for the aging of his white wines that it gained nationwide recognition. His Weißburgunder, and above all his red wines, are often among the best in the Pfalz in their respective categories. As the 1996s and 1997s demonstrate, the white wines can nonetheless be a bit of a disappointment. Many of them tasted of slightly unripe fruit, even the Spätlese. Since the weather in 1995 made it almost impossible to produce great red wines, the Knipser range appeared rather lean that year. The 1996 reds, on the other hand, were a revelation! We tasted eleven excellent red wines from that vintage, including two that were among the finest in Germany. It is not surprising that for many wine writers Knipser has become the quintessential red wine producer of the region.

1996 Grauer Burgunder
Tafelwein trocken ***
33 DM, 33%, ♀ till 2001 **86**

1996 Chardonnay
Tafelwein trocken ***
37 DM, 14%, ♀ till 2001 **86**

——— Red wines ———

1996 Großkarlbacher Osterberg
Sankt Laurent trocken
35 DM, 13%, ♀ till 2003 **89**

1996 Großkarlbacher Burgweg
Spätburgunder trocken
35 DM, 13%, ♀ till 2002 **89**

1996 Lemberger
trocken
29 DM, 13%, ♀ till 2002 **89**

1996 Cabernet Franc
trocken
39 DM, 13%, ♀ till 2003 **89**

1996 Großkarlbacher Burgweg
Spätburgunder Spätlese trocken
38 DM, 13.5%, ♀ till 2002 **89**

1996 Cabernet & Merlot
trocken
41 DM, 13%, ♀ till 2005 **91**

1996 Großkarlbacher Burgweg
Spätburgunder Auslese trocken
41 DM, 13.5%, ♀ till 2004 **91**

KNIPSER
1582
1996
Großkarlbacher Osterberg
Riesling Spätlese trocken
11,5% vol
PFALZ
0,75 l
Qualitätswein mit Prädikat - AP-Nr 5 128 029 013 97
Gutsabfüllung Weingut Knipser, Johannishof
D-67229 Laumersheim/Pfalz

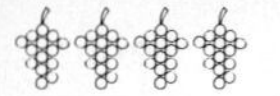

WEINGUT KOEHLER-RUPRECHT

Owner: Bernd Philippi
Manager: Ulrich Meyer
Winemaker: Jan Kux
67169 Kallstadt, Weinstraße 84
Tel. (0 63 22) 18 29, Fax 86 40
Directions: A 61 to A 6 in the direction of Kaiserslautern, exit Grünstadt
Sales: Bernd Philippi
Opening hours: Mon.–Fri. 9 a.m. to 11:30 a.m. and 1 p.m. to 6 p.m.
Tastings by appointment
Restaurant: "Weincastell zum Weißen Roß," closed Mon. and Tue.
Specialties: Palatinate pork belly
History: Owned by the family since 1680
Worth seeing: Old estate buildings with vaulted cellars from 1556

> Vineyard area: 10 hectares
> Annual production: 70,000 bottles
> Top sites: Kallstadter Saumagen, Steinacker and Kronenberg
> Soil types: Limestone detritus, sandy loam, partly with gravel
> Grape varieties: 60% Riesling, 16% Spätburgunder, 7% Weißburgunder, 3% each of Chardonnay, Grauburgunder, Dornfelder and Cabernet Sauvignon, 5% other varieties
> Average yield: 67 hl/ha
> Best vintages: 1993, 1994, 1997
> Member: VDP, Deutsches Barrique Forum

Bernd Philippi certainly belongs to the exceptional growers of the Pfalz. His wines have a perfectly baroque weight, not least because Philippi insists on taking his time making them. Although they can be very puzzling when young, they are very long-lived, developing enormous power and body with age. The 1996s, which spent a year on their fine lees, were very much of this tradition. We had always been great admirers of the mature wines, but had sometimes doubted that the younger wines of recent vintages would develop comparable richness. Although Philippi is still a bit skeptical, the 1997s prove us to be doubting Thomases. This is the finest vintage he has bottled since 1994!

1996 Chardonnay
Tafelwein trocken "Philippi"
30 DM, 13%, ♀ till 2002 **89**

1997 Kallstadter Saumagen
Riesling Spätlese halbtrocken
15 DM, 11.5%, ♀ till 2003 **89**

1996 Chardonnay
Tafelwein trocken "Philippi R"
Not yet for sale, 14%, ♀ till 2004 **91**

1996 Grauer Burgunder
Tafelwein trocken "Philippi R"
Not yet for sale, 14%, ♀ till 2003 **91**

1997 Kallstadter Saumagen
Riesling Spätlese
18 DM, 10%, ♀ till 2007 **91**

1997 Kallstadter Saumagen
Riesling Auslese "R"
Not yet for sale, 11.5%, ♀ till 2010 **94**

1997 Kallstadter Saumagen
Riesling Eiswein
60 DM/0.375 liter, 8%, ♀ till 2012 **94**

1997 Kallstadter Saumagen
Riesling Beerenauslese
45 DM/0.375 liter, 11%, ♀ till 2012 **94**

——— Red wine ———

1996 Spätburgunder
Tafelwein trocken "Philippi RR"
Not yet for sale, 14%, ♀ till 2005 **89**

WEINGUT LEININGERHOF

Owner: Volker Benzinger
67281 Kirchheim, Weinstraße Nord 24
Tel. (0 63 59) 13 39, Fax 23 27
e-mail: Weingut.Leiningerhof.Kirchheim@t-online.de
Directions: A 6, exit Grünstadt, in the direction of Bad Dürkheim on the B 271
Sales: Benzinger family
Opening hours: Mon.–Fri. 8 a.m. to noon and 1 p.m. to 5 p.m. or by appointment

Vineyard area: 13 hectares
Annual production: 100,000 bottles
Top sites: Bockenheimer Schloßberg, Kirchheimer Geißkopf
Soil types: Loess and loam
Grape varieties: 16% Riesling, 13% Portugieser, 11% Grauburgunder, 9% each of Kerner and Scheurebe, 8% Weißburgunder, 7% each of Dornfelder and Müller-Thurgau, 6% each of Spätburgunder and Bacchus, 8% other varieties
Average yield: 80 hl/ha
Best vintages: 1993, 1996, 1997

The imposing baroque mansion in the middle of the old village of Kirchheim is a reminder of the feudal past of the Leiningerhof. The estate's vineyards lie scattered at the foot of the Palatinate woods, where they rise upwards from the plains of the Rhine valley. One doesn't generally have high expectations of wines from such locations; and, indeed, it is not this estate's intent to produce anything exceptional, but rather fresh, fruity wines for everyday consumption. Fermented at low temperatures, reductive in style and marked by their fine lees, they all show the impact of modern cellar techniques. The wines aged in small oak barrels, on the other hand, require more polish. Nonetheless, this is an interesting discovery!

1996 Bockenheimer Schloßberg
Riesling Kabinett trocken
6 DM, 10.5%, ♀ now **80**

1997 Bockenheimer Schloßberg
Riesling Spätlese trocken
9.50 DM, 12%, ♀ till 2000 **80**

1996 Kirchheimer Geißkopf
Grauer Burgunder Spätlese trocken
9.50 DM, 12%, ♀ now **80**

1997 Kirchheimer Kreuz
Gewürztraminer Spätlese trocken
9.50 DM, 12.5%, ♀ now **82**

1996 Kirchheimer Kreuz
Weißer Burgunder Spätlese trocken
9 DM, 12%, ♀ now **82**

1997 Kirchheimer Schwarzerde
Weißer Burgunder Auslese trocken
21.50 DM, 14%, ♀ till 2000 **82**

1997 Bockenheimer Schloßberg
Riesling Spätlese
9.50 DM, 10%, ♀ till 2001 **82**

1996 Kirchheimer Steinacker
Kerner Spätlese trocken
8.50 DM, 12%, ♀ till 2000 **84**

——— Red wines ———

1997 Kirchheimer Steinacker
Portugieser trocken
7.30 DM, 12%, ♀ now **80**

1997 Kirchheimer Steinacker
Dornfelder trocken
7.70 DM, 12.5%, ♀ till 2000 **80**

Pfalz
LEININGERHOF
Kirchheim an der Weinstrasse
Grauer Burgunder
Spätlese trocken
1996
Kirchheimer Geißkopf
Qualitätswein mit Prädikat - A. P. Nr. 5 125 107 10 97
0,75 l Gutsabfüllung Weingut Leiningerhof, D-67281 Kirchheim, Tel. 0 63 59/13 39 12% vol

WEINGUT W. LERGENMÜLLER SÖHNE

Owner: Lergenmüller family
Winemaker: Jürgen Lergenmüller
76835 Hainfeld, Weinstraße 16
Tel. (0 63 41) 9 63 33, Fax (0 63 23) 6 07 09
Directions: A 65, exit Landau-Nord or Edenkoben
Sales: Lergenmüller family
Opening hours: By appointment
Restaurant: 5 p.m. to 11 p.m. except Thur.

Vineyard area: 65 hectares
Annual production: 400,000 bottles
Top sites: Hainfelder Kapelle and Letten, Godramsteiner Münzberg
Soil types: Heavy chalky loam and loess
Grape varieties: 20% Riesling, 10% each of Müller-Thurgau and Spätburgunder, 9% each of Portugieser and Dornfelder, 7% each of Weißburgunder and Grauburgunder, 5% each of Silvaner, Kerner and Scheurebe, 4% each of Sankt Laurent and Chardonnay, 5% other varieties
Average yield: 70 hl/ha
Best vintages: 1992, 1993, 1996

This once rising star from the southern Pfalz has achieved acclaim for its unexpectedly dense red wines; and the very dark-colored reds are, in fact, generally better than the overcrafted whites. Prolonged fermentation on the skins, combined with an immense deployment of oak, often results in massive red wines that are overdone in many respects. The 1996 were again rather straightforward, but of higher quality than in the past. The 1997 whites are also attractive; even the red wines appear to be gaining character and are no longer simply one-dimensional explosions.

1996 Gewürztraminer
Spätlese trocken
12.50 DM, 12.5%, 🍷 now **80**

1997 Riesling
Kabinett halbtrocken "Selektion"
12.50 DM, 10%, 🍷 now **80**

1996 Chardonnay
Spätlese trocken
19.80 DM, 13%, 🍷 now **82**

1997 Grauer Burgunder
Spätlese trocken "Selektion"
16.50 DM, 13%, 🍷 now **82**

1997 Gewürztraminer
Spätlese trocken "Selektion"
12.50 DM, 13%, 🍷 now **82**

1997 Chardonnay
Spätlese trocken "Selektion"
23 DM, 13%, 🍷 till 2000 **84**

Red wines

1996 Spätburgunder
trocken "Angiolino"
21 DM, 13%, 🍷 now **82**

1996 "Selektion"
trocken
29.50 DM, 13%, 🍷 till 2000 **84**

1996 "Philipp L"
trocken
54 DM, 13.5%, 🍷 till 2001 **86**

1996 Spätburgunder
Spätlese trocken "Selektion"
32 DM, 14%, 🍷 till 2001 **86**

WEINGUT LINGENFELDER

Owners: Hermann and Rainer-Karl Lingenfelder
Winemaker: Rainer-Karl Lingenfelder
67229 Großkarlbach, Hauptstraße 27
Tel. (0 62 38) 7 54, Fax 10 96
Directions: A 61 via A 6, in the direction of Kaiserslautern, exit Grünstadt
Opening hours: Mon.–Sat. 8 a.m. to 7 p.m.

Vineyard area: 15 hectares
Annual production: 110,000 bottles
Top sites: Freinsheimer Goldberg and Musikantenbuckel, Großkarlbacher Osterberg and Burgweg
Soil types: Limestone, loess, loam and sand
Grape varieties: 40% Riesling, 20% Spätburgunder, 10% each of Müller-Thurgau and Scheurebe, 8% Dornfelder, 5% each of Silvaner and Kerner, 2% Portugieser
Average yield: 85 hl/ha
Best vintages: 1990, 1993, 1994

After Rainer-Karl Lingenfelder returned home from years of working in Australia, New Zealand and France, this estate quickly rose from obscurity, as did the relatively unknown village of Großkarlbach where he was born. A clever winemaker, Rainer is keen on Riesling and – with increasing enthusiasm – Scheurebe. In 1994 the grapes were not only picked at the highest sugar levels ever attained in the estate's history, but Lingenfelder also produced an abundance of appealing wines. The 1995s, on the other hand, left much to be desired. The 1996 and 1997 ranges were again far from uniform: the Rieslings lacked polish and the Scheurebe was a bit rustic. This estate is certainly capable of making better wines.

1996 Freinsheimer Musikantenbuckel
Riesling Kabinett trocken
9 DM, 12%, 🍷 now **80**

1996 Freinsheimer Musikantenbuckel
Riesling Kabinett halbtrocken
9 DM, 11%, 🍷 now **80**

1996 Freinsheimer Goldberg
Riesling Spätlese trocken
10.50 DM, 12.5%, 🍷 now **82**

1996 Freinsheimer Musikantenbuckel
Scheurebe Spätlese trocken
12 DM, 13.5%, 🍷 now **84**

1996 Freinsheimer Goldberg
Riesling Auslese trocken
15 DM, 13%, 🍷 now **84**

1996 Großkarlbacher Osterberg
Riesling Spätlese halbtrocken
10.50 DM, 11.5%, 🍷 till 2000 **84**

1996 Freinsheimer Musikantenbuckel
Scheurebe Spätlese
12 DM, 12%, 🍷 till 2000 **86**

——— Red wine ———

1996 Großkarlbacher Burgweg
Spätburgunder Weißherbst trocken
10.50 DM, 13%, 🍷 now **82**

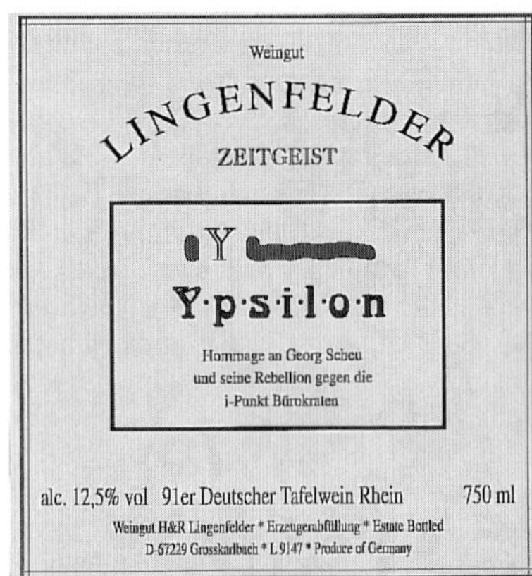

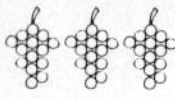

WEINGUT LUCASHOF – PFARRWEINGUT

Owner: Klaus Lucas
Manager: Hans Lucas
67147 Forst, Wiesenweg 1a
Tel. (0 63 26) 3 36, Fax 57 94
Directions: On the wine route B 271, between Neustadt and Bad Dürkheim
Sales: Christine Lucas
Opening hours: Mon.–Fri. 8 a.m. to noon and 1 p.m. to 7 p.m., Sat. 8 a.m. to 4 p.m. Sun. by appointment

Vineyard area: 14 hectares
Annual production: 110,000 bottles
Top sites: Forster Ungeheuer, Pechstein, Musenhang and Stift, Deidesheimer Herrgottsacker
Soil types: Loess, loam and sand
Grape varieties: 90% Riesling, 10% other varieties
Average yield: 74 hl/ha
Best vintages: 1993, 1994, 1996

Klaus Lucas and his wife, Christine, who was born into the Weis family of the Sankt Urbanshof estate on the Mosel, have gradually expanded their property in Forst to 14 hectares; and for years they have produced attractive Rieslings. The positive evolution of the estate continued even in the difficult 1995 vintage. The 1996 range presented an abundance of very ripe fruit. Indeed, the wines seemed almost plump and were not particularly marked by the tell-tale acidity of the vintage. A bit more liveliness would have been desirable. The 1997s have a touch less vibrant character, but even the liter bottlings are appealing. This estate is making wines of very sound quality – all the while cultivating its own distinctive style. Despite this track record, Lucashof is still relatively unknown. And given the fact that the wines are sold at such modest prices, this is a bargain hunter's dream.

1997 Forster Ungeheuer
Riesling Spätlese trocken
13.50 DM, 12%, ♀ till 2001 **86**

1996 Forster Pechstein
Riesling Spätlese trocken
12.50 DM, 12%, ♀ now **86**

1996 Forster Pechstein
Riesling Auslese trocken
16 DM, 12.5%, ♀ till 2000 **86**

1996 Forster Ungeheuer
Riesling Spätlese halbtrocken
13 DM, 11%, ♀ till 2000 **86**

1997 Forster Pechstein
Riesling Spätlese trocken
18 DM, 12%, ♀ till 2002 **88**

1996 Forster Ungeheuer
Riesling Spätlese trocken
12.50 DM, 12%, ♀ till 2000 **88**

1996 Forster Ungeheuer
Riesling Spätlese
11 DM, 10.5%, ♀ till 2002 **88**

1997 Forster Stift
Riesling Auslese
19 DM, 9%, ♀ till 2005 **89**

1996 Forster Stift
Riesling Eiswein
60 DM/0.375 liter, 10%, ♀ till 2008 **92**

WEINGUT HERBERT MESSMER

Owner: Meßmer family
Winemaker: Gregor Meßmer
76835 Burrweiler, Gaisbergstraße 132
Tel. (0 63 45) 27 70, Fax 79 17
Directions: A 65, exit Edenkoben, via Edesheim and Hainfeld
Sales: Meßmer family
Opening hours: Mon.–Fri. 9 a.m. to 11:30 a.m. and 1:30 p.m. to 5 p.m.
Sat. 9 a.m. to 4 p.m.

Vineyard area: 22 hectares
Annual production: 180,000 bottles
Top sites: Burrweiler Schäwer, Schloßgarten and Altenforst
Soil types: Slate, sandy loam, loess, red sandstone and heavy chalky clay and loam
Grape varieties: 45% Riesling, 13% Spätburgunder, 10% Weißburgunder, 6% Sankt Laurent, 5% Grauburgunder, 21% other varieties
Average yield: 65 hl/ha
Best vintages: 1990, 1992, 1993
Member: VDP

In 1960 Herbert Meßmer bought this estate in the idyllic village of Burrweiler. The vineyards were replanted in 1974 and are now at the peak of their maturity. Among them is the Burrweiler Schäwer, the only vineyard with slate soils in the Pfalz. Here, as elsewhere, Meßmer cultivates his sites organically. His ambitious son Gregor is now responsible for the wines; and since 1990 he has abandoned the use of cultivated yeasts and ferments his wines at low temperatures in stainless steel tanks. In the early 1990s he was on a winning streak. In a fine vintage such as 1996, though, we expected a touch more from this estate. And the white Burgundian varieties from 1997 are slightly sweet and laced with carbon dioxide. The red wines from 1995 and 1996 are equally modest. This estate could probably be producing better wines.

1997 Burrweiler Schloßgarten
Weißer Burgunder Spätlese trocken "S"
19.50 DM, 13.5%, ♀ till 2000 **86**

1996 Burrweiler Schloßgarten
Weißer Burgunder Spätlese trocken "Selection"
19 DM, 13%, ♀ till 2000 **86**

1996 Burrweiler Schloßgarten
Grauer Burgunder Spätlese trocken "Selection"
19 DM, 13%, ♀ now **86**

1996 Burrweiler Schäwer
Riesling Spätlese trocken "Selection"
17 DM, 11.5%, ♀ now **86**

1997 Burrweiler Schloßgarten
Grauer Burgunder Spätlese trocken "S"
19 DM, 14%, ♀ till 2001 **88**

1997 Burrweiler Schloßgarten
Muskateller Kabinett trocken
12 DM, 13%, ♀ now **89**

——— Red wines ———

1996 Burrweiler Schloßgarten
Spätburgunder trocken "S"
32 DM, 13%, ♀ till 2000 **86**

1995 Burrweiler Schloßgarten
Spätburgunder trocken "Selection"
30 DM, 13%, ♀ now **86**

WEINGUT THEO MINGES

Owner: Theo Minges
76835 Flemlingen, Bachstraße 11
Tel. (0 63 23) 9 33 50
Directions: A 65, exit Landau-Nord
Sales: Theo Minges
Opening hours: Mon.–Sat. 9 a.m. to 6 p.m.
Worth seeing: Cellar from the 15th century

Vineyard area: 14 hectares
Annual production: 100,000 bottles
Top sites: Gleisweiler Hölle, Flemlinger Vogelsprung
Soil types: Limestone, heavy chalky loam, loess and loam
Grape varieties: 30% Riesling, 13% Dornfelder, 11% Grauer Burgunder, 10% each of Spätburgunder and Scheurebe, 5% Kerner, 21% other varieties
Average yield: 73 hl/ha
Best vintages: 1992, 1993, 1997

Until the 16th century this property belonged to the Counts von der Layen, but for the past six generations the Minges family have managed the estate. Despite the fact that it has received seven major state prizes, it was only four years ago that we were given the address by an attentive reader. The wines from the difficult 1995 vintage proved that Theo Minges understands his trade; a fact that was confirmed again by the 1996 and 1997 ranges. Nothing here is modern, nothing an imitation. The wines are in the finest sense of the word "old-fashioned." Even the red wines, although some might dismiss them as plain or dull, are actually quite appealing and provide an interesting introduction to the Pfalz.

1997 Flemlinger Bischofskreuz
Grauer Burgunder Kabinett trocken
8 DM, 12%, 🍷 now **80**

1997 Flemlinger Zechpeter
Riesling Kabinett
7.20 DM, 9%, 🍷 now **80**

1997 Gleisweiler Hölle
Riesling Kabinett trocken
8 DM, 11.5%, 🍷 now **82**

1997 Flemlinger Bischofskreuz
Grauer Burgunder Spätlese trocken
10.40 DM, 13%, 🍷 now **82**

1996 Gleisweiler Hölle
Riesling Spätlese trocken
10 DM, 11%, 🍷 till 2000 **82**

1996 Flemlinger Bischofskreuz
Grauer Burgunder Spätlese trocken
10 DM, 13.5%, 🍷 now **82**

1996 Gleisweiler Hölle
Riesling Spätlese
10 DM, 9.5%, 🍷 till 2002 **82**

1997 Gleisweiler Hölle
Riesling Spätlese trocken
10.40 DM, 12.5%, 🍷 till 2000 **84**

1997 Flemlinger Herrenbuckel
Grauer Burgunder Auslese trocken
20 DM, 15%, 🍷 till 2000 **84**

1996 Flemlinger Herrenbuckel
Grauer Burgunder Auslese trocken
20 DM/0.5 liter, 14%, 🍷 till 2000 **84**

Theo Minges
Pfalz

1996er Gleisweiler Hölle
Riesling trocken
Qualitätswein mit Prädikat Spätlese - A. P. Nr. 5025 066 21 97
Weingut Theo Minges. D-76835 Flemlingen
11,0 % vol. Erzeugerabfüllung 750 ml e

WEINGUT GEORG MOSBACHER

Owner: Mosbacher family
General Manager: Jürgen Düringer
Winemaker: Richard Mosbacher
67147 Forst, Weinstraße 27
Tel. (0 63 26) 3 29, Fax 67 74
Directions: On the wine route B 271, between Neustadt and Bad Dürkheim
Sales: Sabine Mosbacher-Düringer
Opening hours: Mon.–Fri. 8 a.m. to noon and 1:30 p.m. to 6 p.m.
Sat. 9 a.m. to 1 p.m.
Worth seeing: Vaulted sandstone cellars under the Art Nouveau estate buildings

Vineyard area: 11.3 hectares
Annual production: 100,000 bottles
Top sites: Forster Ungeheuer, Freundstück, Pechstein and Musenhang, Deidesheimer Mäushöhle
Soil types: Sandy loam, weathered limestone, partly with basalt and clay
Grape varieties: 84% Riesling, 16% other varieties
Average yield: 68 hl/ha
Best vintages: 1994, 1996, 1997
Member: VDP

Richard Mosbacher is an unassuming man. Despite the numerous prizes he has won, he seldom makes much of a fuss about either himself or his wines. They, in any case, speak for themselves: limpid, pure Rieslings, just as we like to drink them! After completing her studies at Geisenheim, his daughter Sabine has returned to the estate with her husband, Jürgen Düringer, an experienced winemaker from Ihringen in Baden. Together with her father they have taken this estate to the front ranks of the Pfalz. The 1996 range was perfectly stunning, even the liter bottling was excellent. All of the wines had enormous vigor. They may not have had the weight and body of the wines from other estates, but they made up for it with immensely delicate fruit. The 1997s are also very good, but the rather light style of the vintage was certainly not easy for a producer who excels in elegance.

1996 Forster Pechstein
Riesling Spätlese trocken
16 DM, 12.5%, ♀ till 2000 **89**

1996 Forster Ungeheuer
Riesling Spätlese trocken
18 DM, 13%, ♀ till 2003 **89**

1997 Forster Ungeheuer
Riesling Spätlese trocken
"Erstes Gewächs"
27 DM, 12.5%, ♀ till 2003 **89**

1996 Forster Elster
Riesling Spätlese
14 DM, 10.5%, ♀ till 2004 **89**

1996 Deidesheimer Mäushöhle
Riesling Spätlese trocken
14.50 DM, 12.5%, ♀ till 2003 **90**

1996 Forster Ungeheuer
Riesling Spätlese trocken ***
27 DM, 13%, ♀ till 2006 **90**

1997 Forster Ungeheuer
Riesling Spätlese
26 DM, 11%, ♀ till 2004 **91**

1997 Forster Pechstein
Riesling Auslese
28 DM/0.5 liter, 10%, ♀ till 2007 **92**

1996 Forster Ungeheuer
Riesling Auslese
27 DM, 12%, ♀ till 2006 **92**

1996 Forster Freundstück
Riesling Eiswein
80 DM/0.375 liter, 9%, ♀ till 2016 **95**

WEINGUT
GEORG MOSBACHER
FORST
PFALZ
1996er Forster Ungeheuer
Riesling Spätlese trocken
0,75 l
13% vol
Produce of Germany

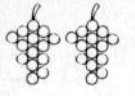

WEINGUT EUGEN MÜLLER

Owner: Kurt Müller
Winemaker: Jürgen Meißner
67147 Forst, Weinstraße 34a
Tel. (0 63 26) 3 30, Fax 68 02
e-mail:
weingut.eugen.müller@t-online.de
Directions: On the wine route, between Neustadt and Bad Dürkheim
Sales: Elisabeth, Kurt and Stefan Müller
Opening hours: Mon.–Fri. 8 a.m. to noon and 1:30 p.m. to 6 p.m.
Sat. 9 a.m. to 4 p.m.
Sun. by appointment

Vineyard area: 17.8 hectares
Annual production: 160,000 bottles
Top sites: Forster Kirchenstück, Jesuitengarten, Ungeheuer, Pechstein and Musenhang
Soil types: Calcareous loam, sandstone detritus, partly with basalt and clay
Grape varieties: 76% Riesling, 10% Grauer and Weißer Burgunder, 14% red varieties
Average yield: 74 hl/ha
Best vintages: 1994, 1996, 1997

"It's better to care about quality in the vineyard than to mount a rescue operation in the cellar." This is the maxim of the prudent Kurt Müller, whose wines we first tasted a few years ago. In 1994 he produced a very wide array of outstanding wines; and despite poor conditions, even the 1995 vintage was a success. Due to a late harvest and the aging of the young wines on their lees, Kurt Müller was also able to capture the fruity acidic structure of the 1996 vintage while retaining enormous extract. The quality approached that of the excellent 1994s. Even though there were a number of appealing wines, the 1997s were not nearly as successful.

1997 Forster Ungeheuer
Riesling Spätlese trocken
11.80 DM, 12%, ♀ till 2000 **82**

1996 Forster Kirchenstück
Riesling Spätlese trocken
14 DM, 13%, ♀ now **82**

1997 Forster Kirchenstück
Riesling Auslese trocken
17.90 DM/0.5 liter, 13%, ♀ till 2000 **84**

1996 Forster Kirchenstück
Riesling Auslese
18 DM/0.5 liter, 10.5%, ♀ till 2006 **84**

1996 Forster Kirchenstück
Riesling Auslese trocken
18 DM/0.5 liter, 13.5%, ♀ till 2000 **86**

1996 Forster Ungeheuer
Riesling Spätlese
11 DM, 10.5%, ♀ till 2003 **86**

1997 Forster Kirchenstück
Riesling Auslese
16.90 DM/0.5 liter, 10%, ♀ till 2002 **86**

1996 Forster Stift
Riesling Eiswein
43 DM/0.375 liter, 8.5%, ♀ till 2005 **88**

1996 Forster Stift
Riesling Eiswein
43 DM/0.375 liter, 9%, ♀ till 2015 **92**

WEINGUT HERBERT MÜLLER ERBEN

Owner: Ulrich Müller
Winemaker: Ulrich Müller
67433 Neustadt-Haardt,
Mandelring 169
Tel. (0 63 21) 6 60 67, Fax 6 07 85
Directions: Haardt is a suburb on the edge of Neustadt
Sales: Ralf Müller
Opening hours: Mon.–Fri. 8 a.m. to 6 p.m., Sat. 8 a.m. to 3 p.m. or by appointment

Vineyard area: 9.25 hectares
Annual production: 95,000 bottles
Top sites: Haardter Herzog and Herrenletten
Soil types: Sandy loam, heavy chalky loam with clay
Grape varieties: 43% Riesling, 13% each of Spätburgunder and Portugieser, 8% Kerner, 7% Scheurebe, 16% other varieties
Average yield: 73 hl/ha
Best vintages: 1990, 1996, 1997

The 17th-century estate buildings with their historic vaulted cellars have, in recent years, been not only renovated but also expanded, providing the Müller family with perfect conditions for professional winemaking. The vineyards are managed organically; the cellar is modern in style. Both Ulrich Müller as well as his brother Ralf, who worked for the Reichsrat von Buhl estate until 1995, studied their craft at Geisenheim. Their wines were perhaps a touch Alsatian in style, but a tart acidic structure conserved the freshness of their 1996 range. The 1997s are even better! The best is certainly yet to come.

1996 Haardter Bürgergarten
Riesling halbtrocken
6.75 DM/1.0 liter, 10.5%, ♀ now **80**

1996 Haardter Herzog
Riesling Spätlese trocken
12 DM, 12%, ♀ now **82**

1997 Haardter Herzog
Riesling Kabinett halbtrocken
8.50 DM, 11%, ♀ now **82**

1996 Haardter Herzog
Riesling Kabinett halbtrocken
8.50 DM, 12%, ♀ till 2000 **82**

1996 Haardter Herrenletten
Riesling Spätlese
10 DM, 11%, ♀ till 2002 **82**

1997 Haardter Herrenletten
Riesling Kabinett trocken
8.50 DM, 11.5%, ♀ now **84**

1997 Haardter Herzog
Riesling Spätlese trocken
11.50 DM, 12%, ♀ till 2000 **84**

1997 Haardter Herzog
Chardonnay Spätlese trocken
13.50 DM, 12.5%, ♀ till 2000 **84**

1996 Haardter Herzog
Riesling Spätlese halbtrocken
13 DM, 12%, ♀ till 2002 **84**

1997 Haardter Herzog
Scheurebe Auslese
20 DM/0.5 liter, 11.5%, ♀ till 2003 **86**

1996
RIESLING
TROCKEN
Müller
Haardter Mandelring A.P.Nr. 5 174 123 01 97 Qualitätswein b.A.
Weingut Herbert Müller Erben D-67433 Neustadt-Haardt Gutsabfüllung
11,5% vol Pfalz 1,0l

WEINGUT MÜLLER-CATOIR

Owner: Jakob Heinrich Catoir
General Manager: Hans-Günter Schwarz
67433 Haardt, Mandelring 25
Tel. (0 63 21) 28 15, Fax 48 00 14
Directions: A 65, exit Neustadt-Lambrecht, follow signs to Haardt
Sales: Ms. Schöttinger
Opening hours: Mon.–Fri. 8 a.m. to noon and 1 p.m. to 5 p.m.
History: Wine estate dates back to 1744
Worth seeing: 19th-century tasting room

Vineyard area: 20 hectares
Annual production: 135,000 bottles
Top sites: Haardter Herrenletten, Bürgergarten and Herzog, Gimmeldinger Mandelgarten, Mußbacher Eselshaut
Soil types: Loamy gravel, clay
Grape varieties: 60% Riesling, 9% Scheurebe, 8% each of Weißburgunder and Rieslaner, 4% each of Muskateller and Grauburgunder, 7% other varieties
Average yield: 55 hl/ha
Best vintages: 1993, 1996, 1997

For many years this picturesquely situated property at the foot of the Haardt mountains was virtually alone at the peak of quality in the Pfalz. Underpinning this privileged position was the reserved but uncompromising owner, Jakob Heinrich Catoir, and his ambitious cellarmaster, Hans-Günter Schwarz. Schwarz regularly conjures up magical wines, both from Weißburgunder and Grauburgunder as well as from Rieslaner and Muskateller. The uncannily spicy Rieslings are a story of their own. It is not surprising that Schwarz became a role model for a whole generation of young growers in the Pfalz. After problems with hail in 1994 and 1995, this estate made a spectular comeback with outstanding ranges from both the 1996 and 1997 vintages. All of the wines have tremendous extract and weight. This is tradition at its finest! Unfortunately for the average consumer, the wines are already sold out.

1997 Haardter Bürgergarten
Muskateller Kabinett trocken
17 DM, 12%, ♀ till 2000 **89**

1996 Haardter Herrenletten
Riesling Spätlese trocken
19 DM, 12.5%, ♀ till 2003 **90**

1997 Haardter Herrenletten
Riesling Spätlese
21 DM, 11%, ♀ till 2005 **91**

1996 Haardter Herzog
Riesling Spätlese
21 DM, 10%, ♀ till 2006 **91**

1997 Haardter Bürgergarten
Riesling Auslese
32 DM, 10%, ♀ till 2007 **94**

1996 Haardter Bürgergarten
Rieslaner Auslese
25 DM/0.375 liter, 8.5%, ♀ till 2010 **94**

1997 Mußbacher Eselshaut
Rieslaner Auslese
26 DM/0.375 liter, 9%, ♀ till 2007 **95**

1996 Haardter Bürgergarten
Riesling Eiswein
70 DM/0.375 liter, 10%, ♀ till 2016 **95**

1996 Haardter Mandelring
Scheurebe Eiswein
80 DM/0.375 liter, 9.5%, ♀ till 2013 **96**

WEINGUT MÜNZBERG

Owners: Lothar Keßler and sons
Winemakers: Gunter and Rainer Keßler
76829 Landau-Godramstein
Tel. (0 63 41) 6 09 35, Fax 6 42 10
Directions: A 65, exit Landau-Nord, on B 10 in the direction of Pirmasens, exit Godramstein
Sales: Keßler family
Opening hours: Mon.–Fri. 8 a.m. to noon and 1:30 p.m. to 6 p.m.
Sat. 9 a.m. to 4 p.m., by appointment

Vineyard area: 12 hectares
Annual production: 100,000 bottles
Top site: Godramsteiner Münzberg
Soil types: Loess and loam, clay and sand over fossil limestone
Grape varieties: 25% Weißburgunder, 20% Riesling, 15% Spätburgunder, 10% each of Müller-Thurgau, Dornfelder and Silvaner, 6% Grauburgunder, 4% other varieties
Average yield: 83 hl/ha
Best vintages: 1994, 1996, 1997

A few years ago Lothar Keßler, who first began to market his bottled wines in the late 1970s, moved this once small winery from the middle of Godramstein to the slopes of the Münzberg vineyard just outside the village. His two sons Günter and Rainer have now joined the family business and given the style of their wines an increasingly recognizable signature; as a rule the Burgundian varieties are better than the other wines. The Keßlers are also on a learning curve in their work with small oak barrels and have turned out a robust performance with both the fine 1996 and excellent 1997 vintages. Although the lesser wines are sometimes lean and tart, all of them are appealing and honest in style. By abandoning individual vineyard designations and decreasing the number of grape varieties, the estate has also brought clarity into its portfolio.

1996 Grauer Burgunder
Kabinett trocken
8 DM, 11%, ♀ now **84**

1997 Riesling
Spätlese trocken
13 DM, 12%, ♀ till 2000 **84**

1995 Chardonnay
Tafelwein trocken
20 DM, 12.5%, ♀ now **86**

1997 Gewürztraminer
Spätlese trocken
14 DM, 12.5%, ♀ till 2001 **86**

1997 Riesling
Auslese trocken
19 DM, 13%, ♀ till 2001 **86**

1996 Weißer Burgunder
Auslese trocken
18 DM, 13%, ♀ now **86**

1997 Weißer Burgunder
Spätlese trocken
12 DM, 12.5%, ♀ till 2002 **88**

1997 Chardonnay
Spätlese trocken "Selektion"
20 DM, 13%, ♀ till 2002 **89**

1997 Weißer Burgunder
Auslese trocken
18 DM, 13.5%, ♀ till 2002 **89**

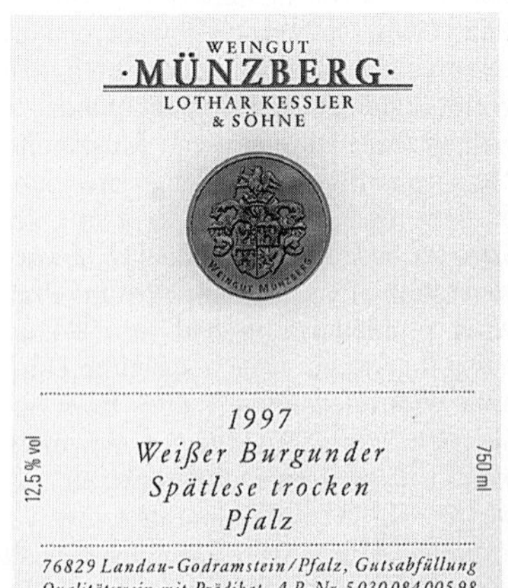

WEINGUT
·MÜNZBERG·
LOTHAR KESSLER
& SÖHNE
1997
Weißer Burgunder
Spätlese trocken
Pfalz
12,5 % vol
750 ml
76829 Landau-Godramstein/Pfalz, Gutsabfüllung
Qualitätswein mit Prädikat, A.P.-Nr. 5 030 084 005 98

WEINGUT NECKERAUER

Owner: Klaus Neckerauer
Winemaker: Arnd Neckerauer
67256 Weisenheim am Sand,
Ritter-von-Geißler-Straße 9
Tel. (0 63 53) 80 59, Fax 66 99
Directions: A 61 to A 6, in the direction of Kaiserslautern, exit Grünstadt
Sales: Klaus and Arnd Neckerauer
Opening hours: Mon.–Fri. 8 a.m. to 7 p.m., Sat. 8 a.m. to 6 p.m. or by appointment

Vineyard area: 16 hectares
Annual production: 120,000 bottles
Top sites: Weisenheimer Hahnen, Halde and Hasenzeile
Soil types: Sandy loam
Grape varieties: 39% Riesling, 21% Portugieser, 10% Müller-Thurgau, 4% each of Kerner, Grauburgunder and Siegerrebe, 18% other varieties
Average yield: 55 hl/ha
Best vintages: 1989, 1992

Weisenheim am Sand is situated in the northern Pfalz; and the Neckerauer family, who began marketing their bottled wines about 50 years ago, have been settled here for over 500 years. Since Robert Parker Jr. began praising their wines, the estate has recorded growing demand from both the States and England. In Germany the Neckerauer's wines remain essentially unknown. This is not difficult to understand, as their finest wines are only seldom of the highest quality. In the course of 1997 the estate sold a portion of its vineyards, "so that we can do a better job of managing the 16 hectares that remain." The most appealing wines from the 1996 vintage were the fruity Spätlese and Auslese made from Scheurebe. The Rieslings were rather strange, and the dry wines, as a whole, tasted tart, malty and bittersweet. Nonetheless, the 1996 range was clearly superior to that of the previous vintage. The 1997s, on the other hand, were less successful.

1996 Weisenheimer Halde
Riesling Spätlese trocken
13.25 DM, 13%, ♀ till 2000 **80**

1997 Weisenheimer Altenberg
Gewürztraminer Spätlese halbtrocken
12.70 DM, 13.5%, ♀ now **80**

1997 Weisenheimer Hasenzeile
Riesling Auslese
16.20 DM/0.5 liter, 11%, ♀ now **80**

1996 Weisenheimer Hahnen
Riesling Spätlese halbtrocken
11.75 DM, 11.5%, ♀ till 2002 **82**

1996 Weisenheimer Halde
Riesling Kabinett
8 DM, 10%, ♀ till 2000 **82**

1996 Weisenheimer Hasenzeile
Scheurebe Spätlese
10.75 DM, 10.5%, ♀ till 2000 **84**

1994 Weisenheimer Rosenbühl
Gewürztraminer Beerenauslese
39.20 DM/0.5 liter, 9.5%, ♀ till 2000 **84**

1996 Weisenheimer Goldberg
Scheurebe Auslese
16.25 DM, 11.5%, ♀ till 2003 **86**

1994 Dirmsteiner Schwarzerde
Müller-Thurgau Trockenbeerenauslese
66.20 DM/0.375 liter, 6%, ♀ till 2003 **88**

WEINGUT PFEFFINGEN – FUHRMANN-EYMAEL

Owner: Doris Eymael
Winemaker: Rainer Gabel
67098 Bad Dürkheim,
Pfeffingen an der Weinstraße
Tel. (0 63 22) 86 07, Fax 86 03
Directions: On the wine route between Bad Dürkheim and Ungstein
Sales: Doris and Karl Fuhrmann
Opening hours: Mon.–Fri. 7 a.m. to 7 p.m., Sat. 9 a.m. to 5 p.m.
Sun. 9 a.m. to noon
Worth seeing: Stone sarcophagus in the courtyard

Vineyard area: 10.5 hectares
Annual production: 90,000 bottles
Top sites: Ungsteiner Herrenberg, Weilberg and Honigsäckel
Soil types: Heavy chalky loam with loess, clay and sand
Grape varieties: 67% Riesling, 12% Scheurebe, 7% Spätburgunder, 6% Gewürztraminer, 4% Müller-Thurgau, 2% each of Silvaner and Weißburgunder
Average yield: 71 hl/ha
Best vintages: 1990, 1996, 1997
Member: VDP

A delightful courtyard in the middle of the vineyards of Pfeffingen has housed for years one of the model properties of the Pfalz. This was and is the lifelong passion of Karl Fuhrmann, whose daughter Doris manages the estate today. The excellent 1990 vintage was the last great work of art for the estate. Forced to gradually replant their vineyards, the Fuhrmann family found it difficult to maintain their quality aspirations. The vines are now again about ten years old. The 1996 range was the best that we had tasted since 1990. The 1997s are perhaps even a touch better. All of the wines show both depth of fruit and spice, and are at the same time crisp, delicate and almost animated. This estate is on its way back into the big leagues.

1997 Ungsteiner Herrenberg
Scheurebe Spätlese
13 DM, 10.5%, 🍷 till 2001 **88**

1997 Ungsteiner Herrenberg
Chardonnay Spätlese trocken
16 DM, 12.5%, 🍷 till 2001 **89**

1996 Ungsteiner Herrenberg
Riesling Spätlese trocken
16 DM, 12.5%, 🍷 till 2003 **89**

1997 Ungsteiner Herrenberg
Riesling Spätlese halbtrocken
14 DM, 13%, 🍷 till 2003 **89**

1996 Ungsteiner Herrenberg
Riesling Spätlese halbtrocken
12 DM, 12%, 🍷 till 2003 **89**

1997 Ungsteiner Herrenberg
Riesling Spätlese
14 DM, 11.5%, 🍷 till 2005 **89**

1996 Ungsteiner Herrenberg
Riesling Spätlese
12 DM, 12%, 🍷 till 2006 **89**

1997 Ungsteiner Weilberg
Riesling Auslese
25 DM/0.375 liter, 11%, 🍷 till 2007 **89**

1996 Ungsteiner Weilberg
Riesling Auslese
23 DM, 10.5%, 🍷 till 2010 **91**

1996 Ungsteiner Herrenberg
Scheurebe Beerenauslese
30 DM/0.375 liter, 10%, 🍷 till 2012 **91**

WEINGUT ÖKONOMIERAT REBHOLZ

Owner: Hansjörg Rebholz
76833 Siebeldingen, Weinstraße 54
Tel. (0 63 45) 34 39, Fax 79 54
Directions: A 65, exit Landau-Nord, then B 10 to Siebeldingen
Sales: Rebholz family
Opening hours: Mon.–Sun. 9 a.m. to noon and 2 p.m. to 6 p.m. or by appointment
History: Wine estate is over 300 years old

Vineyard area: 10 hectares
Annual production: 70,000 bottles
Top sites: Birkweiler Kastanienbusch, Siebeldinger im Sonnenschein, Godramsteiner Münzberg
Soil types: Loess-loam, fossil limestone, gravel, reddish soil
Grape varieties: 43% Riesling, 22% Spätburgunder, 7% each of Weißburgunder, Grauburgunder and Muskateller, 14% other varieties
Average yield: 63 hl/ha
Best vintages: 1994, 1996, 1997
Member: VDP

While the southern Pfalz as a whole still focuses on sweeter wines, this estate has long been one of the few champions of completely dry wines. The friendly Hansjörg Rebholz has followed the example established by his father and grandfather and continues to produce highly individual, often uncompromising wines. In their youth they sometimes seem edgy and awkward, but generally develop astonishingly well. Lean and reductive in style, the wines often exhibit a powerful acidity. It is thus understandable that some of the wines are aged in cask and released only when fully mature. In 1996 Rebholz was right on the mark. The fruit extract provided many of the wines with what appeared to be a touch of sweetness; others were almost Alsatian in style. Although much easier to fathom in their youth, the 1997s are of similar quality.

1997 Siebeldinger Rosenberg
Grauer Burgunder Spätlese trocken
16 DM, 13%, 🍷 till 2001 — **88**

1997 Birkweiler Kastanienbusch
Riesling Kabinett
12 DM, 8.5%, 🍷 till 2003 — **88**

1997 Siebeldinger im Sonnenschein
Riesling Spätlese trocken
16.50 DM, 12%, 🍷 till 2002 — **89**

1997 Godramsteiner Münzberg
Muskateller Spätlese trocken
19 DM, 14%, 🍷 till 2002 — **89**

1996 Siebeldinger im Sonnenschein
Riesling Spätlese trocken
16 DM, 12%, 🍷 till 2003 — **89**

1996 Godramsteiner Münzberg
Muskateller Spätlese trocken
17.50 DM, 14%, 🍷 till 2003 — **89**

1996 Weißer Burgunder
Spätlese trocken "R"
27 DM, 15%, 🍷 till 2002 — **89**

1996 Chardonnay
Spätlese trocken "R"
29 DM, 14.5%, 🍷 till 2003 — **91**

1996 Weißer Burgunder
Spätlese trocken "R"
25 DM, 15%, 🍷 till2000 — **91**

——— Red wine ———

1996 Spätburgunder
Spätlese trocken "R"
35 DM, 13%, 🍷 till 2003 — **89**

WEINGUT KARL SCHAEFER

Owners: Dr. Wolf Fleischmann and Gerda Lehmeyer
Winemaker: Thorsten Rotthaus
67098 Bad Dürkheim, Weinstraße Süd 30
Tel. (0 63 22) 21 38, Fax 87 29
Directions: Located at the southern end of Bad Dürkheim, direction Neustadt
Sales: Mr. Koob and Mr. Sebastian
Opening hours: Mon.–Fri. 8 a.m. to noon and 1 p.m. to 6 p.m., Sat. 9 a.m. to noon
History: Owned by the family since 1843

Vineyard area: 16 hectares
Annual production: 100,000 bottles
Top sites: Dürkheimer Michelsberg and Spielberg, Wachenheimer Gerümpel and Fuchsmantel
Soil types: Chalky loam, partially interspersed with sand
Grape varieties: 86% Riesling, 14% other varieties
Average yield: 67 hl/ha
Best vintages: 1993, 1996, 1997
Member: VDP

The predominately dry wines produced by this estate are characterized by their distinct individuality and are often among the best of the region. Today the property is run in the fourth generation by the chemist Dr. Wolf Fleischmann and his daughter Gerda Lehmeyer. Fleischmann knows well that Riesling "belongs only in the best sites," and his are of noble origin, situated on the steepest terraces along the Haardt. This estate's quality aspirations are equally high, as the must weights of the Kabinetts are often of Spätlese level. The 1994 and 1995 ranges, however, left much to be desired. The 1996s were very closed, but the estate had a great deal of confidence in the vintage; they have in fact developed well. Nonetheless, we are left with the impression that this estate, however good some of the wines might appear, has been underperforming. The 1997s put some of our criticism back into perspective, but even these wines are not up to those of this estate's heyday.

1997 Forster Pechstein
Riesling Kabinett trocken
12.50 DM, 12%, 🍷 till 2000 **84**

1996 Dürkheimer Spielberg
Riesling Kabinett halbtrocken
11.50 DM, 11%, 🍷 till 2000 **84**

1996 Wachenheimer Fuchsmantel
Riesling Kabinett
9.50 DM, 11%, 🍷 till 2000 **84**

1997 Wachenheimer Gerümpel
Riesling Kabinett trocken
12.50 DM, 12%, 🍷 till 2000 **86**

1997 Wachenheimer Gerümpel
Riesling Spätlese trocken
15 DM, 12%, 🍷 till 2001 **86**

1996 Wachenheimer Fuchsmantel
Riesling Spätlese trocken
16 DM, 12.5%, 🍷 till 2000 **86**

1996 Dürkheimer Spielberg
Riesling Spätlese
15.50 DM, 11%, 🍷 till 2002 **86**

1997 Ungsteiner Herrenberg
Riesling Spätlese trocken
15 DM, 12%, 🍷 till 2002 **88**

1996 Wachenheimer Gerümpel
Riesling Spätlese trocken
15.50 DM, 12.5%, 🍷 till 2000 **88**

1997 Dürkheimer Spielberg
Riesling Spätlese
16.50 DM, 11%, 🍷 till 2004 **88**

PFALZ
GUTS-
ABFÜLLUNG
WEINGUT KARL SCHAEFER
DR. WOLF FLEISCHMANN · D-67098 BAD DÜRKHEIM
1996er
Wachenheimer Fuchsmantel
12,5% vol
Riesling Spätlese Trocken
0,75 l
Qualitätswein mit Prädikat
A. P. Nr. 5 160 256 14 97

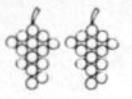

WEINHOF SCHEU

Owners: Günter and Klaus Scheu
Winemaker: Klaus Scheu
76889 Schweigen-Rechtenbach, Hauptstraße 33
Tel. (0 63 42) 72 29, Fax 91 99 75
Directions: A 65, exit Landau-Süd, in the direction of Bad Bergzabern and Weißenburg
Sales: Günter and Klaus Scheu
Opening hours: Mon.–Fri. by appointment, Sat. and Sun. 10 a.m. to 6 p.m.

Vineyard area: 11.5 hectares
Annual production: 60,000 bottles
Top site: Schweigener Sonnenberg
Soil types: Sandy loam, heavy chalky loam and clay
Grape varieties: 25% Riesling, 20% Weißburgunder, 10% Müller-Thurgau, 8% each of Spätburgunder, Grauburgunder and Gewürztraminer, 21% other varieties
Average yield: 75 hl/ha
Best vintages: 1996, 1997

Klaus Scheu, who now runs this property with his father, made some remarkable wines on his "virgin flight" in 1994. We are confident that these well-made and tightly structured wines from the southern Pfalz will mature gracefully. The 1995s were also quite satisfactory – hearty but refreshing. The 1996s, too, were limpid, fresh and lively; but nothing to date has been as good as the 1997s, which even begin to show a touch of character. And once again the crisp Riesling in the liter bottle proves that the ambitious young Scheu knows how to fashion appealing wines for everyday consumption at very reasonable prices.

1997 Schweigener Sonnenberg
Weißer Burgunder Kabinett trocken
6.70 DM, 12%, 🍷 now **82**

1997 Schweigener Sonnenberg
Grauer Burgunder Kabinett trocken
7 DM, 12.5%, 🍷 now **82**

1997 Schweigener Sonnenberg
Riesling Kabinett trocken
6.70 DM, 11.5%, 🍷 now **82**

1997 Schweigener Sonnenberg
Weißer Burgunder Spätlese trocken
9.20 DM, 13%, 🍷 till 2000 **84**

1997 Schweigener Sonnenberg
Grauer Burgunder Spätlese trocken
9.80 DM, 13%, 🍷 till 2000 **84**

1996 Schweigener Sonnenberg
Gewürztraminer Auslese trocken
13.50 DM, 15%, 🍷 till 2000 **84**

1997 Schweigener Sonnenberg
Riesling Spätlese halbtrocken
9 DM, 12%, 🍷 till 2000 **84**

1997 Schweigener Sonnenberg
Gewürztraminer Spätlese
9.50 DM, 12%, 🍷 till 2001 **84**

1997 Schweigener Sonnenberg
Rieslaner Auslese
13 DM, 12%, 🍷 till 2003 **86**

WEINGUT GEORG SIBEN ERBEN

Owner: Siben family
Manager: Andreas Johannes Siben
67143 Deidesheim, Weinstraße 21
Tel. (0 63 26) 98 93 63, Fax 98 93 65
Directions: On the wine route between Neustadt and Bad Dürkheim
Sales: Siben family
Opening hours: Mon.–Fri. 8 a.m. to noon and 2 p.m. to 6 p.m.
Sat. 9 a.m. to noon and 2 p.m. to 5 p.m.
Sun. by appointment
Worth seeing: Cellar built in 1595, tasting room in the sandstone-columned hall

Vineyard area: 17.3 hectares
Annual production: 120,000 bottles
Top sites: Deidesheimer Grainhübel and Kalkofen, Forster Ungeheuer, Ruppertsberger Hoheburg and Reiterpfad
Soil types: Sandy loess and loam, partly with clay and gravel
Grape varieties: 75% Riesling, 15% Burgundian varieties, 10% other varieties
Average yield: 58 hl/ha
Best vintages: 1993, 1994, 1995
Member: VDP, Naturland

Hendrijk Siben came to Deidesheim from his native Holland in 1700. The current owner, Wolfgang Georg Siben, is an advocate of classic Rieslings aged in casks that often require time to develop. Although the majority of his wines are vinified in a full-bodied, dry style, he is no opponent of Riesling with natural residual sugars. In 1988 Siben began to pursue organic viticulture; in 1991 he revamped his entire vineyard and is now a member of the Naturland organization. In contrast to the results of most of his colleagues, his 1995 range was clearly superior to its predecessor. After a lackluster performance in 1996, the finest of the 1997s are again quite pleasant. Nonetheless, the bulk of his wines still lack a touch of freshness and taste rather simple.

1996 Deidesheimer Langenmorgen
Riesling Kabinett halbtrocken
10 DM, 11.5%, ♀ now **80**

1996 Deidesheimer Langenmorgen
Riesling Kabinett trocken
10 DM, 11.5%, ♀ now **82**

1997 Forster Ungeheuer
Riesling Spätlese trocken
13.60 DM, 12.5%, ♀ now **82**

1996 Deidesheimer Leinhöhle
Riesling Spätlese trocken
13.75 DM, 12%, ♀ now **82**

1996 Forster Ungeheuer
Riesling Spätlese halbtrocken
13.75 DM, 12%, ♀ now **82**

1997 Forster Ungeheuer
Riesling Spätlese
13.80 DM, 9.5%, ♀ till 2000 **84**

1996 Deidesheimer Kalkofen
Riesling Auslese
20 DM, 11.5%, ♀ till 2002 **84**

1997 Deidesheimer Leinhöhle
Riesling Spätlese
15 DM, 10%, ♀ till 2002 **86**

1997 Deidesheimer Grainhübel
Riesling Spätlese
25.60 DM, 11.5%, ♀ till 2000 **86**

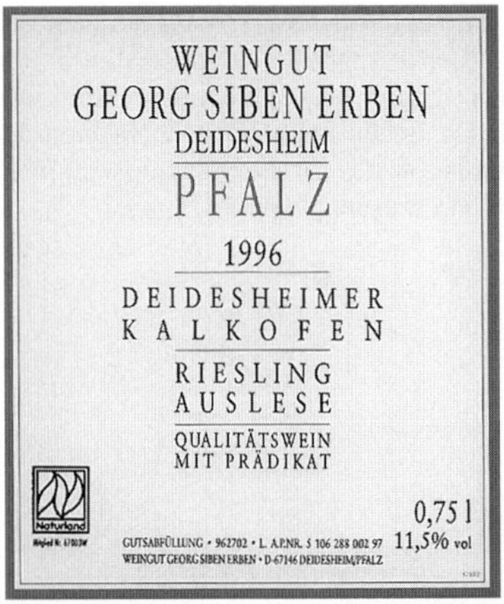

WEINGUT SIEGRIST

Owner: Thomas Siegrist
76829 Leinsweiler, Am Hasensprung 4
Tel. (0 63 45) 13 09, Fax 75 42
Directions: A 65, exit Landau-Nord, via B 10, southern wine route, exit in Birkweiler
Sales: Siegrist and Schimpf families
Opening hours: Mon.–Fri. 8 a.m. to noon and 1:30 p.m. to 6 p.m.
Sat. only to 5 p.m. or by appointment
Worth seeing: Tithe cellar

Vineyard area: 12.5 hectares
Annual production: 80,000 bottles
Top site: Leinsweiler Sonnenberg
Soil types: Heavy chalky loam, loess, weathered red sandstone
Grape varieties: 25% Riesling, 15% Müller-Thurgau, 17% Spätburgunder, 10% each of Weißburgunder and Chardonnay, 8% Silvaner, 5% Dornfelder, 5% Grauburgunder, 5% other varieties
Average yield: 78 hl/ha
Best vintages: 1995, 1996, 1997
Member: Deutsches Barrique Forum

The white wines of Thomas Siegrist are almost always vinified in a dry style; however, the estate is better known for its red wines, the best of which are aged in small oak barrels. And his often belittled Dornfelder can be splendid! Siegrist's grasp of the white Burgundian varieties and even Riesling has improved in recent years as a more modern style has replaced the rather rustic, old-fashioned tradition of the past. The current wines are more limpid and better structured, although they sometimes still lack finesse and elegance. Be that as it may, this estate is on an upward curve, as the 1997s well document. This is perhaps the finest range that Siegrist has ever produced.

1997 Chardonnay
Kabinett trocken
11 DM, 12%, ♀ till 2000 **84**

1996 Leinsweiler Sonnenberg
Weißer Burgunder Kabinett trocken
8.50 DM, 12%, ♀ now **84**

1996 Leinsweiler Sonnenberg
Riesling Spätlese trocken
12 DM, 12%, ♀ now **84**

1996 Chardonnay
Spätlese trocken
20 DM, 13%, ♀ till 2000 **84**

1997 Silvaner
Spätlese trocken
12 DM, 12.5%, ♀ till 2000 **86**

1997 Grauer Burgunder
Spätlese trocken
22 DM, 13%, ♀ till 2000 **86**

1996 Grauer Burgunder
Spätlese trocken
20 DM, 13%, ♀ till 2000 **86**

1997 Leinsweiler Sonnenberg
Riesling Spätlese
13.50 DM, 11%, ♀ till 2002 **86**

Weingut Thomas Siegrist
D-76829 Leinsweiler
Südliche Weinstraße
1996
PFALZ
LEINSWEILER SONNENBERG
WEISSBURGUNDER
KABINETT TROCKEN
GUTSABFÜLLUNG
QUALITÄTSWEIN MIT PRÄDIKAT
A.P.NR. 5 051 045 6 97
0,75 l
12 % vol

WEINGUT HEINRICH VOLLMER

Owner: Heinrich Vollmer
67158 Ellerstadt,
Gönnheimer Straße 52
Tel. (0 62 37) 66 11, Fax 83 66
Directions: A 61 to "Kreuz Ludwigshafen," to A 650, in the direction of Bad Dürkheim
Opening hours: Mon.–Fri. 8 a.m. to 5 p.m., Sat. 8 a.m. to 4 p.m. or by appointment
Worth seeing: Roman tower

Vineyard area: 110 hectares
Annual production: 1.2 million bottles
Top sites: Ellerstadter Bubeneck and Kirchenstück, Freinsheimer Rosenbühl
Soil types: Sandy loam and gravel, also rich in chalk
Grape varieties: 34% Portugieser, 21% Riesling, 10% each of Spätburgunder and Dornfelder, 9% Weißburgunder, 6% Gewürztraminer, 10% other varieties
Average yield: 89 hl/ha
Best vintages: 1990, 1992, 1993

After his training in France, Heinrich Vollmer, a rough-hewn young vintner from Durbach in Baden, founded this small estate in Ellerstadt in 1969; 25 years later it comprises over 100 hectares. In the early 1970s he began planting red grapes instead of the traditional white varieties and in 1973 was one of the first winemakers in Germany to introduce barrel aging. Today his very typically German styled red wines are considerably better than the whites. A few years ago this ambitious mountain climber also acquired an estate in Argentina. The 1996 range constituted a new style for Vollmer: intentionally reductive, yet still a touch rustic and slightly tart. Due to poor weather, the few 1997s that he produced were somewhat less attractive. With such wines Vollmer is on the same quality level as the leading cooperatives of the Pfalz.

1996 Ellerstadter Kirchenstück
Chardonnay Spätlese trocken
11.25 DM, 12.5%, ♀ now **77**

1996 Dürkheimer Nonnengarten
Riesling Spätlese trocken
11.25 DM, 12%, ♀ now **77**

1996 Ellerstadter Sonnenberg
Chardonnay Spätlese trocken
12 DM, 12.5%, ♀ now **80**

1996 Erpolzheimer Kirschgarten
Riesling Spätlese trocken
11.25 DM, 12%, ♀ now **80**

1996 Ellerstadter Bubeneck
Gewürztraminer Auslese trocken
20 DM, 13%, ♀ now **80**

1996 Ellerstadter Sonnenberg
Gewürztraminer Spätlese
10 DM, 12%, ♀ now **80**

1996 Ellerstadter Kirchenstück
Grauer Burgunder Auslese trocken
21.25 DM, 13.5%, ♀ till 2000 **82**

——— Red wines ———

1996 Ellerstadter Kirchenstück
Spätburgunder Spätlese trocken
16.50 DM, 12%, ♀ now **80**

1996 Cabernet Sauvignon
Tafelwein trocken
15 DM, 12%, ♀ till 2000 **82**

WEINGUT WEEGMÜLLER

Owner: Stefanie Weegmüller-Scherr
General Manager: Richard Scherr
Winemaker: Stefanie Weegmüller-Scherr
67433 Neustadt-Haardt, Mandelring 23
Tel. (0 63 21) 8 37 72, Fax 48 07 72
Directions: A 65, exit Neustadt-Lambrecht, follow signs to Haardt
Sales: Stefanie Weegmüller-Scherr
Opening hours: Mon.–Fri. 8 a.m. to noon and 1 p.m. to 5 p.m.
Sat. 9 a.m. to 2 p.m. or by appointment

Vineyard area: 14.5 hectares
Annual production: 110,000 bottles
Top sites: Haardter Herrenletten and Herzog
Soil types: Sandy loam, clay with some heavy chalky loam
Grape varieties: 60% Riesling, 6% Scheurebe, 5% each of Grauer Burgunder, Weißer Burgunder, Gewürztraminer, Kerner and Dornfelder, 9% other varieties
Average yield: 71 hl/ha
Best vintages: 1994, 1996, 1997

This estate was founded in 1685 and is run in the twelfth generation by Stefanie Weegmüller and her husband, Richard Scherr. As the one of three daughters, she had to learn her profession from scratch. She first worked at the neighboring Bassermann-Jordan estate and later pursued her studies at the wine college in Württemberg. At the age of 25 she took over full responsibility for the cellars, which until that time were still run by her father. Since then the estate has been making steady progress. Our attention was first drawn to the estate four years ago when we tasted the successful 1994s. The crisp 1996s and well-balanced 1997s are even better. It would appear that this estate is on the verge of a breakthrough.

1997 Haardter Herrenletten
Scheurebe Kabinett trocken
10.50 DM, 11.5%, ♀ now **82**

1997 Haardter Herzog
Weißer Burgunder Kabinett trocken
10.50 DM, 11%, ♀ now **82**

1996 Haardter Bürgergarten
Riesling Spätlese trocken
15 DM, 12%, ♀ now **82**

1997 Haardter Herrenletten
Grauer Burgunder Spätlese trocken
13.50 DM, 13%, ♀ till 2000 **84**

1997 Haardter Bürgergarten
Riesling Spätlese trocken
15 DM, 13%, ♀ now **84**

1997 Haardter Bürgergarten
Gewürztraminer Spätlese trocken
14 DM, 13.5%, ♀ till 2000 **84**

1996 Haardter Herrenletten
Riesling Spätlese trocken
12.50 DM, 12%, ♀ till 2000 **84**

1997 Haardter Herrenletten
Riesling Auslese
14.50 DM/0.375 liter, 10%, ♀ till 2003 **88**

1996 Haardter Mandelberg
Scheurebe Auslese
15 DM/0.375 liter, 10%, ♀ till 2003 **88**

1996 Haardter Bürgergarten
Riesling Eiswein
60 DM/0.375 liter, 9.5%, ♀ till 2010 **92**

WEINGÜTER GEHEIMRAT J. WEGELER ERBEN GUTSHAUS DEIDESHEIM

Owner: Rolf Wegeler family
General Manager: Heinz Bauer
Winemaker: Ludwig Molitor
67146 Deidesheim, Weinstraße 10
Tel. (0 63 26) 2 21, Fax 79 20
Directions: On the wine route between Neustadt and Bad Dürkheim
Opening hours: By appointment with Heinz Bauer

Vineyard area: 10.5 hectares
Annual production: 85,000 bottles
Top sites: Forster Ungeheuer, Deidesheimer Herrgottsacker, Ruppertsberger Linsenbusch
Soil types: Loess and loam over basalt, weathered red sandstone
Grape varieties: 94% Riesling, 6% Müller-Thurgau
Average yield: 66 hl/ha
Best vintages: 1993, 1995, 1997
Member: VDP

This property represents that portion of the Dr. Deinhard estate that has been leased to the Wegeler family for the past 25 years. The two estates cultivate different vineyards, but the wines are made by the same team under the direction of Heinz Bauer. The management of the wines of the Wegeler properties, though, is in the hands of the estate director, Norbert Holderrieth, who oversees the vinification. As a result, these are the only wines from the Pfalz that are so close in style to those of the Rheingau, yet without attaining the depth or finesse of their northern neighbor. Both the 1994 and 1995 ranges turned out well. The 1996s, on the other hand, were rather lean, acidic and less attractive. The 1997s are pleasant, but nothing to write home about. The decision to restrict the production to only a few wines each vintage is commendable. Unfortunately, there is no clear brand profile as each of the wines has a different label.

1997 Riesling
trocken
10 DM, 11%, ♀ now **80**

1996 Riesling
trocken
10 DM, 11%, ♀ now **80**

1997 Ruppertsberger Linsenbusch
Weißer Burgunder Kabinett trocken
12 DM, 12.5%, ♀ now **80**

1997 Forster Ungeheuer
Riesling Kabinett halbtrocken
13.50 DM, 10.5%, ♀ now **80**

1996 Deidesheimer Herrgottsacker
Riesling Kabinett trocken
13 DM, 11%, ♀ now **82**

1996 Ruppertsberger Linsenbusch
Weißer Burgunder Spätlese trocken
20 DM, 13%, ♀ now **82**

1996 Forster Ungeheuer
Riesling Kabinett halbtrocken
13.50 DM, 10.5%, ♀ now **82**

1997 Forster Ungeheuer
Riesling Spätlese trocken
19.50 DM, 12.5%, ♀ now **84**

1996 Forster Ungeheuer
Riesling Spätlese trocken
19.50 DM, 12.5%, ♀ till 2000 **84**

WEINGUT DR. WEHRHEIM

Owner: Karl-Heinz Wehrheim
76831 Birkweiler, Weinstraße 8
Tel. (0 63 45) 35 42, Fax 38 69
e-mail: Dr.Wehrheim@t-online.de
Directions: A 65, exit Landau-Nord, via B 10 to Birkweiler
Sales: Wehrheim family
Opening hours: Mon.–Fri. 9 a.m. to noon and 2 p.m. to 6 p.m., Sat. 10 a.m. to 4 p.m. or by appointment

Vineyard area: 10 hectares
Annual production: 70,000 bottles
Top sites: Birkweiler Kastanienbusch, Mandelberg and Rosenberg
Soil types: Red sandstone, porphyry, heavy chalky loam, stony clay, sandy loam, fossil limestone
Grape varieties: 40% Riesling, 20% Weißburgunder, 12% Spätburgunder, 10% Silvaner, 8% Sankt Laurent, 10% other varieties
Average yield: 67 hl/ha
Best vintages: 1993, 1996, 1997
Member: VDP

The Wehrheim family's estate at the foot of the Hohenberg has been among the most respected producers of the southern wine route in the Pfalz for many years. As long ago as 1960 Dr. Heinz Wehrheim was cultivating his vineyards using natural farming practices; and while the rest of Germany was still entranced by sweeter styles, they were already making dry wines here. The white wines have always been rich, sumptuous and full of character, especially those from the Kastanienbusch vineyard. Karl-Heinz Wehrheim, Heinz's son, has seldom bottled such a range of first-class Weißburgunder as in 1996. The wines are both limpid and lush, but at the same time elegantly fruity, exhibiting a pronounced ripe acidity. He believes that the exuberant 1997s are even better. This is classic Pfalz at its best. And both the 1993 and 1996 Spätburgunder, which are the finest red wines that we have ever tasted from this estate, are still for sale.

1996 Birkweiler Rosenberg
Chardonnay Spätlese trocken
19.40 DM, 13%, ♀ till 2003 **88**

1996 Birkweiler Kastanienbusch
Grauer Burgunder Spätlese trocken
17 DM, 13%, ♀ till 2002 **88**

1997 Birkweiler Kastanienbusch
Grauer Burgunder Auslese trocken
20 DM, 13.5%, ♀ till 2001 **88**

1997 Birkweiler Rosenberg
Chardonnay Auslese trocken
21 DM/0.5 liter, 13.5%, ♀ till 2001 **88**

1997 Birkweiler Mandelberg
Weißer Burgunder Auslese
22.50 DM, 14%, ♀ till 2003 **89**

1996 Birkweiler Mandelberg
Weißer Burgunder Auslese trocken
18 DM, 14%, ♀ till 2002 **90**

1996 Birkweiler Rosenberg
Chardonnay Spätlese trocken
17 DM/0.5 liter, 13%, ♀ till 2003 **91**

Red wines

1993 Birkweiler Kastanienbusch
Spätburgunder Auslese trocken
21 DM/0.5 liter, 13.2%, ♀ till 2000 **89**

1996 Birkweiler Kastanienbusch
Spätburgunder Auslese trocken
23 DM/0.5 liter, 13.5%, ♀ till 2002 **91**

WEINGUT WEIK

Owners: Dominique Runck and Bernd Weik
Winemaker: Bernd Weik
67435 Neustadt-Mußbach, Lutwitzistraße 10
Tel. (0 63 21) 6 68 38, Fax 6 09 41
Directions: A 65, exit Neustadt-Nord, in the direction of Mußbach
Sales: Dominique Runck
Opening hours: Fri. 1 p.m. to 6 p.m. Sat. 10 a.m. to 4 p.m. or by appointment
Wine bar: "Weik's Vinorant" in town
Worth seeing: Large vaulted cellars

Vineyard area: 5.1 hectares
Annual production: 40,000 bottles
Top sites: Königsbacher Idig, Haardter Herzog, Mußbacher Eselshaut
Soil types: Loamy sand and loess
Grape varieties: 45% Riesling, 11% Sankt Laurent, 7% Weißburgunder, 6% Spätburgunder, 5% Dornfelder, 26% other varieties
Average yield: 58 hl/ha
Best vintages: 1993, 1996, 1997

Based in an idyllically situated property in Mußbach, this estate has been owned by the same family for decades. It is located close to the Eselshaut vineyard, which constitutes the largest portion of their holdings. For the past several years Dominique Runck and Bernd Weik have been running the estate together: Dominique Runck looks after the vineyards, while Bernd Weik oversees the vinification. The 1994 and 1995 vintages were quite palatable, the 1996s and 1997s even better. The fresh, fruity wines of these two vintages indicate that this young couple have now set their sights higher.

1997 Mußbacher Eselshaut
Weißer Burgunder Spätlese trocken
9.80 DM, 12.5%, ♀ till 2000 **82**

1997 Mußbacher Glockenzehnt
Riesling Spätlese trocken
9.80 DM, 12.5%, ♀ till 2000 **84**

1996 Mußbacher Eselshaut
Weißer Burgunder Spätlese trocken
10 DM, 12.5%, ♀ till 2000 **84**

1996 Mußbacher Eselshaut
Silvaner Spätlese trocken
9 DM, 12.5%, ♀ now **84**

1997 Gimmeldinger Schlössel
Riesling Auslese trocken
13 DM, 13%, ♀ till 2001 **84**

1996 Mußbacher Glockenzehnt
Riesling Auslese trocken
11 DM, 12%, ♀ till 2000 **84**

1996 Königsbacher Idig
Riesling Auslese halbtrocken ***
14 DM, 12.5%, ♀ till 2001 **84**

1997 Mußbacher Eselshaut
Gewürztraminer Auslese
13 DM, 11%, ♀ till 2002 **84**

1996 Königsbacher Idig
Riesling Auslese
14 DM, 11%, ♀ till 2005 **86**

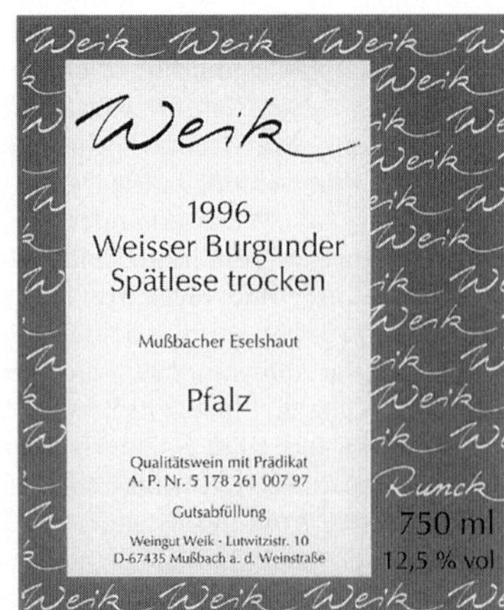

Weik
1996
Weisser Burgunder
Spätlese trocken
Mußbacher Eselshaut
Pfalz
Qualitätswein mit Prädikat
A. P. Nr. 5 178 261 007 97
Gutsabfüllung
Weingut Weik · Lutwitzistr. 10
D-67435 Mußbach a. d. Weinstraße
Runck
750 ml
12,5 % vol

WEINGUT WERLÉ ERBEN

Owner: Werlé family
Managers: Hardy and Claus Werlé
67147 Forst, Forster Schlössel
Tel. (0 63 26) 89 30, Fax 67 77
Directions: On the wine route between Neustadt and Bad Dürkheim
Sales: Hardy Werlé
Opening hours: Mon.–Fri. 9 a.m. to noon and 2 p.m. to 5 p.m. or by appointment

Vineyard area: 12.8 hectares
Annual production: 85,000 bottles
Top sites: Forster Kirchenstück, Jesuitengarten and Ungeheuer, Deidesheimer Leinhöhle and Grainhübel, Ruppertsberger Hoheburg, Reiterpfad and Nußbien
Soil types: Weathered red sandstone, basalt, gravel, loess and loam
Grape varieties: 90% Riesling, 6% Spätburgunder, 2% Silvaner, 2% other varieties
Average yield: 58 hl/ha
Best vintages: 1994, 1996, 1997

Since 1794 the Werlé family have been living in the Forster Schlössel, an attractive castle of noble ancestry dating back to the 16th century. In 1904 the great-grandfather of the current owners began to bottle the estate's wines. For years, and in accordance with principles of natural winemaking, only "Prädikatsweine" were sold. This dogmatic approach has not been adhered to quite so rigidly of late, but in order to make a clear distinction between the two tiers, the "Qualitätsweine" are marketed only in liter bottles and without vineyard designations. Although they are still relatively unknown in Germany, the wines enjoy a good reputation in the English-speaking world. A rather patchy 1995 vintage followed on the heels of the fine 1994s; the 1996s were not that much better. The 1997s are a cut above. All of the wines are well made, but the dry Rieslings nonetheless lack fruit; the sweeter wines lack true expression. This may well be a question of styles. The brothers, in any case, maintain that they produce their wines for their clients, not for journalists.

1997 Deidesheimer Mäushöhle
Riesling Kabinett halbtrocken
12 DM, 11%, ♀ now **80**

1997 Forster Jesuitengarten
Riesling Kabinett trocken
14.50 DM, 11.5%, ♀ till 2000 **82**

1996 Forster Jesuitengarten
Riesling Spätlese trocken
18 DM/0.5 liter, 12%, ♀ now **82**

1996 Forster Pechstein
Riesling Spätlese trocken
16 DM, 12%, ♀ now **82**

1996 Ruppertsberger Hoheburg
Riesling Kabinett
12 DM, 10.5%, ♀ now **82**

1997 Forster Pechstein
Riesling Spätlese halbtrocken
16 DM, 12%, ♀ till 2001 **84**

1996 Forster Ungeheuer
Riesling Spätlese
16 DM, 11%, ♀ now **84**

1996 Deidesheimer Mäushöhle
Riesling Spätlese
16 DM, 10.5%, ♀ till 2000 **84**

1997 Forster Kirchenstück
Riesling Spätlese
28 DM/0.5 liter, 8.5%, ♀ till 2003 **86**

1997 Forster Ungeheuer
Riesling Auslese
45 DM/0.5 liter, 10.5%, ♀ till 2007 **88**

WEINGUT WILHELMSHOF

Owner: Roth family
Winemaker: Herbert Roth
76833 Siebeldingen, Queichstraße 1
Tel. (0 63 45) 91 91 47, Fax 91 91 48
e-mail: Wilhelmshofwein@t-online.de
Directions: A 65 to exit Landau-Nord, on B 10 to Siebeldingen
Sales: Christa Roth-Jung
Opening hours: Mon.–Fri. 8 a.m. to 6 p.m., Sat. 9 a.m. to 5 p.m. or by appointment
Worth seeing: Riddling cellar

Vineyard area: 12.5 hectares
Annual production: 80,000 bottles, of which 25,000 bottles are sparkling wine
Top site: Siebeldinger im Sonnenschein
Soil types: Heavy chalky loam, weathered red sandstone, fossil limestone
Grape varieties: 30% Riesling, 20% Spätburgunder, 25% Weißburgunder, 10% Grauburgunder, 8% Dornfelder, 7% other varieties
Average yield: 71 hl/ha
Best vintages: 1994, 1996, 1997

In 1975 Herbert Roth – originally from the Hunsrück mountains in central Germany – married into the Jung family, who have owned the Wilhelmshof for generations. In only a short period of time he established a name for himself with his bottle-fermented sparkling wines. Justifiably so, since some of them outclass quite a few Champagnes. The 1995 white wines from the Burgundian varieties were, like the previous two vintages, extremely tasty. Even though many of the 1996s and 1997s seemed perhaps a touch plump and heavy, they are a touch better than their predecessors. The Rieslings have also improved; and the red wines are quite pleasant as well. The 1996 and 1997 Weißburgunder Spätlese are the two best dry wines that we have ever tasted from this estate.

1997 Siebeldinger im Sonnenschein
Riesling Spätlese trocken
13 DM, 12%, ♀ now **82**

1996 Siebeldinger im Sonnenschein
Grauer Burgunder Spätlese trocken
14 DM, 13.5%, ♀ till 2000 **84**

1997 Siebeldinger im Sonnenschein
Weißer Burgunder Spätlese trocken
14 DM, 13%, ♀ till 2000 **86**

1996 Siebeldinger im Sonnenschein
Weißer Burgunder Spätlese trocken
13.50 DM, 13%, ♀ till 2000 **86**

1997 Siebeldinger im Sonnenschein
Silvaner Eiswein
50 DM/0.375 liter, 12.5%, ♀ till 2007 **89**

——— Red wines ———

1996 Siebeldinger Königsgarten
Dornfelder trocken
26 DM, 12.5%, ♀ till 2000 **84**

1996 Siebeldinger im Sonnenschein
Spätburgunder Spätlese trocken
26 DM, 13%, ♀ now **84**

1996 "Cuvée Wilhelmshof"
Tafelwein trocken
26 DM/0.5 liter, 15%, ♀ till 2000 **84**

WEINGUT J. L. WOLF

Owners: JLW GmbH and Sturm family
Managers: Ernst Loosen and Christoph Hinderfeld
Winemaker: Günter Deeters
67157 Wachenheim, Weinstraße 1
Tel. (0 63 22) 98 97 95, Fax 98 97 96
Directions: In the Mittelhaardt, on the wine route between Neustadt and Bad Dürkheim
Sales: Christoph Hinderfeld
Opening hours: By appointment
Worth seeing: Villa Wolf and its vaulted cellars are historic monuments

Vineyard area: 9.5 hectares
Annual production: 50,000 bottles
Top sites: Forster Jesuitengarten, Ungeheuer and Pechstein, Deidesheimer Leinhöhle, Wachenheimer Belz, Gerümpel and Goldbächel
Soil types: Sandy loam, basalt, volcanic rock
Grape varieties: 93% Riesling, 5% Grauburgunder, 2% Spätburgunder
Average yield: 44 hl/ha
Best vintages: 1996, 1997

Built in 1843 according to the plans of the celebrated architect Eisenlohn from Karlsruhe, the Villa Wolf was laid out as a country mansion. The estate itself was founded in 1756. By the time Ernst Loosen (of the outstanding estate Dr. Loosen in Bernkastel) took over this property in partnership with Christoph Hunderfeld on the July 1, 1996, its brilliant past had already faded. With his first two vintages Loosen has shown that he is capable of producing appealing wines in the Pfalz as well. Interestingly enough, the fruity Rieslings are more impressive than the dry wines; while the style drifts somewhere between that of the Mosel and the Pfalz. This estate will need another vintage or two in order to establish a track record, but it will certainly be a force to reckon with in the near future.

1997 Forster Pechstein
Riesling Spätlese trocken
19.50 DM, 12%, ♀ till 2000 **84**

1997 Forster Ungeheuer
Riesling Auslese trocken
21 DM, 12.5%, ♀ till 2000 **84**

1997 Forster Stift
Riesling Kabinett halbtrocken
15 DM, 10%, ♀ till 2001 **84**

1996 Forster Pechstein
Riesling Kabinett halbtrocken
15 DM, 10.5%, ♀ till 2000 **84**

1997 Wachenheimer Gerümpel
Riesling Spätlese
19.50 DM, 10.5%, ♀ till 2002 **86**

1996 Wachenheimer Gerümpel
Riesling Spätlese
16.50 DM, 11%, ♀ till 2002 **86**

1996 Forster Stift
Riesling Kabinett
15 DM, 9%, ♀ till 2002 **88**

1997 Wachenheimer Belz
Riesling Auslese
26 DM, 10.5%, ♀ till 2005 **88**

1996 Wachenheimer Gerümpel
Riesling Eiswein
47 DM/0.375 liter, 7%, ♀ till 2010 **92**

Spätlese or "first growth?"

In no other region in Germany is Riesling as dominant as it is in the Rheingau. Over 80 percent of the 3,250 hectares of vineyards are planted with this most regal of grape varieties. Only in the vicinity of Assmannshausen does it step aside to make way for Pinot Noir. Already in Roman times there were vines planted on the southerly slopes north of the Rhine; and it is said that it was Charlemagne who ordered the first vines to be planted on the legendary Johannisberg hillside. From his residence at Ingelheim he noticed that the snow thawed first on the opposite side of the river, so it is hardly surprising that a few centuries later the first Spätlese – or "late harvest" – was brought in from this same vineyard. When the Abbot's messenger, authorizing harvest to begin, was delayed, the obedient monks of the Johannisberg monastery left the grapes on the vines until he arrived. The resulting crush of highly botrytisized grapes was the first recorded production of the nectar that we know today as Spätlese.

The major tourist attraction of the Rheingau is undoubtedly the Cistercian monastery of Eberbach, one of the best-preserved medieval monastic sites in Germany. The complex is now part of the State Winery of Hesse and plays host to thousands and thousands of visitors each year at wine tastings and auctions. The monastery was always a cultural center, and still is an inspiring setting for classical music concerts.

Indeed, one of the secrets of the Rheingau's success is that monasteries, noble estates and independent peasants have engaged – side by side – in wine production for centuries, catering to an extremely broad clientele. Today there are quite a few family properties among the almost 1,100 wineries in the region that are challenging the status of the large traditional estates; and given the fact that almost all of the noble estates, with their fancy-sounding names, are sadly underperforming, at least a dozen of these newcomers in the Rheingau have already surpassed the old guard in quality!

Normally we don't attach much weight to growers' assertions that their latest vintage is their best, but at the Wilhelm Weil estate in Kiedrich it's another matter. In spite of the stellar quality of the outstanding 1995 vintage, the 1996s were certainly the finest wines that this estate has ever produced. The 1997s are also good, but not nearly as ethereal. Weil has also achieved a record on another front. A bottle of his phenomenal 1995 Kiedricher Gräfenberg Riesling Trockenbeerenauslese, which we gave our highest rating in that year, was auctioned at Kloster Eberbach for a price of 3,300 marks, a new world record for a young wine!

The 1996 vintage in the Rheingau, with its extremely high acidity levels, quite

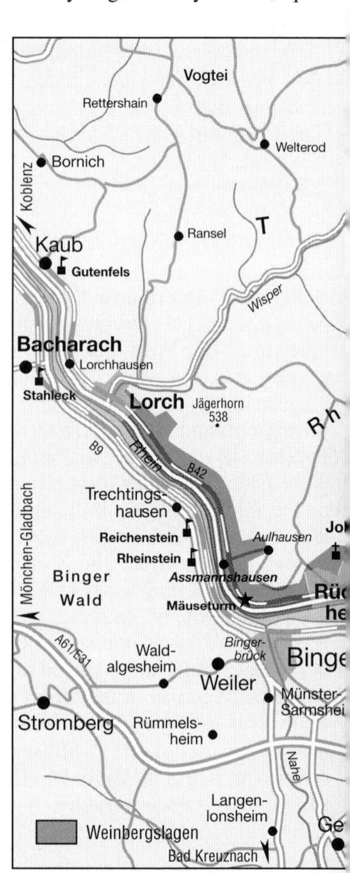

clearly separated the wheat from the chaff. 1997 was a more consistent year in quality; and yields were up by almost twenty percent from the short 1996 vintage, which will make it somewhat easier to find a bottle of the better wines. These two vintages saw the inexorable rise of the Kühn estate in Oestrich. Almost overnight Peter Jakob Kühn has advanced to the very top ranks of the region's growers. In fact, alongside Weil, he presented one of the finest ranges in both of the past two vintages. Bernhard Breuer's dry Rieslings remain inimitable, but his fruity Auslese have not been quite as stunning as those of his two colleagues. Other highly esteemed estates such as Schloß Rheinhartshausen, Franz Künstler and Johannishof maintained their solid reputations. Hot on their heels are J. B. Becker, August Kesseler and Josef Leitz.

For years an ambitious group of the region's best vintners has sought to obtain special status for the most renowned sites in the Rheingau and the right to label the Rieslings produced there as "first growths" rather than mere "Spätlese." The late Erwein Graf Matuschka-Greiffenclau was, notable for his absence, not among them. Those who attended the first combined presentation of the so-called first growths from 1996 saw the emergence of a quartet of top producers: Wilhelm Weil's Gräfenberg and Bernhard Breuer's Berg Schloßberg, followed by Gerko Knyphausen's Marcobrunn and Hans Lang's Schönhell. Although Gunter Künstler has now joined their ranks, the repeat performance in 1997 cemented Bernhard Breuer's position as first among

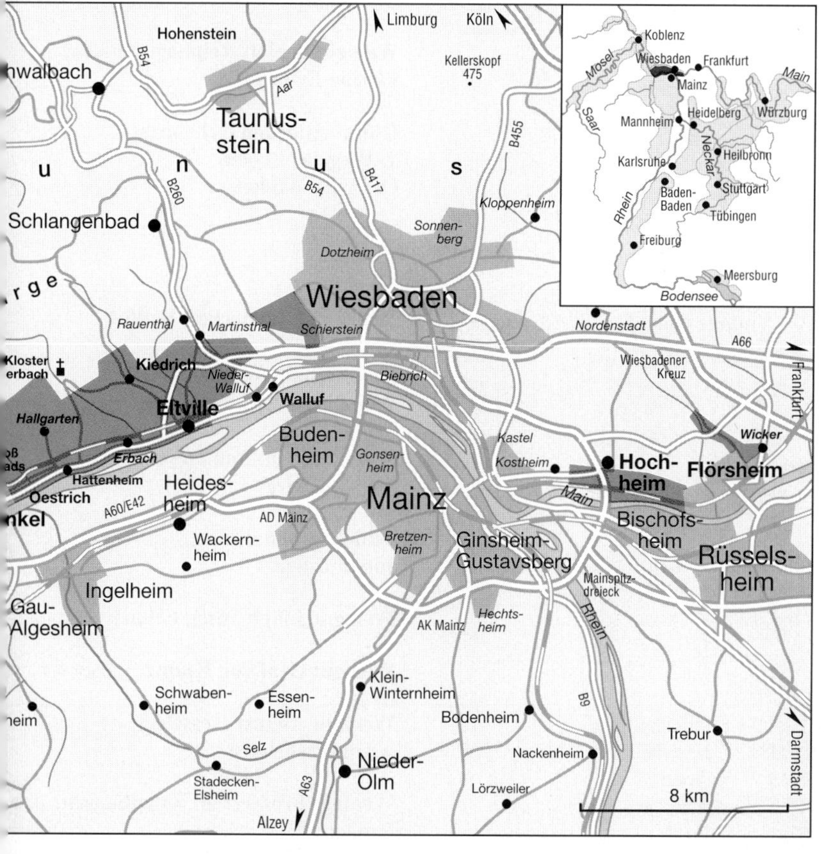

equals in this discipline. Alongside these five there were, however, many Rieslings of only modest quality. Whether the three Romanesque arches, which are the symbol for "first growth" on the label, represent a genuine marketing statement or a standard of quality is still unclear.

Over the last decade a gastronomic tradition has evolved between Lorch and Hochheim, which the other German wine regions, with the exception of Baden, must envy. The annual spring "Rheingauer Schlemmerwoche" has developed into a popular food and wine fair akin to an Oktoberfest, while the more up-market "Rheingau Gourmet Festival" offers a wonderful complement to the well-established music festival.

Vintage chart for the Rheingau

vintage	quality	drink
1997	🍇🍇🍇	till 2004
1996	🍇🍇🍇🍇	till 2005
1995	🍇🍇🍇🍇	till 2004
1994	🍇🍇🍇🍇	till 2004
1993	🍇🍇🍇🍇🍇	till 2005
1992	🍇🍇🍇🍇	till 2000
1991	🍇🍇🍇	now
1990	🍇🍇🍇🍇🍇	till 2005
1989	🍇🍇🍇	now
1988	🍇🍇🍇🍇	now

🍇🍇🍇🍇🍇 : Outstanding
🍇🍇🍇🍇 : Excellent
🍇🍇🍇 : Good
🍇🍇 : Average
🍇 : Poor

The leading estates of the Rheingau

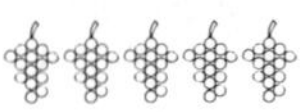

Weingut Georg Breuer, Rüdesheim

Weingut Robert Weil, Kiedrich

Weingut Johannishof, Johannisberg

Weingut Peter Jakob Kühn, Oestrich

Weingut Franz Künstler, Hochheim

Weingut Schloß Reinhartshausen, Eltville-Erbach

Gutsverwaltung Geheimrat J. Wegeler Erben, Oestrich-Winkel

Weingut J. B. Becker, Walluf

Domdechant Werner'sches Weingut, Hochheim

Weingut Prinz von Hessen, Johannisberg

Schloß Johannisberg, Johannisberg

Weingut Jakob Jung, Erbach

Weingut Graf von Kanitz, Lorch

Weingut August Kesseler, Assmannshausen

Weingut Freiherr zu Knyphausen, Erbach

Weingut Robert König, Assmannshausen

Weingut Krone, Assmannshausen

Weingut Hans Lang, Eltville-Hattenheim

Weingut Josef Leitz, Rüdesheim

Weingut Prinz, Hallgarten

Weingut Wilfried Querbach, Oestrich-Winkel

Weingut Balthasar Ress, Hattenheim

Staatsweingut Assmannshausen, Assmannshausen

Hessische Staatsweingüter Kloster Eberbach, Eltville

Weingut Fritz Allendorf, Oestrich-Winkel

Weingut August Eser, Oestrich-Winkel

Weingut Toni Jost – Hahnenhof, Bacharach

Weingut Freiherr Langwerth von Simmern, Eltville

Weingut Dr. Heinrich Nägler, Rüdesheim

Weingut W. J. Schäfer, Hochheim

Domänenweingut Schloß Schönborn, Hattenheim

Weingut Schloß Vollrads, Oestrich-Winkel

Weingut Hans Barth, Hattenheim

Weingut Joachim Flick, Flörsheim-Wicker

Weingut der Forschungsanstalt Geisenheim

Weingut Alexander Freimuth, Geisenheim-Marienthal

Weingut Hupfeld – "Königin-Viktoriaberg," Oestrich-Winkel

von Mumm'sches Weingut, Johannisberg

Weingut Adam Nass-Engelmann, Hallgarten

Weingut Freiherr von Zwierlein Schloß Kosakenberg, Geisenheim

Rating scale for the estates

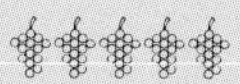

Highest rating: These producers belong to the world's finest.

Excellent estates: These producers are among Germany's best.

Very good producers, known for their consistently high quality.

Good estates, offering better than average quality.

Reliable producers that offer well-made standard quality.

Other notable producers

Weingut Aschrott
☞ *See below, page 354*

Weingut Diefenhardt
65344 Martinsthal, Hauptstraße 11
Tel. (0 61 23) 7 14 90, Fax 7 48 41

Weingut Anton Doufrain
☞ *See below, page 359*

Winzer von Erbach
65346 Erbach, Ringstraße 28
Tel. (0 61 23) 6 24 14, Fax 47 99

Weingut Fürst Löwenstein
65375 Hallgarten, Niederwaldstraße 8
Tel. (0 67 23) 99 97 70, Fax 99 97 71

Weingut Heinz Nikolai
65346 Erbach, Ringstraße 16
Tel. (0 61 23) 6 27 08, Fax 8 16 19

Weingut Detlev Ritter von Oetinger
65346 Erbach, Rheinallee 1–3
Tel. (0 61 23) 6 25 28, Fax 6 26 91

Weingut Johannes Ohlig & Sohn
65375 Oestrich-Winkel, Hauptstraße 68
Tel. (0 67 23) 20 12, Fax 8 78 72

Weingut Speicher-Schuth
65399 Kiedrich, Suttonstraße 23
Tel. (0 61 23) 8 14 21, Fax 6 16 15

Weingut der Stadt Eltville
☞ *See below, page 391*

WEINGUT FRITZ ALLENDORF

Owner: Lotte Allendorf
Manager: Josef Schönleber
Sales Manager: Ulrich Allendorf
Winemaker: Mathias Ganswohl
65375 Oestrich-Winkel,
Kirchstraße 69
Tel. (0 67 23) 9 18 50, Fax 91 85 40
Directions: B 42, second Winkel exit, in the direction of Schloß Vollrads, follow the signs
Sales: Ms. Wucherpfennig
Opening hours: Mon.–Fri. 8 a.m. to 5 p.m., Sat. 10 a.m. to 4 p.m.
Restaurant: Open in April, May, June, September and October
Fri. from 4 p.m.
Sat., Sun. and holidays from noon
Specialties: Food and wine pairings

Vineyard area: 55 hectares
Annual production: 580,000 bottles
Top sites: Winkeler Jesuitengarten and Hasensprung, Rüdesheimer Berg Rottland, Assmannshäuser Höllenberg
Soil types: Loam, loess-loam, slate
Grape varieties: 78% Riesling, 15% Spätburgunder, 5% Müller-Thurgau, 2% other varieties
Average yield: 78 hl/ha
Best vintages: 1990, 1994, 1995
Member: Charta

The Rheingau mourned when Fritz Allendorf, one of the prominent personalities of the region, died in August of 1996. In parting he left a lovely 1995 range, his finest vintage of the decade. The quality of the 1996s refuted the prophecy that managing the business would be too much for his widow, Lotte Allendorf, who now runs the estate with her son Ulrich and son-in-law Josef Schönleber. The lovely 1996 ice wine will surely remind his descendants of old Fritz's last vintage for decades to come. The 1997s, on the other hand, were less convincing.

1997 Winkeler Jesuitengarten
Riesling Kabinett halbtrocken
10.60 DM, 11.5%, ♀ till 2001 **84**

1997 Winkeler Jesuitengarten
Riesling Kabinett
10.60 DM, 9.5%, ♀ till 2002 **84**

1996 Geisenheimer Mönchspfad
Riesling trocken
7.50 DM, 10.5%, ♀ till 2000 **86**

1996 Rüdesheimer Berg Rottland
Riesling Spätlese trocken
16.60 DM, 11%, ♀ now **86**

1996 Geisenheimer Mönchspfad
Riesling halbtrocken
6.50 DM, 10%, ♀ till 2000 **86**

1997 Winkeler Jesuitengarten
Riesling Auslese
22 DM/0.5 liter, 8%, ♀ till 2003 **86**

1996 Winkeler Jesuitengarten
Riesling Kabinett halbtrocken
10.50 DM, 9.5%, ♀ till 2001 **88**

1996 Winkeler Jesuitengarten
Riesling Kabinett
10.50 DM, 8.5%, ♀ till 2001 **88**

1996 Winkeler Hasensprung
Riesling Eiswein
Not yet for sale, 6%, ♀ 2000 till 2015 **95**

WEINGUT ASCHROTT

Owner: Gunter Künstler
Manager: Otto Völker
Winemaker: Gunter Künstler and Frank Fischer
65239 Hochheim, Kirchstraße 38
Tel. (0 61 46) 8 38 60, Fax 57 67
Directions: Exit Hochheim, B 40 to the center of town, left past the Madonna
Sales: Frank Fischer, Franz-Josef Grieß
Opening hours: Mon.–Thur. 8 a.m. to noon and 1 p.m. to 5 p.m.
Fri. 8 a.m. to noon
History: Former property of the bishops of Mainz, in 1823 bought by the banker Herz Seligmann Aschrott
Worth seeing: 500-year-old mansion with its vaulted cellars

Vineyard area: 6 hectares
Annual production: 45,000 bottles
Top sites: Hochheimer Domdechaney, Kirchenstück and Hölle
Soil types: Loamy clay, heavy chalky loam
Grape varieties: 92% Riesling, 8% Spätburgunder
Average yield: 67 hl/ha
Best vintages: 1991, 1993, 1996
Member: VDP

This venerable old estate, despite its potential, had been producing rather indifferent wines in recent years. In 1996 Gunter Künstler and Wolfgang Trautwein took over the estate and put it back on its feet. Shortly before harvest they renovated the cellar, installed stainless steel tanks and set the course for a better future. The whole of the 1996 range was of surprising quality; the ice wine from the Kirchenstück vineyard was stunning. Given this turnaround, the property's reemergence was hardly a surprise. However, the owners' further plans were unclear; and the plan behind their leasing six hectares of vineyards to Künstler's own estate remained a mystery. Trautwein has now left the partnership and it appears that Aschrott has become nothing more than Künstler's second label.

1996 Hochheimer Stielweg
Riesling Kabinett halbtrocken
11.90 DM, 9.5%, ♀ till 2000 **84**

1996 Hochheimer Kirchenstück
Riesling Spätlese trocken
25 DM, 11.5%, ♀ till 2002 **86**

1996 Riesling
7.50 DM, 8.5%, ♀ till 2001 **86**

1996 Hochheimer Stielweg
Riesling Spätlese trocken
22 DM, 11%, ♀ till 2001 **88**

1996 Hochheimer Hölle
Riesling Kabinett
12.80 DM, 7%, ♀ till 2002 **88**

1996 Hochheimer Hölle
Riesling Spätlese
19.80 DM, 7%, ♀ till 2010 **89**

1996 Hochheimer Kirchenstück
Riesling Eiswein
110 DM/0.375 liter, 6.5%, ♀ till 2012 **96**

——— Red wines ———

1996 Hochheimer Stielweg
Spätburgunder trocken
14.50 DM, 12.5%, ♀ till 2003 **82**

WEINGUT HANS BARTH

Owner: Norbert Barth
65347 Eltville-Hattenheim,
Bergweg 20
Tel. (0 67 23) 25 14, Fax 43 75
Directions: Via B 42, exit Hattenheim
Sales: Norbert Barth
Opening hours: Mon.–Fri. 2 p.m. to 6 p.m., Sat. 10 a.m. to 5 p.m. or by appointment
Worth seeing: Sparkling-wine facility using hand riddling

Vineyard area: 11.5 hectares
Annual production: 100,000 bottles
Top sites: Hattenheimer Wisselbrunnen, Hallgartener Jungfer, Assmannshäuser Frankenthal
Soil types: Loess, loam and weathered slate
Grape varieties: 77% Riesling, 18% Spätburgunder, 2% Weißburgunder, 3% other varieties
Average yield: 78 hl/ha
Best vintages: 1993, 1996, 1997
Member: Charta

When it comes to sales, Norbert Barth is never at a loss for ideas. His newsletter is always packed with special offers. For years he has been taking his clients for long walks through the vineyards. For 145 marks wine lovers buy their own vines and receive in exchange a bottle of wine for the following 15 years. Guests often come and feast here during the Christmas market and summer festival, tasting the new wines directly from casks. With such a bubbly spirit, his sparkling wine shouldn't be a disappointment; and the 35,000-bottle-a-year production is an important part of the estate's business. Most of the sparkling wine is made by the classic method of bottle fermentation; the special cuvée "Ultra" can be excellent. After two rather mediocre years, the 1996 and 1997 ranges brought a return to the quality levels of the very successful 1993 vintage. If this trend can be sustained, we will hear more from this estate.

1997 Hattenheimer Schützenhaus
Riesling Spätlese trocken
16 DM, 11.5%, ♀ till 2001 **82**

1996 Riesling
halbtrocken
8 DM, 10.5%, ♀ till 2001 **84**

1996 Riesling
Spätlese halbtrocken
14.50 DM, 10%, ♀ till 2003 **86**

1996 Hattenheimer Schützenhaus
Riesling Auslese
19 DM/0.5 liter, 12.5%, ♀ till 2003 **86**

1997 Hattenheimer Wisselbrunnen
Riesling
18.50 DM, 12%, ♀ till 2003 **88**

1996 Hattenheimer Schützenhaus
Riesling Eiswein
48 DM/0.25 liter, 9.5%, ♀ till 2008 **92**

——— Red wines ———

1996 Assmannshäuser Frankenthal
Spätburgunder trocken
16.80 DM, 13%, ♀ till 2002 **82**

1996 Spätburgunder
trocken
24.50 DM, 13%, ♀ till 2004 **84**

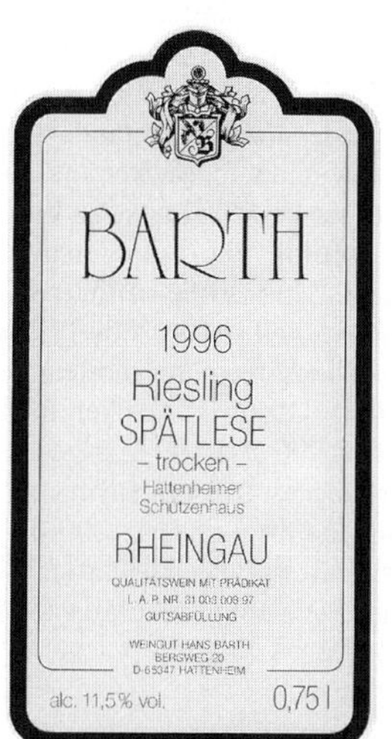

WEINGUT J. B. BECKER

Owner: Maria and Hans-Josef Becker
Winemaker: Hans-Josef Becker
65396 Walluf, Rheinstraße 6
Tel. (0 61 23) 7 25 23, Fax 7 53 35
Directions: A 66, exit Walluf, in village center down to the Rhine
Sales: Maria Becker
Opening hours: Mon.–Fri. 9 a.m. to noon and 2 p.m. to 5 p.m.
Sat. and Sun. by appointment
Restaurant: "Der Weingarten," May to October open Mon.–Fri. from 5 p.m. to midnight, Sat. and Sun. 3 p.m. to midnight
Specialties: Fresh cheese and pretzels
Worth seeing: Foundations of a Roman tower fortress

Vineyard area: 12 hectares
Annual production: 80,000 bottles
Top sites: Wallufer Walkenberg, Eltviller Rheinberg
Soil types: Deep loess and loam
Grape varieties: 81% Riesling, 17% Spätburgunder, 2% Müller-Thurgau
Average yield: 54 hl/ha
Best vintages: 1992, 1994, 1995

Hans-Josef Becker is no typical vintner. Among the many highly individual winemakers of the Rheingau, this small man with a mustache similar to that of Salvador Dalí is one of the most unusual. He has his own ideas about how his dry wines should taste and understands well who will be buying them. Becker ages his white wines in casks for almost an entire year before bottling; the red wines are aged two years. This is one of the reasons his dry wines develop more slowly than comparable wines from his colleagues. The 1995 whites showed Becker in his best light; the 1996 and 1997 ranges were not quite as successful. For lovers of mature Rieslings he offers nearly 100 fine wines from the last two decades at very moderate prices. We are particularly fond of the 1983 Bildstock Spätlese.

1996 Wallufer Walkenberg
Riesling Kabinett trocken
12 DM, 10.5%, ♀ till 2001 **88**

1997 Riesling
Spätlese trocken
16 DM, 12.5%, ♀ till 2005 **88**

1997 Wallufer Walkenberg
Riesling Spätlese trocken
20 DM, 13%, ♀ till 2005 **88**

1997 Wallufer Oberberg
Riesling Kabinett halbtrocken
11.50 DM, 10%, ♀ till 2004 **88**

1997 Martinsthaler Rödchen
Riesling Kabinett
12.50 DM, 10.5%, ♀ till 2000 **88**

1996 Eltviller Rheinberg
Riesling Spätlese trocken
18 DM, 11.5%, ♀ till 2003 **89**

1996 Wallufer Walkenberg
Riesling Spätlese trocken
20 DM, 12.5%, ♀ till 2002 **89**

1996 Wallufer Walkenberg
Riesling Spätlese halbtrocken
19 DM, 11%, ♀ till 2002 **89**

1997 Wallufer Walkenberg
Riesling Auslese
35 DM, 10.5%, ♀ till 2010 **94**

——— Red wines ———

1996 Wallufer Walkenberg
Spätburgunder trocken
17 DM, 12.5%, ♀ till 2005 **88**

750 ml
alc. 12,0% by vol.
SEIT
1893
J. B. BECKER
Rheingau
1996er Riesling Spätlese trocken
Wallufer Walkenberg
A. P. Nr. 37030 006 97
Product of Germany
Qualitätswein mit Prädikat · Erzeugerabfüllung Weingut J. J. Becker, D-65396 Walluf

WEINGUT GEORG BREUER

Owners: Bernhard and Heinrich Breuer
Winemaker: Hermann Schmoranz
65385 Rüdesheim, Grabenstraße 8
Tel. (0 67 22) 10 27, Fax 45 31
e-mail: georg-breuer@t-online.de
Directions: Via B 42, in the center of Rüdesheim
Sales: Bernhard Breuer
Opening hours: Easter to November: Mon.– Sat. 10 a.m. to 5:30 p.m.
November to Easter:
Mon.–Sat. 9:30 a.m. to 4:30 p.m.
Restaurant: "Weinbistro Berg Schloßberg," open evenings, closed Wed.
Specialties: Regional dishes
Worth seeing: Historic vaulted cellar

Vineyard area: 23 hectares
Annual production: 80,000 bottles
Top sites: Rüdesheimer Berg Schloßberg and Berg Rottland, Rauenthaler Nonnenberg
Soil types: Taunus quartz with slate deposits, stony phyllite
Grape varieties: 89% Riesling, 4% Grauburgunder, 7% other varieties
Average yield: 36 hl/ha
Best vintages: 1993, 1994, 1995
Member: Charta, VDP, Deutsches Barrique Forum

Bernhard Breuer's dedication to the Rheingau is exemplary. He remains one of the defining assets of the Charta association and has, for many years, supported the attempt to classify the region's top vineyard sites. Since 1990 his wines have improved to an extraordinary degree, which was why we honored him as our "Rising Star" in a recent guide. While neither the rich 1995s, the racy, tightly structured 1996s nor the well-balanced 1997s perhaps quite reach the highest standards of the excellent preceding vintages, they belong among the best not only of the Rheingau, but of all of Germany. Weil's succulent Auslese are without doubt often better, but no one makes finer dry wines with Breuer's regularity.

1997 Rauenthaler Nonnenberg
Riesling "Erstes Gewächs"
42 DM, 12.5%, ♀ till 2004 **90**

1996 Rüdesheimer Berg Schloßberg
Riesling trocken
45 DM, 12%, ♀ till 2003 **90**

1997 Rüdesheimer Bischofsberg
Riesling Auslese – 15 –
30 DM/0.375 liter, 10%, ♀ till 2006 **91**

1997 Rüdesheimer Berg Schloßberg
Riesling "Erstes Gewächs"
46 DM, 12.5%, ♀ till 2006 **91**

1996 Rüdesheimer Berg Schloßberg
Riesling Auslese
90 DM/0.375 liter, 8.5%, ♀ till 2006 **92**

1997 Rüdesheimer Berg Rottland
Riesling Auslese Goldkapsel
45 DM/0.375 liter, 9.5%, ♀ till 2010 **92**

1996 Rüdesheimer Bischofsberg
Riesling Eiswein – 17 –
190 DM/0.375 liter, 9.5%, ♀ till 2012 **95**

1997 Rüdesheimer Bischofsberg
Riesling Beerenauslese
120 DM/0.375 liter, 9%, ♀ till 2012 **95**

1997 Rüdesheimer Bischofsberg
Riesling Trockenbeerenauslese
240 DM/0.375 liter, 8%, ♀ till 2010 **95**

DOMDECHANT WERNER'SCHES WEINGUT

Owner: Dr. Franz-Werner Michel
Manager and Winemaker: Michael Bott
65234 Hochheim,
Rathausstraße 30, Mailbox 12 05
Tel. (0 61 46) 83 50 37, Fax 83 50 38
Directions: A 66 Wiesbaden–Darmstadt, exit Hochheim-Süd, towards the center of town, after 100 meters turn right into the vineyards
Sales: Oda Michel
Opening hours: Mon.–Fri. 8 a.m. to 6 p.m. Sat. 8 a.m. to 1 p.m. by appointment
History: The name is derived from Domdechant Dr. Franz Werner, who acquired the estate in 1780
Worth seeing: Old estate buildings, family wine museum

Vineyard area: 12.3 hectares
Annual production: 90,000 bottles
Top sites: Hochheimer Domdechaney, Kirchenstück and Hölle
Soil types: Chalk, loam and loess
Grape varieties: 98% Riesling, 2% Spätburgunder
Average yield: 62 hl/ha
Best vintages: 1990, 1994, 1996
Member: VDP

Dr. Franz-Werner Michel, the seventh generation of this estate's family, places a great deal of emphasis on export. At least half of his production goes abroad, particularly those wines made in the lush sweet style that is the hallmark of this estate. The other half is made in a drier style that finds its way into professional hands among the wine merchants and restaurant owners in Germany. Regrettably, the quality of recent vintages has been most irregular. After the excellent 1994s, the 1995s were rather mediocre. The 1996 Domdechaney Spätlese provoked memories of the fabulous 1994 Kirchenstück Spätlese; the superb 1996 ice wine from the Domdechaney led us to believe that this estate was again upwardly mobile. The 1997s, however, did not live up to our expectations. With more continuity, this could be one of the leading estates of the Rheingau.

1997 Hochheimer Hölle
Riesling Spätlese trocken
16.80 DM, 11.5%, ♀ till 2002 **84**

1996 Hochheimer Domdechaney
Riesling Kabinett halbtrocken
12.80 DM, 10%, ♀ till 2001 **84**

1997 Hochheimer Hölle
Riesling Kabinett
12.50 DM, 10%, ♀ till 2004 **84**

1997 Hochheimer Kirchenstück
Riesling Spätlese
21.50 DM, 8.5%, ♀ till 2004 **86**

1997 Hochheimer Domdechaney
Riesling Auslese
38 DM, 8.5%, ♀ till 2004 **86**

1997 Hochheimer Domdechaney
Riesling Spätlese
23.75 DM, 8.5%, ♀ till 2005 **88**

1996 Hochheimer Hölle
Riesling Kabinett
12.20 DM, 8.5%, ♀ till 2004 **89**

1996 Hochheimer Domdechaney
Riesling Spätlese
21.10 DM, 7.5%, ♀ till 2006 **92**

1996 Hochheimer Domdechaney
Riesling Eiswein
120 DM/0.5 liter, 8%, ♀ 2000 till 2010 **96**

WEINGUT ANTON DOUFRAIN

Owner: Anton Doufrain
65347 Hattenheim,
Eberbacher Straße 11–13
Tel. (0 67 23) 24 28, Fax 30 41
Directions: From Wiesbaden B 42, in the direction of Rüdesheim, exit Hattenheim
Sales: Doufrain family
Opening hours: Mon.–Sat. 9 a.m. to 6 p.m. or by appointment
Restaurant: Open during *Rheingau gourmet week* in May
History: Family estate since 1724
Worth seeing: Beautiful old cask cellar, vaulted cellar from the 13th century

Vineyard area: 6 hectares
Annual production: 50,000 bottles
Top sites: Hattenheimer Nußbrunnen, Engelmannsberg
Soil types: Gravel, loam, fossil limestone and loess
Grape varieties: 80% Riesling, 20% Spät- and Frühburgunder
Average yield: 65 hl/ha
Best vintages: 1993, 1994, 1995

Anton Doufrain is a man of few words. If you ask him about his philosophy in the vineyard and cellar, he replies succinctly: "average yields, good quality, reasonable prices." His solid work, paired with the long winemaking tradition in the family, has been honored repeatedly with major state prizes. His bottle-fermented sparkling wines, too, have won numerous awards in recent years. He uses his Spätburgunder grapes to make both rosé and red wines; we even preferred the 1996 rosé to the Rieslings. The quality of the 1996 range as a whole was slightly inferior to that of the three vintages preceding it. The 1997s were even less successful.

1997 Hattenheimer Nußbrunnen
Riesling Kabinett halbtrocken
11 DM, 9.5%, ♀ till 2000 **75**

1997 Hattenheimer Engelmannsberg
Riesling trocken
9 DM, 10%, ♀ till 2000 **75**

1996 Hattenheimer Deutelsberg
Riesling Kabinett trocken
9.40 DM/1.0 liter, 10.5%, ♀ now **77**

1997 Hattenheimer Schützenhaus
Riesling Spätlese
15 DM, 9.5%, ♀ till 2000 **77**

1996 Hattenheimer Engelmannsberg
Riesling Kabinett trocken
11.50 DM, 10.5%, ♀ now **80**

1996 Hattenheimer Hassel
Riesling halbtrocken
9 DM/1.0 liter, 11%, ♀ now **80**

1996 Hattenheimer Nußbrunnen
Riesling Kabinett halbtrocken
12.50 DM, 11%, ♀ till 2001 **82**

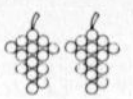

WEINGUT AUGUST ESER

Owners: Joachim and Renée Eser
Manager: Joachim Eser
Winemaker: Joachim Eser
65375 Oestrich-Winkel,
Friedensplatz 19
Tel. (0 67 23) 50 32, Fax 8 74 06
Directions: B 42, exit Oestrich, to the old village center, across from "Hotel Grüner Baum" to Friedensplatz
Sales: Joachim and Renée Eser
Opening hours: Mon.–Fri. 9 a.m. to noon and 1 p.m. to 5 p.m.
Sat. 9 a.m. to noon

Vineyard area: 10 hectares
Annual production: 85,000 bottles
Top sites: Oestricher Lenchen and Doosberg, Rauenthaler Rothenberg, Winkeler Hasensprung, Hattenheimer Wisselbrunnen and Nußbrunnen, Hallgartener Schönhell
Soil types: Tertiary heavy chalky loam
Grape varieties: 96% Riesling, 4% Spätburgunder
Average yield: 65 hl/ha
Best vintages: 1990, 1992, 1993
Member: Charta, VDP

The friendly Joachim Eser is one of the more unassuming growers of the Rheingau. In order not to be confused with his numerous namesakes, he adorned his label with a large golden key that allegedly opens the door to Rheingau Rieslings. Today the label depicts an abstracted key that is harder to recognize. In the early 1990s Eser's wines were among the best of the Rheingau. In the 1994 vintage, however, several wines were not quite up to par; the 1995s were even less alluring. The 1996 and 1997 ranges marked a further drop in overall quality, for which we have little explanation. Quo vadis?

1997 Oestricher Lenchen
Riesling Kabinett trocken
10 DM, 11.5%, ♀ till 2000 **82**

1996 Oestricher Klosterberg
Riesling halbtrocken
8.20 DM, 10.5%, ♀ till 2000 **82**

1996 Rauenthaler Rothenberg
Riesling Spätlese
16.50 DM, 9.5%, ♀ now **82**

1997 Oestricher Lenchen
Riesling Spätlese trocken
16 DM, 11.5%, ♀ till 2002 **84**

1997 Oestricher Doosberg
Riesling Kabinett halbtrocken
10 DM, 10.5%, ♀ till 2003 **84**

1997 Rauenthaler Rothenberg
Riesling Kabinett
10.50 DM, 9.5%, ♀ till 2002 **84**

1997 Rauenthaler Rothenberg
Riesling Spätlese
16.50 DM, 10.5%, ♀ till 2002 **84**

1997 Oestricher Lenchen
Riesling Auslese
60 DM, 10.5%, ♀ till 2002 **84**

1997 Erbacher Siegelsberg
Riesling "Erstes Gewächs"
18 DM, 12%, ♀ till 2002 **88**

1996 Oestricher Lenchen
Riesling Eiswein
90 DM/0.5 liter, 8.5%, ♀ till 2005 **89**

WEINGUT JOACHIM FLICK

Owner: Reiner Flick
65439 Flörsheim-Wicker, Straßenmühle
Tel. (0 61 45) 76 86, Fax 5 43 93
Directions: A 66, exit Flörsheim
Opening hours: Mon.–Fri. 10 a.m. to noon and 1 p.m. to 7 p.m.
Sat. 10 a.m. to 2 p.m.
Restaurant: March to July and September to November
Open Wed.–Sun. from 4 p.m. to 11 p.m.
Closed Mon. and Tue.
History: Estate in the family since 1775

Vineyard area: 10 hectares
Annual production: 80,000 bottles
Top sites: Wickerer Mönchsgewann and Stein, Hochheimer Hölle
Soil types: Loess, loam and limestone
Grape varieties: 81% Riesling, 10% Spätburgunder, 4% each of Weißburgunder and Grauburgunder, 1% Traminer
Average yield: 75 hl/ha
Best vintages: 1992, 1994, 1997

Reiner Flick is one of this region's assets. He is not only the chairman of the young-growers' association in the Rheingau, but also a nimble patron of the initiative to produce "Rheingauer Leichtsinn," an alternative to the very successful Italian sparkling wine Prosecco. Not surprisingly, with an annual production of 10,000 bottles, sparkling wine also plays an important part in his own business. His vineyards still demand a lot of manual work, and he tries to improve the quality during harvest by means of selection. One fifth of his production is sold through the estate's own wine bar. The 1996s were, across the board, of only mediocre quality. Flick, however, bounced back with a much more successful 1997 collection. With a touch of continuity, this estate could become a more serious factor in the region.

1997 Wickerer Mönchsgewann
Riesling Kabinett trocken
7.50 DM, 11.5%, ♀ till 2000 **80**

1997 Wickerer Stein
Riesling Kabinett halbtrocken
6.80 DM, 11%, ♀ till 2000 **80**

1996 Wickerer Stein
Riesling Spätlese
11.50 DM, 10.5%, ♀ till 2000 **82**

1997 Hochheimer Stielweg
Riesling Spätlese halbtrocken
22.50 DM, 13%, ♀ till 2004 **84**

1997 Wickerer Mönchsgewann
Riesling "Charta"
12 DM, 11%, ♀ till 2001 **84**

1997 Hochheimer Hölle
Riesling Spätlese
25 DM/0.375 liter, 8.5%, ♀ till 2005 **89**

1997 Hochheimer Hölle
Riesling Eiswein – 11 –
35 DM/0.375 liter, 8%, ♀ till 2006 **92**

1997 Hochheimer Hölle
Riesling Beerenauslese
45 DM/0.375 liter, 8%, ♀ till 2008 **92**

1996 Wickerer Mönchsgewann
Riesling Eiswein
85 DM/0.375 liter, 7.5%, ♀ till 2008 **95**

WEINGUT DER FORSCHUNGSANSTALT GEISENHEIM

Owner: State of Hesse
Winemaker: Karl Engelmann
65366 Geisenheim, Kirchspiel
Tel. (0 67 22) 50 21 71, Fax 50 21 70
e-mail:
akost@geisenheim.fa.fh-wiesbaden.de
Directions: B 42 from Wiesbaden or Koblenz, follow signposts to "Fachgebiet Kellerwirtschaft"
Sales: Anika Kost
Opening hours: Mon.–Thur. 8 a.m. to noon and 1 p.m. to 5 p.m., Fri. 8 a.m. to 1 p.m., or by appointment
History: College founded by the king of Prussia in 1872

> Vineyard area: 20 hectares
> Annual production: 150,000 bottles
> Top sites: Geisenheimer Rothenberg, Kläuserweg and Mäuerchen
> Soil types: Sandy loam and loess
> Grape varieties: 71% Riesling, 8% Spätburgunder, 7% Müller-Thurgau, 14% other varieties
> Average yield: 58 hl/ha
> Best vintages: 1992, 1993, 1994
> Member: Charta, Deutsches Barrique Forum, VDP

The college of Geisenheim has a worldwide reputation as a training ground for young winemakers. The school also produces some 150,000 bottles of wine per year from its experimental plantings. Riesling constitutes about two-thirds of the total production, but ten percent is made from entirely new varieties. The 1996 and 1997 ranges were, as a whole, of decent quality, yet we can't help wondering why more isn't made of this estate's potential. The Chardonnay is improving, the Weißburgunder is becoming more interesting with each passing year and even the red Frühburgunder can also be surprising. On the other hand, we are often less than impressed by the Rieslings. The civil servants of wine are no better than their political counterparts.

1997 Geisenheimer Mäuerchen
Riesling Spätlese trocken
11 DM, 12%, 🍷 till 2002 — **80**

1997 Riesling
trocken "Von Lade"
11 DM, 11%, 🍷 till 2000 — **80**

1996 Riesling
trocken "Von Lade"
11 DM, 11.5%, 🍷 till 2000 — **82**

1996 Weißer Burgunder
Spätlese trocken
15 DM, 12%, 🍷 till 2000 — **82**

1996 Geisenheimer Kläuserweg
Riesling Spätlese trocken
11 DM, 12.5%, 🍷 till 2000 — **82**

1996 Chardonnay
trocken
15 DM, 12%, 🍷 till 2001 — **84**

1996 Geisenheimer Rothenberg
Riesling Spätlese
12.50 DM, 11.5%, 🍷 till 2000 — **84**

——— Red wine ———

1996 Geisenheimer Fuchsberg
Frühburgunder Spätlese
22.50 DM, 13%, 🍷 till 2005 — **86**

WEINGUT ALEXANDER FREIMUTH

Owner: Alexander Freimuth
65366 Geisenheim-Marienthal,
Am Rosengärtchen 25
Tel. (0 67 22) 98 10 70, Fax 98 10 71
Directions: B 42, exit Geisenheim, in the direction of Marienthal, on southern edge of the village in the vineyards
Sales: Karin Freimuth
Opening hours: Mon.–Sat. by appointment

Vineyard area: 6.7 hectares
Annual production: 35,000 bottles
Top site: Geisenheimer Kläuserweg, Rüdesheimer Bischofsberg
Soil types: Deep loess and loam
Grape varieties: 70% Riesling, 20% Spätburgunder, 5% each of Müller-Thurgau and Weißburgunder
Average yield: 62 hl/ha
Best vintages: 1993, 1994, 1996
Member: Charta

"Nature makes the vintage, the grower can only offer a helping hand," is Alexander Freimuth's simple credo. For many years he has used no chemical fertilizers, no herbicides and hardly any insecticides; and although he now adheres to all of the principles of the organic growers' association, he has deliberately chosen not to become a member. His wines are fermented at low temperatures in steel tanks using cultured yeasts and, for that reason, retain naturally a large amount of lively carbon dioxide. In the cellar Freimuth doesn't tamper with natural processes much either: "The less I interfere, the better it is." The estate's strengths usually lie among the dry and off-dry wines, which make up about 90 percent of production. This was particulary true of the 1996s. Across the board that vintage was quite successful for Freimuth, crowned by a concentrated ice wine. The estate appeared to be on the rise. The 1997s, however, were much less exhilarating.

1997 Geisenheimer Kläuserweg
Riesling Kabinett trocken
12 DM, 11%, 🍷 till 2000 **80**

1997 Geisenheimer Mäuerchen
Riesling Kabinett halbtrocken
11.50 DM, 10%, 🍷 till 2000 **82**

1997 Rüdesheimer Bischofsberg
Riesling Spätlese
14.50 DM, 10.5%, 🍷 till 2001 **82**

1996 Geisenheimer Mönchspfad
Riesling Kabinett trocken – 14 –
11.50 DM, 10%, 🍷 till 2000 **84**

1996 Rüdesheimer Kirchenpfad
Riesling Kabinett halbtrocken
11.50 DM, 10%, 🍷 till 2000 **84**

1996 Geisenheimer Mäuerchen
Riesling Kabinett halbtrocken
11.50 DM, 10.5%, 🍷 till 2001 **86**

1996 Geisenheimer Mönchspfad
Riesling Charta
12 DM, 11.5%, 🍷 till 2001 **86**

1996 Rüdesheimer Bischofsberg
Riesling Eiswein
78 DM/0.375 liter, 11%, 🍷 till 2008 **94**

WEINGUT PRINZ VON HESSEN

Owner: Moritz Landgraf von Hessen
Winemaker: Karl Klein
65366 Johannisberg, Grund 1
Tel. (0 67 22) 81 72, Fax 5 05 88
Directions: B 42, in the direction of Wiesbaden, exit Industriegebiet Geisenheim, in the direction of Johannisberg, at village entrance first house on the left
Opening hours: Mon.–Fri. 8 a.m. to 5 p.m., first Sat. each month 10 a.m. to 1 p.m. or by appointment

Vineyard area: 50 hectares
Annual production: 400,000 bottles
Top sites: Winkeler Hasensprung and Jesuitengarten, Johannisberger Klaus, Kiedricher Sandgrub
Soil types: Deep loess and loam over gravel, tertiary heavy chalky loam, slate
Grape varieties: 91% Riesling, 8% Spätburgunder, 1% Merlot
Average yield: 63 hl/ha
Best vintages: 1994, 1995, 1996
Member: VDP, Charta

This estate long traded as the Landgräflich Hessisches Weingut. Today most of the wines are marketed without vineyard designation under the Prinz von Hessen label. The best wines of any given vintage bear a red label with the signature of the proprietor, Moritz Landgraf von Hessen. Klaus Herrmann, the talented new general manager, produced a 1996 ice wine from the Geisenheimer Kläuserweg that was one of the finest noble sweet Rieslings from Germany in that vintage. Moreover, the Johannisberger Klaus Auslese, which has a touch of ice-wine character, was also an extremely successful wine. This estate had the makings of a rising star. Unfortunately, Herrmann has left the estate. The 1997s are certainly not of the same stature.

1997 Eltviller Langenstück
Riesling Kabinett halbtrocken
11.10 DM, 12%, 🍷 till 2001 **84**

1997 Riesling
Kabinett Charta
16.30 DM, 12.5%, 🍷 till 2000 **84**

1997 Johannisberger Klaus
Riesling Kabinett
11.40 DM, 11%, 🍷 till 2002 **86**

1996 Geisenheimer Kläuserweg
Riesling Kabinett trocken
11.30 DM, 11%, 🍷 till 2000 **88**

1996 Winkeler Hasensprung
Riesling Kabinett
12 DM, 10.5%, 🍷 till 2002 **88**

1997 Johannisberger Klaus
Riesling Spätlese
16 DM, 10%, 🍷 till 2003 **88**

1996 Johannisberger Klaus
Riesling Spätlese
15.90 DM, 10%, 🍷 till 2005 **91**

1996 Johannisberger Klaus
Riesling Auslese
34 DM, 8.5%, 🍷 till 2006 **92**

1996 Geisenheimer Kläuserweg
Riesling Eiswein
230 DM, 7%, 🍷 2000 till 2020 **98**

PRINZ VON HESSEN
1996
RIESLING SPÄTLESE
trocken
Winkeler Jesuitengarten
RHEINGAU

WEINGUT HUPFELD – "KÖNIGIN-VICTORIABERG"

Owners: Henning and Wolfram Hupfeld
65375 Oestrich-Winkel, Rheingaustraße 113
Tel. (0 67 23) 99 92 39 and 13 98, Fax 99 92 59
e-mail: weingut.hupfeld@t-online.de
Directions: B 42 towards Rüdesheim, exit Mittelheim, turn left and follow the road signs
Opening hours: Mon.–Sat. 9:30 a.m. to 7 p.m., by appointment
Worth seeing: Monument in Tudor style in the Königin-Victoriaberg vineyard in Hochheim

Vineyard area: 12 hectares
Annual production: 100,000 bottles
Top sites: Hochheimer Königin-Victoriaberg, Winkeler Jesuitengarten and Hasensprung
Soil types: Deep loess and loam
Grape varieties: 90% Riesling, 6% Spätburgunder, 4% other varieties
Average yield: 65 hl/ha
Best vintages: 1990, 1992, 1997
Member: Charta, VDP

Irmgard Hupfeld brought a dowry of five hectares of the world-famous Hochheimer Königin-Victoriaberg to her marriage. The parcel was given this name in honor of a visit by Queen Victoria to Hochheim in 1845. The estate's other vineyards lie in Johannisberg, Mittelheim, Oestrich and Winkel. Today, Irmgard's sons Henning and Wolfram manage the property. The wines are now vinified in stainless steel tanks, but are still occasionally aged in casks. The quality of the Rieslings from the past few vintages had not developed in a very positive fashion. The 1994s and 1995s were fairly patchy; nor was the 1996 range any better. The 1997s, however, are much more successful, particularly those from Hochheim. We would like to believe that this will prove to be a trend.

1997 Hochheimer Königin-Victoriaberg
Riesling Kabinett trocken
12.50 DM, 10.5%, ♀ till 2001 **82**

1996 Hochheimer Königin-Victoriaberg
Riesling Kabinett trocken
12 DM, 10%, ♀ now **82**

1997 Winkeler Jesuitengarten
Riesling Kabinett halbtrocken
9.50 DM, 10%, ♀ till 2000 **82**

1996 Riesling
Kabinett Charta
11 DM, 10%, ♀ till 2000 **82**

1997 Mittelheimer Edelmann
Riesling halbtrocken
7.70 DM, 10.5%, ♀ till 2001 **82**

1997 Hochheimer Königin-Victoriaberg
Riesling Spätlese trocken
18 DM, 12%, ♀ till 2002 **84**

1997 Hochheimer Königin-Victoriaberg
Riesling Spätlese
18 DM, 9.5%, ♀ till 2003 **84**

1996 Hochheimer Königin-Victoriaberg
Riesling Kabinett
12 DM, 9%, ♀ till 2001 **86**

1997 Hochheimer Königin-Victoriaberg
Riesling Kabinett
12.50 DM, 9%, ♀ till 2005 **88**

1996 Mittelheimer Edelmann
Riesling Kabinett
9 DM, 9%, ♀ till 2003 **88**

SCHLOSS JOHANNISBERG

Manager: Wolfgang Schleicher
General Manager: Heiner Gietz
Winemaker: Hans Kessler
65366 Johannisberg, Schloß
Tel. (0 67 22) 7 00 90, Fax 70 09 33
Directions: B 42, exit Industriegebiet Geisenheim, follow signs
Sales: Heribert Heyn and Frank Schuber
Opening hours: Mon.–Fri. 10 a.m. to 1 p.m. and 2 p.m. to 6 p.m.
Sat. and Sun. 11 a.m. to 6 p.m.
Restaurant: Open daily from 11:30 a.m. to 11 p.m., Tel. (0 67 22) 9 60 90, Fax 73 92
History: Benedictine cloister founded in 1100
Worth seeing: Baroque castle from the 18th century, basilica from the 12th century, castle cellars of 1721

Vineyard area: 35 hectares
Annual production: 250,000 bottles
Top sites: Schloß Johannisberg
Soil types: Taunus quartz, loess soils of moderate depth
Grape varieties: 100% Riesling
Average yield: 62 hl/ha
Best vintages: 1993, 1994, 1996
Member: VDP

The Schloß Johannisberg dominates the Rhine valley near Geisenheim in an absolutely majestic fashion. Legendary wines have been produced here and a few of them are still cellared in the castle's "Bibliotheca subterranea" wine treasury. The whites are fermented at controlled temperatures in a battery of stainless steel tanks that was installed to produce more vivacious wines. The 1994 range brought new life to the estate; unfortunately, many of the 1995s couldn't match them in quality. The 1996s, on the other hand, were the finest wines that we have tasted from this estate in many years. It looked as if Schloß Johannisberg were rising from the ashes. The 1997s, though, brought more humble pie. Few of the wines bear tribute to the estate's reputation.

1997 Schloß Johannisberg
Riesling Kabinett halbtrocken
21.50 DM, 10.5%, 🍷 till 2002 **84**

1997 Schloß Johannisberg
Riesling Spätlese trocken
34.90 DM, 12%, 🍷 till 2002 **86**

1997 Schloß Johannisberg
Riesling Spätlese
34.90 DM, 11.5%, 🍷 till 2005 **86**

1996 Schloß Johannisberger
Riesling Kabinett halbtrocken
19.90 DM, 10.5%, 🍷 till 2004 **88**

1996 Schloß Johannisberger
Riesling Spätlese
32.50 DM, 10.5%, 🍷 till 2005 **88**

1996 Schloß Johannisberger
Riesling Spätlese trocken
32.50 DM, 12%, 🍷 till 2002 **90**

1996 Schloß Johannisberger
Riesling Auslese
50 DM/0.5 liter, 8.5%, 🍷 till 2008 **92**

1997 Schloß Johannisberg
Riesling Beerenauslese
200 DM/0.375 liter, 11%, 🍷 till 2015 **92**

1996 Schloß Johannisberger
Riesling Eiswein
175 DM/0.5 liter, 8%, 🍷 till 2008 **94**

1996 Schloß Johannisberger
Riesling Beerenauslese
160 DM/0.375 liter, 9%, 🍷 till 2008 **94**

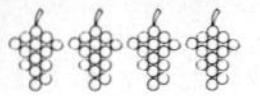

WEINGUT JOHANNISHOF

Owners: Hans Hermann and Elfriede Eser
Winemaker: Johannes Eser
65366 Johannisberg, Grund 63
Tel. (0 67 22) 82 16, Fax 63 87
Directions: B 42, exit Geisenheim, in the direction of Johannisberg, 500 meters after the village entrance, turn left
Sales: Elfriede Eser, Sabine Eser
Opening hours: Mon.–Fri. 8 a.m. to noon and 1 p.m. to 6 p.m., Sat. 10 a.m. to 3 p.m. or by appointment
History: Family estate founded in 1685
Worth seeing: Old vaulted cellar and treasury

Vineyard area: 17.7 hectares
Annual production: 120,000 bottles
Top sites: Geisenheimer Kläuserweg, Johannisberger Hölle, Rüdesheimer Berg Rottland
Soil types: Loess, loam, slate and weathered quartz
Grape varieties: 100% Riesling
Average yield: 62 hl/ha
Best vintages: 1992, 1993, 1995
Member: VDP, Charta

The sympathetic Hans Hermann Eser is the only member of his family who does not live in Oestrich-Winkel. With 14 hectares of vineyards he had been the largest proprietor among his relations for a long time. In 1996 he further increased his holdings by acquiring another 4.5 hectares in the steep vineyards of Rüdesheim from the former Grönesteyn estate. Their quality potential was well shown in the Kabinett from Kirchenpfad and the Spätlese from Berg Rottland from that vintage. Across the board, though, the 1996s weren't a match for the 1995s. Above all, the dry wines had musty undertones and were marked by a tart acidity. The 1997s are good, but certainly not up to our high expectations. This estate will have to produce fireworks next year to maintain its reputation.

1996 Rüdesheimer Kirchenpfad
Riesling Kabinett halbtrocken
12.50 DM, 10%, ♀ till 2003 **88**

1997 Johannisberger Goldatzel
Riesling Kabinett
12.50 DM, 10%, ♀ till 2004 **88**

1996 Johannisberger Goldatzel
Riesling Kabinett
12 DM, 8.5%, ♀ till 2004 **88**

1997 Rüdesheimer Berg Rottland
Riesling Spätlese
19 DM, 9%, ♀ till 2005 **88**

1997 Johannisberger Klaus
Riesling Spätlese
17.50 DM, 9%, ♀ till 2007 **88**

1996 Rüdesheimer Berg Rottland
Riesling Spätlese
18 DM, 9%, ♀ till 2005 **89**

1997 Rüdesheimer Berg Rottland
Riesling Spätlese ***
36 DM, 8%, ♀ till 2007 **92**

1997 Rüdesheimer Berg Rottland
Riesling Auslese
26 DM/0.375 liter, 8%, ♀ till 2012 **95**

1996 Johannisberger Goldatzel
Riesling Eiswein
190 DM/0.5 liter, 7.5%, ♀ till 2010 **95**

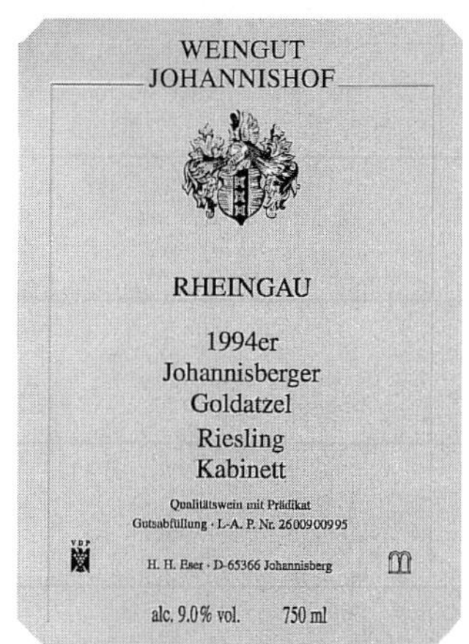

WEINGUT
JOHANNISHOF
RHEINGAU
1994er
Johannisberger
Goldatzel
Riesling
Kabinett
Qualitätswein mit Prädikat
Gutsabfüllung · L-A. P. Nr. 2600900995
H. H. Eser · D-65366 Johannisberg
alc. 9.0% vol. 750 ml

WEINGUT TONI JOST – HAHNENHOF

Owner: Peter Jost
55422 Bacharach, Oberstraße 14
Tel. (0 67 43) 12 16, Fax 10 76
Directions: A 61, exit Rheinböllen to Bacharach, estate in the town center
Sales: Linde and Peter Jost
Opening hours: By appointment
Worth seeing: Wine-tasting room in old German style

Vineyard area: 3.2 hectares
Annual production: 25,000 bottles
Top sites: Wallufer Walkenberg, Martinsthaler Rödchen
Soil types: Loess, loam and gravel
Grape varieties: 85% Riesling, 15% Spätburgunder
Average yield: 62 hl/ha
Best vintages: 1990, 1993, 1995
Member: VDP

Since 1953 the Jost property in Bacharach has also owned vineyards in the Rheingau. Peter Jost's great-grandfather ran a mill in Walluf, where he also owned two hectares of vineyards. These are managed today by an employee living in Walluf. After harvest, the grapes are immediately transported to Bacharach, crushed that evening and vinified with the same care that Jost devotes to his own wines. With a wide array of sweet Auslese, the 1989 vintage generated the finest wines of the last decade; the 1990s were marked by a glorious acidity. A more modest period followed until the 1995 vintage, from which we particularly liked the superb Goldkapsel Auslese. The 1996 range was again of rather modest quality, which Peter Jost attributed to the green cover crops in these vineyards. To bring down the resulting drought stress, he ploughed up the cover crop in every second row. The 1997s are better, but not yet fit for a match with his wines from the Mittelrhein.

1996 Martinsthaler Rödchen
Riesling trocken
9.30 DM, 10.5%, ♀ till 2002 **84**

1997 Wallufer Walkenberg
Riesling Kabinett trocken
11.20 DM, 11%, ♀ till 2001 **84**

1996 Wallufer Walkenberg
Riesling Kabinett halbtrocken
10.80 DM, 9.5%, ♀ till 2002 **84**

1997 Wallufer Walkenberg
Riesling Spätlese trocken
16.80 DM, 11%, ♀ till 2002 **86**

1997 Wallufer Walkenberg
Riesling Spätlese halbtrocken
16.50 DM, 11%, ♀ till 2003 **88**

1997 Wallufer Walkenberg
Riesling Spätlese
18 DM, 9.5%, ♀ till 2005 **88**

Red wines

1996 Wallufer Walkenberg
Spätburgunder trocken
18.80 DM, 12%, ♀ till 2002 **82**

1995 Wallufer Walkenberg
Spätburgunder trocken
18.80 DM, 12%, ♀ till 2002 **82**

WEINGUT TONI JOST
HAHNENHOF
RHEINGAU
1996er
Wallufer Walkenberg
Riesling Kabinett
trocken
alc 10,5%vol
Gutsabfüllung
750 ml
Qualitätswein mit Prädikat · A. P. Nr. 3701900697
Weingut Toni Jost · Hahnenhof · D-55422 Bacharach

WEINGUT JAKOB JUNG

Owner: Ludwig Jung
65346 Erbach, Eberbacher Straße 22
Tel. (0 61 23) 90 06 20, Fax 90 06 21
Directions: B 42, exit Erbach-Mitte
Sales: Brunhilde Jung
Opening hours: Mon.–Fri. 3:30 p.m. to 7 p.m., Sat. 10 a.m. to 5 p.m. Sun. by appointment
History: Estate in the family since 1799
Worth seeing: 200-year-old cellar in the cliffs, eight meters underground

Vineyard area: 7.5 hectares
Annual production: 70,000 bottles
Top sites: Erbacher Hohenrain, Steinmorgen and Michelmark
Soil types: Deep loess and loam, heavy tertiary soils of chalky loam
Grape varieties: 82% Riesling, 14% Spätburgunder, 4% other varieties
Average yield: 70 hl/ha
Best vintages: 1994, 1995, 1997
Member: Charta, VDP

Ludwig Jung, who was just 18 years old when he took over this estate from his late father in 1969, is typical of the dependable, hard-working growers of the region. Fifteen years ago, before there was any talk of an association for ecologically conscious viticulture, Ludwig Jung was already practicing it. This involves both planting a green cover crop between the rows of vines and a complete renunciation of herbicides. His motto was simple: "Everything begins in the vineyard." Following ancient tradition, the wines spend a long time on their lees to give them more body and extract. Before the 1992 and 1993 vintages Ludwig Jung was seldom noticed outside the Rheingau. In 1994 and 1995 he produced even more astonishing wines. The 1996s, however, were not quite as good. Apart from the excellent ice wine from the Hohenrain, all the wines had a flavor of unripe acidity. The 1997s are much more succesful, and all of his wines continue to offer good value for money. Jung's private clientele continues to reward him for this with their loyalty.

1997 Erbacher Steinmorgen
Riesling Spätlese trocken
13.50 DM, 12.5%, ♀ till 2002 **88**

1997 Erbacher Hohenrain
Riesling Kabinett halbtrocken
8.60 DM, 11%, ♀ till 2003 **88**

1996 Riesling
Kabinett Charta
12 DM, 11.5%, ♀ till 2002 **88**

1997 Erbacher Michelmark
Riesling Spätlese
12.50 DM, 11.5%, ♀ till 2006 **88**

1997 Erbacher Hohenrain
Riesling "Erstes Gewächs"
20 DM, 13%, ♀ till 2003 **88**

1996 Erbacher Hohenrain
Riesling trocken
20 DM, 12%, ♀ till 2000 **89**

1997 Erbacher Hohenrain
Riesling Spätlese trocken
16 DM, 13%, ♀ till 2003 **89**

1997 Erbacher Michelmark
Riesling Spätlese halbtrocken
13 DM, 12%, ♀ till 2004 **89**

1996 Erbacher Michelmark
Riesling Eiswein
75 DM/0.375 liter, 8.5%, ♀ till 2010 **94**

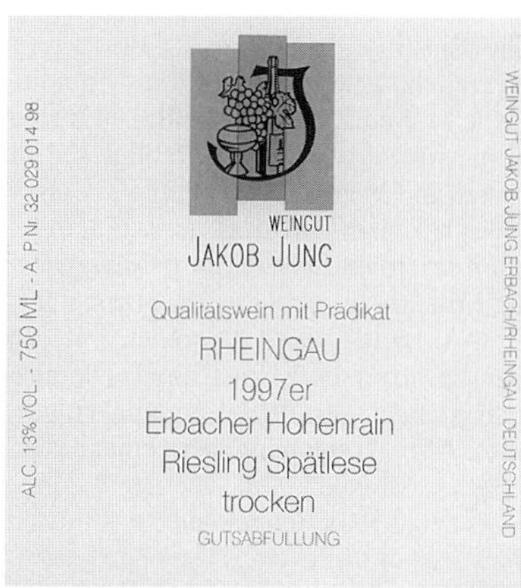

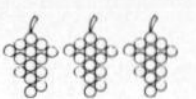

WEINGUT GRAF VON KANITZ

Owner: Count Carl Albrecht von Kanitz
Manager: Ralf Bengel
Winemaker: Jochen Drück
65391 Lorch, Rheinstraße 49
Tel. (0 67 26) 3 46, Fax 21 78
Directions: B 42, between Rüdesheim and the Loreley, signposted at Lorch exit
Sales: Ralf Bengel
Opening hours: Mon.–Fri. 9 a.m. to 5 p.m., Sat. noon to 4 p.m.
Restaurant: "Das Hilchenhaus," April–October from noon to 11 p.m., November–March from 5 p.m. to 11 p.m., closed Thur.
Specialties: Trout from Wispertal
History: Mentioned in the 13th century, later owned by the Baron vom Stein, since 1926 the property of the Counts of Kanitz
Worth seeing: The Hilchenhaus, a Renaissance structure of 1546

Vineyard area: 13.5 hectares
Annual production: 80,000 bottles
Top sites: Lorcher Bodental-Steinberg, Kapellenberg and Krone
Soil types: Quartz, weathered slate and sandy loam
Grape varieties: 91% Riesling, 5% Spätburgunder, 4% Müller-Thurgau
Average yield: 44 hl/ha
Best vintages: 1995, 1996,1997
Member: VDP, Charta, BÖW

The Rieslings from Lorch have a very special character; and the wines from the estate of the Count von Kanitz, produced from vines grown on soils composed of quartz and weathered slate, have a juicy style that, paired with their firm acidity, often resemble those from the neighboring Mittelrhein. As a rule they need a few years in bottle to come round, but can then be surprisingly long-lived. The new management introduced organic viticulture. After convincing performances in 1994, 1995 and 1996, the 1997 range proves that Ralf Bengel has consolidated the status of this estate as one of the most reliable producers from the Rheingau.

1997 Lorcher Schloßberg
Riesling Spätlese trocken
15.70 DM, 12.5%, ♀ till 2003 **86**

1996 Lorcher Bodental-Steinberg
Riesling Kabinett
11.20 DM, 10%, ♀ till 2000 **86**

1997 Lorcher Kapellenberg
Riesling Kabinett halbtrocken
11.60 DM, 11.5%, ♀ till 2004 **88**

1997 Lorcher Bodental-Steinberg
Riesling Spätlese
15.70 DM, 10.5%, ♀ till 2005 **88**

1996 Lorcher Krone
Riesling Spätlese
25 DM, 10.5%, ♀ till 2003 **88**

1997 Lorcher Kapellenberg
Riesling Beerenauslese
94 DM/0.5 liter, 10%, ♀ till 2006 **88**

1997 Lorcher Krone
Riesling Spätlese
29 DM, 11%, ♀ till 2004 **89**

1996 Lorcher Kapellenberg
Riesling Auslese
63 DM/0.5 liter, 10%, ♀ till 2006 **91**

WEINGUT AUGUST KESSELER

Owner: August Kesseler
Winemaker: Velten Tiemann
65385 Assmannshausen,
Lorcher Straße 16
Tel. (0 67 22) 25 13, Fax 4 74 77
Directions: B 42, exit Assmannshausen, in the village center, left near the church
Sales: Beate Kesseler
Opening hours: Mon.–Fri. 8 a.m. to 5 p.m., Sat. by appointment
Worth seeing: Old wine cellar of 1793 in the slate hills

Vineyard area: 16 hectares
Annual production: 90,000 bottles
Top sites: Assmannshäuser Höllenberg, Rüdesheimer Berg Schloßberg and Berg Roseneck
Soil types: Phyllite slate and quartz
Grape varieties: 50% Spätburgunder, 40% Riesling, 10% Silvaner
Average yield: Red wine 35 hl/ha, white wine 55 hl/ha
Best vintages: 1990, 1993, 1996
Member: VDP, Charta

For ten years August Kesseler has worked to reinvent the venerable image of the red wines from Assmannshausen by using small oak barrels – and has achieved astonishing success. There is hardly a fine restaurant in Germany that doesn't have his Spätburgunder on its list. Kesseler, whose main job is that of managing the estate of Schloß Reinhartshausen in Erbach, has now taken leave of extreme methods and today employs new oak discreetly for specific wines. He has also expanded his commitment to more luscious sweet Rieslings. The 1996 range offered the finest wines in that style that this estate has ever produced. Also superb was the rosé Beerenauslese from the Höllenberg. Although the yields were quite small, the red wines from 1995 and 1996 were of very good quality. The 1997 vintage wasn't any different: a spring frost wrecked much of the potential crop. That the resulting wines turned out so well is almost a miracle.

1996
Riesling
13.30 DM, 10.5%, ♀ till 2003 **88**

1996 Rüdesheimer Berg Roseneck
Riesling Kabinett
21 DM, 8.5%, ♀ till 2003 **88**

1997 Riesling
trocken
13.30 DM, 11.5%, ♀ till 2002 **88**

1997 Rüdesheimer Berg Roseneck
Riesling Spätlese
26.90 DM, 11%, ♀ till 2005 **89**

1996 Rüdesheimer Berg Rottland
Riesling Spätlese
36 DM, 9.5%, ♀ till 2006 **89**

1996 Rüdesheimer Bischofsberg
Riesling Auslese
32 DM/0.375 liter, 8%, ♀ till 2007 **92**

1996 Rüdesheimer Bischofsberg
Riesling Trockenbeerenauslese
207 DM/0.375 liter, 7.5%, ♀ till 2012 **94**

1996 Assmannshäuser Höllenberg
Spätburgunder Weißherbst Beerenauslese
72 DM/0.375 liter, 8%, ♀ till 2006 **94**

——— Red wines ———

1996 Assmannshäuser Höllenberg
Spätburgunder Spätlese trocken ***
73 DM, 12.5%, ♀ till 2007 **91**

1996 Assmannshäuser Höllenberg
Spätburgunder Spätlese trocken **
65.50 DM, 13%, ♀ till 2006 **92**

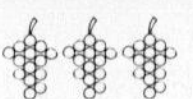

WEINGUT FREIHERR ZU KNYPHAUSEN

Owner: Gerko Freiherr zu Innhausen and Knyphausen
Winemaker: Rainer Rüttiger
65346 Erbach, Klosterhof Drais
Tel. (0 61 23) 6 21 77, Fax 43 15
Directions: A 66, exit Eltville-West, in the direction of Erbach, first house on the left
Opening hours: Mon.–Fri. 8 a.m. to noon and 2 p.m. to 6 p.m., Sat. 10 a.m. to noon and 2 p.m. to 4 p.m. or by appointment
History: Monastic buildings founded by Cistercian monks in 1141, bought in 1818 by the Freiherr von Bodelschwingh
Worth seeing: Estate buildings of 1727, wine columns with carvings

Vineyard area: 22 hectares
Annual production: 130,000 bottles
Top sites: Erbacher Marcobrunn, Steinmorgen, Hohenrain and Siegelsberg, Hattenheimer Wisselbrunnen
Soil types: Mica with tertiary heavy chalky loam, partly loess
Grape varieties: 96% Riesling, 4% Spätburgunder
Average yield: 56 hl/ha
Best vintages: 1992, 1994, 1997
Member: VDP, Charta

Gerko zu Knyphausen is among the least assuming men in this region. He makes little fuss about his beautifully situated estate nor much about himself either. For years the ascetic baron has cultivated classic Rheingau Riesling; but there are now some concessions to the spirit of the times being made. Malolactic fermentation, for example, is used to soften the popular wine "Knippie," which is sold in trendy white Bordeaux bottles. The vineyards are divided principally between Erbach and Kiedrich, but Knyphausen also owns smaller parcels in Hattenheim and Eltville. In good vintages his wines are always racy and elegant. After two less spectacular years, Knyphausen has again produced a solid range of 1997s. This is a reliable estate that deserves more attention.

1997 Erbacher Steinmorgen
Riesling Kabinett trocken
12 DM, 11.5%, 🍷 till 2001 **86**

1997 Erbacher Michelmark
Riesling Spätlese halbtrocken
20 DM, 11.5%, 🍷 till 2001 **86**

1996 Eltviller Taubenberg
Riesling Charta
11 DM, 10.5%, 🍷 till 2000 **86**

1997 Erbacher Steinmorgen
Riesling Kabinett
12 DM, 10%, 🍷 till 2004 **88**

1997 Hattenheimer Wisselbrunnen
Riesling "Erstes Gewächs"
30 DM, 12.5%, 🍷 till 2002 **88**

1996 Erbacher Marcobrunn
Riesling trocken
27 DM, 12%, 🍷 till 2001 **89**

1996 Kiedricher Sandgrub
Riesling Spätlese
18.50 DM, 9%, 🍷 till 2004 **89**

1997 Hattenheimer Wisselbrunnen
Riesling Auslese
43.50 DM/0.5 liter, 8.5%, 🍷 till 2006 **89**

1997 Erbacher Steinmorgen
Riesling Spätlese
22 DM, 8.5%, 🍷 till 2007 **91**

1996 Erbacher Siegelsberg
Riesling Eiswein Goldkapsel
130 DM/0.5 liter, 7%, 🍷 till 2010 **91**

VERITAS VINCIT
BARON ZU KNYPHAUSEN
1997er Erbacher Marcobrunn
Riesling Spätlese
Gutsabfüllung Weingut Freiherr zu Knyphausen
Klosterhof Drais · Erbach im Rheingau · Deutschland
RHEINGAU
Alc. 9.5% vol.
750 ml

WEINGUT ROBERT KÖNIG

Owner: Robert König Sr.
Winemaker: Robert König Jr.
65385 Assmannshausen,
Landhaus Kenner
Tel. (0 67 22) 10 64, Fax 4 86 56
Directions: Via Aulhausen, follow signs to parking lot Mühlberg
Opening hours: By appointment
Restaurant: Open during the *Rheingau gourmet week*
History: Estate founded in 1704

Vineyard area: 8 hectares
Annual production: 50,000 bottles
Top sites: Assmannshäuser Höllenberg, Frankenthal and Rüdesheimer Berg Schloßberg
Soil types: Weathered Taunus quartz, weathered phyllite slate
Grape varieties: 90% Spätburgunder, 5% Riesling, 2% Weißburgunder, 2% Frühburgunder, 1% other varieties
Average yield: 48 hl/ha
Best vintages: 1990, 1993, 1996
Member: VDP

Although grandfather Josef König expanded the vineyards to two hectares in the 1960s and 1970s, wine was only a hobby for this estate until a few years ago. At that time the family's attention was focused on their flourishing building business, which was their principal source of income. Robert König and his son abandoned construction in 1987 and are now full-time vintners. Robert Jr., a young graduate of the Geisenheim college, thirsts for action and has the talent to succeed. The 1996s and 1997s are all of reliable quality. This estate is definitely on an upward trend!

1996 Assmannshäuser Höllenberg
Spätburgunder Weißherbst Auslese
28.50 DM/0.5 liter, 8%, ♀ till 2006 **91**

Red wines

1997 Assmannshäuser Höllenberg
Spätburgunder Kabinett trocken
17.90 DM, 12%, ♀ till 2003 **84**

1996 Assmannshäuser Höllenberg
Spätburgunder trocken
14.95 DM, 12%, ♀ till 2003 **86**

1997 Assmannshäuser Höllenberg
Spätburgunder Auslese trocken
42 DM/0.5 liter, 14%, ♀ till 2005 **88**

1996 Assmannshäuser Frankenthal
Spätburgunder Kabinett trocken
16 DM, 12%, ♀ till 2005 **88**

1997 Assmannshäuser Höllenberg
Spätburgunder Spätlese trocken
23.90 DM, 13%, ♀ till 2004 **88**

1997 Assmannshäuser Höllenberg
Frühburgunder Spätlese trocken
32.95 DM, 14%, ♀ till 2005 **89**

1996 Assmannshäuser Höllenberg
Spätburgunder Spätlese trocken
22.50 DM, 13%, ♀ till 2006 **89**

1996 Assmannshäuser Höllenberg
Frühburgunder Spätlese trocken
33.50 DM, 13%, ♀ till 2006 **91**

WEINGUT KRONE

Owner: Dr. Hufnagel-Ullrich family
Winemaker: Peter Perabo
65385 Assmannshausen,
Rheinuferstraße 10
Tel. (0 67 22) 40 30, Fax 4 83 46
Directions: B 42 from Rüdesheim in the direction of Koblenz, Assmannshausen exit, parallel to B 42 to the Hotel Krone
Opening hours: By appointment
Worth seeing: Historic Krone hotel, wine cellars carved into the cliffs in the Frankenthal vineyard

Vineyard area: 3.4 hectares
Annual production: 16,500 bottles
Top sites: Assmannshäuser Höllenberg and Frankenthal, Rüdesheimer Berg Schloßberg
Soil types: Slate
Grape varieties: 100% Spätburgunder
Average yield: 40 hl/ha
Best vintages: 1994, 1996, 1997

Experienced growers know that this estate owns the finest parcels in the celebrated Höllenberg vineyard in Assmannshausen. The red wines, which in their succulent style are often reminiscent of fine Burgundy, have little in common with the commercial style of Assmannshausen so beloved by tourists. Since Peter Perabo, an outstanding young grower from Lorch, has been responsible for vinification, the red wines have become even more full bodied. He fosters malolactic fermentation and is revitalizing the *barrique* aging of the estate's wines. The interesting 1996 Auslese, following on the heels of an equally fine 1995, showed such quality that we were led to expect even more from these luscious rosés in the future. The 1997s were no disappointment. Quite the contrary! This is the finest range of wines that we have ever tasted from this estate. Almost the entire production is sold at the estate's own hotel or to its clients. In the superbly restored historic inn you will find an extensive assortment of the estate's wines at reasonable prices. We particularly recommend the 1989s and 1990s.

1996 Assmannshäuser Höllenberg
Spätburgunder Weißherbst Auslese
42 DM/0.375 liter, 8%, ♀ till 2001 **88**

1997 Assmannshäuser Höllenberg
Spätburgunder Weißherbst Auslese
60 DM, 9%, ♀ till 2005 **89**

1995 Rüdesheimer Berg Schloßberg
Spätburgunder Weißherbst Auslese
38 DM, 8.5%, ♀ till 2006 **92**

——— Red wines ———

1995 Assmannshäuser Frankenthal
Spätburgunder
21 DM, 12.5%, ♀ till 2001 **84**

1995 Assmannshäuser Frankenthal
Spätburgunder
24 DM/0.5 liter, 13%, ♀ till 2002 **84**

1995 Assmannshäuser Höllenberg
Spätburgunder
28 DM, 13%, ♀ 2000 till 2004 **88**

1996 Assmannshäuser Höllenberg
Spätburgunder Spätlese **
50 DM, 13%, ♀ till 2004 **88**

1996 Assmannshäuser Höllenberg
Spätburgunder Spätlese
40 DM, 13%, ♀ till 2002 **88**

1996 Assmannshäuser Höllenberg
Spätburgunder Spätlese *
45 DM, 13%, ♀ till 2004 **89**

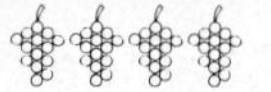

WEINGUT PETER JAKOB KÜHN

Owner: Peter Jakob Kühn
65375 Oestrich, Mühlstraße 70
Tel. (0 67 23) 22 99, Fax 8 77 88
Directions: B 42, exit Oestrich, fifth street on the right, after 600 meters it's the last house
Sales: Angela Kühn, Peter Kühn
Opening hours: Mon.–Sat. by appointment
Restaurant: For four weekends in May and 2nd, 3rd and 4th weekends in Sept., as well as one weekend in Dec. Open Fri.–Sun. from 2 p.m. to 10 p.m.
Specialties: Ham in Riesling with herb cream, Oestrich onions

Vineyard area: 12 hectares
Annual production: 82,000 bottles
Top sites: Oestricher Lenchen and Doosberg
Soil types: Clay loam and gravelly loam
Grape varieties: 83% Riesling, 17% Spätburgunder
Average yield: 61 hl/ha
Best vintages: 1995, 1996, 1997

This previously little-known estate first stepped into the limelight with its victory in the competition for the best dry Riesling of 1991 organized by the magazine *Feinschmecker*. Since then Peter Jakob Kühn has convincingly proven that this award was not won by chance. Each successive vintage was better than the one that preceded it, as if Mother Nature played only a secondary role. From liter bottlings up to Trockenbeerenauslese, the wines are of astonishing quality, generally characterized by full-bodied depth paired with tangy acidity. Although the noble sweet Rieslings were the finest wines from the 1996 vintage, 80 percent of the wines are vinified dry and sold directly to consumers. All count among the best examples of their style. The 1997s were of similar stature. This estate is, without doubt, one of the finest producers in the Rheingau at present.

1996 Oestricher Doosberg
Riesling Spätlese trocken
16 DM, 11.5%, ♀ till 2003 **89**

1997 Oestricher Lenchen
Riesling Kabinett
12 DM, 9.5%, ♀ till 2006 **89**

1997 Oestricher Lenchen
Riesling Spätlese
20 DM, 10.5%, ♀ till 2007 **92**

1997 Riesling
Auslese
45 DM/0.375 liter, 10%, ♀ till 2008 **95**

1996 Riesling
Auslese
44 DM/0.375 liter, 10%, ♀ till 2008 **95**

1996 Riesling
Eiswein
160 DM/0.375 liter, 7%, ♀ till 2015 **98**

1997 Riesling
Beerenauslese
100 DM/0.375 liter, 8%, ♀ till 2015 **98**

1996 Riesling
Trockenbeerenauslese
190 DM/0.375 liter, 7%, ♀ till 2015 **98**

Peter Jakob Kühn Riesling
1997
Oestricher
Lenchen
Kabinett
Gutsabfüllung
M. Kloos
RHEINGAU
Qualitätswein mit Prädikat
D-65375 Oestrich · A.P.Nr. 29 248 013 98
alc. 9.5 % vol.
750 ml

WEINGUT FRANZ KÜNSTLER

Owner: Gunter Künstler
Manager: Otto Völker
Winemaker: Gunter Künstler and Frank Fischer
65239 Hochheim,
Freiherr-vom-Stein-Ring 3 / Kirchstraße 38
Tel. (0 61 46) 8 25 70 and 8 38 60, Fax 57 67
Directions: A 66 Mainz–Wiesbaden, exit Hochheim/B 40
Sales: Frank Fischer, Franz-Josef Grieß
Opening hours: Kirchstraße 38: Mon.–Thur. 8 a.m. to noon and 1 p.m. to 5 p.m., Fri. 8 a.m. to noon
Freiherr-vom-Stein-Ring: Mon.–Fri. 2 p.m. to 7 p.m., Sat. 9 a.m. to 3 p.m.
Worth seeing: 500-year-old estate building with vaulted cellars from 1456

Vineyard area: 24 hectares
Annual production: 150,000 bottles
Top sites: Hochheimer Hölle, Kirchenstück and Domdechaney
Soil types: Light clay and loam
Grape varieties: 85% Riesling, 15% Spätburgunder
Average yield: 67 hl/ha
Best vintages: 1995, 1996, 1997
Member: VDP, Charta

Over the past decade this estate has been one of the most successful producers in the Rheingau. It was founded by Künstler's father in 1965; Gunter has established its current reputation by the most painstaking attention to detail. With the purchase in October 1996 of the neighboring Aschrott estate, with its excellent vineyards and lovely buildings, he vastly expanded his possibilities. Given the lack of space at the old winery, which will now be used only to store bottled wines, the newly refurbished facilities at the Aschrott estate will be used to vinify both of the estate's wines. Given the demand for Künstler's own wines, six hectares planted with old vines in the choicest parcels of the Kirchenstück, Hölle and Domdechaney vineyards were incorporated into the Künstler property. The quality of both the 1996 and 1997 vintages prove that Künstler's investment was well made.

1997 Hochheimer Stielweg
Riesling Auslese trocken
45 DM, 13%, ♀ till 2004 **91**

1997 Hochheimer Hölle
Riesling Spätlese halbtrocken
25 DM, 11%, ♀ till 2005 **91**

1996 Hochheimer Reichestal
Riesling Kabinett
15 DM, 7%, ♀ till 2006 **91**

1996 Hochheimer Kirchenstück
Riesling Spätlese
25 DM, 7.5%, ♀ till 2006 **91**

1997 Hochheimer Kirchenstück
Riesling Spätlese
25 DM, 8.5%, ♀ till 2008 **92**

1997 Hochheimer Hölle
Riesling Beerenauslese
86 DM/0.375 liter, 7.5%, ♀ till 2010 **94**

1996 Hochheimer Hölle
Riesling Beerenauslese
90 DM/0.375 liter, 7.5%, ♀ till 2008 **94**

1996 Hochheimer Reichestal
Riesling Eiswein
138 DM/0.375 liter, 6%, ♀ till 2012 **96**

WEINGUT HANS LANG

Owner: Johann Maximilian Lang
65347 Eltville-Hattenheim,
Rheinallee 6
Tel. (0 67 23) 24 75, Fax 79 63
e-mail: langwein@t-online.de
Internet: www.lang-wein.com
Directions: B 42, exit Hattenheim
Sales: Mr. Moos, Mr. and Ms. Lang
Opening hours: Mon.–Fri. 7:30 a.m. to 5 p.m., Sat. 9 a.m. to 1 p.m. or by appointment

Vineyard area: 15 hectares
Annual production: 120,000 bottles
Top sites: Hattenheimer Wisselbrunnen and Hassel, Hallgartener Schönhell, Assmannshäuser Höllenberg
Soil types: Gravelly loam, slate, loess and loam
Grape varieties: 80% Riesling, 10% Spätburgunder, 3% Weißburgunder, 7 % other varieties
Average yield: 67 hl/ha
Best vintages: 1994, 1996, 1997
Member: Charta, VDP, Deutsches Barrique Forum

Hans Lang is one of the most self-critical men of his profession. Every year he deliberates on how he can improve on the quality that he has already achieved. In 1992, for example, he started experiments with whole-cluster pressing. Although quantity would be diminished by around ten percent, Lang felt justified by promising a considerable reduction in bitter extract in the resulting wines. His specialties include bottle-fermented sparkling wine as well as white and red wines that are aged in small oak barrels; and all three are often among the best in their respective styles that you can find in the Rheingau. His main focus of attention, however, remains – as it has always been – Riesling. The 1996 range was quite convincing. The 1997s are even better! Lang has made another step towards the head of his class.

1996 Hallgartener Schönhell
Riesling trocken
18 DM, 12%, ♀ till 2001 **89**

1996 Weißer Burgunder
Spätlese trocken
15.80 DM, 12%, ♀ till 2002 **90**

1996 Chardonnay
trocken
20.80 DM, 12.5%, ♀ till 2002 **90**

1997 Riesling
Spätlese
16.90 DM, 8.5%, ♀ till 2006 **91**

1997 Hattenheimer Wisselbrunnen
Riesling "Erstes Gewächs"
28 DM, 12.5%, ♀ till 2003 **91**

1997 Hattenheimer Wisselbrunnen
Riesling Spätlese Goldkapsel
29 DM, 8.5%, ♀ till 2005 **92**

1996 Hattenheimer Schützenhaus
Riesling Auslese
37 DM/0.5 liter, 7.5%, ♀ till 2008 **92**

1997 Hattenheimer Wisselbrunnen
Riesling Auslese Goldkapsel
39.50 DM, 7.5%, ♀ till 2007 **92**

1996 Hattenheimer Schützenhaus
Riesling Beerenauslese
87 DM/0.5 liter, 7.5%, ♀ till 2007 **92**

WEINGUT FREIHERR LANGWERTH VON SIMMERN

Owner: Georg-Reinhard Freiherr Langwerth von Simmern
Winemaker: Peter Barth
65343 Eltville, Kirchgasse
Tel. (0 61 23) 9 21 10, Fax 92 11 33
Directions: From Eltville towards Wiesbaden, on the right between fortress and church
Sales: Mr. Müglich, Ms. Ettingshaus
Opening hours: Mon.–Thur. 8 a.m. to noon and 1:30 p.m. to 5 p.m, Fri. to 4 p.m.
Restaurant: "Gelbes Haus," open from 4 p.m., Wed. closed
Specialties: Rheingau dishes
History: In 1464 the Herzog von Pfalz-Zweibrücken gave the estate to his chancellor Johann Langwerth von Simmern
Worth seeing: Langwerther Hof with park

> Vineyard area: 32 hectares
> Annual production: 200,000 bottles
> Top sites: Erbacher Marcobrunn, Hattenheimer Wisselbrunn, Mannberg and Nußbrunnen, Rauenthaler Baiken
> Soil types: Tertiary heavy chalky loam, loess rich in limestone, sandy loam
> Grape varieties: 96% Riesling, 2% Spätburgunder, 2% other varieties
> Average yield: 57 hl/ha
> Best vintages: 1989, 1990, 1992
> Member: VDP

This very traditional estate has been in a phase of consolidation since 1991. While the noble sweet Rieslings sometimes justify our erstwhile estimation of this property, the dry and off-dry wines are at best adequate. When one considers the superlative vineyards owned by the baron in Rauenthal, Kiedrich, Eltville, Erbach and Hattenheim, it is clear that the estate's potential is not being fully exploited. We recall with nostalgia the excellent Rieslings from the 1960s and 1970s, when this estate almost single-handedly set the standards of quality in the Rheingau. The last few vintages have offered little or nothing of similar quality.

1997 Hattenheimer Mannberg
Riesling Kabinett halbtrocken
12.35 DM, 12%, 🍷 till 2002 — **84**

1997 Rauenthaler Baiken
Riesling Kabinett
15.65 DM, 11.5%, 🍷 till 2003 — **84**

1997 Erbacher Marcobrunn
Riesling Spätlese
26.55 DM, 11%, 🍷 till 2003 — **84**

1997 Kiedricher Sandgrub
Riesling trocken
9.45 DM, 12%, 🍷 till 2001 — **84**

1996 Erbacher Marcobrunn
Riesling Spätlese trocken
25.80 DM, 11%, 🍷 till 2001 — **86**

1996 Erbacher Marcobrunn
Riesling Kabinett
15.20 DM, 9.5%, 🍷 till 2002 — **86**

1997 Rauenthaler Baiken
Riesling Spätlese
26.55 DM, 10.5%, 🍷 till 2004 — **86**

1997 Erbacher Marcobrunn
Riesling Auslese
65 DM, 10.5%, 🍷 till 2004 — **86**

1996 Rauenthaler Baiken
Riesling Beerenauslese
414 DM/0.375 liter, 10%, 🍷 till 2007 — **91**

1996 Eltviller Sonnenberg
Riesling Eiswein
130 DM/0.375 liter, 6.5%, 🍷 till 2008 — **98**

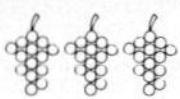

WEINGUT JOSEF LEITZ

Owner: Leitz family
Manager: Johannes Leitz
Winemaker: Johannes Leitz
65385 Rüdesheim,
Theodor-Heuss-Straße 5
Tel. (0 67 22) 22 93 and 4 87 11,
Fax 4 76 58
Directions: From Wiesbaden, at the entrance to Rüdesheim, take direction of Kloster Hildegard
Sales: Johannes Leitz
Opening hours: Mon.–Fri. 9 a.m. to 6 p.m., Sat. 9 a.m. to noon
By appointment
Restaurant: "Zur Hufschmiede," open November to March from 4 p.m. to midnight
Specialties: Regional dishes
Worth seeing: Restored 17th-century forge

Vineyard area: 5.5 hectares
Annual production: 30,000 bottles
Top sites: Rüdesheimer Berg Schloßberg, Berg Roseneck and Berg Rottland
Soil types: Weathered slate
Grape varieties: 91% Riesling, 9% Spätburgunder
Average yield: 59 hl/ha
Best vintages: 1992, 1993, 1995
Member: VDP

After his apprenticeship at the Johannishof estate of Hans Hermann Eser, Johannes Leitz continued his studies at the college in Eltville. Leitz ferments his musts using only wild yeasts and leaves the young wines on their fine lees until the following spring, a technique he acquired from friends in Meursault. The 1995 range was one of the most interesting in the whole of the Rheingau and is, to date, the high point of his meteoric career. Given our rising expectations, the 1996s and 1997s, although still most appealing, were somewhat disappointing. Be that as it may, few in the Rheingau make finer wines than Leitz.

1997 Rüdesheimer Berg Roseneck
Riesling Spätlese trocken
18 DM, 12%, 🍷 till 2002 **86**

1996 Rüdesheimer Berg Schloßberg
Riesling Spätlese halbtrocken
32 DM, 11%, 🍷 till 2000 **86**

1996 Rüdesheimer Magdalenenkreuz
Riesling Kabinett
9.80 DM, 8%, 🍷 till 2002 **86**

1997 Rüdesheimer Berg Rottland
Riesling Auslese trocken
32 DM, 13%, 🍷 till 2004 **88**

1997 Rüdesheimer Magdalenenkreuz
Riesling Kabinett
9.80 DM, 8.5%, 🍷 till 2005 **88**

1997 Rüdesheimer Berg Roseneck
Riesling Spätlese
22 DM, 8.5%, 🍷 till 2004 **88**

1997 Rüdesheimer Berg Rottland
Riesling Spätlese
18 DM, 10%, 🍷 till 2006 **89**

1997 Rüdesheimer Berg Rottland
Riesling Auslese
45 DM, 10%, 🍷 till 2006 **89**

1997 Rüdesheimer Berg Schloßberg
Riesling Beerenauslese
100 DM/0.375 liter, 10%, 🍷 till 2010 **94**

VON MUMM'SCHES WEINGUT

Owner: Fürst von Metternich GbR
Manager: Wolfgang Schleicher
General Manager: Heiner Gietz
Winemaker: Hans Kessler
65366 Johannisberg,
Management Schloß Johannisberg,
Schulstraße 32
Tel. (0 67 22) 7 00 90, Fax 70 09 33
Directions: B 42, exit Industriegebiet Geisenheim, towards Johannisberg
Sales: Heribert Heyn, Frank Schuber
Opening hours: Mon.–Sat. 10 a.m. to 1 p.m. and 2 p.m. to 6 p.m.
In winter by appointment
Restaurant: "Burghotel Schwarzenstein," Mon.–Fri. by appointment
Tel. (0 67 22) 9 95 00, Fax 99 50 99

Vineyard area: 65 hectares
Annual production: 700,000 bottles
Top sites: Johannisberger Mittelhölle and Klaus, Assmannshäuser Höllenberg
Soil types: Gravelly and chalky loess, Taunus quartz
Grape varieties: 85% Riesling, 15% Spätburgunder
Average yield: 59 hl/ha
Best vintages: 1992, 1994, 1996

In the late 1970s the Mumm estate enjoyed considerable success while launching a range of dry wines. They were among the first to realize that the popularity of "nouvelle cuisine" would lead to a greater demand for such wines of German origin. With great panache the Rieslings were marketed in Burgundy bottles, annointed with labels reminiscent of Dom Pérignon – and sold with ease. Similar labels are still being used today. The 1996s were of dependable quality. Although investments in the harvesting methods and cellar equipment were meant to lead to even higher quality, the 1997s fell short of all expectations.

1997 Johannisberger Klaus
Riesling Kabinett halbtrocken
12.80 DM, 11%, ♀ till 2002 **82**

1997 Johannisberger
Riesling trocken
10.90 DM/1.0 liter, 12%, ♀ till 2000 **82**

1997 Johannisberger Hansenberg
Riesling trocken
13.50 DM, 12%, ♀ till 2001 **82**

1996 Riesling
Kabinett trocken
14.50 DM, 10.5%, ♀ till 2000 **84**

1997 Johannisberger Klaus
Riesling Spätlese trocken
21.50 DM, 11.5%, ♀ till 2002 **84**

1996 Geisenheimer Kläuserweg
Riesling halbtrocken
11 DM, 11%, ♀ till 2001 **86**

1996 Johannisberger Mittelhölle
Riesling Kabinett
12.50 DM, 9%, ♀ till 2002 **86**

1996 Rüdesheimer Berg Rottland
Riesling Spätlese
15.50 DM, 11%, ♀ till 2002 **88**

WEINGUT DR. HEINRICH NÄGLER

Owners: Dr. Heinrich and Wiltrud Nägler
Winemaker: Tilbert Nägler
65385 Rüdesheim, Friedrichstraße 22
Tel. (0 67 22) 28 35, Fax 4 73 63
e-mail: h.naegler@t-online.de
Directions: From Wiesbaden at the entrance to Rüdesheim, right on Hildegardis Street
Sales: Wiltrud Nägler
Opening hours: Mon.–Fri. 9 a.m. to 6 p.m., Sat. 10 a.m. to 6 p.m.
Sun. by appointment

Vineyard area: 8 hectares
Annual production: 58,000 bottles
Top sites: Rüdesheimer Berg Schloßberg, Berg Rottland and Berg Roseneck
Soil types: Weathered slate and quartz
Grape varieties: 90% Riesling, 7% Ehrenfelser, 3% Spätburgunder
Average yield: 51 hl/ha
Best vintages: 1989, 1992, 1995
Member: VDP

This estate of eight hectares, run by Dr. Heinrich Nägler and his wife, Wiltrud, is particularly well known in the Rheingau for its dry Rieslings. The estate rose to prominence ten years ago when a dry 1985 Rüdesheimer Berg Schloßberg Spätlese took second place at the "Riesling Olympiade" organized by Gault Millau in Paris. At other blind tastings their wines have performed equally well. At the annual competition for the best dry Rieslings organized by the magazine *Feinschmecker* at the Hotel Krautkrämer in Münster, for example, wines from Nägler have thrice emerged among the top five. The 1996s and 1997s, however, show uncharacteristic irregularity. While the fruity Riesling are appealing, the dry wines seem almost rustic.

1997 Rüdesheimer Berg Rottland
Riesling Spätlese trocken
17.10 DM, 12%, ♀ till 2002 **82**

1997 Rüdesheimer Berg Roseneck
Riesling
9.90 DM, 11.5%, ♀ till 2000 **82**

1996 Rüdesheimer Berg Rottland
Riesling Kabinett trocken
12.90 DM, 11%, ♀ till 2000 **84**

1996 Rüdesheimer Berg Rottland
Riesling Spätlese trocken
20 DM, 12%, ♀ till 2001 **84**

1997 Rüdesheimer Berg Rottland
Riesling Kabinett halbtrocken
12.80 DM, 10.5%, ♀ till 2003 **84**

1996 Rüdesheimer Bischofsberg
Riesling halbtrocken
9.80 DM, 10.5%, ♀ till 2000 **86**

1996 Rüdesheimer Berg Rottland
Riesling Kabinett halbtrocken
12.90 DM, 10.5%, ♀ till 2001 **86**

1997 Rüdesheimer Berg Rottland
Riesling Spätlese halbtrocken
17.10 DM, 12%, ♀ till 2002 **86**

1996 Rüdesheimer Berg Roseneck
Riesling Spätlese
17.30 DM, 9%, ♀ till 2002 **86**

1996 Rüdesheimer Berg Roseneck
Riesling Kabinett
12.50 DM, 9.5%, ♀ till 2003 **88**

WEINGUT ADAM NASS-ENGELMANN

Owner: Karl-Josef Naß
Winemakers: Karl-Josef and Oliver Naß
65375 Hallgarten, Hallgartener Platz 2
Tel. (0 67 23) 33 66 and 41 12, Fax 8 81 37
Directions: B 42, exit Hattenheim or Oestrich-Winkel, in the direction of Hallgarten
Sales: Karl-Josef Naß
Opening hours: By appointment
History: The estate buildings were constructed in 1755

Vineyard area: 7 hectares
Annual production: 50,000 bottles
Top sites: Hallgartener Jungfer and Schönhell
Soil types: Deep loess
Grape varieties: 90% Riesling, 5% each of Spätburgunder and Portugieser
Average yield: 72 hl/ha
Best vintages: 1992, 1994, 1996
Member: VDP

Founded in 1697, this estate recently celebrated its 300th anniversary. The courtyard itself was constructed in 1755 by Jakob Engelmann. Originally managed separately, the estates of Karl Franz Engelmann and Adam Naß were united in 1985 by Karl-Josef Naß; however, the wines continue to be vinified, labelled and marketed separately. Naß is an advocate of cultivating cover crops between the vines and has renounced all use of herbicides. The wines are vinified traditionally and bottled only on demand. The 1996s were clearly superior to the 1995s and, in quality, harkened back to the successful vintages of 1992 and 1994. Due to overcropping, few of the 1997s were of similar interest.

1996 Hallgartener Würzgarten
Riesling halbtrocken
7 DM, 9.5%, ♀ now **80**

1997 Hallgartener Hendelberg
Riesling Kabinett halbtrocken
9 DM, 10.5%, ♀ till 2000 **80**

1996 Hallgartener Jungfer
Riesling Spätlese trocken
11 DM, 11%, ♀ now **82**

1996 Hallgartener Hendelberg
Riesling Kabinett halbtrocken
9 DM, 10%, ♀ till 2000 **82**

1996 Hallgartener Schönhell
Riesling Spätlese halbtrocken
10.50 DM, 10.5%, ♀ till 2000 **82**

1997 Hallgartener Jungfer
Riesling Spätlese
12.50 DM, 8%, ♀ till 2004 **82**

1996 Hallgartener Jungfer
Riesling Kabinett
9 DM, 9%, ♀ till 2001 **84**

1996 Hallgartener Jungfer
Riesling Spätlese
11 DM, 8.5%, ♀ till 2003 **86**

1997 Hallgartener Jungfer
Riesling Eiswein
60 DM/0.5 liter, 8.5%, ♀ till 2008 **89**

WEINGUT PRINZ

Winemaker: Fred Prinz
65375 Hallgarten, Im Flachsgarten 5
Tel. (0 67 23) 99 98 47, Fax 99 98 48
Directions: B 42, exit Hattenheim, in the direction of Hallgarten, at village entrance follow the ring, fifth street on left
Sales: Sabine Prinz
Opening hours: Mon.–Sat. by appointment

Vineyard area: 1.58 hectares
Annual production: 10,000 bottles
Top sites: Hallgartener Jungfer and Schönhell
Soil types: Loess, loam, gravel and red slate
Grape varieties: 90% Riesling, 10% Spätburgunder
Average yield: 55 hl/ha
Best vintages: 1994, 1995, 1997

Since this estate of not even two hectares was initially run as a lark, it is one of the most unusual discoveries that we have made in the Rheingau recently. For years Fred Prinz worked with Bernhard Breuer in Rüdesheim and learned a great deal in the process, not just in marketing and sales, but also in the secrets of vinification. The quality that Prinz attained in his first trio of vintages – 1991, 1992 and 1993 – was remarkable. The 1994 vintage was, to date, certainly this tiny estate's finest; but the 1995s were also first class. The surprising 1996 range, despite the Goldkapsel ice wine, did not quite match its predecessors. The 1997s are again excellent. Prinz is certainly the best hobby winemaker in the Rheingau, but he is also the most expensive. The majority of his production, which is scarcely 10,000 bottles, is sold to restaurants, the rest purchased by merchants. Wines that don't meet his high standards are sold in cask.

1997 Hallgartener Schönhell
Riesling Kabinett trocken
13 DM, 11.5%, 🍷 till 2002 **86**

1997 Hallgartener Hendelberg
Riesling halbtrocken
9 DM, 11%, 🍷 till 2002 **86**

1997 Hallgartener Schönhell
Riesling Spätlese trocken
18 DM, 12.5%, 🍷 till 2004 **88**

1996 Hallgartener Jungfer
Riesling Kabinett
13 DM, 9%, 🍷 till 2002 **88**

1997 Hallgartener Jungfer
Riesling Kabinett
13 DM, 9%, 🍷 till 2005 **89**

1997 Hallgartener Jungfer
Riesling Spätlese
19 DM, 9.5%, 🍷 till 2007 **91**

1997 Hallgartener Jungfer
Riesling Auslese Goldkapsel – 10 –
35 DM/0.375 liter, 9%, 🍷 till 2007 **91**

1996 Hallgartener Jungfer
Riesling Auslese Goldkapsel
26 DM, 8%, 🍷 till 2005 **91**

1997 Hallgartener Jungfer
Riesling Spätlese Goldkapsel
23 DM, 9%, 🍷 till 2008 **92**

1996 Hallgartener Jungfer
Riesling Eiswein Goldkapsel
150 DM/0.375 liter, 6%, 🍷 till 2008 **94**

WEINGUT WILFRIED QUERBACH

Owner: Wilfried Querbach
Manager and winemaker: Wilfried and Peter Querbach
65375 Oestrich-Winkel, Dr.-Rody-Straße 2
Tel. (0 67 23) 38 87, Fax 8 74 05
Directions: B 42, exit Oestrich, from village center follow signs
Sales: Resi Querbach
Opening hours: Mon.–Fri. 8 a.m. to noon and 1 p.m. to 6 p.m.
Sat. and Sun. by appointment

> Vineyard area: 9 hectares
> Annual production: 70,000 bottles
> Top sites: Oestricher Lenchen and Doosberg, Winkeler Hasensprung
> Soil types: Clay, loam and loess
> Grape varieties: 86% Riesling, 14% Spätburgunder
> Average yield: 64 hl/ha
> Best vintages: 1993, 1994, 1995
> Member: Charta

For years Wilfried Querbach has been producing interesting wines and selling them at comparatively modest prices. In all that time his vineyards have been cultivated along ecological lines. The Riesling is now harvested by machine, the Spätburgunder still by hand. The vinification of the predominately dry and off-dry wines is exceptionally gentle. Allowed to settle naturally, the young wines are only lightly filtered just before bottling. Encouraged by his wife, Resi, who is as charming as she is determined, the ambitious Querbach is striving to improve the standing of his estate. His slogan is "Quality begins with a Q, as in Querbach." Their son – who was largely responsible for the delectable 1994s – has now completed his winemaking studies and is working full-time at the estate. Although a tart acidity ran like a thread through the whole range, the 1996s were fully up to our expectations. The 1997s are equally good.

1996 Hallgartener Schönhell
Riesling trocken
8.80 DM, 11.5%, ♀ till 2001 **86**

1996 Oestricher Lenchen
Riesling trocken
9.50 DM, 11.5%, ♀ till 2000 **86**

1996 Oestricher Doosberg
Riesling trocken
20 DM, 11.5%, ♀ till 2001 **86**

1996 Hallgartener Schönhell
Riesling Kabinett trocken
9.50 DM, 10%, ♀ till 2000 **86**

1996 Riesling
halbtrocken
8.50 DM/1.0 liter, 10.5%, ♀ till 2002 **86**

1996 Oestricher Lenchen
Riesling halbtrocken
8.90 DM, 11%, ♀ till 2002 **86**

1997 Oestricher Doosberg
Riesling Spätlese
15.50 DM, 11.5%, ♀ till 2003 **86**

1997 Oestricher Doosberg
Riesling "Erstes Gewächs"
22 DM, 11.5%, ♀ till 2002 **88**

1997 Oestricher Lenchen
Riesling Auslese
19 DM/0.375 liter, 10%, ♀ till 2008 **89**

1997 Oestricher Lenchen
Riesling Eiswein
65 DM/0.375 liter, 7.5%, ♀ till 2010 **91**

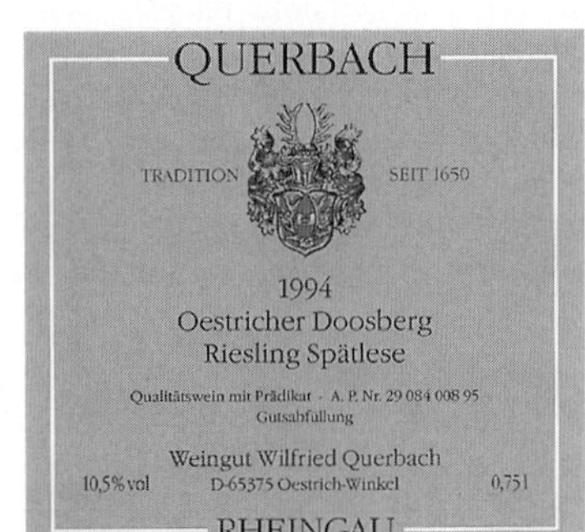

WEINGUT SCHLOSS REINHARTSHAUSEN

Owner:
Friedrich Nikolaus Prince of Prussia
General Manager: August Kesseler
Winemaker: Günter Kanning
65346 Eltville-Erbach,
Hauptstrasse 41
Tel. (0 61 23) 67 63 33, Fax 42 22
Directions: B 42, exit Erbach
Sales: Gerda Kruger
"Vinothek," Tel. (0 61 23) 67 63 99
Opening hours: Tue.–Fri. 9 a.m. to 6 p.m.
Sat., Sun. and holidays 11 a.m. to 5 p.m.
History: Founded 1337, castle with banqueting hall from 1800, acquired in 1855 by Princess Marianne of Prussia
Worth seeing: Hotel Schloß Reinhartshausen, Mariannenaue island

Vineyard area: 100 hectares
Annual production: 500,000 bottles
Top sites: Erbacher Marcobrunn and Schloßberg
Soil types: Deep tertiary chalky loam soils and loess
Grape varieties: 88% Riesling, 4% Weißburgunder, 3% each of Chardonnay and Spätburgunder, 2% other varieties
Average yield: 50 hl/ha
Best vintages: 1992, 1994, 1996
Member: VDP, Charta, BÖW

This is, without doubt, one of the estates with the greatest quality potential in the Rheingau. In an effort to restore it to its former glory, Willi Leibbrand, who recently past away, invested enormous sums in the estate. Part of the funds were spent acquiring the Tillmann property in Erbach. Since Dr. Zerbe left to work at the state domaine, August Kesseler has been managing the winery. Under his guidance the estate has focused its attention on its finest vineyards in Erbach and Hattenheim, which are now the only sites named on any label. The 1996s were not only very successful, the dry Spätlese from the Marcobrunn vineyard was one of the best wines of the vintage. The rather baroque 1997s are almost as fine, although none of the wines quite make the all-star cut for the vintage.

1997 Erbacher Marcobrunn
Riesling Spätlese trocken
40 DM, 12.5%, 🍷 till 2004 **89**

1997 Erbacher Marcobrunn
Riesling Spätlese
40 DM, 9%, 🍷 till 2007 **89**

1996 Erbacher Marcobrunn
Riesling Spätlese
38.60 DM, 8.5%, 🍷 till 2003 **89**

1997 Erbacher Schloßberg
Riesling "Erstes Gewächs"
45 DM, 11.5%, 🍷 till 2006 **89**

1996 Erbacher Marcobrunn
Riesling Spätlese trocken
40 DM, 11.5%, 🍷 till 2004 **91**

1997 Erbacher Schloßberg
Riesling Auslese
29 DM, 8.5%, 🍷 till 2004 **91**

1996 Erbacher Schloßberg
Riesling Auslese
90 DM, 9%, 🍷 till 2008 **92**

1997 Hattenheimer Wisselbrunnen
Riesling Beerenauslese
124 DM/0.375 liter, 8.5%, 🍷 till 2008 **94**

1996 Erbacher Siegelsberg
Riesling Beerenauslese
124 DM/0.375 liter, 10%, 🍷 till 2006 **94**

1996 Erbacher Siegelsberg
Riesling Trockenbeerenauslese
207 DM/0.375 liter, 10%, 🍷 till 2010 **95**

WEINGUT BALTHASAR RESS

Owner: Stefan Ress
Manager: Markus Boor
Winemaker: Bruno Klüpfel
65347 Hattenheim, Rheinallee 7
Tel. (0 67 23) 9 19 50, Fax 91 95 91
e-mail: weingut@ress-wine.com
Directions: B 42, exit Hattenheim, coming from Eltville take second Hattenheim exit, after the Shell petrol station turn right, then first street on the right
Sales: Stefan Ress in the Vinothek
Opening hours: Mon.–Fri. 10 a.m. to 5 p.m., Sat. 11 a.m. to 2 p.m. or by appointment
Worth seeing: Modern art collection

Vineyard area: 33 hectares
Annual production: 220,000 bottles
Top sites: Hattenheimer Wisselbrunnen and Nußbrunnen, Rüdesheimer Berg Schloßberg and Berg Rottland
Soil types: Loess, tertiary chalky loam and quartz
Grape varieties: 91% Riesling, 6% Spätburgunder, 3% other varieties
Average yield: 60 hl/ha
Best vintages: 1993, 1994, 1995
Member: VDP, Charta

In 1978 the congenial Stefan Ress was the first German producer to commission a well-known artist to design a label for a special wine. Following the example of Château Mouton-Rothschild, he also published a copiously illustrated book about the labels. In addition to his own vineyards, Ress also manages the four hectares of the former ecclesiastical property of Schloß Reichartshausen, which surrounds the European Business School. In the castle there is a vaulted cellar used for tastings. As chairman of the Rheingau chapter of the VDP, Ress has remodelled the former winery in Hattenheim as a facility that can be used for diverse purposes. His wines of both the 1996 and 1997 vintages were again of reliable quality.

1997 Hattenheimer Schützenhaus
Riesling Kabinett
12.50 DM, 9%, 🍷 till 2005 **86**

1997 Hattenheimer Nußbrunnen
Riesling Spätlese
31.50 DM, 9.5%, 🍷 till 2003 **86**

1997 Rüdesheimer Berg Rottland
Riesling Auslese
28.50 DM/0.375 liter, 10%, 🍷 till 2003 **86**

1997 Schloß Reichartshausen
Riesling Spätlese
27 DM, 10%, 🍷 till 2005 **88**

1997 Oestricher Doosberg
Riesling Auslese
30 DM/0.375 liter, 9.5%, 🍷 till 2006 **88**

1997 Oestricher Doosberg
Riesling Beerenauslese
105 DM/0.375 liter, 7%, 🍷 till 2005 **88**

1996 Hallgartener Hendelberg
Riesling Eiswein
Not yet for sale, 10%, 🍷 till 2006 **91**

1996 Rüdesheimer Berg Rottland
Riesling Beerenauslese
180 DM/0.375 liter, 11%, 🍷 till 2006 **91**

1996 Oestricher Doosberg
Riesling Beerenauslese
Not yet for sale, 11.4%, 🍷 till 2006 **91**

1997 Oestricher Doosberg
Riesling Trockenbeerenauslese
210 DM/0.375 liter, 7%, 🍷 till 2006 **91**

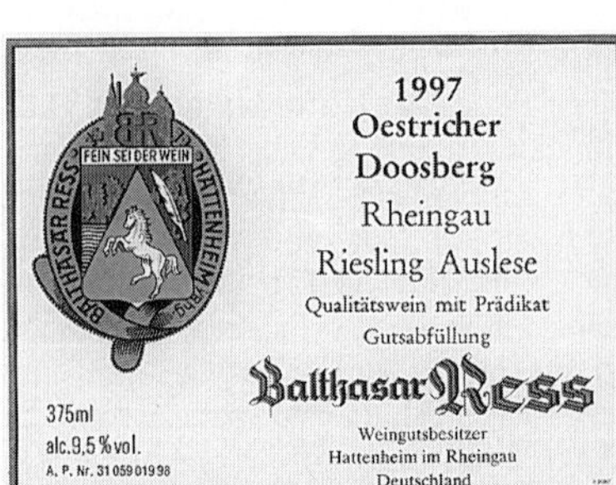

WEINGUT W. J. SCHÄFER

Owner: Josef Schäfer
65239 Hochheim, Elisabethenstraße 4
Tel. (0 61 46) 21 12, Fax 6 15 60
Directions: Exit Hochheim, via the ring to Delkenheimer Straße, towards town center, sixth street on the right
Sales: Josef Schäfer, Wilhelm J. Schäfer
Opening hours: Mon.–Fri. 10 a.m. to 8 p.m., Sat. 9 a.m. to 6 p.m. or by appointment

Vineyard area: 6 hectares
Annual production: 50,000 bottles
Top sites: Hochheimer Domdechaney, Kirchenstück and Hölle
Soil types: Loam, sandy loam
Grape varieties: 85% Riesling, 10% Spätburgunder, 5% Gewürztraminer
Average yield: 65 hl/ha
Best vintages: 1993, 1996, 1997

We first came across this estate by chance at a wine fair in Wiesbaden. The 1996s impressed us so much that we included them in this guide. The 1997s make it clear that this estate has not only considerable potential but is also beginning to show continuity. Do the unusual aromatic qualities of the Rieslings stem from a touch of Gewürztraminer? In Hochheim, in any case, such smug insinuations about Schäfer senior have never ceased. Be that as it may, Wilhelm-Josef Schäfer was able to build his estate to its present size, with parcels in all of the best vineyards of Hochheim; in addition, he is also a committed local historian. Much of the success of the last two years, however, is due to his son Josef, who studied at Geisenheim with Joachin Heger from Baden. Given the estate's wealth in 40- and 50-year-old vines, we would not be surprised if this property soon gave the better estates in the Rheingau a run for their money.

1997 Hochheimer Hofmeister
Riesling Kabinett trocken
9.50 DM, 12%, ♀ till 2001 **84**

1996 Hochheimer Hölle
Riesling Spätlese halbtrocken
14 DM, 11.5%, ♀ till 2001 **84**

1996 Hochheimer Stielweg
Riesling Kabinett
9 DM, 8.5%, ♀ till 2001 **86**

1997 Hochheimer Kirchenstück
Riesling Spätlese trocken
14 DM, 13%, ♀ till 2002 **88**

1996 Hochheimer Reichestal
Riesling Spätlese
11 DM, 11.5%, ♀ till 2004 **88**

1997 Hochheimer Stielweg
Riesling Spätlese halbtrocken
12 DM, 12%, ♀ till 2004 **89**

1997 Hochheimer Hölle
Riesling Spätlese
12 DM, 10%, ♀ till 2005 **89**

1997 Hochheimer Domdechaney
Riesling Auslese
15 DM/0.5 liter, 9%, ♀ till 2006 **89**

1996 Hochheimer Domdechaney
Riesling Spätlese
12 DM/0.5 liter, 8.5%, ♀ till 2005 **91**

1997 Hochheimer Hofmeister
Riesling Eiswein
40 DM/0.375 liter, 10%, ♀ till 2005 **91**

DOMÄNENWEINGUT SCHLOSS SCHÖNBORN

Owner: Dr. Karl Graf von Schönborn-Wiesentheid
General Manager: Günter Thies
Manager: Volker Faust
Winemaker: Gerhard Kirsch
65347 Hattenheim, Hauptstraße 53
Tel. (0 67 23) 9 18 10, Fax 91 81 91
Directions: B 42, exit Hattenheim
Sales: Günter Thies
Opening hours: Mon.–Thur. 8 a.m. to 4:30 p.m., Fri. 8 a.m. to noon
Sat. and Sun. by appointment
History: Documented as being the property of the Schönborn family since 1349
Worth seeing: 500-year-old cask cellar

Vineyard area: 50 hectares
Annual production: 300,000 bottles
Top sites: Erbacher Marcobrunn, Hattenheimer Pfaffenberg and Nußbrunnen, Rüdesheimer Berg Schloßberg and Rottland, Hochheimer Domdechaney
Soil types: Clay, loess, heavy chalky loam
Grape varieties: 91% Riesling, 6% Spätburgunder, 3% Weißburgunder
Average yield: 54 hl/ha
Best vintages: 1990, 1992
Member: VDP, Charta

No other estate in the Rheingau possesses such a bevy of fine vineyards as this highly traditional property in Hattenheim. From Hochheim to Lorchhausen, the Schönborn family owns first-class parcels of land in 12 villages. Unfortunately, the quality has been on the wane here for years, the worst vintages being 1993 and 1994. The wines from the 1995 vintage set the stage for a qualitative relaunch, which has been further consolidated by the 1996s and to a certain extent the 1997s. Although the dry "first growths" are slowly improving, the fruity Rieslings are generally still more appealing; however, the noble late harvest Rieslings from both vintages could have been better. With a bit more regularity this estate might soon be back in the big leagues.

1996 Hattenheimer Pfaffenberg
Riesling Kabinett halbtrocken
11.80 DM, 10.5%, ♀ till 2000 **84**

1997 Hattenheimer Pfaffenberg
Riesling Kabinett
11.90 DM, 10%, ♀ till 2003 **84**

1997 Hattenheimer Pfaffenberg
Riesling Spätlese
18.30 DM, 9.5%, ♀ till 2004 **86**

1996 Erbacher Marcobrunn
Riesling Spätlese
23.70 DM, 8.5%, ♀ till 2001 **86**

1997 Johannisberger Klaus
Riesling Kabinett "Jubiläum"
17.40 DM, 8.5%, ♀ till 2006 **88**

1997 Hattenheimer Pfaffenberg
Riesling Spätlese "Jubiläum"
32.50 DM, 8%, ♀ till 2008 **88**

1997 Erbacher Marcobrunn
Riesling Auslese
39.50 DM/0.5 liter, 8.5%, ♀ till 2005 **88**

1997 Erbacher Marcobrunn
Riesling "Erstes Gewächs"
42 DM, 12.5%, ♀ till 2003 **88**

1996 Rüdesheimer Berg Schloßberg
Riesling Beerenauslese
138 DM/0.5 liter, 7.5%, ♀ till 2007 **91**

1996 Erbacher Marcobrunn
Riesling Trockenbeerenauslese
287 DM/0.5 liter, 7%, ♀ till 2008 **92**

STAATSWEINGUT ASSMANNSHAUSEN

Owner: State of Hesse
General Manager: Friedrich Dries
Winemaker: Oliver Dries
65385 Assmannshausen, Höllenbergstraße 10
Tel. (0 67 22) 22 73, Fax 4 81 21
Directions: B 42, exit Assmannshausen, in the direction of Aulhausen
Sales: Mr. Dries
Opening hours: Mon.–Thur. 8 a.m. to noon and 1 p.m. to 4:30 p.m.
Fri. 8 a.m. to noon and 1 p.m. to 4 p.m.
Sat. 10 a.m. to 4 p.m.
History: In 1108 the Assmannshäuser Höllenberg was owned by the Cistercian monks from Marienhausen

Vineyard area: 20 hectares
Annual production: 120,000 bottles
Top sites: Assmannshäuser Höllenberg and Frankenthal
Soil types: Taunus phyllite and slate
Grape varieties: 98% Spätburgunder, 2% other varieties
Average yield: 41 hl/ha
Best vintages: 1990, 1994, 1996
Member: VDP

This marvellously situated property has had a checkered history over the past two centuries. Today it belongs to the State of Hesse and claims that it is the sole winery in Germany that produces only red wines and rosés. The soils of phyllite and slate provide these wines with a unique character: delicately structured, they are nonetheless full of personality and can age extremely well. The estate's speciality is its rosé ice wine, which it has produced since 1966. The 1995 reds were not quite of the quality of the previous vintage, but the 1996s were again more convincing. A hailstorm that reduced the crop size to a mere 25 hectoliters per hectare made it difficult for the estate to improve the quality of its wines in 1997.

1997 Assmannshäuser Höllenberg
Spätburgunder Weißherbst Eiswein
125.50 DM/0.375 liter, 7%, ♀ till 2010 **92**

——— Red wines ———

1996 Assmannshäuser Höllenberg
Spätburgunder Kabinett trocken
22.50 DM, 11.5%, ♀ till 2004 **86**

1995 Assmannshäuser Höllenberg
Frühburgunder Kabinett trocken
21 DM, 11%, ♀ till 2006 **86**

1996 Assmannshäuser Höllenberg
Spätburgunder Spätlese trocken – 16 –
29.50 DM, 12%, ♀ till 2008 **86**

1995 Assmannshäuser Höllenberg
Spätburgunder trocken – 13 –
19 DM, 12%, ♀ till 2006 **88**

1996 Assmannshäuser Höllenberg
Spätburgunder Spätlese halbtrocken
29.50 DM, 11.5%, ♀ till 2010 **88**

1996 Assmannshäuser Höllenberg
Spätburgunder Spätlese trocken – 14 –
29.50 DM, 13%, ♀ till 2006 **88**

1995 Assmannshäuser Höllenberg
Spätburgunder Spätlese trocken
27.50 DM, 12.5%, ♀ till 2006 **88**

HESSISCHE STAATSWEINGÜTER KLOSTER EBERBACH

Owner: State of Hesse
Manager: Dr. Karl-Heinz Zerbe
Winemakers: Martin Kölble, Fred Prinz
65343 Eltville, Schwalbacher Straße 56–62
Tel. (0 61 23) 9 23 00, Fax 92 30 90
Directions: A 66 Wiesbaden–Rüdesheim, exit Martinsthal/Eltville
Sales: Ms. Kunz, Fred Prinz
Opening hours: Mon.–Fri. 9 a.m. to noon and 1 p.m. to 6 p.m., Sat. 10 a.m. to 4 p.m.
Restaurant: "Gästehaus Kloster Eberbach," open daily from 10 a.m. to 10 p.m.
Specialties: Sander in sauerkraut
History: 850-year-old tradition of Cistercian winemaking
Worth seeing: Cloister Eberbach with Cistercian museum

Vineyard area: 130 hectares
Annual production: 900,000 bottles
Top sites: Steinberger, Rauenthaler Baiken, Erbacher Marcobrunn, Rüdesheimer Berg Schloßberg, Hochheimer Domdechaney
Soil types: Weathered slate, phyllite and heavy chalky loam
Grape varieties: 99.5% Riesling, 0.5% Weißburgunder
Average yield: 60 hl/ha
Best vintages: 1990, 1995, 1997
Member: VDP, Charta

Kloster Eberbach, a historic monastery founded in 1135, is a stunning showcase for the state domaine of Hesse. After initial difficulties, director Dr. Karl-Heinz Zerbe has now taken firm control of this enormous property, Germany's largest. After numerous indifferent vintages, the superb 1995 range first brought the estate back into the limelight. Although attractive, the 1996s were not only less uniform, they were also of slightly inferior quality. The 1997s are again much better. It would be a great boon for the Rheingau if this estate were able to continue its qualitative ascent.

1997 Rauenthaler Baiken
Riesling Kabinett trocken
15.30 DM, 10.5%, ♀ till 2003 **88**

1997 Rauenthaler Baiken
Riesling Spätlese trocken
25.50 DM, 11.5%, ♀ till 2003 **88**

1997 Steinberger
Riesling Kabinett
16.90 DM, 8.5%, ♀ till 2005 **88**

1997 Rauenthaler Baiken
Riesling Spätlese
25.50 DM, 8.5%, ♀ till 2006 **88**

1997 Erbach Siegelsberg
Riesling "Erstes Gewächs"
30 DM, 13.5%, ♀ till 2002 **88**

1997 Rauenthaler Baiken
Riesling Auslese Goldkapsel
104.40 DM, 9%, ♀ till 2006 **89**

1997 Erbacher Marcobrunn
Riesling Auslese
63.80 DM, 8.5%, ♀ till 2010 **92**

1997 Erbacher Marcobrunn
Riesling Eiswein
117 DM/0.375 liter, 9.5%, ♀ till 2012 **92**

1996 Steinberger
Riesling Eiswein
590 DM, 7%, ♀ till 2009 **95**

WEINGUT DER STADT ELTVILLE

Owner: Georg Müller Foundation
General Manager: Roland Broßmann
65347 Eltville-Hattenheim,
Eberbacher Straße 7–9
Tel. (0 67 23) 20 20, Fax 20 35
Directions: B 42, exit Hattenheim
Opening hours: Mon.–Fri. 9 a.m. to 5 p.m., Sat. by appointment

Vineyard area: 8.9 hectares
Annual production: 60,000 bottles
Top sites: Hattenheimer Nußbrunnen and Wisselbrunnen
Soil types: Clay, loam and chalk
Grape varieties: 95% Riesling, 3% Spätburgunder, 2% Müller-Thurgau
Average yield: 74 hl/ha
Best vintages: 1990, 1992, 1993
Member: VDP

In 1913 Georg Müller, one of the former proprietors of the sparkling wine company Matheus-Müller, founded this estate in Hattenheim, where they own vineyards in such exceptional sites as Nußbrunnen and Wisselbrunnen. Municipal reforms in 1972 made Hattenheim a part of Eltville, which explains the estate's current name. Riesling is king here, occupying 95 percent of the surface area; half the wines are made in a dry style. In the cellar Roland Broßmann opts for a swift and careful processing of the grapes, ferments them with cultivated yeasts in plastic tanks and racks the wines for the first time immediately after fermentation. After several irregular vintages, the estate produced a far better range of 1996s; the 1997s, however, are less successful. Although small quantities continue to be sold in bulk, two-thirds of the wines are sold directly to private clients.

1997 Hattenheimer Schützenhaus
Riesling trocken
7.50 DM, 11%, 🍷 till 2000 — **75**

1996 Hattenheimer Schützenhaus
Riesling trocken
7.50 DM, 10.5%, 🍷 now — **77**

1997 Hattenheimer Schützenhaus
Riesling Spätlese trocken
13.50 DM, 11.5%, 🍷 till 2000 — **77**

1997 Hallgartener Jungfer
Riesling Kabinett halbtrocken
9.20 DM, 10%, 🍷 till 2000 — **77**

1997 Hattenheimer
Riesling Beerenauslese
60 DM/0.375 liter, 7%, 🍷 till 2000 — **80**

1996 Hattenheimer Schützenhaus
Riesling Kabinett trocken
9.20 DM, 10%, 🍷 now — **82**

1997 Hattenheimer Nußbrunnen
Riesling Spätlese
15 DM, 9%, 🍷 till 2001 — **82**

1996 Hattenheimer Schützenhaus
Riesling Kabinett
9.20 DM, 9%, 🍷 till 2000 — **84**

1996 Hallgartener Schönhell
Riesling Kabinett halbtrocken
9.20 DM, 10%, 🍷 till 2002 — **88**

——— Red wines ———

1996 Hattenheimer Engelmannsberg
Spätburgunder Weißherbst halbtrocken
8.50 DM, 10.5%, 🍷 till 2000 — **84**

WEINGUT SCHLOSS VOLLRADS

Owner: Nassauische Sparkasse
Director: Gerd Wendling
Winemaker: Ralph Herke
65375 Oestrich-Winkel, Schloß Vollrads
Tel. (0 67 23) 6 60, Fax 66 66
Directions: B 42, exit Winkel, follow signs to Vollrads
Sales: Meike Schygulla
Opening hours: Mon.–Fri. 8 a.m. to noon and 1 p.m. to 5 p.m.
Sat. 2 p.m. to 5 p.m. (November and December)
Sat., Sun. and holidays 11 a.m. to 6. pm.
Restaurant: Open May–September from noon to 11 p.m., closed Wed. October to April closed Wed. and Thur.
History: First documented wine sales in 1211

Vineyard area: 48 hectares
Annual production: 400,000 bottles
Top site: Schloß Vollrads
Soil types: Loam, loess
Grape varieties: 100% Riesling
Average yield: 65 hl/ha
Best vintages: 1985, 1990, 1995
Member: VDP, Charta

It is a tragedy that the gifted Erwein Graf Matuschka-Greiffenclau was no longer able to bear his estate's financial burden and chose instead to end his life. At present, it is still unclear exactly what will become of Schloß Vollrads. Graf Matuschka was a powerful personality who did a great deal for the German wine industry. For years, and at the four corners of the globe, he almost singlehandedly championed the cause of celebrating Riesling as a worthy accompaniment to a fine meal. With wit and charm he moderated countless wine tastings, steadily winning new admirers for the cause of German wine. Nonetheless, he bequeathed the world only an adequate, at best, range of wines in 1996. Nor are the 1997s any better.

1997 Riesling
Spätlese trocken
23.20 DM, 11%, ♀ till 2002 **84**

1997 Riesling
Kabinett
15.90 DM, 8.5%, ♀ till 2002 **84**

1996 Riesling
Spätlese
23 DM, 10%, ♀ till 2004 **84**

1997 Riesling
halbtrocken
13.70 DM, 11%, ♀ till 2001 **84**

1997 Riesling
trocken
13.70 DM, 12%, ♀ 2001 **84**

1997 Riesling
Spätlese halbtrocken
23.20 DM, 11%, ♀ till 2003 **86**

1997 Riesling
Spätlese
23.20 DM, 9.5%, ♀ till 2003 **86**

1996 Riesling
Eiswein
380 DM/0.5 liter, 7.5%, ♀ till 2008 **86**

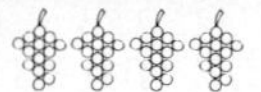

GUTSVERWALTUNG GEHEIMRAT J. WEGELER ERBEN

Owner: Rolf Wegeler family
General Manager: Norbert Holderrieth
Winemaker: Wolfgang Beck
65375 Oestrich-Winkel,
Friedensplatz 9–11
Tel. (0 67 23) 70 31, Fax 14 53
Directions: B 42, exit Oestrich, to village center
Sales: Peter Springer
Opening hours: By appointment

Vineyard area: 55 hectares
Annual production: 440,000 bottles
Top sites: Rüdesheimer Berg Schloßberg, Berg Rottland, Berg Roseneck, Winkeler Jesuitengarten
Soil types: Weathered slate, loess and loam
Grape varieties: 99% Riesling, 1% other varieties
Average yield: 62 hl/ha
Best vintages: 1990, 1993, 1995
Member: VDP, Charta

Norbert Holderrieth has made substantial contributions to the German wine industry. His greatest success was the creation of the premium brand "Geheimrat J," a dry Spätlese that is on the wine list of every top German restaurant today. In its wake he generated second labels such as "Geheimrat Wegeler Deinhard" and, most recently, the sparkling Riesling "Geheimrat J." The Wegeler estate has maintained a remarkably consistent level of quality over the past decade. Other than small quantities of noble late harvest Rieslings, almost all of the wines are made in dry and off-dry styles, which are sold to professional customers in Germany as well as in the export market. The 1996s, with their succulently juicy fruit, were reminiscent of the lively 1994s; the 1997s are softer and appear better balanced, similar in style to the 1995s.

1997 Riesling
Spätlese trocken "Geheimrat J"
32.50 DM, 12.5%, ♀ till 2005 **89**

1996 Riesling
Spätlese trocken "Geheimrat J"
32.50 DM, 12%, ♀ till 2002 **89**

1996 Geisenheimer Rothenberg
Riesling Spätlese
18 DM, 10%, ♀ till 2004 **89**

1997 Oestricher Lenchen
Riesling Auslese
40 DM, 9%, ♀ till 2005 **89**

1997 Rüdesheimer Berg Schloßberg
Riesling "Erstes Gewächs"
23 DM, 12%, ♀ till 2005 **89**

1996 Oestricher Lenchen
Riesling Auslese
49 DM, 10%, ♀ till 2008 **92**

1996 Winkeler Hasensprung
Riesling Eiswein
140 DM/0.5 liter, 7.5%, ♀ till 2007 **94**

1996 Oestricher Lenchen
Riesling Eiswein
170 DM/0.5 liter, 7%, ♀ till 2010 **95**

1997 Oestricher Lenchen
Riesling Trockenbeerenauslese
200 DM/0.375 liter, 7%, ♀ till 2015 **95**

1997 Geisenheimer Rothenberg
Riesling Trockenbeerenauslese
200 DM/0.375 liter, 6.5%, ♀ till 2018 **96**

WEINGUT ROBERT WEIL

Owner: SG-Weingüterverwaltungs-gesellschaft
Estate Director: Wilhelm Weil
Administrator: Clemens Schmitt
Winemakers: Michael Thrien and Christian Engel
65399 Kiedrich, Mühlberg 5
Tel. (0 61 23) 23 08, Fax 15 46
e-mail: info@weingut-robert-weil.com
Internet:
http://www.weingut-robert-weil.com
Directions: A 66, afterwards B 42, exit Eltville-Mitte, in the direction of Kiedrich
Sales: Ms. Weil, Stefan Maas, Jochen Becker-Köhn
Opening hours: Mon.–Fri. 8 a.m. to 5 p.m., Sat. and Sun. by appointment
History: Estate buildings constructed by an English nobleman, Baron Sutton, and purchased in 1879 by Dr. Robert Weil
Worth seeing: Buildings in English country house style with beautiful park

Vineyard area: 53 hectares
Annual production: 360,000 bottles
Top sites: Kiedricher Gräfenberg and Wasseros
Soil types: Stony phyllite soils, with a touch of loess and loam
Grape varieties: 97% Riesling, 3% Spätburgunder
Average yield: 51 hl/ha
Best vintages: 1995, 1996, 1997
Member: VDP, Charta

It has been breathtaking to witness how this estate has succeeded in climbing to the very summit of the Rheingau in just ten years. This cannot be explained solely by the substantial investments that have been made, nor by the resolve of Wilhelm Weil to achieve this goal. It was, at least in part, also possible because many of the more traditional estates in the Rheingau were going through a critical period of decline during that time. That is, though, not to belittle Weil's achievement. With its sumptuous 1995s, this estate joined the elite of the Mosel, Saar and Ruwer and is today undoubtedly one of the world's absolute best producers of white wine! Named two years ago as "Germany's finest estate" in this guide, Wilhelm Weil has not been resting on his laurels. The 1996 range was the finest collection of his young but brilliant career. The 1997s, if not quite of the same caliber, are nonetheless excellent for the vintage.

1997 Riesling
Spätlese trocken
28 DM, 12%, ♀ till 2001 **89**

1996 Kiedricher Gräfenberg
Riesling Spätlese trocken
33 DM, 12%, ♀ till 2002 **89**

1997 Riesling
Spätlese halbtrocken
28 DM, 11%, ♀ till 2003 **89**

1997 Riesling
Kabinett
19 DM, 8.5%, ♀ till 2004 **89**

1996 Kiedricher Gräfenberg
Riesling trocken
45 DM, 12.5%, ♀ till 2002 **90**

1997 Riesling
Spätlese
28 DM, 9%, ♀ till 2005 **91**

1997 Kiedricher Gräfenberg
Riesling Spätlese
42 DM, 8%, ♀ till 2006 **92**

1997 Kiedricher Gräfenberg
Riesling Auslese
44 DM/0.375 liter, 8%, ♀ till 2006 **92**

1996 Kiedricher Gräfenberg
Riesling Spätlese
40 DM, 8.5%, ♀ till 2006 **94**

1996 Kiedricher Gräfenberg
Riesling Auslese
80 DM, 8%, ♀ till 2007 **94**

1997 Kiedricher Gräfenberg
Riesling Beerenauslese
165 DM/0.375 liter, 8%, ♀ till 2008 **95**

1997 Kiedricher Gräfenberg
Riesling Beerenauslese Goldkapsel
580 DM/0.375 liter, 8%, 🍷 till 2008 **95**

1997 Kiedricher Gräfenberg
Riesling Auslese Goldkapsel
290 DM/0.375 liter, 8%, 🍷 till 2008 **96**

1997 Kiedricher Gräfenberg
Riesling Eiswein
218 DM/0.375 liter, 7.5%, 🍷 till 2010 **96**

1996 Kiedricher Gräfenberg
Riesling Beerenauslese
147 DM/0.375 liter, 8%, 🍷 till 2010 **96**

1997 Kiedricher Gräfenberg
Riesling Trockenbeerenauslese Goldkapsel
Not yet for sale, 6%, 🍷 till 2010 **96**

1996 Kiedricher Gräfenberg
Riesling Auslese Goldkapsel
207 DM/0.375 liter, 8%, 🍷 till 2010 **98**

1996 Kiedricher Wasseros
Riesling Eiswein
199 DM/0.375 liter, 7%, 🍷 till 2012 **98**

1996 Kiedricher Gräfenberg
Riesling Eiswein
199 DM/0.375 liter, 6.5%, 🍷 till 2020 **98**

1996 Kiedricher Gräfenberg
Riesling Beerenauslese Goldkapsel
350 DM/0.375 liter, 8%, 🍷 till 2015 **98**

1996 Kiedricher Gräfenberg
Riesling Trockenbeerenauslese
294 DM/0.375 liter, 6.5%, 🍷 till 2015 **99**

RHEINGAU · RIESLING
1996
KIEDRICH GRÄFENBERG
TROCKENBEERENAUSLESE
WEINGUT
ROBERT
WEIL
Qualitätswein mit Prädikat
Erzeugerabfüllung
D-65399 Kiedrich/Rheingau
A. P. Nr. 3400300997
e 750 ml · alc. 6.5% by vol.

WEINGUT FREIHERR VON ZWIERLEIN SCHLOSS KOSAKENBERG

Owner: Mathias Decker-Horz
65366 Geisenheim, Bahnstraße 1
Tel. (0 67 22) 98 05 06, Fax 98 05 07
Directions: B 42, second Geisenheim exit to the railway station
Opening hours: Tue.–Sun. noon to 3 p.m. and 6 p.m. to 11 p.m. or by appointment
Restaurant: Open Tue.–Sun. from noon to 3 p.m. and 6 p.m. to 11 p.m.
Worth seeing: Schloß Kosakenberg with Renaissance doorway that is a historic monument, old park

Vineyard area: 12 hectares
Annual production: 100,000 bottles
Top sites: Geisenheimer Kläuserweg, Rothenberg, Mäuerchen and Schloßgarten, Winkeler Jesuitengarten
Soil types: Loam, loess, sandy banks of the Rhine
Grape varieties: 90% Riesling, 10% Spätburgunder
Average yield: 78 hl/ha
Best vintages: 1990, 1995, 1996
Member: VDP

After many lackluster years, this once renowned estate bounced back with a successful range of wines in 1995. Although the dry Kabinetts often display a tart acidity, the 1996s and 1997s were, as a whole, of comparable quality. Our favorite wine in both vintages was the fruity Geisenheimer Kläuserweg Kabinett. The overall improvement in performance is due to Mathias Decker-Horz, who in 1991 was entrusted with the responsibility of the estate Schloß Kosakenberg by his mother, Gisela Wegeler. She had inherited the property in the 1970s from a descendant of the Freiherr von Zwierlein. The impressive castle was constucted by Graf von Ingelheim in 1681. After an extensive modernization of the winery, the new proprietor can now display the knowledge that he acquired at several notable wineries, not the least of them Deinhard.

1997 Geisenheimer Kläuserweg
Riesling Kabinett trocken
12 DM, 12%, 🍷 till 2000 **80**

1996 Geisenheimer Kläuserweg
Riesling Kabinett trocken
12 DM, 10%, 🍷 till 2000 **80**

1996 Geisenheimer Kläuserweg
Riesling Kabinett halbtrocken
12 DM, 10%, 🍷 till 2000 **82**

1996 Winkeler Jesuitengarten
Riesling Spätlese
14 DM, 10%, 🍷 till 2001 **82**

1997 Geisenheimer Kläuserweg
Riesling Kabinett halbtrocken
12 DM, 11.5%, 🍷 till 2002 **84**

1996 Geisenheimer Rothenberg
Riesling Kabinett halbtrocken
11 DM, 10%, 🍷 till 2001 **84**

1997 Geisenheimer Kläuserweg
Riesling Kabinett
12 DM, 11%, 🍷 till 2004 **86**

1996 Geisenheimer Kläuserweg
Riesling Kabinett
12 DM, 8.5%, 🍷 till 2002 **86**

Out of the shadows of the past

Every fourth bottle of German wine emerges from the vast vineyards of Rheinhessen. Alongside Müller-Thurgau and Silvaner, numerous other modern hybrids attain programmed commercial yields on the fertile loam and loess soils of the rolling hills between Bingen, Mainz and Worms. This is the home of Liebfrauenmilch! Many consumers think that Riesling plays only a minor role here; yet hidden behind the other varieties are 2,400 hectares of Riesling, much of it on the "Rheinfront" between Nackenheim and Oppenheim. Amazing as this may seem, Rheinhessen actually produces as much Riesling as the Rheingau! And much of it is very good.

Many of the younger growers, who prefer producing drier wines, are anxious to step out of the sweet shadows cast by their forefathers. After a prolonged period of self-imposed modesty, they have launched a new marketing offensive to attract a younger clientele. Designer bottles, artist's labels and fashionable accessories are the order of the day. Nonetheless, only 40 or 50 of the some 3,000 wineries in Rheinhessen merit serious attention.

More classical efforts are also being made using the theme of "Selection." Werner Hiestand, for example, markets his better wines in an elegant, slender bottle with the slogan "old vines, classic varieties, hand picked" and he is quite pleased with the results. His dry wines are sold without vineyard designation or Prädikat, even though they are produced from the finest grapes of the vintage. Whether most consumers are ready to pay higher prices for such wines has yet to be proven. Many of them still believe that only a Spätlese or Auslese is worth more than ten marks a bottle.

With the better vintages between 1988 and 1994 the growers in Rheinhessen appear to have emerged rather successfully from the wretched years of the early 1980s. The 1995 vintage, however, offered unforeseen problems, especially on the "Rheinfront," where the finest wines are normally produced. Some of the top vineyards were damaged up to three times by hailstorms. A cool damp September sealed the coffin; good wines were the exception. The 1996 and 1997 vintages saw a return to better quality in Nierstein and its surrounding area. Heyl zu Herrnsheim bounced back after a dismal performance in 1995; G. A. Schneider and Franz Karl Schmitt, both also from Nierstein, made equally splendid comebacks. Seebrich has also improved his quality dramatically. Nonetheless, Fritz Hasselbach from neighboring Nackenheim is still first among equals along the Rhine.

Klaus Keller, the uncrowned king of the Wonnegau, confirmed his status as the leading grower in Rheinhessen in 1996. From his dry Riesling Spätlese to the magnificent Rieslaner ice wine, he produced a range of wines that no other estate could match. The 1997s were even better! Five of his wines were among the top of their class in that vintage, a phenomenal performance. Even Fritz Hasselbach from Gunderloch, who has been the most consistent vintner in Rheinhessen over the past four vintages, had fewer trumps in his hand.

The improved quality of the wines from lesser-known estates such as Schales, Michel-Pfannebecker, Göhring and Scherner-Kleinhanß proves that, beyond Keller, something of note is definitely happening in the southern part of this region, which has for years been unduly neglected by wine lovers. The red wine enclave in Ingelheim is also enjoying a modest renaissance, as is the northwest corner of the region near Bingen. With its successful 1996s and even better 1997s, the once-renowned estate of Villa Sachsen produced its two best collections in years.

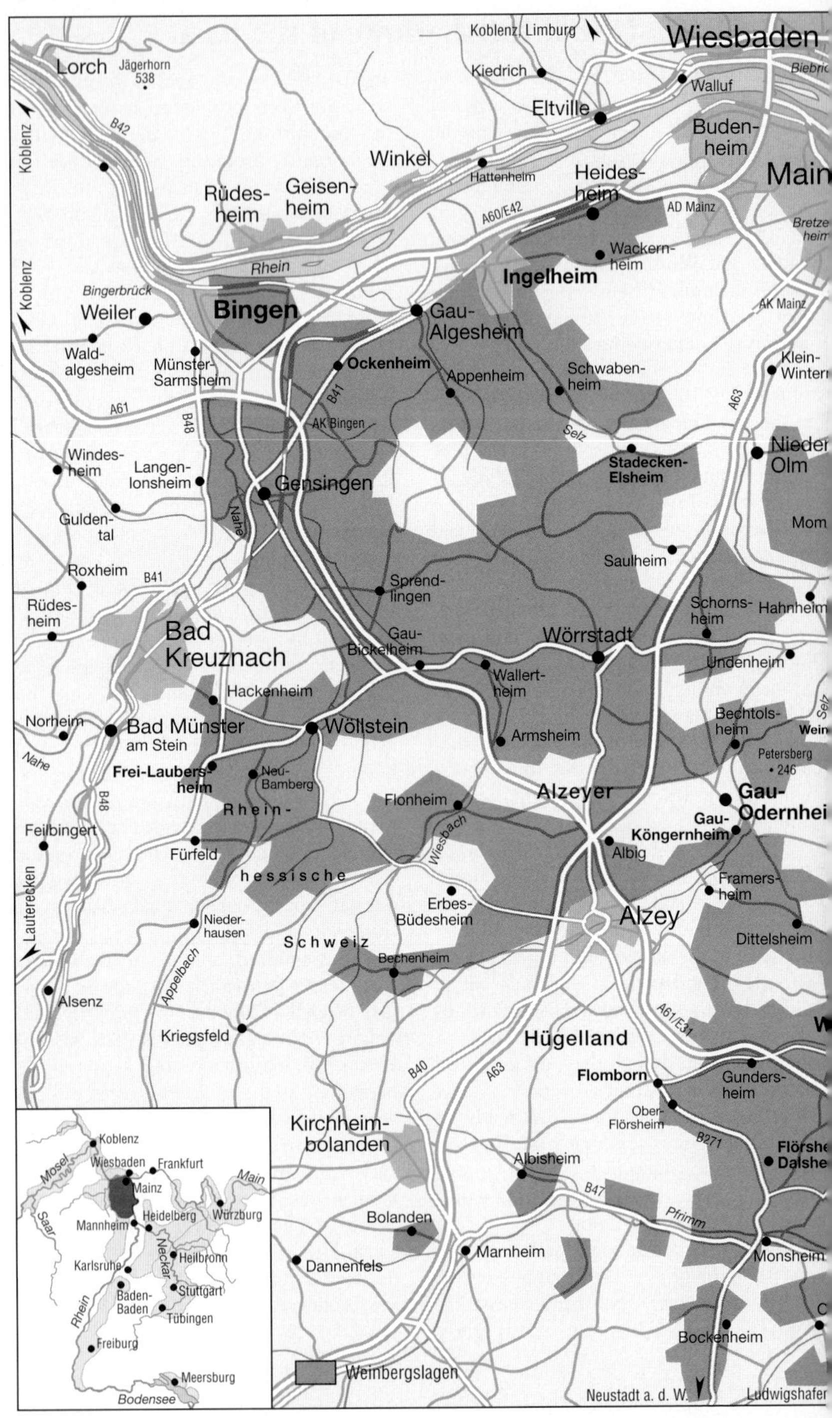
Wiesbaden
Koblenz, Limburg
Lorch
Jägerhorn 538
Kiedrich
Walluf
Eltville
Buden-heim
Mainz
Winkel
Hattenheim
Heides-heim
Rüdes-heim
Geisen-heim
A60/E42
AD Mainz
Wackern-heim
Rhein
Ingelheim
Bingerbrück
Weiler
Bingen
Gau-Algesheim
AK Mainz
Wald-algesheim
Münster-Sarmsheim
Ockenheim
Appenheim
Schwaben-heim
Klein-Winter
A61
B48
B41
AK Bingen
A63
Selz
Windes-heim
Langen-lonsheim
Gensingen
Stadecken-Elsheim
Nieder-Olm
Gulden-tal
Nahe
Saulheim
Roxheim
B41
Sprend-lingen
Schorns-heim
Hahnheim
Rüdes-heim
Bad Kreuznach
Gau-Bickelheim
Wörrstadt
Undenheim
Wallert-heim
Hackenheim
Norheim
Bad Münster am Stein
Wöllstein
Bechtols-heim
Armsheim
Petersberg 246
Nahe
Frei-Laubersheim
Neu-Bamberg
Alzeyer
Gau-Odernheim
B48
Rhein-
Flonheim
Gau-Köngernheim
Feilbingert
Fürfeld
Wiesbach
Albig
hessische
Framers-heim
Lauterecken
Erbes-Büdesheim
Alzey
Nieder-hausen
Dittelsheim
Schweiz
Bechenheim
Appelbach
Alsenz
A61/E31
Kriegsfeld
Hügelland
B40
A63
Flomborn
Gunders-heim
Ober-Flörsheim
Kirchheim-bolanden
B271
Albisheim
B47
Bolanden
Pfrimm
Marnheim
Monsheim
Dannenfels
Bockenheim
Weinbergslagen
Neustadt a. d. W.
Ludwigshafen
Koblenz
Wiesbaden
Frankfurt
Mosel
Mainz
Main
Saar
Heidelberg
Würzburg
Mannheim
Neckar
Karlsruhe
Heilbronn
Baden-Baden
Stuttgart
Rhein
Tübingen
Freiburg
Meersburg
Bodensee

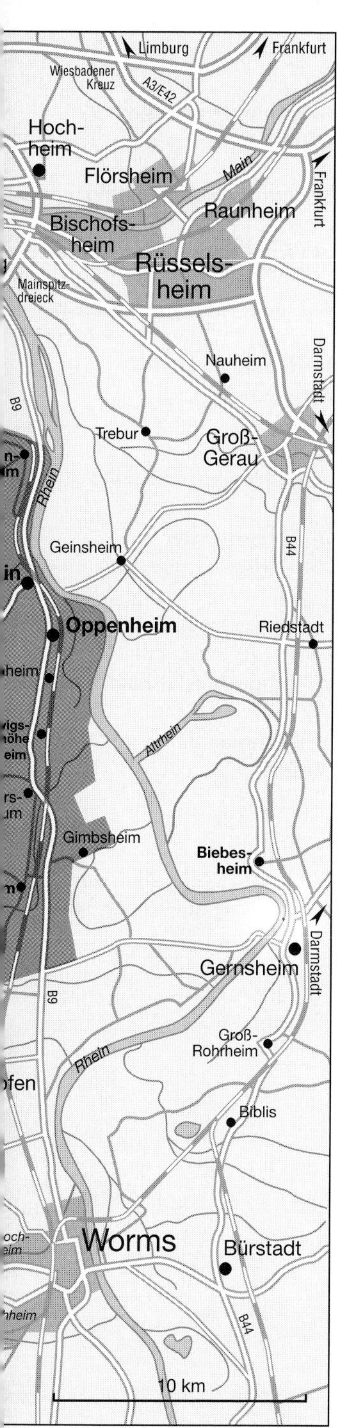

The leading estates of Rheinhessen

Weingut Keller, Flörsheim-Dalsheim

Weingut Gunderloch, Nackenheim

Weingut Freiherr Heyl zu Herrnsheim, Nierstein

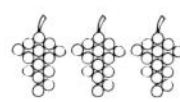

Weingut Michel-Pfannebecker, Flomborn

Weingut Sankt Antony, Nierstein

Weingut Schales, Flörsheim-Dalsheim

Rating scale for the estates

Highest rating: These producers belong to the world's finest.

Excellent estates: These producers are among Germany's best.

Very good producers, known for their consistently high quality.

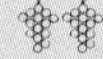

Good estates, offering better than average quality.

Reliable producers that offer well-made standard quality.

Weingut Franz Karl Schmitt, Nierstein

Weingut Georg Albrecht Schneider, Nierstein

Weingut Heinrich Seebrich, Nierstein

Weingut Villa Sachsen, Bingen

Weingut Balbach, Nierstein

Wein- und Sektgut Ch. W. Bernhard, Frei-Laubersheim

Weingut Jean Buscher, Bechtheim

Weingut Göhring, Flörsheim-Dalsheim

Weingut K. F. Groebe, Biebesheim

Weingut Kissinger, Uelversheim

Weingut Kühling-Gillot, Bodenheim

Weingut Manz, Weinolsheim

Weingut Meiser, Gau-Köngernheim

Weingut J. Neus, Ingelheim

Weingut Posthof – Doll & Göth Stadecken-Elsheim

Weingut Scherner-Kleinhanss, Flörsheim-Dalsheim

Staatliche Weinbaudomäne Oppenheim, Oppenheim

Weingut J. & H. A. Strub, Nierstein

Weingut Wittmann, Westhofen

Weingut Brüder Dr. Becker, Ludwigshöhe

Brennersches Weingut, Bechtheim

Weingut Geil, Eimsheim

Weingut Louis Guntrum, Nierstein

Weingut Hedesheimer Hof, Stadecken-Elsheim 1

Weingut Kapellenhof Ökonomierat Schätzel Erben, Selzen

Weingut Bürgermeister Carl Koch Erben, Oppenheim

Weingut Merz, Ockenheim

Weingut Rappenhof, Alsheim

Weingut Stallmann-Hiestand, Uelversheim

Vintage chart for Rheinhessen

vintage	quality	drink
1997	🍇🍇🍇	till 2003
1996	🍇🍇🍇🍇	till 2004
1995	🍇🍇🍇	now
1994	🍇🍇🍇	now
1993	🍇🍇🍇🍇	till 2002
1992	🍇🍇🍇🍇	now
1991	🍇🍇	now
1990	🍇🍇🍇🍇	till 2003
1989	🍇🍇🍇	now
1988	🍇🍇🍇🍇	now

🍇🍇🍇🍇🍇 : Outstanding
🍇🍇🍇🍇 : Excellent
🍇🍇🍇 : Good
🍇🍇 : Average
🍇 : Poor

Other notable producers

Weingut Heinrich Braun
55283 Nierstein, Glockengasse 5 + 9
Tel. (0 61 33) 51 39 und 51 30,
Fax 5 98 77

Weingut Hof Dätwyl – Hans Albert Dettweiler
67587 Wintersheim, Hauptstraße 11
Tel. (0 67 33) 426, Fax 82 10

Weingut Kurt Erbeldinger und Sohn
67595 Bechtheim-West 3
Tel. (0 62 44) 49 32, Fax 71 31

Weingut Gerhard Gutzler
67599 Gundheim, Roßgasse 19
Tel. (0 62 44) 90 52 21, Fax 90 52 41

Weingut Walter Hauck
55234 Bermersheim vor der Höhe, Sonnenhof
Tel. (0 67 31) 12 72 oder 31 95,
Fax 4 56 52

Weingut Hildegardishof
55234 Bermersheim vor der Höhe, Obergasse 5
Tel. (0 67 31) 4 29 99, Fax 4 65 18

Weingut Georg Jakob Keth
67591 Offstein, Wormser Straße 35–37
Tel. (0 62 43) 75 22, Fax 77 51

Weingut Köster-Wolf
55234 Albig, Langgasse 62
Tel. (0 67 31) 25 38, Fax 4 64 74

Weingut Krug'scher Hof
☞ *See below, page 418*

Oberstleutnant Liebrecht'sche Weingutsverwaltung
55294 Bodenheim, Rheinstraße 30
Tel. (0 61 35) 23 01, Fax 82 21

Weingut Karlheinz Milch und Sohn
67590 Monsheim, Rüstermühle
Tel. (0 62 43) 3 37, Fax 67 07

Kommerzienrat P. A. Ohler'sches Weingut
55411 Bingen, Gaustraße 10
Tel. (0 67 21) 1 48 07, Fax 1 42 11

Weingut Schlamp-Schätzel
55283 Nierstein, Oberdorfstraße 34
Tel. (0 61 33) 55 12, Fax 6 01 59

Weingut Adolf Schick
55270 Jugenheim, Kreinergasse 1
Tel. (0 61 30) 2 56, Fax 82 11

Weingut Dr. Alex Senfter
55283 Nierstein, Wörrstädter Straße 10
Tel. (0 61 33) 54 78, Fax 6 04 08

Weingut E. Weidenbach
55218 Ingelheim, Bahnhofstraße 86
Tel. (0 61 32) 21 73, Fax 4 14 18

Weingut Eckhard Weitzel
55218 Ingelheim 4, Backesgasse 7
Tel. (0 61 30) 4 47, Fax 84 38

Schloß Westerhaus – von Opel
55218 Ingelheim, Schloß Westerhaus
Tel. (0 61 30) 66 74 u. 2 18, Fax 66 08

WEINGUT BALBACH

Owner: Fritz Hasselbach
General Manager: Toni Biondino
55283 Nierstein, Mainzer Str. 64
Tel. (0 61 33) 23 41, Fax 24 31
Directions: From Mainz on B 9 towards Worms
Sales: Friedrich and Agnes Hasselbach
Opening hours: By appointment

Vineyard area: 12.6 hectares
Annual production: 100,000 bottles
Top sites: Niersteiner Pettental, Hipping and Oelberg
Soil types: Reddish soil, loess and loam
Grape varieties: 58% Riesling, 22% Müller-Thurgau, 8% Silvaner, 7% Kerner, 3% Weißburgunder, 2% Grauburgunder
Average yield: 75 hl/ha
Best vintages: 1996, 1997

The quality of the wines from this old estate in Nierstein had been on the wane for years when it was leased in the summer of 1996 to Fritz Hasselbach. Lacking descendants, Friedel Bohn offered him this renowned estate with its superb vineyards. As they had sufficient work on their hands at the estate in Nackenheim, Agnes and Fritz Hasselbach hesitated for some time. However, after inspecting the excellent vineyards in Nierstein, they could not resist the temptation. It is a long-term leasehold with a right to buy. The vineyards are now looked after by the same team that manages those of Gunderloch; and although the cellar conditions are not yet at the level of those in Nackenheim, the wines will continue to be made separately in Nierstein. The results of the first vintage made it clear that Hasselbach has already breathed new life into this venerable estate. He was less pleased with the 1997s, and even considered selling a large part of the crop in bulk, but his criticism is merely the mirror of his extremely high standards. This is an estate to follow!

1996 Niersteiner Pettental
Riesling Kabinett
11.50 DM, 10%, ♀ till 2000 **84**

1996 Niersteiner Rehbach
Riesling Spätlese
17.50 DM, 10%, ♀ till 2002 **84**

1997 Niersteiner Pettental
Riesling Spätlese trocken “Maitre B”
19.50 DM, 12.5%, ♀ till 2003 **86**

1996 “Antoine B”
Riesling
8.50 DM, 10.5%, ♀ till 2000 **86**

1997 Niersteiner Pettental
Riesling Kabinett
11.50 DM, 10.5%, ♀ till 2002 **86**

1997 Niersteiner Pettental
Riesling Spätlese
17.50 DM, 10.5%, ♀ till 2007 **89**

1997 Niersteiner Pettental
Riesling Auslese
29 DM, 10.5%, ♀ till 2010 **89**

1996 Niesteiner Hipping
Riesling Auslese
29 DM, 10%, ♀ till 2006 **89**

1996 Niersteiner Oelberg
Riesling Eiswein
60 DM/0.375 liter, 9%, ♀ till 2007 **91**

WEINGUT BRÜDER DR. BECKER

Owner: Lotte Pfeffer-Müller, Hans Müller
Manager: Hans Müller
Winemakers: Hans Müller and Lotte Pfeffer-Müller
55278 Ludwigshöhe, Mainzer Str. 3–7
Tel. (0 62 49) 84 30, Fax 76 39
Internet: www.ecovin.de Brüder-Dr-Becker
Directions: 25 kilometers south of Mainz, via B 9
Sales: Lotte Pfeffer-Müller, Hans Müller
Opening hours: By appointment
History: Wine estate founded in late 19th century
Worth seeing: Wooden casks in vaulted cellar, organic estate

Vineyard area: 10.5 hectares
Annual production: 70,000 bottles
Top sites: Dienheimer Tafelstein, Ludwigshöher Teufelskopf
Soil types: Loess, loam
Grape varieties: 42% Riesling, 18% Silvaner, 17% Scheurebe, 10% Spätburgunder, 13% other varieties
Average yield: 62 hl/ha
Best vintages: 1990, 1993
Member: VDP, BÖW

In the late 1960s, long before it became fashionable, Dr. Becker's vineyards were already cultivated on organic lines; and to this day there is little hectic activity at this estate, either in the vineyards or in the cellars. Instead, priority is given to allowing the wines to evolve naturally; all interventions are made cautiously. The finer wines are nurtured in casks, the simpler wines in stainless steel tanks. The original label of the estate shows each grape variety printed in large red cursive script. After the mediocre 1994 vintage, Lotte Pfeffer herself spoke of the 1995s "as the most difficult and least impressive vintage of the last ten years." Neither the 1996s nor the 1997s are particularly exhilarating either, but the estate is performing in a stable fashion.

1996 Riesling
trocken
8.50 DM/1.0 liter, 11%, ♀ now **80**

1997 Dienheimer Tafelstein
Riesling Kabinett trocken
10.20 DM, 12%, ♀ now **80**

1997 Dienheimer Paterhof
Riesling Spätlese trocken
14.50 DM, 12.5%, ♀ now **80**

1996 Ludwigshöher Teufelskopf
Silvaner Spätlese trocken
17.20 DM, 11.5%, ♀ now **80**

1997 Riesling
trocken "Selection"
18 DM, 12.5%, ♀ now **82**

1996 Dienheimer Falkenberg
Riesling Kabinett halbtrocken
9.60 DM, 9.5%, ♀ now **82**

1997 Dienheimer Tafelstein
Riesling Spätlese
15.20 DM, 10%, ♀ now **82**

1996 Dienheimer Tafelstein
Scheurebe Spätlese
14.20 DM, 11%, ♀ till 2000 **84**

1997 Dienheimer Falkenberg
Riesling Auslese
20 DM, 10%, ♀ till 2000 **84**

1996 Riesling
trocken Selection
18 DM/0.5 liter, 12%, ♀ till 2000 **86**

Brüder Dr. Becker
1996
Riesling
Spätlese trocken
Dienheimer Tafelstein
Alc. 11,0% vol. Rheinhessen 750 ml

WEIN- UND SEKTGUT CH. W. BERNHARD

Owner: Hartmut Bernhard
55546 Frei-Laubersheim,
Philipp-Wehr-Straße 31–33
Tel. (0 67 09) 62 33, Fax 61 60
Directions: A 61, exit Gau-Bickelheim, B 420 in the direction of Wöllstein and Frei-Laubersheim
Opening hours: Mon.–Sat. 8 a.m. to 8 p.m.
History: 400-year-old traditional estate

Vineyard area: 8.7 hectares
Annual production: 70,000 bottles
Top sites: Hackenheimer Kirchberg, Frei-Laubersheimer Fels and Rheingrafenberg
Soil types: Porphyry, clay and sandy loam
Grape varieties: 33% Riesling, 14% Silvaner, 10% Spätburgunder, 9% Kerner, 7% Portugieser, 6% each of Müller-Thurgau and Weißburgunder, 15% other varieties
Average yield: 81 hl/ha
Best vintages: 1989, 1996, 1997

The unusual placement of Hartmut Bernhard's vineyards finds expression in his wines. In particular the Rieslings grown on porphyry soils belong in style to the neighboring Nahe valley. The Bernhards, who in the Middle Ages were weavers in Dutch Brabant, have always made the best of their situation. In 1830 the best cask of each vintage was brought by horse-drawn cart to Darmstadt, where senior officials and officers were among their most loyal customers. What others see as a drawback is for Bernhard often a challenge. He has planted the appropriate grape variety on six different soil types so that he can offer the perfect wine for every taste. His showpiece is a 50-year-old vineyard where the rare Auxerrois grape is planted. Of late, the estate has shown signs of improvement. The 1996 range was certainly the best that we had tasted in years. Although Bernhard compares the 1997s to the legendary 1953s and 1949s, we were less impressed.

1997 Hackenheimer Kirchberg
Riesling Spätlese halbtrocken
9.70 DM, 11%, ♀ till 2001 **82**

1997 Hackenheimer Kirchberg
Riesling Kabinett
7.80 DM, 10%, ♀ till 2000 **82**

1996 Frei-Laubersheimer Fels
Riesling halbtrocken
6.90 DM, 10%, ♀ till 2000 **84**

1996 Frei-Laubersheimer Fels
Auxerrois Kabinett halbtrocken
8.60 DM, 10%, ♀ till 2000 **84**

1996 Hackenheimer Kirchberg
Riesling Kabinett
9.20 DM, 8%, ♀ now **84**

1997 Hackenheimer Kirchberg
Riesling Spätlese
9.50 DM, 10.5%, ♀ till 2002 **84**

1996 Hackenheimer Kirchberg
Scheurebe
7 DM, 9%, ♀ till 2002 **86**

1996 Frei-Laubersheimer Kirchberg
Kerner Spätlese
7.80 DM, 9.5%, ♀ till 2001 **86**

1996 Hackenheimer Kirchberg
Riesling Spätlese
7.80 DM, 8.5%, ♀ till 2003 **86**

WEINGUT
CH. W. BERNHARD
D-55546 FREI-LAUBERSHEIM · TELEFON: 0 67 09 - 62 33
1993
HACKENHEIMER
KIRCHBERG
Silvaner
KABINETT TROCKEN
QUALITÄTSWEIN MIT PRÄDIKAT
10.5% vol
A. P. NR. 4 726 016 05 94
GUTSABFÜLLUNG
750 ml
RHEINHESSEN

BRENNERSCHES WEINGUT

Owner: Christian Brenner
67595 Bechtheim, Pfandturmstraße 20
Tel. (0 62 42) 8 94, Fax 8 74
Directions: Via B 9 or A 61, exit Gundersheim/Westhofen
Opening hours: Mon.–Fri. 8 a.m. to 11:30 a.m. and 1 p.m. to 5 p.m. Weekends by appointment
Worth seeing: Old cask cellar, attractive presshouse

Vineyard area: 10 hectares
Annual production: 90,000 bottles
Top sites: Bechtheimer Geyersberg, Rosengarten, Hasensprung and Heilig Kreuz
Soil types: Loess with heavy chalky loam
Grape varieties: 40% Weißburgunder, 20% Riesling, 15% Spätburgunder, 5% each of Silvaner, Portugieser, Chardonnay, Grauburgunder and Müller-Thurgau
Average yield: 74 hl/ha
Best vintages: 1992, 1995, 1996

Christian Brenner is one of the few growers who doesn't moan about his fate; he has taken fortune into his own hands. Long before others made the discovery that placing wines in good restaurants is a cost-free but image-generating form of public relations, Brenner's dry wines were present on many wine lists. A slight drop in quality in the course of the 1980s couldn't restrain Brenner's wealth of ideas and enthusiasm for innovation. The "creative thinker of Bechtheim," as he is often called, marketed the best wines of each new vintage in unusual bottles with labels designed by Professor Franz Müller. In recent years the yields have dropped, and the 1995s showed a considerable improvement in quality, above all in the Burgundian varieties. The 1996s are a touch better. Even the Rieslings have gained in stature. In spite of the less impressive 1997s, this estate is clearly on an upward curve!

1997 Bechtheimer Heilig Kreuz
Silvaner Spätlese trocken
8.90 DM, 12%, 🍷 now **82**

1997 Weißer Burgunder
Spätlese trocken
13.90 DM, 13%, 🍷 now **82**

1996 Bechtheimer Rosengarten
Riesling Spätlese trocken
9.90 DM, 11.5%, 🍷 now **82**

1996 Bechtheimer Geyersberg
Weißer Burgunder Spätlese trocken
10.90 DM, 12%, 🍷 now **82**

1996 Bechtheimer Gotteshilfe
Riesling Kabinett trocken
7.90 DM, 11%, 🍷 now **84**

1996 Bechtheimer Geyersberg
Weißer Burgunder Spätlese trocken – 15 –
12.90 DM, 12%, 🍷 till 2001 **86**

1996 Weißer Burgunder
trocken Selection
16 DM, 12.5%, 🍷 till 2000 **88**

——— Red wines ———

1996 Bechtheimer Hasensprung
Spätburgunder trocken
16.50 DM, 13%, 🍷 till 2000 **84**

1996 Bechtheimer Hasensprung
Spätburgunder trocken
16.50 DM, 13%, 🍷 till 2002 **88**

AMTLICHE PRÜFUNGSNUMMER 4 257 034 015 97
RHEINHESSEN
QUALITÄTSWEIN MIT PRÄDIKAT
BRENNER
0,75 l · 12% vol
1996er Weißer Burgunder
Spätlese Trocken
Bechtheimer Geyersberg
GUTSABFÜLLUNG
BRENNER'SCHES WEINGUT · D-67595 BECHTHEIM

WEINGUT JEAN BUSCHER

Owner: Michael Buscher
General Manager: Rudolf Leiblein
Winemaker: Rudolf Leiblein
67595 Bechtheim, Wormser Straße 4
Tel. (0 62 42) 8 72, Fax 8 75
Directions: B 9 Mainz–Worms, A 61, exit Gundersheim
Sales: Michael Buscher
Opening hours: Mon.–Fri. 8 a.m. to 5 p.m. or by appointment
History: Founded 1844
Worth seeing: Old vaulted cellars with casks

Vineyard area: 15 hectares
Annual production: 160,000 bottles
Top sites: Bechtheimer Geyersberg, Stein and Hasensprung
Soil types: Loess and loam
Grape varieties: 48% red wine varieties, 24% Riesling, 9% Weißburgunder, 6% each of Kerner and Silvaner, 7% other varieties
Average yield: 79 hl/ha
Best vintages: 1994, 1996, 1997

Michael Buscher has proven himself to be a marketing genius. For ten years he has commissioned artists to design a label embossed in metal, which he launches with a "Vinissage" in the estate's cellars. Again and again this opportunist has managed to be seated with prominent people at his side, from soccer star Uwe Seeler to the director of the NASA space agency. The dubious high point of his originality to date was a label floating inside the bottle. Some find so much gimmickry rather discomfiting; but the wines are good and, in recent years, have even improved in quality. Traditional wooden casks are still retained for about 90 percent of the production in the cellar, where Rudolf Leiblein has been in charge for 45 years. He rules over an abundance of different grape varieties, half of which produce red wines and rosés.

1996 Bechtheimer Geyersberg
Riesling Spätlese trocken
12.50 DM, 11%, 🍷 till 2000 **84**

1996 Bechtheimer Stein
Weißer Burgunder Spätlese trocken
13 DM, 12%, 🍷 now **84**

1997 Bechtheimer Stein
Riesling Auslese trocken
16.50 DM, 12%, 🍷 till 2000 **84**

1996 Bechtheimer Hasensprung
Grauer Burgunder Kabinett halbtrocken
8.60 DM, 9.5%, 🍷 till 2000 **84**

1996 Bechtheimer Stein
Muskateller
8.80 DM, 9%, 🍷 till 2001 **84**

——— Red wines ———

1997 Bechtheimer Stein
Spätburgunder Spätlese trocken
13.50 DM, 12%, 🍷 now **82**

1997 Bechtheimer Stein
Spätburgunder Auslese trocken
22.50 DM/0.5 liter, 13.5%, 🍷 till 2000 **84**

1996 Bechtheimer Rosengarten
Schwarzriesling Spätlese trocken
15.50 DM, 12%, 🍷 till 2000 **84**

1997 Bechtheimer Rosengarten
Schwarzriesling Auslese trocken
25 DM/0.5 liter, 13.5%, 🍷 till 2001 **86**

WEINGUT GEIL

Owner: Thomas Geil
55278 Eimsheim, Mittelstraße 14
Tel. (0 62 49) 23 80, Fax 76 18
Directions: B 9, exit Guntersblum
Sales: Wilfried and Thomas Geil
Opening hours: By appointment
History: Owned by the Geil family since 1760
Worth seeing: Buildings constructed in 1774 in typical Franconian style, cross-vaulted stable with wine bar

Vineyard area: 20 hectares
Annual production: 130,000 bottles
Top sites: Mettenheimer Schloßberg and Michelsberg, Eimsheimer Sonnenhang and Hexelberg
Soil types: Loess and loam
Grape varieties: 27% Silvaner, 25% Riesling, 14% Müller-Thurgau, 7% Burgundian varieties, 6% red wine varieties, 5% Huxelrebe, 16% other varieties
Average yield: 78 hl/ha
Best vintages: 1993, 1996, 1997

Winemaking had little appeal for Thomas Geil when he was a young man. He made the decision to take over the parental estate only about ten years ago while doing practical training at the Nahe state domaine in Niederhausen. Since 1993 he has been responsible for the estate's cellars, in which he produces increasingly well-made wines. Not surprisingly, he has also steadily lowered the yields in the vineyards, which lie in a side valley near the Rhine. About half of the harvest is still done manually. In the cellar his motto is simple: "Intervene only when absolutely necessary." The 1996 range confirmed the success of the previous vintage; the ice wine was of exceptional quality. The 1997s are by and large equally appealing. It appears that we will be hearing more from this estate in the years to come.

1997 Eimsheimer Sonnenhang
Riesling Kabinett trocken
7.55 DM, 11.5%, ♀ now **82**

1996 Eimsheimer Hexelberg
Grauer Burgunder Kabinett trocken
8.40 DM, 10.5%, ♀ now **82**

1997 Eimsheimer Hexelberg
Weißer Burgunder Spätlese trocken
8.50 DM, 12.5%, ♀ till 2000 **82**

1997 Eimsheimer Hexelberg
Grauer Burgunder Spätlese trocken
9.50 DM, 13%, ♀ till 2000 **82**

1997 Mettenheimer Schloßberg
Riesling Kabinett halbtrocken
8 DM, 11%, ♀ till 2001 **82**

1996 Mettenheimer Schloßberg
Riesling Kabinett halbtrocken
7.90 DM, 10.5%, ♀ till 2000 **82**

1997 Eimsheimer Hexelberg
Silvaner Spätlese trocken "Selection"
12 DM, 12.5%, ♀ till 2000 **84**

1996 Mettenheimer Michelsberg
Gewürztraminer Kabinett
7.90 DM, 10%, ♀ till 2001 **84**

1997 Mettenheimer Michelsberg
Riesling Spätlese
11 DM, 11%, ♀ till 2002 **84**

1996 Eimsheimer Römerschanze
Riesling Eiswein
35 DM/0.375 liter, 11%, ♀ till 2006 **91**

SELECTION
Geil
1996 RIESLING SPÄTLESE TROCKEN
METTENHEIMER MICHELSBERG QUALITÄTSWEIN MIT PRÄDIKAT 11,5% vol.
GUTSABFÜLLUNG A.P.Nr. 4351 022 1297 PRODUCE OF GERMANY 750 ml
WEINGUT GEIL D-55278 EIMSHEIM RHEINHESSEN

WEINGUT GÖHRING

Owners: Wilfried and Marianne Göhring
Winemakers: Gerd and Wilfried Göhring
67592 Flörsheim-Dalsheim, Alzeyer Straße 60
Tel. (0 62 43) 4 08, Fax 65 25
Directions: A 61, exit Worms-Mörstadt, to Flörsheim-Dalsheim, then Nieder-Flörsheim
Sales: Marianne and Wilfried Göhring
Opening hours: Mon.–Sat. 8 a.m. to 7 p.m., Sun. 10 a.m. to noon
By appointment
History: Estate owned by the family since 1819

Vineyard area: 14 hectares
Annual production: 100,000 bottles
Top sites: Nieder-Flörsheimer Frauenberg and Goldberg, Dalsheimer Sauloch
Soil types: Loess, loam, clay and fossil limestone
Grape varieties: 18% Riesling, 13% each of Müller-Thurgau and Portugieser, 11% Burgundian varieties, 7% Dornfelder, 7% each of Kerner and Huxelrebe, 24% other varieties
Average yield: 88 hl/ha

Although the Göhrings cultivate vines not only on the Silberberg but also on the Goldberg, they have not been spared the general depression so prevalent in Rheinhessen. Here, too, we find at first glance the same picture encountered at hundreds of other estates in the region. Prices are extremely low and the list of grapes planted reads like an index of new varieties. Yet it is encouraging to see that some undeterred family estates – with hard work and the spirit of enterprise – are succeeding in dragging the growers of Rheinhessen out of their anonymity. The 1994 range from this estate was the first that attracted our attention. Although the wines of the following year were not quite as good, the 1996s and 1997s show marked improvement.

1996 Nieder-Flörsheimer Goldberg
Grauer Burgunder Spätlese trocken
8.20 DM, 12.5%, ♀ now **82**

1997 Nieder-Flörsheimer Goldberg
Riesling Spätlese trocken
8.10 DM, 11.5%, ♀ till 2000 **84**

1996 Nieder-Flörsheimer Frauenberg
Riesling Spätlese trocken
9.70 DM, 12%, ♀ till 2000 **84**

1997 Dalsheimer Bürgel
Weißer Burgunder Auslese trocken
11.70 DM, 13.5%, ♀ till 2000 **84**

1996 Nieder-Flörsheimer Goldberg
Riesling Kabinett halbtrocken
6.70 DM, 10%, ♀ till 2000 **84**

1996 Dalsheimer Sauloch
Gewürztraminer Kabinett
7.20 DM, 10%, ♀ till 2000 **84**

1997 Nieder-Flörsheimer Frauenberg
Riesling Spätlese
8.50 DM, 10%, ♀ till 2001 **84**

1997 Nieder-Flörsheimer Frauenberg
Huxelrebe Spätlese
7.90 DM, 10%, ♀ till 2001 **86**

1996 Nieder-Flörsheimer Frauenberg
Albalonga Auslese
13 DM, 10%, ♀ till 2005 **89**

Weingut Göhring
1997
Riesling
Spätlese Trocken
Nieder-Flörsheimer Goldberg
Qualitätswein mit Prädikat
A. P. Nr. 4 274 049 04 98
Erzeugerabfüllung
750 ml
alc. 11,5% vol.
Produce of Germany
Rheinhessen
D-67592 FLÖRSHEIM-DALSHEIM · ALZEYER STRASSE 60 · TELEFON (0 62 43) 4 08

WEINGUT K. F. GROEBE

Owners: Friedrich and Marianne Groebe
Winemaker: Friedrich Groebe
64584 Biebesheim, Bahnhofstraße 68–70
Tel. (0 62 58) 67 21, Fax 8 16 02
Directions: A 67, exit Biebesheim
Sales: Friedrich Groebe
Opening hours: By appointment
History: Founded in 1625; since 1763 the family coat of arms has taken the form of ancient Christian symbols for wine
Worth seeing: 500-year-old vaulted cellar and the "villa rustica" in the Kirchspiel vineyard

Vineyard area: 7 hectares
Annual production: 50,000 bottles
Top sites: Westhofener Kirchspiel, Aulerde and Steingrube
Soil types: Loess, loam and limestone
Grape varieties: 60% Riesling, 12% Silvaner, 10% each of Spätburgunder and Grauburgunder, 8% other varieties
Average yield: 70 hl/ha
Best vintages: 1990, 1993, 1996

This is an unusual estate: the administration is located on one side of the Rhine in Biebesheim, the vineyards they cultivate on the opposite bank in Westhofen, which is also where the crushing facilities and cask cellars are located. The range of grape varieties is also unusual: an impressive 60 percent of the vineyards are planted with Riesling; various other classic varieties such as Silvaner, Spätburgunder and Grauburgunder make up the rest. The wines are all aged in casks, a few in small oak barrels. In contrast to the two preceding vintages, all of the 1996s show clear fruit. There was no trace of the phenolic tones that we had detected in earlier vintages. Although the 1997s are not quite as good, this estate now seems to be coming of age.

1996 Westhofener
Riesling trocken
7.50 DM/1.0 liter, 10.5%, ♀ now **82**

1997 Westhofener Aulerde
Riesling Kabinett trocken
10 DM, 10.5%, ♀ till 2000 **82**

1997 Westhofener Aulerde
Riesling Kabinett
9.50 DM, 9%, ♀ now **82**

1997 Westhofener Kirchspiel
Riesling Spätlese trocken
14 DM, 11.5%, ♀ till 2000 **84**

1997 Westhofener Kirchspiel
Riesling Spätlese
16 DM, 8%, ♀ till 2001 **84**

1996 Westhofener Aulerde
Riesling Kabinett
10 DM, 9%, ♀ till 2002 **86**

1996 Westhofener Kirchspiel
Kerner Kabinett
9 DM, 9.5%, ♀ now **86**

1997 Westhofener Kirchspiel
Riesling Auslese
16 DM/0.375 liter, 7%, ♀ till 2003 **86**

1996 Westhofener Kirchspiel
Riesling Spätlese
18 DM, 9%, ♀ till 2003 **88**

1996 Westhofener Aulerde
Riesling Auslese
30 DM, 7.5%, ♀ till 2005 **88**

WEINGUT GUNDERLOCH

Owners: Fritz and Agnes Hasselbach
Manager: Toni Biondino
Winemaker: Fritz Hasselbach
55299 Nackenheim,
Carl-Gunderloch-Platz 1
Tel. (0 61 35) 23 41, Fax 24 31
e-mail: Weingut@Gunderloch.de
Directions: A 60, exit Nierstein, B 9, exit Nackenheim, left on entering village
Sales: Agnes Hasselbach-Usinger
Opening hours: By appointment
Restaurant: Open Mon.–Fri. from 6 p.m., Sat. from 4 p.m., Sun. from noon
Specialties: Regional dishes
History: Wine estate founded in 1890 by the banker Carl Gunderloch

Vineyard area: 12.5 hectares
Annual production: 84,000 bottles
Top sites: Nackenheimer Rothenberg, Niersteiner Pettental and Hipping
Soil types: Red clay and slate
Grape varieties: 80% Riesling, 5% Silvaner, 6% Burgundian varieties, 9% other varieties
Average yield: 40 hl/ha
Best vintages: 1993, 1994, 1997
Member: VDP

With a string of highly successful vintages in the late 1980s Fritz and Agnes Hasselbach established their estate as one of the finest of the region; since 1992 they have also earned merited praise from the international wine press. Their efforts to ensure high quality are colossal: the steep vineyards of the excellent Rothenberg are cultivated almost entirely by hand, and yields are kept to no more than 40 hectoliters per hectare. Fritz Hasselbach devotes special attention to a slow and careful vinification of his young Rieslings, which takes place in temperature-controlled stainless steel tanks. The wines then need time to show their full potential. In July 1996, he leased the entire estate of Balbach Erben, with its superlative vineyards in Nierstein. In spite of the double load, the wines of that vintage did not disappoint our expectations. The 1997s are, in spite of his reticence, perhaps even better!

1997 Riesling
Kabinett halbtrocken "Jean Baptiste"
12 DM, 10%, ♀ till 2002 **88**

1997 Riesling
Spätlese
13.50 DM, 9.5%, ♀ till 2003 **89**

1996 Nackenheimer Rothenberg
Riesling Spätlese
25 DM, 9.5%, ♀ till 2004 **89**

1997 Nackenheimer Rothenberg
Riesling trocken "Erstes Gewächs"
39 DM, 13.5%, ♀ till 2007 **90**

1997 Nackenheimer Rothenberg
Riesling Spätlese
18 DM, 9.5%, ♀ till 2004 **92**

1996 Nackenheimer Rothenberg
Riesling Auslese Goldkapsel
60 DM, 9%, ♀ till 2007 **92**

1997 Nackenheimer Rothenberg
Riesling Auslese
35 DM, 9.5%, ♀ till 2007 **94**

1997 Nackenheimer Rothenberg
Riesling Auslese Goldkapsel
60 DM, 8.5%, ♀ till 2010 **95**

WEINGUT LOUIS GUNTRUM

Owner: Hanns Joachim Louis and Louis Konstantin Guntrum
General Manager: Udo Loos
Manager: Gerhard Müller
55283 Nierstein, Rheinallee 62
Tel. (0 61 33) 9 71 70, Fax 97 17 17
e-mail:
weingut-louis-guntrum@t-online.de
Directions: On B 9 between Nierstein and Oppenheim, near the Rhine ferry
Sales: Hanns Joachim Louis Guntrum, Angelika Hamm
Opening hours: Mon.–Thur. 7 a.m. to 4:15 p.m., Fri. 7 a.m. to noon or by appointment
History: Family arms granted through imperial warrant in 1545, estate owned by the family since 1648

Vineyard area: 22 hectares
Annual production: 300,000 bottles
Top sites: Niersteiner Pettental, Oelberg and Orbel, Oppenheimer Herrenberg and Sackträger, Nackenheimer Rothenberg
Soil types: Reddish slate, loam, loess, heavy chalk and clay
Grape varieties: 58% Riesling, 19% Müller-Thurgau, 7% each of Kerner and Scheurebe, 9% other varieties
Average yield: 59 hl/ha
Best vintages: 1993, 1996

Although this well-known estate in Nierstein has languished in the overall torpor of the Rheinhessen for all too long, there are signs of a return to its former glories. This first became apparent with the surprising 1995 range; the 1996s were also good. Although the bread-and-butter wines are of similar quality, the 1997 range lacks real highlights. Its revival is partially due to a shrinking of the vineyard holdings to one third of the former surface area. Hanns Joachim Guntrum was just not willing to stand idly by while his estate came to the same inglorious end as those of Sittmann and Gustav Adolf Schmitt, which have now been dissolved. The owners also operate a negociant business, which has had great success in selling wines in red bottles to Japan; the blue ones go to Sweden.

1997 Oppenheimer Sackträger
Silvaner Spätlese
12.50 DM, 10%, 🍷 now **80**

1997 Oppenheimer Sackträger
Riesling Kabinett trocken "Classic"
14.75 DM, 12.5%, 🍷 now **82**

1997 Oppenheimer Sackträger
Riesling Spätlese trocken "Jubilee 350"
9.95 DM/0.5 liter, 12.5%, 🍷 till 2000 **82**

1996 Oppenheimer Schützenhütte
Riesling Kabinett halbtrocken
11.90 DM, 10.5%, 🍷 till 2001 **82**

1997 Niersteiner Bergkirche
Riesling Kabinett "Jubilee 350"
9.40 DM/0.5 liter, 9.5%, 🍷 now **82**

1996 Oppenheimer Herrenberg
Riesling Kabinett halbtrocken
11 DM, 10.5%, 🍷 till 2000 **84**

1996 Niersteiner Oelberg
Riesling Kabinett halbtrocken
14.75 DM, 11.5%, 🍷 till 2001 **84**

1996 Oppenheimer Herrenberg
Silvaner Eiswein
145 DM/0.5 liter, 10%, 🍷 till 2006 **91**

WEINGUT HEDESHEIMER HOF

Owner: Jürgen Beck
Winemakers: Jürgen and Michael Beck
55271 Stadecken-Elsheim 1
Tel. (0 61 36) 24 87, Fax 92 44 13
Directions: Via A 63, exit Nieder-Olm, to Stadecken
Opening hours: By appointment

Vineyard area: 19.4 hectares
Annual production: 130,000 bottles
Top sites: Stadecker Lenchen and Spitzberg, Elsheimer Bockstein and Blume
Soil types: Heavy clay, loam with loess deposits
Grape varieties: 25% Riesling, 30% red wine varieties, 10% Müller-Thurgau, 8% each of Silvaner and Grauburgunder, 7% each of Kerner and Scheurebe, 5% Weißburgunder
Average yield: 80 hl/ha
Best vintages: 1994, 1996, 1997

We admire the fact that Jürgen Beck has shied away from flashy marketing and has now given his labels an easily recognizable appearance. Thanks to their reliable quality, his wines have also regularly emerged well in comparative tastings. They usually have an appealing fruitiness on the nose and an unmistakably reductive style. Beck prunes his vines severely, has abandoned fertilizers in favor of cover crops and does without harvesting machines. Riesling accounts for a quarter of the production, but he also has a substantial proportion of Burgundian varieties. The majority of his wines, half of which are made in a dry style, are sold to private customers. Although the 1995 range did not match the quality of the two previous vintages, the 1996s and 1997s showed far better. This estate is certainly capable of even more.

1997 Stadecker Lenchen
Grauer Burgunder Spätlese trocken
9.50 DM, 13.5%, 🍷 now **82**

1997 Elsheimer Bockstein
Silvaner Spätlese trocken
10.50 DM, 13.5%, 🍷 now **82**

1996 Stadecker Lenchen
Grauer Burgunder trocken "Selection"
15.50 DM, 12.5%, 🍷 till 2000 **84**

1996 Stadecker Lenchen
Grauer Burgunder Spätlese trocken
9.50 DM, 12.5%, 🍷 now **84**

1996 Stadecker Spitzberg
Riesling trocken "Selection"
15.50 DM, 11.5%, 🍷 till 2000 **86**

1997 Stadecker Spitzberg
Riesling Spätlese trocken
9 DM, 12.5%, 🍷 till 2001 **86**

1996 Stadecker Spitzberg
Riesling Spätlese trocken
8.50 DM, 11.5%, 🍷 till 2001 **86**

1996 Stadecker Spitzberg
Riesling Kabinett halbtrocken
7 DM, 10%, 🍷 till 2000 **86**

1997 Stadecker Lenchen
Riesling Spätlese halbtrocken
9 DM, 11.5%, 🍷 till 2002 **86**

SEIT 1736
Hedesheimer Hof
WEINGUT
1994er
Weißer Burgunder
Kabinett
12,0% vol trocken 0,75 l
RHEINHESSEN
Stadecker Lenchen
Gutsabfüllung · Qualitätswein mit Prädikat · A.P.Nr. 4394195 012 95
DIPL.-ING. J. BECK · D-55271 STADECKEN-ELSHEIM · TEL. (0 61 36) 24 87

WEINGUT FREIHERR HEYL ZU HERRNSHEIM

Owner: Ahr family foundation
Director: Markus Winfried Ahr
Manager: Michael Burgdorf
Winemaker: Bernd Kutschik
55283 Nierstein, Langgasse 3
Tel. (0 61 33) 51 20, Fax 5 89 21
Internet: www.heyl-zu-herrnsheim.de
Directions: B 9, between Mainz and Worms, in Nierstein from Marktplatz into the Langgasse
Sales: Michael d'Aprile, Karoline Kloske
Opening hours: Mon.–Fri. 8 a.m. to 5 p.m., Sat. by appointment
Worth seeing: Estate buildings from the 16th century

Vineyard area: 37.2 hectares
Annual production: 200,000 bottles
Top sites: Niersteiner Brudersberg, Pettental, Oelberg, Hipping and Orbel
Soil types: Reddish slate
Grape varieties: 60% Riesling, 18% Silvaner, 12% Müller-Thurgau, 10% Weißburgunder
Average yield: 56 hl/ha
Best vintages: 1993, 1996, 1997
Member: VDP, Naturland

For decades this property had been producing wines of inimitable character with surprising regularity, and for many wine lovers it remains the leading estate of the region. Four years ago there was a change in ownership: the Ahr family from Westphalia acquired a share of the estate, which they now own fully. The 1995 vintage, though, must have come as a disappointment to the new partners. A late spring frost destroyed many of the buds and then, in the summer, their finest vineyards were severely damaged by hailstorms. That vintage was certainly the estate's nadir. The 1996s were of incomparably better quality and certainly among the finest of the vintage in Rheinhessen. The 1997s are perhaps a touch better, setting the course for the future. This estate has an admirable collection of excellent vineyards and is certainly to be counted among the top three of the region.

1996 Niersteiner Brudersberg
Riesling trocken
32 DM, 12%, ♀ till 2004 **89**

1997 Niersteiner Brudersberg
Riesling trocken "Erstes Gewächs"
32 DM, 12%, ♀ till 2004 **89**

1997 Niersteiner Pettental
Riesling Spätlese
28 DM, 10.5%, ♀ till 2005 **89**

1997 Niersteiner Orbel
Riesling Spätlese
28 DM, 10.5%, ♀ till 2007 **89**

1996 Niersteiner Brudersberg
Riesling Spätlese
26 DM, 10%, ♀ till 2004 **89**

1996 Niersteiner Oelberg
Riesling Spätlese Selection
24 DM, 9.5%, ♀ till 2002 **89**

1997 Niersteiner Pettental
Riesling trocken "Erstes Gewächs"
29 DM, 12.5%, ♀ till 2007 **90**

1996 Niersteiner Hipping
Weißer Burgunder Spätlese trocken
24 DM, 12.5%, ♀ till 2004 **91**

1996 Niersteiner Pettental
Riesling Auslese
32 DM, 10%, ♀ till 2004 **91**

1997 Niersteiner Pettental
Riesling Auslese
32 DM, 11.5%, ♀ till 2010 **92**

WEINGUT KAPELLENHOF ÖKONOMIERAT SCHÄTZEL ERBEN

Owner: Thomas Schätzel
55278 Selzen, Kapellenstraße 18
Tel. (0 67 37) 2 04, Fax 86 70
Directions: From north A 60, from south A 63
Opening hours: Mon.–Fri. 8 a.m. to 7 p.m., Sat. 9 a.m. to 6 p.m.
History: A former church estate that has been owned by the family for 200 years
Worth seeing: Small wine museum, old vaulted cellar, Art Nouveau buildings, spacious park
Restaurant: "Weinstube Kapellenhof"
Specialties: Regional fare

Vineyard area: 17 hectares
Annual production: 120,000 bottles
Top sites: Hahnheimer Knopf, Selzener Osterberg and Gottesgarten
Soil types: Clay, loam
Grape varieties: 33% Riesling, 13% each of Müller-Thurgau and Silvaner, 10% each of red wine and Burgundian varieties, 5% Kerner, 16% other varieties
Average yield: 85 hl/ha
Best vintages: 1992, 1995, 1996

Over the past few years numerous changes have taken place at this beautifully located property in Selzen. After a phase of brightly colored labels, the estate now markets itself more subtly. In the vineyard the estate employs extensive natural green cover; and athough 60 percent of the cellar capacity is in tanks, fermentation still takes place in casks. Some 85 percent of the wines are made in a dry and off-dry style. In contrast with the two previous vintages, the quality of the 1995s was certainly better. This may have been due to the fact that the harvesting machine had been sold and most of the grapes were again being picked by hand. The 1996 range was of a similar quality level. Above all the Rieslings, despite their crisp acidity, were most attractive. The 1997s are appealing, but little more.

1996 Sörgenlocher Moosberg
Grauer Burgunder Spätlese trocken
9.60 DM, 12%, ♀ now **80**

1997 Selzener Osterberg
Riesling Spätlese trocken
8.90 DM, 11.5%, ♀ now **82**

1997 Hahnheimer Knopf
Weißer Burgunder Spätlese trocken
9.80 DM, 12%, ♀ now **82**

1997 Selzener Gottesgarten
Grauer Burgunder Spätlese trocken
9.80 DM, 12%, ♀ now **82**

1996 Hahnheimer Knopf
Weißer Burgunder Spätlese trocken
9.60 DM, 12%, ♀ now **82**

1997 Riesling
trocken "Selection"
16.20 DM, 12%, ♀ till 2002 **84**

1996 Hahnheimer Knopf
Riesling Spätlese trocken
8.70 DM, 12%, ♀ till 2000 **84**

1996 Riesling
trocken Selection "Oekonomierat E"
16 DM, 12%, ♀ till 2000 **86**

1996 Hahnheimer Knopf
Riesling Spätlese halbtrocken
8.70 DM, 10.5%, ♀ till 2000 **86**

Weinbau
Seit 1350
Kapellenhof
1995
Spätburgunder Weissherbst
halbtrocken
Selzener Gottesgarten
Qualitätswein
A. P. Nr. 4 390 100 03 96
Product of Germany
0,75 l
Rheinhessen
10,0 % vol
Gutsabfüllung
Oekonomierat Schätzel Erben · D-55278 Selzen

WEINGUT KELLER

Owners: Klaus and Hedwig Keller
67592 Flörsheim-Dalsheim,
Bahnhofstraße 1
Tel. (0 62 43) 4 56, Fax 66 86
Directions: A 61, exit Worms-Nord, via Mörstadt to Flörsheim and Dalsheim
Opening hours: Mon.–Sat. 8 a.m. to noon and 1 p.m. to 6 p.m. or by appointment
History: The Keller family has run the estate since 1789 – today in the eighth generation

Vineyard area: 12.5 hectares
Annual production: 100,000 bottles
Top sites: Dalsheimer Hubacker, Sauloch and Steig
Soil types: Loam and clay
Grape varieties: 35% Riesling, 30% Grau- and Weißburgunder and Chardonnay, 25% red wine varieties, 10% Rieslaner and Huxelrebe
Average yield: 75 hl/ha
Best vintages: 1994, 1996, 1997

Without overrating the significance of awards, we noted that this estate earned the highest prize ever conferred at the federal wine show, "gold upon gold." We might add, "upon gold!" Klaus Keller is an advocate of pure varietal vinification in stainless steel tanks, and he strives for crystal clear fruit flavors in his wines. For that reason the reductively structured dry wines generally require time to develop their full potential. The 1996s and 1997s were again of superb quality, the dry 1997 Auslese the best of its class! The fruity Spätlese and the outstanding Auslese are simply stunning. The Trockenbeerenauslese and ice wine are not only the finest examples in Rheinhessen, they belong to the best produced in all of Germany. For many it is unfathomable that a producer from the backwaters of Rheinhessen should be listed among the finest producers in Germany. Tasting is believing! Son Klaus-Peter has now graduated from Geisenheim and returned home to help his father, preparing the way for a new generation in Dalsheim.

1997 Dalsheimer Hubacker
Riesling Kabinett halbtrocken
12.80 DM, 12%, ♀ till 2002 **89**

1997 Dalsheimer Hubacker
Riesling Auslese trocken
18.50 DM, 13%, ♀ till 2003 **92**

1996 Dalsheimer Hubacker
Riesling Spätlese – 26 –
22.50 DM, 9.5%, ♀ till 2008 **93**

1997 Dalsheimer Hubacker
Riesling Spätlese – 26 –
25 DM, 9.5%, ♀ till 2007 **94**

1997 Dalsheimer Hubacker
Riesling Auslese ***
55 DM/0.375 liter, 8.5%, ♀ till 2010 **96**

1996 Dalsheimer Hubacker
Riesling Auslese ***
55 DM/0.375 liter, 8%, ♀ till 2009 **96**

1997 Dalsheimer Hubacker
Riesling Eiswein
112 DM/0.375 liter, 8%, ♀ till 2012 **96**

1996 Dalsheimer Hubacker
Riesling Trockenbeerenauslese
150 DM/0.375 liter, 7.5%, ♀ 2002 till 2015 **96**

1996 Dalsheimer Hubacker
Riesling Eiswein Goldkapsel
148 DM/0.375 liter, 6.5%, ♀ till 2008 **98**

1997 Dalsheimer Hubacker
Riesling Trockenbeerenauslese
165 DM/0.375 liter, 7%, ♀ till 2020 **98**

WEINGUT KISSINGER

Owner: Jürgen Kissinger
Winemaker: Jürgen Kissinger
55278 Uelversheim, Römerstraße 11
Tel. (0 62 49) 74 48, Fax 79 89
Directions: Via B 9 to Dienheim, right in the direction of Uelversheim
Sales: Jürgen Kissinger
Opening hours: Mon.–Fri. by appointment, Sat. 9 a.m. to 5 p.m.
Worth seeing: Cask cellar dating from 1722

Vineyard area: 9.7 hectares
Annual production: 55,000 bottles
Top sites: Dienheimer Tafelstein, Uelversheimer Tafelstein and Oppenheimer Herrenberg
Soil types: Loess and loam
Grape varieties: 27% Riesling, 16% red wine varieties, 15% each of Silvaner and Burgundian varieties, 9% Kerner, 5% Müller-Thurgau, 13% other varieties
Average yield: 77 hl/ha
Best vintages: 1994, 1996, 1997

Since Jürgen Kissinger took over this estate, the wine quality has been steadily improving. In the renowned Dienheimer Tafelstein, which slopes steeply towards the Rhine, he has the perfect Riesling vines to bring him fruit of excellent quality. Furthermore, this young grower observes his distinguished colleagues closely and compares his wines with theirs in blind tastings, learning from experience how to improve his own quality. In the vineyard he concerns himself with extracting healthy and fully ripe grapes; in the cellar he does carefully monitored fermentation in small volumes. The disappointing results in 1995 can be largely attributed to the difficult weather conditions that year. The 1996 range was reminiscent of the much finer 1992 and 1994 vintages. The 1997s are again of similar quality. The local rivalry with the neighboring Stallmann-Hiestand estate in Uelversheim has thus, for the moment, been decided in his favor.

1997 Uelversheimer Tafelstein
Weißer Burgunder Spätlese trocken
8.60 DM, 13%, ♀ till 2000 **84**

1997 Oppenheimer Herrenberg
Riesling Kabinett halbtrocken
6.90 DM, 11.5%, ♀ till 2000 **84**

1997 Uelversheimer Tafelstein
Riesling Spätlese trocken
8.60 DM, 12.5%, ♀ till 2001 **86**

1996 Uelversheimer Tafelstein
Riesling Spätlese trocken
8.40 DM, 12%, ♀ till 2000 **86**

1997 Oppenheimer Sackträger
Riesling Auslese trocken
14.20 DM, 13%, ♀ till 2002 **86**

1997 Dienheimer Kreuz
Riesling Spätlese halbtrocken
8.60 DM, 12%, ♀ till 2000 **86**

1997 Dienheimer Kreuz
Riesling Spätlese
8.60 DM, 10.5%, ♀ till 2002 **86**

1996 Oppenheimer Herrenberg
Riesling Kabinett halbtrocken
6.60 DM, 10.5%, ♀ till 2000 **88**

1996 Uelversheimer Tafelstein
Riesling Spätlese halbtrocken
8.40 DM, 11%, ♀ till 2001 **88**

WEINGUT BÜRGERMEISTER CARL KOCH ERBEN

Owner: Carl Hermann Stieh-Koch
55276 Oppenheim, Wormser Straße 62
Tel. (0 61 33) 23 26, Fax 41 32
Directions: Via B 9 in the direction of city center, opposite the wine museum
Opening hours: Mon.–Fri. 8 a.m. to 5 p.m., Sat. and Sun. by appointment
Worth seeing: Winery in the former mansion of the noble Rodenstein family from the 14th century; garden with medieval town wall

Vineyard area: 12.5 hectares
Annual production: 80,000 bottles
Top sites: Oppenheimer Sackträger, Kreuz, Herrenberg
Soil types: Heavy chalky loam, with substantial clay content
Grape varieties: 35% Riesling, 19% Silvaner, 10% Müller-Thurgau, 9% Spätburgunder, 6% Weißburgunder, 5% each of Kerner and Gewürztraminer, 11% other varieties
Average yield: 75 hl/ha
Best vintages: 1993, 1994, 1997

Although this estate has been bottling its own wines since 1921, it has hardly come to the notice of the general public. With its beautiful buildings, the classic labels and the general quality of the wines, it could be a jewel of the region. The young, somewhat shy owner, Carl Hermann Stieh-Koch, cultivates classic grape varieties, uses modern techniques carefully and allows the wines plenty of time to develop naturally. The early 1990s brought a steady improvement in quality. The 1994 vintage was particularly good! However, after the weak 1995s, the 1996 and 1997 ranges show only scarce improvement. Is this estate losing its momentum?

1997 Oppenheimer Kreuz
Weißer Burgunder Spätlese trocken
10 DM, 12.5%, 🍷 till 2000 **82**

1996 Oppenheimer Kreuz
Weißer Burgunder Spätlese trocken
9 DM, 11.5%, 🍷 now **82**

1996 Oppenheimer Sackträger
Grauer Burgunder Auslese trocken
12 DM, 12.5%, 🍷 till 2000 **82**

1997 Dienheimer Tafelstein
Riesling Kabinett halbtrocken
6.80 DM, 11%, 🍷 till 2002 **82**

1997 Oppenheimer Kreuz
Riesling Kabinett
7.80 DM, 10%, 🍷 till 2000 **82**

1996 Oppenheimer Kreuz
Riesling Kabinett
7.20 DM, 9%, 🍷 till 2001 **82**

1996 Oppenheimer Kreuz
Silvaner Kabinett
6.90 DM, 8%, 🍷 till 2000 **84**

1996 Oppenheimer Kreuz
Riesling Spätlese
8.20 DM, 10%, 🍷 till 2001 **84**

1997 Oppenheimer Sackträger
Riesling Auslese
15 DM, 10.5%, 🍷 till 2002 **84**

WEINGUT KRUG'SCHER HOF

Owner: Menger-Krug family
General Manager: Eugen Birk
Winemaker: Erich Acker
55239 Gau-Odernheim,
Am grünen Weg 15
Tel. (0 67 33) 13 37, Fax 17 00
Directions: A 63, exit Alzey, in the direction of Gau-Odernheim
Opening hours: By appointment
History: Estate in the family for five generations

Vineyard area: 60 hectares
Annual production: 500,000 bottles (including the sparkling-wine property Menger-Krug)
Top sites: Alzeyer Römerberg, Gau-Köngernheimer Vogelsang
Soil types: Loamy clay
Grape varieties: 30% Weißburgunder, 20% Riesling, 20% Spätburgunder, 20% Chardonnay, 5% Grauburgunder, 5% other varieties
Average yield: 80 hl/ha
Best vintages: 1993, 1994, 1995

Thanks to the commitment of Regina and Klaus Menger, this property has attracted a great deal of attention in recent years. One often finds their wines served by Lufthansa and the German railways. The sparkling wines from the Menger-Krug property in the Rheinhessen and the Pfalz region – the ten-hectare Motzenbäcker estate – are sold to specialized merchants and restaurants by the German subsidiary of Rémy-Cointreau. The estate places particular value on healthy fruit, which is pressed quickly and gently, before it is put through a temperature-controlled fermentation. The wines are almost all made in a dry style; but in 1996 it was the off-dry Grauburgunder Kabinett that we liked the best. As a whole, the wines were more focused and pure in fruit than in previous vintages. If they could produce wines of this quality regularly, the estate's reputation would improve. The 1997s were less successful.

1995 Chardonnay
trocken "Charly"
10.50 DM, 12%, ♀ till 2000 **82**

1996 Weißer Burgunder
trocken
9.60 DM, 11.5%, ♀ now **84**

1996 Riesling
Kabinett trocken
8.60 DM, 11%, ♀ till 2000 **84**

1995 Chardonnay
Spätlese trocken
20 DM, 12.5%, ♀ till 2001 **84**

1996 Weißer Burgunder
Spätlese trocken
14.20 DM, 12%, ♀ till 2000 **84**

1996 Grauer Burgunder
Kabinett halbtrocken
8.60 DM, 10.5%, ♀ till 2002 **86**

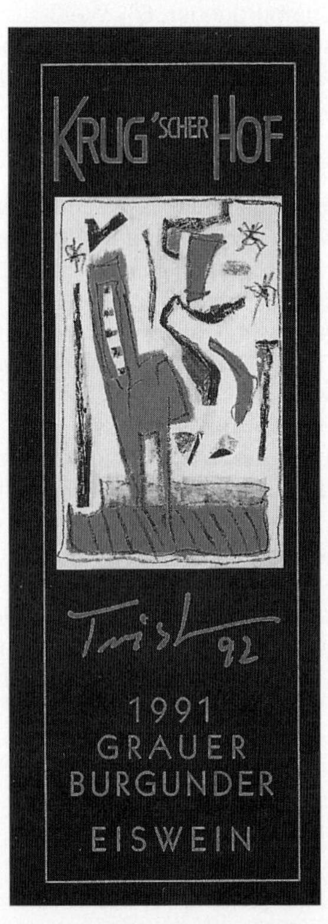

WEINGUT KÜHLING-GILLOT

Owners: Roland and Gabi Gillot
Winemaker: Roland Gillot
55294 Bodenheim, Ölmühlstraße 25
Tel. (0 61 35) 23 33, Fax 64 63
Directions: From Mainz via B 9, in the old village center of Bodenheim
Opening hours: Mon.–Fri. 9 a.m. to noon and 2 p.m. to 5 p.m., Sat. 10 a.m. to noon, Sun. by appointment
Restaurant: June to September, open Fri.–Sun. from 5 p.m.
Specialties: Cream cheese, smoked salmon, lamb
Worth seeing: Park and garden with Art Nouveau pavilion, collection of Mediterranean and exotic trees

Vineyard area: 8.5 hectares
Annual production: 80,000 bottles
Top sites: Oppenheimer Sackträger and Herrenberg, Bodenheimer Burgweg
Soil types: Deep loess and loam
Grape varieties: 40% Riesling, 13% Portugieser, 11% Spätburgunder, 10% Scheurebe, 7% each of Grauburgunder and Chardonnay, 12% other varieties
Average yield: 72 hl/ha
Best vintages: 1992, 1994, 1996
Member: VDP

This estate was created in 1970 when two old properties on the Rhine were merged. It soon made a name for itself through numerous prizes in various competitions. Roland Gillot also feels honored that his estate has now been admitted to the VDP. In spite of this success, he continues to make unusual wines that seldom correspond to popular stereotypes. They often, as was the case in 1996, turn out broad and rather high in alcohol. Nonetheless, the 1996 range was among the best of the last decade. Although he himself was very pleased with the 1997s, they are certainly not as successful as either the 1996s or 1994s. In spite of this, we expect to even hear more from the ambitious Roland Gillot in the near future.

1997 Oppenheimer
Riesling Kabinett trocken
8.50 DM, 12%, ♀ till 2000 **84**

1997 Oppenheimer
Riesling Kabinett halbtrocken
9 DM, 11%, ♀ till 2002 **84**

1997 Oppenheimer Sackträger
Riesling trocken “Erstes Gewächs”
28 DM, 12%, ♀ till 2002 **86**

1996 Oppenheimer Herrenberg
Riesling Spätlese
13 DM, 11%, ♀ till 2002 **88**

1996 Oppenheimer Sackträger
Riesling Spätlese
15 DM, 10%, ♀ till 2005 **88**

1996 Oppenheimer Sackträger
Riesling trocken
30 DM, 11.5%, ♀ till 2001 **89**

1996 Oppenheimer Sackträger
Riesling Auslese ***
50 DM, 9%, ♀ till 2004 **89**

1996 Oppenheimer Sackträger
Riesling Trockenbeerenauslese
Not yet for sale, 10.5%, ♀ till 2006 **91**

WEINGUT MANZ

Owner: Erich Manz
55278 Weinolsheim, Lettengasse 6
Tel. (0 62 49) 79 81 and 71 86,
Fax 8 00 22
Directions: A 61 or A 63, exit Gau-Bickelheim/Wörrstadt, onto the B 420
Opening hours: By appointment

Vineyard area: 7.5 hectares
Annual production: 60,000 bottles
Top sites: Weinolsheimer Kehr and Hohberg, Ülversheimer Schloß
Soil types: Clay, loess and loam
Grape varieties: 25% Dornfelder, 16% Riesling, 12% each of Huxelrebe and Kerner, 8% Portugieser, 7% Müller-Thurgau, 5% each of Weiß- and Spätburgunder, 10% other varieties
Average yield: 75 hl/ha
Best vintages: 1995, 1996, 1997

When someone like Erich Manz operates an estate as a hobby, he can take an easy-going attitude. “After our bottling operation became more and more profitable, my father actually wanted to give up the estate.” Manz now turns out three million bottles each year for others and does not need to depend on his estate for a living. Yet after his recent successes, including a commendable ranking at the Pro-Riesling competition in 1995, Manz has expanded his property. The plan is that after his son Eric has completed his years of study and travel, he will devote his full attention to the estate. The 1996s confirmed the positive impression that we had of the previous vintage. The 1997s are the finest wines that we have ever tasted from this estate. The range is very market driven. As a result there is a wide variety of bottles and labels and even a “Kollektion Manz” for the estate’s best wines.

1997 Weinolsheimer Kehr
Riesling Kabinett trocken
6 DM, 11.5%, ♀ now **82**

1997 Weinolsheimer Kehr
Chardonnay Spätlese trocken
12.50 DM, 12.5%, ♀ till 2000 **84**

1996 Weinolsheimer Kehr
Riesling Spätlese trocken
9 DM, 11.5%, ♀ now **84**

1997 Weinolsheimer Kehr
Riesling Kabinett halbtrocken
6 DM, 11%, ♀ till 2001 **84**

1996 Weinolsheimer Kehr
Riesling Kabinett
6 DM, 9%, ♀ till 2001 **84**

1997 Weinolsheimer Kehr
Kerner Spätlese
6.50 DM, 10.5%, ♀ till 2000 **84**

1997 Weinolsheimer Kehr
Riesling Spätlese trocken
9.50 DM, 11.5%, ♀ till 2002 **86**

1996 Weinolsheimer Kehr
Kerner Spätlese
6.50 DM, 10%, ♀ till 2003 **86**

1997 Weinolsheimer Kehr
Riesling Eiswein
18.50 DM/0.375 liter, 10%, ♀ till 2007 **91**

WEINGUT MEISER

Owners: Erich and Frank Meiser
55239 Gau-Köngernheim,
Alzeyer Straße 131
Tel. (0 67 33) 5 08, Fax 83 26
Directions: A 63, exit Biebelnheim, or A 61, exit Alzey
Opening hours: By appointment
Restaurant: "Poppenschenke" in an old mill with a lovely courtyard, open Fri., Sat. and Mon. from 6 p.m. Sun. from 11 a.m.
Specialties: Rheinhessisch dishes

Vineyard area: 19.5 hectares
Annual production: 150,000 bottles
Top sites: Alzeyer Rotenfels and Römerberg, Westhofener Steingrube, Bechtheimer Hasensprung, Weinheimer Kirchenstück and Hölle
Soil types: Weathered limestone, loess, loam and reddish slate
Grape varieties: 14% each of Riesling and Huxelrebe, 11% Bacchus, 8% Dornfelder, 7% Spätburgunder, 6% Müller-Thurgau, 5% each of Weißburgunder, Chardonnay and Ortega, 25% other varieties
Average yield: 86 hl/ha
Best vintages: 1993, 1996, 1997

This is a very typical estate from the hills of Rheinhessen: the range of grape varieties is enormous and the yields are often close to 100 hectoliters per hectare. Nonetheless, Erich Meiser has been able to distance himself from the army of nameless growers in the region. Today he is supported by his son Frank, whose experience, obtained at the venerable estate of Bassermann-Jordan in the Pfalz, stands him in good stead. Over two-thirds of the wines are sold to specialist merchants, a stable business relationship that Erich Meiser has nurtured since the 1960s. Little by little the two are discarding inferior varieties and reducing the yields. After appealing results in 1995 and 1996, the 1997s are even better. And at less than ten marks a bottle, the Riesling Auslese is bargain!

1996 Alzeyer Rotenfels
Riesling Hochgewächs
5 DM, 9.5%, ♀ till 2000 **82**

1997 Gau-Köngernheimer Vogelsang
Weißer Burgunder Spätlese trocken
6.70 DM, 12.5%, ♀ till 2001 **84**

1997 Gau-Köngernheimer Vogelsang
Chardonnay Spätlese trocken
7.90 DM, 12.5%, ♀ till 2002 **84**

1997 Bechtheimer Hasensprung
Huxelrebe Auslese trocken
9.50 DM, 14.5%, ♀ till 2002 **84**

1996 Gau-Köngernheimer Vogelsang
Weißer Burgunder Kabinett halbtrocken
5.30 DM, 10.5%, ♀ till 2000 **84**

1997 Weinheimer Kirchenstück
Riesling Spätlese trocken
6.60 DM, 11.5%, ♀ till 2002 **86**

1997 Gau-Köngernheimer Vogelsang
Huxelrebe Spätlese
6.80 DM, 11.5%, ♀ till 2003 **88**

1997 Alzeyer Rotenfels
Riesling Eiswein
35 DM/0.5 liter, 8.5%, ♀ till 2010 **88**

1996 Weinheimer Kapellenberg
Huxelrebe Spätlese
6.50 DM, 10%, ♀ till 2002 **89**

1997 Alzeyer Römerberg
Riesling Auslese
9.50 DM, 8%, ♀ till 2005 **89**

WEINGUT MERZ

Owners: Karl and Lyslotte Merz
55437 Ockenheim, Mainzer Straße 43
Tel. (0 67 25) 23 87, Fax 50 69
Directions: Via A 60, exit Ingelheim-West, in the direction of Gau-Algesheim (B 41); via A 61, exit Bad Kreuznach, in the direction of Gensingen, Gau-Algesheim (B 41)
Opening hours: Fri. 5 p.m. to 8 p.m., Sat. 10 a.m. to 6 p.m. or by appointment
History: Estate founded in 1833
Worth seeing: Old stone vaulted cellar, historic press

Vineyard area: 7 hectares
Annual production: 65,000 bottles
Top sites: Ockenheimer Laberstall and Hockenmühle
Soil types: Clay and heavy chalky loam
Grape varieties: 42% Riesling, 22% Silvaner, 8% each of Kerner and Chardonnay, 7% Müller-Thurgau, 13% other varieties
Average yield: 70 hl/ha
Best vintages: 1994, 1996, 1997

At their estate in Ockenheim, not far from Bingen, Karl and Lyslotte Merz produce appealing wines from little-known vineyards such as Ockenheimer Laberstall and Hockenmühle. The yields are kept low through short pruning, but the age of the vines as well as the late harvesting have also had their effect on the improved quality. Following the slow fermentation in tanks, the young wines are aged in oak casks. The fruitier Rieslings are bottled with relatively little residual sugar. The 1995 range was a touch disappointing. Apart from the mediocre Silvaners, the 1996 range was better, reminding us of the finer vintages 1992 and 1994. The 1997s are equally successful. Dry wines remain the current wave here, of which private customers purchase about 90 percent.

1996 Ockenheimer Hockenmühle
Riesling Spätlese trocken
8.95 DM, 11%, 🍷 till 2000 **80**

1997 Ockenheimer Klosterweg
Riesling Spätlese
9.95 DM, 10%, 🍷 now **80**

1997 Ockenheimer Laberstall
Riesling Kabinett trocken
7.25 DM, 11%, 🍷 now **82**

1997 Ockenheimer Laberstall
Riesling Spätlese trocken
8.75 DM, 12%, 🍷 now **82**

1997 Ockenheimer Hockenmühle
Riesling Spätlese trocken
8.95 DM, 12%, 🍷 now **82**

1996 Chardonnay
Spätlese trocken
13.95 DM, 12%, 🍷 till 2002 **82**

1996 Ockenheimer Klosterweg
Riesling Kabinett halbtrocken
6.95 DM, 11%, 🍷 till 2001 **82**

1996 Chardonnay
Auslese halbtrocken
28 DM, 12%, 🍷 till 2003 **86**

1996 Ockenheimer Laberstall
Riesling Auslese
19.95 DM, 11%, 🍷 till 2004 **86**

SEIT 1833
GUTSABFÜLLUNG
WEINGUT MERZ
D-55437 OCKENHEIM b. BINGEN
1996er
OCKENHEIMER LABERSTALL
AUSLESE
RIESLING
- IM HOLZFASS GEREIFT -
QUALITÄTSWEIN MIT PRÄDIKAT A. P. Nr. 4 386 129 004 97
alc. 11% by vol. RHEINHESSEN 750 ml e

WEINGUT MICHEL-PFANNEBECKER

Owners: Heinfried and Gerold Pfannebecker
55234 Flomborn, Langgasse 18/19
Tel. (0 67 35) 3 55 and 13 63, Fax 83 65
e-mail: wgtmi.pfa@t-online.de
Directions: A 61, exit Gundersheim, in the direction of Kirchheimbolanden, on the Hauptstraße
Opening hours: Mon.–Sat. 8 a.m. to 7 p.m. or by appointment

Vineyard area: 10 hectares
Annual production: 62,000 bottles
Top sites: Westhofener Steingrube, Flomborner Feuerberg and Goldberg
Soil types: Loess, loam and heavy chalk
Grape varieties: 16% each of Riesling and Burgundian varieties, 15% Silvaner, 14% Müller-Thurgau, 10% each of Portugieser and Scheurebe, 19% other varieties
Average yield: 73 hl/ha
Best vintages: 1995, 1996, 1997

Once separately managed estates in Flomborn, the Michel-Pfannebecker domaine has created an entirely new profile for itself in the last three years. The brothers Heinfried and Gerold have succeeded well in balancing their commercial existence with their striving for better quality. As long as the wines were sold at modest prices, one could hardly expect the estate to reduce the yields. Yet this was exactly necessary to improve quality. Yields of 150 hectolitres per hectare – as in 1989 and 1992 – have never been the basis for above-average wines. In 1995 yields were 68 hectoliters per hectare, in 1996 only 66 hectoliters were cropped; and these two vintages were the best we had ever tasted from this estate. But the 1997s were even better, by far the finest wines this estate has ever produced! And who would ever have thought that an unknown producer from the wrong side of the tracks would bottle two of the finest wines from the 1997 vintage? These farmers are becoming gentlemen!

1997 Flomborner Goldberg
Weißer Burgunder Spätlese trocken
9.80 DM, 12.5%, ♀ till 2000 **84**

1997 Eppelsheimer Felsen
Riesling Spätlese trocken
9.40 DM, 11.5%, ♀ till 2001 **86**

1997 Flomborner Feuerberg
Grauer Burgunder Spätlese trocken
10.50 DM, 13%, ♀ till 2000 **86**

1996 Flomborner Goldberg
Chardonnay Spätlese trocken
13.50 DM, 12.5%, ♀ till 2000 **86**

1996 Westhofener Steingrube
Riesling Spätlese halbtrocken
8.40 DM, 11%, ♀ till 2001 **86**

1997 Westhofener Steingrube
Riesling Auslese
13.50 DM, 9.5%, ♀ till 2002 **88**

1997 Westhofener Steingrube
Riesling Spätlese trocken
9.70 DM, 12%, ♀ till 2002 **89**

1997 Flomborner Goldberg
Chardonnay Spätlese trocken
13.50 DM, 13%, ♀ till 2002 **89**

1997 Flomborner Feuerberg
Scheurebe Eiswein
34 DM/0.375 liter, 9.5%, ♀ till 2005 **91**

WEINGUT J. NEUS

Owner: Burchards family
55218 Ingelheim, Bahnhofstraße 96
Tel. (0 61 32) 7 30 03, Fax 26 90
Directions: A 60, exit Ingelheim-Ost, in the direction of the city center
Sales: Ulrich Burchards
Opening hours: Mon.–Fri. 8:30 a.m. to noon and 1 p.m. to 6 p.m.
Sat. 9 a.m. to noon
Worth seeing: Old vaulted cellar with oak casks

Vineyard area: 12 hectares
Annual production: 80,000 bottles
Top sites: Ingelheimer Sonnenberg (sole owners), Pares and Horn
Soil types: Loess, loam, fossil limestone
Grape varieties: 60% Spätburgunder, 19% Portugieser, 5% Riesling, 16% other varieties
Average yield: 67 hl/ha
Best vintages: 1995, 1996, 1997
Member: VDP

This estate is managed today by Ulrich Burchards, the great-grandson of the founder. Cultural events celebrating wine are held each year in the attractive estate buildings. The vineyards are cultivated according to the guidelines of ecological viticulture. The estate leaves only a small number of buds during pruning; by picking manually, they also try to harvest a ripe but healthy crop. For their reds, the owners believe in traditional fermentation on the skins followed by cask-aging, which results in full-bodied yet only slightly tannic Spätburgunder. The 1995 reds were of reliable quality, the 1996 whites quite pleasant. The 1997s are also quite good. In recent years we have only rarely tasted such wines from this estate.

1997 Ingelheimer Horn
Riesling Kabinett trocken
8.80 DM, 11.5%, ♀ till 2000 **84**

1996 Ingelheimer Schlossberg
Weißer Burgunder Kabinett trocken
9 DM, 11.5%, ♀ till 2000 **86**

——— Red wines ———

1996 Ingelheimer Pares
Spätburgunder trocken
11.50 DM, 12%, ♀ till 2001 **84**

1996 Ingelheimer Horn
Spätburgunder trocken
11 DM, 12%, ♀ till 2000 **84**

1996 Ingelheimer Pares
Spätburgunder Kabinett trocken
14 DM, 11.5%, ♀ till 2000 **84**

1995 Ingelheimer Sonnenberg
Spätburgunder trocken
11.50 DM, 11.5%, ♀ till 2000 **84**

1995 Ingelheimer Burgberg
Spätburgunder halbtrocken
9.50 DM, 11%, ♀ now **84**

1996 Ingelheimer Sonnenberg
Spätburgunder Kabinett trocken
14.70 DM, 11.5%, ♀ till 2001 **86**

1995 Ingelheimer Pares
Spätburgunder trocken
11.20 DM, 11.5%, ♀ till 2000 **86**

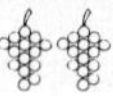

WEINGUT POSTHOF DOLL & GÖTH

Owners: Karl Theo and Roland Doll
Winemakers: Karl Theo and Roland Doll
55271 Stadecken-Elsheim, Kreuznacher Straße 2
Tel. (0 61 36) 30 00, Fax 60 01
Directions: A 60 Mainz–Kaiserslautern, exit Stadecken-Elsheim
Sales: Christel Doll, Erika Doll
Opening hours: By appointment
History: Buildings were formerly an imperial mail post founded in 1883

Vineyard area: 15 hectares
Annual production: 120,000 bottles
Top sites: Stadecker Lenchen and Spitzberg
Soil types: Loam, clay
Grape varieties: 25% Riesling, 11% Dornfelder, 10% each of Silvaner, Portugieser, Grau- and Weißburgunder, 8% each of Kerner, Spätburgunder and Scheurebe
Average yield: 85 hl/ha
Best vintages: 1996, 1997

Although Erika Göth and Roland Doll married in 1988, these two qualified winemakers decided to merge their estates only in 1993. The elder Karl-Heinz Göth still manages the vineyards in Gau-Bischofsheim; however, the vinification of the wines now takes place entirely at the Doll property in Stadecken-Elsheim. There was once an imperial mail post here, which accounts for the name "Posthof." Exceptional for the region is the fact that all of the harvesting is done by hand, which certainly explains the precise expression of the wines. The 1996 range was of surprising quality; and once again the sparkling wine, made from a 1994 Scheurebe, was included in our selection of Germany's finest. The 1997s are perhaps even better: clean, crisp and pure. We expect to hear even more from this estate in the years to come.

1997 Stadecker Lenchen
Weißer Burgunder Kabinett trocken
7.30 DM, 12%, ♀ now **82**

1996 Gau-Bischofsheimer Kellersberg
Riesling Kabinett halbtrocken
6.70 DM, 10.5%, ♀ till 2000 **82**

1997 Stadecker Spitzberg
Riesling Spätlese trocken
11.50 DM, 11.5%, ♀ till 2000 **84**

1997 Grauer Burgunder
Spätlese trocken
8.30 DM, 13%, ♀ till 2000 **84**

1997 Gau-Bischofsheimer Kellersberg
Riesling Kabinett trocken
7 DM, 11.5%, ♀ till 2001 **86**

1996 Grauer Burgunder
Spätlese halbtrocken
8.30 DM, 11.5%, ♀ till 2001 **86**

1996 Riesling
Spätlese
8 DM, 9%, ♀ till 2003 **86**

1997 Gau-Bischofsheimer Glockenberg
Riesling Spätlese
11.50 DM, 10%, ♀ till 2002 **88**

1997 Stadecker Spitzberg
Silvaner Auslese
14 DM, 9.5%, ♀ till 2002 **88**

WEINGUT RAPPENHOF

Owners: Dr. Reinhard Muth and Klaus Muth
General Manager: Klaus Muth
Manager: Hermann Muth
Winemaker: Serge da Cruz
67577 Alsheim, Bachstraße 47
Tel. (0 62 49) 40 15, Fax 47 29
Directions: Via B 9 from Mainz or Worms; A 61, exit Worms-Nord or Alzey
Sales: Ms. Muth
Opening hours: Mon.–Fri. 8 a.m. to 5 p.m. or by appointment
History: Owned by the family for 400 years

Vineyard area: 53 hectares
Annual production: 350,000 bottles
Top sites: Niersteiner Pettental and Oelberg, Oppenheimer Sackträger, Alsheimer Fischerpfad
Soil types: Red clay and slate, rich loam and loess over limestone
Grape varieties: 41% Riesling, 12% Weißburgunder, 11% Spätburgunder, 7% each of Kerner and Müller-Thurgau, 22% other varieties
Average yield: 78 hl/ha
Best vintages: 1993, 1996, 1997
Member: VDP, Deutsches Barrique-Forum

Dr. Muth's Rappenhof has been very growth oriented over the past decade. As the vineyard area expanded to an impressive 53 hectares, his family had little difficulty selling its production. Dr. Reinhard Muth, who runs the property with his son Klaus, is also the mayor of Alsheim and was, for years, the president of the association of German wine growers. He is also one of the leading viticultural experts of the region. Dr. Muth was one of the first to plant Chardonnay and to experiment with the barrel aging of his wines. In a tribute to Beaujolais, each November he releases a young wine made from Portugieser. The 1996 range, like that of the preceding vintages, was adequate, but little more. The 1997s are even a touch less successful. The wines of this estate could have more finesse and personality.

1997 Alsheimer Frühmesse
Riesling trocken
6.50 DM, 12%, ♀ now **80**

1997 Dienheimer Siliusbrunnen
Weißer Burgunder Spätlese trocken
10.50 DM, 12%, ♀ now **80**

1997 Alsheimer Frühmesse
Grauer Burgunder Spätlese trocken
10.50 DM, 12.5%, ♀ now **80**

1996 Niersteiner Ölberg
Riesling Spätlese trocken
15 DM, 11%, ♀ now **80**

1996 Alsheimer Sonnenberg
Riesling
6.80 DM, 10%, ♀ till 2000 **80**

1997 Alsheimer Frühmesse
Riesling Spätlese trocken
11 DM, 12%, ♀ now **82**

1996 Alsheimer Fischerpfad
Riesling Kabinett
8 DM, 8%, ♀ till 2001 **82**

1997 Alsheimer Fischerpfad
Riesling Spätlese
11 DM, 9.5%, ♀ till 2000 **82**

1996 Niersteiner Oelberg
Riesling Spätlese
14 DM, 8%, ♀ till 2002 **84**

1996 Alsheimer Fischerpfad
Riesling Spätlese
12 DM, 8.5%, ♀ till 2000 **86**

WEINGUT SANKT ANTONY

Owner: MAN AG, Munich
General Manager: Dr. Alexander Michalsky
Winemaker: Günter Ewert
55283 Nierstein,
Wörrstädter Straße 22
Tel. (0 61 33) 54 82, Fax 5 91 39
e-mail: St.Antony@com
Directions: Via B 9 or B 420
Sales: Ms. Cersovsky, Ms. Gabler
Opening hours: Mon.–Thur. 8 a.m. to noon and 2 p.m. to 4 p.m.
Fri. 8 a.m. to noon or by appointment

Vineyard area: 23 hectares
Annual production: 140,000 bottles
Top sites: Niersteiner Orbel, Oelberg, Pettental and Hipping
Soil types: Red slate
Grape varieties: 63% Riesling, 12% Silvaner, 10% red wine varieties, 15% other varieties
Average yield: 54 hl/ha
Best vintages: 1992, 1996, 1997
Member: VDP

Until 1985 this property, which now belongs to the large MAN corporation in Munich, traded as the Gutehoffnungshütte Estate. In recent years Sankt Antony has concentrated its efforts on the top vineyards in Nierstein, where the ambitious Dr. Alexander Michalsky now harvests his best Rieslings. The dry wines are fermented slowly in stainless steel tanks and then transferred to traditional casks, which still account for 65 percent of the cellar capacity. Our critical view of the 1993 and 1994 vintages was not shared by the estate's management. Be that as it may, the 1996 range was better than the 1995 and the first in recent years to measure up to the quality of the 1990 and 1992 vintages, which were the best that this estate had ever produced. The 1997s are also quite good, but will need time to develop. Given the increasing emphasis on the so-called first-growth vineyards, Sankt Antony will again be releasing wines under Nierstein's small Großlagen Rehbach and Auflangen.

1997 Niersteiner Auflangen
Riesling trocken
12 DM, 12%, ♀ till 2002 **88**

1996 Niersteiner Rosenberg
Riesling Kabinett trocken
13 DM, 10.5%, ♀ till 2000 **88**

1997 Niersteiner Pettental
Riesling Spätlese trocken
24 DM, 12.5%, ♀ till 2002 **88**

1996 Niersteiner Auflangen
Riesling Spätlese trocken
17 DM, 12.5%, ♀ till 2000 **88**

1996 Niersteiner Auflangen
Riesling Spätlese
16 DM, 10%, ♀ till 2003 **88**

1996 Niersteiner Oelberg
Riesling trocken
33 DM, 12%, ♀ till 2001 **89**

1997 Niersteiner Oelberg
Riesling trocken "Erstes Gewächs"
33 DM, 12.5%, ♀ till 2003 **89**

1996 Niersteiner Oelberg
Riesling Beerenauslese
60 DM, 11%, ♀ till 2007 **92**

WEINGUT SCHALES

Owners: Arno, Kurt and Heinrich Schales
Manager: Ralph Bothe
Winemaker: Kurt Schales
67592 Flörsheim-Dalsheim, Alzeyer Straße 160
Tel. (0 62 43) 70 03, Fax 52 30
e-mail: weingut.schales@t-online.de
Directions: A 61, exit Worms-Nord/ Mörstadt, to Dalsheim on the B 271
Sales: Arno Schales, Ralph Bothe
Opening hours: Mon.–Fri. 8 a.m. to noon and 1 p.m. to 6 p.m., Sat. 9 a.m. to 1 p.m., Sun. by appointment
History: Owned by the family since 1783
Worth seeing: Small wine museum, cask cellar, old wooden press

Vineyard area: 48 hectares
Annual production: 300,000 bottles
Top sites: Dalsheimer Bürgel, Sauloch and Steig
Soil types: Weathered fossil limestone, with a large proportion of clay
Grape varieties: 30% Riesling, 18% Müller-Thurgau, 15% Weißburgunder, 8% red wine varieties, 29% other varieties
Average yield: 72 hl/ha
Best vintages: 1993, 1996, 1997

The Schales brothers look after a small wine museum, regularly publish booklets about grape varieties with information on wine and food pairings, organize auctions and hold tastings of rare wines. In 1989 they ceased using village and vineyard names on their labels, emphasizing only the grape varietal and the Prädikat. Since 1993 the yields have been reduced to about 72 hectoliters per hectare, which has greatly benefitted the quality of the wines. The 1996s were similar in style to those of the previous vintage. The 1997s are also quite good; in particular the dry wines remain convincing. In order to satisfy demand, the brothers have added 12 hectares to their estate's holdings.

1997 Riesling
trocken
18.60 DM, 12.5%, ♀ till 2000 **86**

1997 Grauer Burgunder
Spätlese trocken
9.90 DM, 11.5%, ♀ till 2000 **86**

1997 Weißer Burgunder
Spätlese trocken
10.50 DM, 11.5%, ♀ till 2000 **86**

1997 Silvaner
Spätlese trocken
20.90 DM, 11%, ♀ till 2000 **86**

1997 Gewürztraminer
Spätlese trocken
10.50 DM, 12%, ♀ till 2002 **88**

1997 Riesling
Auslese trocken
16.25 DM, 12.5%, ♀ till 2002 **88**

1997 Weißer Burgunder
Auslese trocken
13.95 DM, 13%, ♀ till 2000 **88**

1997 Rieslaner
Auslese
16.25 DM, 10%, ♀ till 2005 **89**

1996 Grauer Burgunder
Spätlese trocken
9.80 DM, 11.5%, ♀ till 2000 **90**

1996 Riesling
Eiswein
55.20 DM, 9%, ♀ till 2008 **91**

Schales
seit 1783
1994
Gewürztraminer Spätlese
Rheinhessen
Qualitätswein mit Prädikat
Product of Germany
Alc.9,5 % vol.
A. P. Nr. 4 275 092 010 95
750 ml
Gutsabfüllung · Weingut Schales
D-67592 Flörsheim-Dalsheim

WEINGUT SCHERNER-KLEINHANSS

Owner: Klaus R. Scherner
67592 Flörsheim-Dalsheim,
Alzeyer Straße 10
Tel. (0 62 43) 4 35, Fax 56 65
Directions: A 61, exit Worms-Mörstadt
Sales: Monika Bank-Scherner
Opening hours: By appointment
Worth seeing: 16th-century timbered house

Vineyard area: 12.5 hectares
Annual production: 55,000 bottles
Top sites: Nieder-Flörsheimer Frauenberg and Steig, Monsheimer Rosengarten, Dalsheimer Bürgel and Sauloch
Soil types: Loam, sand, gravel, chalky loess
Grape varieties: 20% each of Riesling and Müller-Thurgau, 20% red wine varieties, 10% Weißburgunder, 7% Huxelrebe, 23% other varieties
Average yield: 82 hl/ha
Best vintages: 1995, 1996, 1997

This family has a long tradition as wine producers. In the 16th century the Petitjean family fled from Beaune in Burgundy to the Rhine and translated their French name as Kleinhanß. Joseph Jodokus Scherner founded his property in Dalsheim in 1726. In 1954 the two families were united by marriage. Today Klaus Scherner is the ninth generation of his family to run the winery. Before beginning work here, he garnered experience abroad. After graduating from Geisenheim, he worked for four years as a cellarmaster on the west coast of North America. His 1996 range was of astonishing quality, clearly the best that we had ever tasted from this estate. From the liter bottlings, through the dry white Prädikat wines, the rosé and the Frühburgunder, there wasn't a disappointing wine among the lot. Although softer in style, the 1997s are of similar quality.

1997 Nieder-Flörsheimer Frauenberg
Riesling Spätlese trocken
8.70 DM, 11.5%, 🍷 till 2000 **84**

1997 Nieder-Flörsheimer Steig
Riesling Spätlese
8 DM, 10%, 🍷 till 2000 **84**

1996 Nieder-Flörsheimer Frauenberg
Weißer Burgunder Kabinett trocken
7.40 DM, 11.5%, 🍷 now **86**

1996 Nieder-Flörsheimer Frauenberg
Riesling Spätlese trocken
8.50 DM, 11.5%, 🍷 till 2000 **86**

1996 Dalsheimer Sauloch
Huxelrebe Spätlese trocken
9.50 DM, 13.5%, 🍷 till 2000 **88**

1997 Monsheimer Rosengarten
Rieslaner Auslese
15.50 DM, 10.5%, 🍷 till 2004 **88**

— Red wines —

1997 Nieder-Flörsheimer Frauenberg
Frühburgunder Auslese trocken
17.50 DM, 13.5%, 🍷 now **84**

1996 Nieder-Flörsheimer Frauenberg
Frühburgunder Auslese trocken
14.50 DM, 13.5%, 🍷 till 2002 **88**

WEINGUT
Scherner-Kleinhanß
1995
Nieder-Flörsheimer Frauenberg
Weißer Burgunder
- TROCKEN -
QUALITÄTSWEIN
Gutsabfüllung - A. P. Nr. 4 274 136 16 96
D-67592 FLÖRSHEIM-DALSHEIM
11,5%vol RHEINHESSEN 0,75 l

WEINGUT FRANZ KARL SCHMITT

Owner: Franz Karl Schmitt
55283 Nierstein, Mainzer Straße 48
Tel. (0 61 33) 53 14, Fax 5 06 09
Directions: From Mainz on B 9 towards Worms
Opening hours: By appointment

Vineyard area: 11 hectares
Annual production: 60,000 bottles
Top sites: Niersteiner Oelberg, Orbel, Hipping and Pettental
Soil types: Red clay, slate, loess and loam
Grape varieties: 75% Riesling, 15% Müller-Thurgau, 10% Silvaner, Kerner and Schwarzriesling
Average yield: 52 hl/ha
Best vintages: 1995, 1996, 1997

Franz Karl Schmitt cultivates vineyards in some of the most outstanding sites of Nierstein. At the turn of the century his grandfather produced the first Trockenbeerenauslese in Rheinhessen; their finest wines from the 1930s and 1940s are still in superb condition. The current owner continues to build on this tradition. For Schmitt, it is the vineyards – where he seeks viticultural material of the highest quality – that give the wines their character. Riesling, planted on selected rootstocks that ensure low yields, is the principal focus of his attention. Until 1993 the estate regularly produced some of the finest wines in Nierstein. The 1994s, however, were disappointing. The 1995 and 1996 ranges were again quite successful, putting the estate back on track. The 1997s are of similar quality. Although Schmitt is a Riesling specialist, his Gewürztraminers can also be excellent.

1996 Niersteiner Oelberg
Riesling Spätlese trocken
11 DM, 12%, ♀ till 2001 **86**

1996 Niersteiner Kranzberg
Riesling Kabinett halbtrocken
7.60 DM, 11%, ♀ till 2003 **88**

1997 Niersteiner Oelberg
Riesling Spätlese
11 DM, 10%, ♀ till 2004 **88**

1997 Niersteiner Hipping
Riesling Spätlese
12 DM, 10%, ♀ till 2005 **88**

1996 Niersteiner Oelberg
Riesling Spätlese
11 DM, 9%, ♀ till 2005 **88**

1997 Niersteiner Kranzberg
Gewürztraminer Auslese
17 DM, 10%, ♀ till 2005 **88**

1997 Niersteiner Pettental
Riesling Auslese
18 DM, 8%, ♀ till 2007 **89**

1996 Niersteiner Kranzberg
Gewürztraminer Auslese
15 DM, 10.5%, ♀ till 2006 **89**

1996 Niersteiner Pettental
Riesling Auslese
18 DM, 7.5%, ♀ till 2008 **91**

WEINGUT GEORG ALBRECHT SCHNEIDER

Owner: Albrecht Schneider
55283 Nierstein, Wilhelmstraße 6
Tel. (0 61 33) 56 55, Fax 54 15
e-mail:
Schneider-Nierstein@t-online.de
Directions: Via B 9 towards Bad Kreuznach, third street on the right
Sales: Ulrike and Albrecht Schneider
Opening hours: By appointment

Vineyard area: 17 hectares
Annual production: 90,000 bottles
Top sites: Niersteiner Hipping, Oelberg, Orbel, Pettental
Soil types: Red clay, slate, loess and loam
Grape varieties: 45% Riesling, 25% Müller-Thurgau, 8% Kerner, 22% other varieties
Average yield: 60 hl/ha
Best vintages: 1993, 1996, 1997

After all the improvements over the past decade, the Schneider estate was unable to retain its high ranking within Rheinhessen's second tier of top wine producers in 1995. That vintage was of such modest quality that we hung a question mark over the estate. We suspected rightly that the weather conditions along the Rheinfront were largely responsible for the poor result in that vintage. We were not mistaken, for the 1996 range exhibited the same great appeal as did its better predecessors, restoring the fine reputation of this estate. The 1997s are even better. The Hipping Spätlese is a steal for less than 12 marks! The vineyards are spread out across the best sites in Nierstein and the flavor profile of the wines reflect the location of each parcel. For the past twenty years the Schneiders have employed natural green crop covers in their vineyards and reduced their use of fertilizers. They also enhance quality by using whole-cluster pressing, careful handling of the must and lengthy fermentations. This estate is a sleeper.

1997 Niersteiner Hipping
Riesling Spätlese trocken
11.50 DM, 12%, ♀ till 2002 **88**

1997 Niersteiner Oelberg
Riesling Spätlese halbtrocken
11.50 DM, 10.5%, ♀ till 2002 **88**

1996 Niersteiner Pettental
Riesling Spätlese halbtrocken
11.80 DM, 11.5%, ♀ till 2002 **88**

1997 Niersteiner Paterberg
Riesling Kabinett
8.50 DM, 9%, ♀ till 2002 **88**

1996 Niersteiner Bildstock
Riesling Kabinett
8.20 DM, 8%, ♀ till 2005 **88**

1996 Niersteiner Rosenberg
Riesling Spätlese
11 DM, 9%, ♀ till 2006 **88**

1996 Niersteiner Hipping
Riesling Spätlese
11.50 DM, 8.5%, ♀ till 2006 **89**

1996 Niersteiner Orbel
Riesling Spätlese
11.50 DM, 9.5%, ♀ till 2004 **89**

1997 Niersteiner Hipping
Riesling Spätlese
11.50 DM, 9%, ♀ till 2005 **91**

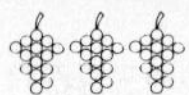

WEINGUT HEINRICH SEEBRICH

Owner: Heinrich Seebrich
Winemaker: Heinrich Seebrich
55283 Nierstein, Schmiedgasse 3
Tel. (0 61 33) 6 01 50, Fax 6 01 65
Directions: From Mainz on B 9 towards Worms
Opening hours: Mon.–Fri. 8 a.m. to 5 p.m., by appointment
History: Wine estate founded in 1783 by the family
Worth seeing: Old vaulted cask cellar

Vineyard area: 10 hectares
Annual production: 85,000 bottles
Top sites: Niersteiner Heiligenbaum, Oelberg and Hipping
Soil types: Red clay and slate
Grape varieties: 35% Riesling, 23% Müller-Thurgau, 13% red varieties, 9% Kerner, 6% Silvaner, 14% other varieties
Average yield: 70 hl/ha
Best vintages: 1993, 1996, 1997

Heinrich Seebrich is a specialist in fruity Rieslings, and such wines from the celebrated red slate vineyards in Nierstein often turn out particularly well, for they are endowed not only with a lush sweetness but also an assertive acidity. The 1993 and 1994 vintages were amazingly successful, establishing the estate's current reputation. The 1995 range, however, was – due to poor weather conditions – disappointing. The 1996s are closer in style to such fine vintages as 1990 and 1993. The 1997s are even better. If such quality can be maintained, this estate may one day be seen as one of the finer producers in Rheinhessen. After his apprenticeship, son Jochen has joined the parental estate. He is now attending the technical college in Oppenheim to complete his training.

1996 Niersteiner Oelberg
Riesling Spätlese trocken
10.20 DM, 11.5%, ♀ till 2001 **88**

1997 Niersteiner Rehbach
Riesling Spätlese halbtrocken
10.30 DM, 11%, ♀ till 2002 **88**

1996 Niersteiner Rehbach
Riesling Spätlese halbtrocken
10.50 DM, 11%, ♀ till 2002 **88**

1996 Niersteiner Oelberg
Riesling Kabinett
8.20 DM, 9%, ♀ till 2002 **88**

1997 Niersteiner Hipping
Riesling Spätlese
10.50 DM, 9.5%, ♀ till 2003 **89**

1997 Niersteiner Oelberg
Riesling Spätlese
10.50 DM, 9.5%, ♀ till 2004 **89**

1996 Niersteiner Hipping
Riesling Spätlese
10.80 DM, 9%, ♀ till 2004 **89**

1997 Niersteiner Hipping
Riesling Auslese
16.50 DM, 9%, ♀ till 2007 **89**

WEINGUT
HEINRICH SEEBRICH
NIERSTEIN/RHEIN
1993er
NIERSTEINER HIPPING
RIESLING
SPÄTLESE
ERZEUGERABFÜLLUNG
PRODUCE OF GERMANY
D-6505 NIERSTEIN
QUALITÄTSWEIN MIT PRÄDIKAT
A.P.Nr. 4 382 261 14 94
RHEINHESSEN
750 ml alc. 10.0% vol.

STAATLICHE WEINBAU-DOMÄNE OPPENHEIM

Owner: State of Rheinland-Pfalz
Domain Director: Dr. Peter Fuchß
Manager: Gunter Schenkel
Winemaker: Arndt Reichmann
55276 Oppenheim,
Wormser Straße 162
Tel. (0 61 33) 93 03 05, Fax 93 03 23
Directions: Via B 9 to Oppenheim
Sales: Ms. Christ
Opening hours: Mon.–Thur. 9 a.m. to noon and 1 p.m. to 4 p.m., Fri. to 6 p.m. Sat. by appointment
History: Founded in 1895 by the Grand Duke Ludwig of Hessen as an experimental estate
Worth seeing: Estate buildings, a historic monument in Art Nouveau style

Vineyard area: 23 hectares
Annual production: 125,000 bottles
Top sites: Niersteiner Oelberg and Glöck (sole owners), Nackenheimer Rothenberg
Soil types: Red clay, slate, limestone, heavy chalky loam and loess
Grape varieties: 52% Riesling, 12% Silvaner, 8% red wine varieties, 6% Müller-Thurgau, 4% Scheurebe, 18% other varieties
Average yield: 74 hl/ha
Best vintages: 1990, 1996, 1997
Member: VDP

In the early 1990s long overdue investments were finally made so that this estate could again concentrate on its role as a model property for Rheinhessen, in particular in its policy of ecologically sensitive viticulture in the vineyards. The wines are fermented slowly in stainless steel tanks and then aged in classic oak casks. The 1996s surpassed by far the quality of the previous vintages, especially among the noble sweet wines. The 1997s are again of solid character. This domain is now poised to restore its tarnished reputation.

1997 Oppenheimer Herrenberg
Riesling Kabinett halbtrocken
8 DM, 10.5%, ♀ till 2000 **84**

1997 Riesling
trocken "Selection"
16 DM, 12%, ♀ till 2000 **86**

1997 Silvaner
trocken "Selection"
15 DM, 12%, ♀ till 2000 **86**

1996 Niersteiner Oelberg
Riesling Spätlese halbtrocken
10 DM, 11.5%, ♀ till 2002 **86**

1997 Oppenheimer Herrenberg
Riesling Spätlese
10 DM, 9%, ♀ till 2002 **86**

1997 Oppenheimer Sackträger
Riesling Auslese
12 DM/0.5 liter, 8.5%, ♀ till 2003 **88**

1996 Niersteiner Oelberg
Riesling Auslese
10 DM/0.5 liter, 8.5%, ♀ till 2006 **88**

1996 Niersteiner Glöck
Scheurebe Beerenauslese
50 DM/0.5 liter, 8.5%, ♀ till 2006 **91**

1996 Bodenheimer Reichsritterstift
Riesling Eiswein
80 DM/0.5 liter, 8.5%, ♀ till 2010 **94**

WEINGUT STALLMANN-HIESTAND

Owner: Werner Hiestand
55278 Uelversheim, Eisgasse 15
Tel. (0 62 49) 84 63 and 8 02 33, Fax 86 14
Directions: Via A 61, exit Gau-Bickelheim or Gundersheim; via B 9, exit Guntersblum or Dienheim
Opening hours: Mon.–Sat. 8 a.m. to 6 p.m., by appointment
Worth seeing: Large vaulted cellar from the 18th century

Vineyard area: 16.5 hectares
Annual production: 120,000 bottles
Top sites: Dienheimer Tafelstein and Kreuz, Guntersblumer Kreuzkapelle
Soil types: Loess, loam and clay
Grape varieties: 25% Riesling, 17% Silvaner, 16% red wine varieties, 13% Weißburgunder, 8% Rivaner, 6% Kerner, 15% other varieties
Average yield: 70 hl/ha
Best vintages: 1990, 1993, 1997

This estate first began to bottle its wines in 1973. At the same time Werner Hiestand – who is the current president of the association of Rheinhessen wine growers – was one of the first in the region to vinify dry wines, which today account for 85 percent of his total production. A native of Guntersblum, he has gradually reduced the proportion of new grape varieties and now focuses on the classics, in particular Weißburgunder and Grauburgunder. Viticultural practices at his estate include planting natural green cover crops for good soil ventilation and bunch-thinning to control yields. The wines of the last few vintages, however, were far from convincing. Indeed, the 1996s could only be described as frail; many of them even have phenolic tones. The 1997s are marginally better, restoring to an extent the reputation of this estate.

1997 Dienheimer Tafelstein
Riesling Spätlese
11.50 DM, 10.5%, ♀ now **77**

1997 Dienheimer Tafelstein
Riesling Spätlese trocken
11 DM, 12%, ♀ now **80**

1997 Uelversheimer Aulenberg
Weißer Burgunder Spätlese trocken
11 DM, 13%, ♀ now **80**

1996 Dienheimer Tafelstein
Riesling Spätlese trocken
10 DM, 12%, ♀ now **80**

1997 Dienheimer Tafelstein
Riesling Spätlese halbtrocken
10 DM, 11.5%, ♀ now **80**

1997 Dienheimer Tafelstein
Grauer Burgunder Spätlese trocken
11.50 DM, 12%, ♀ till 2000 **82**

——— Red wines ———

1995 Dornfelder & Dunkelfelder
trocken
13 DM, 12.5%, ♀ till 2000 **80**

1996 Dornfelder & Dunkelfelder
trocken
13 DM, 12.5%, ♀ till 2000 **82**

WEINGUT J. & H. A. STRUB

Owner: Walter Strub
55283 Nierstein, Rheinstraße 42
Tel. (0 61 33) 56 49, Fax 55 01
Internet:
http://www.vinonet.com/strub.htm
Directions: From Mainz via B 9; from the west via A 61 and B 420, in old village center near the market
Sales: Margit and Walter Strub
Opening hours: Mon.–Fri. 8 a.m. to 5 p.m. and Sat. 9 a.m. to noon
By appointment
History: Estate run by 11th generation
Worth seeing: Vaulted cellar and timbered house from the 17th century

Vineyard area: 18.2 hectares
Annual production: 100,000 bottles
Top sites: Niersteiner Orbel, Oelberg, Hipping and Pettental
Soil types: Red clay, slate, loess, loam and chalk
Grape varieties: 68% Riesling, 15% each of Müller-Thurgau and Silvaner, 2% other varieties
Average yield: 70 hl/ha
Best vintages: 1994, 1995, 1996

The 1993s and 1994s brought this old estate back into focus; and the 1995 range demonstrated that it was possible to make decent wines from Nierstein's vineyards even in a very difficult vintage. The 1996s and, to an extent, the 1997s were again of impeccable quality. Some are perhaps too sweet, but Walter Strub's residual sugars are all natural. He prefers lengthy fermentations, which sometimes never finish. This often occurs with the Rieslings, which since 1993 have been pressed as whole clusters. This varietal clearly takes center stage here, accounting for a good two-thirds of the total production. Müller-Thurgau and Silvaner are mostly sold in cask. The relation between price and quality of the bottled wines at this estate remains very appealing – often a poor man's paradise!

1997 Niersteiner Orbel
Riesling Kabinett
8.80 DM, 9.5%, ♀ till 2000 **84**

1996 Niersteiner Paterberg
Riesling Kabinett
8.80 DM, 8.5%, ♀ till 2000 **86**

1996 Niersteiner Pettental
Riesling Kabinett
9.50 DM, 8.5%, ♀ till 2000 **86**

1996 Niersteiner Oelberg
Riesling Spätlese – 10 –
16 DM, 8%, ♀ till 2003 **86**

1996 Niersteiner Rosenberg
Riesling Kabinett
9.50 DM, 9%, ♀ till 2001 **88**

1996 Niersteiner Hipping
Riesling Spätlese – 6 –
17 DM, 7.5%, ♀ till 2003 **89**

1996 Niersteiner Orbel
Riesling Spätlese
15 DM, 7.5%, ♀ till 2003 **89**

1996 Niersteiner Oelberg
Riesling Spätlese – 9 –
17 DM, 7.5%, ♀ till 2004 **93**

WEINGUT VILLA SACHSEN

Owners: Michael Prinz zu Salm-Salm and partners
General Manager: Rolf Schregel
Winemaker: Klaus Mindnich
55411 Bingen, Mainzer Straße 184
Tel. (0 67 21) 99 05 75, Fax 1 73 86
Directions: A 61, exit Bingen, in the direction of car ferry, white villa on the left between Bingen-Kempten and Bingen
Sales: Rolf Schregel
Opening hours: By appointment
History: Country mansion built in 1843, bought in 1899 by a manufacturer from Leipzig, who started with viniculture
Worth seeing: Estate buildings with park, cross-shaped vaulted cellar

Vineyard area: 22 hectares
Annual production: 130,000 bottles
Top sites: Binger Scharlachberg and Kirchberg
Soil types: Weathered slate, sandy loam
Grape varieties: 54% Riesling, 8% each of Müller-Thurgau and Kerner, 6% Silvaner, 4% each of Grauburgunder and Weißburgunder, 16% other varieties
Average yield: 52 hl/ha
Best vintages: 1995, 1996, 1997
Member: VDP

Until the 1960s this was not only the leading estate at the confluence of the Rhine and the Nahe rivers, it also belonged to the top producers of the whole region. Despite considerable investments in the 1970s and 1980s, the estate never returned to its former glory. The nadir came in the early 1990s when the property went into receivership. While the charming villa is now in Japanese hands, Prince Salm – the chairman of the VDP – and three partners acquired the vineyards. The business is now run from the Salm estate in Wallhausen on the Nahe. After teething problems, the 1996 vintage was the first to show the tremendous potential of the vineyards in Bingen. The 1997s are the finest wines that we have tasted from this estate in years!

1997 Binger Scharlachberg
Riesling Spätlese trocken
15 DM, 12%, ♀ till 2002 **88**

1996 Binger Scharlachberg
Riesling Spätlese trocken
16 DM, 12.5%, ♀ till 2002 **88**

1997 Binger Scharlachberg
Riesling Spätlese halbtrocken
15 DM, 11.5%, ♀ till 2002 **88**

1997 Binger Scharlachberg
Riesling Spätlese
15 DM, 9.5%, ♀ till 2002 **88**

1996 Binger Scharlachberg
Riesling Spätlese
18 DM, 9%, ♀ till 2004 **88**

1996 Binger Scharlachberg
Riesling Beerenauslese
45 DM/0.375 liter, 11%, ♀ till 2008 **88**

1997 Binger Scharlachberg
Riesling trocken "Erstes Gewächs"
28 DM, 12.5%, ♀ till 2005 **89**

1996 Binger Scharlachberg
Riesling Auslese
25 DM, 9%, ♀ till 2006 **89**

1997 Binger Scharlachberg
Riesling Beerenauslese
45 DM/0.375 liter, 8%, ♀ till 2003 **91**

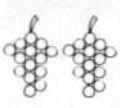

WEINGUT WITTMANN

Owner: Günter Wittmann
Winemakers: Günter and Philipp Wittmann
67593 Westhofen, Mainzer Straße 19
Tel. (0 62 44) 90 50 36, Fax 55 78
Directions: A 61, exit Gundersheim/Westhofen
Sales: Elisabeth Wittmann
Opening hours: By appointment
History: Documents from 1663 mention the ancestors as hereditary owners of the royal harbor in Westhofen
Worth seeing: Large vaulted cellar, Mediterranean garden

Vineyard area: 17 hectares
Annual production: 130,000 bottles
Top sites: Westhofener Morstein, Steingrube and Aulerde
Soil types: Clay with chalky loam, weathered limestone and loess
Grape varieties: 35% Riesling, 16% Müller-Thurgau, 10% each of Silvaner and Weißburgunder, 8% Huxelrebe, 6% Früh- and Spätburgunder, 6% Chardonnay, 9% other varieties
Average yield: 78 hl/ha
Best vintages: 1994, 1995, 1996
Member: Naturland

Günter Wittmann is one of those marketing geniuses in the Rheinhessen region who can make an event out of the simplest matter. It is thus not surprising that the Riesling here is called White Riesling; and the unsophisticated Silvaner is, sure enough, Green Silvaner. The East European laborers who help with the harvest – which is still largely done by hand – have been promoted to the "international harvesting department." Nor has Wittmann neglected to bring forth a range of artist series' labels. It once appeared that winemaking was just a hobby here, but in recent years the quality has steadily improved. The 1996s were the third in a string of fine vintages, narrowing the gap in quality between this estate and the head of the pack. The 1997s, in spite of the sumptuous Trockenbeerenauslese, are not quite as appealing.

1997 Westhofener Steingrube
Riesling trocken
8.90 DM, 11.5%, ♀ till 2000 **84**

1996 Weißer Burgunder
trocken
9.80 DM, 12%, ♀ now **84**

1997 Westhofener Morstein
Riesling Spätlese trocken
14.50 DM, 11.5%, ♀ till 2000 **84**

1997 Westhofener Morstein
Riesling Spätlese
14.50 DM, 8.5%, ♀ till 2002 **84**

1996 Westhofener Aulerde
Chardonnay trocken
14.50 DM, 12%, ♀ till 2000 **86**

1996 Westhofener Morstein
Riesling Spätlese trocken
14.50 DM, 11.5%, ♀ till 2001 **88**

1997 Westhofener Morstein
Riesling Spätlese
12.90 DM, 9.5%, ♀ till 2003 **88**

1996 Westhofener Morstein
Riesling Spätlese
12.90 DM, 9.5%, ♀ till 2002 **88**

1997 Westhofener Aulerde
Riesling Trockenbeerenauslese
125 DM/0.375 liter, 10.5%, ♀ till 2010 **92**

1997 Westhofener Aulerde
Chardonnay Trockenbeerenauslese
125 DM/0.375 liter, 10%, ♀ till 2007 **92**

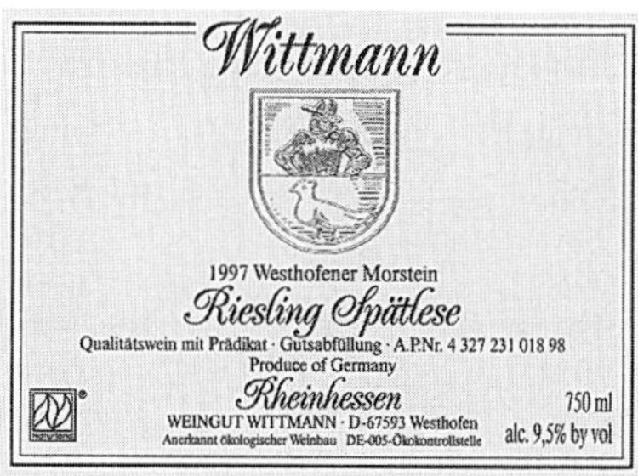

Saale-Unstrut

Southerly slopes and river valleys

The region of Saale and Unstrut in the greater province of Saxony is the most northerly wine-producing zone in all of Europe. The harsh continental climate and the frequent spring frosts restrict the cultivation of vines to just a few selected sites. Viticulture is possible only where early-ripening varieties profit from the microclimatic advantages offered by the southerly slopes along the river valleys of Saale and Unstrut.

The overwhelming majority of vines are planted on fossil limestone soils in the valleys near the Burgendreieck, or "castle corner." There, not far from the towns of Freyburg, Naumburg and Bad Kösen, is the confluence of the two little rivers, Saale and Unstrut. Barely 50 kilometers to the north lies another small wine region along the Süßer See, or "sweet lake," near Eisleben.

Along the middle stretches of the Saale and the upper reaches of the Unstrut viticulture was already solidly established in medieval times. The first documentary evidence records a license to plant vines granted by Emperor Otto II to the monastery in Memleben in 998. However, the monks of the Cistercian Pforta monastery, which was founded in 1137, were the true apostles of winemaking in the region. The vineyards reached their zenith shortly before the Thirty Years' War, when vast expanses of vines were to be found in and around both monasteries and towns.

After shrinking to a mere 75 hectares, the vineyard area expanded to more than 500 hectares after World War II. The preferred varieties of the region are Müller-Thurgau, Silvaner and Weißburgunder. More noble varieties such as Riesling or Traminer represent merely three percent of the surface planted.

The leading producer in the area is Lützkendorf, who is capable of making wines as good as most estates in the west of Germany. However, neither the 1995 nor the 1996 vintage permitted father Udo and son Uwe to show their true talent. None of the other estates, though, produced anything nearly as good as this pair. 1997 was a touch better, but severe winter frosts reduced yields to a mere 15 hectoliters per hectare, an economic catastrophe for many an aspiring young vintner in the region.

With 260 hectares of vineyards, the cooperative of Freyburg-Unstrut produces about two-thirds of all the wine from this region. The only other major player is the state property of Kloster Pforta, which cultivates a high proportion of the finest vineyard sites on the Saale and Unstrut. The remaining properties, some 30 in all, are tiny and often run as a hobby. Despite the relatively high prices that they fetch for often questionable quality, almost all of the producers still enjoy strong demand for their wines. However, the first signs of dissatisfaction are beginning to surface.

Vintage chart for Saale-Unstrut

vintage	quality	drink
1997	🍇🍇	till 2000
1996	🍇	now
1995	🍇🍇	now
1994	🍇🍇🍇	till 2000
1993	🍇🍇	now
1992	🍇🍇🍇	now
1991	🍇🍇	now
1990	🍇🍇	now

🍇🍇🍇🍇🍇 : Outstanding
🍇🍇🍇🍇 : Excellent
🍇🍇🍇 : Good
🍇🍇 : Average
🍇 : Poor

The leading estates of Saale-Unstrut

Weingut Günter Born, Höhnstedt

Weingut Lützkendorf, Bad Kösen

Other notable producers

Weingut Klaus Böhme

06636 Kirchscheidungen
Tel. (03 44 62) 2 03 95, Fax 2 03 95

Weingut Deckert

06632 Freyburg,
Ehrauberg 9
Tel. (03 44 64) 2 74 78

Weingut André Gussek

06618 Naumburg,
Kösener Straße 66
Tel. (0 34 45) 77 84 28

Landesweingut Kloster Pforta

06628 Bad Kösen,
Saalhäuser
Tel. (03 44 63) 30 00, Fax 3 00 25

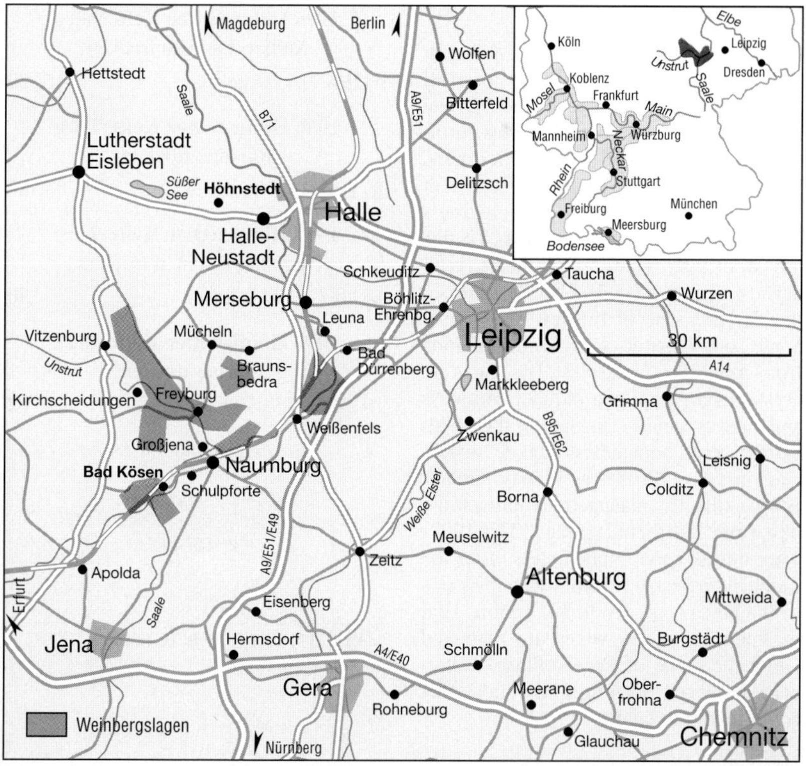

WEINGUT GÜNTER BORN

Owner: Günter Born
Winemaker: Günter Born and Lars Wellhöfer
06179 Höhnstedt, Wanslebener Straße 3
Tel. (03 46 01) 2 29 30, Fax 2 00 39
Directions: Near the "Süße See," from Halle via the B 80 in the direction of Eisleben
Sales: The Born family
Opening hours: Mon.–Sun. 10 a.m. to 8 p.m.

Vineyard area: 6.3 hectares
Annual production: 30,000 bottles
Top sites: Höhnstedter Kreisberg
Soil types: Red sandstone
Grape varieties: 30% Müller-Thurgau, 20% Weißburgunder, 15% each of Riesling and Kerner, 10% Silvaner, 5% Portugieser, 5% other varieties
Average yield: 40 hl/ha
Best vintages: 1994, 1995

Günter Born's life is not easy. With just 50 hectares of vineyards in a small district in the hills above the "Sweet Lake," the Süße See forms the most northerly viticultural zone in all of Germany. On the slopes of the village of Höhnstedt he and his father founded the region's first private wine estate in 1990. To this day all of their wines are vinified to total dryness. The quality of the 1996s proved that Born is one of the few vintners in Saale and Unstrut who need not hide from colleagues in the west. His wines are crystal clear, display a piquant fruitiness and a robust acidity. In spite of their high extract, they nonetheless lacked weight and ripeness. Be that as it may, Günter Born skillfully managed to extract the best from a difficult vintage. The 1997s were not as good. Nonetheless, after the Lützkendorf estate, Born's winery is one of the best properties in the region. That the majority of his wines are marketed under the name of the Großlage Kelterberg, however, does little to validate his commitment to quality.

1997 Höhnstedter Kelterberg
Müller-Thurgau Kabinett trocken
10 DM, 11.5%, ♀ now **77**

1997 Höhnstedter Kelterberg
Weißer Burgunder Kabinett trocken
13 DM, 11.5%, ♀ now **77**

1997 Höhnstedter Kelterberg
Kerner Spätlese trocken
15 DM, 13%, ♀ now **77**

1997 Höhnstedter Kreisberg
Silvaner Spätlese trocken
16 DM, 12.5%, ♀ now **77**

1996 Höhnstedter Kelterberg
Kerner trocken
12 DM, 11%, ♀ now **80**

1996 Höhnstedter Kelterberg
Weißer Burgunder trocken
11.50 DM, 11%, ♀ now **80**

1996 Höhnstedter Kelterberg
Müller-Thurgau trocken
9 DM, 11%, ♀ now **80**

1996 Höhnstedter Kelterberg
Riesling trocken
15 DM, 11.5%, ♀ now **80**

1997 Höhnstedter Kelterberg
Riesling Kabinett trocken
16 DM, 11%, ♀ now **80**

1996 Höhnstedter Kelterberg
Silvaner trocken
10 DM, 12%, ♀ now **82**

0,75 l
SAALE-UNSTRUT
11,5 % vol.
1995er
GUTEDEL
HÖHNSTEDTER KELTERBERG
QUALITÄTSWEIN b.A. TROCKEN
ERZEUGERABFÜLLUNG
WEINGUT GÜNTER BORN
WANSLEBENER STRASSE 3 · D-06179 HÖHNSTEDT
TELEFON (034601) 22930

WEINGUT LÜTZKENDORF

Owner: Uwe Lützkendorf
06628 Bad Kösen, Saalberge 31
Tel. (03 44 63) 6 10 00, Fax 6 10 01
e-mail:
weingut.luetzkendorf@t-online.de
Directions: A9 from Leipzig, exit Naumburg, via B 180 and B 87
Sales: Udo Lützkendorf
Opening hours: Mon.–Sun. 10 a.m. to 8 p.m.
Restaurant: Open daily from 10 a.m. to 8 p.m.
Specialties: Homemade Thüringer sausage

Vineyard area: 9 hectares
Annual production: 37,000 bottles
Top sites: Karsdorfer Hohe Gräte, Pfortener Köppelberg
Soil types: Clay with stone and slate, weathered fossil limestone, clay and chalk
Grape varieties: 48% Silvaner, 24% Riesling, 8% each of Traminer and Spätburgunder, 7% Weißburgunder, 5% other varieties
Average yield: 31 hl/ha
Best vintages: 1993, 1994, 1997
Member: VDP

For over two decades Udo Lützkendorf was in charge of the state-owned Naumburg winery in East Germany. After reunification he and his son Uwe have resurrected their family business. They erected a new cellar and tasting room, have enlarged their vineyard holdings to almost ten hectares and are now considered to be one of the finest producers in the former GDR. However, neither the 1995 nor 1996 range was thoroughly convincing: the wines rarely displayed fine aromas, and all were marked by a tart acidity. Given the severe frost that the region experienced, Lützkendorf was nonetheless reasonably happy with the outcome. Although perhaps not as good as the fine 1994s, the 1997s were much better than either the 1995s or the 1996s. Sadly, yields were not even half of a normal crop.

1997 Pfortener Köppelberg
Riesling trocken
17 DM, 11.5%, ♀ till 2000 **80**

1996 Karsdorfer Hohe Gräte
Silvaner trocken
13.50 DM, 12%, ♀ now **80**

1996 Karsdorfer Hohe Gräte
Riesling trocken
16.50 DM, 11.5%, ♀ now **82**

1996 Freyburger Schweigenberg
Traminer trocken
16.50 DM/0.5 liter, 11%, ♀ now **82**

1997 Karsdorfer Hohe Gräte
Silvaner Spätlese trocken
15 DM/0.5 liter, 12%, ♀ till 2000 **82**

1997 Karsdorfer Hohe Gräte
Weißer Burgunder Spätlese trocken
19 DM/0.5 liter, 12%, ♀ now **82**

1997 Karsdorfer Hohe Gräte
Riesling Spätlese trocken
18.50 DM/0.5 liter, 12%, ♀ till 2001 **84**

1997 Karsdorfer Hohe Gräte
Silvaner Beerenauslese
89 DM/0.375 liter, 11%, ♀ till 2003 **86**

1996 Pfortener Köppelberg
Silvaner Beerenauslese
88 DM/0.375 liter, 8.5%, ♀ till 2003 **86**

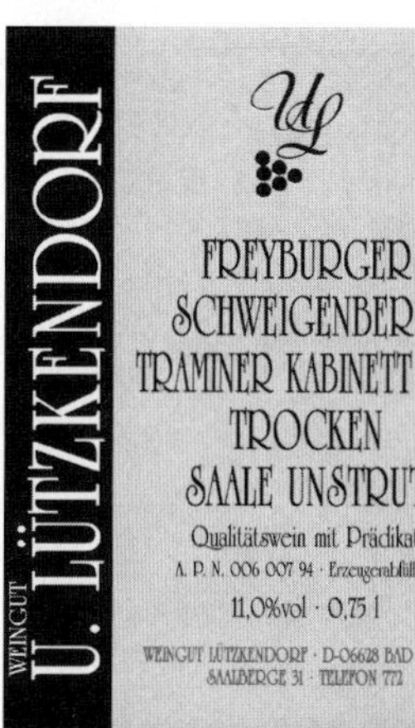

The discreet charm of the Elbe

The steep vineyards along the banks of the Elbe – from Pirna, south of Dresden, to Seußlitz, north of Meißen – form the most eastern wine-growing region of Germany. As do Saale and Unstrut, Saxony also endures a harsh climate, with hot summers and cold winters. In the spring, late frosts often lead to a drastic reduction of yields. In 1996 the average production of the whole region was a mere 34 hectoliters per hectare; in 1997 it was only 20! That is why the cultivation of the vine is restricted to the very few southerly slopes that enjoy a benevolent microclimate. Near Meißen the soils are of weathered granite, while between Radebeul and Dresden they are composed of weathered gneiss. In other localities, limestone, clay, loess, sand and porphyry are also encountered.

Documents trace winemaking in Saxony, or "Sachsen" as it is called in German, back to the Middle Ages. In Napoleonic times, when the vineyards along the Elbe covered over 1,500 hectares, the first viticultural college in Europe was established in Meißen. War and plaque damage caused the vineyard area to shrink to a mere 70 hectares. Today it has expanded again to 300 hectares and is likely to grow further.

The most important grape variety in Saxony is Müller-Thurgau, which occupies almost 40 percent of the vineyard area. Nonetheless, the more noble varieties have a significant presence. Weißburgunder and Traminer now account for 15 percent of the area under vine; Riesling with seven percent and Grauburgunder with six are also more commonly encountered here than in the Saale and Unstrut region. However, that does not mean that the quality of the wines is superior. A few estates have been investing money in their operations,

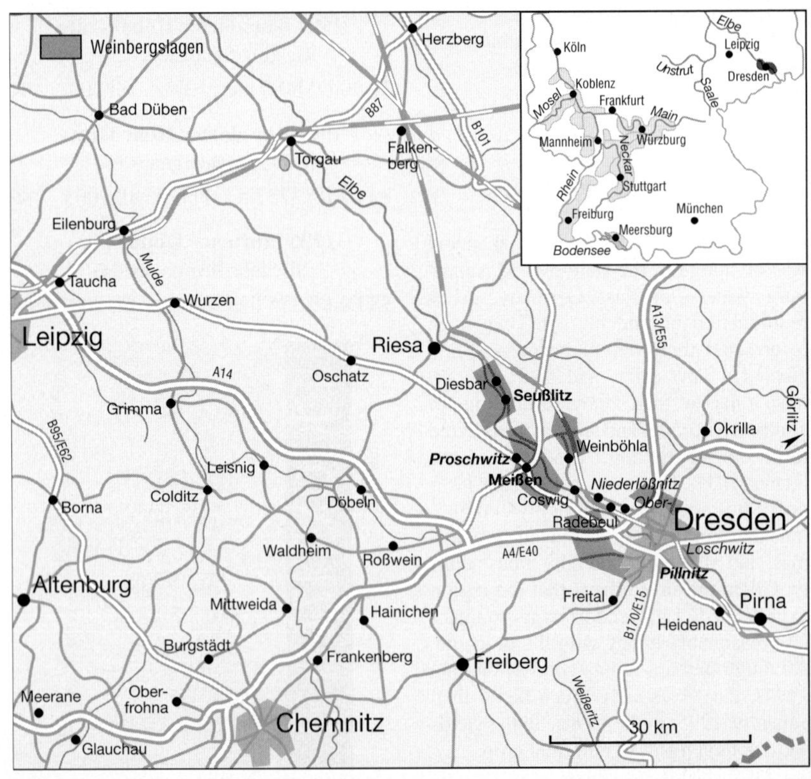

but it will take years before there is any dramatic improvement in overall quality. Most wines have yet to attain international standards.

The cooperative, with its some 2,500 adherents cultivating 120 hectares, handles over one-third of the total production. However, their wines are scarcely worth mentioning. The state winery at Schloß Wackerbarth owns almost all of the remaining vineyards. Though it had made little headway in terms of quality until the 1997 vintage, its production now offers a ray of hope for the future. There is, though, little room left for independent producers to exploit. Joachim Lehmann in Seußlitz, who produces appealing wines from one and a half hectares, is a typical example of the region's some 25 wineries. Klaus Zimmerling in Dresden, the most aspiring vintner in the region, cultivates two hectares and has planted two more. Vincenz Richter, whose restaurant in the former guildhall of the weavers in Meißen enjoys a high reputation, owns three hectares. Klaus Seifert in Radebeul, on the other hand, doesn't even own a telephone. Dr. Georg Prince of Lippe from Schloß Proschwitz near Meißen was the first independent grower to make much headway here. His estate, the leading producer in Saxony, has now expanded to some 50 hectares of vineyards and was the first in former East Germany to be admitted to the VDP. Yet even he seldom produces wines of great interest.

As severe winter frosts restricted yields both in 1996 and 1997, Saxony brought in the smallest crop in all of Germany. And the quality could hardly be regarded as exemplary. A late harvest was absolutely necessary, and at that, most estates produced only wines of modest quality. A lack of physiological ripeness is the hallmark of both vintages. At their best, the wines are no more than light and refreshing.

Anyone who wishes to become better acquainted with the wines of the region should visit the "Weingalerie" on the square in front of the cathedral near the Albrecht Castle in Meißen.

The leading estates of Sachsen

Weingut Schloß Proschwitz, Proschwitz via Meißen

Weingut Klaus Zimmerling, Dresden-Pillnitz

Other notable producers

Weinstube Joachim Lehmann
☞ *See below, page 444*

Weingut Vincenz Richter
01662 Meißen, Dresdener Straße 147a
Tel. (01 77) 2 15 50 36,
Fax (0 35 21) 45 37 63

Sächsisches Staatsweingut Schloß Wackerbarth
01445 Radebeul, Postfach 02 01 61
Tel. (03 51) 72 27 28, Fax 7 46 51

Weingut Klaus Seifert
01445 Radebeul, Weinbergstraße 26

Vintage chart for Sachsen

vintage	quality	drink
1997	🍇🍇	till 2000
1996	🍇	now
1995	🍇🍇	now
1994	🍇🍇🍇	till 2000
1993	🍇🍇	now
1992	🍇🍇🍇	now
1991	🍇🍇	now
1990	🍇🍇	now

🍇🍇🍇🍇🍇 : Outstanding
🍇🍇🍇🍇 : Excellent
🍇🍇🍇 : Good
🍇🍇 : Average
🍇 : Poor

WEINSTUBE JOACHIM LEHMANN

Owner: Joachim Lehmann
01612 Seußlitz, An der Weinstraße 26
Tel. (03 52 67) 5 02 36
Directions: A4 Dresden–Leipzig, via Meißen
Sales: Joachim and Waltraut Lehmann
Opening hours: Mon.–Sun. 9 a.m. to 10 p.m., except Thur.
Wine bar: "Seußlitzer Weinstuben," open Mon.–Fri. from 5 p.m. to 11 p.m., except Thur., Sat. and Sun from noon to 11 p.m.
Specialties: Saxon dishes

Vineyard area: 2 hectares
Annual production: 10,000 bottles
Top site: Seußlitzer Heinrichsburg
Soil types: Loess and weathered granite
Grape varieties: 30% Müller-Thurgau, 15% each of Weißburgunder and Grauburgunder, 10% each of Riesling, Gewürztraminer and Spätburgunder, 8% Portugieser, 2% other varieties
Average yield: 50 hl/ha
Best vintages: 1993, 1994, 1996

Even during the Communist reign Joachim Lehmann was an independent grower who supplied the cooperative with his harvest. Since almost the entire production of this small estate is now sold at its own bar, it is best to sample these refreshing wines in the summer while seated on the terrace beneath the shady chestnut trees. If you drink one glass too many, help is at hand: there are also five guest rooms at your disposal. Lehmann does everything with considerable craftsmanship, both in the vineyards and in the cellars. Be that as it may, the 1995s were not as good as the ostensibly more difficult 1996s. Nor were the 1997s any great shakes. The white wines have perhaps become more limpid and fresh; in particular the Grauburgunder turned out well. But Lehmann's reds would be better if elaborated as rosés.

1996 Seußlitzer Heinrichsburg
Müller-Thurgau trocken
12.50 DM, 10.5%, 🍷 now **77**

1996 Seußlitzer Heinrichsburg
Weißer Burgunder Kabinett trocken
16.50 DM, 9%, 🍷 now **77**

1996 Seußlitzer Heinrichsburg
Traminer trocken
16.50 DM, 10.5%, 🍷 now **80**

1996 Seußlitzer Heinrichsburg
Grauer Burgunder trocken
16 DM, 10.5%, 🍷 now **82**

——— Red wine ———

1996 Seußlitzer Heinrichsburg
Blauer Zweigelt trocken
16.50 DM, 12%, 🍷 now **75**

Sachsen
1996er
Seußlitzer
Heinrichsburg
Traminer
trocken
Qualitätswein b. A.
Erzeugerabfüllung
Weinstube Joachim Lehmann
D - 01612 D.-Seußlitz/Elbe
L/A.P.Nr. 0307.97
10,5% Vol. 0,75l

WEINGUT SCHLOSS PROSCHWITZ

Owner: Dr. Georg Prinz zur Lippe
Winemaker: Martin Scharz
01665 Proschwitz via Meißen, Reichenbach 2
Tel. (0 35 21) 45 20 96, Fax 45 20 96
Directions: A4 Dresden–Chemnitz, exit Wilsdruff, via Meißen
Sales Manager: Peter Bohn
Opening hours: By appointment
Wine bar: "Weingalerie" on Domplatz in Meißen's Albrechtsburg, open April to November, Wed.–Sat. from 10 a.m. to 6 p.m.
History: The oldest wine estate in Saxony

Vineyard area: 51 hectares
Annual production: 200,000 bottles
Top sites: Schloß Proschwitz, Seußlitzer Heinrichsburg
Soil types: Granite cliffs with significant layers of loam and loess
Grape varieties: 20% Grauburgunder, 15% Müller-Thurgau, 10% each of Riesling, Weiß- and Spätburgunder, 9% each of Traminer and Elbling, 7% Goldriesling, 6% Dornfelder, 4% other varieties
Average yield: 20 hl/ha
Best vintages: 1995, 1996, 1997
Member: VDP

Long producers of fine wines, the Princes of Lippe once belonged to the most respected aristocratic families in eastern Germany. Their heirs, however, lost everything during the communist era. After reunification, Dr. Georg Prinz zur Lippe succeeded in reacquiring the old family estate located opposite the Burgberg in Meißen. Since then a new winery has been constructed close to the vineyards. In 1995 it was clear that the delicate wines from Schloß Proschwitz were the best in Saxony. The 1996s, too, were pure in expression, fresh and lively. The 1997s are perhaps even a touch better. Unfortunately, frost in both vintages meant that the harvest was very, very small. In spite of its large vineyard holdings, the estate must now buy grapes to meet demand.

1996 Schloß Proschwitz
Weißer Burgunder trocken
16 DM, 12%, ♀ now **80**

1996 Müller-Thurgau
trocken "Edition Meißen"
12 DM, 11%, ♀ now **80**

1997 Schloß Proschwitz
Scheurebe Kabinett trocken
17 DM, 11.5%, ♀ now **80**

1997 Seußlitzer Heinrichsburg
Traminer Spätlese trocken
23.50 DM, 12.5%, ♀ now **80**

1996 Schloß Proschwitz
Grauer Burgunder trocken
16.50 DM, 12%, ♀ now **82**

1996 Schloß Proschwitz
Müller-Thurgau trocken
13.50 DM, 11.5%, ♀ now **82**

1997 Weißer Burgunder
Spätlese trocken "Edition Meißen"
18.50 DM, 12.5%, ♀ now **82**

1997 Schloß Proschwitz
Grauer Burgunder Spätlese trocken
21.50 DM, 13%, ♀ till 2000 **84**

WEINGUT KLAUS ZIMMERLING

Owner: Klaus Zimmerling
01326 Dresden-Pillnitz, Bergweg 27
Tel. (03 51) 2 61 87 52
Directions: Via Dresden to Pillnitz
Opening hours: By appointment

Vineyard area: 4 hectares
Annual production: 5,000 bottles
Top sites: Pillnitzer Königlicher Weinberg
Soil types: Sand and loam over weathered rock
Grape varieties: 22% Riesling, 18% each of Traminer, Grauburgunder and Kerner, 12% each of Bacchus and Müller-Thurgau
Average yield: 20 hl/ha
Best vintages: 1993, 1995, 1997

Having studied mechanical engineering, Klaus Zimmerling came to wine through the back door. After a year as an apprentice at the Wachau estate of Nikolaihof in 1990, he decided to set up his own winery in Dresden. His first vintage was 1992. Since then, the quality of his wines has steadily improved. The 1996 range was truly appealing: characterful wines with limpid fruit, mineral acidity and solid structure. His estate is now four hectares in size, but only one and a half are currently in production. All of his wines are sold as table wines, as he does not want to have anything to do with the wine authorities: "It takes too much time, money and bottles, and I lack all three." The 1997 vintage was a small one. Frost of minus 22 degrees Celsius damaged the vines and curtailed the yield to little more than a thousand bottles. The packaging of the wines is extremely original. Each year the picture of a sculpture by the Polish artist Malgorzata Chodakowska adorns the bottle. She also just happens to be his wife.

1995 Kerner
Landwein trocken
18 DM/0.5 liter, 12%, 🍷 now **80**

1996 Müller-Thurgau
Landwein trocken
15 DM/0.5 liter, 10%, 🍷 now **80**

1996 Bacchus
Landwein trocken
16 DM/0.5 liter, 11%, 🍷 now **80**

1997 Kerner
Landwein trocken
24 DM/0.375 liter, 13.5%, 🍷 now **82**

1995 Grauer Burgunder
Landwein trocken
18 DM/0.375 liter, 11.5%, 🍷 now **82**

1997 Riesling
Landwein trocken
24 DM/0.5 liter, 10.5%, 🍷 till 2000 **84**

1995 Traminer
Landwein trocken
30 DM/0.375 liter, 12.5%, 🍷 now **84**

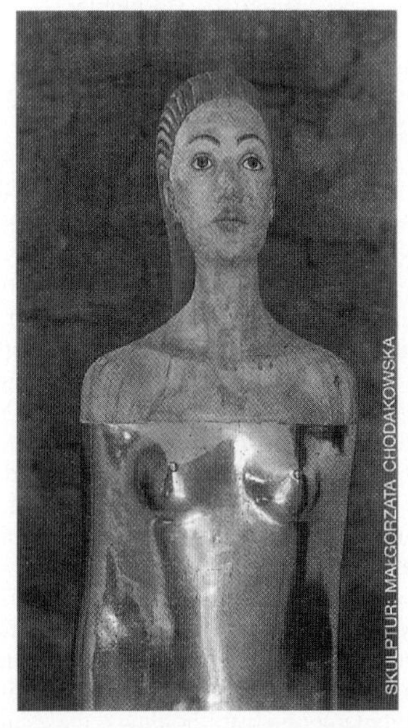
SKULPTUR: MAŁGORZATA CHODAKOWSKA

Württemberg

Red wines and black forests

Württemberg produces 40 percent of Germany's red wine. The two most widely planted varieties are Trollinger and Schwarzriesling. Higher-quality grapes such as Lemberger and Spätburgunder account, respectively, for only eight and three percent of the total planting, but they produce almost all of the interesting wines. Riesling is, with 24 percent of the surface area, the most widely planted white variety, but few vintners understand the intricacies of this grape; Müller-Thurgau, Kerner and Silvaner follow in its shadow.

Württemberg is divided into six regions, with a total of 210 single vineyards. These are scattered between Lake Constance and the Tauber, with their main centers near Stuttgart and Heilbronn. Around Heilbronn on the middle stretch of the Neckar valley lie three-quarters of the vineyards and most of the best sites. They are sheltered by the Black Forest and the Swabian mountains, and their soil composition – stony clay, loess, loam, and gypsum as well as scattered fossil limestone along the Neckar and its tributaries – is ideal for viticulture. At least two-thirds of the vines are planted on steep slopes, partly in terraced sites that are extremely hard to cultivate.

Although none of them are truly in top form at present, the three best-known estates of the region belong to Count von Neipperg, Count Adelmann and Prince zu Hohenlohe-Öhringen. The Neipperg estate has been the most consistent over the past several years, but Adelmann's performance with the 1997 vintage appears to indicate that he is now back on track. These large noble properties, with a wealth of fine vineyards, are being given a run for their money by the surprising Dautel estate and, increasingly, by the ambitious Hans-Peter Wöhrwag in Untertürkheim. While Dautel's best card is his Weißburgunder, Wöhrwag trumps with his Rieslings. In addition, Albrecht Schwegler in Korb, who makes wine only as a hobby, produces the finest reds of the region. Only a dozen more of the over 500 other wineries merit serious attention.

Given the strong demand in Württemberg – the locals knock back almost 40 liters of wine per person each year, twice the national average – prices have remained stable. However, producers who once had to allocate their wines must now "export" them to other parts of Germany; prices are coming under pressure. The cooperatives, which account for 85 percent of the total production, are understandably having a more difficult time. Justifiably so, for with the exception of Grantschen and, to some extent, Flein, quality is seldom their calling card.

In order to secure a higher profile for the region in general, some estates are discussing the issue of vineyard classification. The noble estates of Neipperg, Hohenlohe and Adelmann have founded a group known as "Württemberg Klassisch." Using only classic grape varieties planted in the best vineyard sites, the group is trying to push the quality level to new heights in order to regain the lost reputation of the region.

That has been a tall order of late, even in the finest of vineyard sites. Since 1990, Mother Nature has allotted Württemberg only one reasonable vintage. 1996, like 1993, turned out to be a fine year for the reds, but it was certainly not a great vintage for white wines. 1997 may be the year of the decade, but for most of the vintners it has been a long, long wait.

To date the most attractive aspect of Württemberg is its Wine Route. Whoever experiences the Swabian friendliness and excellent regional cooking accompanied by a quarter liter of wine will want to return for more. We also recommend a stroll through some of the lovely little villages of the region, which despite the business acumen of the Swabians, have lost nothing of their old-fashioned charm.

The leading estates of Württemberg

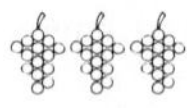

Weingut Graf Adelmann, Kleinbottwar

Weingut Ernst Dautel, Bönnigheim

Schloßgut Graf von Neipperg, Schwaigern

Weingut Albrecht Schwegler, Korb

Weingut Wöhrwag, Untertürkheim

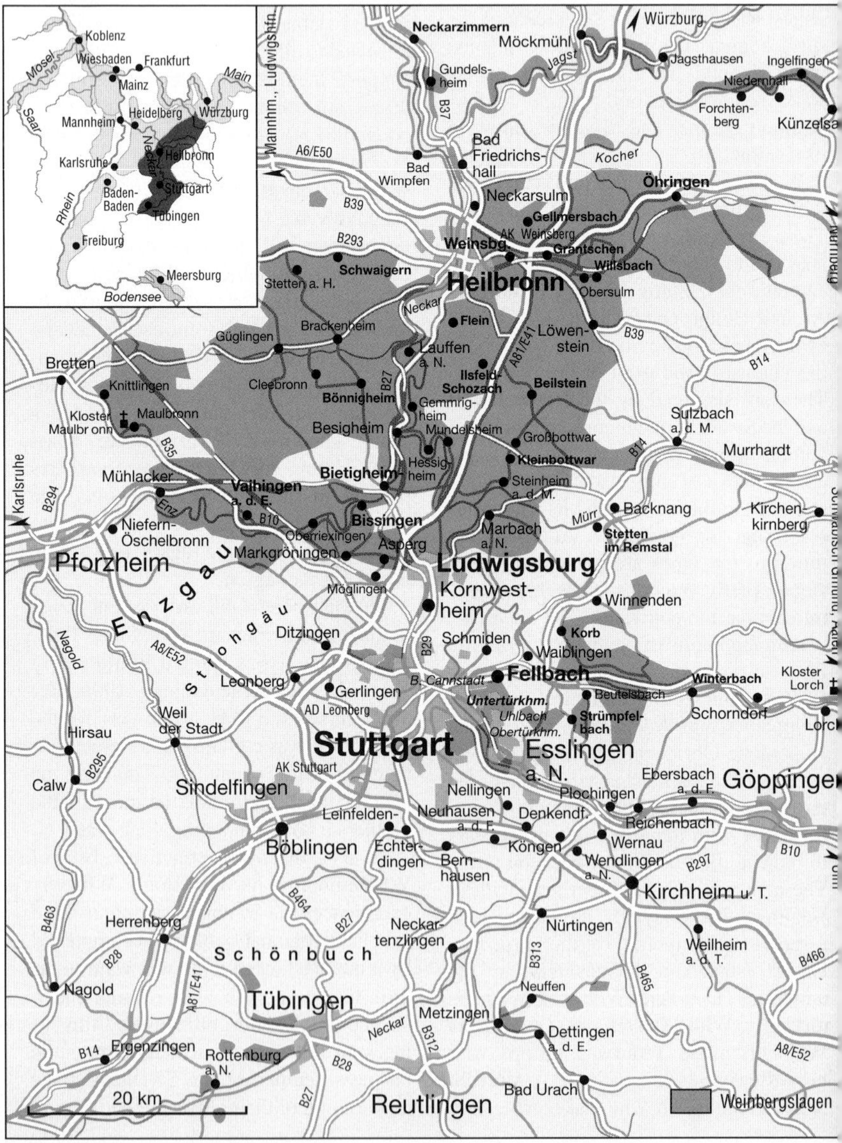

Weingut Gerhard Aldinger, Fellbach

Weingut Drautz-Able, Heilbronn

Weingut Jürgen Ellwanger, Winterbach

Weinmanufaktur Feindert, Bietigheim-Bissingen

Weingut Karl Haidle, Kernen im Remstal

Weingut G. A. Heinrich, Heilbronn

Weingut Fürst zu Hohenlohe-Oehringen, Öhringen

Weingut des Hauses Württemberg Hofkammerkellerei, Ludwigsburg

Weingut Amalienhof, Heilbronn

Weingut Graf von Bentzel-Sturmfeder, Ilsfeld-Schozach

Weingärtnergenossenschaft Flein-Talheim, Flein

Weingärtnergenossenschaft Grantschen, Weinsberg-Grantschen

Weingut Erich Hirth, Obersulm-Willsbach

Schloßgut Hohenbeilstein, Beilstein

Weingut Kistenmacher-Hengerer, Heilbronn

Weingut Kuhnle, Weinstadt-Strümpfelbach

Weingut Gerhard Leiss, Gellmersbach

Weingut Sonnenhof – Bezner-Fischer, Vaihingen-Enz

Staatsweingut Weinsberg, Weinsberg

Rating scale for the estates

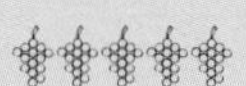

Highest rating: These producers belong to the world's finest.

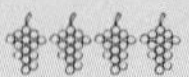

Excellent estates: These producers are among Germany's best.

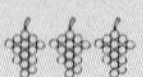

Very good producers, known for their consistently high quality.

Good estates, offering better than average quality.

Reliable producers that offer well-made standard quality.

Other notable producers

Weingut Bader "Im Lehen"
71394 Kernen, Albert-Moser-Straße 100
Tel. (0 71 51) 4 28 28, 4 54 97

Weingut Dr. Baumann – Schloß Affaltrach
74182 Obersulm,
Am Ordenschloß 15–21
Tel. (0 71 30) 5 57, Fax 93 65

Weingut Beurer
71394 Stetten im Remstal
Langestraße 67
Tel. (0 71 51) 4 21 90, Fax 4 21 90

Weingut und Schloßkellerei Burg Hornberg
74865 Neckarzimmern, Burg Hornberg
Tel. (0 62 61) 50 01, Fax 23 48

Weingut Robert Drautz
74072 Heilbronn, Ludwig-Pfau-Straße 11
Tel. (0 71 31) 8 95 02, Fax 62 01 89

Weingut Kusterer
73728 Esslingen, Untere Beutau 44
Tel. (07 11) 35 79 09, Fax 3 50 81 05

Weingärtnergenossenschaft Lauffen
74348 Lauffen, Im Brühl 48
Tel. (0 71 33) 1 85-0, Fax 1 85 60

Weingut Medinger
71394 Kernen-Stetten, Brühlstraße 6
Tel. (0 71 51) 4 45 13, Fax 4 17 37

Weingut Schäfer-Heinrich
74074 Heilbronn, Im Letten 3
Tel. (0 71 31) 16 24 54, Fax 16 56 59

Weingut Rainer Schnaitmann
70734 Fellbach, Untertürkheimer Straße 4
Tel. (07 11) 57 46 16, Fax 57 46 16

Vintage chart for Württemberg

vintage	quality	drink
1997	🍇🍇🍇	till 2002
1996	🍇🍇🍇	now
1995	🍇🍇🍇	now
1994	🍇🍇🍇	now
1993	🍇🍇🍇🍇	now
1992	🍇🍇🍇	now
1991	🍇🍇	now
1990	🍇🍇🍇🍇	now
1989	🍇🍇🍇🍇	now
1988	🍇🍇🍇	now

🍇🍇🍇🍇🍇 : Outstanding
🍇🍇🍇🍇 : Excellent
🍇🍇🍇 : Good
🍇🍇 : Average
🍇 : Poor

WEINGUT GRAF ADELMANN

Owner: Count Michael Adelmann
General Manager: Peter Albrecht
71711 Kleinbottwar, Burg Schaubeck
Tel. (0 71 48) 66 65, Fax 80 36
Directions: A 81 Stuttgart–Heilbronn, exit Großbottwar
Opening hours: Mon.–Fri. 9 a.m. to noon and 2 p.m. to 6 p.m.
Sat. 9 a.m. to 1 p.m.
History: Independent county until 1803
Worth seeing: Idyllic Schaubeck castle with its 13th-century courtyard

Vineyard area: 17 hectares
Annual production: 110,000 bottles
Top sites: Kleinbottwarer Süßmund and Oberer Berg
Soil types: Clay with stone and slate, red chalky loam
Grape varieties: 29% Riesling, 18% Trollinger, 10% Lemberger, 8% Samtrot, 6% Clevner, 5% each of Spätburgunder and Muskattrollinger, 4% each of Silvaner and Muskateller, 11% other varieties
Average yield: 54 hl/ha
Best vintages: 1993, 1996, 1997
Member: VDP, Deutsches Barrique Forum, Hades

In order to have a viable alternative to his Rieslings, Count Michael employs "Cuvées." The "Lion of Schaubeck" consists of a third each of Riesling, Grauburgunder and Silvaner; the red wine is known as "The Walls of Schaubeck." Although somewhat uneven in quality, this estate remains for many wine lovers the best in Württemberg. After splendid performances in 1989 and 1990, the 1991 and 1992 vintages were little more than average, and the 1993 and 1994 vintages irregular in quality. With the white 1995s and the fine 1996 reds a discernible improvement took place. The 1997s set the stage for a comeback. No one produced better Rieslings in Württemburg, and the barrel-aged reds are among the finest in Germany. Perhaps one day soon this estate will again be without peer in the region.

1997 Kleinbottwarer Süßmund
Riesling Kabinett trocken
17.50 DM, 11.5%, ♀ till 2000 **86**

1997 Kleinbottwarer Süßmund
Riesling Spätlese
34.50 DM, 11%, ♀ till 2005 **86**

1997 Kleinbottwarer Oberer Berg
Riesling Kabinett trocken
17.50 DM, 11%, ♀ till 2001 **88**

1997 Kleinbottwarer Süßmund
Riesling Spätlese trocken
"Brüsseler Spitze"
31.50 DM, 12.5%, ♀ till 2003 **89**

1996 Kleinbottwarer Oberer Berg
Muskateller Auslese
45 DM, 11.5%, ♀ till 2003 **89**

——— Red wines ———

1996 "Der Löwe von Schaubeck"
Lemberger trocken
24.50 DM, 12.5%, ♀ till 2002 **86**

1996 Samtrot
Spätlese trocken "Brüsseler Spitze"
35 DM, 11.5%, ♀ till 2003 **88**

1996 "Cuvée Vignette"
Tafelwein trocken
45 DM, 12%, ♀ till 2005 **89**

WEINGUT GERHARD ALDINGER

Owner: Gert Aldinger
70734 Fellbach, Schmerstraße 25
Tel. (07 11) 58 14 17, Fax 58 14 88
Directions: From Stuttgart via B 14, exit Fellbach-Süd
Opening hours: Mon.–Fri. 8 a.m. to noon and 2 p.m. to 6 p.m., Sat. 8 a.m. to noon, Sun. by appointment
Restaurant: "Weinstube Germania," closed Sun. and Mon.
Specialties: Swabian dishes, game, lobster and asparagus
History: Wine estate owned by the family since 1492

Vineyard area: 20 hectares
Annual production: 160,000 bottles
Top sites: Untertürkheimer Gips, Fellbacher Lämmler, Stettener Pulvermächer
Soil types: Gypsum and clay with stone and slate, red clay with stone and slate, weathered sandstone
Grape varieties: 37% Trollinger, 30% Riesling, 10% Spätburgunder, 5% Lemberger, 3% each of Müller-Thurgau, Dornfelder, Schwarzriesling, Cabernet, Chardonnay and Kerner
Average yield: 85 hl/ha
Best vintages: 1990, 1993, 1996
Member: VDP

The Aldinger estate on the outskirts of Stuttgart is best known in Swabia for its thirst-quenching Trollinger, a light red wine for lazy afternoons. Wine lovers buying from this estate are understandably more keen on the finest red wines from better vintages. In 1996 Aldinger also made discernible improvements in the quality of his white wines, moving him into the ranks of the most dependable producers from Württemberg. Although appealing, the 1997s do not have the same luster. If the congenial Gert Aldinger could maintain his quality levels, he might soon be regarded as one of the best vintners in the region.

1996 Untertürkheimer Gips
Riesling Spätlese trocken
17.75 DM, 11.5%, ♀ till 2000 **84**

1996 Untertürkheimer Gips
Gewürztraminer Spätlese
18.75 DM, 12%, ♀ till 2002 **86**

1996 Riesling
Eiswein
66 DM/0.375 liter, 7.5%, ♀ till 2008 **89**

——— Red wines ———

1997 Untertürkheimer Gips
Samtrot Spätlese trocken
19.75 DM, 12.5%, ♀ till 2000 **84**

1996 Untertürkheimer Gips
Spätburgunder Auslese trocken
23 DM, 12.5%, ♀ till 2002 **84**

1995 Untertürkheimer Gips
Spätburgunder Auslese trocken
30 DM, 12.5%, ♀ till 2002 **84**

1996 "Cuvée C"
trocken
30 DM, 12.5%, ♀ till 2002 **86**

1995 "Cuvée C"
trocken
30 DM, 12.5%, ♀ till 2003 **88**

ROTWEIN
1996
IM BARRIQUE GEREIFT
GA
GUTSABFÜLLUNG
WEINGUT ALDINGER
D-70734 FELLBACH
WÜRTTEMBERG
QUALITÄTSWEIN · A.P.NR. 403 044 97 · 13,0% VOL · 0,75 L

WEINGUT AMALIENHOF

Owner: Strecker family
74074 Heilbronn,
Lukas-Cranach-Weg 5
Tel. (0 71 31) 25 17 35, Fax 57 20 10
Directions: B 27, exit Heilbronn, following the signs for Sontheim
Sales: Strecker family
Opening hours: Mon.–Fri. 8 a.m. to 6 p.m., Sat. 8 a.m. to 4 p.m.
Sun. by appointment
Worth seeing: The estate in the Beilsteiner Steinberg vineyard

Vineyard area: 29 hectares
Annual production: 250,000 bottles
Top sites: Beilsteiner Steinberg, Fleiner Altenberg, Heilbronner Stiftsberg
Soil types: Heavy clay loam, gypsum, and clay with stone and slate
Grape varieties: 34% Riesling, 24% Trollinger, 16% Samtrot, 7% Lemberger, 4% each of Muskat-lemberger and Schwarzriesling, 11% other varieties
Average yield: 70 hl/ha
Best vintages: 1990, 1993, 1994

The lion's share of the Amalienhof's vineyard holdings lie in the Beilsteiner Steinberg, of which it is the sole owner. Working very traditionally, Strecker does all he can here to ensure that the proportion of "Prädikat" wines is always as high as possible. It is thus not unusual for nature to reward the former professor from the wine college in Weinsberg with an abundance of noble late harvest wines from grape varieties that one rarely sees elsewhere: Muskattrollinger, Muskatlemberger and now the experimental variety "No. 112," an offspring of Cabernet Sauvignon produced by the estate's own propagation methods. A staunch individualist, Strecker vinifies the majority of his wines in an off-dry style; his red wines are generally slightly sweet. Because he bottles late, it is often difficult to assess his young wines accurately; but it does appear that there has been a slight improvement in quality in the last two vintages.

1996 Beilsteiner Steinberg
Riesling Kabinett trocken
9.50 DM, 11%, 🍷 till 2002 **80**

1996 Beilsteiner Steinberg
Kerner Kabinett
8.25 DM, 11.5%, 🍷 now **80**

1997 Beilsteiner Steinberg
Riesling Spätlese
15.60 DM, 12%, 🍷 till 2002 **80**

——— Red wines ———

1996 Beilsteiner Steinberg
Dornfelder trocken
10 DM, 12.5%, 🍷 now **80**

1996 Beilsteiner Steinberg
Lemberger
11.50 DM, 11%, 🍷 now **80**

1995 Beilsteiner Steinberg
Lemberger Spätlese trocken
18.50 DM, 12%, 🍷 now **82**

1996 Beilsteiner Steinberg
Samtrot Auslese trocken
28 DM, 13%, 🍷 till 2002 **82**

1996 Beilsteiner Steinberg
Muskat-Lemberger Auslese
15.75 DM, 13%, 🍷 till 2002 **82**

1996 Beilsteiner Steinberg
Muskat-Lemberger Auslese trocken
31.50 DM, 13.5%, 🍷 till 2002 **84**

WEINGUT GRAF VON BENTZEL-STURMFEDER

Owner: Count Kilian von Bentzel-Sturmfeder
General Manager: Hermann Blankenhorn
Winemaker: Peter Titus
74360 Ilsfeld-Schozach, Sturmfederstraße 4
Tel. (0 71 33) 96 08 94, Fax 96 08 95
e-mail: sturmfeder@wein.com
Directions: A 81 Stuttgart–Heilbronn, exit Ilsfeld
Sales: Hermann Blankenhorn
Opening hours: Mon.–Fri. 9 a.m. to 6 p.m., Sat. 10 a.m. to 1 p.m. or by appointment
History: Owned by the family since the year 1396
Worth seeing: Cellar built in 1711

Vineyard area: 15.5 hectares
Annual production: 120,000 bottles
Top site: Schozacher Roter Berg (sole owners)
Soil types: Gypsum and clay with stone and slate over a fossil limestone subsoil
Grape varieties: 25% Riesling, 26% Spätburgunder, 17% Samtrot, 17% Lemberger, 5% each of Traminer and Müller-Thurgau, 5% other varieties
Average yield: 80 hl/ha
Best vintages: 1990, 1993, 1996
Member: VDP

Since the old count resided in the distant Thurn castle, general manager Hermann Blankenhorn was safely entrusted with his position as manager of this estate for over thirty years. The younger Count Kilian, on the other hand, has learned the vintner's trade and now manages the estate. The furnishings in his cellar are just as simple as the estate's credo: "If it ain't broke, don't fix it." It is curious that the family has not planted a single vine of Württemberg's most popular grape variety, Trollinger. Although the wines often lack body, they are generally delicately fruity. The 1990 Lemberger Spätlese, which was auctioned recently, shows that the estate is capable of producing better wines in good vintages.

1996 Schozacher Roter Berg
Riesling trocken
8.25 DM/1.0 liter, 11.5%, ♀ now **80**

1996 Riesling
trocken
8.50 DM, 11.5%, ♀ now **80**

1997 Schozacher Roter Berg
Riesling Kabinett trocken
9.90 DM, 11%, ♀ now **80**

— Red wines —

1996 Schozacher Roter Berg
Lemberger trocken
10 DM, 12%, ♀ till 2000 **80**

1996 Schozacher Roter Berg
Samtrot trocken
10 DM, 12%, ♀ till 2000 **80**

1996 Lemberger
trocken
9.75 DM, 12%, ♀ till 2000 **82**

1997 Schozacher Roter Berg
Lemberger Kabinett trocken
13.50 DM, 11.5%, ♀ till 2000 **82**

1997 Schozacher Roter Berg
Samtrot Spätlese trocken
19 DM, 12.5%, ♀ till 2000 **84**

WEINGUT ERNST DAUTEL

Owner: Ernst Dautel
74357 Bönnigheim, Lauerweg 55
Tel. (0 71 43) 87 03 26, Fax 87 03 27
Directions: A 81 Heilbronn–Stuttgart, exit Mundelsheim, via Kirchheim to Bönnigheim
Opening hours: By appointment
History: Wine estate in the family since 1510

Vineyard area: 10 hectares
Annual production: 70,000 bottles
Top sites: Besigheimer Wurmberg, Bönnigheimer Sonnenberg
Soil types: Fossil limestone, clay with stone and slate
Grape varieties: 20% Riesling, 16% each of Trollinger and Lemberger, 10% each of Schwarzriesling and Spätburgunder, 7% Kerner, 6% Weißburgunder, 4% Chardonnay, 3% Müller-Thurgau, 8% other varieties
Average yield: 66 hl/ha
Best vintages: 1993, 1996, 1997
Member: Deutsches Barrique Forum

With the 1996 vintage yielding only 45 hectoliters per hectare, Ernst Dautel harvested – especially when compared to the norm in Württemberg – only an extremely modest sized crop. By doing multiple selections in each vineyard, he was able to bring in a small amount of Spätlese and several Kabinetts. All of his 1996s had not only a healthy extract, but also significant potential for further development; in their youth, however, they were very difficult to assess, much less enjoy. 1997 brought not only a larger crop, but also somewhat better and certainly more pleasant wines. The Chardonnay was the best dry white wine produced in Württemberg in 1997 and the "Kreation" one of the best reds from the 1996 vintage! Nonetheless, a number of the wines were excessively marked by new oak. In spite of this fact, Dautel's estate remains the leader in Württemberg; and his dry wines are often some of the best produced in Germany in any given vintage.

1997 Besigheimer Wurmberg
Riesling trocken ***
18.50 DM, 12%, ♀ till 2000 **88**

1997 Weißer Burgunder
trocken ****
20 DM, 12.5%, ♀ till 2001 **88**

1996 Weißer Burgunder
Tafelwein trocken
28 DM, 12%, ♀ till 2000 **89**

1997 Chardonnay
trocken ****
29 DM, 12.5%, ♀ till 2002 **89**

1997 Bönnigheimer Sonnenberg
Riesling Auslese
29 DM, 11%, ♀ till 2002 **89**

——— Red wines ———

1996 Lemberger
trocken ****
32 DM, 12%, ♀ till 2005 **88**

1996 Spätburgunder
trocken ****
31 DM, 12%, ♀ till 2003 **88**

1995 "Kreation"
Tafelwein trocken
35 DM, 12.5%, ♀ till 2005 **89**

1996 "Kreation"
trocken
44 DM, 12.5%, ♀ till 2005 **89**

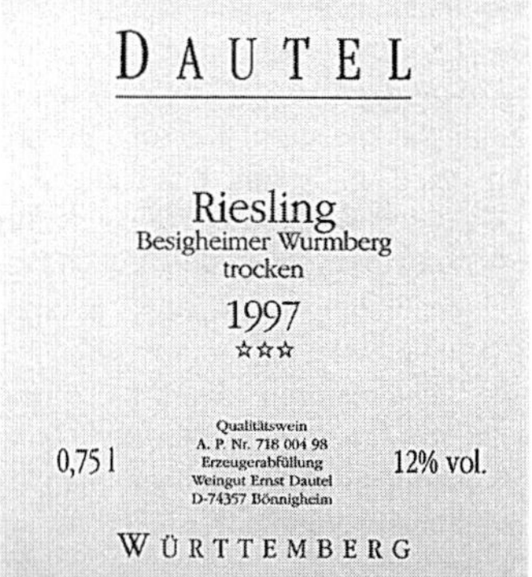

WEINGUT DRAUTZ-ABLE

Owners: Christel Able and Richard Drautz
Winemakers: Richard Drautz and Thomas Gramm
74074 Heilbronn, Faißtstraße 23
Tel. (0 71 31) 17 79 08, Fax 94 12 39
e-mail: wgda@wein.com
Directions: On the outskirts of Heilbronn
Sales: Monika Drautz and Christel Able
Opening hours: Mon.–Fri. 8 a.m. to noon and 1:30 p.m. to 6 p.m.
Sat. 9 a.m. to 4 p.m.
History: Family coat of arms bestowed in 1496

Vineyard area: 16 hectares
Annual production: 140,000 bottles
Top sites: Heilbronner Stiftsberg and Wartberg, Neckarsulmer Scheuerberg
Soil types: Heavy clay loam, clay with stone and slate, weathered sandstone
Grape varieties: 32% Trollinger, 21% Riesling, 9% Lemberger, 8% Spätburgunder, 7% each of Schwarzriesling and Kerner, 4% Dornfelder, 12% other varieties
Average yield: 92 hl/ha
Best vintages: 1990, 1993, 1997
Member: VDP, Deutsches Barrique Forum, Hades

The bearded bard, Richard Drautz, is the epitome of a Swabian vintner. Together with his sister Christel Able he has taken this old family estate to new heights. Although some of the wines lack personality, his 1996s and 1997s were all very well made. The dry white wines are a touch light, those aged in casks often overcrafted and the Auslese irksomely sweet. When aged in small oak barrels the Lemberger from the finest great vintages – 1996 will be a case in point when released – often leave wine lovers in rapture, but the everyday wines are often quite simple and seldom display as much charm. Nonetheless, with over 30 such wines on the list at under ten marks per bottle, these generally represent the best value for money.

1997 Neckarsulmer Scheuerberg
Silvaner Spätlese trocken
16.85 DM, 12.5%, ♀ now **82**

1995 Grauer Burgunder
Tafelwein trocken "Hades"
28 DM, 11%, ♀ now **84**

1997 Heilbronner Stiftsberg
Riesling Auslese
21 DM, 11%, ♀ till 2002 **84**

1997 Neckarsulmer Scheuerberg
Gewürztraminer Auslese
23.25 DM, 11.5%, ♀ till 2002 **86**

——— Red wines ———

1997 Lemberger
trocken
9.50 DM, 13%, ♀ till 2001 **84**

1997 Neckarsulmer Scheuerberg
Spätburgunder Spätlese trocken
27.90 DM, 13%, ♀ till 2001 **86**

1997 Heilbronner Stiftsberg
Frühburgunder Auslese trocken
23.25 DM, 13%, ♀ till 2002 **86**

1996 Dornfelder
Tafelwein trocken "Hades"
24.50 DM, 12%, ♀ till 2003 **86**

1994 Spätburgunder Rotwein
Tafelwein trocken "Jodokus"
50 DM, 13%, ♀ till 2004 **89**

WEINGUT JÜRGEN ELLWANGER

Owner and manager: Jürgen Ellwanger
Winemaker: Andreas Ellwanger
73650 Winterbach, Bachstraße 21
Tel. (0 71 81) 4 45 25, Fax 4 61 28
Directions: From Stuttgart via B 14, exit Waiblingen, in the direction of Schorndorf
Sales: Sieglinde Ellwanger
Opening hours: Mon.–Fri. 9 a.m. to 7 p.m., Sat. 8 a.m. to 3 p.m. or by appointment

Vineyard area: 17 hectares
Annual production: 120,000 bottles
Top sites: Winterbacher Hungerberg, Grunbacher Berghalde and Klingle, Schnaiter Altenberg, Hebsacker Lichtenberg
Soil types: Heavy clay with stone and slate, and pebbly sand
Grape varieties: 20% Trollinger, 18% Riesling, 15% Lemberger, 14% Kerner, 7% each of Spätburgunder and Zweigelt, 5% Weißer and Grauer Burgunder, 4% Dornfelder, 10% other varieties
Average yield: 70 hl/ha
Best vintages: 1993, 1996, 1997
Member: VDP, Deutsches Barrique Forum, Hades

Until recently this estate was best known for its easy-to-drink Trollinger. Today it is one of the few serious red wine producers in Württemberg. On the other hand, although the oak-aged "Nicodemus" range has been improving from year to year, Jürgen Ellwanger has never been particularly esteemed for his rather simple white wines. The barrel-aged red wines that he makes with his son Andreas remain the top attraction at this estate and more than make up for the lack of firepower on the white wine front. The Blauer Zweigelt, a grape of Austrian origin, merits particular attention.

1997 Winterbacher Hungerberg
Weißer Burgunder Auslese trocken
20 DM, 13%, ♀ till 2000 **82**

1997 Schorndorfer Grafenberg
Riesling Spätlese
15 DM, 12%, ♀ till 2001 **82**

1997 Winterbacher Hungerberg
Traminer Auslese
22 DM, 13%, ♀ till 2002 **84**

——— Red wines ———

1997 Schnaiter Burghalde
Lemberger Spätlese trocken
17 DM, 12%, ♀ till 2001 **84**

1996 Spätburgunder
Tafelwein trocken "Hades"
29 DM, 12.5%, ♀ till 2000 **84**

1995 Spätburgunder
Tafelwein trocken "Hades"
29 DM, 12.5%, ♀ till 2002 **86**

1996 Zweigeltrebe
Tafelwein trocken "Hades"
29 DM, 12%, ♀ till 2001 **88**

1995 Zweigeltrebe
Tafelwein trocken "Hades"
29 DM, 12.5%, ♀ till 2003 **89**

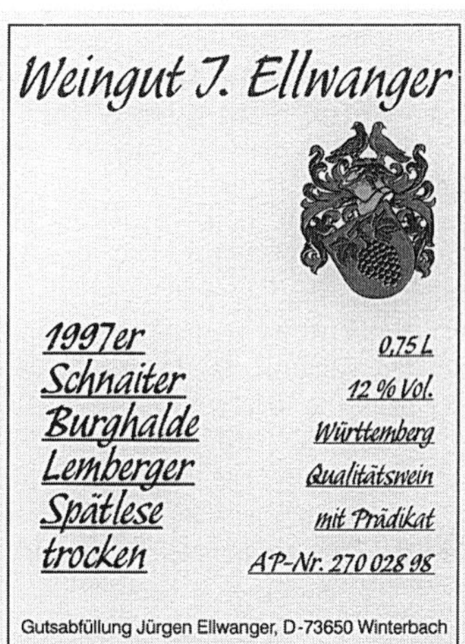

WEINMANUFAKTUR FEINDERT

Owners: Joachim F. and Ilga Feindert
74321 Bietigheim-Bissingen, Olgastraße 23
Tel. (0 71 42) 98 89 24, Fax 98 89 25
e-mail: weinmanufaktur.feindert@t-online.de
Directions: A 81 Heilbronn–Stuttgart, exit Ludwigsburg-Nord, B 27 in the direction of Bietigheim-Bissingen
Sales: Joachim and Ilga Feindert
Opening hours: By appointment

Vineyard area: 2 hectares
Annual production: 3,000 bottles
Top sites: No single vineyard names are used
Soil types: Fossil limestone
Grape varieties: 65% Trollinger, 25% Riesling, 5% each of Schwarzriesling and Silvaner
Average yield: 15 hl/ha
Best vintages: 1995, 1996

It was only after finishing his apprenticeship as a mechanic that Joachim Feindert discovered his love of wine. Changing careers, he became a grower's apprentice, studied viticulture at Geisenheim and then went to Switzerland as the technical director of a large winery. His decision to set up his own business was courageous, for he owned neither vineyards nor cellar equipment. Today he manages one and a half hectare along the banks of the Neckar and Enz. He harvests only ice wines, which are aged in brand-new small oak barrels in cellars beneath the castle at Freiberg on the Neckar. His model, in opulence of style as well as in price, is Chateau d'Yquem. With 13 to 15 percent alcohol and distinct oak flavors, the wines differ from the local norm. For that reason, most of his colleagues shake their heads when they hear his name. Quite a few describe him as a utopian or even a madman. Whether his ideas will work in the market remains to be seen.

1995 Riesling
Eiswein
95 DM/0.25 liter, 11%, 🍷 till 2010 **89**

1995 Schiller
Eiswein "Genius"
300 DM/0.5 liter, 🍷 till 2010 **91**

1995 Riesling
Eiswein "Primus inter pares"
295 DM/0.5 liter, 10.5%, 🍷 till 2010 **91**

1995 Rosé
Eiswein "Primus inter pares"
248 DM/0.5 liter, 🍷 till 2010 **89**

1995 "Primus inter pares"
Rosé Eiswein
250 DM/0.5 liter, 11%, 🍷 till 2010 **89**

1995 Schillerwein
Rosé Eiswein "Genius"
300 DM/0.5 liter, 12%, 🍷 till 2010 **91**

HEDON
Württemberg
1995
Eiswein Riesling
Qualitätswein mit Prädikat

11,0 % vol
0,25 l
A.P.Nr. 0138 001 97

Flasche Nr.

Abfüller:
WEINMANUFAKTUR
J.F. FEINDERT KG
D-74321 Bietigheim-Bissingen
- Product of Germany -

WEINGÄRTNER GENOSSENSCHAFT FLEIN-TALHEIM

Chairman: Martin Göttle
General Manager: Helmut Ebert
Winemaker: Roland Hönnige
74223 Flein, Römerstraße 14
Tel. (0 71 31) 5 95 20, Fax 59 52 50
Directions: A 81 Heilbronn–Stuttgart, exit Heilbronn-Süd
Sales: Martin Söhner
Opening hours: Mon.–Fri. 8 a.m. to noon and 1 p.m. to 5 p.m.
Sat. 8 a.m. to noon
History: Founded in 1923

Vineyard area: 295 hectares
Number of adherents: 400
Annual production: 3 million bottles
Top sites: Fleiner Eselsberg, Altenberg, Sonnenberg and Schloßberg
Soil types: Clay with stone and slate, fossil limestone, reed sandstone
Grape varieties: 50% Riesling, 32% Schwarzriesling, 6% Samtrot, 3% each of Kerner and Spätburgunder, 6% other varieties
Average yield: 90 hl/ha
Best vintages: 1990, 1993, 1997

This cooperative can boast that it was the first in Württemberg to win a federal gold medal; and it remains to this day one of the two or three leading cooperatives in the region. The adherents understand their marketing well, selling an upscale range of wines, both still and sparkling, with a modern label under the name "Sankt Veit." The liter bottlings often turn out well and are generally appealing in style. Apart from these, though, the 1996s were disappointing – simple wines with an excessive dose of sweetness. The 1997s, in particular the Rieslings, are much better.

1997 Fleiner Altenberg
Riesling Spätlese trocken
10 DM, 12.5%, ♀ now **80**

1997 Fleiner Altenberg
Riesling Auslese trocken "Sankt Veit"
23.25 DM, 13.5%, ♀ till 2000 **82**

1997 Fleiner Altenberg
Riesling Auslese
17.50 DM, 11.5%, ♀ till 2003 **84**

1997 Fleiner Altenberg
Riesling Eiswein
40.75 DM/0.375 liter, 9.5%, ♀ till 2005 **88**

——— Red wines ———

1996 Fleiner Kirchenweinberg
Spätburgunder Kabinett
8.75 DM, 9.5%, ♀ now **77**

1997 Fleiner Kirchenweinberg
Spätburgunder Spätlese
12.50 DM, 11%, ♀ now **77**

1997 Fleiner Kirchenweinberg
Samtrot Spätlese
13.75 DM, 11%, ♀ now **77**

1995 "Sankt Veit"
trocken
28.75 DM, 13%, ♀ now **80**

1997 Fleiner Kirchenweinberg
Lemberger trocken
7.90 DM, 12.5%, ♀ till 2000 **82**

WEINGÄRTNER GENOSSENSCHAFT GRANTSCHEN

Chairman: Friedrich Wirth
General Manager: Bruno Bolsinger
Winemaker: Fritz Herold
74189 Weinsberg-Grantschen,
Wimmentaler Straße 36
Tel. (0 71 34) 9 80 20, Fax 98 02 22
Directions: A 81 Heilbronn–Stuttgart, exit Weinsberg-Ellhofen
Sales: Wolfgang Dämon
Opening hours: Mon.–Fri. 9 a.m. to 5 p.m., Sat. 9 a.m. to 12:30 p.m.
History: Founded 1947

Vineyard area: 140 hectares
Number of adherents: 217
Annual production: 1.2 million bottles
Top sites: Grantschener Wildenberg
Soil types: Weathered clay, stone and slate
Grape varieties: 28% Riesling, 25% Trollinger, 22% Lemberger, 15% Schwarzriesling, 5% Kerner, 5% other varieties
Average yield: 100 hl/ha
Best vintages: 1990, 1993, 1997
Member: Deutsches Barrique Forum

With the exception of some of the reds, the wines from Grantschen have been at best mediocre for the past three vintages; and as neither the "SM" nor the often superb "Grandor" – their two top red cuvées – were produced in 1995 or 1996, and only the "SM" in 1997, the range of wines shown here is nothing to write home about. Nonetheless, this cooperative remains one of the most reliable in the area. Among the best known of its wines, and rightly so, are the red Lembergers aged in small Swabian oak barrels, which, like all of the cooperative's wines, are marketed with only discreet mentions of the individual vineyards on the back label. In addition, the growers produce their own marc, which is not only well made but also sold in very distinctive bottles.

1997 Riesling
Spätlese trocken
17.50 DM, 12.5%, ♀ till 2000 **80**

1997 Gewürztraminer
Auslese
14.50 DM, 12.5%, ♀ till 2002 **82**

1997 Gewürztraminer
Eiswein
99.75 DM/0.5 liter, 10.5%, ♀ till 2005 **88**

Red wines

1997 Lemberger
trocken
8.95 DM, 12.5%, ♀ till 2000 **80**

1997 Schwarzriesling
Spätlese
10 DM, 11.5%, ♀ till 2000 **82**

1997 Lemberger
Spätlese trocken
25.80 DM, 12.5%, ♀ till 2002 **82**

1997 Samtrot
Auslese
15 DM, 12.5%, ♀ till 2001 **84**

1997 "SM"
trocken
21.50 DM, 12%, ♀ till 2002 **86**

WEINGUT KARL HAIDLE

Owner: Hans Haidle
71394 Kernen im Remstal, Hindenburgstraße 21
Tel. (0 71 51) 94 91 10, Fax 4 63 13
Directions: From Stuttgart via B 14 into the Rems valley
Sales: Haidle family
Opening hours: Mon.–Fri. 8 a.m. to noon and 1 p.m. to 6 p.m.
Sat. 8 a.m. to 1 p.m.
Worth seeing: Ruins of Yburg castle above the property

Vineyard area: 17.6 hectares
Contracted growers: 5.2 hectares
Number of adherents: 25
Annual production: 135,000 bottles
Top sites: Stettener Pulvermächer, Häder and Mönchberg, Schnaiter Burghalde
Soil types: Clay with stone and slate
Grape varieties: 48% Riesling, 14% Trollinger, 11% Kerner, 5% Spätburgunder, 22% other varieties
Average yield: 58 hl/ha
Best vintages: 1990, 1992, 1997
Member: VDP

The terraced vineyards below the Yburg have gradually recovered from the hailstorm that devastated them four years ago. The 1996 whites were considerably better than the 1995s. Opulent, if somewhat attenuated on the nose, even the liter bottlings were perfectly respectable. Given the difficult 1995 vintage experienced in Württemberg, the three red wines of that year were also very successful. Although we are not totally convinced by the overall quality, Hans Haidle considers the 1997 vintage to be even better, his finest since 1992. Undoubtedly one of the best estates in the region, Haidle is harking back to his golden years in the early 1990s.

1997 Stettener
Weißburgunder Spätlese trocken
19.90 DM, 13%, ♀ till 2001 **82**

1996 Stettener Pulvermächer
Riesling Spätlese trocken
20 DM, 12%, ♀ till 2002 **84**

1997 Stettener Pulvermächer
Riesling Spätlese
22 DM, 12%, ♀ till 2000 **84**

1997 Stettener Pulvermächer
Riesling Auslese
32 DM, 12.5%, ♀ till 2002 **86**

——— Red wines ———

1995 Schnaiter Burghalde
Spätburgunder Spätlese trocken
20 DM, 12.5%, ♀ till 2002 **86**

1996 Schnaiter Burghalde
Spätburgunder Auslese trocken
30 DM/0.5 liter, 13.5%, ♀ till 2000 **86**

1996 Schnaiter Burghalde
Spätburgunder Auslese trocken
26 DM/0.5 liter, 13.5%, ♀ till 2002 **86**

1995 Lemberger Rotwein
trocken
29 DM, 12.5%, ♀ till 2003 **88**

WEINGUT G. A. HEINRICH

Owner: Martin Heinrich
74076 Heilbronn, Riedstraße 29
Tel. (0 71 31) 17 59 48, Fax 16 63 06
Directions: Winery at the foot of the Wartberg in Heilbronn
Sales: Christel Heinrich
Opening hours: Mon.–Fri. 9 a.m. to noon and 1:30 p.m. to 6 p.m.
Sat. 9 a.m. to noon or by appointment
Restaurant: In November from 11 a.m. to midnight
Specialties: Swabian ravioli, boiled beef

Vineyard area: 11.7 hectares
Annual production: 80,000 bottles
Top sites: Heilbronner Wartberg and Stiftsberg
Soil types: Clay with stone and sand, weathered sandstone, loess and loam
Grape varieties: 25% Trollinger, 24% Riesling, 20% Lemberger, 5% each of Schwarzriesling and Spätburgunder, 4% Scheurebe, 3% each of Clevner and Samtrot, 11% other varieties
Average yield: 85 hl/ha
Best vintages: 1993, 1996, 1997

In recent years this old estate in Heilbronn, now directed by Martin Heinrich, has emerged from the shadows of the better-known producers in Württemberg. Their red wine called "GA 1" has set new quality standards. With the 1993 vintage this industrious Swabian winemaker set off on a new path. Although the 1994 and 1995 ranges were a bit of a disappointment, Heinrich made a comeback with the 1996s and 1997s. It's true that the Müller-Thurgau and the Trollinger are rather simple wines, but there are other very appealing wines in the collection. We look forward to tasting the top 1996 and 1997 reds next year, for it would appear that this estate has not yet pulled out all the stops.

1997 Heilbronner Stiftsberg
Riesling
7.80 DM, 11%, ♀ till 2000 **80**

1997 Heilbronner Stiftsberg
Riesling Spätlese
15 DM, 11.5%, ♀ till 2002 **82**

1995 Heilbronner Stiftsberg
Gewürztraminer trocken
16 DM/0.5 liter, 12%, ♀ till 2000 **84**

1995 Heilbronner Stiftsberg
Weißer Burgunder trocken
16 DM/0.5 liter, 12%, ♀ till 2000 **84**

1997 Heilbronner Stiftsberg
trocken "GA 2"
25 DM, 12.5%, ♀ till 2001 **84**

1997 Heilbronner Stiftsberg
Gewürztraminer Auslese
20 DM/0.5 liter, 9%, ♀ till 2004 **88**

1995 Heilbronner Stiftsberg
Clevner Beerenauslese
50 DM/0.5 liter, 10%, ♀ till 2008 **89**

——— Red wines ———

1995 Heilbronner Stiftsberg
Lemberger & Trollinger trocken
13 DM, 12%, ♀ now **82**

1997 Heilbronner Stiftsberg
Lemberger trocken
19 DM, 12.5%, ♀ till 2002 **86**

WEINGUT ERICH HIRTH

Owner: Erich Hirth
74182 Obersulm-Willsbach,
Löwensteiner Straße 76
Tel. (0 71 34) 36 33, Fax 86 22
Directions: A 81 Heilbronn–Stuttgart, junction Weinsberg, exit Ellhofen in the direction of Obersulm
Sales: Gudrun Hirth
Opening hours: Mon.–Fri. 4 p.m. to 6 p.m., except Wed., Sat. 9 a.m. to noon or by appointment

> Vineyard area: 8.5 hectares
> Annual production: 70,000 bottles
> Top site: Willsbacher Dieblesberg
> Soil types: Clay with stone and sand
> Grape varieties: 38% Riesling, 19% Lemberger, 17% Trollinger, 14% Schwarzriesling, 6% Spätburgunder, 2% Chardonnay, 4% other varieties
> Average yield: 80 hl/ha
> Best vintages: 1990, 1993, 1997

Trained at Geisenheim, Erich Hirth was for years cellarmaster at the cooperative in Flein before setting up on his own in 1986. Since then he has gradually made a name for himself through unusual marketing; he has also steadily improved the quality of his wines. Above all his red wines, with their varietal purity and absence of new oak, are appreciated by his Swabian clientele. Never short of humor, often with a pun in the local dialect, Erich Hirth uses well-chosen one liners to add spice to his price lists. As a description of this 1997 Lemberger, for example, Hirth writes "love at first drink." Jokes aside, though, his red wines often lack character and weight of fruit; nor would the quality of his whites entice us to uncork a second bottle. His 1996s could have had more substance and elegance; the 1997s, which Hirth considers to be his finest since 1990 and 1993, are much better. All remain both quaffable and sensibly priced.

1996 Willsbacher Dieblesberg
Riesling trocken
7 DM/1.0 liter, 12%, ♀ now **77**

Red wines

1996 Willsbacher Dieblesberg
Lemberger trocken
9.25 DM, 12.5%, ♀ now **80**

1996 Willsbacher Dieblesberg
Spätburgunder Kabinett trocken
8.50 DM, 12%, ♀ till 2000 **80**

1997 Willsbacher Dieblesberg
Dornfelder trocken
8.50 DM, 12.5%, ♀ till 2000 **82**

1997 Willsbacher Dieblesberg
Spätburgunder Kabinett trocken
8.70 DM, 12%, ♀ till 2000 **82**

1997 Willsbacher Dieblesberg
Lemberger Kabinett trocken
9.90 DM, 12%, ♀ till 2000 **82**

1997 Willsbacher Dieblesberg
Schwarzriesling Spätlese trocken
9.80 DM, 12.5%, ♀ till 2000 **82**

1997 Willsbacher Dieblesberg
Lemberger trocken
9.30 DM, 12.5%, ♀ till 2002 **84**

1997 Willsbacher Dieblesberg
Samtrot Spätlese trocken
13.10 DM, 12.5%, ♀ till 2002 **84**

Württemberg
1993 Willsbacher Dieblesberg
Riesling Kabinett trocken
Qualitätswein mit Prädikat
A. P. Nr. 786 010 94 0,75 l 12,0% vol.
Abfüller: Weingut Erich Hirth · D-7104 Willsbach · Löwensteiner Str. 76 · Tel. 07134/3633

SCHLOSSGUT HOHENBEILSTEIN

Owner: Hartmann Dippon
71717 Beilstein, Im Schloß
Tel. (0 70 62) 43 03, Fax 2 22 84
Directions: A 81 Heilbronn–Stuttgart
Opening hours: Mon.–Fri. 9 a.m. to 11:30 a.m., Sat. 9 a.m. to 11:30 a.m.
Worth seeing: Ruins of Langhans

> Vineyard area: 12.5 hectares
> Annual production: 80,000 bottles
> Top site: Hohenbeilsteiner Schloßwengert (sole owners)
> Soil types: Clay with stone and slate
> Grape varieties: 25% Riesling, 20% Trollinger, 12% Lemberger, 9% Spätburgunder, 8% Samtrot, 6% Schwarzriesling, 5% Kerner, 4% each of Weißburgunder, Muskattrollinger and Silvaner, 3% other varieties
> Average yield: 72 hl/ha
> Best vintages: 1989, 1990, 1993
> Member: VDP, Deutsches Barrique Forum, Naturland

Beneath the ruins of the former Langhans castle from the 12th century stands the Hohenbeilstein estate, which has been in the hands of the Dippon family since 1959. After training at the local Weinsberg college and then in California, Hartmann Dippon took over this modern winery from his father, Eberhard, and runs it according to environmentally sound principles. He has earned a reputation for the Lembergers that he ages in barrels. “This wine needs the freedom of wooden barrels in order to breathe, space in which to shape itself,” says Hartmann Dippon, who learned that lesson from Joe Heitz in California. However, the majority of the wines produced here are simple, quaffable Trollingers and Rieslings, which is the way they like them in Württemberg. Since the 1990 vintage we have, apart from the 1993 Spätlese, tasted few wines that make any greater demands on the palate. It’s a pity, since the potential at this estate is considerable.

1996 Silvaner
Kabinett trocken
12.25 DM, 11%, 🍷 now — **80**

1997 Weißer Burgunder
Spätlese trocken
15.10 DM, 12.5%, 🍷 now — **80**

1997 Riesling
Spätlese trocken
16.25 DM, 12%, 🍷 now — **82**

1997 Silvaner
Spätlese trocken
12.80 DM, 12.5%, 🍷 now — **82**

1997 Riesling
Kabinett
11.40 DM, 11.5%, 🍷 till 2000 — **82**

1996
trocken
15.10 DM, 12%, 🍷 till 2000 — **82**

——— Red wines ———

1996 Samtrot
trocken
15.10 DM, 11.5%, 🍷 till 2001 — **82**

1995 Hohenbeilsteiner Schloßwengert
Spätburgunder trocken
12.75 DM, 12%, 🍷 now — **84**

1995 Hohenbeilsteiner Schloßwengert
Samtrot Kabinett trocken
14 DM, 12 %, 🍷 now — **84**

1997
TROLLINGER QUALITÄTSWEIN
TROCKEN
Schloßgut Hohenbeilstein
WÜRTTEMBERG
GUTSABFÜLLUNG
0,75 l 12,0% vol

WEINGUT FÜRST ZU HOHENLOHE-OEHRINGEN

Owner: Fürst Krafft zu Hohenlohe-Oehringen
Manager: Siegfried Röll
74613 Öhringen, Im Schloß
Tel. (0 79 41) 9 49 10, Fax 3 73 49
Directions: A 6 Heilbronn–Nürnberg, exit Öhringen
Sales: Siegfried Röll
Opening hours: Mon.–Fri. 8 a.m. to 5 p.m., Sat. 9 a.m. to noon
Restaurant: "Schloßhotel Friedrichsruhe"
Specialties: Refined Swabian cooking
History: Wine estate founded in 1360

Vineyard area: 19 hectares
Annual production: 180,000 bottles
Top site: Verrenberger Verrenberg (sole owners)
Soil types: Clay with stone and slate, fossil limestone
Grape varieties: 50% Riesling, 12% each of Lemberger and Spätburgunder, 8% Trollinger, 6% Weißburgunder, 4% each of Kerner, Silvaner and Schwarzriesling
Average yield: 62 hl/ha
Best vintages: 1995, 1996, 1997
Member: VDP, Deutsches Barrique Forum, Hades

Not only are the castle cellars from the 17th century well worth seeing, the finest red wines from the Verrenberger Verrenberg vineyard have also won their merited place on the wine lists of top German restaurants. However, we have never found the whites to be very convincing; and they again left a great deal to be desired in both 1996 and 1997. As expected, the red wines from the 1995 and 1996 vintages fared much better; the 1995 "Ex flammis orior" and 1996 "In scenio" were two of the finest red wines produced in Germany from those vintages. In short, as a white wine producer this estate is hardly worth mentioning; as a red wine specialist it deserves particular recognition.

1997 Verrenberger Verrenberg
Weißer Burgunder trocken
24 DM, 12.5%, ♀ now **82**

1997 Verrenberger Verrenberg
Riesling Spätlese trocken
18.75 DM, 12%, ♀ till 2000 **82**

1997 Verrenberger Verrenberg
Chardonnay trocken
22 DM, 12.5%, ♀ till 2000 **84**

——— Red wines ———

1996 Verrenberger Verrenberg
Samtrot Spätlese trocken
16 DM, 11.5%, ♀ till 2000 **84**

1997 Verrenberger Verrenberg
Lemberger Auslese trocken
45 DM, 13%, ♀ till 2002 **86**

1996 Lemberger
Tafelwein trocken "Hades"
32 DM, 13%, ♀ till 2000 **86**

1996 "Ex flammis orior"
Tafelwein trocken
41 DM, 13%, ♀ till 2004 **88**

1996 "In scenio"
Tafelwein trocken
45 DM, 13%, ♀ till 2005 **89**

1995 "Ex flammis orior"
Tafelwein trocken
41 DM, 13%, ♀ till 2003 **89**

WEINGUT KISTENMACHER-HENGERER

Owner: Hans Hengerer
74074 Heilbronn,
Eugen-Nägele-Straße 23–25
Tel. (0 71 31) 17 23 54, Fax 17 23 50
Directions: On the outskirts of Heilbronn
Sales: Hans Hengerer
Opening hours: Mon.–Fri. 4 p.m. to 6:30 p.m., Sat. 9 a.m. to 11 a.m. and 1 p.m. to 4 p.m.
History: Wine estate owned by the family since 1504

Vineyard area: 7 hectares
Annual production: 65,000 bottles
Top sites: Heilbronner Wartberg and Stiftsberg
Soil types: Clay with stone and slate, weathered sandstone
Grape varieties: 30% Trollinger, 20% Riesling, 10% each of Schwarzriesling and Spätburgunder, 8% each of Kerner and Lemberger, 5% each of Samtrot and Muskattrollinger, 4% other varieties
Average yield: 87 hl/ha
Best vintages: 1993, 1996, 1997

For almost 500 years the Kistenmacher family has been cultivating vines in Heilbronn. Although the property has been in its present form since the early 1960s, its growing reputation was established only four years ago, when son Hans took over. He spends a great deal of time caring for the vineyards – from canopy management to the harvest, almost everything is done by hand. In the cellar Hengerer particularly values the malolactic fermentation, which in his view brings a more harmoniously integrated acidity to the wine. Indeed his wines, although not comparable to the finest from the region, are fun to drink; they are also reasonably priced. This property is a good example of what small and unknown estates in the region could and should be doing.

1997 Heilbronner Stiftsberg
Riesling Kabinett trocken
8.70 DM, 12%, ♀ now **80**

1997 Heilbronner Stiftsberg
Riesling Spätlese trocken
9.90 DM, 12.5%, ♀ till 2000 **82**

1996 Heilbronner Stiftsberg
Riesling Spätlese
10 DM, 11.5%, ♀ till 2000 **82**

1996 Heilbronner Stiftsberg
Riesling Eiswein
35 DM/0.375 liter, 10%, ♀ till 2015 **92**

——— Red wines ———

1996 Heilbronner Stiftsberg
Spätburgunder trocken
10 DM, 12.5%, ♀ till 2000 **80**

1996 Weinsberger Salzberg
Samtrot trocken
8.75 DM, 12%, ♀ now **80**

1995 Heilbronner Stiftsberg
Lemberger trocken
9.50 DM, 12.5%, ♀ now **82**

1997 Heilbronner Stiftsberg
Samtrot Spätlese
12.90 DM, 12.5%, ♀ till 2000 **82**

1997 Heilbronner Stiftsberg
Lemberger Spätlese trocken
12.90 DM, 12.5%, ♀ till 2001 **84**

WEINGUT KUHNLE

Owners: Werner and Margret Kuhnle
71384 Weinstadt-Strümpfelbach, Hauptstraße 49
Tel. (0 71 51) 6 12 93, Fax 61 07 47
Directions: B 14 from Stuttgart via Fellbach
Sales: Margret Kuhnle
Opening hours: Fri. 4 p.m. to 7 p.m. or by appointment
History: Located in a 16th-century forester's house

Vineyard area: 14 hectares
Annual production: 100,000 bottles
Top sites: Stettener Pulvermächer, Strümpfelbacher Altenberg and Nonnenberg, Schnaiter Burghalde
Soil types: Heavy clay loam and red sandstone
Grape varieties: 22% Trollinger, 20% Riesling, 9% Chardonnay, 8% each of Spätburgunder and Kerner, 5% each of Müller-Thurgau, Schwarzriesling and Gewürztraminer, 18% other varieties
Average yield: 70 hl/ha
Best vintages: 1993, 1995, 1997

The village of Strümpfelbach lies in a narrow valley between vineyards and orchards. The parents of Margret Kuhnle were members of the local cooperative. After many years as a cellarmaster at another cooperative, Werner Kuhnle and his wife, Margret, opted for independence, taking into their own hands everything from viticulture to the marketing of their bottled wines. Numerous awards indicate that the estate is gradually earning local recognition. However, the quality of several of the latest vintages did not mirror this development. Most of what we tasted between 1994 and 1996 were simple quaffing wines, but not much more. In particular the whites seemed rather dull, probably as a result of deacidification. In 1997 the general quality has significantly improved. Kuhnle is now planning to extend his cellars. If he finds room for a few more barrels, it would certainly stand his red wines in good stead.

1997 Strümpfelbacher Nonnenberg
Riesling Auslese trocken
22 DM, 13.5%, 🍷 till 2000 **82**

1997 Strümpfelbacher Nonnenberg
Kerner Auslese
16 DM, 11%, 🍷 till 2002 **84**

1997 Strümpfelbacher Nonnenberg
Chardonnay Auslese trocken
22 DM, 13%, 🍷 till 2000 **86**

——— Red wines ———

1996 Lemberger
trocken "Feuerwand"
10 DM, 12.5%, 🍷 now **77**

1997 Strümpfelbacher Altenberg
Dornfelder trocken
8.50 DM, 13%, 🍷 till 2000 **80**

1996 Stettener Mönchberg
Dornfelder trocken
8 DM, 13%, 🍷 now **80**

1997 Schnaiter Sonnenberg
Samtrot Auslese trocken
22 DM, 13.5%, 🍷 till 2000 **80**

1997 Strümpfelbacher Nonnenberg
Schwarzriesling Auslese trocken
24 DM, 13%, 🍷 till 2000 **82**

1997 Lemberger
Spätlese trocken "Feuerwand"
20 DM, 12%, 🍷 till 2002 **84**

1993er
Schnaiter Burghalde
Spätburgunder Spätlese „trocken"
Qualitätswein mit Prädikat
A. P. Nr. 570 007 94
Weingut Kuhnle
12%vol Gutsabfüllung · Württemberg 0,75l
Weingut Kuhnle · Hauptstraße 49 · D-71384 Weinstadt-Strümpfelbach · Tel. (0 7151) 6 12 93

WEINGUT GERHARD LEISS

Owner: Gerhard Leiss
Winemaker: Wolf-Peter Leiss
74189 Gellmersbach,
Lennacher Straße 7
Tel. (0 71 34) 1 43 89, Fax 2 06 21
Directions: A 81 Heilbronn–Stuttgart, exit Weinsberg
Sales: Christa Leiss
Opening hours: Mon.–Fri. 5:30 p.m. to 7 p.m., Sat. 9 a.m. to 6 p.m.
Restaurant: "Besenwirtschaft"
Specialties: Regional fare

Vineyard area: 10 hectares
Annual production: 95,000 bottles
Top site: Gellmersbacher Dezberg
Soil types: Clay with stone and slate
Grape varieties: 26% Riesling, 22% Trollinger, 19% Schwarzriesling, 10% Lemberger, 6% Kerner, 4% Müller-Thurgau and Gewürztraminer, 9% other varieties
Average yield: 80 hl/ha
Best vintages: 1993, 1997

Over the past few years this estate, run by the industrious Gerhard Leiss, has developed – albeit without much fanfare – in an extremely positive fashion. In particular the quality of the wines has improved considerably. The estate was founded in 1959 by his parents; through hard work and an instinctive feeling for his wines, he has expanded his vineyard holdings from less than one to almost ten hectares. Unassuming as he is, Leiss does not place too much value on the fact that he has won major provincial prizes no fewer than three times. Indeed the estate is little known within Württemberg, much less in other parts of Germany. It's true that the quality of his wines is still far behind the head of the pack, but Württemberg has all too few delicately fruity wines for easy drinking that are offered at such attractive prices. The 1996s were again appealing wines for everyday consumption. The 1997s are even better; and they remain inexpensive.

1997 Gellmersbacher Dezberg
Kerner Spätlese
9 DM, 11.5%, ♀ till 2000 **80**

1997 Erlenbacher Kayberg
Riesling Kabinett trocken
7.50 DM, 12%, ♀ now **82**

1996 Erlenbacher Kayberg
Muskateller
9 DM, 11%, ♀ now **82**

1997 Gellmersbacher Dezberg
Riesling Kabinett
7.50 DM, 11%, ♀ till 2000 **82**

1997 Erlenbacher Kayberg
Muskateller Spätlese
13 DM, 11.5%, ♀ till 2001 **84**

1996 Erlenbacher Kayberg
Traminer Spätlese
12 DM, 11%, ♀ now **84**

Red wines

1997 Gellmersbacher Dezberg
Spätburgunder Spätlese trocken
13 DM, 12.5%, ♀ till 2000 **80**

1995 Erlenbacher Kayberg
Lemberger trocken
9.50 DM, 12.5%, ♀ now **82**

1997 Gellmersbacher Dezberg
Samtrot Spätlese
13.50 DM, 12.5%, ♀ till 2000 **82**

SCHLOSSGUT GRAF VON NEIPPERG

Owner: Karl Eugen Erbgraf zu Neipperg
General Manager: Matthias Boss
Winemaker: Bernd Supp
74190 Schwaigern, Im Schloß
Tel. (0 71 38) 50 81, Fax 40 07
Directions: A 61, exit Bad Rappenau
Sales: Ms. Binkele
Opening hours: Mon.–Fri. 8 a.m. to 11:30 a.m. and 1 p.m. to 4 p.m. Sat. 9 a.m. to 11:30 a.m.
Restaurant: "Zum Alten Rentamt"
History: Wine estate founded in 1248
Worth seeing: Staufer fortress in Neipperg, castle in Schwaigern

Vineyard area: 28 hectares
Annual production: 180,000 bottles
Top sites: Schwaigerner Ruthe, Neipperger Schloßberg
Soil types: Clay with stone and slate, weathered reed-sandstone
Grape varieties: 26% Riesling, 25% Lemberger, 18% Schwarzriesling, 8% Trollinger, 5% Müller-Thurgau, 4% Gewürztraminer, 4% Muskateller, 4% Spätburgunder, 6% other varieties
Average yield: 50 hl/ha
Best vintages: 1990, 1993, 1997
Member: VDP

This estate is one of the most consistent producers in Württemberg; even the liter bottlings for everyday consumption are often appealing! Riesling and Lemberger generally produce their finest wines, but few other estates in the region work with equal ease with such a wide variety of both white and red varietals. In 1994 and with certain whites in 1995 the estate's performance suffered from poor weather conditions after it was severely struck by hail. The 1996 and 1997 whites are higher in quality, as are the reds from the last three vintages; but yields that were often as low as a mere 27 hectoliters per hectare mean that the choicest wines are on allocation.

1997 Neipperger Schloßberg
Riesling
10.45 DM, 12%, ♀ till 2001 **86**

1997 Neipperger Schloßberg
Muskateller Spätlese
19.50 DM, 11%, ♀ till 2002 **86**

1996 Schwaigerner Ruthe
Riesling Spätlese trocken
18.50 DM, ♀ till 2000 **88**

1997 Schwaigerner Ruthe
Riesling Spätlese
18.65 DM, 11.5%, ♀ till 2003 **88**

——— Red wines ———

1997 Neipperger Schloßberg
Spätburgunder Spätlese trocken
23.20 DM, 11.5%, ♀ till 2001 **84**

1997 Neipperger Schloßberg
Schwarzriesling Spätlese ***
23.20 DM, 12%, ♀ till 2002 **86**

1996 Neipperger Schloßberg
Lemberger trocken ***
30.15 DM, 12.5%, ♀ till 2001 **88**

1997 Neipperger Schloßberg
Lemberger Spätlese trocken ***
26.70 DM, 12.5%, ♀ till 2003 **88**

1995 Neipperger Schloßberg
Lemberger trocken
26 DM, 11%, ♀ till 2001 **88**

WEINGUT ALBRECHT SCHWEGLER

Owner: Albrecht Schwegler
71404 Korb, Steinstraße 35
Tel. (0 71 51) 3 48 95, Fax 3 49 78
Directions: B 14 Stuttgart–Nürnberg, exit Korb
Sales: Andrea Schwegler
Opening hours: By appointment

Vineyard area: 0.65 hectares
Annual production: 4,000 bottles
Top sites: Korber Hörnle and Sommerhalde
Soil types: Clay with stone and slate
Grape varieties: 55% Blauer Zweigelt, 30% Lemberger, 15% Merlot
Average yield: 45 hl/ha
Best vintages: 1990, 1993, 1994

After years working as an oenologist and winemaker in – among other places – South Africa and New Zealand, Albrecht Schwegler returned home in 1990. He had grown tired of pumping millions of liters through large wineries. Today he is the managing partner of a technological company based in Korb that sells parts to Mercedes. As a hobby, he runs the smallest but also one of the finest independent estates in Germany. As a rule he produces just one red wine, called "Saphir," a blend of Blauer Zweigelt and Lemberger. In top vintages he also bottles a small quantity of a wine called "Granat." Our most recent tastings confirm our view that this wine needs time; extremely closed in its youth, it begins to blossom only after five or six years. The sublime 1990 "Granat" is now sold out, but the 1994 is an excellent replacement. For everyday drinking the "simple" Beryll, which was first made in 1992, is recommended. The top 1995s, that we have not retasted since bottling, will be released only after this book goes to press; the 1996s and 1997s are still in barrel. Admittedly Schwegler produces very little wine, but it is worth looking for!

Red wines

1995 "Beryll"
trocken
12.50 DM, 12.5%, 🍷 till 2002 **84**

1994 "Saphir"
trocken
21 DM/0.375 liter, 12.5%, 🍷 till 2003 **84**

1993 "Saphir"
trocken
35.50 DM, 12.5%, 🍷 till 2005 **88**

1992 "Saphir"
trocken
21 DM/0.375 liter, 12.5%, 🍷 till 2003 **89**

1993 "Granat"
trocken
29.50 DM/0.375 liter, 13%, 🍷 till 2003 **89**

1994 "Granat"
trocken
53.50 DM, 13%, 🍷 till 2004 **91**

AS
ALBRECHT SCHWEGLER
GRANAT
1990
ABFÜLLER: ALBRECHT SCHWEGLER
STEINSTRASSE 35 · 71404 KORB
QUALITÄTSWEIN WÜRTTEMBERG
AP 418 001 92
0,75 l 12,5 Vol.%

WEINGUT SONNENHOF – BEZNER-FISCHER

Owners: Albrecht W. and Charlotte Fischer
Winemaker: Andreas Schuch
71665 Vaihingen-Enz, Ortsteil Gündelbach, Sonnenhof
Tel. (0 70 42) 2 10 38, Fax 2 38 94
e-mail: Weingut.Sonnenhof@t-online.de
Directions: A 81 Heilbronn–Stuttgart, exit Vaihingen-Enz, follow the B 10
Opening hours: Mon.–Fri. 8 a.m. to noon and 1 p.m. to 6 p.m., Sat. 9 a.m. to noon and 1 p.m. to 5 p.m.
History: Wine estate since 1522

Vineyard area: 29 hectares
Annual production: 250,000 bottles
Top sites: Gündelbacher Wachtkopf, Hohenhaslacher Kirchberg
Soil types: Clay with stone and slate, mostly heavy chalky loam
Grape varieties: 23% each of Trollinger and Riesling, 17% Lemberger, 9% Schwarzriesling, 8% Spätburgunder, 20% other (14) varieties
Average yield: 75 hl/ha
Best vintages: 1990, 1993, 1997
Member: Deutsches Barrique Forum, Hades

Within twenty years the Sonnenhof estate at the foot of the Wachtkopf vineyard has grown to an impressive 29 hectares. After the early death of his partner Helmut Bezner, Albrecht Fischer and his wife, Charlotte – born a Bezner – are now in sole charge of the property. A considerable proportion of their vineyards are located in steep southerly sites with up to 30 percent grades; two-thirds of the vines planted are red grape varieties. Although the estate helped to found the Hades association, nothing that we had tasted here since the appealing 1993 range much attracted our attention until the 1997 vintage. Interestingly enough though, the Spätlese appear to be better than the Auslese. The finest reds from that vintage, generally his best, have yet to be released. If Fischer can repeat this performance, his reputation will certainly improve.

1997 Gündelbacher Wachtkopf
Müller-Thurgau Auslese
18 DM, 12%, ♀ till 2002 **82**

1997 Gündelbacher Wachtkopf
Riesling Spätlese trocken
13.20 DM, 12%, ♀ till 2000 **84**

1997 Gündelbacher Wachtkopf
Riesling Auslese
15.50 DM, 11.5%, ♀ till 2003 **84**

1997 Gündelbacher Wachtkopf
Muskateller Spätlese
14.20 DM, 11.5%, ♀ till 2003 **86**

1997 Gündelbacher Wachtkopf
Riesling Spätlese
13.20 DM, 10.5%, ♀ till 2005 **86**

——— Red wines ———

1996 Gündelbacher Stromberg
Lemberger trocken
9 DM, 12.5%, ♀ now **77**

1997 Gündelbacher Wachtkopf
Lemberger Spätlese
18 DM, 11.5%, ♀ till 2000 **82**

1997 Gündelbacher Wachtkopf
Spätburgunder Auslese
23 DM, 12%, ♀ till 2002 **82**

1997 Hohenhaslacher Kirchberg
Lemberger Spätlese trocken
18 DM, 12.5%, ♀ till 2001 **84**

STAATSWEINGUT WEINSBERG

Owner: State of Baden-Württemberg
Manager: Dr. Günter Bäder
Winemaker: Gerhard Wächter
74189 Weinsberg, Traubenplatz 5
Tel. (0 71 34) 5 04 67, Fax 5 04 68
Directions: A 81 Heilbronn–Stuttgart, exit Weinsberg
Sales: Ilona Liepelt, Martin Schwegler
Opening hours: Mon.–Fri. 8 a.m. to noon and 1 p.m. to 4 p.m. or by appointment
History: Oldest winemaking college in Germany

Vineyard area: 40 hectares
Annual production: 300,000 bottles
Top sites: Burg Wildeck (sole owners), Weinsberger Schemelsberg (sole owners), Gundelsheimer Himmelreich
Soil types: Gypsum clay with stone and slate, heavy chalky loam, fossil limestone, Neckar gravel
Grape varieties: 20% Riesling, 14% Lemberger, 12% Trollinger, 8% Spätburgunder, 6% Samtrot, 40% other varieties
Average yield: 65 hl/ha
Best vintages: 1990, 1993, 1997
Member: VDP, Deutsches Barrique Forum, Hades, Naturland

Founded as a wine-research center in 1868 by the King of Württemberg, this university is the oldest institution of its kind in Germany; it is also one of the largest wine estates in Swabia. Since 1995 the wines have been sold under the name "Staatsweingut Weinsberg." Since the estate owns such excellent vineyards as Schemelsberg, Himmelreich and Burg Wildeck, the potential for quality exists. Over the years, however, the estate had seldom made the most of it. The 1996s and the 1997s show a trend towards improved quality; in particular the Rieslings are more appealing. The new director has promised that the coming vintages will be even better.

1996 Chardonnay
Tafelwein trocken "Hades"
26.90 DM, 11.5%, ♀ till 2001 **82**

1997 Riesling
Kabinett
12 DM, 11%, ♀ till 2002 **84**

1997 Riesling
Spätlese trocken
15.80 DM, 12%, ♀ till 2001 **86**

——— Red wines ———

1996 Samtrot
Kabinett trocken
12.50 DM, 12.5%, ♀ now **80**

1996 Lemberger
trocken
11.60 DM, 12%, ♀ till 2000 **80**

1995 Gundelsheimer Himmelreich
Lemberger trocken
11.25 DM, 12.5%, ♀ now **82**

1997 Gundelsheimer Himmelreich
Schwarzriesling Spätlese trocken
16.50 DM, 12.5%, ♀ till 2000 **82**

1996 Dornfelder
trocken
13.60 DM, 12%, ♀ now **82**

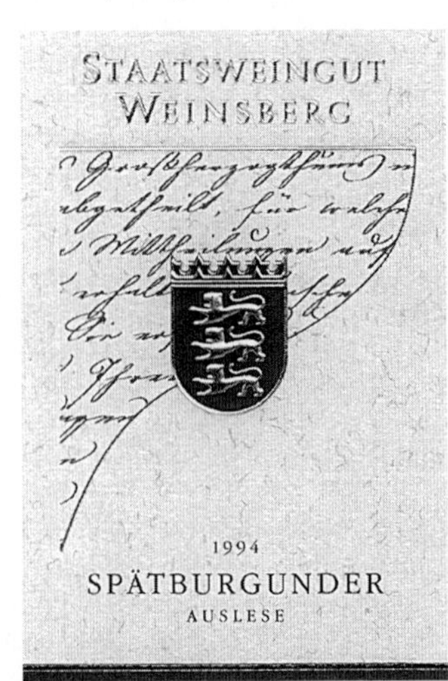

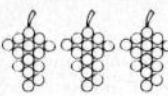

WEINGUT WÖHRWAG

Owner: Hans-Peter Wöhrwag
70327 Untertürkheim,
Grunbacherstraße 5
Tel. (07 11) 33 16 62, Fax 33 24 31
e-mail:
hans-peter.woehrwag@t-online.de
Directions: Via B 10, exit Untertürkheim
Sales: Christin Wöhrwag
Opening hours: Mon.–Fri. 8 a.m. to noon and 4 p.m. to 6:30 p.m.
Sat. 9 a.m. to 1 p.m.

Vineyard area: 17 hectares
Annual production: 150,000 bottles
Top site: Untertürkheimer Herzogenberg (sole owners)
Soil types: Clay with sand and slate, heavy chalky loam
Grape varieties: 40% Riesling, 35% Trollinger, 6% Lemberger, 5% Spätburgunder, 4% each of Grauburgunder and Weißburgunder, 3% Müller-Thurgau, 3% other varieties
Average yield: 63 hl/ha
Best vintages: 1993, 1996, 1997

Long before Mercedes produced its first car here, wooden casks were being rolled out of the cellars of the Wöhrwag family in Untertürkheim. Since leaving the local cooperative in 1959, the estate had not made much of a stir outside of Württemberg. After completing his education at Geisenheim, son Hans-Peter Wöhrwag has done much to change that fact in just a few years. The stunning 1993s, in particular the late harvested Rieslings, first caught our attention; and the 1996 ice wine was adequate proof of his ability to make such wines on a regular basis. However, the rest of the wines were not always so successful. Wöhrwag, like many of his colleagues in Swabia, had to cope with three very modest vintages. That he did so well is a tribute to his craft, which he plies better than almost all others in the region. The much finer 1997 vintage made his life easier. This is the most appealing range of wines that we have tasted here since 1993!

1997 Untertürkheimer Herzogenberg
Weißer Burgunder Spätlese trocken
20 DM, 13.5%, ♀ till 2001 **86**

1997 Untertürkheimer Herzogenberg
Riesling Kabinett trocken "Goldkapsel"
14 DM, 12%, ♀ till 2002 **88**

1997 Untertürkheimer Herzogenberg
Riesling Kabinett trocken "SC"
16 DM, 12%, ♀ till 2003 **88**

1997 Untertürkheimer Herzogenberg
Grauer Burgunder Spätlese trocken
20 DM, 13.5%, ♀ till 2002 **88**

1996 Untertürkheimer Herzogenberg
Riesling Eiswein
50 DM/0.375 liter, 8%, ♀ till 2010 **94**

——— Red wines ———

1997 "Moritz"
trocken
16 DM, 12.5%, ♀ till 2002 **86**

1996 Untertürkheimer Herzogenberg
Spätburgunder Spätlese trocken "R"
32 DM, 12.5%, ♀ till 2000 **86**

1996 "Philipp"
trocken
25 DM, 12.5%, ♀ till 2003 **88**

WEINGUT DES HAUSES WÜRTTEMBERG HOFKAMMERKELLEREI

Owner: Carl Herzog von Württemberg
General Manager: Dr. Jürgen Dietrich
Winemaker: Bernhard Idler
71634 Ludwigsburg, Schloß Monrepos
Tel. (0 71 41) 22 55 25, Fax 22 55 30
Directions: A 81 Heilbronn–Stuttgart, exit Ludwigsburg-Nord
Sales: Hartmut Otter and Hilde Meyer-Trump
Opening hours: Mon.–Fri. 9 a.m. to 6 p.m.
History: Since 1677 the estate of the House of Württemberg
Worth seeing: Monrepos castle grounds with lake

Vineyard area: 39.6 hectares
Annual production: 400,000 bottles
Top sites: Stettener Brotwasser, Maulbronner Eilfingerberg and Klosterstück, Untertürkheimer Mönchberg, Gündelbacher Steinbachhof and Wachtkopf
Soil types: Reed-sandstone, fossil limestone, gypsum clay with stone and slate, and heavy chalky loam
Grape varieties: 53% Riesling, 24% Trollinger, 15% Lemberger, 4% Spätburgunder, 4% other varieties
Average yield: 65 hl/ha
Best vintages: 1990, 1996, 1997
Member: VDP

In 1677 the Hofkammerkellerei was established as the private wine estate of the House of Württemberg; in 1981 the winery moved to a new home near the king's Monrepos Castle. After a string of mediocre vintages, the new general manager Dr. Jürgen Dietrich and his ambitious young cellarmaster Bernhard Idler are again producing interesting wines, and vow to do even better. In comparison with those from previous years, the wines have already gained in purity and intensity. Over the next few years further efforts will be devoted to the vineyards, which are among the finest in Swabia. This is an estate to keep an eye on.

1997 Stettener Brotwasser
Riesling Kabinett trocken
14.50 DM, 11.5%, 🍷 till 2001 **84**

1996 Untertürkheimer Mönchberg
Riesling Auslese trocken
35 DM, 12.5%, 🍷 till 2000 **84**

1997 Untertürkheimer Mönchberg
Riesling Spätlese halbtrocken
18.50 DM, 11.5%, 🍷 till 2002 **84**

1997 Asperger Berg
Riesling Spätlese trocken
19.50 DM, 12.5%, 🍷 till 2002 **86**

1997 Untertürkheimer Mönchberg
Riesling Auslese trocken
25 DM, 13%, 🍷 till 2002 **86**

1996 Stettener Brotwasser
Riesling Eiswein
90 DM/0.375 liter, 6.5%, 🍷 till 2015 **89**

——— Red wines ———

1996 Maulbronner Eilfingerberg
Lemberger trocken
12.60 DM, 12%, 🍷 till 2001 **82**

1997 Hohenhaslacher Kirchberg
Trollinger trocken
9.50 DM, 12%, 🍷 till 2000 **82**

1996 Untertürkheimer Mönchberg
Spätburgunder Spätlese trocken
26 DM, 12%, 🍷 till 2000 **82**

1996 Untertürkheimer Mönchberg
Spätburgunder Spätlese trocken
24.50 DM, 12.5%, 🍷 till 2002 **84**

WEINGUT DES HAUSES WÜRTTEMBERG
HOFKAMMERKELLEREI
1994er
MAULBRONNER EILFINGERBERG
LEMBERGER TROCKEN
WÜRTTEMBERG
11,0% VOL 0,75 L

The Best Sparkling Wines

Worth a closer look

At the turn of the century Germany's sparkling Rieslings enjoyed worldwide recognition. Some, indeed, were sold at higher prices than Champagne. Over the past decade attempts have been made to revive the standards of those days. In some regions producers' associations have been formed. With their assistance, many growers have begun to produce their own sparkling wines by traditional methods.

Well into the 1980s, sparkling wine producers could legally sell products made from cheap Italian and French base wines as German sparkling wine. This deception has been eliminated. Today German sparkling wine must be produced from German wines. Only *Sekt* without the addition of *Deutsch* is allowed to be elaborated from non-German base wines.

Schaumwein is the simplest category. It is not subject to official inspection and bears no official coding. *Sekt* is identical to *Qualitätsschaumwein* and can bear an official coding. *Sekt bestimmter Anbaugebiete* is the same as *Qualitätsschaumwein bestimmter Anbaugebiete* and must be officially inspected. Both the base wine and the final *dosage* must come from one and the same region of production.

Moreover, the following terms define the amount of residual sugar in the Sekt:

Extra Brut	0–6 grams
Brut	0–15 grams
Extra Trocken	12–20 grams
Trocken	17–35 grams
Halbtrocken	33–50 grams
Mild	over 50 grams

A Sekt with five grams of residual sugar can be labeled Brut or Extra Brut; a sparkling wine with 13 grams of residual sugar can be marketed either as Brut or as Extra Trocken. While a dry wine may have no more than nine grams of residual sugar, a Sekt can have as much as 35 grams and still be sold as *trocken.*

This does not mean that production methods are not of great significance for the quality of each individual sparkling wine. One prerequisite for sparkling wine production is secondary fermentation, which is provoked by inoculating the fermented base wine with special yeasts. Tank fermentation rapidly imparts a sparkle to the wine, but the result is regarded in knowledgeable circles as mediocre. The required time for bottle aging of tank-fermented wines is six months, while for bottle-fermented wines it is nine months.

Traditionally, once inoculation has taken place, the bottle is sealed with a crown cap. After the secondary fermentation, the producer cellars the bottles to enable the wine to attain a degree of maturity. Only later is the bottle placed on a rack and riddled over a two-month period, until the murky yeast residue has made its way into the neck of the bottle. Immersion in a cold environment freezes the yeast. When the crown cap is removed in a process known as disgorgement, the residue is ejected. The *dosage* that follows is what determines the degree of sweetness in the finished wine.

The bottle subsequently is corked and fastened with wire. In general, the longer the aging of the wines on the lees, the more elegant the taste of the final product. If only the word *Flaschengärung* – which means "bottle-fermented" in German – appears on the label, it is nonetheless likely that the wine has been made in tanks. Whoever takes the trouble to use the classic methods is more likely to use the term *Traditionelle* or *Klassische Flaschengärung.* Only these terms guarantee to consumers that the *méthode champenoise* has been employed.

WEINGUT KARL KURT BAMBERGER & SOHN

Nahe
55566 Meddersheim,
Römerhofstraße 10
Tel. (0 67 51) 26 24, Fax 21 41

1993 Meddersheimer Paradiesgarten
Riesling trocken

Elegant aromas of pears and nut-butter, lush weight of fruit, complex finish. 13.80 DM, ♀ till 2002 **90**

WEINGUT BERNHARD HUBER

Baden, page 88

1993 Pinot
Rosé Brut

Aroma of wild cherries and brioches, velvety fruit texture, lively Pinot fruit, lush finish. 23 DM, ♀ till 2000 **89**

WEINGUT LINDENHOF

Nahe, page 278

1994 Riesling
Brut

Aromas of Cox apples and apricots, sumptuous body, extremely well integrated acidity. 18 DM, ♀ till 2000 **89**

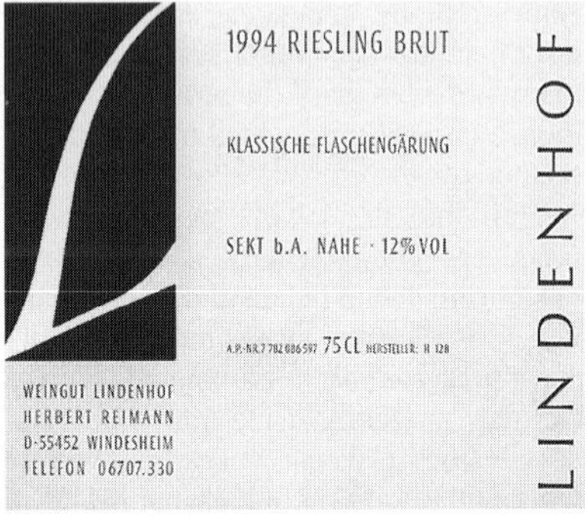

1994 Weißer Burgunder
Brut

Elegant nose of hay and yeast, concentrated but elegant, full-bodied length of flavor. 30 DM, ♀ till 2000 **89**

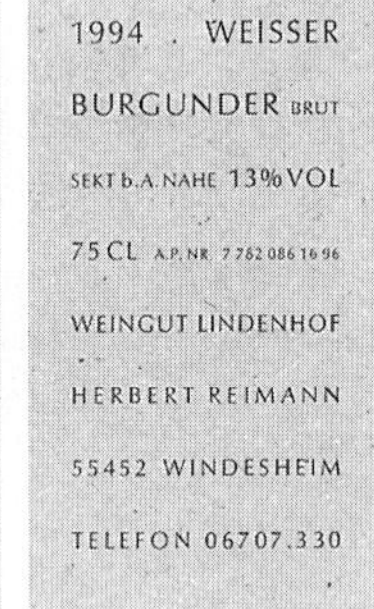

WEINGUT STUDERT-PRÜM

Mosel, page 248

1995 Maximiner Cabinet
Riesling trocken

Aromas of apple compote with cinnamon, sumptuous weight of fruit, elegant aftertaste. 16 DM, 🍷 till 2001 **89**

BISCHÖFLICHE WEINGÜTER

Mosel, page 189

1993 DOM Scharzhofberger
Riesling Brut

Mineral aromas of apricots and green apple, elegant ripe fruitiness, balanced. 18 DM, 🍷 till 1999 **88**

ST. LAURENTIUS-SEKTGUT

Mosel
54340 Leiwen, Laurentiusstraße 2
Tel. (0 65 07) 38 36, Fax 38 96

1995 St. Laurentius
Riesling Brut

Lavish apricot tones on the nose, full body, very impressive finish. 16 DM, 🍷 till 1999 **88**

WEINGUT HEYMANN-LÖWENSTEIN

Mosel, page 205

1994 Riesling
Extra Brut

Lively scent of apples, ample body, balanced play of acidity on the finish. 23 DM, 🍷 till 2000 **88**

WEINGUT BERNHARD HUBER

Baden, page 88

1993 Pinot
Brut

Aromas of ripe pears and vanilla, vinous character, well-integrated acidity, a classic style. 23 DM, 🍷 till 2000 **88**

WEINGUT KOEHLER-RUPRECHT

Pfalz, page 321

1990 Pinot "Philippi"

Aromas of forest floors, nut and caramel, supple fruitiness, very well integrated acidity, highly individual. 25 DM, 🍷 now **88**

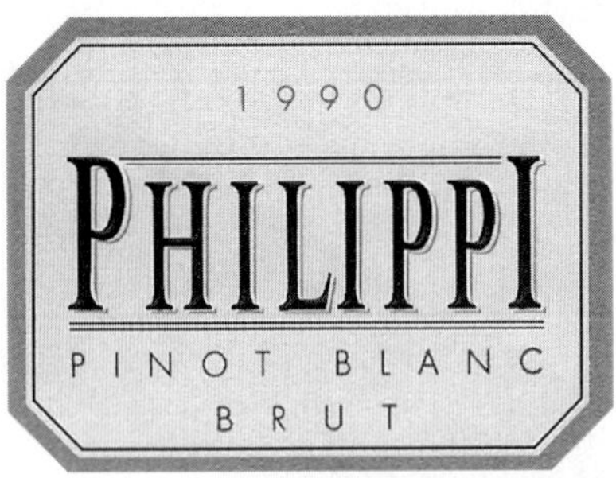

SEKTHAUS VOLKER RAUMLAND

Rheinhessen
67592 Flörsheim-Dalsheim,
Alzeyer Straße 134
Tel. (0 62 43) 90 80 70, Fax 90 80 77

1992 Riesling
Brut

Hearty apple aromas, full-bodied, harmonious play of acidity. 15.50 DM, 🍷 till 1999 **88**

WEINGUT WILHELMSHOF

Pfalz, page 346

1995 Siebeldinger Königsgarten
Blanc de Noirs

Aromas of raspberries and toasted bread, lush weight of fruit, refreshing acidic structure, spicy aftertaste. 25 DM, 🍷 till 2002 **88**

WEINGUT KARL KURT BAMBERGER & SOHN

Nahe
55566 Meddersheim,
Römerhofstraße 10
Tel. (0 67 51) 26 24, Fax 21 41

1993 Meddersheimer Paradiesgarten
Riesling Brut

13.80 DM, ♀ till 2000 **86**

WEIN- UND SEKTGUT CH. W. BERNHARD

Rheinhessen, page 404

1994 Riesling
Brut

18.70 DM, ♀ till 1999 **86**

WEINGUT GEORG BREUER

Rheingau, page 357

1994 Riesling
Brut

25 DM, ♀ till 1999 **86**

1995 Weißer Burgunder
Brut

25 DM, ♀ till 1999 **86**

WEINGUT ANTON DOUFRAIN

Rheingau, page 359

1996 Hattenheimer Heiligenberg
Riesling Brut

15 DM, ♀ till 2000 **86**

WEINGUT JOACHIM FLICK

Rheingau, page 361

1994 Wickerer Stein
Riesling Brut

16 DM, ♀ till 2000 **86**

WEINGUT REINHARD UND BEATE KNEBEL

Mosel, page 216

1995 Winninger Domgarten
Riesling Brut

17.50 DM, ♀ now **86**

WEINHOF HERRENBERG

Mosel
54441 Schoden, Hauptstraße 80
Tel. (0 65 81) 12 58, Fax 12 58

1994 Schodener Herrenberg
Riesling Brut

17.90 DM, ♀ till 2000 **86**

WEINGUT LÄMMLIN-SCHINDLER

Baden, page 95

1994 Mauchener Sonnenstück
Pinot Brut

19.50 DM, ♀ till 2000 **86**

BADEN · SEKT B.A.
1994
Pinot Brut
MAUCHENER
SONNENSTÜCK
11,5 %vol · 0,75 l

WEINGUT HANS LANG
Rheingau, page 377

1993 Johann Maximilian
Riesling Extra Brut
26.80 DM, ♀ now **86**

WEINGUT POSTHOF DOLL & GÖTH
Rheinhessen, page 425

1994 Essenheimer Teufelspfad
Scheurebe extra trocken
13.50 DM, ♀ till 2000 **86**

WEINGUT DR. HEINRICH NÄGLER
Rheingau, page 381

1994 Rüdesheimer Berg Rottland
Riesling Extra Brut
17 DM, ♀ now **86**

SEKTHAUS VOLKER RAUMLAND
Rheinhessen
67592 Flörsheim-Dalsheim,
Alzeyer Straße 134
Tel. (0 62 43) 90 80 70, Fax 90 80 77

1988 Weißer Burgunder
Brut
17.50 DM, ♀ now **86**

WEINGUT SCHÄFER-FRÖHLICH
Nahe, page 287

1995 Bockenauer Stromberg
Riesling trocken
16.50 DM, ♀ till 1999 **86**

WEIN & SEKTGUT REH

Mosel
54340 Schleich, Weierbachstraße 12
Tel. (0 65 07) 9 91 10, Fax 9 91 11

1992 Riesling
trocken

17 DM, 🍷 now **86**

WEINGUT RÖMERHOF

Mosel
54340 Riol, Burgstraße 2
Tel. (0 65 02) 21 89, Fax 2 06 71

1994 Rigodulum
Riesling trocken

15 DM, 🍷 now **86**

WEINGUT JOSEF ROSCH

Mosel, page 239

1995 Weißer Burgunder
Brut

18.50 DM, 🍷 till 1999 **86**

STAATSWEINGUT ASSMANNSHAUSEN

Rheingau, page 389

1995 Assmannshäuser Höllenberg
Spätburgunder Brut

24.50 DM, 🍷 till 2000 **86**

1995 Assmannshäuser Höllenberg
Spätburgunder Weißherbst Brut

23.50 DM, 🍷 till 2000 **86**

STAATSWEINGUT ASSMANNSHAUSEN

Rheingau, page 389

1995 Burgunder
Brut

26.50 DM, 🍷 now **86**

WEINGUT FORSTMEISTER GELTZ – ZILLIKEN

Mosel, page 257

1995 Riesling
Brut

16 DM, 🍷 till 2000 **86**

STAATLICHE LEHR- UND VERSUCHSANSTALT

Nahe
55545 Bad Kreuznach,
Rüdesheimer Straße 68
Tel. (06 71) 82 02 51, Fax 3 63 66

1995 Riesling
Brut

13 DM, 🍷 till 2000 **86**

The Best Marc and Fine

Stimulated by the marketing triumphs of marc and grappa, German wine producers have rediscovered their ancient distilling traditions. Single wines are distilled into *Weinbrand*; the residue left in the press after the crush is distilled into *Tresterbrand* or *Grappa*; the lees are distilled into *Hefebrand*. The best of these products are delicious and often marketed in attractive bottles. Provided they are aged in glass, these spirits remain transparently clear; but if they have been aged in oak casks they take on a hue that ranges from pale yellow to amber.

RIESLING TRESTERBRAND

Mosel-Saar-Ruwer

Weingut Heymann-Löwenstein
Marc de Riesling "As we get it"
64% Vol., 67 DM/0.35 liter

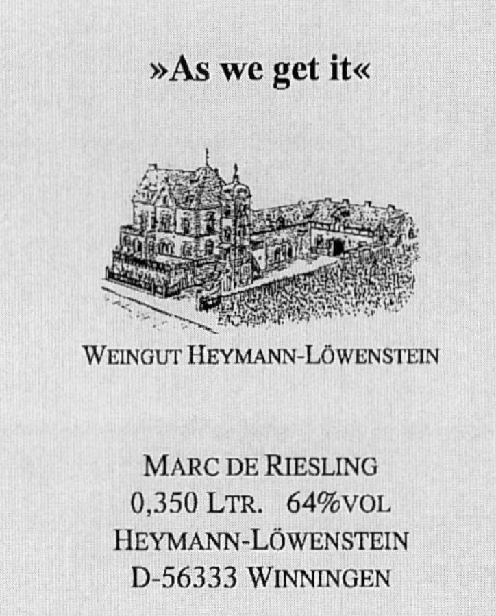

Brennerei Stefan Justen – Meulenhof
Alter Tresterbrand
40% Vol., 18 DM/0.5 liter

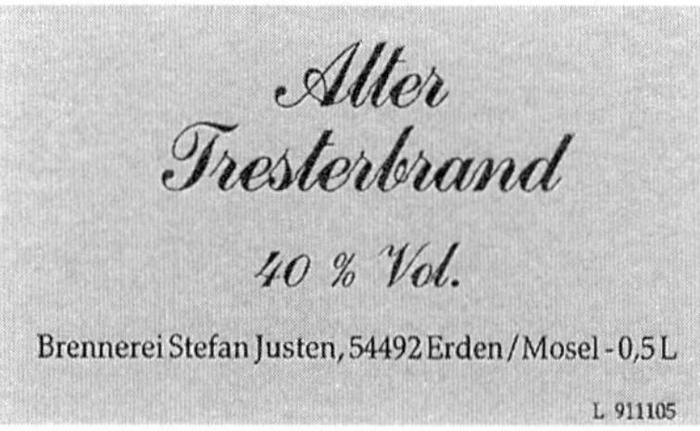

Weingut Lubentiushof
1995 Marc de Moselle
Tresterbrand vom Riesling
40% Vol., 25 DM/0.35 liter

LUBENTIUSHOF MARC DE MOSELLE
TRESTERBRAND VOM RIESLING

1995 — Deutsches Erzeugnis
40% by vol. 35 cl

Weingut Milz – Laurentiushof
Marc vom Riesling
40% Vol., 44 DM/0.5 liter

Weingut Sankt Urbans-Hof
Riesling-Tresterbrand
42% Vol., 40 DM/0.5 liter

Weingut Selbach-Oster
Riesling Trester Brand
40% Vol., 30 DM/0.5 liter

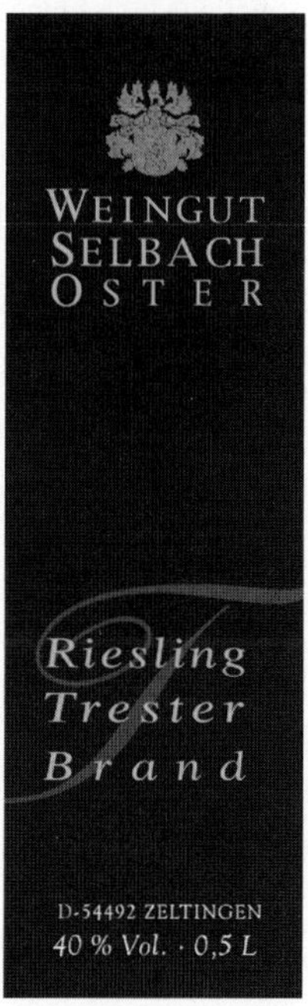

Weingut Heinz Schmitt
1995 Riesling Tresterbrand
42% Vol., 30 DM/0.5 liter

Nahe

Destillerie Steitz
Trester aus Riesling
40% Vol., 25.90 DM/0.5 liter

DESTILLERIE
STEITZ

Trester
aus
Riesling

Anni und Hermann Steitz
D-67811 DIELKIRCHEN-STEINGRUBEN

Vertragsbetrieb Nr. 7008 A BÖW

0,5 l

40 % vol

Weingut Bürgermeister Schweinhardt
Perkello
Riesling Edelbrand aus Weintrester
44% Vol., 28.50 DM/0.5 liter

TRESTERBRAND

Nahe

Weingut Hahnmühle
Traminer Tresterbrand
40% Vol., 30 DM/0.5 liter

Destillerie Steitz
Tester aus Blauem Spätburgunder
40% Vol., 23.50 DM/0.5 liter

DESTILLERIE
STEITZ

Trester
aus
Blauem
Spätburgunder

Anni und Hermann Steitz
D-67811 DIELKIRCHEN-STEINGRUBEN

0,5 l 40 % vol

Weingut Bürgermeister Schweinhardt
Perkello
Burgunder Edelbrand aus Weintrester
44% Vol., 28.50 DM/0.5 liter

Rheinhessen

Groebe & Prinz
Marc vom Burgunder
40% Vol., 56 DM/0.5 liter

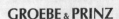

GROEBE & PRINZ

MARC
VOM
BURGUNDER

DEUTSCHES ERZEUGNIS
D-64584 BIEBESHEIM
40 % vol. 500 ml

Weingut Schales
Feiner Tresterbrand
vom Gewürztraminer
40% Vol., 34.50 DM/0.5 liter

Rheingau

Weingut Allendorf
Assmannshäuser Höllenberg
Spätburgunder Trester
43% Vol., 26 DM/0.5 liter

Weingut Allendorf
1994 Trockenbeerenauslese Trester
42% Vol., 100 DM/0.5 liter

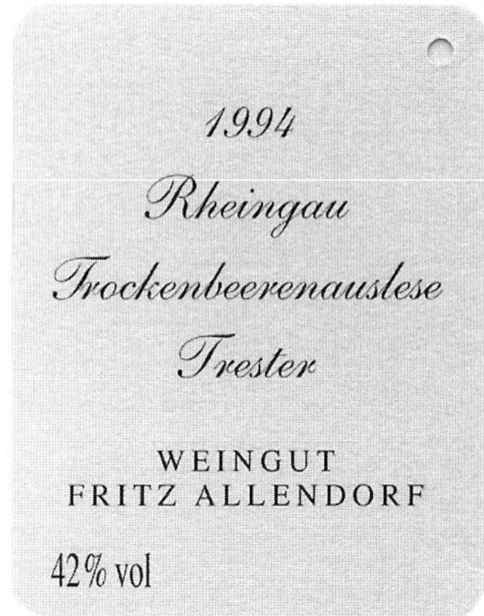

Weingut Doufrain
Spätburgunder Tresterbrand
45% Vol., 25 DM/0.5 liter

Weingut Balthasar Ress
"Von Unserm"
Tresterbrand aus Spätburgunder
42% Vol., 35 DM/0.5 liter

Pfalz

Mäurer's Weingut
Trester aus Pinot
40% Vol., 38 DM/0.5 liter

Weingut Rainer Eymann
Spätburgunder Tresterbrand
40% Vol., 30 DM/0.5 liter

Weingut Becker
Weintresterbrand aus Gewürztraminer
43% Vol., 35 DM/0.7 liter

Weingut Wehrheim
Traminer-Trester
40% Vol., 35 DM/0.5 liter

Württemberg

Weingut G. A. Heinrich
Trester von Gewürztraminer
42% Vol., 45 DM/0.5 liter

Weingut Kistenmacher-Hengerer
Muskateller-Marc
42% Vol., 35 DM/0.5 liter

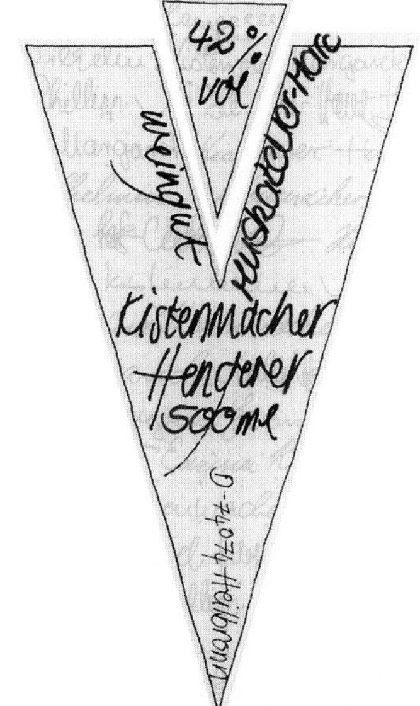

Baden

Weingut Heinrich Männle
Scheurebe Traubentresterbrand 1985
45% Vol., 25 DM/0.5 liter

Weingut Salwey
Marc vom Kaiserstuhl
45% Vol., 17.50 DM/0.35 liter

Franken

Weingut Fürst
Trester vom Spätburgunder
42% Vol., 44 DM/0.5 liter

Weingut Horst Sauer
Trester
40% Vol., 22 DM/0.5 liter

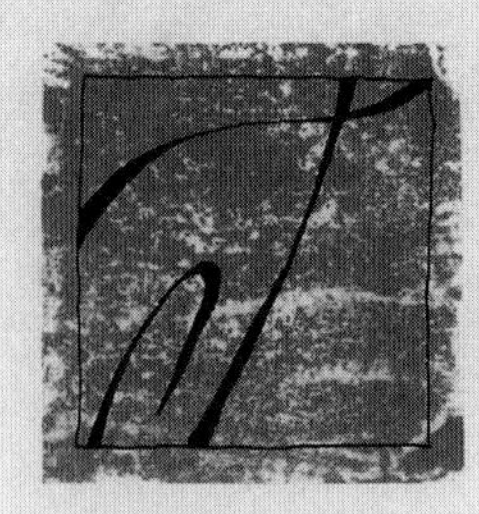

Weingut Wirsching
Fränkischer
Tresterbrand 42% Vol.,
32.50 DM/0.5 liter

Hessische Bergstraße

Bergsträsser Winzer e. G.
Marc vom
Burgunder
Tresterbrand
41% Vol.,
35 DM/0.5 liter

WEINHEFE

Baden

Weingut Salwey
Weinhefe
45% Vol., 12 DM/0.35 liter

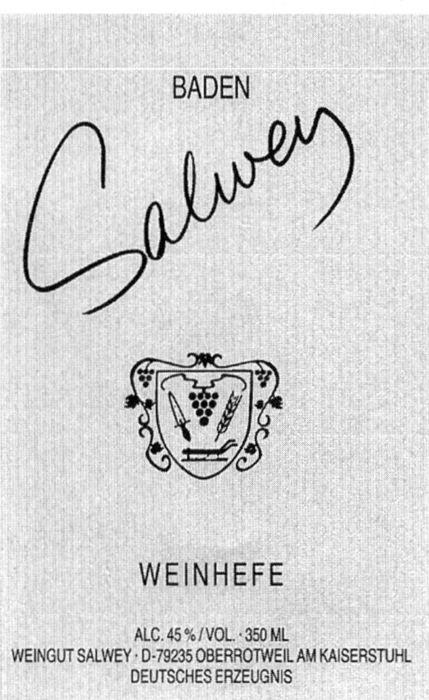

Weingut Wolff Metternich
Durbacher Hefenbrand
45% Vol., 23 DM/0.5 liter

Weingut Seeger
Weinhefebrand
42% Vol., 25 DM/0.35 liter

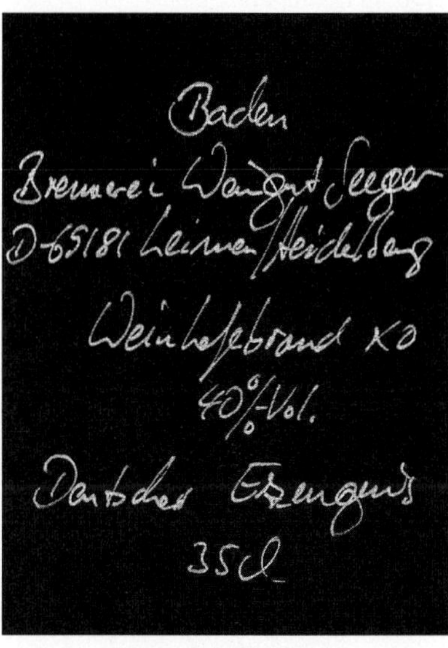

Weingut Kalkbödele
Weinhefe aus dem Holzfäßle
42% Vol., 25 DM/0.7 liter

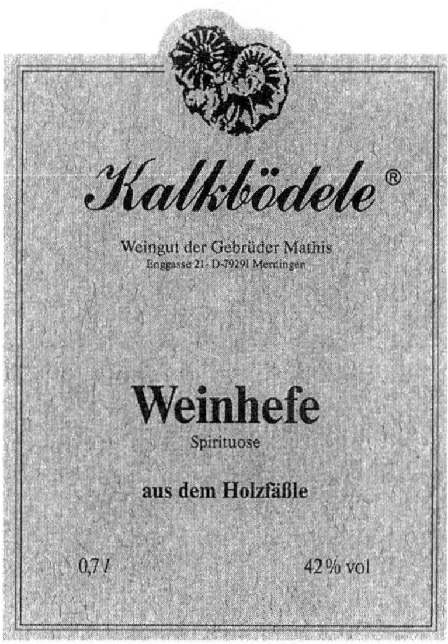

Pfalz

Weingut Georg Mosbacher
Riesling Hefebrand
45% Vol., 22 DM/0.7 liter

Weingut Koehler-Ruprecht
Hefebrand "Philippi"
45% Vol., 50 DM/0.5 liter

Rheingau

Weingut Freiherr zu Knyphausen
Weinhefe-Brand vom Riesling
38% Vol., 30 DM/0.5 liter

Staatsweingut Assmannshausen
1995 Weinhefebrand
vom Spätburgunder
40% Vol., 40 DM/0.5 liter

Rheinhessen

Weingut Weitzel
1994 Weinhefebrand
40% Vol., 17 DM/0.5 liter

Weingut Wittmann
Feiner Brand aus Weinhefe
40% Vol., 25 DM/0.5 liter

TRAUBENBRAND

Pfalz

Weingut Dr. Bürklin-Wolf
Traubenbrand aus Gewürztraminer
40% Vol., 40 DM/0.5 liter

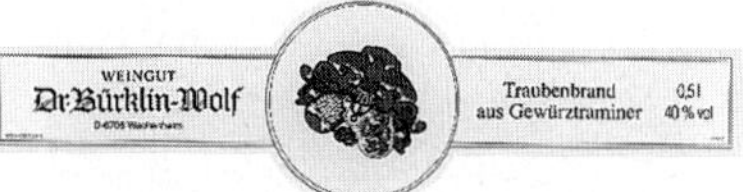

Nahe

Weingut Hahnmühle
Traminer Traubenbrand
40% Vol., 30 DM/0.5 liter

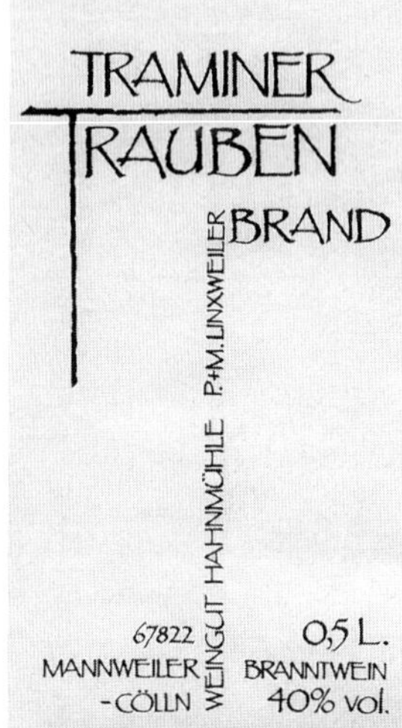

Rheinhessen

Weingut H. L. Menger
Traubenbrand aus Gewürztraminer
40% Vol., 20 DM/0.5 liter

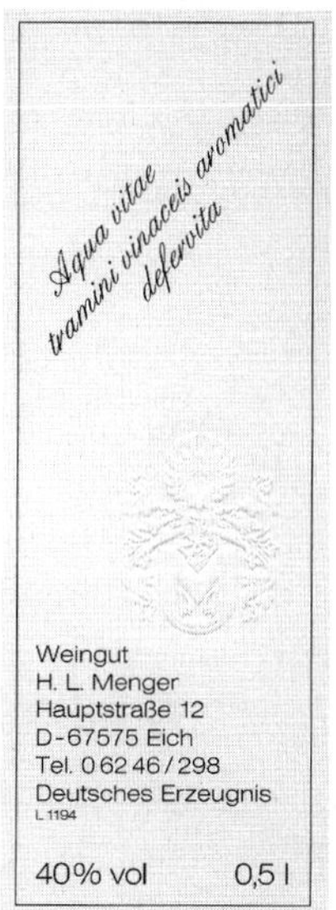

WEINBRAND

Rheingau

Weingut Alexander Freimuth
Rheingau Riesling
Alter Weinbrand XO
38% Vol., 27 DM/0.5 liter

Weingut Balthasar Ress
"Von Unserm"
Alter Weinbrand aus Riesling
38% Vol., 30 DM/0.5 liter

Rheinhessen

Weingut J. Neus, Ingelheim
Spätburgunder Weinbrand
V.S.O.P. Vinum Ingelheim
38% Vol., 32 DM/0.5 liter

Weingut H. L. Menger
Der alte Menger
Sehr alter Weinbrand V.S.O.P.
40% Vol., 35 DM/0.5 liter

Württemberg

Weingut Drautz-Able
Weinbrand
38% Vol., 48 DM/0.5 liter

German Wine Information Bureaus

BELGIUM

Bureau d'Information du vin allemand c/o Primal
Informatiebureau voor duitse wijn c/o Primal
Rue Osseghem 218, B-1080 Bruxelles
Osseghemstraat 218, B-1080 Brussel
Tel.: ++32-2 411 02 22
Fax: ++32-2 411 11 35
E-mail: primal@axl.be
Contact: Mr. Alain Jacobs

BRAZIL

Câmara de Comércio e Indústria Brasil-Alemanha
German-Brasilian Chamber of Commerce
Rua Verbo Divino 1488, 3° Andar
BR-04719-904 São Paulo-SP
Tel.: ++55-11-5181-0677
Fax: ++55-11-5181-7013
E-mail: ahk-brasil@originet.com.br
Internet: http://www. ahkbrasil.com
Contact: Mr. Martin Langewellpott

CANADA

German Wine Information Bureau
160 Bloor Street East * Suite #501
KAN-Toronto, Ontario M4W 1B9
Tel.: ++1 / 416 / 964 8014
Fax: ++1 / 416 / 964 6300
E-mail: germanwine@continental.ca
Contact: Mr. Ron Fiorelli

DENMARK

Deutsch-Dänische Handelskammer Borsen
DK-1217 Kopenhagen K
Tel.: ++45-33-91 33 35
Fax: ++45-33-91 31 16
E-mail: 106623.300@compuserve.com
Contact: Mr. André Minier

FINLAND

Saksan Viinitiedotus
Otavantie 7, 00200 Helsinki
Tel.: ++358-9-682 0830
Fax: ++358-9-682 2040
E-mail: zaraband@co.inet.fi
Contact: Mrs. Monika Halén

GREAT BRITAIN

German Wine Information Service (UK)
1-7 Woburn Walk, London WC1H 0JJ
Tel.: ++44-171 388 2525
Fax: ++44-171 387 6411
E-mail: germanwine@dial.pipex.com
Contact: Miss Nicky Forrest,
Mrs. Anne Whitehurst

IRELAND

German-Irish Chamber of Industry and Commerce
46 Fitzwilliam Square, Dublin 2
Tel.: ++353-1-6762934
Fax: ++353-1-6762595
E-mail: wine@german-irish.ie
Contact: Mrs. Dagmar McGuinness

JAPAN

German Wine Information Service
Aoyama Crystal Building, 6th Floor
Kita-Aoyama 3-chome
Minato-ku, Tokyo 107-8648
Tel.: ++81-3-5413-4606
Fax: ++81-3-3403-0508
E-mail: nakajyo@ozma.co.jp
Contact: Mr. Akio Yamaguchi,
Mr. Yoshihiro Nakajyo, Mrs. Saori Kondo

MEXICO

German-Mexican Chamber of Commerce
B. de Ciruelos 130 - 1202 Col. B. de las Lomas
MEX-11700 Mexico D.F.
Tel.: ++525 / 251 4022
Fax: ++525 / 596 7695
E-mail: investment@ahk-mexiko.com.mx
Contact: Mr. Bernd Rohde

NETHERLANDS

Informatiebureau vorr Duitse wijn
Postbus 189, NL-2250 AD Voorschoten
Tel.: ++31-71-560 20 40
Fax: ++31-71-560 20 20
E-mail: IDW@hulzen.nl
Contact: Mrs. Maaike Buijsman, Mrs. Barbara Luijt

RUSSIA

German Wine Information Service
c/o Rusmarketing
Ul. Kulnewa No. 3, 121170 Moscow
Tel.: ++7501-258 39 05
Fax: ++7095-258 39 09
E-mail: cma@co.ru
Contact: Dr. Ewald Ewering

SWEDEN/NORWAY

Tysk VinInformation
Sagavägen 14, S-181 42 Lidingö
Tel.: ++46-8-765 52 90
Fax: ++46-8-446 01 18
E-mail: tvi@intertrademarketing.se
Contact: Mr. Hansuno Krisch, Mrs. Ingert Krisch

TAIWAN

German Wine Information Service Taiwan
5. Fl., No. 120-2, Chung-Cheng Road
111 Shih-lin Dist., Taipei
Tel.: ++886-2-2836 9944
Fax: ++886-2-2836 9947
E-mail: gut@mail.ht.net.tw
Contact: Mr. Johnny Huang

USA

German Wine Information Bureau
245 Fifth Avenue, Suite 2204
New York, NY 10016
Tel.: ++1-212-896-3336
Fax: ++1-212-896-3342
E-mail: info@germanwineusa.org
Internet: www.germanwineusa.org
Contact: Mrs. Carol Sullivan, Mrs. Robyn Jacob

The Right Glasses

Red Wine Magnum Glass

The long-shouldered elliptical shape of the bowl was designed for complex red wines with high tannin content. This form concentrates the bouquet and makes it easier to discern the refined taste of great aged Bordeaux wines. Spiegelau recommends this glass also for Shiraz, Rioja and Cabernet Sauvignon.

Red Wine Glass

The rounded bowl of this red wine glass was designed especially for full-bodied, rich wines with a high alcohol content, like red Burgundy, Barolo and Barbaresco. The voluminous shape of the bowl exposes a larger surface of wine to the air, allowing it to breathe and develop its bouquet and flavor quickly and completely.

Red Wine Glass

This is a compact glass well suited to wines with normal body and pronounced acidity. Spiegelau recommends this glass as an all-round red wine glass.

'hite Wine Glass

is form is particularly suitable · white wines ripened in oak rrels. This glass gives balance these wines, which often have igh alcohol and low acidity ntent, like Chardonnay.

Weinbrand

Also known as a nosing glass because it was originally used by cognac distillers for the blending of their Cognac-Cuvées. This glass is also used by master distillers and liquor tasters for all digestives such as cognac, brandy, armagnac and whiskey.

›ung White Wine Glass

so called a Riesling glass, this ıss with its petal-lipped rim was nceived for acidic and tangy ite wines like Riesling, Grüner ltliner and Silvaner. The delicate tural carbonic acid gives the ung white wine its freshness. th this glass shape the wine shes onto the tip of the tongue st, where the acidity is not tasted abruptly.

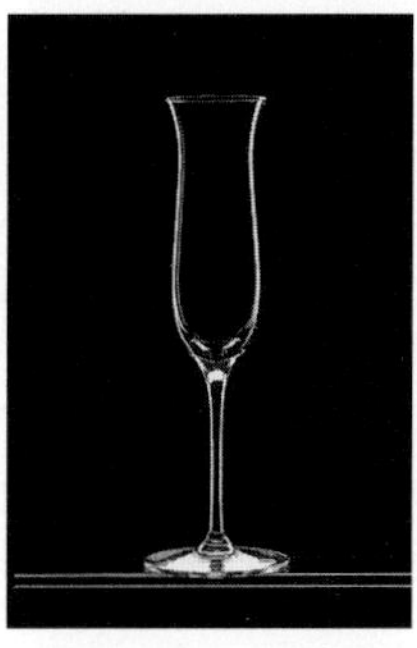

Grappa Glass

This fascinating glass was designed in cooperation with sommeliers and grappa producers. The narrowness of the surface exposed to the air prevents evaporation and so concentrates the aroma. The narrow, petal-lipped rim prevents the fine bouquet from being dominated by the alcohol.

hampagne Glass

is long tulip-shaped glass eases the fine bouquet and arkling fruitiness generously to the tongue and leaves the pression "I am drinking stars," Dom Perignon – one of the coverers of champagne – ce exclaimed!
iegelau recommends this glass nerally for all sparkling wines d especially for vintage ampagnes and Prestige Cuvées.

Cognac/Digestive

A modern cognac glass! Unlike the traditional snifter, this glass diminishes the pungency of the alcohol and enhances the fine aromas evocative of cigar, dried fruit or spices.

S
SPIEGELAU

Index of the Estates

The full presentation of the best estates is to be found on the pages printed in boldface type.

Index of Individuals

Z

English-Language Edition
EDITORS: OWEN DUGAN AND NANCY GRUBB
DESIGNER: CELIA FULLER
PRODUCTION MANAGER: HOPE KOTURO
TRANSLATION: STEPHEN BROOK

EDITOR IN CHIEF, WILHELM HEYNE VERLAG: GERHARD BENZ

 Inquiries should be addressed to Abbeville Publishing Group, 22 Cortlandt Street, New York, N.Y. 10007. The text of this book was set in Times and Helvetica. Printed and bound in Kempten, Germany.

First edition
2 4 6 8 10 9 7 5 3 1

Library of Congress Cataloging-in-Publication Data
Diel, Armin.
[WeinGuide Deutschland. English]
German wine guide / Armin Diel and Joel Payne.
p. cm.
Includes index.
ISBN 0-7892-0577-7
1. Wine and winemaking–Germany. I. Payne, Joel II. Title.
TP559.G3D5413 1999
641.2'2'0943–dc21 99-11481